EXAM CRAM

Cisco CCNA

Routing and Switching 200-120

Fourth Edition

Michael Valentine
Keith Barker

Cisco CCNA Routing and Switching 200-120 Exam Cram, Fourth Edition

ISBN-13: 978-0-7897-5109-6
ISBN-10: 0-7897-5109-7

Library of Congress Cataloging-in-Publication Data: 2013955307

Printed in the United States on America

First Printing: December 2013

Trademarks

All terms mentioned in this book that are known to be trademarks or service marks have been appropriately capitalized. Pearson cannot attest to the accuracy of this information. Use of a term in this book should not be regarded as affecting the validity of any trademark or service mark.

Warning and Disclaimer

Every effort has been made to make this book as complete and as accurate as possible, but no warranty or fitness is implied. The information provided is on an "as is" basis. The author and the publisher shall have neither liability nor responsibility to any person or entity with respect to any loss or damages arising from the information contained in this book or from the use of the CD or programs accompanying it.

Special Sales

For information about buying this title in bulk quantities, or for special sales opportunities (which may include electronic versions; custom cover designs; and content particular to your business, training goals, marketing focus, or branding interests), please contact our corporate sales department at corpsales@pearsoned.com or (800) 382-3419.

For government sales inquiries, please contact governmentsales@pearsoned.com.

For questions about sales outside the U.S., please contact international@pearsoned.com.

Publisher
Paul Boger

Associate Publisher
David Dusthimer

Executive Editor
Brett Bartow

Senior Development Editor
Christopher Cleveland

Managing Editor
Sandra Schroeder

Project Editor
Seth Kerney

Copy Editor
Keith Cline

Indexer
Ken Johnson

Proofreader
Jess DeGabriele

Technical Editors
Brian D'Andrea
Andrew Whitaker

Publishing Coordinator
Vanessa Evans

Multimedia Developer
Lisa Matthews

Book Designer
Mark Shirar

Page Layout
Bumpy Design

Contents at a Glance

Table of Contents

About the Authors

Michael Valentine has been in the IT field for 16 years, focusing on network design and implementation. He is a Cisco Certified Systems Instructor (#31461) and specializes in Cisco Unified Communications instruction and CCNA courses. His accessible, humorous, and effective teaching style has demystified Cisco for hundreds of students since he began teaching in 2002. Michael has a Bachelor of Arts degree from the University of British Columbia and currently holds CCNA, CCDA, CCNP, and CCNP-Voice certifications. In addition to the popular *Exam Cram 2: CCNA* and *CCENT* books, Michael co-authored the *Official Certification Guide for CCNA-Voice* and has contributed to or served as technical editor for the Cisco Press titles *CCNP ONT Official Exam Certification Guide* and *CCNA Flashcards*, among others. Michael has also developed courseware and lab guides for Official Cisco Curriculum courses and custom classes for individuals and corporations.

Keith Barker, CCIE No. 6783 R/S & Security, is a 27-year veteran of the networking industry. He currently works at CBT Nuggets. His past experience includes EDS, Blue Cross, Paramount Pictures, and KnowledgeNET, and he has delivered CCIE-level training for several years. As part of the original set of Cisco VIPs for the Cisco Learning Network, he continues to give back to the community in many ways. He is CISSP, HP, PaloAlto, Brocade, and Juniper certified, loves to teach, and keeps many of his video tutorials at http://www.youtube.com/keith6783. You can reach him on Facebook at "Keith Barker Networking."

About the Technical Editors

Brian D'Andrea started his career working as a bench technician for a large computer manufacturer. He then progressed to a consultant position for various financial and medical institutions across Pennsylvania, New Jersey, and Delaware. He is now a long-time instructor and courseware developer of Cisco courses that include CCNA Routing & Switching, CCDA, CCNA Security, CCNP Routing & Switching, and CCDP. He has been privileged to be part of several Cisco Press published materials. He enjoys sharing his knowledge and 17 years of experience in the information technology field.

Andrew Whitaker (CCNA:Security, CCNP, CCSP, CCVP, CCDP, CCDA, CCENT, CISSP, CEH, CEPT, CPT, LPT, MCT, CEI, CICP, CHFI, ECSA, MCTS, MCSE, CNE, EMCPA, CTP, A+, Network+, Security+, Convergence+, Linux+, CEREA, WAPT, CSSA, LPI-1) is a nationally recognized expert on cybersecurity, an author of best-selling networking and security books, and an award-winning technical trainer. He was also contributing author to previous editions of the *CCNA* and *CCENT Exam Crams*. His work has gained media coverage by NBC, *The Wall Street Journal*, *The Philadelphia Inquirer*, *San Francisco Gate*, *Business Week* magazine, and others. He is a frequent conference speaker and has given talks at GFIRST8, DefCon, TakeDownCon, ChicagoCon, BSides, and SecurePhilly. As an instructor, he is the recipient of both the EC-Council Instructor of Excellence award and the EC-Council Instructor of the Year award.

Dedication

Michael Valentine:
This one is for Andy DeMaria, a good boss and a stalwart friend.

Keith Barker:
To Dan and Johnna Charbonneau and the CBT Nuggets family:
If anyone had the opportunity to be surrounded by such awesome people, even for a few hours, they would never be the same again. Thank you!

Acknowledgments

With this book in its fourth iteration, I have thanked several people several times over. But a few of those people deserve to be thanked every day.

Brett Bartow, Chris Cleveland, Vanessa Evans, and all the unseen warriors at Pearson: You put up with a lot and rarely lose your patience with your authors and their egos. I'm impressed and grateful for your long-suffering help.

The crew at Skyline—Toby, Ed, Marshall and Suad—have taught me, coached me, saved me, and/or kicked my butt as required and been such constant, dependable, professional colleagues, and friends I can't imagine working without. They make me better at what I do.

Andy DeMaria (despite being a fan of a disreputable New York hockey team) is possibly the best boss I have ever had. Through thick and thin, a serious and debilitating injury, border guard zeal, and general gong show snafus, he has been a deep well of patience, logic, perceptive observation, and effective action. If either of us ever has 10 minutes to spare, I owe him (at last count) two fresh salmon and three cases of good Canadian beer. Seriously, Andy: Thanks.

My little girl has grown up seeing me glued to my chair, grinding away on chapters, slides, lab guides, and lectures. She has learned a whole new sign language for when I am not able to talk because I am lecturing, brought me dozens of cups of coffee and meals, and generally been a great kid and assistant. Pretty soon she will be able to type better than I can (not that that is any great challenge) and she can take over while I dictate. Thank you for being a great kid and a big help.

My wonderful wife: You and me, together. Thank you for being the kind of girl who enjoys driving around New Zealand in a hippie van named Vince.

And last of all: You, the reader, the student, the learner, the exam taker. Thanks for all your work. I wish you success.

We Want to Hear from You!

As the reader of this book, *you* are our most important critic and commentator. We value your opinion and want to know what we're doing right, what we could do better, what areas you'd like to see us publish in, and any other words of wisdom you're willing to pass our way.

We welcome your comments. You can email or write us directly to let us know what you did or didn't like about this book—as well as what we can do to make our books better.

Please note that we cannot help you with technical problems related to the topic of this book.

When you write, please be sure to include this book's title and authors as well as your name, email address, and phone number. We will carefully review your comments and share them with the author and editors who worked on the book.

Email: feedback@pearsonitcertification.com

Mail: Pearson IT Certification
ATTN: Reader Feedback
800 East 96th Street
Indianapolis, IN 46240 USA

Reader Services

Visit our website and register this book at http://www.pearsonitcertification.com/register for convenient access to any updates, downloads, or errata that might be available for this book.

Introduction

Welcome to *Cisco CCNA Routing and Switching 200-120 Exam Cram*! Whether this is your first or your fifteenth Exam Cram series book, you'll find information here that will help ensure your success as you pursue knowledge, experience, and certification. This introduction explains Cisco's certification programs in general and talks about how the Exam Cram series can help you prepare for the Cisco CCNA Routing and Switching 200-120 exam. The materials in this book have been prepared with a very clear focus on testable concepts, configurations, and skills. As much extraneous material as possible, beyond what is needed for background comprehension, has been eliminated so that the book is a distillation of the necessary knowledge to take—and pass—the CCNA Routing and Switching 200-120 exam. The two sample tests with answer keys at the end of the book should give you a reasonably accurate assessment of your knowledge. We have also included challenge labs to give you the critical hands-on practice you will need to master the simulator questions on the CCNA Routing and Switching 200-120 exam. Read the book, understand the material, practice the labs, and you'll stand a very good chance of passing the test.

Exam Cram books help you understand and appreciate the subjects and materials you need to pass Cisco certification exams. Exam Cram books are aimed strictly at test preparation and review. They do not teach you everything you need to know about a topic. Instead, we present and dissect the topics and key points we've found that you're likely to encounter on a test. We've worked to bring together as much accurate information as possible about the latest CCNA Routing and Switching 200-120 exam.

Nevertheless, to completely prepare yourself for any Cisco test, we recommend that you begin by taking the Self-Assessment that is included in this book, immediately following this introduction. The Self-Assessment tool will help you evaluate your knowledge base against the requirements for a CCNA under both ideal and real circumstances.

Based on what you learn from the Self-Assessment, you might decide to begin your studies with some classroom training, some practice with the Cisco IOS, or some background reading. On the other hand, you might decide to pick up and read one of the many study guides available from Cisco or third-party vendors on certain topics.

We also recommend that you supplement your study program with visits to http://www.examcram2.com to receive additional practice questions, get advice, and track the CCNA program.

We also strongly recommend that you practice configuring the Cisco devices that you'll be tested on because nothing beats hands-on experience and familiarity when it comes to understanding the questions you're likely to encounter on a certification test. Book learning is essential, but without a doubt, hands-on experience is the best teacher of all!

Taking a Certification Exam

After you've prepared for your exam, you need to register with a testing center. The CCNA exam can be taken in either one or two steps: The single-exam option is the 200-120 exam, and costs $295. The two-exam option requires you to take both the 100-101 ICND1 and 200-101 ICND2 exams, at a cost of $150 each. In the United States and Canada, tests are administered by VUE.

You can sign up for a test or get the phone numbers for local testing centers through the Web at http://www.vue.com.

To sign up for a test, you must possess a valid credit card or contact VUE for mailing instructions to send a check (in the United States). Only when payment is verified or your check has cleared can you actually register for the test.

To schedule an exam, you need to call the number or visit either of the web pages at least 1 day in advance. To cancel or reschedule an exam, you must call before 7 p.m. Pacific standard time the day before the scheduled test time (or you might be charged, even if you don't show up to take the test). When you want to schedule a test, you should have the following information ready:

- Your name, organization, and mailing address
- Your Cisco test ID
- The name and number of the exam you want to take
- A method of payment (As mentioned previously, a credit card is the most convenient method, but alternative means can be arranged in advance, if necessary.)

After you sign up for a test, you are told when and where the test is scheduled. You should try to arrive at least 15 minutes early. You must supply two forms of identification—one of which must be a photo ID—and sign a nondisclosure agreement to be admitted into the testing room.

All Cisco exams are completely closed book. In fact, you are not permitted to take anything with you into the testing area, but you are given a blank sheet of paper and a pen (or in some cases, an erasable plastic sheet and an erasable pen). We suggest that you immediately write down on that sheet of paper all the information you've memorized for the test. In Exam Cram books, this information appears on a tear-out sheet inside the front cover of each book. You are given some time to compose yourself, record this information, and take a sample orientation exam before you begin the real thing. We suggest that you take the orientation test before taking your first exam, but because all the certification exams are more or less identical in layout, behavior, and controls, you probably don't need to do this more than once.

When you complete a Cisco certification exam, the software tells you immediately whether you've passed or failed. If you need to retake an exam, you have to schedule a new test with VUE and pay another $150 or $295.

Note

If you fail a Cisco test, you must wait 5 full days before you can take it again. For example, if you failed on Tuesday, you would have to wait until Monday to take it again.

Tracking Your Certification Status

As soon as you pass the CCNA Routing and Switching 200-120 exam (or both the 100-101 ICND1 and 200-101 ICND2 exams), you are a CCNA. Cisco generates transcripts that indicate which exams you have passed. You can view a copy of your transcript at any time by going to Cisco.com and going to the certifications tracking tool. This tool enables you to print a copy of your current transcript and confirm your certification status.

After you pass the necessary exam, you are certified. Official certification is normally granted after 3 to 6 weeks, so you shouldn't expect to get your credentials overnight. The package for official certification that arrives includes the following:

- A certificate that is suitable for framing, along with a wallet card.
- A license to use the applicable logo, which means that you can use the logo in advertisements, promotions, and documents, as well as on letterhead, business cards, and so on. Along with the license comes information on how to legally and appropriately use the logos.

Many people believe that the benefits of Cisco certification are among the most powerful in the industry. We're starting to see more job listings that request or require applicants to have CCDA, CCNP, and other certifications, and many individuals who complete Cisco certification programs can qualify for increases in pay and/or responsibility. As an official recognition of hard work and broad knowledge, one of the Cisco credentials is a badge of honor in many IT organizations.

How to Prepare for an Exam

Preparing for the CCNA Routing and Switching 200-120 exam requires that you obtain and study materials designed to provide comprehensive information about the product and its capabilities that will appear on the specific exam for which you are preparing. The following list of materials can help you study and prepare:

- The official Cisco study guides by Cisco Press.
- Practicing with real equipment or simulators.
- The CCNA Prep Center on Cisco's website, which features articles, sample questions, games, and discussions to focus and clarify your studies.
- The exam-preparation advice, practice tests, questions of the day, and discussion groups on the http://www.examcram.com e-learning and certification destination website.
- The *CCNA Routing and Switching 200-120 Exam Cram*—This book gives you information about the material you need to know to pass the tests. Seriously, this is a great book.
- Classroom training. Cisco training partners and third-party training companies (such as the Training Camp) offer classroom training for CCENT and CCNA related skills and topics. These companies aim to help you prepare to pass the CCENT and CCNA exams. Although such training can be expensive, most of the individuals lucky enough to partake find this training to be very worthwhile.
- Other publications. There's no shortage of materials available about CCENT and CCNA. Try to remember not to drown yourself in reading material—at some point, you are just ready to test and should go for it.

This set of required and recommended materials represents a good collection of sources and resources about the CCNA exam and related topics. We hope that you'll find that this book belongs in this company.

What This Book Will Not Do

This book will not teach you everything you need to know about networking with Cisco devices, or even about a given topic. Nor is this book an introduction to computer technology. If you're new to networking and looking for an initial preparation guide, check out http://www.quepublishing.com, where you will find a whole section dedicated to Cisco certifications and networking in general. This book will review what you need to know before you take the test, with the fundamental purpose dedicated to reviewing the information needed on the Cisco CCNA exam.

This book uses a variety of teaching and memorization techniques to analyze the exam-related topics and to provide you with ways to input, index, and retrieve everything you need to know to pass the test. Once again, it is not a comprehensive treatise on Cisco networking.

What This Book Is Designed to Do

This book is designed to be read as a pointer to the areas of knowledge you will be tested on. In other words, you might want to read the book one time, just to get an insight into how comprehensive your knowledge of networking with Cisco is. The book is also designed to be read shortly before you go for the actual test and to give you a distillation of the entire field of CCNA knowledge in as few pages as possible. We think you can use this book to get a sense of the underlying context of any topic in the chapters—or to skim read for Exam Alerts, bulleted points, summaries, and topic headings.

We've drawn on material from the Cisco listing of knowledge requirements, from other preparation guides, and from the exams themselves. We've also drawn from a battery of third-party test-preparation tools and technical websites, as well as from our own experience with Cisco equipment and the exam. Our aim is to walk you through the knowledge you will need—looking over your shoulder, so to speak—and point out those things that are important for the exam (Exam Alerts, practice questions, and so on).

The CCNA exam makes a basic assumption that you already have a strong background of experience with the general networking and its terminology. However, because the CCNA is an introductory-level test, we've tried to demystify the jargon, acronyms, terms, and concepts.

About This Book

If you're preparing for the CCNA exam for the first time, we've structured the topics in this book to build upon one another. Therefore, the topics covered in later chapters might refer to previous discussions in earlier chapters.

CCNA Official Exam Topics

The following lists official exam topics for CCNA. Each CCNA chapter will reference a selection of the topics in this list. Be sure to check Cisco.com (http://www.cisco.com/web/learning/certifications/associate/ccna/index.html) for any updates to the ICND1, ICND2, or composite exam.

Operation of IP Data Networks

- Operation of IP data networks.
- Recognize the purpose and functions of various network devices such as routers, switches, bridges, and hubs.
- Select the components required to meet a given network specification.
- Identify common applications and their impact on the network.
- Describe the purpose and basic operation of the protocols in the OSI and TCP/IP models.
- Predict the data flow between two hosts across a network.
- Identify the appropriate media, cables, ports, and connectors to connect Cisco network devices to other network devices and hosts in a LAN.

LAN Switching Technologies

- Determine the technology and media access control method for Ethernet networks.
- Identify basic switching concepts and the operation of Cisco switches:
    - Collision domains
    - Broadcast domains
    - Types of switching
    - CAM table

- Configure and verify initial switch configuration, including remote-access management.
    - Cisco IOS commands to perform basic switch setup
- Verify network status and switch operation using basic utilities such as ping, Telnet, and SSH.
- Identify enhanced switching technologies:
    - RSTP
    - PVSTP
    - EtherChannels
- Describe how VLANs create logically separate networks and the need for routing between them.
- Explain network segmentation and basic traffic management concepts.
- Configure and verify VLANs.
- Configure and verify trunking on Cisco switches:
    - DTP
    - Autonegotiation
- Configure and verify PVSTP operation:
    - Describe root bridge election.
    - Spanning tree mode.

IP Addressing (IPv4 / IPv6)

- Describe the operation and necessity of using private and public IP addresses for IPv4 addressing.
- Identify the appropriate IPv6 addressing scheme to satisfy addressing requirements in a LAN/WAN environment.
- Identify the appropriate IPv4 addressing scheme using VLSM and summarization to satisfy addressing requirements in a LAN/WAN environment.
- Describe the technological requirements for running IPv6 in conjunction with IPv4 such as dual stack.

- Describe IPv6 addresses:
    - Global unicast
    - Multicast
    - Link local
    - Unique local
    - eui 64
    - Autoconfiguration

IP Routing Technologies

- Describe basic routing concepts:
    - CEF
    - Packet forwarding
    - Router lookup process
- Describe the boot process of Cisco IOS routers:
    - POST
    - Router bootup process
- Configure and verify utilizing the CLI to set basic router configuration:
    - Cisco IOS commands to perform basic router setup
- Configure and verify operation status of a device interface, both serial and Ethernet.
- Verify router configuration and network connectivity:
    - Cisco IOS commands to review basic router information and network connectivity
- Configure and verify routing configuration for a static or default route given specific routing requirements.
- Manage Cisco IOS files:
    - Boot preferences
    - Cisco IOS image(s)

- Licensing:
    - Show license
    - Change license
- Differentiate methods of routing and routing protocols:
  - Static vs. dynamic
  - Link state vs. distance vector
  - Administrative distance
  - Split horizon
  - Metric
  - Next hop
  - IP routing table
  - Passive interfaces
- Configure and verify OSPF (single area):
  - Benefit of single area
  - Neighbor adjacencies
  - OSPF states
  - Discuss multi-area
  - Configure OSPF v2
  - Configure OSPF v3
  - Router ID
  - Passive interface
  - LSA types
- Configure and verify EIGRP (single AS):
  - Feasible distance / feasible successors / administrative distance
  - Feasibility condition
  - Metric composition
  - Router ID
  - Autosummary
  - Path selection

- Load balancing:
  - Equal
  - Unequal

Passive interface

- Configure and verify inter-VLAN routing (router on a stick):
  - Subinterfaces
  - Upstream routing
  - Encapsulation
- Configure SVI interfaces.

IP Services

- Configure and verify DHCP (IOS router):
  - Configuring router interfaces to use DHCP
  - DHCP options
  - Excluded addresses
  - Lease time
- Describe the types, features, and applications of ACLs:
  - Standard:
    - Sequence numbers
    - Editing
  - Extended
  - Named
  - Numbered
  - Log option
- Configure and verify ACLs in a network environment:
  - Named
  - Numbered
  - Log option

- Identify the basic operation of NAT:
    - Purpose
    - Pool
    - Static
    - 1 to 1
    - Overloading
    - Source addressing
    - One-way NAT
- Configure and verify NAT for given network requirements.
- Configure and verify NTP as a client.
- Recognize high availability (FHRP):
    - VRRP
    - HSRP
    - GLBP
- Configure and verify syslog:
    - Utilize syslog output.
- Describe SNMP v2 & v3.

Network Device Security

- Configure and verify network device security features such as
    - Device password security
    - Enable secret vs. enable
    - Transport
    - Disable telnet
    - SSH
    - VTYs
    - Physical security
    - Service password
    - Describe external authentication methods

- Configure and verify switch port security features such as
    - Sticky MAC
    - MAC address limitation
    - Static/dynamic
    - Violation modes:
        - Err disable
        - Shutdown
    - Protect restrict
    - Shut down unused ports
    - Err disable recovery
    - Assign unused ports to an unused VLAN
    - Setting native VLAN to other than VLAN 1
- Configure and verify ACLs to filter network traffic.
- Configure and verify an ACLs to limit telnet and SSH access to the router.

Troubleshooting

- Identify and correct common network problems.
- Utilize NetFlow data.
- Troubleshoot and correct common problems associated with IP addressing and host configurations.
- Troubleshoot and resolve VLAN problems:
    - Identify that VLANs are configured
    - Port membership correct
    - IP address configured
- Troubleshoot and resolve trunking problems on Cisco switches:
    - Correct trunk states
    - Correct encapsulation configured
    - Correct VLANs allowed

- Troubleshoot and resolve spanning-tree operation issues:
    - Root switch
    - Priority
    - Mode is correct
    - Port states
- Troubleshoot and resolve routing issues:
    - Routing is enabled
    - Routing table is correct
    - Correct path selection
- Troubleshoot and resolve OSPF problems:
    - Neighbor adjacencies
    - Hello and Dead timers
    - OSPF area
    - Interface MTU
    - Network types
    - Neighbor states
    - OSPF topology database
- Troubleshoot and resolve EIGRP problems:
    - Neighbor adjacencies
    - AS number
    - Load balancing
    - Split horizon
- Troubleshoot and resolve inter-VLAN routing problems:
    - Connectivity
    - Encapsulation
    - Subnet
    - Native VLAN
    - Port mode trunk status

- Troubleshoot and resolve ACL issues:
    - Statistics
    - Permitted networks
    - Direction
    - Interface
- Troubleshoot and resolve WAN implementation issues:
    - Serial interfaces
    - PPP
    - Frame relay
- Troubleshoot and resolve Layer 1 problems:
    - Framing
    - CRC
    - Runts
    - Giants
    - Dropped packets
    - Late collision
    - Input/output errors
- Monitor NetFlow statistics.
- Troubleshoot EtherChannel problems.

WAN Technologies

- Identify different WAN technologies:
    - Metro Ethernet
    - VSAT
    - Cellular 3G/4G
    - MPLS
    - T1/E1
    - ISDN
    - DSL

    - Frame relay
    - Cable
    - VPN
- Configure and verify a basic WAN serial connection.
- Configure and verify a PPP connection between Cisco routers.
- Configure and verify Frame Relay on Cisco routers.
- Implement and troubleshoot PPPoE.

We suggest that you read this book from front to back. You won't be wasting your time because nothing we've written is a guess about an unknown exam. We've had to explain certain underlying information on such a regular basis those explanations are included here.

After you've read the book, you can brush up on a certain area by using the Index or the Table of Contents to go straight to the topics and questions you want to reexamine. We've tried to use the headings and subheadings to provide outline information about each given topic. After you've been certified, we think you'll find this book useful as a tightly focused reference and an essential foundation of CCNA knowledge.

Chapter Formats

Each Exam Cram chapter follows a regular structure, along with graphical cues about especially important or useful material. The structure of a typical chapter is as follows:

- **Cram Savers and Cram Quizzes:** Responding to our readers' feedback, we have added more quizzes and answers. At the beginning of each major topic, you will find a Cram Saver. If these questions are no problem for you, you might be able to back off a little on how hard you cram that section. If you can't get them right, start cramming. Similarly, at the end of each major section, you will find a new Cram Quiz, which serves as an immediate check on your understanding and retention of that topic.
- **Topical coverage:** Each chapter covers topics drawn from the official exam topics as they relate to the chapter's subject.
- **Alerts:** Throughout the topical coverage section, we highlight material most likely to appear on the exam by using a special Exam Alert layout that looks like this:

ExamAlert

This is what an Exam Alert looks like. An Exam Alert stresses concepts, terms, software, or activities that will most likely appear in one or more certification exam question. For that reason, we think any information found offset in Exam Alert format is worthy of unusual attentiveness on your part.

Even if material isn't flagged as an Exam Alert, all the content in this book is associated in some way with test-related material. What appears in the chapter content is critical knowledge.

- **Notes:** This book is an overall examination of basic Cisco networking. Therefore, we dip into many aspects of Cisco networking. Where a body of knowledge is deeper than the scope of the book, we use notes to indicate areas of concern or specialty training, or refer you to other resources.

Note

Cramming for an exam will get you through a test, but it won't make you a competent IT professional. Although you can memorize just the facts you need to become certified, your daily work in the field will rapidly put you in water over your head if you don't know the underlying principles of networking with Cisco gear.

- **Tips:** We provide tips that will help you to build a better foundation of knowledge or to focus your attention on an important concept that will reappear later in the book. Tips provide a helpful way to remind you of the context surrounding a particular area of a topic under discussion.
- **Exam Prep Questions:** This section presents a short list of test questions related to the specific chapter topic. Each question has a following explanation of both correct and incorrect answers. The practice questions highlight the areas we found to be most important on the exam.

The bulk of the book follows this chapter structure, but there are a few other elements that we would like to point out:

- **Practice exams:** The practice exams are very close approximations of the types of questions you are likely to see on the current CCNA Routing and Switching 200-120 exam. The answer key for each practice exam will help you determine which areas you have mastered and which areas you need to study further.
- **Answer keys:** These provide the answers to the sample tests, complete with explanations of both the correct responses and the incorrect responses.

- **Glossary:** This is an extensive glossary of important terms used in this book.
- **Cram Sheet:** This appears as a tear-out sheet, inside the front cover of this Exam Cram book. It is a valuable tool that represents a collection of the most difficult-to-remember facts and numbers we think you should memorize before taking the test. Remember, you can dump this information out of your head onto a piece of paper as soon as you enter the testing room. These are usually facts that we've found require brute-force memorization. You only need to remember this information long enough to write it down when you walk into the test room. Be advised that you will be asked to surrender all personal belongings before you enter the exam room itself.

  You might want to look at the Cram Sheet in your car (no, not while you are driving!) or in the lobby of the testing center just before you walk into the testing center. The Cram Sheet is divided under headings so that you can review the appropriate parts just before each test.
- **CD-ROM:** The CD-ROM contains the Pearson IT Certification Practice Test engine, which provides multiple test modes that you can use for exam preparation. The practice tests are designed to appropriately balance the questions over each technical area (domain) covered by the exam.

Pearson IT Certification Practice Test Engine and Questions on the CD-ROM

The CD-ROM in the back of the book includes the Pearson IT Certification Practice Test engine—software that displays and grades a set of exam-realistic multiple-choice questions. Using the Pearson IT Certification Practice Test engine, you can either study by going through the questions in Study Mode, or take a simulated exam that mimics real exam conditions. You can also serve up questions in a Flash Card Mode, which will display just the question and no answers, challenging you to state the answer in your own words before checking the actual answers to verify your work.

The installation process requires two major steps: installing the software and then activating the exam. The CD in the back of this book has a recent copy of the Pearson IT Certification Practice Test engine. The practice exam—the database of exam questions—is not on the CD.

Note

The cardboard CD case in the back of this book includes the CD and a piece of paper. The paper lists the activation code for the practice exam associated with this book. Do not lose the activation code. On the opposite side of the paper from the activation code is a unique, one-time-use coupon code for the purchase of the Premium Edition eBook and Practice Test.

Install the Software from the CD

The Pearson IT Certification Practice Test is a Windows-only desktop application. You can run it on a Mac using a Windows virtual machine, but it was built specifically for the PC platform. The minimum system requirements are as follows:

- Windows XP (SP3), Windows Vista (SP2), Windows 7, or Windows 8
- Microsoft .NET Framework 4.0 Client
- Pentium class 1GHz processor (or equivalent)
- 512MB RAM
- 650MB disc space plus 50MB for each downloaded practice exam

The software installation process is pretty routine as compared with other software installation processes. If you have already installed the Pearson IT Certification Practice Test software from another Pearson product, there is no need for you to reinstall the software. Simply launch the software on your desktop and proceed to activate the practice exam from this book by using the activation code included in the CD sleeve.

The following steps outline the installation process:

1. Insert the CD into your PC.
2. The media interface that automatically runs allows you to access and use all CD-based features, including the exam engine and sample content from other Cisco self-study products. From the main menu, click the Install the Exam Engine option.
3. Respond to windows prompts as with any typical software installation process.

The installation process gives you the option to activate your exam with the activation code supplied on the paper in the CD sleeve. This process requires that you establish a Pearson website login. You will need this login to activate the exam, so please do register when prompted. If you already have a Pearson website login, there is no need to register again. Just use your existing login.

Activate and Download the Practice Exam

Once the exam engine is installed, you should then activate the exam associated with this book (if you did not do so during the installation process) as follows:

1. Start the Pearson IT Certification Practice Test software from the Windows Start menu or from your desktop shortcut icon.
2. To activate and download the exam associated with this book, from the My Products or Tools tab, click the Activate Exam button.
3. At the next screen, enter the activation key from paper inside the cardboard CD holder in the back of the book. Once entered, click the Activate button.
4. The activation process will download the practice exam. Click Next, and then click Finish.

Once the activation process is completed, the My Products tab should list your new exam. If you do not see the exam, make sure that you have selected the My Products tab on the menu. At this point, the software and practice exam are ready to use. Simply select the exam and click the Open Exam button.

To update a particular exam you have already activated and downloaded, select the Tools tab and click the Update Products button. Updating your exams will ensure you have the latest changes and updates to the exam data.

If you want to check for updates to the Pea Pearson IT Certification Practice Test engine software, simply select the Tools tab and click the Update Application button. This will ensure that you are running the latest version of the software engine.

Activating Other Exams

The exam software installation process, and the registration process, only has to happen once. Then, for each new exam, only a few steps are required. For instance, if you buy another new Pearson IT Certification Cert Guide, extract the activation code from the CD sleeve in the back of that book; you don't even need the CD at this point. From there, all you have to do is start the exam engine (if not still up and running), and perform steps 2 through 4 from the previous list.

Contacting the Authors

We've tried to create a real-world tool that you can use to prepare for and pass the CCNA certification exams. We're interested in any feedback you would care to share about the book, especially if you have ideas about how we can improve it for future test takers. We'll consider everything you say carefully and will respond to all reasonable suggestions and comments. You can reach us via email at examcram@mikevalentine.ca and keithb@hurry.ws

Let us know if you found this book to be helpful in your preparation efforts. We'd also like to know how you felt about your chances of passing the exam before you read the book and then after you read the book. Of course, we'd love to hear that you passed the exam—and even if you just want to share your triumph, we'd be happy to hear from you.

Thanks for choosing us as your personal trainers, and enjoy the book. We would wish you luck on the exam, but we know that if you read through all the chapters and work with the product, you won't need luck—you'll pass the test on the strength of real knowledge!

Self-Assessment

This section helps you to determine your readiness for the Cisco Certified Network Associate (CCNA) certification exam. You will be invited to assess your own skills, motivations, education, and experience and see how you compare against the thousands of CCNA candidates we have met.

> **Tip**
>
> You can also pre-assess your CCNA readiness by using the accompanying DVD.

CCNA in the Real World

The Cisco Certified Network Associate remains one of the most popular certifications in the IT industry. Although Cisco does not publish certification statistics for CCNA, it is safe to say that thousands of new CCNAs are minted each year from all over the world. In the face of a backlash against so-called paper-only certification holders, Cisco has worked hard to maintain the credibility of its certifications by making them difficult to achieve, as well as ensuring that the exams test not only their own products and services but also general networking knowledge. In the past few years, Cisco has added router and switch simulators to computer-based tests to test the applied knowledge of candidates, and we can expect this trend to continue. A Cisco certification is still the gold standard for networking professionals.

A candidate who has passed the CCNA has demonstrated three significant capabilities:

- **A mastery of technical knowledge:** The successful CCNA candidate knows the technical material and has an elevated level of retention and accuracy. The CCNA exam has a pass mark of 849 out of 1,000. Very little room for technical error exists. Successful candidates know their stuff.

- **A demonstrated ability to apply the technical knowledge:** The addition of simulator questions has greatly reduced the possibility that a candidate can simply memorize all the information and pass the exam. A CCNA is supposed to be able to apply basic router and switch configurations; the simulator questions help prove that the candidate can do so.
- **The ability to perform under pressure:** The CCNA exams require that you proceed at a fairly rapid pace, spending about 1 minute per question on average. Many candidates find that they have little time left when they finish, and indeed many run out of time altogether—and some fail as a result. Add to this the stress of being in an exam environment, the potential of having an employer's performance expectations, personal expectations, and possibly financial or career implications pressuring you as well, and the exam turns into a pressure cooker. All of this is intimidating—and unfortunate for the unprepared—so be prepared.

Imagine yourself as an employer looking for a junior networking professional. You want someone who knows his or her stuff, who can reliably do the actual work of setting up and configuring equipment, and who can do all that under the pressures of time, screaming bosses and customers, and critical deadlines. Enter the successful CCNA candidate.

The Ideal CCNA Candidate

Other than a photographic memory, typing speed that would make Mavis Beacon jealous, and nerves of steel, what makes for the "ideal" CCNA candidate? A combination of skills and experience is the short answer. The successful candidates we have seen—and we have seen thousands from classes that we have taught—had a good mix of the following traits:

- **Motivation:** Why are you taking the CCNA? Here are some of the most common answers to this question that we have seen:
    - Because I want to further my career and get a promotion.
    - To expand my knowledge; I'm interested in it.
    - My job is changing, and the company needs me to get the certification.
    - I am unemployed and/or starting a new career.
    - The company needs more Cisco-certified people to gain a certain partner status as a reseller.

- We're just burning the training budget for this year.
- I've heard that the computer industry is a good field and that a CCNA guarantees you $85,000 a year.

So what motivates you? Who is paying for the training and exams? What are the implications if you fail? Successful candidates are highly motivated. If you don't care, your chances of passing drop tremendously.

- **An interest in learning and an ability to learn:** Passing a CCNA exam requires taking on board a great deal of new information, much of it obscure and without a referential pattern to make it easier to recall. Candidates who have acquired the skills to do this—and rest assured, these are skills that can be learned—will do better than those who have trouble retaining information. Candidates who simply enjoy learning will find it easier and will do better as a result.

  If you have trouble retaining and recalling information quickly and accurately, you will find CCNA certification a difficult thing to achieve. This book is not aimed at teaching you these skills; other books are. In the absence of the ability to learn and retain quickly, patience and persistence are a good substitute. If it takes you a year to pass, you have still passed.

- **A decent background in IP networking:** *Decent* is intentionally vague. We have seen candidates with little experience succeed and candidates with extensive experience fail. Experience is not a guarantee, but it absolutely helps. Many CCNA questions test the basics of networking; many others assume that you know the basics and incorporate the requirement of that knowledge into a more advanced question (the old "question-within-a-question" trick). As a guideline, if you have been involved with business-class networks for about a year, you will probably have absorbed enough knowledge to give you an advantage when it comes to the basics. After a certain point, experience can be a weakness: In the immortal words of Han Solo, "Don't get cocky." If you think that CCNA will be easy because you have 10 years of experience, you are in for a rude awakening.

Put Yourself to the Test

Now is the time to take a close look at your education, experience, motivation, and abilities. It's worth being honest with yourself; being aware of your weaknesses is as important as being aware of your strengths. Maybe you know someone who can help you with an objective assessment (a friend, a teacher, or an HR person perhaps). Above all, realize that the following questions and comments simply summarize our experience with CCNA candidates. That experience is pretty solid; we have taught CCNA to more than a thousand people. By the same token, though, there is no magic formula; every person is a different story. Your best plan is to be as prepared as you can be in all respects. Now, time to look inward.

Educational Background

Although in theory anyone can attempt the CCNA exam, in reality some are better prepared than others. Educational background forms a big part of this preparation. These questions will help to identify education and training that will be of benefit:

1. Have you ever taken any computer science courses at a college level?

   Most college-level IT courses include an element of networking theory. Also, if you are taking this kind of course, you are probably already interested in this topic and will find it easier to master the basics and pick up the advanced stuff. If you have never taken an IT course at this level, you have a steeper learning curve and might be at a disadvantage.

2. Did you attend college and major in a computer-related field?

   If so, you should have most of the basics covered—unless you studied programming; in which case, you might not have covered much in the way of networking. Some colleges actually offer the CCNA as part of the curriculum. Doing a college major in IT is not a prerequisite by any means, but it might be helpful.

3. Have you ever held an IT certification?

   If you have been certified before, you have some idea of what is coming in terms of the depth of knowledge required and the examination process; it also implies at least some involvement in computers and networking.

4. Which certifications have you held?

   A previous CCNA will definitely be an asset—but not a guarantee. The CCNA has changed dramatically in the past 3 years. Previous certification in general networking (perhaps a NET+), or an MCSE, will cover the basics, but not the Cisco-specific information. On the flip side, a certification in Visual Basic or Oracle might not be very helpful for CCNA.

5. Do you currently hold any IT certifications?

   Current information is more relevant—especially in the IT world. Some certifications are more relevant than others, of course, as noted previously.

6. Which certifications do you currently hold?

   You might hold other Cisco specialization certifications, or current certifications from Microsoft, CompTIA, or Novell. Again, anything that has tested your networking knowledge will be an asset.

7. Have you ever taken any IT training courses in networking?

   Many people take training courses but do not certify. Any exposure and knowledge gained from these courses will be useful.

8. How much self-study have you done?

   Although it is difficult to do pure self-study and pass the new CCNA, the more you study, the better the chances are that you will retain information. In our experience, it is always more productive to get some training—whether online, with a mentor/tutor, or from a training company—but a significant amount of self-study is always required regardless. The fact that you are holding this book is a very good sign. Read all of it!

9. How long have you been studying for your CCNA?

   This is a tricky equation. The longer you study, the more you are likely to know—but the more you are likely to forget, as well.

10. Is there a formal or informal training plan for you at your workplace?

    Work experience is a great way to gain the knowledge and skills you need for the exam. A training plan can be a good motivator because you might have someone coaching and encouraging you and also because there may be a reward—perhaps a promotion or raise—for completing the program.

Hands-On Experience

It is the rare individual who really understands networks but has never built, broken, and then rebuilt one. For the CCNA exam, a certain amount of hands-on experience is a must. The new simulator questions require you to actually type in router configurations. Ask yourself the following:

1. Does your job allow you to work with Cisco routers and switches on a regular basis?

2. Is there a lab where you can practice? Perhaps at home with borrowed or purchased gear?

3. How long have you been working with Cisco equipment?

4. Are you completely fluent in subnetting?

At a minimum, you should get a simulator that includes lab exercises for you to practice key skills. If you have access to a lab and equipment you can play with, as you become more advanced, you can build more complicated and realistic test networks.

The major skill areas in which you need hands-on experience include the following:

- Basic configuration (IP addresses, passwords)
- Subnetting
- Dynamic routing protocol configuration
- NAT/PAT (Network/Port Address Translation)
- Basic WAN protocols and configuration
- Switching, VLANs, VLAN Trunking Protocol, trunking
- IP access lists

As you think about those areas, picture yourself in front of a Cisco router and assess your level of confidence in being able to quickly and correctly configure it. You should feel no intimidation or uncertainty in being able to tackle these kinds of configurations. Subnetting in particular is heavily emphasized and is one of the main areas where people have difficulty. You must be totally, unequivocally confident with subnetting; otherwise, you will face a serious challenge on your exam.

Testing Your Exam Readiness

The CCNA exam will demand a high degree of technical accuracy, applied skill, and the ability to perform quickly under pressure. You can give yourself experience in this environment by practicing on an exam simulator until you are comfortable. You must become technically accurate to about 90% to 95%, have no difficulty with the simulator tasks, and be able to complete the exam in the appropriate time frame. This can be achieved by repetition, but be careful that you do not simply memorize all the questions in the test pool!

Assessing Your Readiness for the CCNA Exam

There are three "pillars" of success on the CCNA exam: technical excellence, applied skills, and the ability to perform under pressure. Technical excellence is achieved with study, training, and self-testing. Applied skills are learned through practice labs and exams, work experience, and hands-on training and experience. The ability to perform under pressure is gained from situational training such as exam simulators and challenge labs, perhaps with a trainer or mentor. The goal is to increase your confidence level so that you feel as if you own the material and want to be challenged to a duel by the exam.

With a combination of educational and work experience, CCNA-specific training, self-study, and hands-on practice, you will put yourself in the best position to approach the exam with a high degree of confidence—and pass. Good luck; study hard.

CHAPTER ONE

Networking Fundamentals

This chapter covers the following official CCNA Routing and Switching 200-120 exam topics:

- ▶ Recognize the purpose and functions of various network devices such as routers, switches, bridges, and hubs.
- ▶ Select the components required to meet a given network specification.
- ▶ Identify the appropriate media, cables, ports, and connectors to connect Cisco network devices to other network devices and hosts in a LAN.
- ▶ Determine the technology and media access control method for Ethernet networks.

A qualified CCNA is expected to have a broad understanding of different network technologies and a more detailed knowledge of a few specific ones. This chapter introduces the basics of networking and points out some of the concepts that are tested on the CCNA Routing and Switching 200-120 exam.

Essential Terms and Components

- **Network topologies**
- **Ethernet**
- **WAN technologies**

CramSaver

If you can correctly answer these questions before going through this section, save time by skimming the Exam Alerts in this section and then completing the Cram Quiz at the end of the section.

1. Which of the following topologies can apply to Ethernet?
   - **A.** Star
   - **B.** Bus
   - **C.** Cross
   - **D.** Mesh

2. Which of the following are advantages of star-wired, full-duplex Ethernet on UTP? Choose all that apply.
   - **A.** No collisions
   - **B.** Greater throughput
   - **C.** Dedicated communication per link
   - **D.** Microsegmentation
   - **E.** Simultaneous send and receive

Answers

1. A, B, and D are correct. C is wrong because "cross" is not a valid topology type.
2. All answers are correct. Star-wired, full-duplex Ethernet eliminates collisions, provides greater throughput (in no small part because of simultaneous send and receive and zero collisions). Dedicated communication means each port connects to only one host, also known as microsegmentation.

A *network* is a set of devices, software, and cables that enables the exchange of information between them. *Host devices* are computers, servers, laptops, tablets, and smartphones, or anything a person uses to access the network. *Network devices* are hubs, repeaters, bridges, switches, routers, and firewalls (to name a few). Cables can be copper, fiber optic, or even wireless radio (which isn't really a cable, but serves the same purpose). The applications used on a network include those that actually enable network connectivity, such as the Transmission Control Protocol/Internet Protocol (TCP/IP), those that test network links, such as the Internet Control Message Protocol (ICMP), and end-user applications, such as email and File Transfer Protocol (FTP). There are thousands of networkable applications; we are concerned with a small number of them.

Topologies

A topology describes the layout of a network. You need to know several topologies for the exam, including the following:

- **Point to point**: A point-to-point topology involves two hosts or devices that are directly connected to each other and to nothing else; anything sent by one can be received only by the other. Serial communication is usually point to point, but not always.
- **Star**: A star topology is one in which one host or device has multiple connections to other hosts; this is sometimes called hub-and-spoke. In a star topology, if a host wants to send to another host, it must send traffic through the hub or central device. Ethernet, if using a hub or a switch and twisted-pair cabling, is star wired.
- **Ring**: A ring topology is created when one device is connected to the next one sequentially, with the last device being connected to the first. The actual devices don't necessarily form a circle, but the data moves in a logical circle. Fiber Distributed Data Interface (FDDI) and Token Ring are examples of ring topologies.
- **Bus**: A bus topology uses a single coaxial cable, to which hosts are attached at intervals. The term *bus* comes from an electrical bus, which is a point from which electrical power can be drawn for multiple connections. Ethernet that uses coaxial cable creates a bus topology.
- **Mesh**: A *full mesh* is a topology with multiple point-to-point connections that connect each location to the others. The advantage is that you can send data directly from any location to any other location instead of having to send it through a central point. There are more options for sending if one of the connections fails. The disadvantages are that it is expensive and complex to implement a full mesh. You can compromise and build a *partial mesh*, which is when only some locations are connected to the other locations.

Figure 1.1 shows each these topologies in a typical diagram.

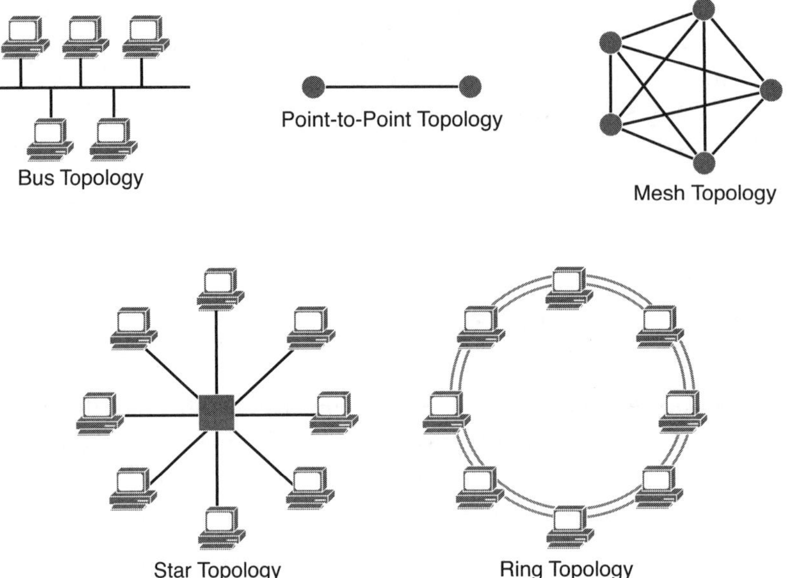

FIGURE 1.1 **Network topologies.**

Ethernet

LAN stands for local-area network. LANs are short-range, high-speed networks typically found in schools, offices, and homes. Over the years, there have been many types of LANs. Currently, Ethernet is king, and it is the only LAN technology you need to know for the CCENT and CCNA exams.

Ethernet is the most common LAN technology in use today. It is a family of implementations, which have evolved into faster and more reliable solutions all based on a common technology.

Ethernet was pioneered by Digital Equipment Corporation, Intel, and Xerox and first published in 1980. The IEEE modified it and gave it the specification 802.3. The way Ethernet works is closely linked to its original connection type: A coaxial cable was used to join all the hosts together. This formed a segment. On a single segment, only one host could use the cable at a time; because the wire was coaxial, with one positive conductor and one negative conductor, it created a single electrical circuit. This single circuit could be energized by only one host at a time, or a conflict would result as two hosts tried to talk at once and nothing got through. Much the same thing happens when you and a friend try to send at the same time using walkie-talkies; all that is heard is noise. This conflict is called a *collision*.

CSMA/CD (carrier sense multiple access with collision detection) is the method Ethernet uses to deal with collisions. When a host wants to transmit, it first listens to the wire to see whether anyone else is transmitting at that moment. If it is clear, it can transmit; if not, it waits for the host that is transmitting to stop. Sometimes, two hosts decide at the same instant that the wire is clear and collide with each other. When this happens, the hosts that were involved with the collision send a special jam signal that advises everyone on that segment of the collision. Then all the hosts wait for a random period of time before they check the wire and try transmitting again. This wait time is tiny—a few thousandths of a second—and is determined by the backoff algorithm. (The backoff algorithm is the mathematical equation a host runs to come up with the random number.) The theory is that if each host waits a different amount of time, the wire should be clear for all of them when they decide to transmit again.

Any Ethernet segment that uses coaxial cable (10BASE-2, 10BASE-5) or a hub with twisted-pair cabling is a collision environment.

Exam**Alert**

When a collision occurs

1. A jam signal is sent.
2. All hosts briefly stop transmitting.
3. All hosts run the backoff algorithm, which decides the random time they will wait before attempting to transmit again.

Collisions have the effect of clogging up a network because they prevent data from being sent. The more hosts you have sharing a wire, and the more data they have to send, the worse it gets. A group of devices that are affected by one another's collisions is called a *collision domain*. As networks grew, it became necessary to break up collision domains so that there were fewer collisions in each one. Devices called bridges and switches did this; these devices are covered in Chapter 6, "Basic Switch Operations and Configuration."

It is possible to eliminate collisions altogether if we can provide separate send and receive circuits; this is more like a telephone (which allows us to speak and hear at the same time) than a walkie-talkie. This requires four conductors—a positive and negative pair for each circuit. The use of twisted-pair cabling (not coax), which has at least four conductors (and more likely eight) allows us to create a full-duplex connection, with simultaneous send and receive circuits. Full-duplex connections eliminate collisions because the host can now send and receive simultaneously. A switch that has a host connected to each port, with full-duplex connections for each host, is said to be *microsegmented*, which is a cool word that means there are no collisions because every segment has only one sender and one receiver (the host and the switch). This is a very good thing to have in a network.

Modern Ethernet is fast, reliable, and collision free if you set it up right. Speeds of up to 40Gbps are possible with the correct cabling.

Table 1.1 summarizes some of the different Ethernet specifications, characteristics, and cable types. This is not all of them—just an idea of how far Ethernet has come.

TABLE 1.1 **Comparing Ethernet Implementations**

IEEE	Cabling	Topology	Speed/Duplex/ Media	Maximum Range
802.3	10BASE-5	Bus	10Mbs Half duplex Thicknet	500m
802.3	10BASE-2	Bus	10Mbs Half duplex Thinnet	185m
802.3	10/100-BASE T	Star	10/100Mbs Half duplex UTP	100m
802.3u	100-BASE T	Star	100Mbs Half/Full duplex UTP	100m
802.3u	100-BASE FX	Star	100Mbs Full duplex Multimode fiber optic	400m
802.3ab	1000-BASE T	Star	1000Mbs Full duplex UTP	100m
802.3z	1000-BASE ZX	Star	1000Mbs Full duplex Single-mode fiber optic	100km

You should be familiar with the contents of Table 1.1.

WAN Technologies

A wide-area network (WAN) serves to interconnect two or more LANs. WAN technology is designed to extend network connectivity to much greater distances than any LAN technology can. Most companies can't afford to build their own WAN, so it is usual to buy WAN service from a service provider. Service providers are in the business of building and selling WAN connectivity; they invest in the equipment, cabling, and training to build transcontinental networks for other businesses to rent. For the CCNA exam, you need to be familiar with four types of WAN connections and the protocols associated with them. WAN connectivity and configuration is covered in detail in Chapter 15, "WAN Operation." The four WAN connection types are outlined in the following sections.

Dedicated Leased-Line Connections

A leased line refers to a connection that is installed and provisioned for the exclusive use of the customer. Essentially, when you order a leased line, you get your very own piece of wire from your location to the service provider's network. This is good because no other customer can affect your line, as can be the case with other WAN services. You have a lot of control over this circuit to do things such as quality of service and other traffic management. The downside is that a leased line is expensive and gets a lot more expensive if you need to connect offices that are far apart.

A leased line is usually a point-to-point connection from the head office to a branch office. So if you need to connect to multiple locations, you need multiple leased lines. Multiple leased lines get even more expensive. Leased-line circuits usually run the Point-to-Point Protocol (PPP), High-Level Data-Link Control Protocol (HDLC), or possibly Serial Line Internet Protocol (SLIP). (These protocols are covered in detail in Chapter 15).

Circuit-Switched Connections

A circuit-switched WAN uses the phone company as the service provider, either with analog dialup or digital ISDN connections. With circuit-switching, if you need to connect to the remote LAN, a call is dialed, and a circuit is established. The data is sent across the circuit, and the circuit is taken down when it is no longer needed. Circuit-switched WANs usually use PPP, HDLC, or SLIP, and they tend to be really slow—anywhere from 19.2K for analog dialup to 128K for ISDN using a Basic Rate Interface (BRI). They can also get expensive because most contracts specify a pay-per-usage billing.

Packet-Switched Connections

Packet-switched WAN services allow you to connect to the provider's network in much the same way as a PC connects to a hub: When connected, your traffic is affected by other customers' and theirs by you. This can be an issue sometimes, but it can be managed. The advantage of this shared-bandwidth technology is that with a single physical connection from your router's serial port (usually), you can establish virtual connections to many other locations around the world. So, if you have a lot of branch offices and they are far away from the head office, a packet-switched solution is a good idea. Packet-switched circuits usually use Frame Relay or possibly X.25.

Cell-Switched Connections

Cell switching is similar to packet switching; the difference is that with packet-switched networks, the size of the units of data being sent (called *frames*) is variable. Cell-switched units (*cells*) are of a constant size. This makes dealing with heavy traffic loads easier and more efficient. Cell-switched solutions such as Asynchronous Transfer Mode (ATM) tend to be big, fast, and robust.

Wireless Networks

The impact of wireless networks for both LAN and WAN applications has, of course, been huge. The IEEE 802.11 standard, known as Wi-Fi (a play on Hi-Fi or *high fidelity*, wireless fidelity becomes Wi-Fi) specifies an ever-expanding set of standards for short-range, high-speed wireless systems that are good for everything from mobile device connectivity to home media center systems. The advantages are the elimination of cables and the freedom of movement. The disadvantages are in range, reliability, and security. Wireless is a good WAN choice for moderate distances (less than 15 kilometers, typically) with line-of-sight between them (for example, between buildings in a campus). Special antennas are used to make the wireless signal directional and increase the range, often to more than 20 kilometers.

The Internet as a WAN

We are all aware of the impact of the Internet on our culture. Its impact on our technical world has been similarly dramatic. Among other things, it has bent the definition of WAN away from the traditional services of leased lines and packet- or circuit-switched circuits to one that includes virtual private networks (VPNs), digital subscriber line (DSL), cable, and wireless LTE (a.k.a. 4G)—and it keeps evolving. Now there are many people who have never accessed the Internet using a "traditional" WAN, and others who have never used a

traditional WAN at all. It is increasingly likely that your WAN service is an Ethernet connection to the Internet. The Internet is an entirely valid choice as a WAN provision, and in fact has some advantages in terms of speed, lower cost, and wider availability than many traditional WAN services.

Cram Quiz

1. What technology is fast superseding Frame Relay as a low-cost, high-bandwidth WAN option?

   ❍ **A.** Satellite

   ❍ **B.** Over-the-Horizon longwave radio

   ❍ **C.** X.25

   ❍ **D.** Wi-Fi

   ❍ **E.** VPN over the Internet

2. Gary is showing off his home network, which is wired using thinnet coaxial cabling. Which of the following are characteristic of coaxial-cabled Ethernet? Choose three.

   ❍ **A.** Collisions

   ❍ **B.** Full duplex

   ❍ **C.** Half duplex

   ❍ **D.** Jam sessions

   ❍ **E.** Backoff algorithms

   ❍ **F.** Microsegmentation

Cram Quiz Answers

1. E is correct. A is wrong because satellite is neither low-cost nor high-bandwidth. B can be high bandwidth, but at spectacular cost. X.25 is not high bandwidth, and is largely obsolete so probably not available regardless of cost. Wi-Fi has reasonable bandwidth, and at low cost, but its range is very limited, making it unsuitable for most WAN applications.
2. A, C and E are the correct answers. B is wrong because coaxial Ethernet cannot be full duplex. (It has only a single circuit.) D is wrong, perhaps you thought or read “jam signals.” Jam sessions are different, generally involving musical instruments and endless versions of 12-bar blues. Microsegmentation is only possible on a switch using star-wired UTP, not coax.

Review Questions

1. Your boss asks you to explain what happens when a collision occurs on an Ethernet segment. Which of the following are accurate? Choose three.
   - ❍ **A.** Every device stops transmitting for a short time.
   - ❍ **B.** When it is safe to transmit again, the devices that collided get priority access to the wire.
   - ❍ **C.** The collision starts a random backoff algorithm.
   - ❍ **D.** A jam signal is sent to alert all devices of the collision.
   - ❍ **E.** Only the devices involved in the collision stop transmitting briefly to clear the wire.

2. How is equal access to the wire managed in a collision-oriented environment such as Ethernet?
   - ❍ **A.** The hosts are given equal access based on the circulation of a token; hosts can only transmit when they hold the token.
   - ❍ **B.** Hosts are given prioritized access to the wire based on their MAC address.
   - ❍ **C.** Hosts are given equal access to the wire by being allowed to transmit at specified time intervals.
   - ❍ **D.** Hosts signal their desire to transmit by sending a contention alert.
   - ❍ **E.** Hosts check the wire for activity before attempting to send; if a collision happens, they wait a random time period before attempting to send again.

3. Which of the following are commonly used WAN protocols? Choose three.
   - ❍ **A.** WEP
   - ❍ **B.** WING
   - ❍ **C.** Frame Relay
   - ❍ **D.** HDLC
   - ❍ **E.** AAA
   - ❍ **F.** PPP

4. Which of the following are IEEE specifications for Gigabit Ethernet? Choose two.
   - ❍ **A.** 802.1d
   - ❍ **B.** 802.11
   - ❍ **C.** 802.3z
   - ❍ **D.** 802.1Q
   - ❍ **E.** 802.3ab

5. Which technology is cell switched?

❍ **A.** Token Ring
❍ **B.** FDDI
❍ **C.** Ethernet
❍ **D.** Frame Relay
❍ **E.** ATM
❍ **F.** PPP

6. Which devices were designed to segment collision domains? Choose two.

❍ **A.** Hubs
❍ **B.** Repeaters
❍ **C.** MAUs
❍ **D.** Bridges
❍ **E.** Switches

7. You have just acquired some new office space in a building across the street from your current space, about 350 meters away. You want to arrange for high-speed (10Mbs) network connectivity between them; which of the following choices is a valid connection option?

❍ **A.** Analog dialup
❍ **B.** ISDN BRI
❍ **C.** Ethernet using 100BASE-TX cabling
❍ **D.** An Ethernet connection to a cable Internet service that supports a site-to-site VPN

8. Which WAN technology is the best choice if you have many remote offices that are in different states, you need always-on connectivity, and you don't have money to burn?

❍ **A.** Circuit switched
❍ **B.** Leased line
❍ **C.** Packet switched
❍ **D.** Wireless

Answers to Review Questions

1. Answers A, C, and D are correct. B is incorrect because there is no method to prioritize access to the wire in Ethernet. Answer E is incorrect because all devices stop transmitting in the event of a collision.
2. Answer is E correct. CSMA/CD is the technology that enables hosts to send if the wire is available and to wait a random time to try again if a collision happens. Answer A is incorrect because it describes Token Ring, not Ethernet. Answers B, C, and D are incorrect because they are fictitious.
3. Answers C, D, and F are correct. The big three WAN protocols are PPP, Frame Relay, and HDLC. There are others, but CCNA does not cover them. Answer A is incorrect because WEP is Wired Equivalent Privacy, a security scheme for wireless networks. Answer B is incorrect because it is fictional. Answer E is incorrect because AAA stands for authentication, authorization, and accounting, a scheme to manage access and activities on networked devices.
4. Answers C and E are correct. 802.3z specifies 1Gb on fiber, and 802.3ab specifies 1Gb on copper. Answers A, B, and D are incorrect; those are the specs for STP, Wi-Fi, and Inter-Switch VLAN tagging, respectively.
5. Answer E is correct. ATM is a cell-switched technology. Answers A, B, C, D, and F are incorrect because they use variable-sized frames, not cells.
6. Answers D and E are correct. Bridges and switches segment collision domains. Answers A and B are incorrect because hubs and repeaters have the opposite effect: They make collision domains bigger and more of a problem.
7. Answer D is correct. A cable Internet connection with a 10BASE-T or 100BASE-T Ethernet interface that supports a VPN is a valid choice. Answers A and B are incorrect because analog and ISDN BRI do not provide the required bandwidth. Answer C is incorrect because 100BASE-TX is copper cabling, which has a maximum range of 100 meters. (You might be able to go with Ethernet over fiber-optic cabling, but it is expensive—and it is not one of the offered choices here anyway.)
8. Answer C is the correct answer. Packet-switched networks are a good choice in this context. Answer A is incorrect; circuit-switched connections are a poor choice because they are not usually always on, and they get expensive the longer they are connected. Answer B is incorrect because leased lines have always-on connectivity, but at a prohibitive cost. Answer D is incorrect; wireless does not have the range to cover interstate distances.

What Next?

If you want more practice on this chapter's exam topics before you move on, remember that you can access all of the Cram Quiz questions on the CD. You can also create a custom exam by topic with the practice exam software. Note any topic you struggle with and go to that topic's material in this chapter.

CHAPTER TWO

Network Models

This chapter covers the following official CCNA Routing and Switching 200-120 exam topics:

- Describe the purpose and basic operation of the protocols in the OSI and TCP/IP models.
- Predict the data flow between two hosts across a network.
- Identify common applications and their impact on the network.

Any complex operation requires a certain degree of structure to be understood. When dealing with millions of individuals all designing and building programs, protocols, and equipment that is intended to network together, the use of a theoretical model as a basis for understanding and interoperability is critical. This chapter reviews the Open Systems Interconnection (OSI) model and compares it to the TCP/IP model. In addition, the chapter also mentions the Cisco three-layer hierarchical model. All of these models are tested, and a strong understanding of the OSI model is necessary for success on the exam (in addition to being useful in the real world).

Cisco Hierarchical Design

CramSaver

1. What are two advantages of a hierarchical network design? Choose two.
   - **A.** Broadcast domain segmentation
   - **B.** Scalability
   - **C.** Volume pricing discounts on equipment purchases
   - **D.** Easier troubleshooting

2. In the traditional three-layer hierarchical model, in which layer are routers most likely to be located?
   - **A.** Access
   - **B.** Distribution
   - **C.** Core

Answers

1. Answers B and D are correct. A is wrong because although broadcast domain segmentation is a good thing, it is not a specific advantage related to the three-layer hierarchical model. C is wrong because although less-expensive equipment is also a good thing, it too is not a specific advantage related to the three-layer hierarchical model.
2. Answer B is correct. In the traditional three-layer hierarchical model, routers are most likely to be located in the Distribution layer.

Cisco has created a reference model for the functions its equipment performs. The three-layer hierarchical model describes the major functional roles in any network and provides a basis for understanding and troubleshooting scalable networks. Figure 2.1 shows a representation of the three-layer model with switches and routers in their typical layers. The following sections describe each layer in more detail.

Access Layer

The access layer is the point that connects end users to the network. This can be achieved by a hub or switch to which PCs are connected, a wireless access point, a remote office connection, a dialup service, or a virtual private network (VPN) tunnel from the Internet into the corporate network.

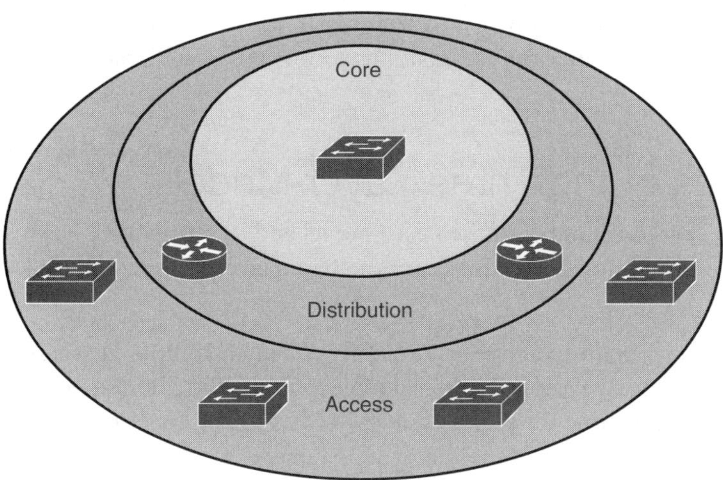

FIGURE 2.1 **The three-layer hierarchical design.**

Distribution Layer

The distribution layer provides routing, packet filtering, WAN access, and QoS (quality of service). The access layer devices (usually switches) connect to a router so that traffic can be routed to another network. Packet filtering refers to the use of access control lists to identify certain types of traffic and control where it might go—or block it altogether. (We look at ACLs in detail in Chapter 13, "Advanced Router Operation.")

Traditional WAN access usually involves a specialized interface—perhaps a serial port or Integrated Services Digital Network (ISDN) Primary Rate Interface controller. These specialized functions are found on distribution layer devices such as routers. If our network needs to use QoS features to make it run well, these features are typically first implemented at the distribution layer.

If our network includes different LAN technologies (Token Ring, Fiber-Distributed Data Interchange, and Ethernet, for example), the translation between these different media types is usually done by a distribution layer device. Because these devices are typically routers and Layer 3 switches, this is also where broadcast domain segmentation happens.

Core Layer

The core layer is all about speed. Here, we typically find big, fast switches that move the data from the distribution layer to centralized resources such as mail and database servers, or to other distribution layer devices, as quickly as possible. The core does not usually do any routing or packet filtering, but it might do QoS if that is an important part of the network (if using Voice over IP [VoIP], for example).

Advantages of the Three-Layer Model

The exam focuses on the benefits of the Cisco model and its particulars. Keep the following points in mind as advantages of the Cisco layered approach to networks:

- **Scalability:** If we want to add users, it is easy to put an additional access layer device in place, without having to replace all the distribution and core devices at the same time. It is easier to add extended functionality to one layer at a time as needed instead of all at once.
- **Cost savings:** An access layer device is much cheaper than a distribution or core device; also, by upgrading only one layer, we do not have to upgrade all three layers at once, incurring unnecessary costs.
- **Easier troubleshooting:** If a component at one layer fails, it will not affect the entire system. It is also easier to find the problem if the failed device affects only one layer.

Cram Quiz

1. Which of the following can be considered a typical access-layer connection? Choose all that apply:

   ❍ **A.** Frame-Relay

   ❍ **B.** WiFi

   ❍ **C.** Ethernet

   ❍ **D.** PPP leased line

2. In the traditional three-layer hierarchical model, in which layer would you apply security policies?

   ❍ **A.** Access

   ❍ **B.** Distribution

   ❍ **C.** Core

Cram Quiz Answers

1. Answers B and C are correct. A and D are wrong; Frame Relay and PPP leased lines are WAN services, not usually used as access layer connections. Don't get snarled up with ideas like "What if I used the PPP link to access the network, making it a part of an access layer connection?" Just answer the question.
2. Answer B is correct. In the traditional three-layer hierarchical model, you would apply security policies in the distribution layer. Although modern security principles and practices recommend additional security configurations at every layer, because the question is framed in the "traditional three-layer hierarchical model" context, it is safe to choose the simple answer, particularly because the other two are not as good.

OSI Model

CramSaver

1. Which three of the following are physical layer components?
   - **A.** Switch
   - **B.** NIC
   - **C.** RJ-45 connector
   - **D.** Hub
   - **E.** STP
2. True or false? Layer 3 provides hierarchical addressing.
3. What is the correct order of PDUs?
   - **A.** Packet, bits, frame, data, segment
   - **B.** Segment, data, frame, packet, bits
   - **C.** Data, segment, frame, packet, bits
   - **D.** Bits, frame, packet, segment, data
   - **E.** Data, segment, packet, bits, frame

Answers

1. Answers B, C and D are correct. Answer A is wrong because a switch is a Layer 2 device. Answer E is wrong because STP is a Layer 2 protocol.
2. True. Unlike Layer 2 (MAC) addressing. which is "flat," Layer 3 IP addressing provides for hierarchical address assignment.
3. Answer D is correct. Know this backward and forward!

The International Standards Organization (ISO) defined a seven-layer model to standardize networking processes. The Open Systems Interconnection (OSI) model facilitates the understanding of the complexities of networking by defining what happens at each step of the process.

You should be clear that the OSI model does not impose rules on network equipment manufacturers or protocol developers; rather, it sets guidelines for functions so that intervendor operability is possible and predictable.

Each of the seven layers in the model communicates with the layers above and below, using standardized coding at the beginning of the message that can be interpreted by another device regardless of who made it. So if a vendor decides that they want to build a network device, they have the option of building a unique, proprietary system and trying to convince people to buy it; or, they can build a device that works with other devices according to the OSI model.

The seven different layers break up the process of networking, making it easier to understand and to troubleshoot problems. It is possible to test the functionality of each layer in sequence, to determine where the problem is and where to begin repairs.

The seven layers, in order, are as follows:

7. Application
6. Presentation
5. Session
4. Transport
3. Network
2. Data link
1. Physical

ExamAlert

You must know the names of the layers, in order. Start memorizing! You could use a mnemonic; there are several, some of them unprintable, but this one works pretty well:

"All People Seem To Need Data Processing."

I don't know if Dave Minutella made that one up, but I'll give him the credit because he taught it to me.

Let's examine what happens at each layer as we send data to another computer.

Layer 7: The Application Layer

If you are using any program or utility that can store, send, or retrieve data over a network, it is a Layer 7 application. Layer 7 is sometimes called the user interface layer; for example, when you launch a web browser and type in an address, you are working with a network-aware application and instructing it what to do on the network—that is, go and retrieve this web page. The same thing happens when you save a document to a file server or start a Telnet connection—you create some data that is to be sent over the network to another computer. Some applications or protocols are "hidden" from the user; for example, when you send and receive email, you might use Microsoft Outlook, Eudora, or any other mail program you care to name, but the protocols that send and receive your mail are almost always going to be SMTP and POP3, or perhaps IMAP.

Be aware of the difference between an application that you use and the application layer of the OSI and TCP/IP models. Applications such as a web browser, Microsoft Word, and so on operate "above" the application layer of the OSI or TCP/IP model, but they send data down to the application layer to move it across the network.

The application layer protocols (and deciphered acronyms) that you should know are as follows:

- **HTTP (Hypertext Transfer Protocol):** Browses web pages.
- **FTP (File Transfer Protocol):** Reliably sends/retrieves all file types.
- **SMTP (Simple Mail Transfer Protocol):** Sends email.
- **POP3 (Post Office Protocol 3):** Retrieves email.
- **IMAP (Internet Message Access Protocol):** Sends and retrieves email with additional features/functionality.
- **NTP (Network Time Protocol):** Synchronizes networked device clocks.
- **SNMP (Simple Network Management Protocol):** Communicates status and allows control of networked devices.
- **TFTP (Trivial File Transfer Protocol):** Simple, lightweight file transfer.
- **DNS (Domain Naming System):** Translates a website name (easy for people) to an IP address (easy for computers).
- **DHCP (Dynamic Host Configuration Protocol):** Assigns IP, mask, and DNS server (plus a bunch of other stuff) to hosts.
- **Telnet:** Provides a remote terminal connection to manage devices to which you are not close enough to use a console cable.

ExamAlert

You should be ready to name any of the application layer protocols, as well as recognize them either by name or by acronym. This gets easier the more experience you have, because they are constantly mentioned in the context of everyday networking.

Layer 6: The Presentation Layer

The presentation layer is responsible for formatting data so that application layer protocols (and then the users) can recognize and work with it. If you think about file extensions—such as .doc, .jpg, .txt, .avi, and so on—you realize that each of these file types is formatted for use by a particular type of application. The presentation layer does this formatting, taking the application layer data and marking it with the formatting codes so that it can be viewed reliably when accessed later. The presentation layer can also do some types of encryption, but that is not as common as it used to be since there are better ways to encrypt that are easier on CPU and RAM resources.

Layer 5: The Session Layer

The session layer deals with initiating and terminating network connections. It provides instructions to connect, authenticate (optionally), and disconnect from a network resource. Common examples are the login part of a Telnet or SQL session (not the actual data movement) and Remote Procedure Call (RPC) functions. The actual movement of the data is handled by the lower layers.

Layer 4: The Transport Layer

The transport layer is possibly the most important layer for exam study purposes. A lot is going on here, and it is heavily tested.

The transport layer deals with exactly how two hosts are going to send data. The two main methods are called *connection-oriented* and *connectionless*. Connection-oriented transmission is said to be *reliable*, and connectionless is *unreliable*. Every network protocol stack will have a protocol that handles each style; in the TCP/IP stack, reliable transmission is done by *TCP*, and unreliable by *UDP*. Now, don't get too wrapped up in the term *unreliable*. This doesn't mean that the data isn't going to get there; it only means that it isn't *guaranteed* to get there.

Think of your options when you are sending a letter: You can pop it in an envelope, throw a stamp on it, and put it in the mailbox. Chances are good that it will get where it's supposed to go, but there is no guarantee, and stuff does go missing once in a while. However, it's cheap.

Your other choice is to use a courier—FedEx's motto used to be "When it absolutely, positively has to be there overnight." For this level of service, you have to buy a fancy envelope and put a bunch of extra labels on it to track where it is going and where it has been. But, you get a receipt when it is delivered, you are guaranteed delivery, and you can keep track of whether your shipment got to its destination. All of this costs you more—but it is reliable!

This analogy works perfectly when describing the difference between UDP and TCP: UDP is the post office, and TCP is FedEx. Let's look at this more closely, starting with TCP.

Reliable Communication with TCP

The key to reliable communication using TCP is the use of sequence and acknowledgment numbers. These numbers are attached to the various segments of information that are sent between two hosts to identify what order they should be assembled in to re-create the original data and to keep track of whether any segments went missing along the way. When a host sends a segment of data, it is labeled with a *sequence number* that identifies that segment and where it belongs in the series of segments being sent. When the receiving host gets that segment, it sends an acknowledgment back to the sender with an *acknowledgment number*; the value of this number is the sequence number of the last segment it received, plus one. In effect, the receiver is saying, "I got your last one, now I am ready for the next one."

The first step in establishing a reliable connection between hosts is the *three-way handshake*. This initial signaling allows hosts to exchange their starting sequence numbers and to test that they have reliable communication between them. Figure 2.2 illustrates the three-way handshake in TCP communication.

From this point, the sender continues to send segments of data. A process known as *PAR (positive acknowledgment and retransmission)* makes sure that all the segments get where they are going. Following are the three main elements of PAR:

1. The sender starts a timer when it sends a segment, and will retransmit that segment if the timer expires before an acknowledgment is received for that segment.

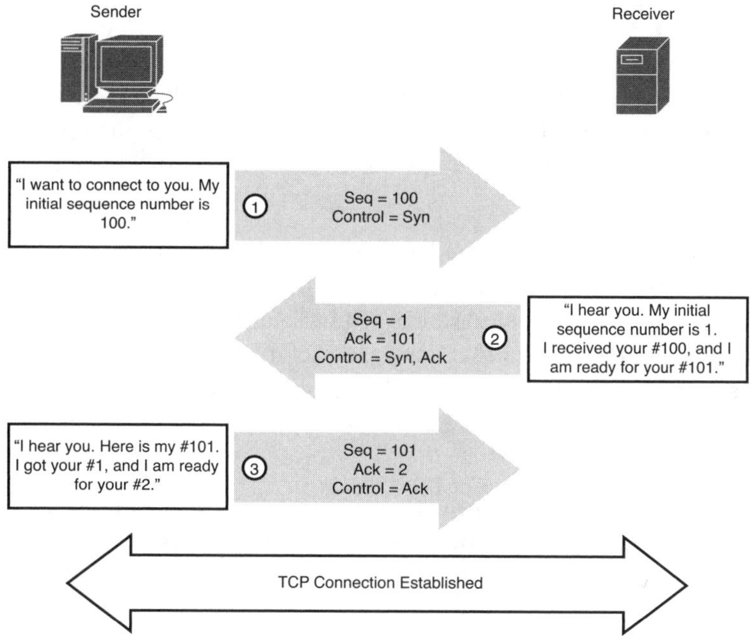

FIGURE 2.2 **The TCP three-way handshake.**

2. The sender keeps a record of all segments sent and expects an acknowledgment of each one.
3. The receiving device acknowledges the receipt of a segment by sending a segment back to the sender indicating the next sequence number it expects.

If any of the segments of data should go missing—perhaps due to interference, collisions, or a link failure—the sender will not receive an acknowledgment of it and will retransmit it. The sequence number enables the receiver to put all the segments back in the correct order.

> Exam**Alert**
>
> Know how the three-way handshake works.
>
> Know the elements of PAR.
>
> Understand that in TCP reliability is guaranteed by sequence and acknowledgment numbers and the ability to retransmit missing segments.

The TCP Sliding Window

Sometimes a receiver can get very busy—imagine a web server that is getting millions of hits an hour. If it receives more segments than it can handle, it might be forced to drop (discard) some; this is not desirable because the senders would then have to retransmit them; this wastes time and bandwidth and increases delay.

The receiver has a method to tell the sender(s) to slow down the transmission rate. It's called the *sliding window*. The window size indicates how many segments can be sent before an acknowledgment will be sent. If the receiver is not busy, it can handle a large number of segments and send a single acknowledgment. If the receiver gets very busy, it can make the window size very small, allowing the sender(s) to send only a few segments before an acknowledgment is sent.

The window size of the sender and receiver is included in the segment header and can change during the lifetime of the conversation. Figure 2.3 shows how the sliding window feature of TCP operates.

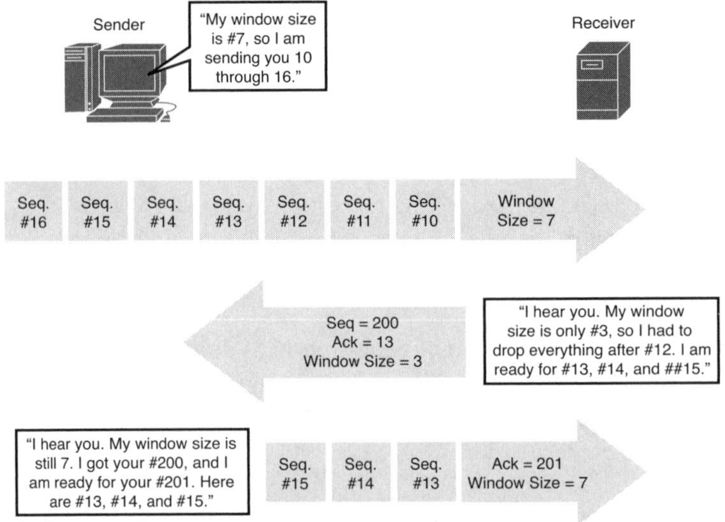

FIGURE 2.3 **The TCP sliding window controls how much data is sent before an acknowledgment is needed.**

ExamAlert

You must understand the definition and advantages of the TCP sliding window.

Port Numbers

Imagine a server that performs a number of functions—for example, email, web pages, FTP, and DNS. The server has a single IP address, but can perform all these different functions for all the hosts that want to connect to it. The transport layer (Layer 4) uses port numbers to distinguish between different types of traffic that might be headed for the same IP address.

Port numbers are divided into ranges by the Internet Assigned Naming Authority (IANA). The following are the current port ranges. (Note that the real world may ignore these ranges, but they are correct for exam purposes.)

0–1023	Well-Known—For common TCP/IP functions and applications
1024–49151	Registered—For applications built by companies
49152–65535	Dynamic/private—For dynamic connections or unregistered applications

Port numbers are used by both TCP and UDP protocols. Table 2.1 lists some of the common port numbers you should know for the CCNA exam.

TABLE 2.1 **Common TCP and UDP Port Numbers**

	TCP	UDP	
FTP	20, 21	DNS	53
Telnet	23	DHCP	67, 68
SMTP	25	TFTP	69
DNS	53	NTP	123
HTTP	80	SNMP	161
POP	110		
NNTP	119		
HTTPS	443		

Exam**Alert**

Know your port numbers! You will either be asked outright for the correct ports (and whether the protocol uses TCP or UDP), or you will need to know them to do something else, perhaps an access list question.

When a host sends a segment, it specifies the *destination port* that matches the service to which it wants to connect. It also includes a *source port* (a random port number from the dynamic range) that acts as a "return address" for that connection. In this way, a single host can have multiple—possibly hundreds—of connections with the same server, and the server can track each of them because of the different source port numbers for each connection. When the server sends its replies back to the host, the host source ports become the server's destination ports. This system enables the transport layer to *multiplex* connections—meaning, support multiple connections between the same two hosts.

To understand this better, look at Figure 2.4. Suppose that Host A wants to start a Telnet session to Server Z. A will send a segment to Z's IP address, with the destination port of 23 and a random source port number (generated by the host operating system) from the dynamic range—let's choose 55440.

When Server Z receives the segment, it looks at the destination port of 23 and realizes that this segment is intended for its Telnet application, so it sends the data (which, in this case, is a request to start a Telnet session) to its Telnet application. When the Telnet application answers, the server sends a reply back to the host. The destination port of this reply is the original source port of the host, and the source port is the original segment, it specifies the *destination port* that destination port of the host. Figure 2.4 shows this exchange in action.

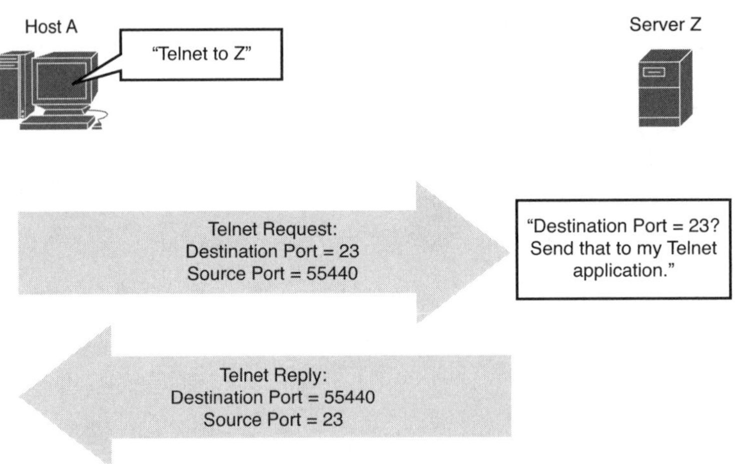

FIGURE 2.4 **Source and destination ports in action.**

Using TCP means that we have to include a lot of information with each segment: the sequence number, the acknowledgment number, the source and destination ports, and the window size. All this information is contained in the Layer 4 header. A *header* is a label attached to the beginning of the data being sent that contains all the control information; once the header is attached, the data is called a *segment*. Figure 2.5 shows the fields in a TCP header.

Source Port	Destination Port
Sequence Number	
Acknowledgement Number	
Misc. Flags	Window Size
Checksum	Urgent
Options	

FIGURE 2.5 **The TCP header.**

Unreliable Communication with UDP

When you look at all the control information that TCP needs to work, and factor in the need to do the three-way handshake before any data is sent, you begin to realize that TCP is a pretty high-overhead operation. For every unit of data being sent, a ton of control information needs to be sent along with it. For some types of communication, we don't need all that control—sometimes, just dropping a postcard in the mail is fine. That is where UDP comes in.

UDP does not use any of the control and reliability features we just discussed in TCP. In fact, if you look at Figure 2.6, which shows what the UDP header looks like, you can see that the only elements in common are the port numbers and the checksum.

Source Port	Destination Port
Length	Checksum

FIGURE 2.6 **The UDP header is a lightweight.**

There is no sequencing, no acknowledgments, no window size—and no three-way handshake, either. So you can see that *much* less control information is sent with each segment. With UDP, there is no PAR. You ask for something, and then you get it. If it doesn't work, you have to ask all over again. Most applications, such as a TFTP server for example, will handle any errors and retransmissions—which means that the application itself (up at Layer 7) is doing the reliability, not Layer 4.

The typical UDP connection goes something like this:

Host A: "Hey Server Z, what's the IP address of www.google.com?"

Server Z: "www.google.com is 66.102.7.147."

Or perhaps:

Host B: "Hey Server Z, send me that file using TFTP."

Server Z: "Here's the file."

UDP is good when reliability is not needed (for DNS lookups or TFTP transfers, for example) or when the overhead of TCP would cause more problems than it solves (for example, when doing VoIP). TCP signaling would introduce so much delay that it would degrade the voice quality—plus, by the time any missing voice segment was retransmitted, it would be too late to use it! VoIP uses UDP because it is faster than TCP, and reliability is less important than minimizing delay.

ExamAlert

You must be able to identify a TCP header on sight, when compared to a UDP header. Be ready for a twist on the wording, such as, "Which provides reliable connections?" So not only do you need to know which header is TCP and which is UDP, but also which one is reliable!

Layer 3: The Network Layer

The network layer deals with logical addressing—in our CCNA world, that means IP addresses, but it could also mean IPv6, IPX, AppleTalk, SNA, and a bunch of others. A logical address is one that is assigned to an interface in software—as opposed to one that is burned onto an interface at the factory (as is the case with MAC addresses, as you will see in a minute).

For two IP hosts to communicate, they must be in the same network. (Chapter 3, "Concepts in IP Addressing," elaborates on this.) If they are in different networks, we need a router to connect the two networks. Finding the way between networks, potentially through hundreds of routers, is called path *determination*. This is the second function of the network layer. Path determination means routing, and routers are a Layer 3 device (so are Layer 3 switches, oddly enough).

The last function of the network layer is to communicate with the layer above (transport) and the layer below (data link). This is achieved by attaching a header to the beginning of the segment that Layer 4 built. The addition of this header makes the segment into a *packet* (sometimes called a datagram, but we like packet better). The packet header has a field that indicates the type of segment it is carrying—TCP or UDP, for example—so that the packet can be sent to the correct function at Layer 4. Communicating with Layer 2 in this case means that an IP packet can be sent to Layer 2 to become an Ethernet frame, Frame Relay, PPP, or almost any other Layer 2 technology. We elaborate on this a little later.

One of the big advantages of a logical addressing scheme is that we can make it *hierarchical*. Hierarchical means "organized into a formal or ranked order." Because all the networks are numbered, and we have control over where those networks are set up, it's easy for us to build a really big system: Big networks are broken into smaller and smaller pieces, with the routers closer to the core knowing the big picture and no details, and the routers at the edge knowing their little set of detailed information but nothing about anyone else's. This makes it easier to organize and find all the millions of different networks, using routers. It's roughly equivalent to a postal address. For example, look at the following address:

24 Sussex Drive
Ottawa, Ontario
Canada K1N 9E6

You could probably find it, eventually, because you would know to get to Canada first, and then to the province of Ontario, and then the city of Ottawa (beautiful place). Grab yourself a map, and soon you'll be standing in front of that address—which happens to be the prime minister's house, so don't be surprised if the Mounties are curious about you being there.

The alternative to a nicely organized hierarchical system like that is a *flat* topology. In a flat system, there is no efficient way to determine where a single address is, because they are not organized. Imagine if the address were this instead:

30000000

Okay, where is it? We have no idea. Unless we can ask everyone at once if it's their address, we don't really stand a chance of finding it. Flat networks (Layer 2) work as long as there are not very many addresses; hierarchical is scalable. Layer 3 is hierarchical, logical addressing that allows us to perform path determination.

You should be familiar with the protocols that exist at Layer 3 as well.

Table 2.2 lists the ones you need to know, along with a very brief description.

TABLE 2.2 **Layer 3 Protocols**

Protocol	Description
IP	IP is the "mother protocol" of TCP/IP, featuring routable 32-bit addressing.
ICMP	Internet Connection Management Protocol. Incorporates ping and traceroute, which are Layer 3 link-testing utilities.
OSPF, EIGRP, RIP, ISIS	Dynamic routing protocols that learn about remote networks and the best paths to them from other routers running the same protocol.
ARP	Address Resolution Protocol. ARP learns what MAC address is associated with a given IP address.

ExamAlert

You should be familiar with Table 2.2.

Remember that Layer 3 is about logical, hierarchical addressing and path determination using that hierarchy—which means routing.

Layer 2: The Data Link Layer

The data link layer is responsible for taking the Layer 3 packet (regardless of which protocol created it—IP, IPX, and so on) and preparing a frame for the packet to be transmitted on the media. There are, of course, many different Layer 2 frame types; in CCNA, we are interested in only the following:

- Ethernet
- Frame Relay
- Point-to-Point Protocol (PPP)
- High-Level Data Link Control protocol (HDLC)
- Cisco Discovery Protocol (CDP)

The type of frame created depends on the type of network service in use; if it is an Ethernet interface, obviously it will be creating Ethernet frames. A router serial port can create several different frame types, including PPP, HDLC, and Frame Relay.

The data link layer uses flat addressing—not hierarchical as in Layer 3. In Ethernet, the addresses in question are MAC addresses. MAC stands for Media Access Control. A MAC address is a number assigned by the manufacturer of a NIC, burned in at the factory. For this reason, it is sometimes called a hardware or physical address, again as opposed to the logical addressing at Layer 3. A valid MAC address will consist of 12 hexadecimal characters, making it 48 bits in length. The first six characters (24 bits) are called the *organizationally unique identifier (OUI)*, and identify the company that made the card. The last six characters (24 bits) are the card serial number. Following are some valid MAC addresses as examples:

```
00-0F-1F-AE-EE-F0
0000.0C01.AACD
0C:60:76:4f:53:4B
```

Note that different formats are used for MAC address representation in different operating systems. Whether separated by dashes, dots, colons, or nothing at all, as long as there are 12 hex characters, the MAC is valid, even if you have to enter it in different formats depending on what machine you are using. A MAC address must be unique within a broadcast domain. This is because one of the functions of Ethernet is that a host will broadcast an ARP request to find out the MAC address of a particular IP; if there are two identical MACs in that broadcast domain, there will be serious confusion.

In other Layer 2 network types, the addresses are not MACs but serve an equivalent purpose. Frame Relay, for example uses DLCIs (data link connection identifiers). A dialup link using regular analog phone or digital ISDN will use the phone number as the Layer 2 address of the IP you are trying to reach. Remember that you must always resolve an IP address down to some type of Layer 2 address, and there will always be a mechanism to do so.

ExamAlert

You must be able to recognize a valid MAC address: 12 valid hex characters.

The first six characters are the OUI or vendor code. All MAC addresses are assigned by the network interface card (NIC) manufacturer and "burned in" at the factory.

MAC addresses are also called hardware or physical addresses.

Layer 2 devices include switches and bridges. These devices read MAC addresses in frames and forward them to the appropriate link. (We go into more detail on switching technology in Chapter 6, "Basic Switch Operations and Configuration.")

Layer 1: The Physical Layer

The last piece of the OSI puzzle is the actual connection between devices. At some point, you have to transmit your signal onto a wire, an optical fiber, or a wireless medium. The physical layer defines the mechanical, procedural, and electrical standards for accessing the media so that you can transmit your Layer 2 frames.

All network signaling at Layer 1 is digital, which means that we are sending binary bits onto the wire. This can mean energizing a copper cable with electricity, where "electricity on" indicates a binary 1 and "electricity off" indicates a binary 0; or, it can mean blinking a laser down an optical fiber where on = 1 and off = 0. Wireless systems do much the same thing.

By defining standards for the physical layer, we can be assured that if we buy an RJ-45 patch cord (for example), it will fit into and work properly in any interface designed to use it.

Sending Data Between Hosts

You also need to understand the flow of information between two networked hosts. The OSI model describes the framework for this flow. As we move down the layers from application to physical, the data is *encapsulated*, which means that headers and trailers are added by each layer. The following section describes the process of creating a piece of data on one host and sending it to another host:

1. At Layer 7, the user generates some *data*, perhaps an email message or a text document. This data is passed down to Layer 6.
2. At Layer 6, the *data* is formatted so that the same application on the other host can recognize and use it. The data is passed down to Layer 5.
3. At Layer 5, the request to initiate a session for the transfer of the *data* is started. The data is passed down to Layer 4.
4. At Layer 4, the data is encapsulated as either a TCP or UDP *segment*. The choice depends on what application generated the data. Source and destination port numbers are added, as are sequence and acknowledgment numbers and window size. The segment is passed down to Layer 3.
5. At Layer 3, the segment is encapsulated with a Layer 3 header and becomes a *packet*. The packet header contains source and destination IP addresses and a label indicating what Layer 4 protocol it is carrying. The packet is passed down to Layer 2.
6. At Layer 2, a header with source and destination MAC addresses is added. This encapsulation creates the *frame*. The trailer at this layer contains an error-checking calculation called the FCS (Frame Check Sequence). The frame header also contains a label indicating which Layer 3 protocol it is carrying (IP, IPX, and so on). The frame is sent to the interface for transmission on to the media (Layer 1).

7. At Layer 1, the binary string that represents the frame is transmitted onto the media, whether electrically, optically, or by radio. *Bits* are transmitted across the media to the network interface of the other host.
8. When received by the other host, the Layer 1 bits are sent up to Layer 2.
9. At Layer 2, the destination MAC is examined to make sure that the frame was intended for this host. The FCS is calculated to check the frame for errors. If there are errors, the frame is discarded. If there are none, the frame is *decapsulated* and the packet is sent to the correct Layer 3 protocol based on the protocol ID in the header.
10. At Layer 3, the destination IP address is checked to see whether it is intended for this host. The packet header is checked to see which Layer 4 protocol to send it to. The packet is decapsulated, and the segment is sent up to Layer 4.
11. At Layer 4, the destination port in the segment header is checked and the segment is decapsulated. The data is sent to the correct upper layer application. Depending on the application, it might go directly to Layer 7 or through 5 and 6.

This process of encapsulation, transmission, and decapsulation makes data flow in an organized and manageable fashion down the OSI stack on the sender, across the transmission media, and up the OSI stack on the receiving host. It is important to understand that Layer 3 on the sender is communicating with Layer 3 on the receiver as well by way of the information in the headers.

ExamAlert

You must be comfortable with visualizing how this process works. You must remember the names of the encapsulations at each layer, in order, backward and forward. These are generically called PDUs (protocol data units):

Layer	PDU
Application	Data
Presentation	Data
Session	Data
Transport	Segment
Network	Packet
Data Link	Frame
Physical	Bits

Try a mnemonic: "Did Sally Pack For Bermuda?"

Cram Quiz

1. Which of the following does TCP use to provide reliability? Choose all that apply.
   - ❍ **A.** Sliding window
   - ❍ **B.** IP addressing
   - ❍ **C.** Secret numbers
   - ❍ **D.** Acknowledgments
   - ❍ **E.** Three-way handshake
   - ❍ **F.** Sequence numbers

2. True or false: Packets contain segments.
   - ❍ **A.** True
   - ❍ **B.** False

3. The OSI model is useful when troubleshooting. Which of the following are true when troubleshooting using the OSI model as a reference?
   - ❍ **A.** If you can consistently ping the host, the cable is probably not faulty.
   - ❍ **B.** If pings fail three out of four times, the cable is definitely faulty.
   - ❍ **C.** If you can consistently ping a host on a remote network, Layer 3 is functioning.
   - ❍ **D.** If you could telnet to the host this morning but now you can't, it is certain that the problem is at Layer 7.
   - ❍ **E.** If you can access the web-based interface of the server, but cannot ping it, the problem is definitely at Layer 3.

Cram Quiz Answers

1. Answers A, D, E, and F are correct. Reliability includes mechanisms to establish contact with the intended receiver (E), identify and acknowledge all the data sent and received (F and D), and manage congestion to avoid data loss (A). B is wrong because IP addressing is handled at Layer 3 and has nothing to do with TCP reliability. Answer C is wrong because there is no such concept associated with TCP.
2. True. Packet is the term used to describe the encapsulation performed at Layer 3, which encapsulates the segment created by the encapsulation at Layer 4.
3. Answers A and C are correct. B is wrong; we cannot be certain that it is the cable, but testing it or replacing it is not a bad idea to eliminate the possibility. Answer D is wrong for much the same reason: We don't have enough information to be certain. A couple other tests would help us decide. Answer E is wrong: If you can ping it, Layer 3 is working, at least intermittently. Again, more tests will narrow the problem down.

TCP/IP Model

CramSaver

1. The OSI model Layer 3 corresponds to which TCP/IP model layer?
   - **A.** Network
   - **B.** Intranet
   - **C.** Transport
   - **D.** Data
   - **E.** Network interface
   - **F.** Internet

2. What are the TCP/IP model layer names in order?
   - **A.** Data, transport, Internet, network interface
   - **B.** Data, Internet, transport, network interface
   - **C.** Network interface, Internet, transport, application
   - **D.** Application, transport, network, network interface

Answers

1. Answer F is correct: Internet. Not Answer A: Network (that's OSI). Not Answer B: intranet. (That's a private web). Read carefully! Not Answers C or D. If you picked one of those, you better read on.
2. Answer C is correct. D is almost correct, but the TCP/IP model calls it Internet, not network. Yes, it matters, and no, it's not the same thing!

Although the TCP/IP protocol can be fit into the OSI model, it actually uses its own model, which differs slightly. Remember that the OSI model is intended to be a standardized framework, and TCP/IP was originated as a proprietary Department of Defense protocol. It stands to reason that some variances will exist from the official OSI stack. The following section describes these differences.

The TCP/IP model has only four layers:

- Application
- Transport
- Internet
- Network interface

OSI Layers 5, 6, and 7 have been amalgamated into a single layer called the application layer. The application layer features all the same protocols as found in OSI Layer 7: Telnet, FTP, TFTP, SMTP, SNMP, and so on. The transport layer is equivalent to OSI Layer 4. TCP and UDP are located here.

The Internet layer corresponds to OSI Layer 3. IP, ARP, and ICMP are the primary protocols here.

Layer 1 and 2 are fused into the network interface layer (sometimes called network access layer). This is confusing because it is illogical to have a protocol software stack define a physical interface; just remember that the TCP/IP model is a logical framework, and the fact that physical standards are included is necessary because it must connect to the media at some point. The TCP/IP model uses the same definitions for network interface standards as the OSI model does for data link and physical layers.

Figure 2.7 directly compares and contrasts the OSI model with the TCP/IP model.

OSI Model	TCP/IP Model
Application	Application
Presentation	
Session	
Transport	Transport
Network	Internet
Data Link	Network Interface
Physical	

FIGURE 2.7 **OSI and TCP/IP models compared.**

ExamAlert

A great deal of overlap exists between the OSI and TCP/IP models, but you must be clear on the differences and watch for what the exam question is asking about; Cisco is fond of trying to trick you into answering with an OSI answer when it is, in fact, a TCP/IP model question.

Cram Quiz

1. The TCP/IP model names TCP and UDP as transport layer protocols to provide reliable and unreliable (respectively) transport. What TCP/IP protocols are used in Layer 4 of the OSI model for the same purposes?

2. The OSI layers 5, 6 and 7 have been amalgamated into which layer in the TCP/IP model?

   ❍ **A.** Data

   ❍ **B.** Application

   ❍ **C.** Transport

   ❍ **D.** Internetwork

3. What is the TCP/IP model equivalent of the OSI Layer 3?

   ❍ **A.** Application

   ❍ **B.** Presentation

   ❍ **C.** Network

   ❍ **D.** Internet

   ❍ **E.** Internetwork

   ❍ **F.** Data

   ❍ **G.** Session

Cram Quiz Answers

1. TCP and UDP. It's a trick question! Get used to it.
2. Correct answer: B: Application Layer.
3. Answer D is correct: Internet.

Review Questions

1. Which protocol will allow you to test connectivity through Layer 7?
   - ❍ **A.** ICMP
   - ❍ **B.** ARP
   - ❍ **C.** RIP
   - ❍ **D.** Telnet

2. Which answer correctly lists the OSI PDUs in order?
   - ❍ **A.** Data, packet, frame, segment, bit
   - ❍ **B.** Bit, data, packet, segment, frame
   - ❍ **C.** Data, segment, packet, frame, bit
   - ❍ **D.** Bit, frame, segment, packet, data

3. Which transport layer protocol provides connection-oriented, reliable transport?
   - ❍ **A.** TFTP
   - ❍ **B.** UDP
   - ❍ **C.** Ethernet
   - ❍ **D.** TCP
   - ❍ **E.** Secure Shell

4. Which of the following are application layer protocols? Choose all that apply.
   - ❍ **A.** Ethernet
   - ❍ **B.** CDP
   - ❍ **C.** FTP
   - ❍ **D.** TFTP
   - ❍ **E.** Telnet
   - ❍ **F.** ARP
   - ❍ **G.** ICMP
   - ❍ **H.** ATM

5. Match the protocol with its port number:

FTP	80
Telnet	69
TFTP	20, 21
DNS	123
SNMP	25
SMTP	110
NTP	161
POP3	53
HTTP	23

6. Which protocols use TCP? Choose all that apply.

❍ **A.** DNS
❍ **B.** SNMP
❍ **C.** SMTP
❍ **D.** FTP
❍ **E.** TFTP
❍ **F.** POP3

7. Which port numbers are used by well-known protocols that use connectionless transport?

❍ **A.** 25
❍ **B.** 53
❍ **C.** 20
❍ **D.** 69
❍ **E.** 161
❍ **F.** 110

8. Which are elements of PAR? Choose all that apply.

❍ **A.** Devices that collide must wait to retransmit.

❍ **B.** The source device starts a timer for each segment and will retransmit that segment if an acknowledgment is not received before the timer expires.

❍ **C.** Devices will broadcast for the hardware address of the receiver.

❍ **D.** Source devices keep a record of all segments sent and expect an acknowledgment for each one.

❍ **E.** The receiving device will drop frames that it cannot buffer.

❍ **F.** The receiving device will acknowledge receipt of a segment by sending an acknowledgment indicating the next segment it expects.

9. Which layer of the TCP/IP model is responsible for interhost data movement and uses either connection-oriented or connectionless protocols?

❍ **A.** Network

❍ **B.** Internet

❍ **C.** Transport

❍ **D.** Network interface

❍ **E.** Application

10. Which of the following depicts a TCP header?

❍ **A.**

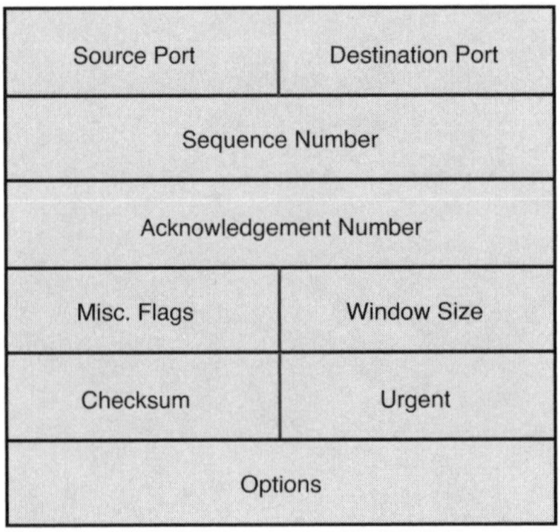

Source Port	Destination Port
Sequence Number	
Acknowledgement Number	
Misc. Flags	Window Size
Checksum	Urgent
Options	

❍ **B.**

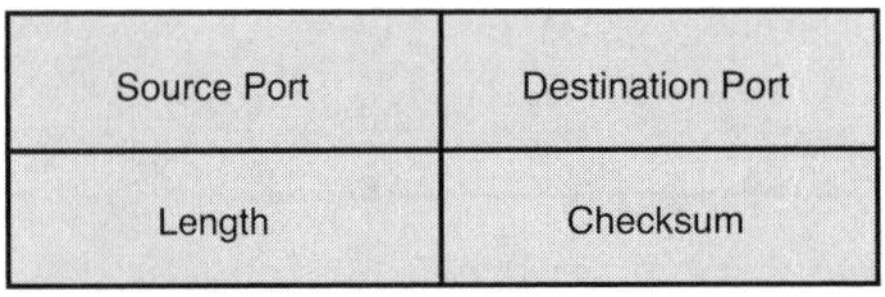

Source Port	Destination Port
Length	Checksum

Answers to Review Questions

1. Answer D is correct. Telnet is the only Layer 7 protocol listed. All the others only operate at Layer 3, so they do not test above Layer 3.
2. Answer C is correct. "Did Sally Pack For Bermuda?"
3. Answer D is correct. TCP is a transport layer protocol that uses sequencing, acknowledgments, and retransmission for reliability. Answers A, C, and E are incorrect because TFTP, Ethernet, and Secure Shell are not transport layer protocols. Answer B is incorrect because UDP does not provide reliability.
4. Answers C, D, and E are correct. Answers A, B, and H are Layer 2 protocols; Answers F and G are Layer 3 protocols.
5. Answer:

FTP	20, 21
Telnet	23
TFTP	69
DNS	53
SNMP	161
SMTP	25
NTP	123
POP3	110
HTTP	80

6. Answers A, C, D, and F are correct. DNS uses both TCP and UDP; B and E use UDP only.
7. Answers B, D, and E are correct. These ports are used by DNS, TFTP, and SNMP—all of which use unreliable/connectionless UDP transport. (Note that DNS uses both TCP and UDP.)
8. Answers B, D, and F are correct; PAR provides reliability by using these three functions. Answer A describes CSMA/CD; Answer C describes ARP. Answer E is a basic hardware function that has nothing to do with the process of PAR, although PAR might react to the lost frames by retransmitting them.
9. Answer C is correct. Connectionless and connection-oriented protocols are found at Layer 4 (transport). Answer A is incorrect because it is an OSI layer name. Answers B, D, and E are incorrect because those layers do not use connection-oriented or connectionless protocols.
10. Answer A is correct. It depicts a TCP header.

CHAPTER THREE

Concepts in IP Addressing

This chapter covers the following official CCNA Routing and Switching 200-120 exam topics:

- Describe the operation and necessity of using private and public IP addresses for IPv4 addressing.
- Identify the appropriate IPv4 addressing scheme using VLSM and summarization to satisfy addressing requirements in a LAN/WAN environment.
- Describe IPv6 addresses.
- Identify the appropriate IPv6 addressing scheme to satisfy addressing requirements in a LAN/WAN environment.
- Describe the technological requirements for running IPv6 in conjunction with IPv4 such as dual stack.

The exam requires a perfect fluency in subnetting. Success requires speed and accuracy in answering the many questions you will see on this topic. The key to this level of fluency is practice—you must work at your skills until they become second nature.

The following sections discuss binary and hexadecimal numbering systems as compared with the more familiar decimal system. An understanding of binary, in particular, is crucial to success on the test as it is fundamental to computer systems in general, and to topics such as subnetting, access lists, routing, and route summarization. This chapter also looks at the relationship between the IP address and subnet mask in more detail, as well as how it can be manipulated for more efficient network functionality using route summarization. Finally, IP Version 6 is introduced and some of its features are explained.

Binary

CramSaver

1. What are the eight binary values found in a single octet of an IP address?
   - **A.** 256 128 64 32 16 8 4 2
   - **B.** 254 62 30 14 6 4 0
   - **C.** 128 64 32 16 8 4 2 1
   - **D.** 0 2 4 6 8 10 12 14

2. What is the decimal value of binary 00001110 ?
   - **A.** 13
   - **B.** 14
   - **C.** 1,110
   - **D.** 16
   - **E.** 15

3. What is the binary value of decimal 256?
   - **A.** 11111111
   - **B.** 1111111111
   - **C.** 100000000
   - **D.** 10000000

Answers

1. Answer C is correct.
2. Answer B is correct.
3. Answer C is correct.

Binary is the language of digital electronic communication. Binary is another name for Base 2 numbering. Our usual numbering system is Base 10, in which a single character or column can represent one of 10 values: 0, 1, 2, 3, 4, 5, 6, 7, 8, or 9. The first column indicates how many ones there are in a given value. To represent a value greater than 9, we need another column, which represents how many "tens" there are; if the value we want to represent is greater than 99, we use another column for the "hundreds," and so on. You might notice that each additional column is ten times greater than the preceding one: ones, tens, hundreds, thousands, and so forth—all "powers of 10": 100, 101, 102, 103, and so on. Base 10 is easy because most of us have 10 fingers and have known how to count from an early age.

In binary, or Base 2, a single character or column can represent one of only two values: 0 or 1. The next column represents how many "twos" there are; the next column how many "fours," and so on. You'll notice here that the value of each additional column is two times greater than the previous—all "powers of 2": 20, 21, 22, 23, and so on. This is not a coincidence.

Given that a Base 2 or binary column can have only two possible values (0 or 1), this makes it easy to represent a binary value as an electrical value: either off (0) or on (1). Computers use binary because it is easily represented as electrical signals in memory or digital values on storage media. The whole system works because computers are quick at computing arithmetic, and as you'll learn, pretty much all computer operations are really just fast binary math.

Let's take a look at some Base 10 (or decimal) to binary conversions. Take the decimal number 176. Those three digits tell us that we have one 100, plus seven 10s, plus six 1s. Table 3.1 illustrates how decimal numbers represent this distribution of values.

TABLE 3.1 **Decimal Values**

100,000s	10,000s	1000s	100s	10s	1s
0	0	0	1	7	6

Notice that we have some 0s in the high-value columns; we can drop those from the beginning if we want to. You will not have to analyze decimal numbers in this way on the exam; we are simply demonstrating how Base 10 works so it can be compared to Base 2 and Base 16 in the same way.

In binary, the columns have different values—the powers of 2. Table 3.2 lists the values of the lowest 8 bits in binary.

TABLE 3.2 **Binary Values**

128	64	32	16	8	4	2	1

Note

The biggest values in a binary string (the 1s at the left) are often called the *high-order* bits because they have the highest value. Similarly, the lowest-value bits at the right are referred to as the *low-order* bits.

Tip

You must know the value of each binary bit position! If you have difficulty memorizing them, try starting at 1 and keep doubling as you go to the left.

To represent the decimal number 176 in binary, we need to figure out which columns (or bit positions) are "on" and which are "off." Now, because this is arithmetic, there are a few different ways to do this.

Start with the decimal number you want to convert:

176

Next, look at the values of each binary bit position and decide if you can subtract the highest column value and end up with a value of 0 or more. Ask yourself: "Can I subtract 128 from 176?" In this case, 176 – 128 = 48.

Yes, you can subtract 128 from 176 and get a positive value, 48. Because we "used" the 128 column, we put a 1 in that column, as shown in Table 3.3.

TABLE 3.3 **Building a Binary String, Part 1**

128	64	32	16	8	4	2	1
1							

Now, we try to subtract the next highest column value from the remainder. We get 176 – 128 = 48. We take the 48 and subtract 64 from it.

Notice that you can't do this without getting a negative number; this is not allowed, so we can't use the 64 column. Therefore, we put a 0 in that column, as shown in Table 3.4.

TABLE 3.4 **Building a Binary String, Part 2**

128	64	32	16	8	4	2	1
1	0						

Move along and do the math for the rest of the columns: 48 – 32 = 16. We then subtract 16 from 16 and get 0.

Note that when you get to 0, you are finished—you need to only fill the remaining bit positions with 0s to complete the 8-bit string. So, we used only the 128 column, the 32 column, and the 16 column. Table 3.5 is what we end up with.

TABLE 3.5 **Completed Binary Conversion**

128	64	32	16	8	4	2	1
1	0	1	1	0	0	0	0

176 decimal = 10110000 binary.

If you add up 128 + 32 + 16, you get 176. That is how you convert from binary to decimal: Simply add up the column values where there is a 1.

ExamAlert

You will see several questions on converting from decimal to binary and back, so prepare accordingly.

Hexadecimal

The CCNA exam will ask you a few questions on the conversion of binary to hexadecimal and back, so you need to understand how it works. An understanding of hex is also a useful skill for other areas of networking and computer science.

Binary is Base 2; decimal is Base 10; hexadecimal is Base 16. Each column in hex can represent 16 possible values, from 0 through 15. To represent a value of 10 through 15 with a single character, hex uses the letters A through F. It is important to understand that the values of 0 through 15 are the possible values of a 4-bit binary number, as shown in Table 3.6.

TABLE 3.6 **Decimal, Binary, and Hex Values Compared**

Decimal	Binary	Hex
0	0000	0
1	0001	1
2	0010	2
3	0011	3
4	0100	4
5	0101	5
6	0110	6
7	0111	7
8	1000	8
9	1001	9
10	1010	A
11	1011	B
12	1100	C
13	1101	D
14	1110	E
15	1111	F

Exam**Alert**

You should be able to reproduce Table 3.6 as a quick reference for the exam.

Conversion Between Binary, Hex, and Decimal

The following sections provide an introduction to converting between binary, hex, and decimal. Again, there is more than one mathematical approach to finding the correct answer, but the method shown is simple and reliable.

Decimal to Hexadecimal Conversions

The easiest way to get from decimal to hexadecimal and back is to go through binary. Take the example we used earlier in which we converted 176 decimal to binary:

176 = 10110000

Given that a single hex character represents four binary bits, all we need to do is to break the 8-bit string 10110000 into two 4-bit strings like this:

1011   0000

Now, simply match the 4-bit strings to their hex equivalent:

1011 = B

0000 = 0

The answer is simply 10110000 = 0xB0.

The 0x in front of the answer is an expression that means "the following is in hex." This is needed because if the hex value was 27, we could not distinguish it from 27 decimal.

Hexadecimal to Decimal Conversions

The reverse of the procedure is easier than it seems, too. Given a hex value of 0xC4, all we need to do is to first convert to binary, and then to decimal.

To convert to binary, take the two hex characters and find their binary value:

C = 1100

0100 = 4

Now, make the two 4-bit strings into one 8-bit string:

11000100

Finally, add the bit values of the columns where you have a 1:

128 + 64 + 4 = 196

ExamAlert

It is critical to polish your skills in binary. You must be confident and quick in conversions, and the better your understanding of binary, the easier subnetting and other advanced IP topics will be for you. Practice, practice, practice!

Cram Quiz

1. Write the following binary IP in dotted-decimal format: 11000000.10101000.00000001.11111110.
2. Write the following subnet mask in binary format: 255.255.255.240.
3. What is 127.0.0.1 in binary?

Cram Quiz Answers

1. 192.168.1.254
2. 11111111.11111111.11111111.11110000
3. 01111111.00000000.00000000.00000001

IP Address Components

CramSaver

1. What class of IP address is 191.168.1.0?
2. What is the range (in decimal) of Class B addresses?
3. What is the range of private Class A addresses?
4. Is the address 172.16.1.0/24 subnetted?

Answers

1. Class B.
2. 128.0.0 .0 to 191.255.255.255
3. 10.0.0.0 to 10.255.255.255
4. Yes. The default mask is /16; /24 is longer so the address is subnetted.

CCNA candidates need to be fluent in their understanding of IP addressing concepts. The following sections detail how IP addresses are organized and analyzed, with a view to answering subnetting questions.

Address Class

Early in the development of IP, RFC 791 designated five classes of IP address: A, B, C, D, and E. These classes were identified based on the pattern of high-order bits (the high-value bits at the beginning of the first octet). The result is that certain ranges of networks are grouped into classes in a pattern based on the binary values of those high-order bits, as detailed in Table 3.7.

TABLE 3.7 **Address Class and Range**

Class	High-Order Bits	1st Octet Range
A	0	1–127
B	10	128–191
C	110	192–223
D	1110	224–239
E	11110	240–255

You might notice that 127 is missing. This is because at some point the address 127.0.0.1 was reserved for the loopback (sometimes called *localhost*) IP—this is the IP of the TCP/IP protocol itself on every host machine.

ExamAlert

You absolutely must be able to identify the class of an address just by looking at what number is in the first octet. This is critical to answering subnetting questions.

Public and Private IP Addresses

As the popularity of TCP/IP increased, many organizations wanted to use it in their own networks, without paying to be connected to the Internet. The IETF published a Recommended Best Practice (RFC 1918) that defined several "private" IP networks that could be used by individuals, corporations, or other organizations without needing to pay to lease them from an Internet service provider (ISP). The tradeoff was that these networks were not routable on the Internet because these addresses were filtered from the route tables on Internet routers and so were unreachable from the Internet. They work exactly the same as any other IP address in every other respect; in fact, if they weren't filtered they would work on the Internet too.

These address ranges will probably be familiar to you already, because every LAN you have ever joined likely used one of them. To access the Internet from a LAN using one of these private, non-routable networks, we have to go through a Network Address Translation (NAT) router. NAT is explained in Chapter 10, "IP Services." Table 3.8 lists the private IP Address ranges. You should commit these to memory and be able to recognize them at a glance.

TABLE 3.8 **Private IP Address Ranges**

Class	Range
A	10.0.0.0 to 10.255.255.255
B	172.16.0.0 to 172.31.255.255
C	192.168.0.0 to 192.168.255.255

Default Subnet Mask

Each class of address is associated with a default subnet mask, as shown in Table 3.9. An address using its default mask defines a single IP broadcast domain—all the hosts using that same network number and mask can receive each other's broadcasts and communicate via IP.

TABLE 3.9 **Address Class and Default Masks**

Class	Default Mask
A	255.0.0.0
B	255.255.0.0
C	255.255.255.0

One of the rules that Cisco devices follow is that a subnet mask must be a contiguous string of 1s followed by a contiguous string of 0s. There are no exceptions to this rule: A valid mask is always a string of 1s, followed by 0s to fill up the rest of the 32 bits. (There is no such rule in the real world, but we will stick to the Cisco rules here; it's a Cisco exam, after all.)

Therefore, the only possible valid values in any given octet of a subnet mask are 0, 128, 192, 224, 240, 248, 252, 254, and 255. Any other value is invalid.

ExamAlert

You should practice associating the correct default subnet mask with any given IP address; this is another critical skill in subnetting.

The Network Field

Every IP address is composed of a network component and a host component. The subnet mask has a single purpose: to identify which part of an IP address is the network component and which part is the host component. Look at a 32-bit IP address expressed in binary, with the subnet mask written right below it. Figure 3.1 shows an example.

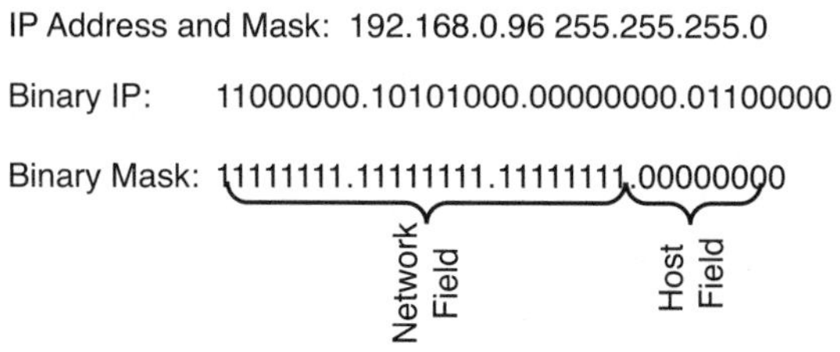

IP Address and Mask: 192.168.0.96 255.255.255.0

Binary IP: 11000000.10101000.00000000.01100000

Binary Mask: 11111111.11111111.11111111.00000000

Network Field

Host Field

FIGURE 3.1 **IP address and mask in binary, showing network and host fields.**

Anywhere you see a binary 1 in the subnet mask, it means "the matching bit in the IP address is part of the network component." In this example, the network part of the address is 192.168.0.X, and the last octet (X) will be the host component.

Because there are 24 bits in a row in the mask, we can also use a shortcut for the mask notation of /24. These examples show how a dotted-decimal mask can be expressed in slash notation:

192.168.1.66 255.255.255.0 = 192.168.1.66 /24

172.16.0.12 255.255.0.0 = 172.16.0.12 /16

10.1.1.1 255.0.0.0 = 10.1.1.1 /8

This slash notation is sometimes called CIDR (classless interdomain routing) notation. For some reason, it's a concept that confuses students, but honestly it's the easiest concept of all: The slash notation is simply the number of 1s in a row in the subnet mask. The real reason to use CIDR notation is simply that it is easier to say and especially to type—and it appears interchangeably with dotted-decimal throughout the exam. CIDR notation also appears in the output of various IOS commands.

Every IP address has a host component and a network component, and the 1s in the mask tell us which bits in the address identify the network component.

The Host Field

If the 1s in the mask identify the network component of an address, the 0s at the end of the mask identify the host component. In the preceding example, the entire last octet is available for the host IP number.

The number of 0s at the end of the mask mathematically define how many hosts can be on any given network or subnet. The 1s in the mask always identify the network component, and the 0s at the end of the mask always identify the host component of any IP address.

Nondefault Masks

At this point, you should be able to recognize what class an address belongs to, and what its default mask is supposed to be. Here's the big secret: If a mask is longer than it is supposed to be, that network has been subnetted. So, it is clearly another critical skill that you be able to spot those nondefault masks.

The Subnet Field

Because we have extended the subnet mask past the default boundary into the bits that were previously host bits, we identify the bits we "stole" from the host part as the subnet field. The subnet field is relevant because those bits mathematically define how many subnets we create. Figure 3.2 uses the same IP address from our previous example, but now we have applied a mask that is longer than the default. Note that this creates the subnet field.

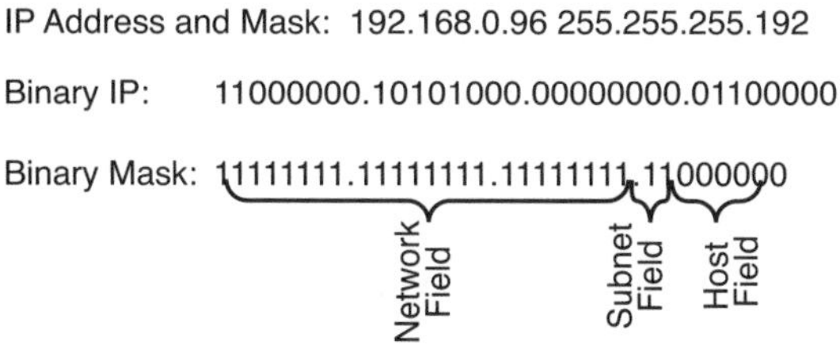

IP Address and Mask: 192.168.0.96 255.255.255.192

Binary IP: 11000000.10101000.00000000.01100000

Binary Mask: 11111111.11111111.11111111.11000000

FIGURE 3.2 **IP address and non-default mask in binary illustrating the subnet field.**

Figure 3.2 identifies the two extra bits past the default boundary as the subnet field—they used to be in the host field, but we subnetted and stole them to become the subnet field.

Cram Quiz

1. If the mask assigned to a private Class C address is 24 bits, is the address subnetted?
2. Which of the following are private IP addresses that can be assigned to a host?
   - ❍ **A.** 12.17.1.45
   - ❍ **B.** 10.255.255.254
   - ❍ **C.** 172.15.255.248
   - ❍ **D.** 192.168.1.5
   - ❍ **E.** 239.0.0.1
3. Why can't Duncan assign the address of 17.21.12.1111 to his Internet web server?

Cram Quiz Answers

1. No. /24 is the default mask, so the address is not subnetted.
2. Answers B and D are correct. The other addresses are not in the private unicast ranges.
3. Because it is not a valid IP address: .1111 in any octet is not a valid IP.

Subnetting

CramSaver

1. How many hosts are on the network 172.16.41.0/27?
   - **A.** 65,534
   - **B.** 32
   - **C.** 254
   - **D.** 30
   - **E.** 27
   - **F.** 14

2. How many subnets are created by the address 192.168.1.0 255.255.255.248?
   - **A.** 1
   - **B.** 2
   - **C.** 4
   - **D.** 8
   - **E.** 16
   - **F.** 32
   - **G.** 64

3. What is the broadcast ID of the seventh subnet created using 172.16.0.0/28?
   - **A.** 172.16.111.0
   - **B.** 172.16.0.0
   - **C.** 172.16.0.7
   - **D.** 172.16.0.96
   - **E.** 172.16.0.110
   - **F.** 172.16.0.111
   - **G.** 172.16.0.112

Answers

1. Answer D is correct. Five 0s at the end of the mask; $(2^5) - 2 = 30$
2. Answer F is correct. 5 bits were stolen to extend the mask: $(2^5) = 32$
3. Answer F is correct. The seventh subnet ranges from the network ID of 172.16.0.96 to the broadcast ID of 172.16.0.111.

Subnetting is not as difficult as it initially seems. Because we are dealing with arithmetic, there is definitely more than one way to do this, but the method shown here has worked well. The following sections work through the process of subnetting. Then, we work on some shortcuts to show how you can subnet quickly because CCNA exam candidates often find that they are pressed for time on the exam.

Address Class and Default Mask

Subnetting happens when we extend the subnet mask past the default boundary for the address we are working with. So it's obvious that we first need to be sure of what the default mask is supposed to be for any given address. Previously, we looked at the RFC791 designations for IP address classes and the number ranges in the first octet that identify those classes. If you didn't pick up on this before, you should memorize those immediately.

When faced with a subnetting question, the first thing to do is decide what class the address belongs to. Here are some examples:

192.168.1.66

The first octet is between 192 and 223: Class C

Default mask for Class C: 255.255.255.0

188.21.21.3

The first octet is between 128 and 191: Class B

Default mask for Class B: 255.255.0.0

24.64.208.5

The first octet is between 1 and 126: Class A

Default mask for Class A: 255.0.0.0

It's important to grasp that if an address uses the correct default mask for its class, it is not subnetted. This means that regardless of how many hosts the 0s at the end of the mask create, all those hosts are on the same network, all in the same broadcast domain. This has some implications for classful networks (ones that use the default mask for the address). Take a Class A for example: A Class A network can have 16,777,214 hosts on it. Almost 17 million PCs on one network would never work—there would be so much traffic from broadcasts alone, never mind regular data traffic, that nothing could get through and the network would collapse under its own size. Even a Class B network has 65,534 possible host IPs. This is still too many. So, either we waste a lot of addresses by not using the whole classful A or B network, or we subnet to make the networks smaller.

This is actually one of the most common reasons we subnet: The default or classful networks are too big, causing issues such as excessive broadcast traffic and wasted IP address space. Subnetting creates multiple smaller subnetworks out of one larger classful network, which allows us to make IP networks the "right" size—big or small—for any given situation.

The Increment

By definition, the process of subnetting creates several smaller classless subnets out of one larger classful one. The size of these subnets, or how many IP addresses they contain, is called the increment. Because we are working with binary numbers, a pattern emerges in which the increment is always one of those powers of 2 again—another good reason to memorize those numbers.

The increment is really easy to figure out. It is simply the value of the last 1 in the subnet mask. Let's look at some examples. Figure 3.3 shows an IP address and subnet mask in binary.

IP Address and Mask: 192.168.21.1 255.255.255.0

Binary IP: 11000000.10101000.00010101.00000001

Binary Mask: 11111111.11111111.11111111.00000000

FIGURE 3.3 **IP address and mask in binary.**

Note that this is a Class C address, and it uses the correct default mask—so it is not subnetted. This means that there is only one network, so there isn't really an increment to worry about here. It's sufficient at this point to recognize that an address that uses its default mask creates one network (no subnets), so there is no subnetted increment to consider.

Let's take the same address and subnet it by extending the mask past the default boundary, as shown in Figure 3.4.

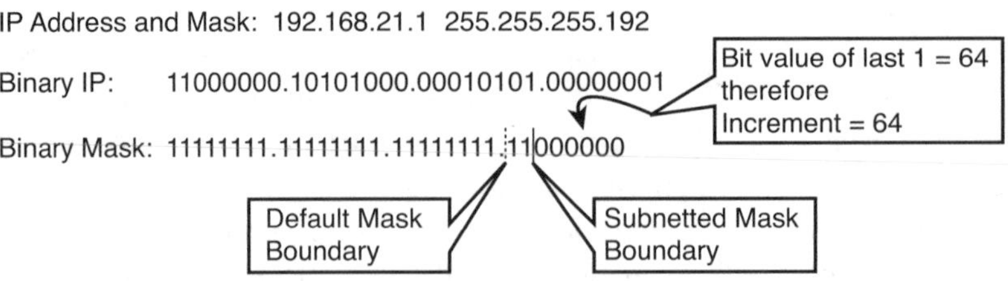

FIGURE 3.4 **IP address and subnetted mask.**

The very last 1 in the subnet mask in the figure is in the bit position worth 64—so the increment in this case is 64, which means that the subnets we made are evenly spaced at 64 IP addresses apart.

Think about this for a second. We are doing the subnetting in the fourth octet—that is where the mask changes from 1s to 0s. (The octet where this happens is sometimes referred to as the *interesting* octet.) The lowest possible value in that fourth octet is 0. If the subnets are 64 IP addresses apart, this means that the first subnet starts at 0, the next one starts at 64, the third at 128, and the fourth at 192—all multiples of the increment. Note that if we add another 64 to that last 192, we get 256—and that is larger than 255, the largest value that is possible in one octet. So this means we only have room for four subnets. Figure 3.5 illustrates this pattern more clearly.

.0	.64	.128	.192
.1	.65	.129	.193
.	.	.	.
.	.	.	.
.	.	.	.
.62	.126	.190	.254
.63	.127	.191	.255

FIGURE 3.5 **Subnets created with increment of 64.**

The multiples of the increment—0, 64, 128, and 192—are the starting addresses of the subnets we created. The subnets are all 64 addresses long, so we have room to make four subnets before we run out of addresses in the fourth octet.

Figure 3.6 shows our IP and subnet mask—note that the value of the last "1" in the mask is 16—and the subnets created with that increment of 16.

192.168.21.0 255.255.255.240

IP: 11000000.10101000.00010101.00000000
Mask: 11111111.11111111.11111111.11110000

Subnets Created with Increment of 16:

.0	.16	.32	.48	.64	.80	.96	.112	.128	.144	.160	.176	.192	.208	.224	.240
.	.	.	.	.	.	.	.	.	.	.	.	.	.	.	.
.	.	.	.	.	.	.	.	.	.	.	.	.	.	.	.
.	.	.	.	.	.	.	.	.	.	.	.	.	.	.	.
.15	.31	.47	.63	.79	.95	.111	.127	.143	.159	.175	.191	.207	.223	.239	.255

FIGURE 3.6 **IP address and subnet mask with increment of 16.**

First of all, you should notice that we are subnetting again—the mask extends past the default boundary. The last 1 in the mask is in the bit position worth 16, so our increment is 16. The multiples of 16 are 0, 16, 32, 48, 64, 80, 96, 112, 128, 144, 160, 176, 192, 208, 224, and 240. Again, we can't make another subnet because 240 + 16 = 256. Be careful not to start doubling as we did with the binary values; here we are just adding the increment value each time. It's easy to get confused!

The increment is really the key to subnetting; if you can determine the increment, you can see how big your subnets are and how many you have created. Remember, the easy way to find the increment is to just determine the bit value of the last 1 in the mask.

Number of Hosts

The number of 0s at the end of the mask always defines the number of hosts on any network or subnet. There is a simple mathematical formula that defines how many IP addresses are available to be assigned to hosts.

> **Note**
>
> Hosts is another word for computers, router interfaces, printers, or any other network component that can be assigned an IP address.

Now, no one expects you to be a big fan of algebra, but you need to see and understand the formula.

The number of binary bits you have to use determines the maximum number of different values you can express using those bits. If you have 3 bits, you can make eight different values—0 through 7, or 000 through 111 in binary; 3 bits, and $2^3 = 8$—this is not a coincidence. The binary values you learned earlier—1, 2, 4, 8, 16, 32, 64, and 128—are all powers of 2 and define the maximum number of different values you can create if the mask ends in that bit position. So it should come as no surprise that the formula for the number of hosts on any network or subnet is $2^H - 2$, where H is the number of 0s at the end of the mask.

But why do we subtract 2 in the formula? It's pretty straightforward: Every network or subnet has two reserved addresses that cannot be assigned to a host. The rule is that no host can have the IP address in which all the host bits are set to 0, and no host can have the IP address in which all the host bits are set to 1. These addresses are called the network ID and the broadcast ID, respectively. They are the first and last IP addresses in any network or subnet. We lose those two IP addresses from the group of values that could be assigned to hosts.

Think of a network or subnet as a street with houses on it. Each house has a unique address, and the street has a name. The network ID is like the street name, and all the houses are hosts on a subnet that is known by its network ID street name. If two hosts have identical network and subnet fields in their addresses, they are on the same network, and can ping each other and exchange data and all that good stuff. If the network and subnet fields are different, even by 1 bit, they are on different networks and can't communicate until we put a router between them. The routers act like street intersections; you must get to the right intersection (router) before you can get on to the street you want (but we'll save that for later).

In a network where there are no routers, devices running TCP/IP make a decision about whether a particular IP address is on the network by performing a logical AND operation. The AND is a Boolean function that works like this:

1 AND 1 = 1

0 AND 1 = 0

1 AND 0 = 0

0 AND 0 = 0

This operation applies to IP networking like this: A host does a logical AND between its own IP and its mask. This determines its network ID. The host can then do an AND between another IP address and its own mask to determine if that second address is on the same network or some other one.

Let's take the IP address and mask of an imaginary host and display them in binary, as shown in Figure 3.7. The AND operation takes each bit in the address and ANDs it with the corresponding bit in the mask below it; the result is the network ID of the host.

IP Address and Mask: 192.16.20.12 255.255.255.0

Binary IP: 11000000.00010000.00010100.00001100

Binary Mask: 11111111.11111111.11111111.00000000

AND Result: 11000000.00010000.00010100.00000000

NetID = 192.16.20.0

FIGURE 3.7 **The AND operation determines the network ID.**

Now the host knows its own network ID and can compare any other host's address to that to see if the other host has the same network ID. If the two network IDs are different, traffic has to be sent through a router to get to the other network—and if there is no router, the two hosts can't communicate.

ExamAlert

Being able to do the AND operation is a useful skill. A lot of test questions center around the network ID, and being able to find it quickly is a big help.

The Broadcast ID

The broadcast ID is the address that represents every host on that network or subnet. Sometimes called a directed broadcast, it is the common address of all hosts on that network ID. This should not be confused with a full IP broadcast to the address of 255.255.255.255, which hits every IP host that can hear it; the broadcast ID hits only hosts on a common subnet.

Let's take the previous example of an increment of 64 and expand on the detail, as shown in Figure 3.8.

Subnets Created with Increment of 64 – NetID and Broadcast ID shown:

.0 N	.64 N	.128 N	.192 N
.1	.65	.129	.193
.	.	.	.
.	.	.	.
.	.	.	.
.62	.126	.190	.254
.63 B	.127 B	.191 B	.255 B

FIGURE 3.8 **Subnets from increment of 64 with network ID and broadcast ID shown.**

Note that all the multiples of the increment—the numbers that mark the start of each subnet—have been identified by an *N* for network ID, and the last IP in every subnet is marked with a *B* for broadcast ID. This leaves us with 62 IPs left over in each subnet, and any of these (but only these) can be assigned to a host.

This leaves us with a range of IP addresses within every network or subnet that can be assigned to hosts. There is an unofficial convention that the gateway or router for a subnet is assigned the first or the last IP address available, but that is entirely arbitrary.

ExamAlert

You need to know exactly what the first and last IP addresses are in any subnet; a lot of questions ask for them, and it's fundamental to understanding what is happening when you subnet.

The first valid IP address is defined as

Network ID + 1

In Figure 3.8, the first valid host IPs in each subnet are .1, .65, .129, and .193.

The last valid host is defined as

Broadcast ID – 1

In Figure 3.8, the last valid host IPs in each subnet are .62, .126, .190, and .254.

Tip

Here are some handy tips to help you keep track of the network ID, first and last hosts, and broadcast ID:

Network ID:	Always even
First host:	Always odd
Last host:	Always even
Broadcast ID:	Always odd

See how the subnetted mask in the previous example has shortened the number of 0s at the end of the mask as compared to the default of 8? We now have only six 0s in the host part, so our formula would be

$2^6 - 2 = 62$

Here's something interesting: It doesn't matter what IP address you use with this mask; that mask will always give you 62 hosts on each subnet. You can pick a Class A address, say 22.1.1.0, and that mask would still make 62 hosts per subnet. The number of 0s at the end of the mask always drives how many hosts are on each subnet, regardless of the address.

So, what happened to all the other host IPs we started with? Remember that subnetting takes a classful A, B, or C network and splits it into several equal-sized pieces. It's just like cutting a pie into pieces; the original amount of pie is still there, but each piece is now separate and smaller.

Remember that the number of 0s at the end at the mask always defines how many hosts are on each subnet, regardless of the address in use.

Number of Subnets

Following on with the pie analogy, we know that we slice a classful network into pieces—but how many pieces? There is a simple mathematical relationship to this as well, but it is slightly more complex because of an old rule that we sometimes have to deal with.

The basic formula for the number of subnets is similar to the hosts formula. It is simply 2^S, where S is the number of bits in the subnet field—that means the number of 1s in the mask past the default boundary for that address. If you look at Figure 3.9, you can see how this works.

The default boundary for that Class C address should be at the 24th bit, where the third octet ends and the fourth begins. The subnetted mask extends that by 2 bits into the fourth octet. So, we have stolen 2 bits, and our formula would look like this:

# of subnets = 2^S

S = 2

$2^2 = 4$

IP Address and Mask: 192.168.21.1 255.255.255.192

Binary IP: 11000000.10101000.00010101.00000001

Binary Mask: 11111111.11111111.11111111.11000000

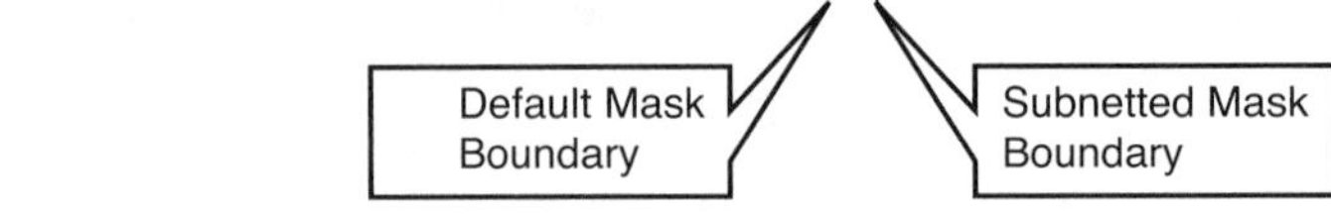

FIGURE 3.9 **Subnetted Class C with increment of 64.**

We made four subnets, as you saw earlier. To figure out how many bits we stole, we first must know where the default boundary is so that we know where to start counting. This is where knowing the address classes and the correct default masks is critical; if you can't figure this out, you will not be able to answer most subnetting questions correctly, and that would be bad.

Now here's where things get tricky. A rule that some older systems use says that the first and last subnets created are invalid and unusable. The rule is known as the Subnet Zero Rule, and obviously if it is in effect, we lose two subnets from the total we create. These two subnets will be referred to from now on as the zero subnets. Newer systems do not use the Zero Subnets Rule, including newer Cisco devices. This is confusing and makes things more difficult—but difficult is not something Cisco shies away from on its certification exams. So if you want your CCNA, pay attention to the question and don't complain about how hard it is.

ExamAlert

Cisco tests might be difficult and tricky, but they are fair; they do not withhold information you need to answer the question. The test question will always tell you whether somehow the Zero Subnets Rule is in effect; yes, both types of questions are asked.

The Cisco IOS supports the use of the zero subnets. The command **ip subnet zero** turns on the ability to use them, so that might be how the question is telling you whether they are in effect. Once you pass your CCNA, you will not likely have to worry about the Zero Subnets Rule again, unless you lose your mind and decide to become a Cisco trainer.

Tip

After you determine whether the zero subnets are available, use the following to get the calculation for the number of subnets right:

Zero subnets not available?	Subtract two subnets: The formula is $2^S - 2$.
Zero subnets available?	Keep all subnets: The formula is 2^S.

Working with Subnetting Questions

ExamAlert

The approach you need to take to any subnetting question is simple. After you become fluent in subnetting, you can take some shortcuts; but to build a solid understanding, you need to be methodical.

Every subnetting question you ever see will revolve around one of three things:

- Number of hosts
- Number of subnets
- The increment

Your task will be to simply figure out what the question is asking for and solve it without getting confused or distracted.

Determining Host Requirements

There are only two scenarios when determining the host requirements: Either you are given a mask and asked how many hosts per subnet this creates or you are given a requirement for a certain number of hosts and asked to provide the appropriate mask. Either way, the number of 0s at the end of the mask drives how many hosts per subnet there will be; the address to which that mask is applied is irrelevant. Your task is to put the correct number of 0s at the end of the mask such that $2^H - 2$ is greater than or equal to the desired number of hosts, or to determine what the value of $2^H - 2$ actually is. From there, you must choose the correct expression of the mask, either in dotted-decimal or CIDR notation.

Determining Subnet Requirements

The scenarios for determining subnet requirements are quite similar to the host questions. Either you are told how many subnets you need and asked to provide the appropriate mask or you are given a mask and asked how many subnets it creates. Note that in both cases (unlike hosts questions), you must know the IP address or at least the class of address you are working with. Creating subnets happens by extending the default mask, so you must know where the mask should end by default—and for that you need to know the class of address. Once you know where to start, simply extend the mask by the correct number of subnet bits such that $2^S - 2$ (or possibly just 2^S) gives you the correct number of subnets.

ExamAlert

Remember that the Zero Subnets Rule might come into play here. Although the majority of questions say that the zero subnets are valid and therefore the formula should be 2^S, it's possible that a few questions may clearly state that zero subnets are not available. Read the question!

Determining Increment-Based Requirements

Increment questions are the most challenging and complex subnetting questions, often requiring you to do a lot of legwork before you can get to the answer.

Increment questions often give you two or more IP addresses and masks, and ask you things such as, "Why can't Host A ping Host B?" The answer could be that A and B are on different subnets. To determine this, you need to understand where those subnets begin and end, and that depends on the increment. Another popular question gives you several IP addresses and masks that are applied to PCs, servers, and routers. The system, as it is described, is not working, and you need to determine what device has been incorrectly configured—perhaps two IPs in different subnets, perhaps a host that is using a network ID or broadcast ID as its address.

The key is to first determine what the increment is or should be; then, carefully plot out the multiples of the increment—the network IDs of all the subnets. Then you can add the broadcast IDs, which are all one less than the next network ID. Now you have a framework into which you can literally draw the host IP ranges, without risk of "losing the picture" if you do this all in your head.

All of these skills take practice. Everyone goes through the same process in learning subnetting: For quite a while, you will have no idea what is going on—then suddenly, the light goes on and you "get it." Rest assured that you will get it. It takes longer for some than others, and you do need practice or you will lose the skill.

The Subnetting Chart

You should now understand concepts and mechanics of subnetting. You can do it and get the right answer almost all of the time, but it takes you a while. This is good—congratulations! If you are not at that point yet, you should practice more before you look at this next section.

What follows is one of many variations of a subnetting chart. This is a good one because it is easy to use under pressure when your brain will behave unpredictably.

ExamAlert

You must be able to re-create this chart exactly and correctly before you start your exam. If you make a simple mistake in creating your chart, you could easily get all of your subnetting questions wrong, and that would probably cause you to fail.

The chart represents the last two octets of a subnet mask, and what effect a 1 or a 0 in the different bit positions will have. It lists the increment, CIDR notation, the mask in decimal, the number of hosts created, and the number of subnets formed from a Class B and C address. Use an acronym to help get the rows correct: "Internet Class May Have Been Canceled." (I = increment, C = CIDR, M = mask, H = host, B = B hosts, C = C hosts). Figure 3.10 shows a completed version.

Subnetting Chart

	32768	16384	8192	4096	2048	1024	512	256									
Increment	128	64	32	16	8	4	2	1	-	128	64	32	16	8	4	2	1
CIDR	/17	/18	/19	/20	/21	/22	/23	/24	-	/25	/26	/27	/28	/29	/30	/31	/32
Mask	128	192	224	240	248	252	254	255	-	128	192	224	240	248	252	254	255
Hosts	32766	16382	8190	4094	2046	1022	510	254	-	126	62	30	14	6	2	0	0
B-Subnet	2	4	8	16	32	64	128	256	-	512	1024	2048	4096	8192	16384	~	~
C-Subnet	1	1	1	1	1	1	1	1	-	2	4	8	16	32	64	~	~

FIGURE 3.10 **The subnetting chart.**

The following are steps to re-create the chart:

1. The first row is simply the binary bit position values—the powers of 2. Start at the right with 1 and keep doubling the value as you go left: 1, 2, 4, 8, 16, 32, 64, 128. Repeat for the third octet.
2. The second row is the CIDR notation—the number of 1s in a row in the mask. Our chart starts at the 17th bit, so number the second row starting at 17, through 32.
3. The third row is the mask in binary. Add consecutive bit values together from left to right to get the valid mask values of 128, 192, 224, 240, 248, 252, 254, and 255. Or you can just memorize them.
4. The fourth row is the number of hosts created. Starting at the right side of the fourth octet, subtract 2 from the increment line (the first line) and enter that value. Do this for the whole fourth octet. When you get to the third octet (the left half of the chart), you will have to change your approach: The value will keep increasing in the same pattern, but subtracting 2 from the top row won't work anymore because the top row resets for the third octet. The simplest approach is to double the last value and add 2. For example, (126 × 2) + 2 = 254, (254 × 2)+2 = 510, and so on.
5. The fifth row is the number of subnets created from a Class B address. Starting at the left side of the chart (the third octet), repeat the values from the first line, but in reverse order. Remember to start at 2!.

Caution

Remember that the Zero Subnets Rule will change your answers and how you use your chart. If the zero subnets are not allowed, simply deduct 2 from the values in lines 5 and 6 of your chart in the appropriate octet.

6. The sixth row of the chart is the number of subnets created from a Class C address. Remember, with a Class C, we do not make any subnets (that is, we have only one network) in the third octet, so we have all 1s there. For the fourth octet, the numbers are the same as in row 5; just start them in the fourth octet instead. The same caution and tactic about the zero subnets applies.

Provided you have built it correctly, your chart is a huge help in answering subnetting questions quickly and accurately. All you need to do is determine what the question is asking for, and then look up that value on your chart. All of the answers you need will be in the same column. Practice building and using the chart until it becomes something you can do without thinking. You will need your brain for other more complicated problems.

Cram Quiz

1. What is the ideal mask to use on point-to-point serial links?
2. Is 172.16.255.0/18 a valid host IP?
3. Julie's IP address is 192.168.1.21 255.255.255.240. Joost's IP is 192.168.1.14/28. Their computers are connected together using a crossover Ethernet cable. Why can't they ping each other?
   - ❍ **A.** The subnet masks are different
   - ❍ **B.** They can. This is another trick question.
   - ❍ **C.** Because they are in different subnets.
   - ❍ **D.** Because the router does not support subnetting.
   - ❍ **E.** Because it should be a straight-through cable.

Cram Quiz Answers

1. /30, or 255.255.255.252. That provides two valid host IPs, one for each end of the link.
2. Yes. The subnet's valid host IPs range from 172.16.192.1 to 172.16.255.254 .
3. Answer C is correct. Answer A is incorrect; the masks are the same, just written differently. Answer B is incorrect, sorry. Answers D and E are incorrect. First of all, the question specifically mentions that they are cabled back to back with a crossover; Second, a router that doesn't support subnetting probably came as a prize in a box of cereal. Real routers support subnetting.

VLSM

CramSaver

1. Why is VLSM important to modern IP networks?
   - **A.** Because networks that use the same mask cannot route.
   - **B.** Because every subnet must use a different mask to avoid conflicts.
   - **C.** Because it allows us to uniquely identify each subnet by its mask number.
   - **D.** Because it allows each subnet in a routed system to be correctly sized for the requirement.

2. What must a routing protocol be able to do to support VLSM?
   - **A.** Multicast
   - **B.** Automatically summarize networks to a common mask
   - **C.** Advertise the mask for each subnet in the routing update

Answers

1. Answer D is correct. Answers A and B are simply untrue. Answer C sounds good, but networks are uniquely identified by the network ID, not the mask.
2. Answer C is correct. Answer A is not a requirement. Answer B is effectively the opposite of VLSM

Variable-length subnet masking or VLSM can be defined as the capability to apply more than one subnet mask to a given class of addresses throughout a routed system. Although this is common practice in modern networks, there was a time when this was impossible because the routing protocols in use could not support it. Classful protocols such as RIPv1 do not include the subnet mask of advertised networks in their routing updates; therefore, they cannot possibly learn the existence of more than one mask length. Only classless routing protocols—EIGRP, OSPF, RIPv2, IS-IS, and BGP—include the subnet mask for the networks they advertise in their routing updates and thus publish a level of detail that makes VLSM possible.

The main push for VLSM came from the need to make networks the right size.

Subnetting logically creates the appropriately sized networks, but without the capability for routing protocols to advertise the existence (for example) of both a /26 and a /30 network within the same system. Prior to VLSM-capable routing protocols, the network in our example would have been confined to using only /26 masks throughout the system. The use of VLSM has two main advantages that are closely linked:

- It makes network addressing more efficient.
- It provides the capability to perform route summarization (discussed in the next section).

ExamAlert

Know the definition of VLSM and its two main advantages.

An illustration of the need for VLSM is shown in Figure 3.11.

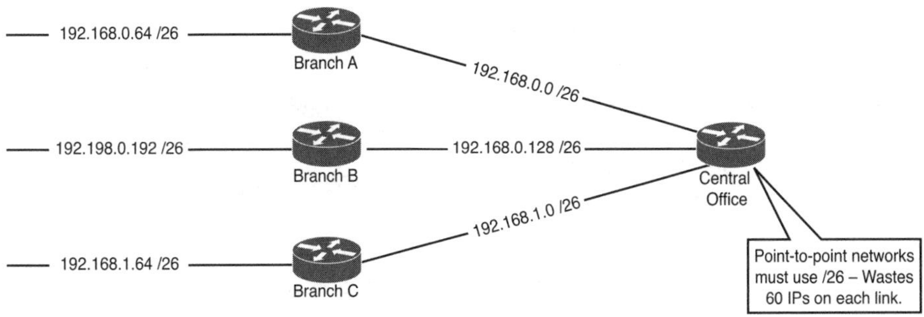

FIGURE 3.11 **Inefficient addressing without VLSM.**

The diagram shows several branch offices using subnetted Class C (/26) addresses that provide each branch with 62 possible host IPs. The branches are connected to the central office via point-to-point WAN links. The ideal mask to use for such a link is /30 because it provides only two hosts, one for each end of the link. The problem arises when the routing protocols are configured: Prior to VLSM, the /30 networks could not be used because the /26 networks existed in the same system and the classful routing protocols could only advertise one mask per class of address. All networks, including the little /30 links, had to use the same mask of /26. This wastes 60 IP addresses on each WAN link.

With the implementation of VLSM-capable routing protocols, we can deploy a /30 mask on the point-to-point links, and the routing protocols can advertise them as /30s along with the /26s in the branches because the subnet mask for each network is included in the routing updates. Figure 3.12 illustrates the preferred, optimized addressing scheme that takes advantage of VLSM.

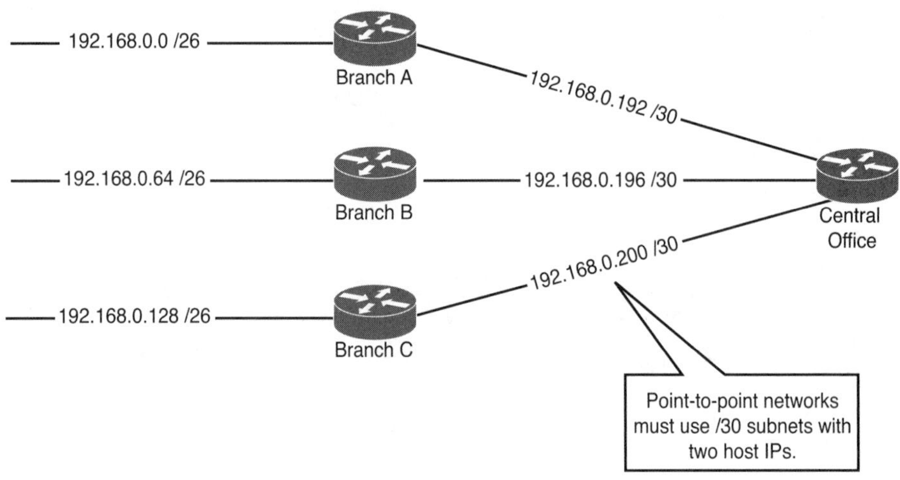

FIGURE 3.12 **Optimized addressing using VLSM.**

Note that using VLSM has allowed us to make the point-to-point link networks the ideal size (two hosts on each) using /30 masks. This has allowed us to use a single subnetted Class C network for all the addressing requirements in this scenario—and as you'll see, it makes a perfect opportunity to summarize these routes. This is what is meant by "more efficient addressing"—in other words, making networks the right size without depleting the limited address space or limiting future growth.

Cram Quiz

1. True or false: It is impossible to subnet a subnet.
2. How does VLSM make IP addressing more efficient?
   - ❍ **A.** By increasing the total number of IP addresses.
   - ❍ **B.** By decreasing the total number of IP addresses
   - ❍ **C.** By creating subnets
   - ❍ **D.** By allowing a routed system to include subnets of different mask lengths to suit requirements

Cram Quiz Answers

1. False. It is not only possible, you can in fact subnet a subnet of a subnet—and keep going as long as there are sufficient bits left in the mask.
2. Answer D is correct. Answers A and B are incorrect: VLSM neither creates nor deletes IP addresses. (You might argue that subnetting reduces the available IPs, but VLSM itself is not necessarily subnetting.) Likewise, Answer C is not correct; VLSM does not create subnets. It is simply the application of different subnet masks within a routed system.

Route Summarization

CramSaver

1. What is the best summary for the following range of subnets? 172.20.32.0/24 to 172.20.47.0/24
2. Why is summarization so important to an efficient routed system?
   - **A.** It adds detail to the route tables of routers.
   - **B.** Summarization sends all subnets as classful networks, eliminating the overhead of transmitting the mask in routing updates.
   - **C.** Summarization reduces the size of route tables, prevents route table instability due to flapping routes, and reduces the size of routing updates.
   - **D.** Summarization enforces router authentication, preventing spurious updates from excessively loading the router.

Answers

1. 172.20.32.0/20 or 172.20.32.0 255.255.240.0
2. Answer C is correct. A is incorrect; that is the opposite effect of summarization. Answer B is incorrect; this describes classful routing protocols (in part). Answer D is completely untrue.

If subnetting is the process of lengthening the mask to create multiple smaller subnets from a single larger network, route summarization can be described as shortening the mask to include several smaller networks into one larger network address. As the network grows large, the number of individual networks listed in the IP route table becomes too big for routers to handle effectively. They get slower, drop packets, and even crash. This, of course, is an undesirable state of affairs. With more than 450,000 routes (at the time of this writing, anyway) known to major Internet routers, some way to reduce the number of entries is not only desirable, but also critical.

In the previous VLSM example, all the subnets for the branches and the WAN links were created from the 192.168.0.0 /24 Class C network. If we take that diagram and put it into context, we can see how route summarization can reduce the number of entries in the route table, as shown in Figure 3.13.

The Central Office router can either send a routing update with all the subnets it knows about listed individually, or it can send a single line in the update that essentially says, “Send anything that starts with 192.168.0 to me.” Both methods work; the issue is one of scalability. No router will ever collapse under the load of advertising six subnets, but make it 6,000 subnets and it makes a huge difference in performance if you summarize as much as possible.

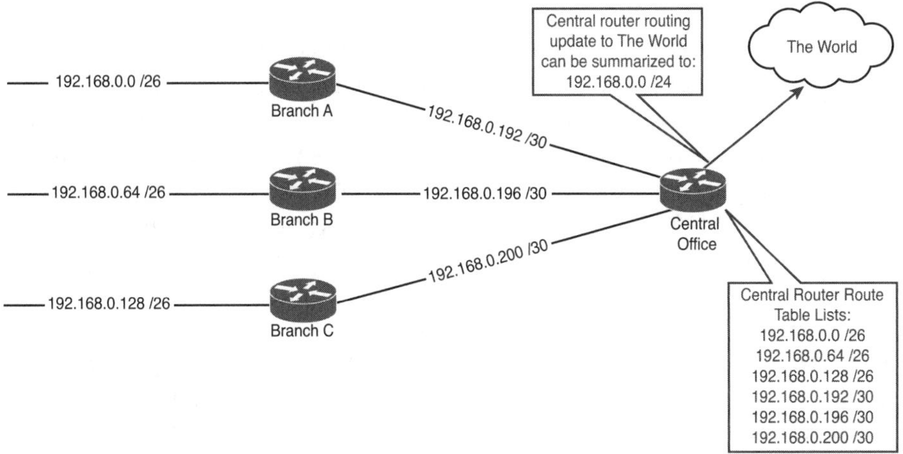

FIGURE 3.13 **Simple route summarization example.**

Route summarization takes a set of contiguous networks or subnets and groups them together using a shorter subnet mask. The advantages of summarization are that it reduces the number of entries in the route table, which reduces load on the router and network overhead, and hides instability in the system behind the summary, which remains valid even if summarized networks are unavailable.

Note

The word *contiguous* sometimes confuses people. It is not a typo of *continuous*; the word means “adjacent or adjoining.” For example, when we make subnets using a 16 increment, the first four network IDs are .0, .16, .32, and .48. Those four subnets are contiguous because they are adjacent to each other. If we take the last four subnets from that same increment (.192, .208, .224, and .240), they are contiguous with each other, but not with the first four—there are a bunch of subnets between the two sets.

ExamAlert

Know the definition and advantages of route summarization.

Summarization Guidelines

It is important to follow a few rules and guidelines when summarizing. Serious routing problems will happen otherwise—such as routers advertising networks inaccurately and possibly duplicating other routers' advertisements, suboptimal or even totally incorrect routing, and severe data loss.

The first rule is to design your networks with summarization in mind, even if you don't need it yet. This means that you will group contiguous subnets together behind the router that will summarize them—you do not want to have some subnets from a summarized group behind some other router. The summary is essentially saying, "I can reach the networks represented by this summary; send any traffic for them through me." If one (or more) of the networks behind the summarizing router is unavailable, traffic will be dropped—but not by the summarizing router, because the individual routes to the networks that were summarized are still valid, and have a longer match entry than the summary. The packet will get routed to the router that connects to the dead network, and dropped there. Advance planning, including making plenty of room for future growth, will give you a solid, scalable network design that readily lends itself to summarizing. Figure 3.14 shows a badly designed network that will be almost impossible to summarize because the subnets are discontiguous, with individual subnets scattered all over the system.

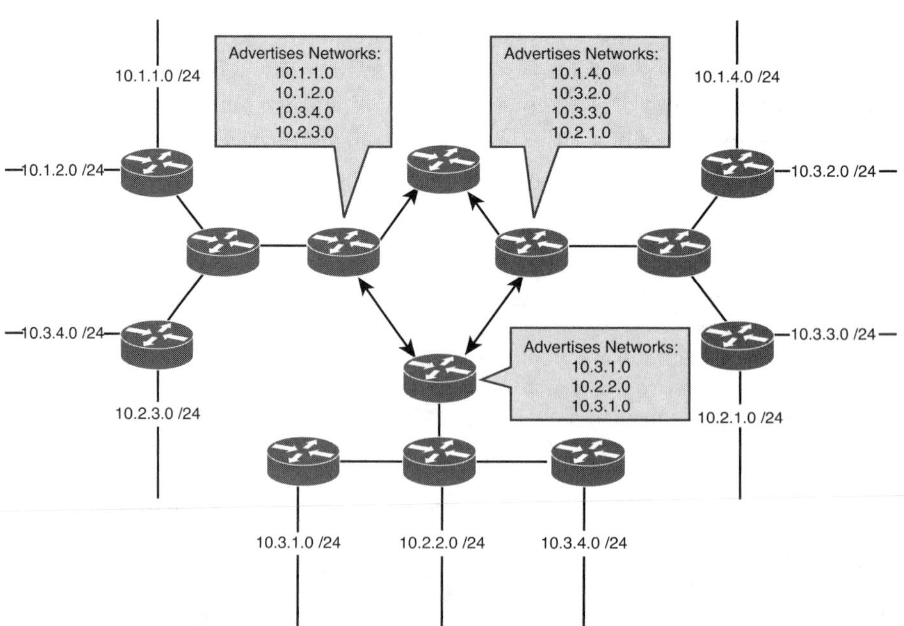

FIGURE 3.14 **Poor planning prevents proper performance.**

The second rule is to summarize into the core of your network. The core is where the bigger, faster, busier routers are—like the Central Office router in the previous example. These routers have the job of dealing with high volumes of traffic headed for all different areas of the network, so we do not want to burden them with big, highly detailed route tables. The further you get from the core, the more detail the routers need to get traffic to the correct destination network. It's much like using a map to drive to a friend's house; you don't need a great deal of detail when you are on the highway, but when you get into the residential areas, you need to know very precise information if you have a hope of finding the place.

Figure 3.15 illustrates the same network after your friendly neighborhood Cisco Certified Internetwork Expert has spent the afternoon re-addressing the network and configuring summarization. This network will scale beautifully and have minimal performance issues (at least because of route table and routing update overhead).

Following these rules will give you one of the additional benefits of summarization as well: hiding instability in the summarized networks. Let's say that one of the branches is having serious spanning-tree problems because Sparky the Junior Woodchuck was allowed to configure a Cisco switch. (This is actually a felony in some states.) That route could be "flapping"—up, down, up, down—as spanning-tree wreaks havoc with your network. The router will be doing its job, sending out updates every time the route flaps. If we were not summarizing, those flapping messages would propagate through the entire corporate system, putting a totally unnecessary and performance-robbing load on the routers. Once you summarize, the summary is stable: It can't flap because it is not a real network. It's just like a spokesperson at a press conference: "The rumors of a fire at the Springfield plant have had no impact on production whatsoever." Meanwhile, the Springfield plant could be a charred hulk. The summary is still valid, and traffic will still be sent to the router connected to the flapping network. This keeps people from asking any more questions about the Springfield fire. However, if someone were to send a shipment to Springfield, it would be hastily redirected to another site (or dropped). All we have done is hide the problem from the rest of the world so that we don't flood the Internet with rapid-fire routing updates.

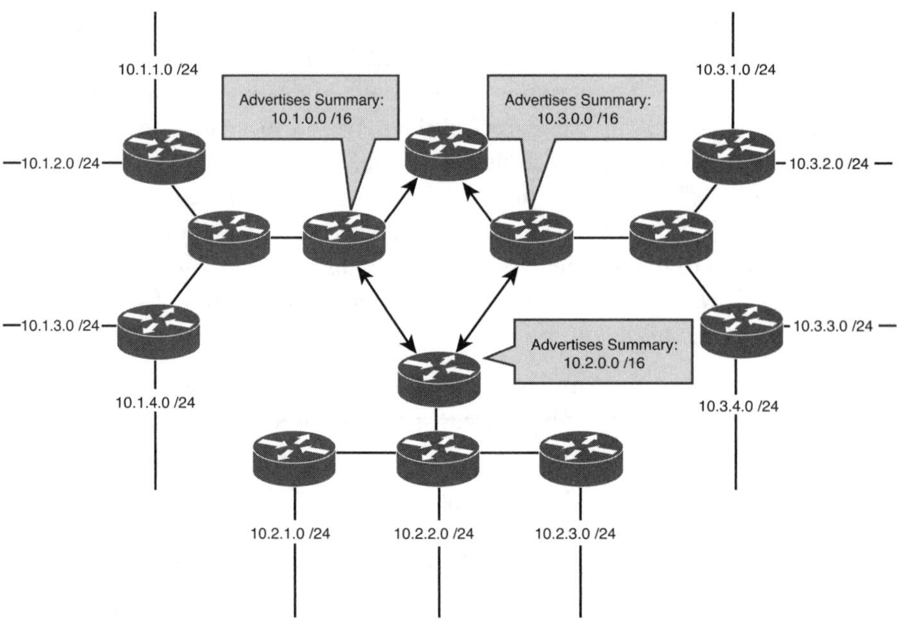

FIGURE 3.15 **Proper planning prevents poor performance.**

Determining Summary Addresses

When using routing protocols in classless configurations, creating summary addresses is a totally manual process. Classful routing protocols perform automatic summarization, but that is not as fancy as it sounds. They simply treat any subnet as the classful address from which it was created, which works if your networks are built with this in mind; however, in reality that is too simplistic and real networks need more customized summarization. The upshot of all this is that you need to understand how to determine the summary address given a set of networks to be summarized, and you also need to be able to figure out if a particular network is included in a given summary.

Remember that summarization is exactly the opposite of subnetting; in fact, another term for summarization is supernetting. (You might also see it called aggregation.) When we subnet, we lengthen the mask, doubling the number of networks each time we add an extra bit to the mask. Supernetting does the opposite: For each bit we retract or shorten the mask, we combine networks into groups that follow the binary increment numbers.

To illustrate this, let's look at the private Class B address space. These networks are listed as follows:

172.16.0.0 /16
172.17.0.0 /16
172.18.0.0 /16
172.19.0.0 /16
172.20.0.0 /16
172.21.0.0 /16
172.22.0.0 /16
172.23.0.0 /16
172.24.0.0 /16
172.25.0.0 /16
172.26.0.0 /16
172.27.0.0 /16
172.28.0.0 /16
172.29.0.0 /16
172.30.0.0 /16
172.31.0.0 /16

If you look carefully, you will notice that the range of networks is identified in the second octet. The octet where the range is happening is referred to as the *interesting octet*. This is your first clue where to begin your summarization.

The next step is to figure out what the binary values of the network's range are. The binary values for the interesting octet are shown in Figure 3.16.

16 = 0 0 0 1 0 0 0 0
17 = 0 0 0 1 0 0 0 1
18 = 0 0 0 1 0 0 1 0
19 = 0 0 0 1 0 0 1 1
20 = 0 0 0 1 0 1 0 0
21 = 0 0 0 1 0 1 0 1
22 = 0 0 0 1 0 1 1 0
23 = 0 0 0 1 0 1 1 1
24 = 0 0 0 1 1 0 0 0
25 = 0 0 0 1 1 0 0 1
26 = 0 0 0 1 1 0 1 0
27 = 0 0 0 1 1 0 1 1
28 = 0 0 0 1 1 1 0 0
29 = 0 0 0 1 1 1 0 1
30 = 0 0 0 1 1 1 1 0
31 = 0 0 0 1 1 1 1 1

FIGURE 3.16 **Binary values for Class B private range second octet.**

You should see a pattern in the binary values: The first 4 bits are all the same. The range is actually happening in the last 4 bits in the second octet; those 4 bits range from 0000 through 1111; the first 4 bits are common for all 16 networks in the range.

The next step is to identify those common bits. While you are learning how to do this, it's a good idea to write out the binary for the range and draw a line that represents the boundary between the common bits and the variable bits in the range. Remember, be absolutely sure that your boundary line is in the right place: For all the networks in the range, everything to the left of the line must be identical, and everything to the right will be the ranging values.

The next step is easy. We are about to summarize: All we need to do is to build a subnet mask that puts a 1 under all of the common bits in the range, and a 0 under everything else—1s to the left of the boundary, and 0s to the right, as shown in Figure 3.17.

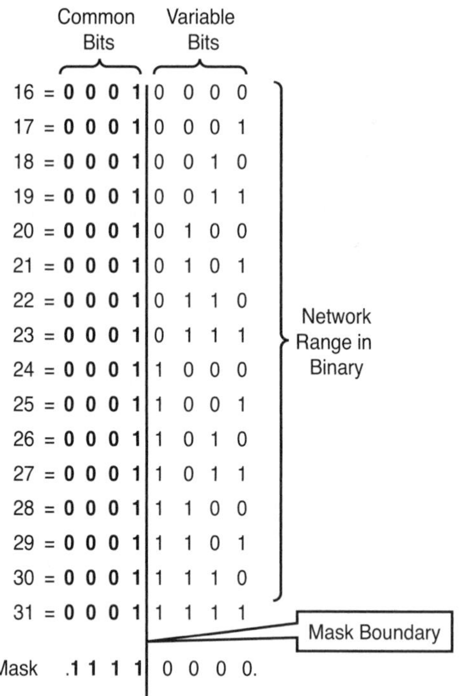

FIGURE 3.17 **Identifying and masking the common bits in a summary.**

The last step is to actually create the summary statement. A summary is always an IP address plus a mask; the IP is usually a network ID, and it should be the first network in the range. In our example, the first network ID is 172.16.0.0 so that is the IP we will use. For the mask, the first octet is the same in the whole range, and we have figured out that the first four bits in the second octet are always the same. Remembering that a mask is always a string of 1s followed by a string of 0s, this means that we should mask all 8 bits in the first octet and the first 4 in the second octet, so our mask looks like this:

```
11111111.11110000.00000000.00000000
```

That can also be expressed as

```
255.240.0.0 or /12
```

So, our summary statement becomes

```
172.16.0.0 255.240.0.0
```

or

```
172.16.0.0 /12
```

Reverse engineering this is the same process. You are given a summary statement and asked what networks it includes. The octet in which the mask changes from 1s to 0s is the interesting one, where the range will be defined. Jot down the address and mask in that octet in binary and see what possible values are in the range. Then check the networks to see if those are in the range. Figure 3.18 gives an example.

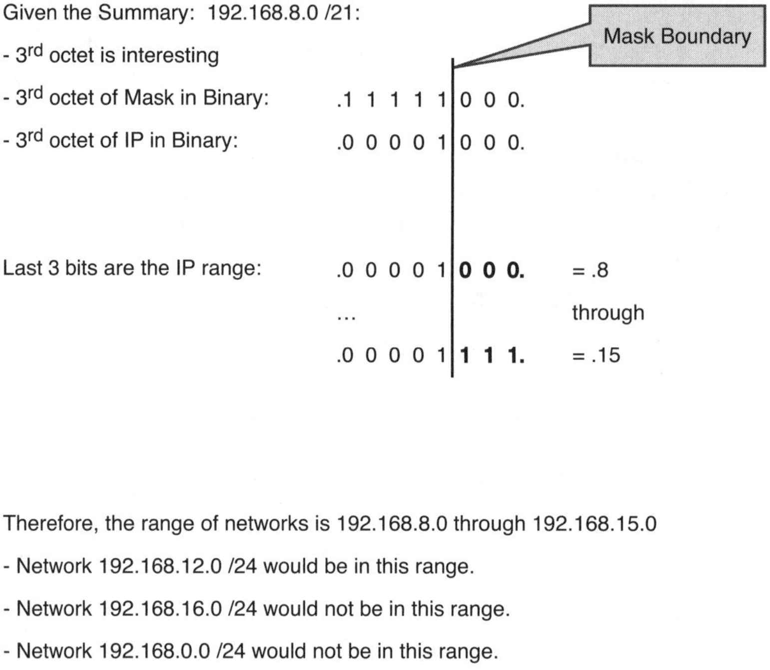

Given the Summary: 192.168.8.0 /21:

- 3rd octet is interesting

- 3rd octet of Mask in Binary: .1 1 1 1 1 | 0 0 0.

- 3rd octet of IP in Binary: .0 0 0 0 1 | 0 0 0.

Mask Boundary

Last 3 bits are the IP range: .0 0 0 0 1 | **0 0 0.** = .8

... through

.0 0 0 0 1 | **1 1 1.** = .15

Therefore, the range of networks is 192.168.8.0 through 192.168.15.0

- Network 192.168.12.0 /24 would be in this range.

- Network 192.168.16.0 /24 would not be in this range.

- Network 192.168.0.0 /24 would not be in this range.

FIGURE 3.18 **Summary address analysis.**

Cram Quiz

1. You are given the following ranges of subnets:

192.168.1.0/29	192.168.1.128/29
192.168.1.8/29	192.168.1.136/29
192.168.1.16/29	192.168.1.144/29
192.168.1.24/29	192.168.1.152/29
192.168.1.32/29	192.168.1.160/29
192.168.1.40/29	192.168.1.168/29
192.168.1.48/29	192.168.1.176/29
192.168.1.56/29	192.168.1.184/29

Your task is to summarize these two ranges of subnets. Do *not* include any subnets not named in the ranges in your summary. (Hint: You may use more than one summary address).

2. Your boss complains that manual route summarization is difficult and complex, and wonders if maybe you should not bother with it. What are the most compelling arguments in favor of route summarization? Choose all that apply.

   ❍ **A.** Utilizes the full RAM and CPU performance capacity of the routers

   ❍ **B.** Can suppress the effects of an unstable or "flapping" interface

   ❍ **C.** Advertises complete and detailed route tables

   ❍ **D.** Increases security by advertising "fake" networks

   ❍ **E.** Reduces the size of the route tables

   ❍ **F.** Reduces the load on RAM, CPU, and bandwidth of routers

Cram Quiz Answers

1. Two summary statements are required. Because these two network ranges are discontiguous, we cannot use a single statement without including the ranges between and after, which is both not allowed in the question and not generally a good idea in practice. The two summary statements are 192.168.1.0/26 and 192.168.1.128/26. The /26 in each statement can also be expressed as 255.255.255.192.

2. Answers B, E, and F are correct. Answer A is incorrect because summarization actually reduces the load on routers, and maxing out your router is not a good idea to begin with. Answer C is incorrect; summarization sends out summary routes that represent the detailed routes. Answer D is incorrect, but tricky: Summarization does in fact send out fake routes, but this does nothing to increase security.

IPv6

CramSaver

1. Which of the following are valid types of IPv6 address? Choose all that apply.
   - **A.** Global unicast
   - **B.** Unique local
   - **C.** Link local
   - **D.** Multicast
   - **E.** Anycast
   - **F.** Broadcast
   - **G.** Directed broadcast

2. Which of the following are valid IPv6 addresses? Choose all that apply.
   - **A.** 2001:0db8:0000:0000:0000:ff00:0042:8329
   - **B.** 2001:db8:0:0:0:ff00:42:8329
   - **C.** 2001:db8::ff00:42:8329
   - **D.** 0000:0000:0000:0000:0000:0000:0000:0001
   - **E.** ::1
   - **F.** ::192:168:1:1

3. Which of the following is a valid command to apply an IPv6 address to a router interface?
   - **A.** **interface fastethernet 1/0 ip address 2001:AB00:00FF:1::/64 eui-64**
   - **B.** **interface fastethernet 1/0 ipv6 address 2001:AB00:00FF:1::/64 eui-64**
   - **C.** **line con 0 ipv6 address 2001:AB00:00FF:1::/64 eui-64**
   - **D.** **interface fastethernet 1/0 ipv6 address 2001:AB00:000FF:1/64 eui-64**

Answers

1. Answers A, B, C, D, and E are correct. IPv6 does not broadcast, so Answers F and G are wrong.
2. All answers are correct! Even F, which looks bogus, is sometimes used (probably to mke the admin feel a little better).
3. Answer B is correct. Answer A is wrong because it uses **ip** instead of **ipv6**. Answer C is wrong because the Console port cannot be given an IPv6 (or IP for that matter) address. Answer D is wrong because the IPv6 address is missing the :: to make it the correct 64-bit length.

Up to this point, when we talked about IP or an IP address, we were referring to IP Version 4. IPv4 was created to build a Defense Department network in the early 1970s. At the time, no one foresaw that the Internet as we know it today was going to happen. The designers of the TCP/IP suite of protocols did not plan for their little project to balloon into the largest network in the world and revolutionize the commercial, cultural, and communications behavior of the whole planet.

But it did, and a couple problems came to light rather quickly when the Internet started to really catch on. One really tricky one was that the address "space" was originally handed out without quite enough thought and planning as to who got what size chunks, and what routers would be responsible for those chunks. At the time it didn't matter; there were plenty of addresses to go around. But as the routers started to get really large route tables, with all these networks being added, they had trouble dealing with it. Routers at the time were relatively small and slow, and when the route tables became so large, they were overloaded, slow to do their jobs, and generally poor performers. Solutions were urgently needed because the Internet was growing very fast and the problem was only getting worse.

The solutions came in things like VLSM-capable protocols, route summarization, a reassignment and redistribution of addresses, and the NAT service. These solutions have allowed the IPv4 address space to continue to function and serve as the address system for the Internet, but the second problem is one we can't get around: The mathematical reality is that there are not enough IP addresses available to meet the demand (especially in Europe and Asia). More people want Internet addresses than there are addresses to hand out.

This is where IPv6 comes in. Whereas an IPv4 address is a 32-bit string, theoretically providing more than 4 billion IP addresses (for the sake of clarity I'll ignore the fact that a large number of theses addresses are not really usable). An IPv6 address is 128 bits long, providing about 3.4×10^{38} possible addresses, or as the story goes, 500,000,000,000,000,000,000,000,000 addresses for each of the 6.5 billion people on the planet. Running out of IPv6 addresses is not expected to be a problem.

Along with the sheer number of addresses available, IPv6 also cleans up a few of the issues with IPv4, making the operation and management of large internetworks easier and more efficient, and adds some useful new functionality as well. So now we can easily envision a world where anything we want can have an Internet IP address (including silly things such as the fridge), where an Internet-enabled mobile phone can keep its IP address as it moves across the globe, and all the difficulty and headache caused by using VPNs through NAT disappears.

IPv6 Address Allocation

An organization called the Internet Corporation for Assigned Network Numbers (ICANN) has the overall responsibility for dividing up the IPv6 address space. They do so with the benefit of a better understanding of the global demand for Internet IP addresses and the luxury of a huge number of addresses to hand out.

The system works like this: First, remember that for the Internet to work well, we need to use route summarization so that the route tables don't get huge and slow the routers down. Route summarization works best if every router is responsible only for its "branch of the tree," with smaller branches feeding into larger and larger ones as we get closer to the core or trunk of the tree. This allows the possibility for a single router to advertise a summary that in effect says, "I can reach all North American routes." That big router connects to other routers that summarize routes for four major Internet service providers (ISPs). Each ISP router connects to smaller ISPs or large enterprise customers, who advertise the summaries that represent the addresses assigned to them. Figure 3.19 gives some idea of how this system works.

The beauty of the system is that it is organized, planned, and executed in advance, with efficient routing in mind. The large number of addresses available also means that changes at or below the ISP level, for example, because of mergers or large customers changing Internet providers, do not affect the global routing information at the core.

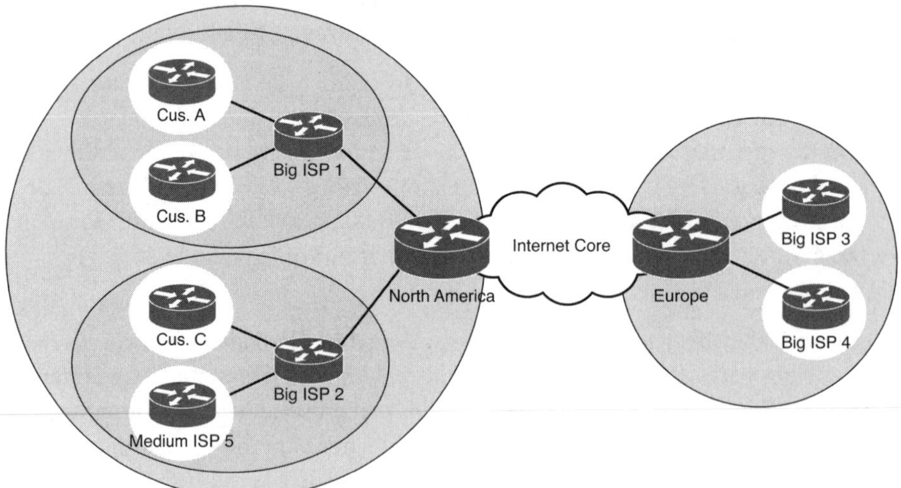

FIGURE 3.19 **Global IPv6 address design.**

IPv6 Address Notation

IPv6 addresses are different in appearance from IPv4. Of course, they are 128 bits long, so even in binary they would be four times longer than a 32-bit IPv4 address, but in notation that humans read and write the format is still different. Instead of using dotted-decimal in four octets, we use hexadecimal in eight sets of four characters separated by colons, like this:

2201:0FA0:080B:2112:0000:0000:0000:0001

The use of hex makes it a little easier to represent all those 128 bits in a shorter format because each character represents 4 bits. But it's still a long thing to type out, and remember that network people are generally lazy—so we have a couple of truncation methods to make the long addresses even shorter. The first method is that we are allowed to drop leading 0s (0s that appear at the beginning of each set), like so:

2201:FA0:80B:2112:0:0:0:1

That makes for a little less typing and a little more clarity. Pay attention to the fact that dropping 0s at the end of each set is not allowed! Dropping leading 0s does not change the value of the set; dropping 0s at the end does (like removing a 0 from the end of your paycheck amount—not good!)

The second truncation method we can use is to condense contiguous groups of all-0 sets. In our example, there are three sets that are all 0s. We can represent these by a double colon, like this:

2201:FA0:80B:2112::1

This is as short as it gets. We are only allowed to do the double-colon trick once in any address, so if you see an address with two double-colons in it, it is not valid. Here's an example:

2201::BCBF::1

One last piece of the addressing notation: the mask. We do not represent the mask as another set of hex characters. Instead, we identify the prefix length with slash notation. This is not as confusing at it seems: The slash notation simply identifies how many bits identify the network part, with the remainder being the host part.

For example, the North American registry ARIN (American Registry for Internet Numbers) was given the block of 2620:0000::/23 in September 2006. This indicates that the first 23 bits of 2620:0000:: identify the block of addresses that the North American routers will advertise to the rest of the world. From this point, ARIN will assign chunks of that space to the Big ISPs; Big ISP1 might get 2620:0100::/24, and Big ISP2 might get 2620:0200::/24. Those ISPs then hand out pieces of their chunk to smaller ISP or big customers, and the prefix length will get bigger as the chunks gets smaller—this should feel familiar because what we are doing here is subnetting. Don't worry, you won't be expected to subnet in IPv6. Not yet at least.

Types of IPv6 Addresses

An IPv6 address will be one of the following types. Some will be familiar, but there is one brand-new one, too.

- **Unicast:** An IPv6 unicast address is the same as an IPv4 unicast address; it is an IP that is assigned to an interface on a host. It can be the source of an IP packet or the destination for one. A packet sent to a unicast address goes to the one host with that address.
- **Global unicast:** A global unicast IPv6 address is the equivalent of a public, registered IP address. They are Internet routable, globally registered IPs that must be leased from an ISP.
- **Unique local:** Equivalent to a private IPv4 address; not registered with an ISP and not Internet routable.
- **Link local:** Every IPv6 interface gives itself a link-local address. The address range is FE80::/10, and usually combines this prefix with the last 64 bits in EUI-64 format. It is roughly equivalent to the Automatic Private IP Address (APIPA) address range of 169.254.0.0/16.
- **Multicast:** Just like in IPv4, a single IPv6 multicast address is assigned to multiple hosts so that a packet sent to the address may be delivered to multiple hosts more or less at the same time. IPv6 multicast addresses always start with the prefix FF00::/8.
- **Anycast:** An anycast address is a single address that is assigned to multiple hosts. This is similar to a multicast, except that a packet for the anycast address will be delivered to the one host that is nearest according to the routing protocol's idea of distance. There is no special prefix for anycast addresses.

There is no such thing as a broadcast in IPv6. Ever. Any requirement for broadcasting is performed by a multicast instead.

ExamAlert

Know the IPv6 address types. Remember that IPv6 cannot broadcast, ever! Any answers with the word broadcast in them are invalid.

IPv6 Address Configuration

For hosts to use IPv6 addresses, an IPv6 protocol stack must be installed. This likely means that you will need to upgrade your router IOS to provide IPv6 support. Then you can choose one of four options for address assignment.

To understand the address assignment choices better, we need to examine the concepts of stateful versus stateless configuration and the EUI-64 address format.

In IPv6, we can use DHCP to assign IP addresses just like in IPv4. The admin must set up the server with a scope of IPv6 addresses to hand out. The mechanisms used to discover and assign addresses are a little different, but the net result is the same. This is called *stateful addressing*, where the DHCP server keeps track of what hosts have been assigned what IPv6 address—in other words, the state of the host DHCP-wise.

There is another option for dynamic addressing in IPv6 called *stateless autoconfiguration*. This feature allows a host to choose and configure an address for itself. The host that wants an address learns what the /64 network prefix is on the local link, then appends its MAC address (in a special 64-bit format called EUI-64), thus generating a 128-bit IPv6 address that is unique to that host because it incorporates the unique MAC of the host.

The EUI-64 format is not so difficult to understand. We simply take the 48-bit MAC address and put a special pattern, FFFE, after the first 24 bits (the six OUI characters), followed by the rest of the six hex characters in the host MAC. The only trick is that according to IPv6 rules, the seventh bit in an EUI-64 address must be 1, which identifies that the burned-in MAC address has been modified. This is a little confusing, to be sure, but you can relax because the host determines and configures its EUI-64 address all by itself, if you tell it to. Here's what an EUI-64 address conversion looks like:

Original MAC:

00-15-C5-CB-42-2B

Original MAC in binary:

00000000-00010101-11000101-11001011-01000010-00101011

7th bit = 0

Change 7th bit to 1:

00000010-00010101-11000101-11001011-01000010-00101011

EUI-64 MAC now:

02-15-C5-CB-42-2B

EUI-64 Address = </64 net_prefix>:0215:C5FF:FECB:422B

So, back to the four choices. The following really simplifies the options:

- **Static configuration:** The administrator chooses and assigns a static IPv6 address to the host NIC. It is the admin's responsibility to choose an address that will function and be valid in the network to which the host is connected.
- **Static configuration using EUI-64:** The administrator manually configures the address with the local /64 network prefix followed by the host's MAC in EUI-64 format.
- **Dynamic configuration using DHCP to assign 128-bit address:** The host is set to obtain its address from DHCP, and the DHCP server is set up to hand out IPv6 addresses from a scope.
- **Dynamic configuration using stateless autoconfiguration with EUI-64:** The host is set to obtain its address automatically, but the DHCP server either does not exist (which works fine by the way), or if it does, it only informs the host of the /64 local network prefix.

IPv6 Router Configuration

Assuming your IOS provides IPv6 support, giving it an IPv6 address is really easy. The command is carried out at the interface configuration prompt:

```
interface fastethernet 1/0
ipv6 address 2001:AB00:00FF:1::/64 eui-64
```

Notice the **eui-64** switch; this tells the router to figure out its own EUI-64 address to follow the /64 prefix provided. Without that, you must provide a full 128-bit address in the command.

To verify your configuration, use the **show ipv6 interface** command at the interface configuration prompt. The following is a sample output (with different addresses applied). You can see multiple addresses in use by the interface for global unicast, link-local, and multiple multicast groups:

```
Router#show ipv6 interface
  Serial1/0 is up, line protocol is up
```

```
  IPv6 is enabled, link-local address is FE80::A8BB:CCFF:FE00:D200
  Global unicast address(es):
    2001:1:33::3, subnet is 2001:1:33::/64 [TENTATIVE]
  Joined group address(es):
    FF02::1
    FF02::1:FF00:3
    FF02::1:FF00:D200
  MTU is 1500 bytes
  ICMP error messages limited to one every 100 milliseconds
  ICMP redirects are enabled
  ND DAD is enabled, number of DAD attempts: 1
  ND reachable time is 30000 milliseconds
Router#
```

IPv6 Features

IPv6 has a couple features that you should keep in mind:

- **IPsec:** Support for IPsec is built in for IPv6; this means that every packet can be protected by IPsec transport on every IPv6 host if so configured.
- **Mobility:** IP mobility is built in, but obviously not mandatory because some hosts are not mobile.
- **Fixed header size:** The IPv6 header is fixed at 40 bytes or 320 bits. Figure 3.20 (in the next section) shows the IPv6 header.
- **ICMP for IPv6 has changed, adding new functionality:** One example of the new tricks it has learned is path MTU (PMTU) discovery: Before transmitting a packet, a host can send an ICMP message to learn what the smallest maximum transmission unit (MTU) on any link is between the sender and the destination. Then, the host sends packets that are no larger than that value. This clever trick relieves routers of having to fragment and reassemble packets over a small-MTU link, which can be a real performance hog. According to RFC 1981, hosts not using PMTU will transmit packets at the minimum IPv6 link MTU, which is actually quite small and likely to be inefficient.
- **IPv6 makes extensive use of Router Solicitation (RS) and Router Advertisement (RA) messages:** These are multicast messages to the addresses FF02::1 and FF00::2, respectively. The RS is sent from a host to all routers on the link as a multicast, and the RA message is sent from a router to all hosts on the link, also as a multicast. This is one way that the hosts learn whether DHCP is supported on the link, and possibly the DHCP server address.

The IPv6 Header

As mentioned in the preceding section, the IPv6 header is fixed at 40 bytes (320 bits) in length. Figure 16.11 shows the header fields and their sizes, and this section identifies what the fields are for.

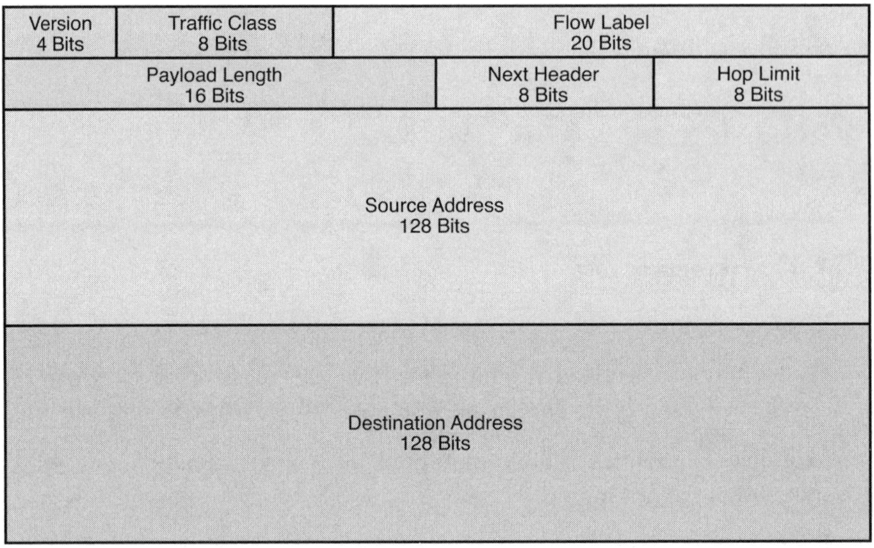

Version 4 Bits	Traffic Class 8 Bits	Flow Label 20 Bits	
Payload Length 16 Bits		Next Header 8 Bits	Hop Limit 8 Bits
Source Address 128 Bits			
Destination Address 128 Bits			

FIGURE 3.20 **The IPv6 header.**

The Version field identifies the IP version of this packet; for IPv6, obviously the version will be 6.

The Traffic Class field is where quality of service (QoS) marking for Layer 3 can be identified. In a nutshell, the higher the value of this field, the more important the packet. Your Cisco routers (and some switches) can be configured to read this value and send a high-priority packet sooner than other lower ones during times of congestion. This is very important for some applications, especially VoIP.

The Flow Label field is a number that identifies this packet as one of a flow of packets in a stream from sender to receiver; a good example is a VoIP call. It's best for VoIP if all the packets in a given call get sent along exactly the same path to the receiving phone, so that they arrive in the same order they were sent. The flow label is one mechanism that IPv6 routers can use to keep track of different application flows and try to make sure that all the packets within a flow get treated the same way.

The Payload Length field indicates how big the payload of this packet is; it can be variable, so the router needs to know where the packet is supposed to end. That way it knows if anything went missing. This is especially important because there is no header checksum, as there used to be in IPv4.

The Next Header field takes over the Options header functions in IPv4. Short codes for extension headers are listed in the Next Header field, and additional information is appended in additional headers after the primary IPv6 header. All of this is designed to speed up the routing of IPv6 packets by preserving the size and content of the primary header, so it can be routed in the "fast switching" path of the router.

The Hop Limit field is a cool one: Whereas in IPv4 there was a TTL field that limited the life of a packet to 255 hops. (The IPv4 TTL value typically starts at 255 and is decremented by at least 1 as a packet is processed by a router. If it reaches 0, the packet is dropped. This prevents the packet from being endlessly misrouted around the Internet, although it could be misrouted up to 255 hops.) IPv6 is smarter: The Hop Limit value is set to the actual number of hops the packet will go through to reach its destination. This hop information comes from the IPv6 routing protocols. The Hop Limit is still decremented by 1 at each router, but the more accurate value means that the packet can't be misrouted even by one hop.

The Source and Destination Address fields are self-explanatory; remember that the full 128-bit address for each is listed.

IPv6 Transition Strategies

Clearly, things are moving toward IPv6. The U.S. government once specified that all federal agencies must deploy IPv6 by 2008; then it was pushed back, ultimately to 2012. The process, though, is not going to affect every single host in these large networks overnight. Cisco wants you to be aware of their strategies for the transition to using IPv6 while still maintaining IPv4 functionality.

Tip

Putting CCNA exam studying aside for a moment, we strongly recommend that you start learning how to use IPv6 in your labs now. It is your big chance to be ready when the boss walks in and says, "We need to deploy IPv6 connectivity because of blah blah blah. Can you do it?" When you say, "Sure, no problem," and gain massive respect, that's when you can send us an email and thank us.

The easiest IPv6 transition choice is called dual stack. Dual stacking means that the host (router, PC, printer, and so on) runs both the IPv4 and IPv6 protocol stacks and can send and receive both types of packets, probably (but not necessarily) on the same interface. The drawbacks here are the additional load on the host and whether an IPv6 stack for that device is available (your old router might not be able to run IPv6).

Tunneling mode creates a tunnel for one protocol through another. You can picture taking an IPv6 packet from the head office, encapsulating it inside an IPv4 packet to transition across the provider network, then decapsulating it on the other side and forwarding the IPv6 packet into the remote branch office. This is known as a 6-to-4 tunnel; these tunnels can be either automatic or manual. 6-to-4 tunnels have a special address range of 2002::/16. Other tunneling strategies include the following:

- **Teredo tunneling:** Named after a particularly ugly species of marine wood-boring clam that makes tunnels in wood, this technology encapsulates IPv6 packets in IPv4 UDP datagrams for routing through the IPv4 network (usually the Internet). Its chief benefit is that it can operate from behind NAT devices. It is considered a “last resort” transition strategy, meaning that you should implement IPv6 natively instead, if possible.
- **ISATAP (Intra-Site Automatic Tunnel Addressing Protocol) tunneling:** This technology uses the IPv4 network (again, this would usually be the Internet) as a virtual NBMA data link layer. IPv6 link layer addressing is derived dynamically from IPv4 addresses, allowing dynamic neighbor discovery on top of IPv4 in addition to simple routability. ISATAP is a native capability in most Windows operating systems, Linux, and most Cisco IOS versions.

Translation means taking an IPv6 packet, removing the IP header, and replacing it with an IPv4 header that approximates the original IPv6 information as much as possible.

Translation is usually associated with a NAT router, and sometimes is known as NAT-PT (for Protocol Translation). What happens here is that the IPv6 packet header is removed and replaced with an IPv4 header (or vice versa), effectively changing from one protocol to the other. The big issues with NAT-PT are latency, performance loading, and the loss of header information in the translation process.

You need to know IPv6 configuration for your test; they may or may not ask you to actually do it (in a sim), but you definitely need to be able to recognize if the configuration they show you is valid.

Cram Quiz

1. Which is a valid alternate expression of FE80:0000:0000:0000:0202:B3FF:0E1E:8329? Choose all that apply.
   - ❍ **A.** FE80::0202:B3FF:0E1E:8329
   - ❍ **B.** FE80::0202:B3FF::E1E:8329
   - ❍ **C.** FE80::202:B3FF:E1E:8329
   - ❍ **D.** FE80::0202:B8FF:0E1E:8329

2. If the router's MAC address is 0012.7feb.6b40, which of the following is the correct EUI-64 format for the IPv6 link-local interface address?
   - ❍ **A.** ::0012:7FEB:6B40
   - ❍ **B.** 2001:DB8::212:7FFF:FEEB:6B40
   - ❍ **C.** 2001:DB8::212:7FFF:FE80:6B40
   - ❍ **D.** 2001:DB8::2012:7FEB:6B40
   - ❍ **E.** 2001:DB8::212:7FFF:0000:6B40

3. Which of the following are valid transition strategies when moving from IPv4 to IPv6? Choose all that apply.
   - ❍ **A.** NAT-PT
   - ❍ **B.** SNARD encapsulation
   - ❍ **C.** 4-in-4-out tunneling
   - ❍ **D.** Short stacking
   - ❍ **E.** 6-to-4 tunneling
   - ❍ **F.** Dual stacking

Cram Quiz Answers

1. Answers A and C are correct. Answer B is incorrect because it uses the "::" twice. Answer D is incorrect because of the B8FF, which should be B3FF:.
2. Answer B is correct. Answer A is incorrect because it omits the network number. Answer C is wrong because it uses the wrong value for the EUI expansion. (It uses FE80 instead of the correct FFFE.) Answer D is incorrect because it uses the wrong link-local network number, adding 0x2 to the end of the link-local identifier.
3. Answers A, E, and F are correct. Answers B, C, and D are incorrect; I just made up those terms.

Review Questions

1. Which of the following are alternate representations of the decimal number 227? Choose two.

   ❍ **A.** 0x227
   ❍ **B.** 11100011
   ❍ **C.** 0x143
   ❍ **D.** 0xE3
   ❍ **E.** 11100110

2. Which of the following are alternate representations of 0xB8? Choose two.

   ❍ **A.** 10110100
   ❍ **B.** 10111111
   ❍ **C.** 10111000
   ❍ **D.** 184
   ❍ **E.** 0x184

3. You have been asked to create a subnet that supports 16 hosts. What subnet mask should you use?

   ❍ **A.** 255.255.255.252
   ❍ **B.** 255.255.255.248
   ❍ **C.** 255.255.255.240
   ❍ **D.** 255.255.255.224

4. Given the mask 255.255.254.0, how many hosts per subnet does this create?

   ❍ **A.** 254
   ❍ **B.** 256
   ❍ **C.** 512
   ❍ **D.** 510
   ❍ **E.** 2

5. You are a senior network engineer at True North Technologies. Your boss, Mr. Martin, asks you to create a subnet with room for 12 IPs for some new managers. Mr. Martin promises that there will never be more than 12 managers, and he asks you to make sure that you conserve IP address space by providing the minimum number of possible host IPs on the subnet. What subnet mask will best meet these requirements?

   ❍ **A.** 255.255.255.12
   ❍ **B.** 255.255.255.0

- ❍ **C.** 255.255.240.0
- ❍ **D.** 255.255.255.240
- ❍ **E.** 255.255.255.224

6. Your boss, Duncan, does not seem to be able to grasp subnetting. He comes out of a management meeting and quietly asks you to help him with a subnetting issue. He needs to divide the Class B address space the company uses into six subnets for the various buildings in the plant, while keeping the subnets as large as possible to allow for future growth. What is the best subnet mask to use in this scenario?

- ❍ **A.** 255.255.0.0
- ❍ **B.** 255.255.248.0
- ❍ **C.** 255.255.224.0
- ❍ **D.** 255.255.240.0
- ❍ **E.** 255.255.255.224

7. You have purchased several brand-new Cisco routers for your company. Your current address space is 172.16.0.0 /22. Because these new routers support the **ip subnet zero** command, you realize you are about to gain back two subnets that you could not use with the old gear. How many subnets total will be available to you once the upgrades are complete?

- ❍ **A.** 4
- ❍ **B.** 2
- ❍ **C.** 32
- ❍ **D.** 62
- ❍ **E.** 64

8. Which of the following are true about the following address and mask pair: 10.8.8.0 /24? Assume that all subnets are available. Choose all that apply.

- ❍ **A.** This is a Class B address.
- ❍ **B.** This is a Class A address.
- ❍ **C.** This is a Class C address.
- ❍ **D.** 16 bits were stolen from the host field.
- ❍ **E.** 24 bits were stolen from the host field.
- ❍ **F.** The default mask for this address is 255.0.0.0.
- ❍ **G.** The mask can also be written as 255.255.255.0.
- ❍ **H.** The mask creates 65,536 subnets total from the default address space.
- ❍ **I.** Each subnet supports 256 valid host IPs.
- ❍ **J.** Each subnet supports 254 valid host IPs.

9. Indy and Greg have configured their own Windows 8 PCs and connected them with crossover cables. They can't seem to share their illegally downloaded MP3 files, however. Given their configurations, what could be the problem?

   Indy's configuration:

   IP:192.168.0.65

   Mask:255.255.255.192

   Greg's configuration:

   IP:192.168.0.62

   Mask:255.255.255.192

   - ❍ **A.** Indy is using a broadcast ID for his IP.
   - ❍ **B.** Greg is using an invalid mask.
   - ❍ **C.** Indy's IP is in one of the zero subnets.
   - ❍ **D.** Greg and Indy are using IPs in different subnets.

10. You are given an old router to practice for your CCNA. Your boss, Dave, has spent a lot of time teaching you subnetting. Now he challenges you to apply your knowledge. He hands you a note that says the following:

    "Given the subnetted address space of 192.168.1.0 /29, give the E0 interface the first valid IP in the eighth subnet. Give the S0 interface the last valid IP in the 12th subnet. The zero subnets are available. You have 10 minutes. Go."

    Which two of the following are the correct IP and mask configurations? Choose two.

    - ❍ **A.** E0: 192.168.1.1 255.255.255.0
    - ❍ **B.** E0: 192.168.1.56 255.255.255.248
    - ❍ **C.** E0: 192.168.1.57 255.255.255.248
    - ❍ **D.** S0: 192.168.1.254 255.255.255.0
    - ❍ **E.** S0: 192.168.1.95 255.255.255.248
    - ❍ **F.** S0: 192.168.1.94 255.255.255.248

11. The following questions are part of a Subnetting SuperChallenge. This monster question will stretch your subnetting skills, especially if you give yourself a time limit. Start with 10 minutes and see if you can get down to 5.

    The Vancouver Sailing Company has four locations: a head office and three branch offices. Each of the branches is connected to the head office by a point-to-point T1 circuit. The branches have one or more LANs connected to their routers. The routers are called Main, Jib, Genoa, and Spinnaker. The company has been assigned the 172.16.0.0/20 address space to work within.

    Your task is to choose the correct IP address and mask for each interface, based on the information provided. Remember that no IP address may overlap with any address in another subnet, and that the required number of hosts for each subnet will affect your decision as to which address to use.

Here are the known IP configurations for the routers:

Main:

S0/0:172.16.0.1 /30

S0/1:172.16.0.5 /30

S0/2:172.16.0.9 /30

Fa1/0:172.16.4.1 /23

Fa1/1:172.16.6.1 /23

Jib:

S0/0: Connects to Main S0/0

Fa1/0: 172.16.8.33/27

Fa1/1: 30 hosts needed

Genoa:

S0/0: Connects to Main S0/1

Fa1/0: 172.16.8.129/26

Fa1/1: 100 hosts needed

Fa2/0: 100 hosts needed

Fa2/1: 172.16.13.0/24.

Spinnaker:

S0/0: Connects to Main S0/2

Fa1/0: 500 hosts needed

Choose the correct IP and mask assignments for each router:

❍ **A.** Jib Fa1/1: 172.16.8.62/27

❍ **B.** Jib Fa1/1: 172. 16.8.64/27

❍ **C.** Jib Fa1/1: 172.16.8.65/28

❍ **D.** Jib Fa1/0: 172.16.8.65/27

❍ **E.** Jib Fa1/1: 172.16.8.65/27

❍ **F.** Genoa S0/0: 172.16.0.2/30

❍ **G.** Genoa S0/0:172.16.0.6/30

❍ **H.** Genoa Fa1/1:172.16.12.1/26

❍ **I.** Genoa Fa1/1:172.16.12.1/25

❍ **J.** Genoa Fa2/0:172.16.12.129/24

❍ **K.** Genoa Fa2/0:172.16.12.129/25

❍ **L.** Genoa Fa2/1:172.16.12.193/25

❍ **M.** Genoa Fa2/1:172.16.13.1/25

❍ **N.** Genoa Fa0/2:172.16.13.1/24

❍ **O.** Spinnaker S0/0: 172.16.0.10/30

- ❍ **P.** Spinnaker S0/0: 172.16.0.12/30
- ❍ **Q.** Spinnaker Fa1/0: 172.16.13.0/23
- ❍ **R.** Spinnaker Fa1/0: 172.16.14.0/23
- ❍ **S.** Spinnaker Fa1/0: 172.16.14.1/23

12. Which of the following is the best summary statement for the following range of networks?

192.168.1.0 /24–192.168.15.0 /24

- ❍ **A.** 192.168.1.0
- ❍ **B.** 192.168.1.0 255.255.240.0
- ❍ **C.** 192.168.1.0 0.0.15.0
- ❍ **D.** 192.168.1.0 255.255.248.0
- ❍ **E.** 192.168.0.0 255.255.240.0

13. Which of the following is the best summary statement for the following range of networks?

192.168.24.0 /24–192.168.31.0 /24

- ❍ **A.** 192.168.24.0 255.255.240.0
- ❍ **B.** 192.168.24.0 /28
- ❍ **C.** 192.168.24.0 /21
- ❍ **D.** 192.168.0.0 /27

14. Which of the following networks are included in the summary 172.16.0.0 /13? Choose all that apply.

- ❍ **A.** 172.0.0.0 /16
- ❍ **B.** 172.16.0.0 /16
- ❍ **C.** 172.24.0.0 /16
- ❍ **D.** 172.21.0.0 /16
- ❍ **E.** 172.18.0.0 /16

15. What are the advantages of route summarization? Choose three.

- ❍ **A.** Ensures job security for network admins because of difficulty of configuration
- ❍ **B.** Reduces routing update traffic overhead
- ❍ **C.** Reduces the impact of discontiguous subnets
- ❍ **D.** Reduces CPU and memory load on routers
- ❍ **E.** Identifies flapping interfaces
- ❍ **F.** Hides network instability

16. Which of the following is a valid IPv6 address format?

- ❍ **A.** G412:AFFA:2001:0000:0000:0000:0000:0001
- ❍ **B.** 2001:8888:EEEE:1010:0000:0000:0000:0001
- ❍ **C.** 2001::8888::1
- ❍ **D.** 2010:2112:5440:1812:1867

17. Which of the following is a valid IPv6 unicast address format?

- ❍ **A.** 2001:8888:EEEE:1010:0000:0000:0000:0001
- ❍ **B.** FF00:0000:0000:0002:00CO:00A8:0001:0042
- ❍ **C.** 2001:8888::2FFE::00A8
- ❍ **D.** FFFF:FFFF:FFFF:FFFF:FFFF:FFFF:FFFF

18. Which of the following are valid IPv6 address formats for the same address? Choose three.

- ❍ **A.** 2001:0000:0000:0200:0222:0000:0000:0001
- ❍ **B.** 2001:0000:0000:02:0222:0000:0000:0001
- ❍ **C.** 2001:0:0:200:222:0:0:1
- ❍ **D.** 2001::200:222::1
- ❍ **E.** 2001:0:0:200:222::1

19. Which of the following is a valid IPv6 unicast address?

- ❍ **A.** FF00:2112:1812:5440::1
- ❍ **B.** 1812:2112:5440:1
- ❍ **C.** 255:255:255:255:255:255:255:255:255
- ❍ **D.** None of the above

Answers to Review Questions

1. Answers B and D are correct. Answer A in decimal would be 551. Answer C in decimal would be 323. Answer E in decimal is 230.
2. Answers C and D are correct. Answer A in hex is 0xB4. Answer B in hex is 0xBF. Answer E is simply an attempt to trick you—the correct decimal answer is incorrectly expressed as a hex value.
3. Answer D is correct. A will only support 2 hosts; B only 6, and C only 14. Watch out for the minus 2 in the host calculation! Answer C creates 16 IP addresses on the subnet, but we lose 2—one for the network ID and one for the broadcast ID.
4. Answer D is correct. The mask 255.255.254.0 gives us nine 0s at the end of the mask; 29 – 2 = 510. Answer A is checking to see if you missed the 254 in the third octet because you are used to seeing 255. Answer B does the same thing plus tries to catch you on not subtracting 2 from the host calculation. Answer C tries to catch you on not subtracting 2, and Answer E is the increment of the given mask that you might pick if you were really off track.
5. Answer D is correct. Disregarding for the moment the possibility that Mr. Martin might be wrong, let's look at the requirements. He says make room for 12 managers, and make the subnets as small as possible while doing so. You need to find the mask that has sufficient host IP space without making it bigger than necessary. Answer A is invalid; 12 is not a valid mask value. Remember, a mask is a continuous string of 1s followed by a continuous string of 0s. In Answer B, the mask is valid, but it is not correct. This mask has eight 0s at the end, which, when we apply the formula 28 – 2 gives us 254 hosts. That makes more than enough room for the 12 managers, but does not meet the "as small as possible" requirement. Answer C has the correct mask value in the wrong octet. That mask gives us eight 0s in the fourth octet, plus another four in the third octet; that would give us 4094 hosts on the subnet. Answer E gives us 30 hosts per subnet, but that only meets half the requirement. This mask does not provide the minimum number of hosts.
6. Answer C is correct. The default mask for a Class B is 255.255.0.0. Answer C extends that mask by three bits, creating eight subnets (23 = 8). Although we only need six of them, we have to use the mask that creates eight because the next smaller mask would only create four, and that isn't enough. Answer A is incorrect because it is the default mask for a Class B and not subnetted at all. Answers B and D are incorrect because although they create sufficient subnets, they do not maximize the number of hosts per subnet and so are not the best answer. Answer E uses the correct mask in the wrong octet.
7. Answer E is correct. With **ip subnet zero** enabled, all 64 subnets created by the mask in use become available. Answers A, B, and C are not even close and are simply distracters. Answer D wants to catch you by subtracting the zero subnets.
8. Answers B, D, F, G, H, and J are correct. Answers A and C are incorrect because this is a Class A address. Answer E is incorrect because only 16 bits were stolen. Answer I is incorrect because it does not subtract the two IPs for the network ID and broadcast ID.

9. Answer D is correct. With that mask, the increment is 64. Greg is in the first subnet, and Indy is in the second. Without a router between them, their PCs will not be able to communicate above Layer 2. Answer A is incorrect; the broadcast ID for Indy would be .63. Answer B is incorrect; nothing is wrong with the mask. Answer C is incorrect; the zero subnets are the first and last created, and Indy is in the second subnet. The question does mention the zero subnets, so we can use them, and in any case Windows 8 fully supports them.

10. Answers C and F are correct. This is an increment question. The increment here is 8, so you should start by jotting down the multiples of 8 (those are all the network IDs), and then noting what 1 less than each of the network IDs is (those are the broadcast IDs). From there, it is easy to find what the first and last IPs in each subnet are. (Remember that Dave says we can use the zero subnets.)

    The eighth subnet network ID is 192.168.1.56; the first valid IP is 192.168.1.57. The twelfth subnet network ID is 192.168.1.88; the last valid IP is 192.168.1.94. Answers A and D are incorrect because they do not use the subnetted address space Dave requested. Answer B is incorrect because it is a network ID. Answer E is incorrect because it is a broadcast ID.

11. SuperChallenge answers:

    A. Incorrect (same subnet as Fa1/0)

    B. Incorrect (network ID)

    C. Incorrect (not enough hosts)

    D. Incorrect (Fa1/0 IP already assigned)

    E. Correct

    F. Incorrect (wrong subnet—not on the same network as the connected interface on Main)

    G. Correct

    H. Incorrect (not enough hosts)

    I. Correct

    J. Incorrect (overlaps with Fa1/1)

    K. Correct

    L. Incorrect (overlaps with Fa2/0)

    M. Incorrect (wrong mask)

    N. Incorrect (no Fa0/2 interface on Genoa)

    O. Correct

    P. Incorrect (network ID)

    Q. Incorrect (overlaps with Genoa)

    R. Incorrect (network ID)

    S. Correct

12. Answer E is correct. Answers A and C use incorrect syntax; Answer D uses the wrong mask. Answer B looks correct, but it does not use the correct network ID; the range should always start at a binary increment (in this case 0, not 1). (In other words, this is a case of "best answer.") Note that the correct summary does include the 192.168.0.0/24 network as well (not just 192.168.1–15.0/24). This is intended to confuse and distract you!
13. Answer C is correct. Answer A uses the wrong mask and summarizes more than the specified networks. Answer B subnets instead of summarizes. Answer D uses the wrong address and mask.
14. Answers B, D, and E are correct. The networks in Answers A and C are out of the range, which is 172.16.0.0 through 172.23.0.0.
15. Answers B, D, and F are correct. Answer A might have an element of truth, but Cisco does not have much of a sense of humor. Answer C is incorrect because discontiguous subnets are a real problem if you intend to summarize. Answer E is incorrect; route summarization does not identify but rather hides the effects of flapping interfaces.
16. Answer B is correct. IPv6 addresses must have (or at least indicate, perhaps with ::) eight sets of four valid hex characters. Answer A is wrong because G is not a valid hex character. Answer C is wrong because it uses the :: notation twice, which is invalid. Answer D is wrong because it uses only five sets.
17. Answer A is correct. IPv6 addresses must have eight sets of four valid hex characters. Answer B is wrong because it starts with FF, which indicates a multicast address, not a unicast. Answer C is wrong because it uses :: twice, which is invalid. Answer D is wrong because there are only seven sets.
18. Answers A, C, and E are correct. These are the same address, represented in three valid notations: A is not truncated, C has dropped leading 0s, and E has compressed the contiguous all-zero groups with the ::. Answer B is wrong because it drops trailing 0s, not leading 1s. D is wrong because it uses the :: twice, which is invalid.
19. Answer D is correct. None of these is a valid unicast format. Answer A is an IPv6 multicast (starts with FF00/8). Answer B has only four sets instead of eight. Note that if there had been a double colon before the last 1, it could have been correct. Answer C uses the decimal 255 to confuse you; it could have been correct except that there are nine sets.

What Next?

If you want more practice on this chapter's exam topics before you move on, remember that you can access all of the Cram Quiz questions on the CD. You can also create a custom exam by topic with the practice exam software. Note any topic you struggle with and go to that topic's material in this chapter.

CHAPTER FOUR
Working with Cisco Equipment

This chapter covers the following official CCNA Routing and Switching 200-120 exam topics:

- ▶ Configure and verify initial switch configuration, including remote access management.
- ▶ Verify network status and switch operation using basic utilities such as ping, telnet, and SSH.
- ▶ Configure and verify utilizing the CLI to set basic router configuration.
- ▶ Configure and verify network device security features.

This chapter introduces you to Cisco equipment. We examine how to connect to it and make initial configurations, in addition to how to connect it to other devices to build a network. We review the different types of network connections available, with particular emphasis on those that are tested on the exam. We also look at where a Cisco device stores the various files it needs for operations, the boot process, and management protocols and tools.

Introducing Your Cisco Gear

CramSaver

If you can correctly answer these questions before going through this section, save time by skimming the Exam Alerts in this section and then completing the Cram Quiz at the end of the section.

1. Which connection is used for local device management?
   - **A.** vty
   - **B.** SSH
   - **C.** Console
   - **D.** Ethernet

2. What kind of cable should you use to connect a router FastEthernet 0/0 interface directly to the NIC on your workstation?
   - **A.** Rollover
   - **B.** USB-to-serial
   - **C.** V.35-to-DB60
   - **D.** Straight-through
   - **E.** Crossover

Answers

1. Answer C is correct. Answers A and B are wrong because *local management* means directly connected, non-network-based connectivity; vty lines are used for Telnet and SSH connections (among others). Answer D is wrong for similar reasons; you can't use Ethernet to manage the router unless the network (IP in our case) is involved.
2. Answer E is correct. Router-to-NIC connections use a crossover. (Disregard, as always, the reality that auto-MDIX capability exists on most newer routers to "cross" or "uncross" the port automatically as needed.) Answers A and B are wrong because rollovers (with or without USB-serial adapters) are used for the console; C is wrong because that cable type is typically used for serial WAN connections (legacy ones at that). Answer D is wrong in the context of CCNA. If you want to argue that it is correct in the real world, that is fine, as long as you get the point about the exam not reflecting reality very much!

The CCNA exam does not test you about product-specific knowledge. That is to say, you are not expected to know what feature cards are available for a 6500 series switch, but you do need to understand the differences between a router and a switch, and you need to understand how their configuration requirements vary.

For our purposes, we use a Catalyst 2960 switch and a 1900 or 2900 series router as example devices. Most of the commands you learn in this chapter also apply to more advanced models.

External Connections

Cisco devices make connections to other devices, and collectively they all create a network. At some point, making a connection means plugging in a cable—even with a wireless system. This section examines some of the various connections found on Cisco routers and switches.

Console

When you first obtain a new Cisco device, it won't be configured. That is to say, it will not do any of the customized functions you might need; it does not have any IP addresses, and it is generally not going to do what you paid for. However, if you buy a 2960 switch, plug in the power, and plug PCs in to it, it will work to connect those PCs with no further configuration, but you are missing out on all the cool stuff and advanced features. Your new router, however, will not be capable of doing much for you at all, even if you plug devices into the interfaces. Routers need basic configuration to function on a network, or they simply consume power and blink at you.

The console port is used for *local management* connections. This means that you must be able to physically reach the console port with a cable that is typically about 6 feet long. The console port looks exactly like an Ethernet port. It uses the same connector, but it has different wiring and is often (but not always) identified with a pale blue label that says CONSOLE. If the device is not configured at all—meaning, if it is new or has had a previous configuration erased—the console port is the only way to connect to it and apply configurations. Figure 4.1 shows what a console port looks like.

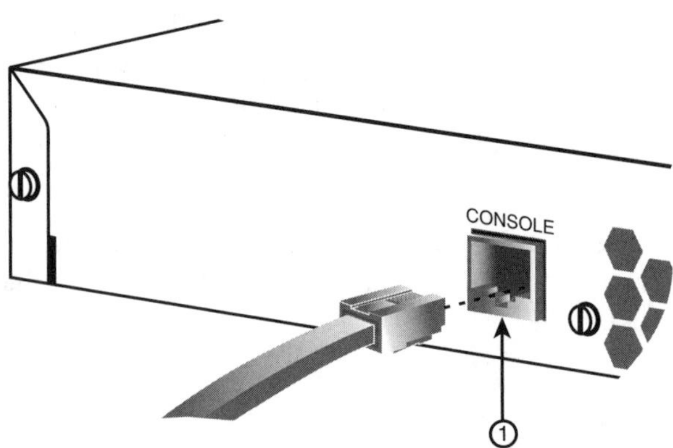

FIGURE 4.1 **The console port (image used with permission from Cisco Systems, Inc.).**

Connecting to the console port is done with a special *rollover* cable; a rollover cable has pins 1 through 8 wired to the opposite number, as shown in Figure 4.2.

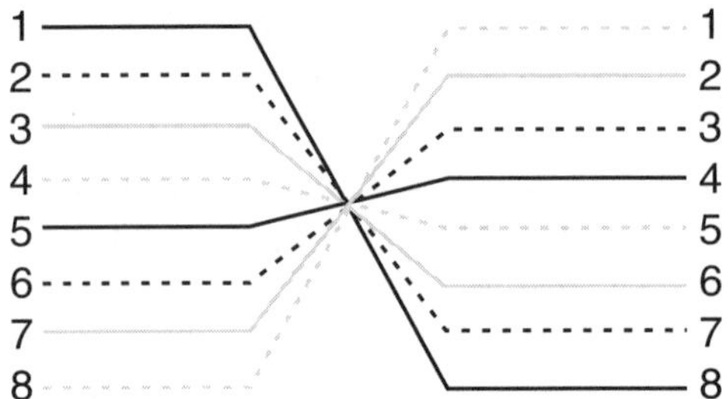

FIGURE 4.2 **Rollover cable pinouts.**

One end of the rollover cable has the RJ-45 connector to connect to the console port; the other has either a molded-in 9-pin serial connector, or another RJ-45 and adapters for 9-pin or 15-pin serial connections. Because many new laptops do not have the EIA/TIA 9- or 15-pin serial connections and feature USB ports only, you might need to buy yourself a USB-to-serial adapter; or you could buy a USB-to-serial console cable (which has the adapter built in) instead. The serial connection on the rollover cable attaches to one of your workstation's serial (COM) ports.

Now that you are plugged in, you need to configure a terminal application to communicate with the Cisco device over the rollover cable. You can use HyperTerminal, Procomm, TeraTerm, SecureCRT, or any of a number of others that support character-based terminal emulation. The settings for your terminal session are as follows:

Baud rate:	9600
Data bits:	8
Parity:	None
Stop bits:	1
Flow control:	None

The COM port number your workstation ends up using for this connection will vary.

AUX Port

The AUX port is really just another console port that is intended for use with a modem, so you can remotely connect and administer the device by phoning it. This is a great idea as long as the modem is connected, powered up, and plugged into the phone system; however, doing so can create some security issues, so make sure that you get advice on addressing those before setting this up. Note that not all routers will have an AUX port.

Ethernet Port

An Ethernet port (which might be a Fast Ethernet or even a Gigabit Ethernet port, depending on your router model) is intended to connect to the LAN. Some routers have more than one Ethernet or Fast Ethernet port; it really depends on what you need and of course what you purchase. The Ethernet port usually connects to the LAN switch with a *straight-through cable*.

A straight-through cable has pin 1 connected to pin 1, 2 to 2, 3 to 3, and so on. It is used to connect routers and hosts to switches or hubs.

If you have two or more Ethernet ports, you can connect the others to a high-speed Internet connection such as a cable modem or digital subscriber line (DSL), or to another separate LAN.

A crossover cable is used to connect two devices that each use the same pins for the transmit and receive functions; this means that if we use a straight-through cable to connect them, the Layer 1 circuit will not come up, and the connection will not work. For example, suppose I want to connect my router's FastEthernet0/1 interface to another router's FastEthernet0/1 interface. If I use a straight-through cable, the link will not work. Instead, I will use a cross-over cable, which changes the pinouts of the transmit and receive pairs so that they line up, respectively, with the receive and transmit pairs on the other device. When I attach the crossover cable, the link lights should come on, and Layers 1 and 2 should change to up.

A crossover cable should be used between two routers, two switches, a switch and a hub, a PC's NIC direct to another PC's NIC—in general, two "like" devices will be connected by a crossover cable. Here's a tricky one, though: To connect a PC's NIC directly to your router's Ethernet interface, you need a crossover cable—even though those two devices are not like. In the real world, some devices sense when a connection needs to be crossed over, and will automatically "rewire" the port to the correct pinouts. This autosensing function is unfortunately not a factor for the CCNA exams, so you will need to know how to correctly set up your connections the old-fashioned way.

Figure 4.3 shows the straight-through and crossover pinouts and examples of where each type of cable is used.

ExamAlert

You must understand how to use rollover, straight-through, and crossover cables, and you must know how to identify them from a diagram of their pinouts.

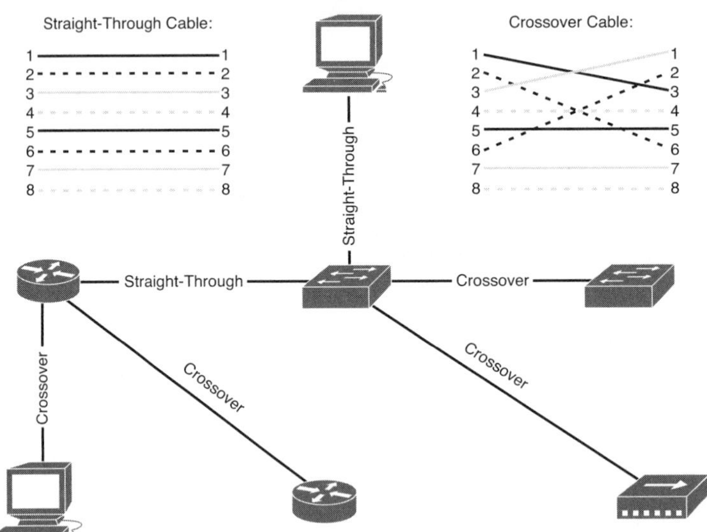

FIGURE 4.3 **Straight-through and crossover cable pinouts and applications.**

Serial Port

A Cisco serial port is a proprietary design, a 60-pin D-sub. This connector can be configured for almost any kind of serial communication. You need a cable that has the Cisco connector on one end and the appropriate type of connector for the service you want to connect to on the other.

Serial ports are almost always used for WAN connections and use one of several Layer 2 protocols, including Frame Relay, PPP, and High-Level Data Link Control (HDLC). Serial ports can also connect to an ISDN Primary Rate Interface (PRI) service or regular analog telephone service. (For a telephone service, you need a special hardware type called an asynchronous serial port and a modem.)

HDLC is the default encapsulation on a Cisco serial port, and the HDLC protocol here is a Cisco proprietary version of the standardized ISO HDLC that can run multiple Layer 3 protocols, which the ISO version can't do.

You might have one or more serial ports depending on what you need and what you buy.

ExamAlert

You will need to know the three WAN encapsulations for a serial port: HDLC, PPP, and Frame Relay. These are discussed in more detail later.

Know that Cisco's proprietary version of HDLC is the default encapsulation for serial ports.

Other Connections

Your router may use a T1 controller card to connect to a T1 WAN service. The controller will probably have a label that reads "T1 CSU/DSU," with a plug that looks like the RJ-45 connector but is actually an RJ-48.

You can also buy ports for high-speed serial communication (perhaps ATM) or even different fiber-optic connections. What you purchase will depend on the services you need to connect to, the model of router you buy, and of course how much money you want to spend.

Although the Other Connections listed here are by no means an exhaustive list of your options, they are the most commonly used. These connection types are not tested, but are included here for your interest.

Cram Quiz

1. Your junior net techs are confused because their laptops do not have a connector like the one on the end of the console cable that came with the new switch. When they get around to asking you what they should do, what will you tell them?

   ❍ **A.** Carefully solder the wires to the USB contacts.

   ❍ **B.** Use the USB-to-serial adapter you gave them earlier.

   ❍ **C.** Build a custom USB-PS2-Parallel-Serial adapter using stuff from the junk box on the workbench.

2. True or False: If your router has a spare Ethernet port, you could use it as a WAN connection.

Cram Quiz Answers

1. Answer B is correct. Answer A will ruin at least the cable and the USB port, and maybe a few other things besides. Answer C might fit together but won't get you anywhere (although I must admit I might tell the juniors to try it just for the laugh).
2. True, and yes, "it depends," but I only asked if you *could*, no specifics. If you figured out that it would only work if your WAN service presented an Ethernet interface to connect to, that's good. By the way, Ethernet (including Fast and Gigabit varieties) are increasingly common for WAN connections.

Connecting and Configuring Cisco Devices

CramSaver

If you can correctly answer these questions before going through this section, save time by skimming the Exam Alerts in this section and then completing the Cram Quiz at the end of the section.

1. Which of the following is typically found in ROM?

   A. IOS image

   B. Startup config

   C. Running config

   D. Bootstrap

2. Your configuration register is currently set to 0x2101. What will your 2921 router boot from?

   A. ROM

   B. NVRAM

   C. RAM

   D. Flash

3. What is the chief advantage of using Telnet over SSH?

   A. Telnet is more secure.

   B. SSH is easier to configure.

   C. IOS 15.x requires special licensing to enable SSH functionality.

   D. SSH is not available outside the EU and North America.

   E. None of the above.

Answers

1. Answer D is correct. IOS is usually found in Flash, startup config in NVRAM, and running config in RAM.
2. Answer D is correct. Newer routers will boot to the first IOS file on Flash with the configuration register set to 0x2101.
3. Answer E is correct. Telnet is less secure, transmitting passwords in clear text. SSH is more complex to configure than Telnet (though not difficult). No additional licensing is needed, and although there are certain restrictions on cryptographic technology, SSH availability certainly extends beyond the EU and North America.

Now that we have examined what our connection options are, we will look at how Cisco devices operate, including the boot sequence, operating system and configuration file location, and basic command-line functions.

Device Memory Locations

A Cisco device has four memory types. Each is used for a specific purpose:

- ROM, or read-only memory, holds the POST, bootstrap, ROMmon, and (on older routers) rxboot microcode. The POST (power-on self test) is a basic inventory and test of the hardware in the device. The bootstrap is responsible for finding an operating system to load. ROMmon is a minimal command set that can be used to connect to a TFTP server and restore a missing or corrupted IOS image. Rxboot is a mini-IOS that has a much more familiar command set than ROMmon and more features, so it is easier to use for IOS restoration from TFTP.
- Flash memory normally stores the IOS image file. Because flash is simply a file storage area, assuming that you have enough space, you could store other files here, as well, perhaps another IOS version or backups of a configuration. Flash can be either SIMM cards on the motherboard or PCMCIA cards either externally accessible or inside the case of the router on the motherboard. Newer routers will also feature USB ports for easily adding external flash memory.
- NVRAM is nonvolatile RAM; this means that it will not lose the data stored in it when the power is turned off or fails. The startup configuration file is stored here, as is the configuration register value (more on this later).
- RAM is similar to RAM on a PC; this very fast memory is where all dynamically learned information is stored, such as routing tables, ARP cache, and buffers. It's important to note that the running config is also stored in RAM, as is the live (as opposed to stored) IOS image.

IOS Startup Process

When you turn on the power, you will see information scrolling down your terminal screen almost immediately. It is a good idea to watch this information, because important messages can be seen here if failures occur during boot.

The IOS startup process is actually more complex than it appears. The basic steps are as follows:

1. Run the POST.
2. Find the IOS.
3. Load the IOS to RAM.
4. Find the configuration.
5. Load the configuration to RAM.

ExamAlert

Know the basic steps in the boot process.

Let's look at the process in more detail. The default behavior for a router or switch is as follows:

1. The POST runs.
2. The configuration register value is checked, and its setting determines the next boot action. (More on the configuration register setting later).
3. Assuming that there are no critical errors with the POST run, the bootstrap checks the startup config file in NVRAM for boot system commands. These commands might have been entered by the router admin to override the default behavior, perhaps to load a different IOS for test purposes.
4. Assuming that there are no boot system commands, the router loads the first valid IOS image it finds in the flash memory.
5. If no valid IOS is found in flash, the router loads the ROM image or bootflash. This very minimal operating system will allow you to manually connect to a TFTP server to download a valid IOS to flash.
6. After an IOS is loaded (except for ROMmon), the router looks for the startup config file in NVRAM. If it is found, it is copied to RAM and renamed running config.
7. If there is no startup config file in NVRAM, the router broadcasts for a TFTP server to see whether there is a configuration file available for it.
8. If that fails, the router launches setup mode.

Note that on most devices, the IOS image is decompressed and copied to RAM to run from there; similarly, the startup config file is copied from NVRAM and renamed running config as it is copied into RAM. You can see the files in flash (including your IOS images) by entering the privileged exec command **show flash**.

Setup Mode

Cisco devices include a feature called setup mode to help you make a basic initial configuration. Setup mode runs only if there is no configuration file in NVRAM—either because the router is brand new or because it has been erased. (It is also possible to manually start setup mode by using the **setup** command). Setup mode asks you a series of questions and applies the configuration to the device based on your answers. You can abort setup mode by pressing CTRL+C or by answering No when asked if you want to enter the initial configuration dialog.

Configuration Register

The configuration register is a four-character hexadecimal value that can be changed to manipulate how the router behaves at boot. The default value is 0x2102.

> **Note**
>
> The characters "0x" indicate that the characters that follow are in hexadecimal. This makes it clear whether the value is "two thousand one hundred and two" or, as in this case, "two one zero two hexadecimal."

The fourth character in the configuration register is known as the boot field. Changing the value for this character will have the following effects:

- 0x2100 = Always boot to ROMmon. There are few good reasons to do this, except possibly for training or a practical joke.
- 0x2101 = Always boot the first valid IOS file in flash.
- 0x2102 through 0x210F = Try each boot system command in the startup config file; if none of them work, load the first valid IOS file in flash.

Password Recovery

The third character in the configuration register can modify how the router loads the configuration file. The setting of 0x2142 causes the router to ignore the startup config file in NVRAM (which is where the password is stored) and proceed without a configuration—as if the router were brand new or had its configuration erased.

This is a useful setting for those times when you do not know the password to enable the router and configure it. Perhaps you forgot the password (we hope not); maybe you bought a used router, or maybe a student configured a password in a previous lab. Perhaps the previous admin quit, got fired, or was hit by a bus. In any event, we need the password to log in and make changes, so we need to bypass the existing password and change it to something we know. This process is called *password recovery*.

The password recovery process is simple and takes about 5 minutes depending on how fast your router boots:

1. Connect to the console port, start your terminal application, and power cycle the router. When you see the boot process beginning, hit the Break sequence. (This is usually Ctrl+Break, but it might differ for different terminal applications.) Doing this interrupts the boot process and drops the router into ROMmon.
2. At the ROMmon prompt, enter the command **confreg 0x2142** to set the configuration register to 0x2142.
3. Restart the router by power cycling it or by issuing the command **reset**.
4. When the router reloads, the configuration register setting of 0x2142 instructs the router to ignore the startup config file in NVRAM. You will be asked if you want to go through setup mode, because the router thinks it has no startup configuration file. Exit from setup mode.
5. Press Return and enter the command **enable** to go into privileged exec command mode. No password is required because the startup config file was not loaded.
6. Load the configuration manually by entering **copy startup-config running-config**.
7. Go into the global configuration mode using the command **configure terminal** and change the privileged exec password with the command **enable password password** or **enable secret password**. (You may need to make changes to other passwords, as well.)

8. Save the new password by entering **copy running-config startup-config**.
9. Go to the global config prompt, and change the configuration register back to the default setting with the command **config-register 0x2102**. Exit back to the privileged exec prompt.
10. Reboot the router using the **reload** command. You will be asked to save your changes; you can do so if you have made additional configuration changes.

That's all there is to it. Don't tell anyone how easy this is.

ExamAlert

Know the following:

- What setup mode is and how to abort it
- The four configuration register settings described previously and what they do

Command-Line Modes

Access to a router or switch command line is referred to as an *exec session*. There are two levels of access: *user exec* and *privileged exec*. In user exec mode, you have limited access to information and diagnostic commands, and you are not able to make configuration changes to the router. Privileged exec mode gives you the complete command set and full authority to change or erase the configuration.

When you connect to a router using the console port, you see a message like this:

```
Router Con0 is now available.

Press RETURN to get started!
```

Pressing Return takes you to the user exec prompt, which looks like this:

```
Router>
```

To go to privileged exec mode, you must enter the command **enable**. The prompt will change from > to #, as shown:

```
Router>enable
Router#
```

From this point, you can enter commands to view the status and settings of the router, make some kinds of changes, and erase, back up, or restore the IOS and configuration files.

To make most kinds of changes, however, you must enter the global configuration mode. This is done by entering the command configure terminal from the privileged exec mode:

```
Router#configure terminal
Router(config)#
```

Notice that the command prompt changes to `Router(config)#`. From this prompt, you can make changes to functions that affect the whole router, or you can enter a more specific configuration mode to work with specialized functions. Some of the possible modes are listed and explained in the following:

```
Router(config)#interface serial 0
Router(config-if)#
```

This is the *interface configuration mode*. Here you can set IP addresses and subnet masks, change speed, duplex, clock rate and bandwidth, or change the Layer 2 encapsulation of the interface. Changes made here affect only the interface you specified in the interface command:

```
Router(config)#line console 0
Router(config-line)#
```

Line configuration mode allows you to set up line parameters. Lines include the console, AUX, TTY, and vty connections. The console and aux lines are the local administration connections. TTY lines are synchronous serial connections, usually for analog dialup access with modems. The vty lines are virtual connections for Telnet and SSH access to the router to perform remote administration over an IP network:

```
Router(config)#router rip
Router(config-router)#
```

The *router configuration mode* is where you set up dynamic routing protocols such as RIP, EIGRP, and OSPF. Chapter 7, "Basic Routing" and Chapter 13, "Advanced Router Operation," covers this material in detail.

It is important to understand—and get used to navigating between—the different configuration modes. Some commands work only at a specific configuration mode, and getting used to the IOS quirks is a big part of being prepared for the CCNA exam and being a capable Cisco admin.

Command Shortcuts

Take a look at this command. It backs up the current configuration and saves it so that the router will use it next time it boots:

```
Router#copy running-config startup-config
```

That's a big hunk of typing. More typing means more time and more errors, so to save time, we can use truncation. As long as the truncation provides enough information for the IOS to figure out what command you are trying to enter, you can reduce the amount of typing you have to do, saving yourself time:

```
Router#copy run start
```

Or even smaller

```
Router#cop ru st
```

That's a big savings in typing effort.

As you get used to working with the IOS, you will develop your own shortcuts.

The IOS will tell you when you make a mistake, too. There are three error messages:

- **Incomplete command:** The IOS needs more command keywords to complete the command. It advises you of the error, and retypes what you entered so that you can complete it. The error looks like this:

```
Router#copy running-config
% Incomplete Command
Router#copy running-config
```

- **Ambiguous command:** The IOS is not sure what command you mean because you truncated too much:

```
Router#co ru st
%Ambiguous command
```

- **Invalid input:** You made a typo or entered a command at the wrong prompt. Notice that the IOS will also show you exactly where the problem happens with a little pointer:

```
Router#cpy run start
         ^
%Invalid input detected at '^' marker
```

Context-Sensitive Help

The IOS has a complete listing of all the commands available. If you get stuck, you can use the question mark (?) to access this help. You can use it in different ways.

On its own, to see a list of all the available command words at a particular prompt

```
Router(config-if)#?
Interface configuration commands:
access-expression    Build a bridge boolean access expression
arp                  Set arp type (arpa, probe, snap) or timeout
backup               Modify dial-backup parameters
bandwidth            Set bandwidth informational parameter
bridge-group         Transparent bridging interface parameters
carrier-delay        Specify delay for interface transitions
cdp                  CDP interface subcommands
cmns                 OSI CMNS
custom-queue-list    Assign a custom queue list to an interface
default              Set a command to its defaults
delay                Specify interface throughput delay
description          Interface specific description
exit                 Exit from interface configuration mode
fair-queue           Enable Fair Queuing on an Interface
help                 Description of the interactive help system
hold-queue           Set hold queue depth
ip                   Interface Internet Protocol config commands
ipx                  Novell/IPX interface subcommands
keepalive            Enable keepalive
llc2                 LLC2 Interface Subcommands
load-interval        Specify interval for load calculation for an
interface
—More—
```

After a command word, to see the next possible command words

```
Router# copy ?
  running-config
  startup-config
  tftp:
  flash:
```

Don't be afraid to use the help, especially when you are learning. The help commands also function (with limited capabilities) in the router simulator questions on the CCNA exam.

Managing IOS Licensing

In the past few years, there was a big change in the way Cisco licenses the IOS. Previously, all you had to do was download the IOS you wanted, copy it to flash, and restart the device. It was possible to do this illegally, stealing copyrighted property from Cisco and installing and using it in violation of several agreements and laws. Millions of people did it; some of them willfully, some out of ignorance, and some because they thought it "didn't really matter." As the author of several copyrighted texts and videos, I can tell you that it does really matter: That's how I and many others make our living. So, if you are reading this having obtained an illegal copy without paying the royalties, you just stole hard-earned money from us, and we don't appreciate it.

Along with the change in licensing came a related change in how Cisco builds IOS files. Using the old way, customers would buy an IOS image file that was built for the specific hardware model or series (2801 model or 2800 series, for example). For each model/series, there would be multiple IOS files, each of which had a different feature set available (Data, Voice or Security, or a combination of those, for example). In other words, if you had the IOS file for your router, you had all the capabilities of that IOS. Load it, and it worked.

Cisco's new licensing strategy makes a fundamental change: Now, the IOS is an "all-in-one" file: All features are built in to a single IOS image file. And to make them work, the other big change is that you must obtain a license to activate the features you want to use. This change applies to the Integrated Services Routers Generation 2 (ISR-G2) and later device model ranges.

You can still download the IOS images from Cisco.com, but now the download area both authenticates you and verifies that your profile has the rights to the IOS you are trying to obtain. If not, the download is denied. Once you have the IOS downloaded, you can copy it to flash on your router. The basic functionality of the IOS is available as a permanent license, which means you don't have to do anything else to enable the IP Base feature set. To activate other features (such as Security, Voice, or Data), you have some work to do.

Cisco offers a free application called Cisco License Manager that automates the Internet-accessed feature license activation process; this utility is primarily intended for larger customers with a lot of licensing issues to administer.

The manual process, which is equally valid but a little more complicated, follows these steps:

1. Obtain a product authorization key (PAK). A PAK is your proof of purchase. When you buy the license you want to activate, either from a value-added reseller (VAR) or from Cisco directly, the PAK is what you get in return. It is simply a cryptographic string of characters that identifies what you bought.
2. Obtain the unique device identifier (UDI) from your router, using the command **show license udi**. The UDI, as the name suggests, is a model and serial number identifier that is unique to your device.
3. Browse to www.cisco.com/go/license (the Cisco License Registration Portal).
4. Input the UDI you obtained in Step 2.
5. Input the PAK.
6. Copy the License Key file generated by the License Portal (or email it to yourself, or both).
7. Make the License Key file available to your router by copying it to flash, by putting it on a USB stick inserted into the device, or by TFTP.
8. At the command line, enter **license install** *<url>*, where the *<url>* variable is the location of the License Key file.
9. Reload the router.
10. Issue the **show license** command to verify the PAK feature has been activated.

Note

Cisco also has a "Right to Use" license feature that allows you to activate any feature for a 60-day trial period.

Remote Management

Having the ability to remotely manage your router is crucial to any network engineer. If you have a WAN that spans across the world, you do not want to have to fly out to a location every time you have a problem with a router. Some of the protocols and tools you can use to help you troubleshoot and remotely manage your routers include the following:

- Telnet
- Secure Shell (SSH)
- Cisco Discovery Protocol (CDP)
- Internet Control Message Protocol (ICMP)
- Network Time Protocol (NTP)
- Syslog
- Simple Network Management Protocol (SNMP)
- NetFlow

Telnet

Telnet operates at the application layer of the OSI model and is used to remotely connect into a router. Configuring Telnet authentication is covered in Chapter 5, "Securing your Cisco Devices." As a review, however, the commands to configure a router to allow Telnet access are as follows. (The password *cisco* is used in this example.)

```
Router(config)#enable secret cisco
Router(config)#line vty 0 4
Router(config-line)#login
Router(config-line)#password cisco
```

You must have an enable password for Telnet access to work. If you do not, you will get the following output when you attempt to access privileged exec mode:

```
Router#telnet 192.168.1.1
Trying 192.168.1.1 ... Open
User Access Verification
Password:
Router>en
% No password set
Router>
```

To close out an active Telnet session, type **exit**.

It is also possible to suspend a Telnet session and resume it later. This is helpful as it keeps you from having to remember the IP address of a router. Instead, you can suspend your Telnet session and resume it later based on its session number, not IP address.

To suspend a Telnet session, press Ctrl+Shift+6, X. (Hold down the Ctrl, Shift, and 6 buttons at the same time. Release them, and then press X.)

To see what sessions you have suspended, execute the **show sessions** command from user exec or privileged exec mode. In the output that follows, there are two Telnet sessions that have been suspended:

```
Router#show sessions
Conn Host                 Address               Byte  Idle Conn Name
   1 192.168.1.1          192.168.1.1              0     0 192.168.1.1
*  2 172.16.0.1           172.16.0.1               0     0 172.16.0.1
```

Entries that have an asterisk (*) next to them indicate the last session you were using. There are four methods of resuming a session:

- **Enter key:** Pressing the Enter key will take you to the last session you were currently using (as shown by the asterisk in the show sessions command).
- **Resume:** Typing **resume** without specifying a session number will allow you to resume the last session you were using. This is the same as pressing the Enter key.
- **Resume #:** Typing **resume** followed by the session number will resume Telnet for that session. For example, typing **resume 1** resumes Telnet for the 192.168.1.1 router.
- **Resume [*IP address* | *hostname*]:** Instead of giving a Telnet session number, you can also give the IP address, or, if you have DNS lookups enabled with a DNS server, you can type in the hostname of the remote router.

ExamAlert

Know the commands you use to resume and close a Telnet session (Ctrl+Shift+6, X; **show sessions**; **resume**; **disconnect**). Also, remember that the **exit** command will close an active session, whereas the **disconnect** command will close a suspended session.

Secure Shell

In addition to Telnet, you can also use Secure Shell (SSH) to remotely manage your routers. Configuring your router for SSH is covered in Chapter 5. Now you will learn how to use your router as an SSH client to connect into other routers.

SSH is preferred by many engineers because it secures your communication to your router when remotely managing it. This is done by encrypting the communication with algorithms such as Triple Data Encryption Standard (3DES) and Advanced Encryption Standard (AES), as well as by securing the authentication to the router through password hashing algorithms such as message digest 5 (MD5) and Secure Hash Algorithm 1 (SHA-1). Encrypting communication and hashing the password prevents malicious hackers from eavesdropping on you when you are configuring your router.

Starting an encrypted SSH session with a router is done with the **ssh** command. This command can be entered from either user exec or privileged exec mode. It has several options, as outlined in Table 4.1.

TABLE 4.1 **SSH Options**

Command Option	Description
-v {**1** | **2**}	This optional parameter specifies whether you are going to use version 1 or version 2. SSH Version 1 had some known vulnerabilities, so you should use version 2 whenever possible.
-c {**3des** | **aes128-cbc** | **aes192-cbc** | **aes256-cbc**}	This optional parameter specifies the encryption you are going to use when communicating with the router. This value is optional; if you choose not to use it, the routers negotiate the encryption algorithm to use automatically.
-l username	This specifies the username to use when logging in to the remote router.
-m {hmac-md5-128 | hmac-md5-96 | hmac-sha1-160 | hmac-sha1-96}	This specifies the type of hashing algorithm to use when sending your password. It is optional and if you do not use it, the routers negotiate what type of hashing to use.
ip-address | **hostname**	You need to specify the IP address or, if you have DNS or static hostnames configured, the name of the router you want to connect to.

For example, if you want to use SSH version 2 to connect to a router at IP address 192.168.0.1 with the username of Admin, using AES256-CBC encryption, and using SHA1 hashing, you type the following:

```
Router#ssh -v 2 -l Admin -c aes256-cbc -m hmac-sha-1-160 192.168.0.1
```

The syntax may appear long at first, but after you start using it on a regular basis to manage your routers, it will become second nature to you. For the exam, you can expect simplified commands—something like this:

```
Router# ssh -l Admin 192.168.0.1
```

Cisco Discovery Protocol

Sometimes when you telnet to another router, you might not know what its IP address is. If this is the case, you can use the CDP to discover the Layer 3 address of neighboring devices.

CDP is a Cisco proprietary Layer 2 (data-link) multicast protocol that is enabled on all Cisco routers and switches. It can be used to discover information about directly connected Cisco devices. Although it is a Layer 2 protocol, it is not forwarded by Cisco switches. (It is by other vendors, however.)

To view what neighboring Cisco devices you have connected to your router or switch, execute the **show cdp neighbors** command from either user exec or privileged exec mode. Following is an example of this output:

```
Router#show cdp neighbors
Capability Codes: R - Router, T - Trans Bridge, B - Source Route
Bridge
                  S - Switch, H - Host, I - IGMP, r - Repeater

Device ID        Local Intrfce      Holdtme     Capability  Platform
Port ID
CoreRouter          Ser 1           144             R         2500
Ser 0
```

Here you see that you are connected to a router named CoreRouter. You are connected to it out of your local interface serial 1. The holdtime indicates how long it will take to flush this entry out should your router stop hearing CDP frames. CDP sends advertisements every 60 seconds by default and will flush out an entry if it fails to hear a CDP advertisement after 180 seconds. (Timers are manipulated with the **cdp timer** global configuration command.) The capability of this device is *R*, which stands for router. In fact, from this output you can see that this is a 2500 series router and it is connected to your router out of its serial 0 interface.

Quite a bit of information gets generated from this command, but it did not tell you the IP address of the 2500 nor did it tell you the IOS version running on the 2500. The two commands you can use to discover the Layer 3 IP address and IOS version are as follows:

- **show cdp neighbors detail**
- **show cdp entry ***

These two commands are functionally equivalent. You can look at a specific device in the **show cdp entry** *command* or use the wildcard asterisk character to view all entries. Following is the output of the **show cdp neighbors detail** command. (The other **show** command generates the same output.)

```
Router#show cdp neighbors detail
-------------------------
Device ID: CoreRouter
Entry address(es):
  IP address: 10.0.0.1
Platform: cisco 2500,  Capabilities: Router
Interface: Serial0,  Port ID (outgoing port): Serial0
Holdtime : 171 sec

Version :
Cisco Internetwork Operating System Software
IOS (tm) 2500 Software (C2500-I-L), Version 12.1(20), RELEASE SOFTWARE
(fc2)
Copyright (c) 1986-2003 by cisco Systems, Inc.
Compiled Thu 29-May-03 22:00 by kellythw
```

ExamAlert

If you need to telnet into a router but do not know its IP address, use CDP. Remember, only the **show cdp neighbors detail** and **show cdp entry *** commands will show you the IP address and IOS version of neighboring devices.

Internet Control Message Protocol

Another useful troubleshooting tool is the ICMP. ICMP is a Layer 3 (network) protocol designed to carry status messages. CCNAs will exercise ICMP via two tools: ping and traceroute. The two messages used by the ping program, echo request and echo reply, test both connectivity and integrity. The responding station's job is to reply and repeat the payload, thus testing the quality of the connection. The **ping** command followed by an IP address or name uses a default payload and primarily tests connectivity.

If a host is unreachable, you get an ICMP Type 3 Destination Unreachable message. If a firewall or access list is blocking ICMP, you get an ICMP Type 3/Code 13 Destination Unreachable:Administratively Prohibited message. Unreachables show a *U* in the output on your screen, whereas a successful ping shows exclamation points (!). Timeouts show a "." (period) in the output.

The extended ping has options to test integrity, such as the capability to change the size and content of the payload to be echoed back. Cisco also supports an extended ping feature that is accessible from privileged exec. To access the extended ping feature, enter privileged exec and type **ping**. Do not enter an IP address, however; instead, press Enter, and you will be presented with a number of questions. With extended ping, you can set the size of your ping messages, source interface, number of pings, and timeout settings. Following is the output of the extended **ping** command. Note that the exclamation mark is an indication of a successful ping:

```
Router#ping
Protocol [ip]:
Target IP address: 10.0.0.1
Repeat count [5]: 1000
Datagram size [100]: 1024
Timeout in seconds [2]:
Extended commands [n]: y
Source address or interface: 172.16.0.1
Type of service [0]:
Set DF bit in IP header? [no]:
Validate reply data? [no]:
Data pattern [0xABCD]:
Loose, Strict, Record, Timestamp, Verbose[none]:
Sweep range of sizes [n]:
Type escape sequence to abort.
Sending 1000, 1024-byte ICMP Echos to 10.0.0.1, timeout is 2 seconds:
!!!!!!!!!!!!!!!!!!!!!!!!!!!!!!!!!!!!!!!!!!!!!!!!!!!!!!!!!!!!
```

Tip

When bringing up a new wide-area network circuit, you can do an extended ping and send out 10,000 pings with a size of 1024 bytes. Watch the results and verify success. If some packets are lost, you know it is not a clean circuit and you should contact your provider.

Traceroute is a technique used when you suspect that a router on the path to an unreachable network is at fault. Traceroute sends out a UDP datagram to a destination with a Time To Live (TTL) of 1. If the first hop is not the destination, an ICMP Type 11/Code 0 (ICMP Time Exceeded) message is sent back, and the response time in milliseconds is recorded. Routers decrement TTL so that a packet will not circulate forever if there is a problem such as a routing loop (covered in Chapter 10, "IP Services"). When a TTL gets to 0, the router drops the packet and returns the unreachable message.

A second packet is then sent out with a TTL value of 2, and if it is not the destination, an unreachable message is sent back and the response time in milliseconds is recorded. This continues until the destination is reached or until the maximum TTL as defined by the vendor is reached. (Cisco uses 30 as its maximum TTL with traceroute, but this is configurable.)

Many devices support traceroute. On Windows machines, the command is **tracert**. On Cisco devices, the command is **traceroute**, but this can be abbreviated as **trace**.

Network Time Protocol

NTP is an IP-based protocol that synchronizes the time setting of networked devices with an external clock source. The external source is commonly a very accurate clock, of which there are many available on the Internet.

Time synchronization is very important for networked devices and applications, so that things like logs can be accurately compared between different devices and email messages do not arrive before they were sent.

Simple Network Management Protocol

SNMP is an IP-based protocol (UDP Port 161) that monitors networked devices for conditions that require administrative attention. Almost any networked device can support an SNMP agent, which is the software that collects and sends relevant info to a network management station (NMS). The NMS aggregates, stores, and displays the data from the SNMP agents, so administrators can view it easily and take any necessary action. The data collected may be different on different devices. (For example, a server may report on a hard drive prefailure warning, a router may report a failed interface, and both might report the current chassis temperature or fan RPM.) The data set that the agent may collect and report on is called the Management Information Base (MIB).

The NMS can request info from the agent with a Get message; it can also send configuration instructions using a Set message. Agents can send Trap and Inform messages to the NMS, either autonomously or in response to Get requests.

Syslog

Syslog is a client/server protocol that uses either TCP or UDP port 514. A logging application collects and redirects system log messages to a central repository (the receiving end of the syslog system is often called syslogd— short for syslog daemon [service]), where they can be stored, archived, reviewed, and sorted easily. Most of the messages that appear on your Cisco device console are syslog messages. By default, they are only sent to the console line, but can easily be redirected to a server that is running a syslog service. Multiple devices can log to the same syslogd, so log entries from one device can be correlated against another's to determine of one event was related to another.

NetFlow

NetFlow is a Cisco-proprietary service that tracks individual packet flows through a device. Statistics on these flows are submitted to a NetFlow collector/analyzer, which makes it possible for administrators to monitor, analyze, and react to various conditions. NetFlow information can be used for traffic analysis and performance benchmarking, for network usage billing or for security design and threat detection, to name just a few.

Basic Switch Configuration

A Cisco switch will function perfectly well right out of the box with no configuration required; however, it's a good idea to do a few basic configurations to personalize, secure, and optimize the device.

Setting the Hostname

The default hostname is Switch, which not only lacks imagination but also is confusing if you have a lot of them. Changing the hostname is simple:

```
Switch(config)#hostname My2960
My2960(config)#
```

Notice that the hostname changed instantly!

Configuring a Management IP And Default Gateway

If you want to telnet to your switch to manage it remotely, have it participate in an SNMP system, or use the integrated HTTP server for monitoring, your switch needs an IP address and gateway address. This IP address is applied to the VLAN1 interface, and the default gateway is a global command on a switch. (Unlike a router, a switch has no physical ports that can be assigned IP addresses, so the virtual interface of VLAN1 (the management VLAN) gets the addresses.)

```
My2960(config)#interface vlan1
My2960(config-if)#ip address 192.168.1.2 255.255.255.0
My2960(config-if)#exit
My2960(config)#ip default-gateway 192.168.1.1
```

Note

A default gateway is an IP address of a router that can connect you to another network. A switch needs a default gateway if it is going to communicate with any device on any IP network other than the one its VLAN1 IP address is in. This is most commonly needed for remote management of the switch using Telnet or SSH, for the switch to participate in SNMP, or any other IP operation that crosses to another network or subnet.

Setting Speed and Duplex on Ethernet Ports

Although the Ethernet interfaces will autodetect the duplex and speed setting on a 2960, it is usually a good idea to hard-code them when you are sure of what you are connecting to (such as a server, a switch, or router):

```
My2960(config)#interface f0/24
My2960(config-if)#speed 100
My2960(config-if)#duplex full
```

Basic Router Configuration

Routers need a little more configuration than switches to function properly; every interface that you want to use needs an IP address and mask, in addition to being enabled. You will probably need to add static routes or perhaps run a dynamic routing protocol. You need to configure your serial port for connectivity as well.

Serial Port Configuration

As mentioned before, a Cisco serial port can run several different Layer 2 encapsulations—meaning that it can connect to different types of networks. You must be sure that the encapsulation type matches that of the device you are connecting to. In CCNA, we are interested only in three serial encapsulations:

HDLC, PPP, and Frame Relay. The command to change the encapsulation is executed at the interface configuration prompt:

```
Router(config)#interface serial 0
Router(config-if)#encapsulation [hdlc | frame-relay | ppp]
```

You might also need to set up the serial speed by configuring a clock rate. Usually this is supplied by the service provider's device (the Data Communication Equipment [DCE]), but in training labs we will hook a router directly to another router with a special back-to-back cable. In this situation, one of the devices must emulate the DCE, and the DCE sets the clock. Only one device needs the clock rate set.

You can also configure a bandwidth statement on the interface. This one is a little tricky; it looks like we are setting the bandwidth (as in bits per second) of the interface, but we really aren't—the clock rate sets the physical data rate. What we are doing with the **bandwidth** command is reporting to the routing protocols about the capacity of the interface (more on this in Chapter 9, "IP Access Lists"). It might have an actual clock rate of 64000 (64K), but we could lie and set the bandwidth to 56K for the purposes of routing information:

```
Router(config-if)#clock rate 64000
Router(config-if)#bandwidth 56
```

Note

Be aware of the syntax for clock rate and bandwidth: Clock rate is in bps, and bandwidth is in kilobits per second (Kbps). I remember it this way: **clock rate** is a longer command and needs a longer number (64000), and **bandwidth**, truncated as **band** so it's short, needs a shorter number (64).

Enabling Interfaces

By default, every interface on a router (whether it is brand new or has had its configuration erased) is in a *shutdown* state. This is also known as *administratively down*; although the interface might have been perfectly configured with an IP and mask, encapsulation, and whatever else is needed, the interface is effectively *off*—even Layer 1 is down. A shutdown interface doesn't send or receive any data at all, and it causes the other end of a serial link to think it is dead altogether. So when you first configure a new router or one that has had its configuration erased, remember to issue the **no shutdown** command at each interface, or none of the interfaces will work!

```
Router(config-if)#no shutdown
```

ExamAlert

Understand that all router interfaces are shut down by default until the **no shut** command is issued. (This is not the case with a switch; all switch interfaces are enabled by default.)

On a router, every interface is a gateway to another network. For this reason, we do not need to supply a default gateway. However, every interface you intend to use will need an IP address and mask. The commands to set an IP are exactly the same as on a switch. Don't forget the **no shutdown** (**no shut** for short):

```
Router(config)#interface s0
Router(config-if)#ip address 10.0.0.1 255.0.0.0
Router(config-if)#no shut
Router(config-if)#interface e0
Router(config-if)#ip address 172.16.0.1 255.255.0.0
Router(config-if)#no shut
```

Cram Quiz

1. Your workstation's IP is 172.16.21.48/24. You attempt to SSH to the switch at 10.14.83.253, but the connection is unsuccessful. You suspect a network problem, but the senior network engineer performs some tests and declares the network healthy, with all devices answering pings between your subnet and the switch's subnet. She does, however, report that the switch itself is not answering pings from remote networks, but it is answering pings from the router on the same subnet. Based on this information, what are the two most likely reasons for the failure of your SSH connection? Choose two.

   ❍ **A.** No crypto license on the switch.

   ❍ **B.** No IP address on the switch.

   ❍ **C.** No default gateway configured on the switch.

   ❍ **D.** An ACL in the path is blocking ICMP traffic.

   ❍ **E.** An ACL in the path is blocking SSH traffic

2. You want to set up a syslog server and configure your network devices to use it. What can you list in the expense approval request as a reason why syslog is needed?

   ❍ **A.** Syslog eliminates the need for network monitoring software.

   ❍ **B.** Syslog reduces the load on the network by taking management traffic out of band.

   ❍ **C.** Syslog centralizes authentication, authorization, and accounting management.

   ❍ **D.** Syslog centralizes all log entries from multiple devices, simplifying device log collection and analysis.

3. What information will the command **show cdp neighbor detail** give you that **show cdp neighbor** will not?

   ❍ **A.** Traffic flows, top talkers, hourly traffic rate analysis

   ❍ **B.** Local and remote port connections

   ❍ **C.** Device capabilities

   ❍ **D.** IOS version and IP addresses

Cram Quiz Answers

1. Answers C and E are correct. Answer A is wrong because SSH does not require any licensing. Answer B is wrong because if the switch can answer pings at all, it must have an IP. Answer D is wrong because the network engineer reports that pings are successful along the entire path.
2. Answer D is correct. Answer A is incorrect; Syslog is a complementary system to network monitoring software, it does no t replace it. Answer B is wrong because syslog actually adds traffic to the network because logged entries are transmitted to the syslogd server instead of being stored locally. Answer C is wrong because syslog is not a AAA system.
3. Answer D is correct. Answer A is wrong because CDP does not collect this information, NetFlow does. Answers B and C are wrong because this information is available in both commands.

Review Questions

1. Bob types in an excellent initial configuration on his new router, but when he tries to ping the interfaces, they don't answer. What could be wrong?
   - ❍ **A.** Bob changed the configuration register to suppress pings.
   - ❍ **B.** Bob needs a new router; this one is clearly defective.
   - ❍ **C.** The router does not support the IP protocol by default.
   - ❍ **D.** Bob neglected to issue the no shut command at each interface.

2. For which of the following connections will you need a crossover cable?
   - ❍ **A.** PC's NIC direct to router Fa0/1
   - ❍ **B.** PC's serial (COM) port to the router's console port
   - ❍ **C.** PC to switch
   - ❍ **D.** Router to switch
   - ❍ **E.** Hub to router
   - ❍ **F.** Hub to switch

3. Which two actions will get you out of setup mode?
   - ❍ **A.** Typing **abort setup**
   - ❍ **B.** Choosing not to, when asked if you want to keep the configuration at the end of setup mode
   - ❍ **C.** Waiting until it times out
   - ❍ **D.** Pressing Ctrl+C

4. What command lists the IOS images stored in flash?
   - ❍ **A.** **show ios**
   - ❍ **B.** **list flash**
   - ❍ **C.** **show flash**
   - ❍ **D.** **show version**

5. Jaine sets her configuration register to 0x2142. What is she up to?
   - ❍ **A.** Changing which IOS image in flash to boot from
   - ❍ **B.** Forcing the router to boot from rxboot
   - ❍ **C.** Forcing the router to boot from ROMmon
   - ❍ **D.** Performing a password recovery

6. Which of the following correctly summarizes the boot sequence?
   - ❍ **A.** Find IOS, load IOS, POST, find config, load config
   - ❍ **B.** Post, find IOS, load IOS, find config, load config
   - ❍ **C.** POST, find config, load config, find IOS, load IOS
   - ❍ **D.** ROMmon, load IOS, load config

7. Match the entries in the list on the left with the descriptions on the right:

ROM	Stores compressed IOS images
RAM	Stores startup config file
FLASH	Stores running config and decompressed IOS
NVRAM	Stores mini-IOS and ROMmon images

8. What command must be entered on the DCE device to enable serial communication at a speed of 64Kbps?
   - ❍ **A.** Router(config)#**clock rate 64000**
   - ❍ **B.** Router(config-if)#**interface-type dce**
   - ❍ **C.** Router(config-if)#**bandwidth 64**
   - ❍ **D.** Router(config-if)#**clock rate 64000**

9. Which of the following features of the IOS for a Cisco 2921 router does not require a feature license to be activated?
   - ❍ **A.** Cryptonomic
   - ❍ **B.** IP Standard
   - ❍ **C.** Voice
   - ❍ **D.** IP Base

10. You are trying to telnet to a router, but do not know its IP address. What commands can you enter to see the IP address of a neighboring router? Select all that apply.
    - ❍ **A.** **show cdp neighbors detail**
    - ❍ **B.** **show cdp neighbors**
    - ❍ **C.** **show cdp entry ***
    - ❍ **D.** **show cdp**
    - ❍ **E.** **show cdp entry neighbors**

Answers to Review Questions

1. Answer D is correct. Until you issue the no shut command at each interface, the interfaces will effectively be switched off. Answer A is incorrect; you can't use the config register to suppress ping. Answer B may be true, but it is unlikely, so it is not the best choice. Answer C is incorrect because it is false; every IOS supports only IP until you upgrade to one that supports other network protocols as well.
2. Answers A and F are correct. Answer B requires a rollover. Answers C, D, and E require a straight-through.
3. Answers B and D are correct. Answer A is not a valid command. Answer C is incorrect because setup mode does not time out.
4. Answer C is correct. Answers A and B, **show ios** and **list flash**, are not valid commands. Answer D, the **show version** command, is incorrect because it lists only the file in use, not all the images in flash.
5. Answer D is correct. 0x2142 is one of the steps in password recovery. Answers A, B, and C (changing which IOS image in flash to boot from, forcing the router to boot from rxboot, and forcing the router to boot from ROMmon) are controlled by the config register, but use values other than 0x2142.
6. Answer B is correct. Answers A, C, and D are either out of order or incorrect.
7.

ROM	Stores mini-IOS and ROMmon images
RAM	Stores running config and decompressed IOS
FLASH	Stores compressed IOS
NVRAM	Stores startup config file

8. Answer D is correct. Answer A is incorrect because it is executed at the wrong command prompt. Answer B is incorrect because it is invalid syntax, and Answer C is incorrect because it sets the bandwidth for routing metrics, not the required DCE clock speed.
9. Answers D is correct. Answers A and B are not valid licensed features. Answer C requires a feature license.
10. Answers A and C are correct. The commands **show cdp neighbors detail** and **show cdp entry *** are functionally equivalent and would show you the Layer 3 IP address of the neighboring router along with platform and IOS version. Answer B is incorrect because this would not give you the IP address of a neighboring router. Answer D shows global CDP statistics but will also not give you the output this question is asking about. Answer E is incorrect because it is not a valid command.

What Next?

If you want more practice on this chapter's exam topics before you move on, remember that you can access all of the Cram Quiz questions on the CD. You can also create a custom exam by topic with the practice exam software. Note any topic you struggle with and go to that topic's material in this chapter.

CHAPTER FIVE

Securing Your Cisco Devices

This chapter covers the following official CCNA Routing and Switching 200-120 exam topics:

- Configure and verify network device security features such as SSH.
- Describe external authentication methods.
- Configure and verify switch port security features.

This chapter deals with securing your Cisco router or switch. It covers some basic device security best practices such as configuring passwords and changing from Telnet to Secure Shell (SSH) for remote management, and it describes external authentication methods and configuring switch port security.

Securing Routers and Switches

CramSaver

If you can correctly answer these questions before going through this section, save time by skimming the Exam Alerts in this section and then completing the Cram Quiz at the end of the section.

1. What command creates an encrypted privileged exec password?
2. What three commands are needed to apply a password to the console line?
3. What does the error "Password required, but none set" mean?

Answers

1. Router(config)#**enable secret** *<password>*
2. Router(config)#**line con 0 Router(config-line)#password** *<password>* **Router(config-line)#login**
3. You have attempted to telnet to a device that has no password applied to the vty lines.

The CCENT and CCNA certifications are not going to make you a security expert; other courses will help you do so if that is your ultimate goal. But just as you don't need to be a Formula 1 driver to operate a car correctly and safely, there are a number of basic operations that you need to know about network and device security without being a security expert. This chapter is about "hardening" the IOS, which simply means making it more difficult to attack or exploit your routers and switches.

Configuring Password Security

Initially, your router or switch will have no passwords at all. Pressing Enter will grant you first user exec. You can then gain privileged exec access by using the **enable** command. The Telnet lines are secured by default; they will refuse connections until they are configured with a password.

The minimum security configuration is to require a password to log in to your devices. Passwords can be applied to the console port, to the vty lines (controlling Telnet/SSH access), and to the privileged exec prompt.

The commands in Example 5.1 illustrate how to apply basic password security to your router or switch, for the console port (user exec), vty lines (for remote user exec administration using Telnet), and the privileged exec prompt. Lines that begin with an exclamation point are informational remarks and do not configure the device:

EXAMPLE 5.1 **Basic Password Configuration**

```
Router(config)#line con 0
!    The console port is always con 0
Router(config-line)#login
!    Requires a password to access user exec over the console port
Router(config-line)#password ExamCram2
!    Specifies the password - Note: passwords are case sensitive.
Router(config)#line vty 0 4
!    There are 5 vty lines, numbered 0 through 4
Router(config-line)#login
Router(config-line)#password 23StanleyCups
!
Router(config)#enable password cisco
!    sets the privileged exec password to 'cisco'
```

A Word About vty Lines

A vty line is used by both Telnet and SSH connections. The vty stands for virtual teletype—*virtual* because there is no associated hardware as there would be with the console port or asynchronous serial (TTY) ports for modems. For our purposes, there are five vty lines, numbered 0, 1, 2, 3, and 4. The command **line vty 0 4** shown previously enables you to configure all of them simultaneously by specifying the range of "0 [through] 4." Some newer switches and routers will show 16 lines, numbered 0 through 15; it's unlikely that this feature will be a factor on your test, however.

Why have so many vty lines, when only one is used by a Telnet session? For that same reason, actually: One Telnet/SSH session uses one vty line. If you telnet in, and then telnet out to some other device, you use two vty lines. It's common to telnet to multiple devices concurrently when you are working on a network; it's also possible that multiple administrators could be working on or from the same device at the same time, each administrator needing at least one vty line.

By the way, there is no easy way to determine or predict to which vty line you are going to connect. They are used in a round-robin fashion. So, setting a different password for each one is probably more of a hassle than a security benefit; you can't be sure which line you just connected to and therefore which password to enter!

These passwords will all appear in your configuration file in plain text; anyone with access to that file could read them. To encrypt your privileged exec password with an MD5 hash, use the **enable secret** command:

```
Router(config)#enable secret squirrel42
```

You can also apply encryption to the other passwords for the console, privileged exec, vty and TTY lines (but *not* the *enable secret* password [this privileged exec password is already encrypted]) using the **service password-encryption** command:

```
Router(config)#service password-encryption
```

ExamAlert

You should know how to apply passwords to the console and vty lines and to the privileged exec prompt (including encrypting all of them). Practice this: Pick three random passwords and type in the full configuration as quickly and accurately as you can, even if you just use Notepad. Can you do it with zero errors in less than a minute?

Cram Quiz

Answer these questions. The answers follow the last question. If you cannot answer these questions correctly, consider reading this section again until you can.

1. Sparky the Junior Woodchuck has been told to encrypt all passwords in the router config. Did he meet the objective by entering the following configuration?

```
Router(config)#line con 0
Router(config-line)#password woodchuck
Router(config-line)#login
Router(config-line)#line vty 0 4 Router(config-line)#password
sparky
Router(config-line)#login
Router(config)#enable password sparkywoodchuck
Router(config)#service password-encryption
```

   ❍ **A.** Yes

   ❍ **B.** No

2. Ewan connects to a router using Telnet. Charley tries to telnet to the same router, but gets the error "Password required but none set." Ewan then terminates his Telnet session. Charley tries again, and this time he can connect using Telnet. What is the likely problem here?

   ❍ **A.** Charley's IP is blocked by an access list.

   ❍ **B.** Charley does not have an account with administrative rights.

   ❍ **C.** There are no passwords configured on the vty lines.

   ❍ **D.** Some of the vty lines do not have passwords.

Cram Quiz Answers

1. Answer A is correct. All the passwords are encrypted: The enable, console, and vty passwords will be given mild encryption by the **service password-encryption** command. But because Sparky used the **enable password** *<password>* command instead of the **enable secret** *<password>* command, the enable password is very weakly encrypted.
2. Answer D is correct: It appears that at least one (and possibly more) of the vty lines have not been set up to require a password. Answer A can't be right because Charley was able to connect the second time. Answer B is wrong because connecting via Telnet does not require privileged exec rights. Answer C must be wrong because both Ewan and Charley were able to connect without getting the "Password required" message.

ExamAlert

Know the password configuration commands cold.

Configuring SSH Access to Your Router

- **Configure and verify network device security features such as SSH.**
- **Configure and verify network device security features such as <describe> external authentication methods.**

CramSaver

If you can correctly answer these questions before going through this section, save time by skimming the Exam Alerts in this section and then completing the Cram Quiz at the end of the section.

1. What is the primary advantage of SSH over Telnet?
2. True or False: SSH uses a VPN for security.
3. True or False: Configuring SSH automatically disables Telnet access.

Answers

1. SSH provides encryption, including of the password.
2. False.
3. False.

Telnet is a simple and effective way to remotely administer your router or switch, but it has one significant disadvantage: It is completely unencrypted, which means that everything you send across the network via Telnet could be read easily if intercepted. That's not a good thing.

Secure Shell, or SSH, is a good alternative. It is slightly more complicated (but not difficult) to set up and provides a secured remote command-line interface using public key exchange and decent encryption. Cisco recommends (and we do too!) that SSH always be used instead of Telnet for security reasons. Your IOS version must include support for crypto features, or this will not work.

The following are the basic steps to set up a router for SSH support:

1. Define a username and password. SSH can't use the line password we created for Telnet access, so we must create a username/password pair for SSH to use. You might choose to make more than one, for different admins.

```
Router(config)#username Admin007 password ExamCram2
```

2. Configure the router to use the username/password. (We could use AAA [authentication, authorization, and accounting] instead of the command shown, but that is quite a large topic that we don't need to get into here.)

```
Router(config-line)#login local
```

3. Set the router's domain name. This does not necessarily have to be the actual domain name of the company, but it makes sense if it is the domain that the router actually operates in. If no defined domain is in use, make one up. (The domain name is used as a factor in generating the encryption key). I used ExamCramLab.local in this example. One other thing: Your router has a default hostname of Router, but you have probably already changed it to something more specific. Just be aware that the hostname is another factor in the encryption key generation too.

```
Router(config)#ip domain-name ExamCramLab.local
```

4. Create the encryption key. Simply put, this command creates the encryption key that will be used to allow secure connections from users supplying the correct credentials. This is the command that will fail if your IOS doesn't support the right crypto features.

```
Router(config)#crypto key generate rsa
```

5. (Optional) Restrict vty line connections to SSH only, instead of both Telnet and SSH. It makes sense to do this, although it is not strictly required for SSH to work.

```
Router(config)#line vty 0 4
Router(config-line)#transport input ssh
```

There's one other catch to using SSH instead of Telnet: You must have an SSH client application. I prefer to use terminal applications such as SecureCRT because they are feature rich and easier to use, in my opinion.

To connect to your router using SSH, launch your SSH client of choice, give it the IP address of the device you want to SSH to, and when prompted, supply the username and password you configured.

ExamAlert

Know the configurations for SSH, as well as why it is preferred over Telnet.

External Authentication Methods

Creating username/password combinations on the router or switch is okay, but it doesn't scale well because you have to repeat the commands on every device. It is also not very secure because the configuration file may expose those accounts to people who shouldn't see them. It's a lot of "administrative overhead"—that's code for "extra work that isn't efficient".

In many network environments, a central resource stores usernames and passwords. Network applications can refer to this resource to verify that the account that is attempting to log in is valid and has the correct password. Some of these systems can also provide information about what the user account is allowed to do (privilege or authorization), and may also track what the account did (auditing or accounting).

Cisco devices can use external authentication provided by AAA protocols such as RADIUS (which stands for Remote Authentication Dial-In User Service, but these days it is used more for on-net rather than dialup access) or DIAMETER, which is a newer, more capable replacement for RADIUS. (DIAMETER isn't an acronym; it's just a play on the word *radius*—as in, it's twice as good. Get it?). You may also encounter Terminal Access Controller Access-Control System Plus (TACACS+), which is an older system developed by Cisco but released as an open standard.

The process is simple: If a Cisco device is configured to use AAA for authentication, when a user attempts to log in that authentication request is relayed to the configured AAA server. The AAA server then performs the authentication and informs the Cisco device whether it was successful; if it was successful the user is granted access; if not, access is denied.

The main advantage to an external authentication system is that it is centrally administered; you build all the accounts once, you manage all the passwords in one place, and an almost limitless number of devices can use the service.

The disadvantages include the following:

- The users end up with the same password on multiple systems, which most security policies identify as a bad practice if the system is not properly secured.
- If the AAA system fails or is otherwise unreachable, nobody can authenticate unless there is a local account.
- Someone needs to know how to set up and maintain the AAA systems, as well as how to configure the devices that use it.

Cram Quiz

Answer these questions. The answers follow the last question. If you cannot answer these questions correctly, consider reading this section again until you can.

1. When using SSH, is a local username/password configuration required?

❍ **A.** Yes

❍ **B.** No

2. Which of the following are recommended security practices for a switch? Choose all that apply.

❍ **A.** Set a very strong password; for ease and consistency of administration, never change it.

❍ **B.** Place all inactive ports in an unused VLAN.

❍ **C.** Treat all passwords securely: difficult to guess, kept secret, changed regularly.

❍ **D.** Disable trunking on inactive interfaces.

Cram Quiz Answers

1. Answer B is correct. SSH can use AAA for user authentication, although a local username/password also works fine.

2. Answers B, C, and D are correct. Answer A is almost right, but you should change passwords regularly.

Switch Port Security

- **Configure and verify switch port security features such as Sticky MAC.**
- **Configure and verify switch port security features such as MAC address limitation.**

CramSaver

If you can correctly answer these questions before going through this section, save time by skimming the Exam Alerts in this section and then completing the Cram Quiz at the end of the section.

1. What is the primary purpose of port security?
2. True or False: All port security allowed MACs must be manually entered.
3. True or False: When port security is configured, all destination MACs are checked.

Answers

1. To control which and how many devices are allowed to send frames into a switch.
2. False. MACs can be dynamically learned and then (optionally) made "sticky" entries in the config.
3. False. All source MACs are checked!

Security Best Practices for Switches

Let's take a moment to talk about best practices for Cisco switch security. We have already mentioned passwords; that's obviously a very important component. You should also realize that the passwords we just configured should be treated like any other password: They should be hard to guess, must be kept a secret, and should be changed on a regular basis.

Shutting down unused ports using the **shutdown** command pretty much solves the security problem: Because all ports on a switch are enabled by default, shutting down ones that are not supposed to be used prevents unauthorized connection to the network. But what happens if the port is reenabled? The default settings are not very secure, so Cisco also recommends taking some steps to secure unused switch ports:

- Assign the port to an unused VLAN using the **switchport access vlan** *<vlan_id>* command. This action prevents a connected device from accessing the rest of the network, even if the port is enabled.

- Disable unauthorized trunk connections using the **switchport mode access** or **switchport nonegotiate** command. This prevents traffic from multiple VLANs from being trunked to an unauthorized device and avoids certain network attacks.
- Change the native VLAN from the default of VLAN 1 to an unused VLAN using the **switchport trunk native vlan** *<vlan_id>* command. This prevents access to the management VLAN of the switch, and may also help prevent a trunk connection from forming with an unauthorized new device.

These settings will help secure a switch port even if it is reenabled, whether unintentionally or purposely. The next section describes a way to further secure switch ports while they are operational.

One of the ways to increase the security of an operational switch ports (and the connected network) is to control which (or how many) devices can connect to it. Cisco switches provide a mechanism called port security that enables you to determine which devices can connect to a switch port and send in frames. Access is granted or denied based on the MAC address of the device that is attempting to forward frames through a switch port. The function also applies even if the device is connected to a different switch: If the port receives a frame with a source MAC that is not allowed (whether the source is directly connected or on a different switch), it drops the frame. The port will (by default) send out alerts and disable itself, but these options are configurable.

You can configure port security in several ways. It is activated per port, and each port can have different settings. The following list identifies some of the configurable options for port security:

- Specific MAC addresses can be statically or permanently identified as permitted, or you can let the port dynamically learn the MAC addresses from inbound frames.
- If the port is dynamically learning MACs, you can specify a limit to how many it is allowed to learn.
- The learned MAC addresses can be made into permanent entries (and can be preserved in the startup-config file by using the copy run start command). This makes administration a little easier, because you don't have to statically enter the MACs; as long as you are certain that only legitimate devices are connecting, all the legitimate MACs can be dynamically learned and made permanent. This capability is called "sticky" learning, because the dynamically learned MACs stick in the MAC table. You can also limit the number of allowed MACs in sticky or static modes.

If a violation occurs (meaning, if a MAC other than an allowed one is detected, or if the maximum number of allowed MACs is exceeded) the port can react in one of three ways:

- **Protect:** Discards frames from disallowed MACs
- **Restrict:** Discards frames from disallowed MACs, and sends out log alerts and SNMP traps about the event
- **Shutdown (default):** Discards frames from disallowed MACs, sends out log alerts and SNMP traps about the event, and places the interface into err-disabled state, effectively disabling it for all traffic until an administrator manually resets it using the **shutdown** and **no shutdown** commands

Configuring Port Security

The steps for configuring port security are as follows:

1. Statically set either access or trunk mode on the port using either **switchport mode access** or **switchport mode trunk**. (These commands are covered in more detail in Chapter 6, “Basic Switch Operations and Configuration.”)
2. Enable port security using the **switchport port-security** command.

> **Note**
>
> Many people miss the second step. You have to enter this command, all by itself, to activate port security. The tricky part is this: The following commands will be accepted but won’t do anything for you until you enter the command **switchport port-security**.

3. If desired, set the maximum number of allowed MAC addresses to something other than the default of one, using the **switchport port-security maximum** *<number>* command.
4. Set the desired violation response. (Protect or Restrict; Shutdown is the default and does not need to be set unless you are changing it back to the default.)
5. If desired, statically identify allowed MACs using the **switchport port-security mac-address** *<mac_address>* command. Re-issue the command for each allowed MAC.

Example 5.2 demonstrates some port security configurations:

EXAMPLE 5.2 Switch Port Security Configuration

```
interface FastEthernet0/1
switchport mode access
! sets port to non-trunking
switchport port-security
! activates port security
switchport port-security mac-address 0c00.aaaa.1111
! statically defines an allowed MAC
switchport port-security violation restrict
! Forwards traffic from the specified MAC
! Drops traffic from non-allowed MACs
! Sends alerts and SNMP traps on violation
!
interface FastEthernet0/2
switchport mode access
! sets port to non-trunking
switchport port-security
! activates port security
switchport port-security mac-address sticky
! sets the port to "sticky" learn MACs
! Violation: Shutdown (default)


interface FastEthernet0/3
switchport mode access
! sets port to non-trunking
switchport port-security
! activates port security using defaults:
! No sticky learning
! No statically-defined MACs
! Violation: Shutdown (default)

interface FastEthernet0/4
switchport mode access
! sets port to non-trunking
switchport port-security
! activates port security
switchport port-security maximum 8
! sets limit of 8 allowed MACs
switchport port-security violation protect
! Discards frames from non-allowed MACs
! Forwards frames from allowed Macs
! Does not send alerts or SNMP traps on violation
```

Verifying Port Security

The port security settings you have applied will show up in the **show running-config** command output. (Sticky-learned MACs will only show up if you do a **copy run start** and then **reload**.) The command **show port-security** <*interface*> will list the current state of and statistics for port security per interface, as demonstrated in Example 5.3.

EXAMPLE 5.3 **Verifying Switch Port Security**

```
Switch#show port-security interface f0/1
Port Security : Enabled
Port Status : Secure-shutdown
Violation Mode : Shutdown
Aging Time : 0 mins
Aging Type : Absolute
SecureStatic Address Aging : Disabled
Maximum MAC Addresses : 1
Total MAC Addresses : 1
Configured MAC Addresses : 1
Sticky MAC Addresses : 0
Last Source Address:Vlan : 00c0.bbbb.2222:1
Security Violation Count : 1

Switch#show port-security interface f0/2
Port Security : Enabled
Port Status : Secure-up
Violation Mode : Restrict
Aging Time : 0 mins
Aging Type : Absolute
SecureStatic Address Aging : Disabled
Maximum MAC Addresses : 1
Total MAC Addresses : 1
Configured MAC Addresses : 1
Sticky MAC Addresses : 1
Last Source Address:Vlan : 0c00.cccc.3333:1
Security Violation Count : 0

Switch#show running-config
(Output truncated for brevity)
interface FastEthernet0/2
switchport mode access
switchport port-security
switchport port-security mac-address sticky
```

Note that in the output of **show port-security interface f0/1** you can see that the port status is **secure-shutdown**, which indicates that a nonallowed MAC has attempted to send a frame through this port. The specific MAC that caused the violation is shown in the line **Last Source Address:Vlan : 00c0.bbbb.2222:1** (where **00c0.bbbb.2222** is the MAC, and **:1** is the VLAN number).

So to sum up: The purpose of port security is to control which devices can send frames into a particular switch port. The allowed devices are identified by their MAC address, either statically or dynamically. A limit of how many MACs a port may learn can be defined, and the dynamically learned MACs can be made sticky (permanent). The port can be configured to respond in three different ways to a violation (that is, a frame from a disallowed MAC arriving at the port).

Cram Quiz

Answer these questions. The answers follow the last question. If you cannot answer these questions correctly, consider reading this section again until you can.

1. Which of the three violation responses available in port security does not send alerts and SNMP traps?

   ❍ **A.** Protect

   ❍ **B.** Restrict

   ❍ **C.** Shutdown

2. What would be the effect of applying the command **switchport port-security maximum 1** if sticky learning is also configured?

   ❍ **A.** Only frames from the most-recent source MAC to send will be denied.

   ❍ **B.** Only frames from the first MAC to send will be denied.

   ❍ **C.** All frames sent from the first MAC will be allowed.

   ❍ **D.** All frames sent to the first MAC will be allowed.

Cram Quiz Answers

1. Answer A is correct. Both Restrict and Shutdown log and trap.
2. Answer C is correct. Answer A is wrong; all frames from any source MAC after the first to send will be denied. Answer B is wrong; only frames from the first MAC to send will be allowed. Answer D is wrong; all frames sent *from*, not sent *to*, the first MAC will be allowed.

Review Questions

You can find the answers to these questions at the end of the chapter.

1. Which of the following applies an encrypted password of cisco to the privileged exec prompt?
   - ❍ **A.** **enable password cisco**
   - ❍ **B.** **enable password cisco encrypted**
   - ❍ **C.** **enable cisco secret**
   - ❍ **D.** **enable secret cisco**

2. What commands apply a password of Vienna to the first five Telnet connections on a router?
   - ❍ **A.** **line vty 5 login password Vienna**
   - ❍ **B.** **line vty 0 4 login password vienna**
   - ❍ **C.** **interface vty 0 4 login password Vienna**
   - ❍ **D.** **line vty 0 4 login password Vienna**

3. True or False: The command **service password-encryption** encrypts the password set by the command **enable password** *<password>*.
   - ❍ **A.** True
   - ❍ **B.** False

4. True or False: SSH is enabled by default.
   - ❍ **A.** True
   - ❍ **B.** False

5. Which of the following are required in an SSH configuration? Choose all that apply.
   - ❍ **A.** Setting the domain name
   - ❍ **B.** Configuring a AAA server
   - ❍ **C.** Configuring a username and password
   - ❍ **D.** Generating an RSA key
   - ❍ **E.** Installing the SSH client on the switch

6. Stephen complains that configuring SSH is overly complex, and he doesn't see the benefit of using it. What is the single most important benefit of using SSH instead of Telnet?

   ❍ **A.** Its complex configuration ensures job security.

   ❍ **B.** Because SSH supports tunneling encapsulation, it converges mission-critical data into a cloud-based dark data store.

   ❍ **C.** SSH supports IPv6.

   ❍ **D.** SSH provides encryption.

7. Which of the following are security best practices for a switch?

   ❍ **A.** Apply passwords and enforce password rules.

   ❍ **B.** Assign inactive ports to an unused VLAN.

   ❍ **C.** Disable trunking on inactive interfaces.

   ❍ **D.** Change the Native VLAN on trunk interfaces.

   ❍ **E.** Change the management VLAN.

   ❍ **F.** All of these answers are correct.

8. Which of the following best describes port security?

   ❍ **A.** Port security is a set of configurations that controls which hosts can send frames through a given switch port.

   ❍ **B.** Port security utilizes 802.1x port-based authentication.

   ❍ **C.** Port security applies packet-inspection rules to uplink ports.

   ❍ **D.** Port security uses client-side digital certificates for port-based authentication

9. True or False: Sticky-learned MACs are permanently stored in the running config across reboots.

   ❍ **A.** True

   ❍ **B.** False

10. Which port security violation configuration drops frames from disallowed MACs, permits frames from allowed MACs, and sends alerts and traps?

   ❍ **A.** Protect

   ❍ **B.** Restrict

   ❍ **C.** Shutdown

   ❍ **D.** Secure

Answers to Review Questions

1. Answers D is correct. Answer A is a valid command, but does not encrypt the password. Answer B is a valid command but does not encrypt the password. Answer C is not a valid command.
2. Answer D is correct. Answer A only applies the password to vty line 5 (if it exists). Answer B uses the wrong password; it's case sensitive. Answer C is an invalid command; there is no **interface vty 0 4**.
3. True.
4. False.
5. Answers A, C, and D are correct. Answer B is not required, but is optional. Answer E is incorrect; the client is installed on the admin workstation, not the switch.
6. Answer D is correct. Answer A may indeed be true in some environments, but can't be said to be the most important benefit. Answer B wins the Buzzword Bingo game, but is otherwise baloney. Answer C happens to be true, but is not the single most important benefit from our perspective.
7. Answer F is correct. All the possible answers here are correct.
8. Answer A is correct. Answer B is false; 802.1x is an entirely different method of securing network access. Answer C is incorrect; a Layer 2 switch here in CCNA land cannot do packet inspection. Answer D is incorrect; port security does nothing more than inspect the source MAC.
9. False. If you do a copy run start and then reload the switch, however, the sticky MACs will become permanent across reboots.
10. Answer B is correct. Protect will discard nonallowed MAC frames, but will not alert or trap. Shutdown will alert and trap, and additionally will err-disable the port. Secure is not a valid option.

What Next?

If you want more practice on this chapter's exam topics before you move on, remember that you can access all of the Cram Quiz questions on the CD. You can also create a custom exam by topic with the practice exam software. Note any topic you struggle with and go to that topic's material in this chapter.

CHAPTER SIX

Basic Switch Operations and Configuration

This chapter covers the following official CCNA Routing and Switching 200-120 exam topics:

- Identify basic switching concepts and the operation of Cisco switches.
- Describe how VLANs create logically separate networks and the need for routing between them.
- Explain network segmentation and basic traffic management concepts.
- Configure and verify trunking on Cisco switches.

This chapter introduces the concepts and modes of Layer 2 switching and physical layer connectivity between switches. We also introduce the Spanning Tree Protocol and its importance to switched systems. From there, we move on to VLANs and trunking.

Bridging and Switching

- **Identify basic switching concepts and the operation of Cisco switches.**
- **Explain network segmentation and basic traffic management concepts.**

CramSaver

1. What are the three operations performed by a bridge or switch?
   - **A.** Filter, copy, frame
   - **B.** Broadcast, multicast, unicast
   - **C.** Filter, forward, flood
   - **D.** Filter, forward, broadcast
2. True or False: A switch populates its MAC address table with the destination MAC address of frames received on each port.
3. What is the definition of *collision domain*?
   - **A.** A DNS domain in which IP address conflicts occur.
   - **B.** A set of devices that hear broadcasts caused by collisions.
   - **C.** Collision domains only exist when using coaxial media.
   - **D.** A set of devices that cause and are affected by one another's collisions.

Answers

1. Answer C is correct. Switches will filter (drop) a frame of the source and destination MAC addresses are on the same port, forward the frame out a single port if the destination MAC is known in the MAC table, or flood the frame out all ports (except the one it was received on) if the destination MAC is not in the MAC table or it is a broadcast frame (or, by default, if it is a multicast frame).
2. False. A switch populates the MAC table using the source MAC address of frames received on each port.
3. Answer D is correct. The only other answer that is remotely true is Answer C; while the part about coaxial media is true, collisions also happen on half-duplex circuits using UTP as well.

Bridges and switches are devices that segment (break up) collision domains. They are important parts of a network infrastructure, and the concepts presented here are heavily tested on the CCNA exams.

Functions of Bridges and Switches

When talking about LANs at the CCNA level, we are almost exclusively interested in Ethernet. You have an idea from Chapter 1, "Networking Fundamentals," of how Ethernet works. This chapter deals with how to make it work at a highly optimized level by using specialized devices to enhance the simple and adaptable Ethernet technology.

In the early implementations of Ethernet, every device connected to a single wire. Thicknet (10BASE-5) and Thinnet (10BASE-2) were the most common physical layer implementations. A little later, hubs were used. All these technologies did effectively the same thing: connect many hosts together so that one of them at a time could transmit on the wire. This created a single, often large, collision domain. As you recall from Chapter 1, the bigger the collision domain, the more collisions and the less data that actually gets sent successfully. In these types of implementations, you can lose 50% to 60% of the available throughput just because of collisions. So, if we had a 10BASE-T hub, not only did we actually end up with only about 4 or 5Mbps instead of 10Mbps, but that reduced bandwidth must also be shared by all the devices on that segment, instead of each device getting the full 10Mbps. Breaking up (segmenting) collision domains is necessary to make them small enough so that devices can reliably transmit data. We can segment using routers, but routers are expensive and difficult to configure; in addition, they don't usually have very many ports on them, so we would need a lot of them to segment effectively.

Bridges were developed to address this issue. A *bridge* isolates one collision domain from another while still connecting them and selectively allowing frames to pass from one to the other. A *switch* is simply a bigger, faster bridge. Every port on a switch or bridge is its own collision domain. The terms bridge and switch can be used interchangeably when discussing their basic operations; we use the term *switch* because switches are more modern and more common.

A business-class switch must do three things:

- Address learning
- Frame forwarding
- Layer 2 loop removal

Note

All the descriptions and references in this book are to transparent bridging (switching). By definition, a *transparent bridge* is invisible to the hosts connected through it. Other bridge types (for example, source route, source route translational, and so on) are used in mixed-media networks, including Token Ring and FDDI, that are no longer relevant to the CCNA test.

Address Learning

Address learning refers to the intelligent capability of switches to dynamically learn the source MAC addresses of devices that are connected to its various ports. These dynamically-learned MAC entries have a default max age timer of 300 seconds; the timer is reset when a new frame from the same MAC arrives on the port. These MAC addresses are stored in RAM in a table that lists the address and the port on which a frame was last received from that address. This enables a switch to selectively forward the frame out the appropriate port(s), based on the destination MAC address of the frame.

Anytime a device that is connected to a switch sends a frame through the switch, the switch records the source MAC address of the frame in its MAC address table (also known as the content-addressable memory [CAM] table) and associates that address with the port the frame arrived on. Figure 6.1 illustrates a switch that has learned the MAC addresses of the three hosts connected to it, as well as the ports to which they are connected.

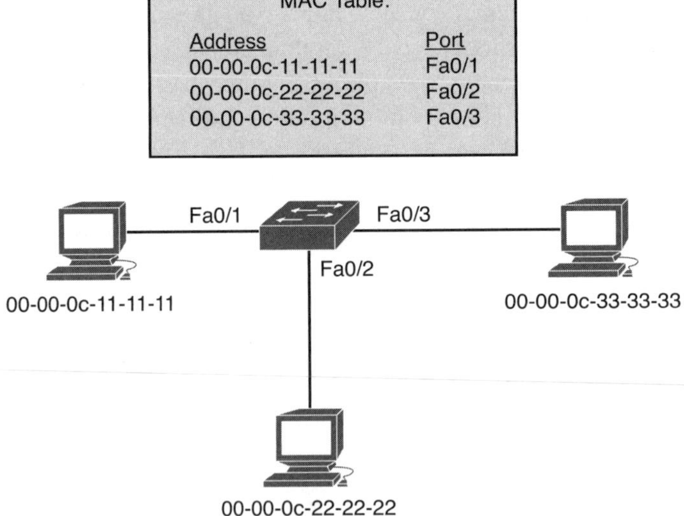

FIGURE 6.1 **A switch with a complete MAC table.**

Frame Forwarding

After a switch has learned the MAC addresses of the devices connected to it, it can intelligently forward unicast frames to the correct host by comparing the destination MAC of the frame with the addresses in its MAC table; when it finds a match, it then sends the frame out the port associated with that entry. Figure 6.2 illustrates the forwarding decision made by the switch.

This is where switches create such a benefit to an Ethernet network: If a switch knows the port to which the destination MAC is connected, the switch will send the frame out that port and only that port. This prevents the traffic from being unnecessarily sent to hosts that it is not intended for, significantly improving the efficiency of the network. This is in sharp contrast to the behavior of a hub, which always sends all frames out all ports except the one it came in on (to avoid a false collision detection by the sending station).

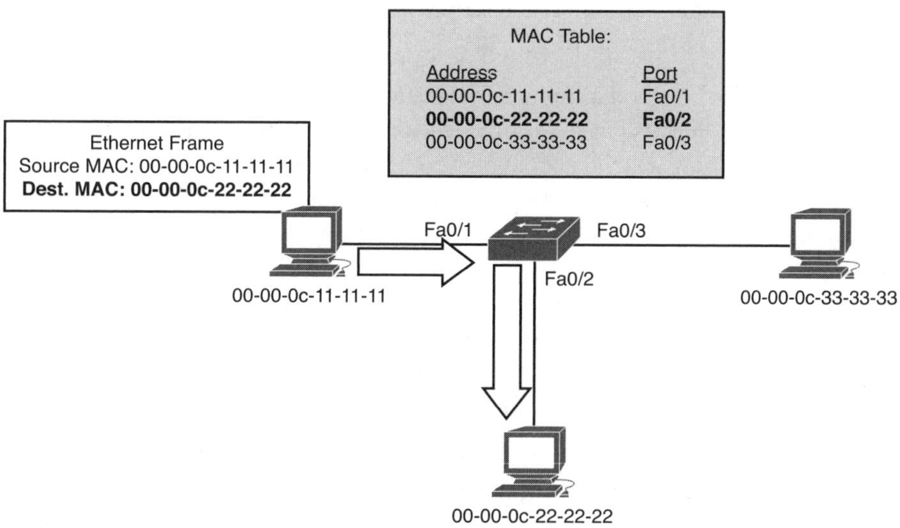

FIGURE 6.2 **The forward decision.**

Sometimes a switch cannot make its forwarding decision, however. Consider the case in which one of the hosts sends out a broadcast. The MAC address for a broadcast is FF-FF-FF-FF-FF-FF; this is effectively the MAC address of all hosts because every host in a broadcast domain must receive all broadcasts. When the switch receives a broadcast frame inbound on one of its ports, it will check that the source MAC is correctly listed in its MAC table (and update it if necessary) and check the destination MAC of the frame for a match in the table. Because FF-FF-FF-FF-FF-FF matches the MAC of all hosts, the switch must *flood* the frame—it sends it out every port (except the one it came in on) so that the broadcast frame will reach all possible hosts. At this point, the switch is behaving like a hub. This also illustrates why switches (by default) do not segment broadcast domains.

Another scenario in which a switch (by default) is unable to be optimally efficient in the delivery of frames is in the case of a multicast. A *multicast* is a message sent by one host and intended for a specific group of other hosts. This group could be a single host or a very large number of hosts in different places. The key here is that a single host transmits a stream of data (perhaps a video of a speech or event) to a group of hosts. By default, the switch will treat this the same way as a broadcast, flooding it out all ports to make sure that it reaches all the possible hosts in the group. This is inefficient because the traffic also hits those hosts who do not want the stream. There are several mechanisms and configurations to set it so that only the hosts in the multicast group receive the multicast, but that is well out of the scope of the CCENT and CCNA exams; the CCNP track covers this topic.

The switch will also flood a frame if it does not have an entry in its MAC table for the destination MAC in the frame. Although this happens rarely, if the switch doesn't know which specific port to send the frame out, it responds by doing the safest thing and flooding that frame so that it has the best chance of reaching the correct destination. Interestingly, after the destination host responds to that first frame, the switch will enter the missing MAC address into its table and the flood probably won't happen again. MAC addresses do "age out" of the MAC address table, too, so in the unlikely event that a host doesn't send a frame into the switch for 300 seconds (the default aging timer), the switch will no longer have that entry in the table.

The last situation we should examine is what happens if the sending and receiving hosts are both connected to the same port on the switch. This is most commonly seen when the two hosts are connected to a hub, which is in turn connected to a switch. From the switch's perspective, the two hosts are on the same port. When the sending host transmits a frame, the hub does its thing and floods it out all ports, including the ones connected to the intended receiver and the switch. The receiver simply receives it; the switch checks the source MAC of the frame, updates its MAC table if necessary, and then checks the destination MAC in its table to see which port it should be sent out. When it discovers that the two MACs are associated with the same port, it *filters* the frame: The switch does not transmit the frame out any ports and assumes that the frame will reach its intended recipient without help from the switch. Figure 6.3 illustrates this process.

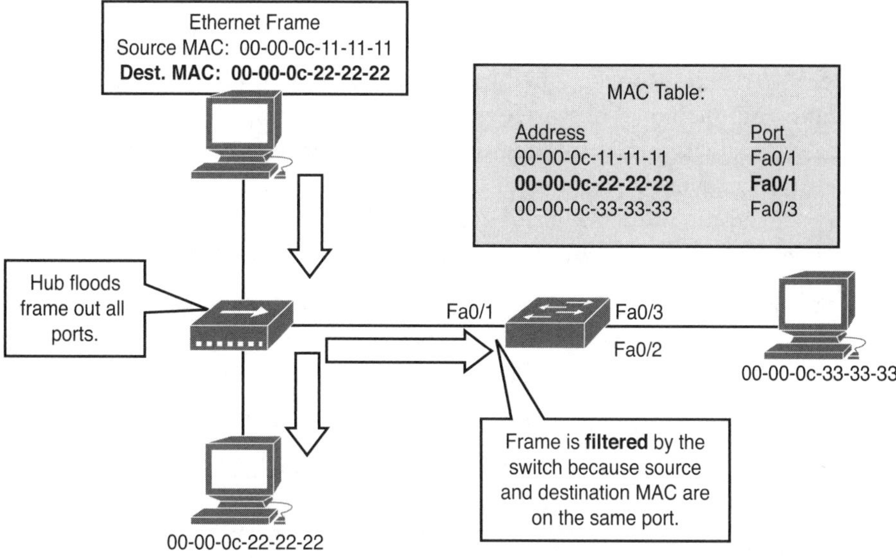

FIGURE 6.3 **The filter decision illustrated.**

ExamAlert

You should understand how a switch responds to unicast, broadcast, and multicast frames, and you must know the filter, forward, and flood decision processes. You should also have a clear understanding of the advantages of switches over hubs.

You have seen how switching gives you a huge efficiency advantage over hubs and coaxial media. Even a low-end switch is preferable to any kind of hub or coax media. You want to be sure that you get the right equipment for the job; different switches run at various speeds, and have diverse limitations on the number of MAC addresses they can support. Although almost any switch is better than any hub, you should take stock of your network, how many hosts, how much and what kind of traffic you expect to support, and then choose the switch that best meets your performance and budget requirements.

The Differences Between Switches and Bridges

We have been using the term *switch* interchangeably with *bridge*, but you need to know about some significant differences between them. The key difference is in the technology. Bridges, which are older, do all the work of frame analysis and decision making in software, using the CPU to analyze data stored in RAM. Switches use ASIC (application-specific integrated circuit) chips. ASICs are specialized processors designed to do one thing—in this case, switch frames. Depending on the model of switch, the speed difference can be astounding: A bridge typically switches around 50,000 frames per second, whereas a lowly 2960 switch can move an average of 12 million frames per second. (This, of course, depends on the frame size.) A big switch, such as the Catalyst 6500 series, could do 10 times that, depending on the hardware configuration.

Switches also tend to have many more ports than bridges; a bridge by definition has at least 2 ports, and they didn't get much bigger than 16 ports. Switches can have hundreds of ports if you buy the appropriate expansion modules.

Other differences include the following:

- Switches support half and full duplex, bridges only half duplex.
- Switches support different port speeds (10 and 100Mbps, for example), but a bridge's ports must all be the same speed.
- Switches support multiple VLANs and an instance of spanning tree for every VLAN (more on this soon).

Table 6.1 summarizes the differences between switches and bridges.

TABLE 6.1 **Switches and Bridges Compared**

Comparison	Switches	Bridges
Switching technology	ASIC (hardware)	Software
Speed	Fast	Slow
Port density	High	Low
Duplex	Full and half	Half only
VLAN aware	Yes	No
Collision domains	1 per port	1 per port
Broadcast domains	1 per VLAN	1
STP instances	1 per VLAN possible	1

Switching Modes

Switches examine the source and destination MAC in a frame to build their MAC table and make their forwarding decision. Exactly how they do that is the topic of this section. You need to be aware of three switching modes: store-and-forward mode, cut-through mode, and fragment-free mode.

Store-and-Forward Mode

Store-and-forward mode is the basic mode that bridges and switches use. It is the only mode that bridges can use, but many switches can use one or more of the other modes as well, depending on the model. In store-and-forward switching, the entire frame is buffered (copied into memory) and a cyclic redundancy check (CRC) is run to compare the frame's FCS value with the CRC output value.

> **Note**
>
> A CRC is a simple mathematical calculation. A sample of the data (in this case, a frame) is used as the variable in an equation. The product of the equation is included as the FCS at the end of the frame as it is transmitted by the source host. When the switch receives it, the same equation is run against the same sample of data. If the CRC product value is the same as the value of the FCS in the frame, the frame is assumed to be good. If the value differs, the frame is assumed to be corrupt or damaged, and the frame is dropped. This analysis happens before the forwarding decision is made.

Cut-Through Mode

Cut-through mode is the fastest switching mode. The switch analyzes the first 6 bytes after the preamble and SOF delimiter of the frame to make its forwarding decision. Those 6 bytes are the destination MAC address, which, if you think about it, is the minimum amount of information a switch has to look at to switch efficiently. After the forwarding decision has been made, the switch can begin to send the frame out the appropriate ports, even if the rest of the frame is still arriving at the inbound port. The chief advantage of cut through switching is speed; no time is spent running the CRC, and the frame is forwarded as fast as possible. The disadvantage is clearly that bad frames will be switched along with the good. Because the CRC/FCS is not being checked, we might be propagating bad frames. This would be a bad thing in a busy network, so some vendors support a mechanism in which the CRCs are still checked but no action is taken until the count of bad CRCs reaches a threshold that causes the switch to change to store and forward mode.

Fragment-Free Mode

Fragment-free mode is a switching method that picks a compromise between the reliability of store-and-forward mode and the speed of cut-through mode. The theory here is that frames that are damaged (usually by collisions) are often shorter than the minimum valid Ethernet frame size of 64 bytes.

Fragment-free mode buffers the first 64 bytes of each frame, updates the MAC table if necessary, reads the destination MAC, and forwards the frame. If the frame is less than 64 bytes, it is discarded. Frames that are smaller than 64 bytes are called *runts*. Fragment-free switching is sometimes called runtless switching for this reason. Because the switch only ever buffers 64 bytes of each frame, Fragment-free mode is a faster mode than store-and-forward mode, but there still exists a risk of forwarding bad frames, so the previously described mechanisms to change to store-and-forward mode if excessive bad CRCs are received are often implemented as well.

Switch Connections

Switches have the capability of connecting to various types of devices: PCs, servers, routers, hubs, other switches, and so on. Historically, their role was to break up collision domains, which meant plugging hubs into them. This meant that the switch port had to be able to connect in the same way as the hub—using carrier sense multiple access with collision detection (CSMA/CD), which in turn implies half duplex.

Half duplex means that only one device can use the wire at a time; much like a walkie-talkie set, if one person is transmitting, the others must listen. If others try to transmit at the same time, all you get is a squawk, which is called a collision in network terms. Hubs can use only half-duplex communication. Some older NICs (network interface cards), whether for PCs or even for older routers such as the Cisco 2500 series, can use only half duplex as well.

Full duplex is more advanced. In this technology, a device can send and receive at the same time because the send wire is connected directly to the receive wire on both connected devices. This means that we get the full bandwidth of the link (whether 10Mbps, 100Mbps, or 1Gbps) for both transmit and receive, at the same time, for every connected device. If we have a 100Mbps Fast Ethernet connection using full duplex, it can be said that the total available bandwidth is 200Mbps. This doesn't mean 200Mbps up or 200Mbps down, but is the sum of the full 100Mbps up and 100Mbps down for that link; some sales documentation might gloss over this point in an effort to make the switch look better on paper.

Full duplex does give us a major boost in efficiency because it allows for a zero-collision environment: If every device connected to a switch can send and receive at the same time, they cannot collide with each other. The only possible conflict (collision is not the right term here) is within the switch itself, and this problem (should it even happen) is handled by the switch's capability to buffer the frames until the conflict is cleared. Setting up a switch so that every device connected to it is running full duplex (and therefore there are no collisions) is sometimes called *microsegmentation* because every device has been segmented into its own collision domain, in which there are no collisions. You might see a reference to the collision detection circuit being disabled on a switch as soon as full duplex is selected for a switch port. Note that full-duplex connections can be only point to point, meaning that one full-duplex device connected to one switch port. Half-duplex connections are considered multipoint, which makes sense when you consider that a hub might be connected to a switch port, and there might be several hosts connected to the hub.

Note that not every NIC, whether on a PC or a router, can support full duplex, although it is rare these days to find a NIC that does not. Most newer NICs have the capability of full duplex, and nearly all switches do as well. Furthermore, most NICs and some switches can perform an autosensing function to determine whether the link is full duplex and set themselves accordingly.

Tip

It is a good practice to set the duplex of certain connections manually to full duplex (or half where necessary), instead of using the Auto function. Connections to other switches, routers, or important servers should be stable and well known enough to set as full duplex. Doing so avoids potential problems in which the duplex negotiation fails, causing a degradation or loss of connectivity. For connections to hosts, where we don't necessarily have control over the NIC settings, the Auto function is useful.

Duplex Configuration

Setting the appropriate duplex mode is done at the interface configuration prompt. The choices you have are Auto, Full, or Half. The default is Auto, so your switch should work in most cases if you do not make any configuration changes at all. Note that if you manually set duplex to Half or Full, the interfaces will be locked to that setting and will no longer use the Auto negotiation to dynamically determine the duplex setting of the links.

Following is an example of a configuration that sets interface FastEthernet 0/1 to full duplex/100Mbps, interface 0/2 to half duplex/10Mbps, and interface 0/3 to Auto duplex/Auto speed:

```
2960#config terminal
2960(config)#interface fastethernet 0/1
2960(config-if)#duplex full
2960(config-if)#speed 100
```

```
2960(config-if)#interface fastethernet 0/2
2960(config-if)#duplex half
2960(config-if)#speed 10
2960(config-if)#interface fastethernet 0/3
2960(config-if)#duplex auto
2960(config-if)#speed auto
```

STP

Earlier, we mentioned that one of the functions of a switch was Layer 2 loop removal. The Spanning Tree Protocol (STP) carries out this function. STP is a critical feature; without it, many switched networks would completely cease to function. Either accidentally or deliberately in the process of creating a redundant network, the problem arises when we create a looped switched path. A *loop* can be defined as two or more switches that are interconnected by two or more physical links.

Switching loops create three major problems:

- **Broadcast storms:** Switches must flood broadcasts, so a looped topology will create multiple copies of a single broadcast and perpetually cycle them through the loop.
- **MAC table instability:** Loops make it appear that a single MAC address is reachable on multiple ports of a switch, and the switch is constantly updating the MAC table.
- **Duplicate frames:** Because there are multiple paths to a single MAC, it is possible that a frame could be duplicated to be flooded out all paths to a single destination MAC.

All these problems are serious and will bring a network to an effective standstill unless prevented.

Figure 6.4 illustrates a looped configuration and some of the problems it can create.

Other than simple error, the most common reason that loops are created is because we want to build a redundant or fault-tolerant network. By definition, redundancy means that we have a backup, separate path for data to follow in the event the first one fails. The problem is that unless the backup path is physically disabled—perhaps by unplugging it—the path creates a loop and causes the problems mentioned previously. We like redundant systems; we do not like loops and the problems they cause. We need a mechanism that automatically detects and prevents loops so that we can build the fault-tolerant physical links and have them become active only when needed. The mechanism is called the *Spanning Tree Protocol*. STP is a protocol that runs on bridges and switches to find and block redundant looped paths during normal operation. STP was originally developed by the Digital Equipment Corporation (DEC), and the idea was adopted and modified by the IEEE to become 802.1D. The two are incompatible, but it is exceedingly rare to find a DEC bridge these days, so the incompatibility is not usually a problem.

Note

We discuss STP at length in Chapter 12, "Advanced Switching Concepts."

ExamAlert

STP eliminates Layer 2 loops in switched networks with redundant paths.

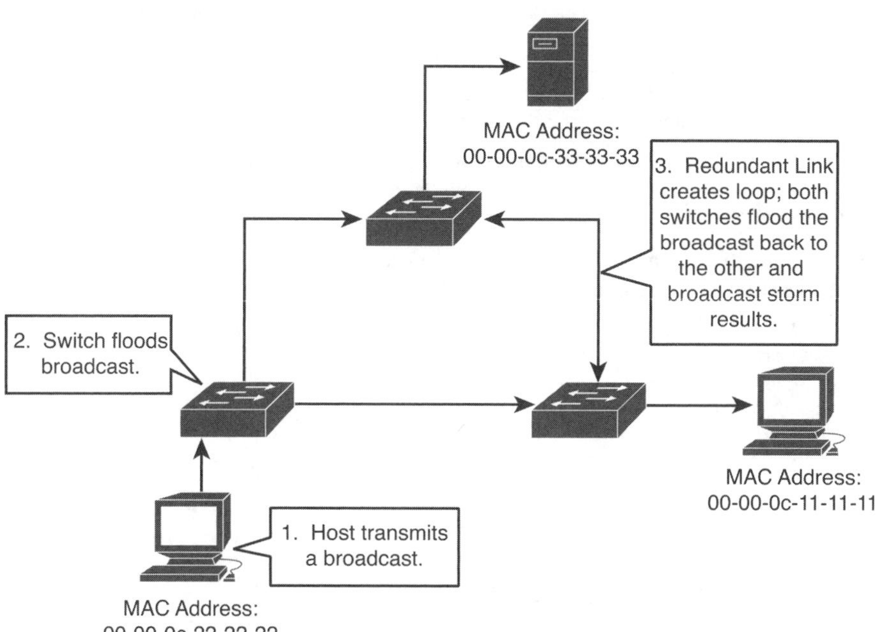
MAC Address:
00-00-0c-33-33-33
3. Redundant Link creates loop; both switches flood the broadcast back to the other and broadcast storm results.
2. Switch floods broadcast.
MAC Address:
00-00-0c-11-11-11
1. Host transmits a broadcast.
MAC Address:
00-00-0c-22-22-22

FIGURE 6.4 **A Layer 2 (switching) loop.**

Cram Quiz

1. Collisions are an expected part of how Ethernet was designed to work. Unfortunately, they cause congestion, loss and delay, especially as the network gets larger and busier. Bridges (and subsequently switches) were designed to eliminate the problem of collisions. How do they do that?

   ❍ **A.** Switches use CSMA/CA to arbitrate which device is allowed to send so that collisions do not happen.

   ❍ **B.** Switches process frames so fast that although collisions still happen, they take less time to clear and their impact is greatly reduced.

   ❍ **C.** Switches filter, forward, or flood frames based on the destination MAC address in the frame received on each port, which completely eliminates collisions.

   ❍ **D.** Switches support full-duplex cabling on UTP, which allows a simultaneous send and receive which completely eliminates collisions.

2. Building a fully redundant switched network involves installing switches with redundant connections. Doing so creates the possibility of switching loops, broadcast storms, duplicate frame transmission, and MAC table instability. What works to avoid these undesirable consequences?

   ❍ **A.** Disconnect redundant links until they are needed upon network failure.

   ❍ **B.** The default STP feature will eliminate switching loops automatically.

   ❍ **C.** The optional Spanning Tree Protocol can be installed and manually configured to respond to switching loops.

   ❍ **D.** Upgrade all switches to Layer 3 switches, a more modern technology that automatically eliminates switching loops.

3. Examine the partial configuration from a switch. Assuming normal operation, will this port experience collisions?

```
Switch#config terminal
Switch(config)#interface fastethernet 0/1
Switch(config-if)#duplex full
Switch(config-if)#speed 100
```

   ❍ **A.** Yes

   ❍ **B.** No

Cram Quiz Answers

1. Answer D is correct. A is incorrect; CSMA/CA is a feature of wireless access points, but not switches. Answer B is incorrect; if collisions are happening, the switch has little to with how fast they are cleared. Answer C is a correct statement but does not answer the question; switches can still function as a switch as described in this answer, while collisions are happening.

2. Answer B is correct. Answer A may be correct, but is really an unacceptable answer and certainly not the best answer. Answer C is incorrect; STP is installed and operating by default. Enhancements and tuning may be manually configured. Answer D is incorrect; upgrading to a Layer 3 switch will not eliminate collisions, although like Layer 2 switches they can be configured to do so.

3. Answer B is correct. Notwithstanding unusual network problems causing errors, setting a properly cabled switch interface to full duplex will eliminate collisions on that port.

VLAN Concepts and Applications

- **Identify basic switching concepts and the operation of Cisco switches.**
- **Describe how VLANs create logically separate networks and the need for routing between them.**
- **Explain network segmentation and basic traffic management concepts.**
- **Configure and verify trunking on Cisco switches.**

CramSaver

1. What are three benefits of using VLANs?
   - **A.** Complexity
   - **B.** Security
   - **C.** Obscurity
   - **D.** Flexibility
   - **E.** Limitation of broadcast impact
   - **F.** Higher speeds
   - **G.** Extended cable range
   - **H.** Better mileage

2. Your CCNA study partner argues that it is okay to have multiple VLANs use the same IP subnet. Are they correct?
   - **A.** Yes
   - **B.** No

3. Which configuration correctly places interface Gi0/24 in VLAN 111?
   - **A.** Switch(config)#**int f0/24**
     Switch(config-if)#**switch port access vlan 111**
   - **B.** Switch(config)#**int f0/24**
     Switch(config-if)#**switchport access vlan 111**
   - **C.** Switch(config)#**int gi0/24**
     Switch(config-if)#**switch port access vlan 111**
   - **D.** Switch(config)#**int gi0/24**
     Switch(config-if)#**switchport access vlan 111**

Answers

1. Answers B, D, and E are correct. Answer A is incorrect; complexity is seldom an advantage. Answer C is wrong; obscurity is not a defined benefit of VLANs. Answers F and G are not related to VLAN configuration. Answer H is a benefit of moderating your driving habits and maintaining proper tire pressure, among other things, and has nothing to do with VLANs.
2. You need to change CCNA study partners; this person is wrong.
3. Answer D is correct. Answer A is wrong because it configures the wrong interface and the **switchport** command has a space in it. Answer B is incorrect because it configures the wrong interface. Answer C is incorrect because **switchport** command has a space in it.

When you plug a bunch of PCs in to a switch and give them all IP addresses in the same network, you create a LAN. A VLAN is a virtual LAN. The difference is that with VLANs, you still connect all the PCs to a single switch but you make the switch behave as if it were multiple, independent switches. Each VLAN is its own broadcast domain and IP subnet. In this way, you get the ability to use switches to segment broadcast domains, which up to this point was possible only with routers. Figure 6.5 illustrates a simple VLAN configuration:

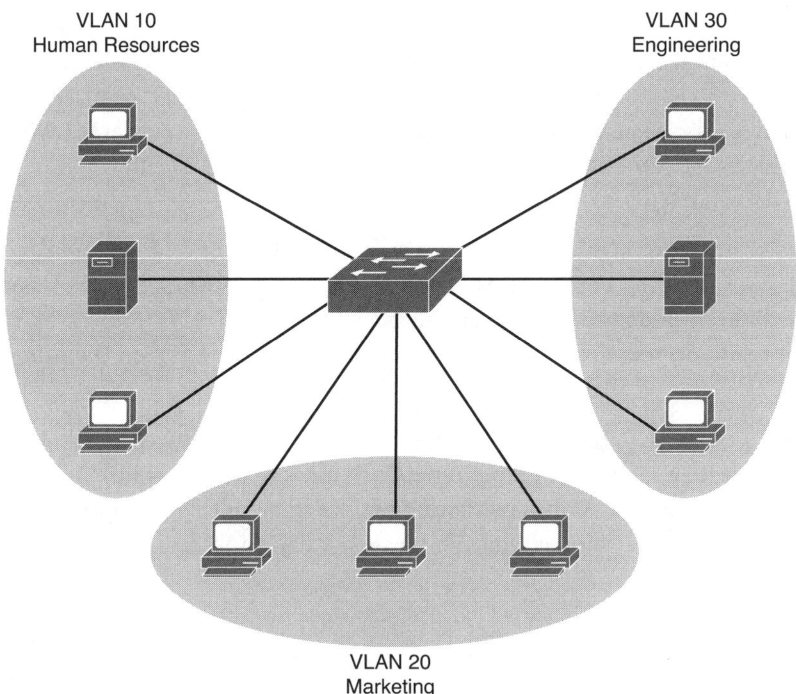

FIGURE 6.5 **VLANs provide a logical segmentation of broadcast domains.**

The Definition of a VLAN

A *VLAN* can be defined as a virtual broadcast domain. Instead of segmenting the broadcast domain with routers at Layer 3, you segment using switches at Layer 2. Each VLAN should be associated with its own IP subnet.

> **ExamAlert**
>
> VLANs logically divide a switch into multiple, independent switches at Layer 2.
>
> Each VLAN is its own broadcast domain.
>
> Each VLAN should be in its own subnet.

Benefits of VLANs

The advantages of using VLANs are as follows:

- VLANs increase the number of broadcast domains while reducing their size: this is the same effect that routers have, but without the need to buy a lot of routers or a big router with a lot of ports, so it's less expensive and easier to administer.
- VLANs provide an additional layer of security: No device in any VLAN can communicate with a device in any other VLAN until you deliberately configure a way for it to do so. An example might be a server in VLAN 10 that holds sensitive employee files for HR; no PCs from other VLANs can access VLAN 10 (or the server in it), unless you specifically configure it to do so.
- VLANs are flexible in terms of how they are used in network equipment: Imagine a building that has LAN cabling and a single switch installed, but four different tenants. You can create four different VLANs, one for each tenant, and no tenant will see or hear from the other tenants on the other VLANs.
- VLANs can span across multiple switches using trunk links: This allows you to create a logical grouping of network users by function instead of location. If you want all the marketing people to be in their own broadcast domain and IP subnet, you can create a VLAN for them on the first

switch; then, you can connect another switch using a trunk link, define the same VLAN on that switch, and the marketing users on the second switch are in the same VLAN and can communicate with the marketing users on the first switch, and are isolated from other VLANs on both switches. This capability can be extended across an enterprise network campus, so that marketing users in the Barker Pavilion could in theory be in a VLAN with other marketing users in the Valentine Pavilion.

- The ability to trunk VLANs across multiple switches makes adding users, moving users, and changing users' VLAN memberships much easier.

ExamAlert

Know the advantages of VLANs:

- Increase the number of broadcast domains while reducing their size.
- Provide additional security.
- Increase the flexibility of network equipment.
- Allow a logical grouping of users by function, not location.
- Make user adds, moves, and changes easier.

Note

Wait, what's a broadcast domain? First of all, don't get this confused with a collision domain. A broadcast domain is a set of devices that are able to receive one another's broadcasts. Just as too many collisions is a bad thing, likewise too many broadcasts is a bad thing. Every device has to stop and inspect every broadcast, to see whether the broadcast might have been intended for itself. So, fewer broadcast is better; one way to achieve fewer broadcasts is to make more broadcast domains, because if the number of devices remains the same, the number in each broadcast domain is less, which means fewer broadcasts.

And whereas a switch (or a bridge) will segment collision domains, it will *not* segment broadcast domains (not by default, at least). To break up broadcast domains, you need a Layer 3 device: a router. Just as every port on a switch is a separate collision domain, every port on a router is a separate broadcast domain.

Figure 6.6 illustrates a multiswitch VLAN system.

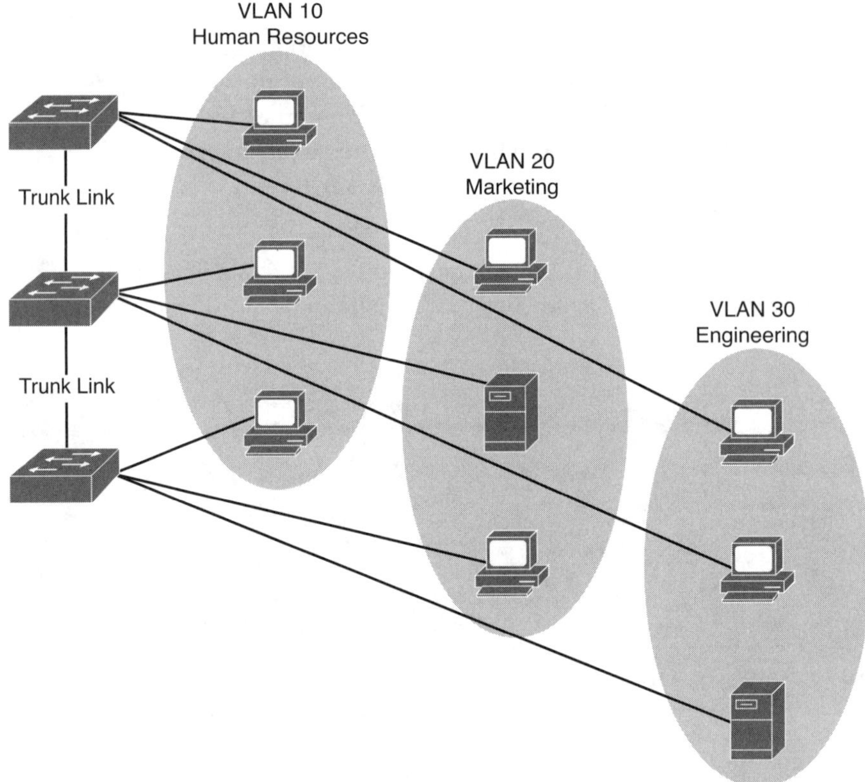

FIGURE 6.6 **VLANs over trunk links allows a logical grouping of users by function.**

Implementing VLANs

Implementing VLANs is done in three steps:

1. Create the VLAN.
2. Name the VLAN (optional, but expected).
3. Assign switch ports to the VLAN.

> **ExamAlert**
>
> Know the three steps in VLAN implementation: Create it, name it, and assign ports to it.

The commands to create a VLAN vary depending on the switch model and IOS version; we stick with the Catalyst 2960 using an IOS later than 12.1(9) as our example.

The command to create a VLAN is simply **vlan** [*vlan_#*]. To name the VLAN, the equally simple command is **name** [*vlan_name*]. These commands are entered starting at the global config prompt.

To create VLAN 10 named HR, VLAN 20 named Marketing, and VLAN 30 named Engineering, the commands look like Example 6.1.

EXAMPLE 6.1 **Creating and Naming VLANs**

```
2960#configure terminal
2960(config)#vlan 10
2960(config-vlan)#name HR
2960(config-vlan)#vlan 20
2960(config-vlan)#name Marketing
2960(config-vlan)#vlan 30
2960(config-vlan)#name Engineering
2960(config-vlan)#exit
2960(config)#exit
2960#
```

The global config prompt changes to the config-vlan prompt when you create the first VLAN; it is okay to stay in that prompt to continue creating VLANs.

With these commands, you can create all your VLANs at once, or you can go back later and add some more as needed. On most of the switches we use in CCNA, the VLAN configuration (names and numbers) is not stored in the running-config or startup config file in NVRAM; rather, it is stored in flash memory in a special file called vlan.dat. This means that it is possible to erase the startup config file, reload the router, and be confused by the reappearance of VLANs that you thought you just deleted. To delete VLANs, you can do it one at a time using the **no vlan** [*vlan_#*] command, or to get rid of all of them at once, you can use the command **delete flash:vlan.dat**, which erases and resets the entire VLAN database.

ExamAlert

The exact syntax for the **delete flash:vlan.dat** command is critical: no space after **flash** or the colon! If you put a space after **flash**, you could delete the entire flash directory, including your IOS. This is a very bad thing to do, and is actually quite an ordeal to fix.

Note

Cisco switches have a few default VLANs preconfigured; these are intended for the management and essential functionality of Ethernet, Token Ring, and FDDI LANs. VLAN 1, for example, is the management VLAN for Ethernet. All switch ports are in VLAN 1 by default. You cannot change or delete these default VLANs.

The Cisco Catalyst 2960 will support up to 255 VLANs defined locally.

VLANs can exist without any ports actually being in them. Adding switch ports to a VLAN is done when you want to put a host into a particular VLAN. Obviously, you need to know which physical ports your hosts are connected to so that you can add the correct port to the correct VLAN; it would be an unpopular move to put a marketing user into the Engineering VLAN; these two groups are mutually hostile.

The commands to add a switch port to a VLAN are executed at the Interface Config prompt—if you think about that, it makes sense because you are putting the port itself into the VLAN. The command is **switchport access vlan** [*vlan_#*]. What you are saying is "this port shall access VLAN X."

Example 6.2 puts ports Fa0/8 into VLAN 10, Fa0/13 into VLAN 20, and Fa0/14 into VLAN 30:

EXAMPLE 6.2 **Assigning VLANs to Switch Ports**

```
2960#config t
2960(config)#interface fa0/8
2960(config-if)#switchport access vlan 10
2960(config-if)#int fa0/13
2960(config-if)#switchport access vlan 20
2960(config-if)#int fa0/14
2960(config-if)#switchport access vlan 30
2960(config-if)#exit
2960(config)#exit
2960#
```

VLAN Membership

The commands in the previous section assign particular ports to a particular VLAN *statically*. (Static VLAN assignment is sometimes called port-based VLAN membership.) When a user changes ports (moves around the office or campus), you need to repeat the commands at the Switch(config-if)# prompt for the correct new interface. As you can imagine, if there are a lot of moves, this can become an administrative pain.

There is an alternative called dynamic VLAN membership. This feature allows you to dynamically assign VLAN membership to switch ports based on the MAC address of the host connecting to the port. You need a little service called the VLAN Membership Policy Server (VMPS) that holds a database of all the MAC addresses and the correct VLAN for each one; then you tell the switch ports to do dynamic VLAN assignment. When a host connects to a switch port configured to do dynamic membership, the switch checks the MAC of the host and asks the VMPS what VLAN that MAC should be in. The switch then changes the VLAN membership of that port dynamically.

This sounds like a wonderful idea, and it can be, but it is difficult to create the VMPS database and to maintain it if your network grows quickly. Imagine having to get and maintain certain knowledge of every MAC address of every host in your network, and then keep the VMPS database updated. Dynamic VLAN membership is a good option if you have a lot of users in a lot of different VLANs moving around to many switch ports, but be ready to wrestle with some administrative issues.

Cram Quiz

1. What is the relationship between VLANs and IP subnets?
   - ❍ **A.** VLANs have no relationship to IP subnets.
   - ❍ **B.** All VLANS must be in the same IP subnet.
   - ❍ **C.** If subnets are in use, VLANs cannot be used.
   - ❍ **D.** Each VLAN must be numbered to match the IP subnet network ID.
   - ❍ **E.** Each VLAN must use a separate IP subnet.
   - ❍ **F.** In a Frame Relay WAN environment, there must be an equal number of VLANs and subnets.

2. True or False: Access between VLANs is not possible without a functioning Layer 3 process.

3. True or False: For security reasons, all switch ports are assigned an unused VLAN by default.

Cram Quiz Answers

1. Answer E is correct. Therefore, Answers A and B are wrong. Answer C is incorrect. Answer D is not required, but we often do this to save confusion. Answer F sounds good, but remember that VLANs do not extend into traditional WAN circuits like Frame Relay.

2. True.

3. False. By default, all switch ports are assigned to VLAN 1, and are fully functional; therefore, VLAN 1 is in use.

Trunking

- **Identify basic switching concepts and the operation of Cisco switches.**
- **Describe how VLANs create logically separate networks and the need for routing between them.**
- **Explain network segmentation and basic traffic management concepts.**
- **Configure and verify trunking on Cisco switches.**

CramSaver

1. Vijay wants to build a trunk interface on his Ethernet 0/24 interface. He tries the following commands without success:

```
Switch(config)#interface Ethernet 0/24
Switch(config-if)#switchport mode trunk
```

   What is the issue?

   A. He is using the incorrect trunk command.

   B. He cannot build a trunk without first enabling the switch.

   C. He cannot create the trunk interface until the corresponding VLAN interface is created.

   D. He must shut the port down first.

   E. Ethernet interfaces do not support trunking on some switches.

2. Guy bets you five bucks that he can create a trunk between two 2960s without configuring the two switches being trunked—all he needs is a crossover cable. Should you take the bet?

3. John explains the concept of the Native VLAN to you. To prove you understand it, choose the correct explanation from the following.

   A. The native VLAN is the VLAN assigned to interface VLAN 1.

   B. The native VLAN is the VLAN into which frames will be switched, if they arrive at a trunk interface untagged.

   C. The native VLAN is the one assigned to the trunk interface.

   D. The native VLAN is not longer supported by Cisco switches.

Answers

1. Answer E is correct. Answer A is incorrect; there is nothing wrong with the trunk command. Answer B is wrong; the switch is clearly enabled as the # prompt indicates. Answer C is incorrect; no relationship exists between a trunk and a VLAN interface. Answer D is not a requirement to configure a port. Confused? It's not a trick, but it is tricky: You usually need to have a Fast Ethernet or Gigabit Ethernet interface to create a trunk. Vijay is using plain old Ethernet, and that is not supported on some switches.

2. Take the bet. Guy is my brother, and he's clever, but he is older than me and probably remembers when switches defaulted to "dynamic desirable." On a 2960, Dynamic Trunking Protocol is running by default, and every port is in DTP mode Dynamic Auto, which will *not* negotiate to trunking together.
3. John is my other brother, and he's just as clever—and he will be disappointed if you don't remember the correct answer, which is Answer B in this case. Answer A is misleading because it is sometimes true—but it is not a requirement or definition of the native VLAN. Answer C cannot be true because by definition a trunk is in all VLANs, it is not an access port that is always assigned to one VLAN. Answer D is just false.

For VLANs to span across multiple switches, you obviously need to connect the switches to each other. Although it is possible to simply plug one switch into another using an Access port just as you would plug in a host or a hub, doing so kills the VLAN-spanning feature and a bunch of other useful stuff too. A switch-to-switch link must be set up as a trunk link for the VLAN system to work properly. A trunk link is a special configuration; the key difference between an ordinary connection (an access port) and a trunk port is that although an access port is only in one data VLAN at a time (although it could simultaneously support the voice VLAN as well), a trunk port has the job of carrying traffic for all VLANs from one switch to another. Any time you connect a switch to another switch, you want to make it a trunk.

Some key points about trunks are as follows:

- ▶ By default, traffic from all VLANs is allowed on a trunk. You can specify which VLANs are permitted (or not) to cross a particular trunk if you have that requirement.
- ▶ Switches (whether trunked or not) are always connected with crossover cables, not straight-through cables. In CCNA land, there is no such thing as an Auto-MDIX port that will autodetect a crossed connection and fix it. In reality, the Catalyst 2960 has such a feature, but the exam will test your knowledge of when to use a crossover cable. For the purposes of your exams, if two switches are not connected with a crossover cable, there will be no connectivity between them.

ExamAlert

By default, all VLANs are permitted across a trunk link. Switch-to-switch trunk links always require the use of a crossover cable, never a straight-through cable.

When creating a trunk, a trunking protocol adds a VLAN identification tag to frames coming into the switch. As those frames are forwarded across the trunk, the VLAN from which the frame originated is identifiable, and the data frame can be distributed to ports in the same VLAN on other switches—and not to different VLANs. This frame tagging and multiplexing function is what enables VLANs to span multiple switches and still keeps each VLAN as a separate broadcast domain. Figure 6.7 illustrates a simple trunk as it multiplexes frames from two separate VLANs across a single Fast Ethernet Trunk.

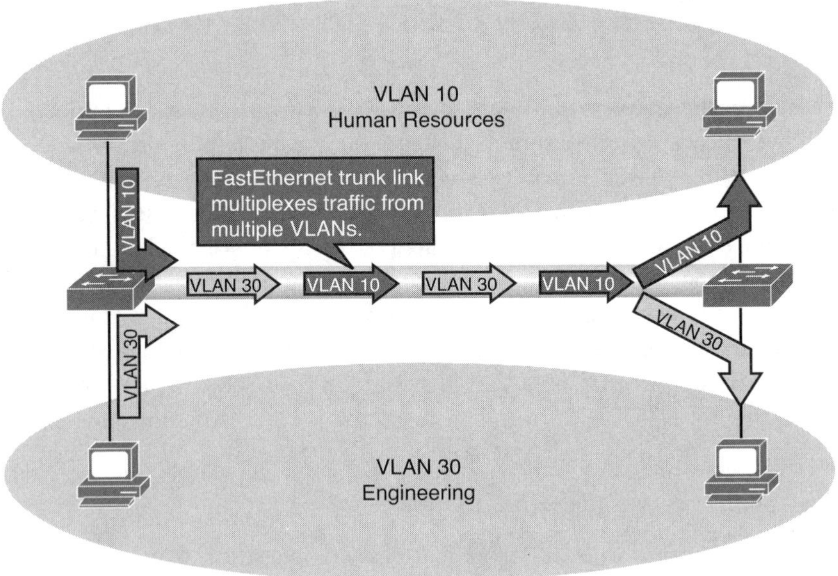

FIGURE 6.7 **Trunks carry traffic from multiple VLANs across a single physical link.**

Cisco supports two trunking protocols, ISL and 802.1Q,but only 802.1Q is tested on the exam. In fact, Cisco has all but eliminated switch support for ISL in favor of 802.1Q.

802.1Q

The IEEE-standard 802.1Q trunk encapsulation has the advantage of being an industry standard, so intervendor operation is much less of a problem. Often referred to as dot1q, this protocol does not re-encapsulate the original frame, but instead inserts a 4-byte tag into the original header. This means that a dot1q frame will be seen as a "baby giant" of 1522 bytes. Most modern NICs will not reject these frames if they mistakenly receive one. Figure 6-8 shows a dot1q-tagged frame.

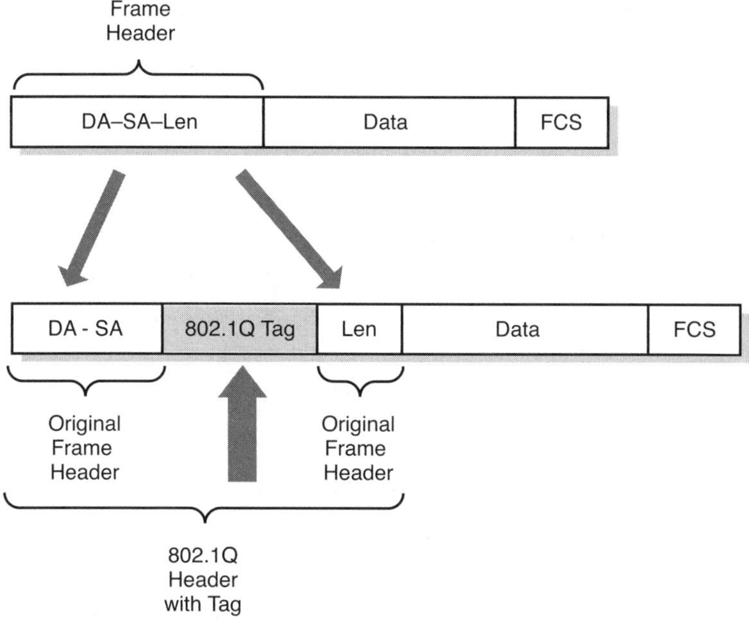

FIGURE 6-8 **802.1Q inserts a 4-byte tag into the existing frame header.**

Configuring Switches for Trunking

Configuring a switch for trunking is fairly straightforward. Once again, we focus on the Catalyst 2960 switch; other switches may have slightly different capabilities and syntax.

> **Note**
>
> Cisco has implemented the Dynamic Trunking Protocol to make setting up trunks easier. DTP can send/receive trunk negotiation frames to dynamically establish a trunk link with a connected switch. DTP is not necessary to establish a trunk link, and like many other automatic functions, many administrators would rather not use it and instead manually configure their trunk links. The CCNA exam is likely to ask about the five port modes, so an explanation is warranted.

A switch port can be in one of five modes:

- **Access (a.k.a. "off"):** In access mode, the port is an access port and will not trunk, even if the neighbor switch wants to. This mode is intended for the connection of single hosts or hubs. DTP frames are not sent or acknowledged. The command to enable this is **switchport mode access**.

- **Trunk (a.k.a. "on"):** In trunk mode, the port will trunk unconditionally, and trunk connectivity will happen if the neighbor switch port is set to Auto, Desirable, or NoNegotiate. DTP frames are sent, but the received trunk will only form if a request is received from the other switch. The command to enable this is **switchport mode trunk**.
- **NoNegotiate:** Disables DTP. A trunk will form only if the neighbor switch port is set to On (mode trunk). DTP frames are not sent or acknowledged. The command to enable this is **switchport nonegotiate**.
- **(Dynamic) Desirable:** This mode actively solicits a trunk connection with the neighbor. DTP frames are sent and responded to if received. A trunk forms if the neighbor is set to On, Desirable, or Auto. If the neighbor is set to NoNegotiate, the trunk will not form because Desirable needs a response from the neighbor, which NoNegotiate will not send. The command to enable this is **switchport mode dynamic desirable**.
- **(Dynamic) Auto:** The port trunks only in response to a DTP request to do so. A trunk forms with a neighbor port set to on or desirable. DTP frames are not sent but are acknowledged if received. The command to enable this is **switchport mode dynamic auto**.

ExamAlert

Know the five switch port modes: On, Off, Desirable, Auto, and NoNegotiate.

Know the command to set permanent trunking mode:

switchport mode trunk

To configure a switch port to trunk, we need to set the mode and choose a trunking protocol (only if the switch supports more than one to choose from). Also, the native VLAN setting for the trunk must match on both switches. The native VLAN defaults to VLAN1, but can be changed with the command **switchport native vlan** *vlan_id*.

The command to set the port mode is **switchport mode**, executed at the interface configuration prompt for the port you want to modify. Remember that to set NoNegotiate mode the command is **switchport nonegotiate**, as demonstrated in Example 6.3.

EXAMPLE 6.3 **Configuring Switch Port Modes**

```
2960(config)#int fa0/1
2960(config-if)#switchport mode     access
                                    Trunk
                                    dynamic auto
                                    dynamic desirable
2960(config-if)#switchport nonegotiate
```

Cram Quiz

1. Rob and Lorena are discussing the behavior and capabilities of trunks. Rob tells Lorena that traffic from all VLANs is allowed across an 802.1Q trunk by default, but when Lorena asks how the traffic is kept in its correct VLAN when it is received at the port at the other end of the trunk, Rob has trouble explaining the mechanism. Which of the following best explains how frames from multiple VLANs are transmitted across a single trunk link and are properly distributed into the correct VLAN at the receiving switch?

   ❍ **A.** Each frame (with the exception of frames in the native VLAN) is marked with its VLAN ID using a 4-byte tag, which also necessitates the recalculation of the FCS. Correct redistribution is accomplished at the receiving end by analysis of the frame header information, in which the tag encodes the destination VLAN.

   ❍ **B.** The frames are each assigned a fragmentation number so they can be easily reassembled in order at the receiving end.

   ❍ **C.** The frames are sent on a clocked circuit; by keeping track of the clock markings on the frames, the correct distribution can be guaranteed.

   ❍ **D.** All frames are assigned a number based on the Copeland-Summers algorithm, which allows them to be properly encoded at the destination

2. Which of the following DTP mode pairings will form a trunk? Choose all that apply.

   ❍ **A.** Trunk and access

   ❍ **B.** Dynamic desirable and NoNegotiate

   ❍ **C.** Dynamic auto and trunk

   ❍ **D.** Dynamic auto and dynamic desirable

3. Is the following configuration for Switch A and Switch B valid for trunking?

```
SwitchA(config)#int f0/24
SwitchA(config-if)#switchport mode trunk
SwitchA(config-if)#switchport native vlan 10
SwitchB(config)#int f0/24
SwitchB(config-if)#switchport mode dynamic desirable
```

❍ **A.** Yes

❍ **B.** No

Cram Quiz Answers

1. Answer A is correct. Answer B is incorrect because fragmentation is done at the packet level and has nothing to do with trunking. Answer C is wrong, intentionally misleading you by mixing in serial WAN terminology. Answer D is fictitious and therefore wrong, although the Copeland-Summers algorithm was an important part of my favorite band.
2. Answers C and D are the pairs that will trunk. Answer A will not because one side is access, which will never trunk. Answer B will not because dynamic desirable needs to hear a response to the negotiation, and NoNegotiate will never respond.
3. No. Although the trunk modes are compatible (though different), Switch A has the native VLAN set to 10, while Switch B will be at the default of 1. The native VLANs must match.

Review Questions

1. What is the most common Layer 2 device?
   - ❍ **A.** Hub
   - ❍ **B.** Repeater
   - ❍ **C.** Router
   - ❍ **D.** Switch
   - ❍ **E.** Bridge

2. What devices and functions can an administrator use to segment the network, assuming that no VLANs are used? Choose all that apply.
   - ❍ **A.** Routers to segment broadcast domains
   - ❍ **B.** Switches to segment broadcast domains
   - ❍ **C.** Switches to increase the number of collision domains
   - ❍ **D.** Bridges to segment collision domains
   - ❍ **E.** Hubs to segment collision domains
   - ❍ **F.** Bridges to segment broadcast domains
   - ❍ **G.** Repeaters to segment broadcast domains

3. How many collision and broadcast domains exist on a 12-port switch with default configuration?
   - ❍ **A.** 2 collision domains, 12 broadcast domains
   - ❍ **B.** 1 collision domain, 12 broadcast domains
   - ❍ **C.** 1 collision domain, 1 broadcast domain
   - ❍ **D.** 12 collision domains, 1 broadcast domain

4. Which of the following are true of switches and bridges? Choose all that apply.
   - ❍ **A.** Switches have fewer ports and switch in software.
   - ❍ **B.** Switches have a higher port density and switch using ASIC hardware.
   - ❍ **C.** Bridges are faster than switches.
   - ❍ **D.** Switches are faster than bridges.
   - ❍ **E.** Switches create only one broadcast domain by default.
   - ❍ **F.** Bridges create only one broadcast domain.

5. Which switching mode sacrifices speed for error-free switching?

❍ **A.** Segment-free mode
❍ **B.** Store-and-forward mode
❍ **C.** Cut-throat mode
❍ **D.** Fragment-free mode
❍ **E.** Cut-through mode

6. What is the function of 802.1D STP?

❍ **A.** Prevents routing loops in redundant topologies
❍ **B.** Prevents Layer 2 loops in networks with redundant switched paths
❍ **C.** Prevents frame forwarding until all IP addresses are known
❍ **D.** Enables the use of multiple routed paths for load-sharing
❍ **E.** Allows the propagation of VLAN information from a central source

7. What happens when a switch receives a frame with the destination MAC address of FF-FF-FF-FF-FF-FF?

❍ **A.** The switch drops the frame and sends a "Destination Unreachable" message back to the source.
❍ **B.** The switch forwards the frame out the port that connects to the host with that MAC address.
❍ **C.** The switch filters the frame because the address is not valid.
❍ **D.** The switch floods the frame out all ports except the one it came in on.

8. Which of the following is an advantage of switches over hubs?

❍ **A.** Switches provide full-duplex microsegmentation of collision domains.
❍ **B.** The low cost of switches compared to hubs makes them an attractive choice for growing businesses.
❍ **C.** Although they cannot segment broadcast domains, the much greater speed of switches still makes them a desirable upgrade.
❍ **D.** Switches are impervious to security threats by definition and provide a secure Layer 2 solution out of the box.

9. Which of the following explains why full-duplex operation is desirable?

❍ **A.** Full duplex allows for the detection of collisions so that data can be retransmitted when the wire is free.
❍ **B.** Full duplex allows simultaneous transmit and receive functions, providing higher overall throughput.
❍ **C.** Full duplex provides inter-VLAN routing capability.
❍ **D.** Full duplex can take advantage of existing coaxial cabling.

10. You currently have seven hubs that form the LAN in your office, to connect 12 servers and 30 users. You have the budget to buy one 24-port switch. What is the most efficient way to utilize your limited switch resources?

❍ **A.** Connect all the hubs to each other, and then connect the string of hubs to one switch port.

❍ **B.** Connect each hub to a single switch port.

❍ **C.** Connect each hub to a single switch port. Move the servers to their own switch ports. Move active user PCs to the remaining switch ports, leaving the less-active PCs attached to hubs. Distribute the remaining PCs evenly across the hubs.

❍ **D.** Connect each hub to the switch with two or three cables to provide additional bandwidth.

Answers to Review Questions

1. Answer D is correct. Switches are by far the most common Layer 2 device in use. Answers A, B, and C are incorrect because hubs, repeaters, and routers are not Layer 2 devices. (Hubs and repeaters are Layer 1; routers are Layer 3.) Answer E is incorrect because switches are much more common than bridges.
2. Answers A, C, and D are correct. Routers segment broadcast domains; switches and bridges segment (increase the number of) collision domains. Answers B, E, F, and G are incorrect. The question stipulates that VLANs are not in use, so a switch does not segment broadcast domains. Hubs and repeaters extend and enlarge, not segment, collision and broadcast domains. Bridges do not segment broadcast domains.
3. Answer D is correct. Each port on a switch is a collision domain. Answers A, B, and C are incorrect; with a default configuration (that is, a single VLAN), a switch creates one broadcast domain.
4. Answers B, D, E, and F are correct. Switches have more ports than bridges and are faster than bridges. Watch out for the trick: Both switches and bridges create only one broadcast domain. Answers A and C are incorrect.
5. Answer B is correct. Store-and-forward mode is the slowest mode but has the advantage of fully error checking every frame for reliability. Answers A, C, D, and E are incorrect. There is no such thing as segment-free or cut-throat switching. Fragment-free mode examines the first 64 bytes of every frame for increased reliability, but is not as fast as cut-through mode.
6. Answer B is correct. STP prevents Layer 2 loops if redundant paths exist. Answers A, C, D, and E are incorrect; STP is not concerned with routing loops, IP addresses, routing in general, or VLAN administration.
7. Answer D is correct. The MAC address shown is the broadcast address, so the switch will perform the flood operation. Answer A is what a router would do to a packet it has no route for. Answer B is what the switch would do with a frame whose address is in the MAC address table, and Answer C, the filter operation, happens only when the source and destination addresses are on the same port.
8. Answer A is correct. Switches, when they are configured correctly, can eliminate collisions from the LAN. This design of creating a single collision domain for each connected device is called microsegmentation. Answer B is incorrect; switches cost more than hubs. Answer C is incorrect; switches can segment broadcast domains through the use of VLANs. Answer D is incorrect; switches are not inherently secure and should have basic security measures applied.
9. Answer B is correct. Full duplex uses two wire pairs or two optical fibers to establish separate send and receive circuits, effectively doubling potential throughput. Answer A is incorrect; full duplex disables the collision-detection circuit because it is no longer required. Answer C is incorrect; inter-VLAN routing capability is a Layer 3 function available only on certain switches and has nothing to do with duplex setting (Layer 1). Answer D is incorrect; full duplex cannot work on coaxial cabling because there is only one pair of conductors, and full duplex requires two.

10. Answer C is correct. Doing this will ensure that the most important devices have the best possible data access speed. Answer A is incorrect; this creates a single large collision domain with minimal bandwidth. Answer B is not wrong, it is just not the best answer; in doing this, you create several collision domains, but do not make the best use of the switch resources. Answer D is incorrect; this could create nasty loops in your network.

What Next?

If you want more practice on this chapter's exam topics before you move on, remember that you can access all of the Cram Quiz questions on the CD. You can also create a custom exam by topic with the practice exam software. Note any topic you struggle with and go to that topic's material in this chapter.

CHAPTER SEVEN

Basic Routing

This chapter covers the following official CCNA Routing and Switching 200-120 exam topics:

- Describe basic routing concepts.
- Configure and verify utilizing the CLI to set basic router configuration.
- Verify router configuration and network connectivity.
- Configure and verify routing configuration for a static or default route given specific routing requirements.
- Differentiate methods of routing and routing protocols.
- Configure and verify OSPF (single area).
- Configure and verify inter-VLAN routing (router on a stick).
- Configure SVI interfaces.

This chapter introduces one of the largest and most challenging topics on the CCNA exam. Routers are a vital component of a functioning network. Understanding how they work, configuring them to work properly, and determining why they don't comprise a core skill set. This chapter covers the theory of routing, basic configurations for connectivity, static and default routing, dynamic routing theory, and inter-VLAN routing, in addition to OSPF configuration, verification, and troubleshooting.

Routing Fundamentals

CramSaver

1. A router has interface f0/0 configured as 192.168.1.1/24 and interface f0/1 configured as 172.16.0.1/16. There are no static, default, or dynamic routes configured on this router. Julie's PC is connected to the same switch as the router's f0/0. Julie's IP address is 192.168.1.127 with a mask of 255.255.255.0 and a default gateway of 192.168.1.1. Joost's MacBook is connected to the same switch as the router's f0/1. Joost's IP configuration is 172.16.0.112 with a mask of 255.255.0.0 and a default gateway of 172.16.0.1. Can Joost ping Julie?

   A. Yes

   B. No

2. Duncan recently read *Static Routes for Dummies*. Despite this, he is having trouble identifying the issue with the following command syntax: **ip route 10.4.4.128 255.255.255.128 10.0.0.0**. What is the problem with the syntax?

   A. The mask is wrong. A 10.x.x.x network uses a 255.0.0.0 mask.

   B. The first IP must be a network ID, not an IP address.

   C. The next hop is not valid.

   D. The mask must be wildcarded.

   E. The next hop address is in the wrong place.

3. Examine the following partial output of **show ip route**: O 172.16.0.0/16 [110/2] via 10.0.0.2, 00:12:35, FastEthernet0/0. Which of the following is true? Choose all that apply.

   A. The *O* stands for observed route.

   B. The *O* stands for other route.

   C. This is an OSPFv3 route.

   D. The administrative distance has been changed from the default.

   E. The metric is 110.

   F. The metric is 55.

   G. The next hop is f0/0.

   H. The next hop is 10.0.0.20.

Answers

1. Yes. A correctly configured router will route between connected networks. All the configurations here are correct.
2. Answer C is correct. 10.0.0.0 is a network ID. The next hop must be either an IP address or in some special cases an exit interface. Answer A is both incorrect and offers incorrect reasoning. The mask must be the subnet mask of the destination network. Answer B is wrong; 10.4.4.128 is a network ID when the mask is 255.255.255.128. Answer D is incorrect; the mask is entered in decimal form and not wildcarded. Answer E is wrong. Everything is in the right place.
3. Answer: None of the above! Is that even allowed? Probably not on the exam. Trust your feelings.

Routing is the process by which a packet gets from one location to another. To route a packet, a router needs to know the destination address and which of its interfaces it should send the traffic out (egress interface). When a packet comes into an interface (ingress interface) on a router, it looks up the destination IP address in the packet header and compares it with its routing table. The routing table, which is stored in RAM, tells the router which outgoing, or egress, interface the packet should go out to reach the destination network.

The Next Hop Concept

It's important to understand that a router cannot send traffic to a remote network destination network it is supposed to go to (unless that network is directly connected to the router). That sounds odd, but what it really means is this: A router sends traffic to *the next router on the best path to the destination*. That next router is called the *next hop*. (Imagine the packet hopping from router to router on the way to its destination.) Because each router in a multirouter system has an interface in the same network as at least one other router, every router has at least one next hop that they can always reach, because it is on the same shared network. This allows each router to relay or hand off a packet to the next hop down the best path, hop by hop, to the final destination network. Sometimes the next hop is not specified, but the *exit interface* is—this would be the interface used to transmit the packet to the next hop.

The real question, then, is this: How does the router know what the correct next hop is?

For the purposes of exam preparation, we will focus on four ways to control routing decisions (which really means determining the correct next hop) on your router:

- Connected networks
- Static routes
- Default routes
- Dynamic routes

The next sections describe each of those processes.

Connected Networks

When you attach a network cable to a router interface, configure an IP address in that network on the interface, and issue the **no shutdown** command, you have created a connected network. By definition, to route a router must have two or more different connected networks; having only one network connected would make it simply a host (like a computer or a printer or something). A router will automatically route traffic between its connected networks; you don't have to configure anything other than the interfaces. Figure 7.1 shows a router with two connected networks. Because the router can always route between its connected networks, Host A can ping Host B and vice versa. No additional router configuration is necessary beyond connecting and configuring the interfaces.

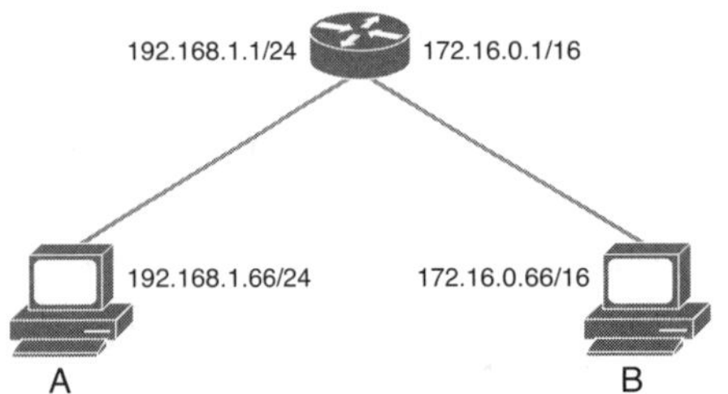

FIGURE 7.1 **Connected networks.**

In a bigger, more complex network with multiple routers, we run into a problem: Not all routers are connected to all networks. In this case, we have to somehow teach the routers about the other networks to which they are *not* directly connected. Figure 7.2 shows a system with two routers; in this system,

Host A cannot ping Host B (and vice versa) because Router 1 is not connected to Host B's network and does not know the next hop to get there; likewise, Router 2 does not know about Host A's network.

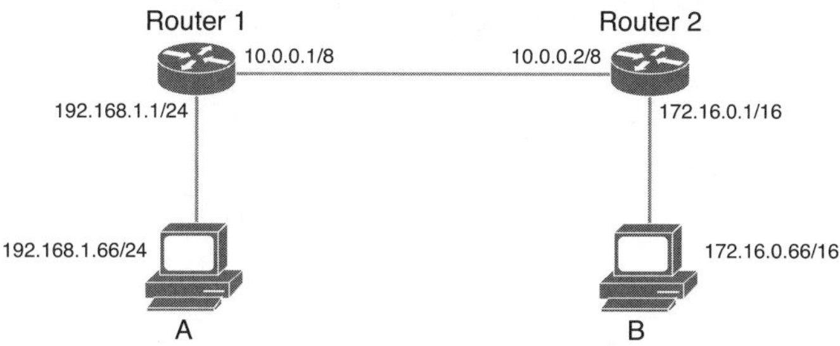

FIGURE 7.2 **Remote networks.**

If we can teach Router 1 about all of Router 2's networks (and vice versa), the whole system works; every router knows the next hop to every remote network. That does not happen automatically. We have to use either static or dynamic routes to tell each router about the remote networks.

Static Routes

Use a static route when you want to manually define the path that the packet will take through your network. Static routes are useful in small networks with rarely changing routes, when you have little bandwidth and do not want the overhead of a dynamic routing protocol, or when you want to manually define all of your routes for security reasons.

Static routes are created in global configuration mode. The syntax for the static route is as follows:

```
ip route [destination_network_address] [subnet_mask] [next-hop-address
| interface] [distance]
```

For example, in Figure 7.3, Carol is trying to get to a web server on a different network. Her computer will be configured to use the Cancun router as its default gateway, but the Cancun router needs to know how to get to the 192.168.100.0/24 network where the web server resides.

Using the Honolulu router as your next hop in the path to the web server, type the following to create a static route on the Cancun router:

```
ip route 192.168.100.0 255.255.255.0 172.16.0.2
```

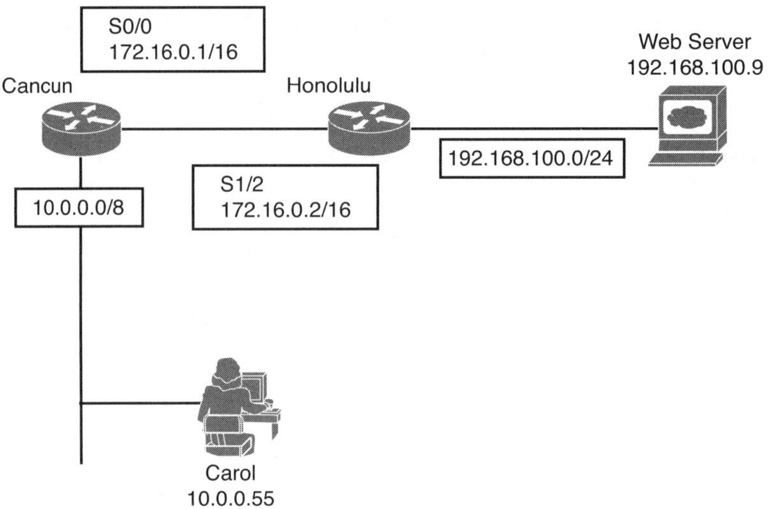

FIGURE 7.3 **Static route example.**

Instead of routing to the next-hop router, you could also create a static route out of an interface. If you did not know the address of the Honolulu router, you could tell the Cancun router to use interface serial 0/0 to get to the 192.168.100.0 network. The syntax would then be ip route 192.168.100.0 255.255.255.0 serial 0/0.

At this point, you have created a route to get to the 192.168.100.0 network attached to the Honolulu router. That will get Carol's data to the web server, but the Honolulu router will also need a route to get traffic back to Carol's network. Using the Cancun router as the next hop, the syntax would be as follows:

```
ip route 10.0.0.0 255.0.0.0 172.16.0.1
```

Remember that when entering the static route the destination is typically a network address, whereas the next hop address is a specific IP address assigned to another router's interface. As noted previously, you can also create a static route to direct your traffic through a specific interface.

Default Routes

A default route can be configured as a static route (or learned from a routing protocol), but instead of configuring a route to a specific network, you are configuring the router to know where to send traffic for any network not found in its routing table. Default routes are used to establish a gateway of last resort for your router.

There are two ways to create a default route. The first is to use the same command that you used for a static route but use the 0.0.0.0 network as your destination with a subnet mask of 0.0.0.0. For example, to establish a default route to send traffic out serial 0/0 destined for any network not learned through dynamic or static means, type the following:

```
ip route 0.0.0.0 0.0.0.0 serial 0/0
```

If you chose to specify the next hop IP address of the router, you could type the following instead (assuming a next hop address of 192.168.1.1):

```
ip route 0.0.0.0 0.0.0.0 192.168.1.1
```

The second method of creating a default route is to use the **ip default-network** command. With this command, any traffic destined for networks not found in the routing table will be sent to the default network. Figure 7.4 illustrates the use of the default network.

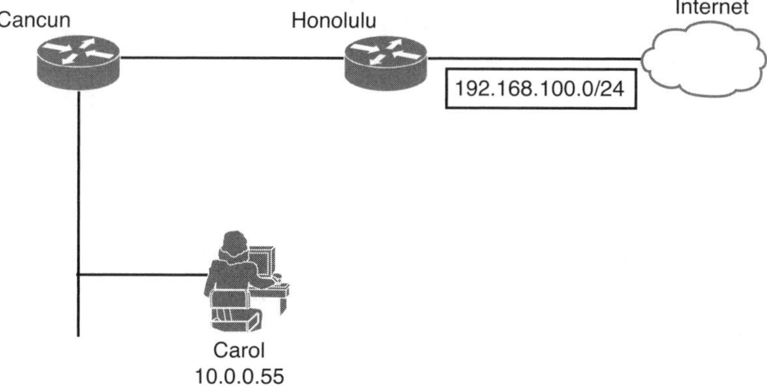

FIGURE 7.4 **Default network example.**

If Carol is trying to access the Internet, a default route could be configured with the following global configuration command on the Honolulu router:

```
Honolulu(config)#ip default-network 192.168.100.0
```

Or, if using OSPF instead of RIP or EIGRP, you could use the following:

```
Router(config-router)# default-information originate
```

Note that you do not include the subnet mask in this command. Routing protocols, such as RIP, can propagate this default network to other routers. When Carol attempts to access the Internet, her computer sends traffic to the Cancun router, which is her default gateway. The Cancun router will see a default network of 192.168.100.0, look up this destination in its routing table, and forward her packets to the Honolulu router. The Honolulu router, in turn, will forward the traffic out its interface connected to the 192.168.100.0 network and on to the Internet.

ExamAlert

Know how to configure a static route, default route, and default network (for EIGRP and OSPF).

Dynamic Routes

Static and default routes are nice, but they are not scalable. If you need a scalable solution, you need to work with dynamic routing protocols. A dynamic routing protocol is a language that routers use to communicate with each other about their own connected networks. When routers tell each other about their connected networks, all of them eventually know about all the networks in the system, as well as the next hop they should use to get traffic to each of them. If there is more than one path to get to any given network, the router will then make a decision about the best path to use, using the administrative distance and metric values described in the following sections.

For the ICND1 exam, you need to know how to configure static, default and OSPF routing. For the CCNA and ICND2 exams, you need to understand the operation and configuration of EIGRP as well. EIGRP is covered in Chapter 13, "Advanced Router Operation."

Before we go much further, you should also understand a couple routing terms that are characteristic of all dynamic routing protocols: administrative distance and metric.

Administrative Distance

Administrative distance is the measure of trustworthiness that a router assigns to how a route to a network was learned. A route can be learned if the network is directly connected, there is a static route to the network, or by various routing protocols as they exchange information about networks between routers. For example, in Figure 7.5, the Jupiter router needs to determine the best route to get to the 10.0.0.0/8 network attached to the Earth router. It has learned of two separate paths; one is learned through EIGRP and the other through OSPF. EIGRP has decided that the best path for a packet destined to the 10.0.0.0/8 network is through Saturn, Mars, and finally Earth. However, OSPF has determined that the best path is through Pluto and then Earth. The Jupiter router needs to decide which routing protocol it should trust, or prefer, over the other. The one preferred will be the one the router listens to when making decisions on how to route.

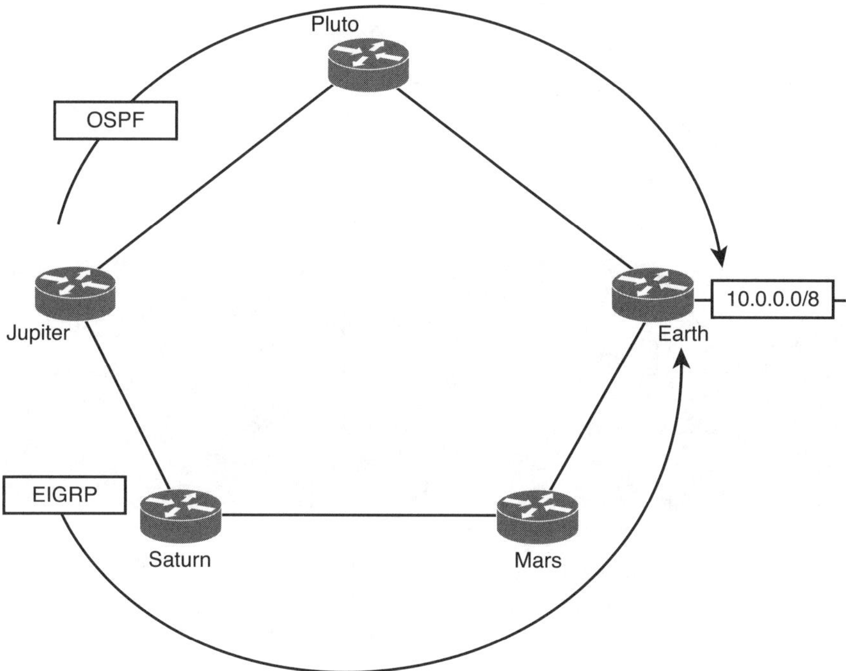

FIGURE 7.5 **Administrative distance decisions.**

To determine which routing source is preferred, Cisco has assigned administrative distances to sources of routing information. A router will choose the route that is learned through the source with the lowest administrative distance. Table 7.1 illustrates the default administrative distance value.

ExamAlert

It is possible to change the administrative distance of a static route by appending a different administrative distance to the end of the command. For example, the following command assigns the administrative distance of 130 to a static route:

```
ip route 10.0.0.0 255.0.0.0 serial 0/0 130
```

Changing the administrative distance of a static route is commonly used when configuring a backup route, called a floating static route. If you do not specify an administrative distance at the end of the static route, the default is being used. For the exam, you should be able to look at the syntax of a static route and know what administrative distance is being used.

TABLE 7.1 **Administrative Distances**

Routing Source	Administrative Distance
Connected	0
Static	1
EIGRP (internal)	90
OSPF	110
RIP (Version 1 and 2)	120
EIGRP (external)	170

Exam**Alert**

Make sure that you memorize this table. You should know both the values and understand the concept of administrative distances. Remember, the lowest number is preferred. It might help you to memorize these by remembering the word Eeyore—E-OR, for EIGRP, OSPF, and RIP. This is the order of the dynamic routing protocols. They are also alphabetic in order. (EIGRP external routes are discussed in Chapter 14, "Advanced IP Services.")

In Figure 7.5, the Jupiter router would take the EIGRP learned path through Saturn and Mars to get to the 10.0.0.0/8 network attached to the Earth router. EIGRP has a lower administrative distance (90) than OSPF (110) and is therefore preferred.

Metrics

In the previous example, two routing protocols run on the routers, but OSPF and EIGRP chose two different paths to get to the Earth router. Each routing protocol has its own algorithm to determine what it considers to be the best path to a destination network. The main factor in deciding the best path is the routing protocol's *metric.*

A metric is the variable used in the algorithm when making routing decisions. Each routing protocol uses a different type of metric. Table 7.2 illustrates the different metrics used by various routing protocols.

TABLE 7.2 **Routing Metrics**

Routing Protocol	Metric	Description
RIP	Hop count	The number of hops, or routers, that a packet has to pass through to reach a destination. The route with the lowest hop count is preferred.
EIGRP	Feasible distance	Calculated based on bandwidth and delay by default, but also can factor reliability and load.
OSPF	Cost	Cost is defined by Cisco as reference bandwidth/interface bandwidth. Default reference bandwidth is 10^8.

Understanding the Router Lookup Process and the IP Route Table

Routers collect information about networks—whether they are connected or remote—and the next hop they should use to get traffic to each network. This information is listed in the IP route table. The route table also lists some details about each route, including the metric, the administrative distance, and the time the entry was last updated (if the route was dynamically learned).

Let's take another look at Figure 7.2 (now called 7.6) to refresh your memory of the networks and connections.

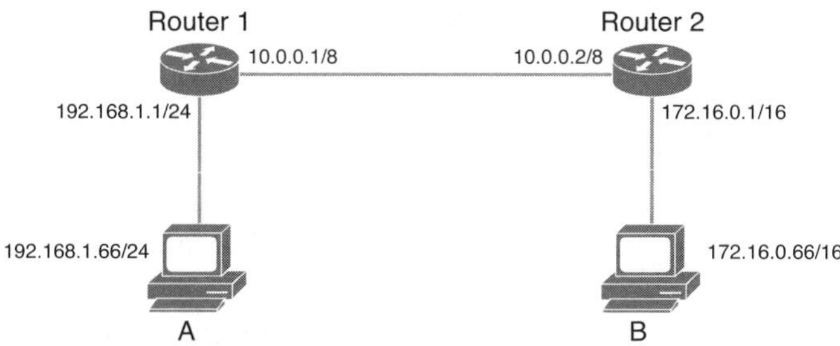

FIGURE 7.6 **Connected networks.**

If we take a look at the output of **show ip route** from Router1 in Figure 7.6, this is what we get:

```
Router1#sh ip route
Codes: L - local, C - connected, S - static, R - RIP, M - mobile, B - BGP
       D - EIGRP, EX - EIGRP external, O - OSPF, IA - OSPF inter area
       N1 - OSPF NSSA external type 1, N2 - OSPF NSSA external type 2
```

```
       E1 - OSPF external type 1, E2 - OSPF external type 2
       i - IS-IS, su - IS-IS summary, L1 - IS-IS level-1, L2 - IS-IS level-2
       ia - IS-IS inter area, * - candidate default, U - per-user static route
       o - ODR, P - periodic downloaded static route, + - replicated route

Gateway of last resort is not set

      10.0.0.0/8 is variably subnetted, 2 subnets, 2 masks
C        10.0.0.0/8 is directly connected, FastEthernet0/0
L        10.0.0.1/32 is directly connected, FastEthernet0/0
      192.168.1.0/24 is variably subnetted, 2 subnets, 2 masks
C        192.168.1.0/24 is directly connected, FastEthernet0/1
L        192.168.1.1/32 is directly connected, FastEthernet0/1
```

The output begins with a list of letter codes that identify how the route was learned. We will cover some of them as we go along, but they are pretty easy to understand anyway. In this case, we can see that Router1 is connected to two networks (as indicated by the *C* at the beginning of the line entry): 10.0.0.0/8 on its F0/0 and 192.168.1.0/24 on F0/1.

Note

You may have noticed the *L* entries, as well, and some of you who have been studying for CCNA for a while might not recognize it. The entry, which signifies a local route, is new for IOS 15. So, what's a local route? Simply put, it is the actual IP address of the interface that is in the connected network. The routes appear as /32 or *host routes* (routes that point to a single IP address as opposed to a network or subnet ID). These entries allow the router to more efficiently route traffic to themselves.

The fact that there is an entry in the route table for each connected network is the technical reason why routers can route between their connected networks. In other words (and this is an important concept), if a router does not find an entry in the route table that matches the destination of the packet, it cannot route the packet. Note that a default route is a match, even though it matches every possible destination.

Let's take a closer look at the two entries for network 192.168.1.0:

```
C        192.168.1.0/24 is directly connected, FastEthernet0/1
L        192.168.1.1/32 is directly connected, FastEthernet0/1
```

Supposing you wanted to send a packet to 192.168.1.66: Router1, having received the packet, looks at the destination IP address of the packet (192.168.1.66) and compares it to the entries in the route table. It looks at the route table and performs a **longest match** analysis. That means that the route table entry that has the longest prefix (the number of bits defined by the mask, e.g. /24) that matches the destination IP of the packet will be selected as the destination.

The Connected entry 192.168.1.0/24 means that the first 24 bits of the destination address must match the entry for it to be a valid next-hop choice. The Local entry for 192.168.1.1/32 means all 32 bits of the destination address must match the entry for it to be a valid next hop choice.

Comparing the destination IP of the packet (192.168.1.66) with the route table entries:

- The 192.168.1.0/24 entry matches the first 24 bits of the destination IP 192.168.1.66 and is a valid choice.
- The 192.168.1.1/32 entry is not a valid choice because not all 32 bits of 192.168.1.66 match 192.168.1.1.

If there are multiple paths to a given network, the route table might list multiple matches. Consider these entries as an example:

- 192.168.0.0/16 via 10.4.99.1, Serial 1/0/0
- 192.168.99.0/24 via 192.168.1.2, Fastethernet 0/1
- 192.168.99.192/26 via 10.20.20.2, GigabitEthernet 1/0
- 192.168.99.248/29 via 10.100.100.2, GigabitEthernet 1/1

If this router needs to route a packet to 192.168.99.250, the route table lookup tells it:

- 192.168.0.0/16 is a valid match; the first 16 bits of 192.168.99.250 match this entry.
- 192.168.99.0/24 is a valid match; the first 24 bits of 192.168.99.250 match this entry.
- 192.168.99.192/26 is a valid match; the first 26 bits of 192.168.99.250 match this entry.
- 192.168.99.248/29 is a valid match; the first 29 bits of 192.168.99.250 match this entry.

In this case, all the entries listed match the destination IP of the packet. Applying the longest match rule, the packet will be forwarded to 10.100.100.2, the next hop specified by the 192.168.99.248/29 entry, via GigabitEthernet 1/1.

Other than the actual route matching process (which is very important, of course), the entries in the route table provide information about the source of the route information, the administrative distance, the metric, and the last update time of the information.

Router1now has OSPF configured, so the route table will show some dynamic routes. Let's take the updated (partial) output of **show ip route** on Router1 and analyze one of the entries:

```
Router1#show ip route
Codes: L - local, C - connected, S - static, R - RIP, M - mobile, B - BGP
       D - EIGRP, EX - EIGRP external, O - OSPF, IA - OSPF inter area
       N1 - OSPF NSSA external type 1, N2 - OSPF NSSA external type 2
       E1 - OSPF external type 1, E2 - OSPF external type 2
       i - IS-IS, su - IS-IS summary, L1 - IS-IS level-1, L2 - IS-IS level-2
       ia - IS-IS inter area, * - candidate default, U - per-user static route
       o - ODR, P - periodic downloaded static route, + - replicated route

Gateway of last resort is not set

      10.0.0.0/8 is variably subnetted, 2 subnets, 2 masks
C        10.0.0.0/8 is directly connected, FastEthernet0/0
L        10.0.0.1/32 is directly connected, FastEthernet0/0
O     172.16.0.0/16 [110/2] via 10.0.0.2, 00:12:35, FastEthernet0/0
      192.168.1.0/24 is variably subnetted, 2 subnets, 2 masks
C        192.168.1.0/24 is directly connected, FastEthernet0/1
L        192.168.1.1/32 is directly connected, FastEthernet0/1
!
! output truncated
```

Let's take the highlighted line from that output and break it down to explain each component:

```
O     172.16.0.0/16 [110/2] via 10.0.0.2, 00:12:35, FastEthernet0/0
```

- **O** indicates the route was learned dynamically from OSPF.
- **172.16.0.0/16** is a learned destination network prefix used for longest-match routing.
- **[110/2]** indicates the administrative distance (110 for OSPF) and the metric (OSPF cost of 2 in this case).
- **via 10.0.0.2** indicates the next hop to which traffic destined for 172.16.0.0/16 should be sent.
- **00:12:35** is the time since the route was last updated (12 minutes and 35 seconds ago).
- **FastEthernet0/0** is the interface from which the route was learned.

ExamAlert

Be completely familiar with how to interpret the output of **show ip route**, including both longest-match analysis and what each component of the entries means.

There are always a few "loose ends" to tie up in a study guide like this—things that Cisco thinks are important enough to include in the exam, but that don't really fit anywhere. So, with that said, the next sections on VLSM and routing, Cisco Express Forwarding, and passive interfaces are presented for your interest.

VLSM and Routing

Variable-length subnet masking (VLSM) was discussed in Chapter 3, "Concepts in IP Addressing." It is important to understand the connection between the concepts of VLSM and how it impacts routing. *VLSM* can be defined as the capability to apply more than one subnet mask to a given class of addresses throughout a routed system. Although this is common practice in modern networks, there was a time when this was impossible because the routing protocols in use could not support it. Classful protocols such as RIPv1 do not include the subnet mask of advertised networks in their routing updates; therefore, they cannot possibly learn the existence of more than one mask length. Only classless routing protocols—EIGRP, OSPF, RIPv2, IS-IS, and BGP—include the subnet mask for the networks they advertise in their routing updates and thus publish a level of detail that makes VLSM possible.

When the route updates (complete with the subnet masks) show up in the route table, that's how we get the possibility of multiple matches with different prefix lengths, including some that might be summaries (with shorter-than-default masks).

Cisco Express Forwarding

Cisco Express Forwarding (CEF) is a recent variation of Cisco's efforts to speed up the routing process. So far, we have talked about routing in terms of the original method that routers used, called *process switching*. Using this method, every packet must be analyzed, compared with the entire route table, the routing decision made, and the frame that will carry the packet across the link to the next hop must be created. All this work takes up a lot of CPU cycles, and if the route table is large, it gets to be a significant performance load. After a few years, Cisco came up with an improved system called *fast switching*. The improvements made by fast switching included building an additional table that listed previously routed packet addresses, and the saved data-link information used to forward those packets on the next-hop link. With these tables, the router didn't have to do the calculation of the routing and switching info for every packet; it just looked it up in a table. In the third iteration of routing technology, CEF added sophistication to how the tables are created a used. The tables are created for all routing table destinations ahead of time (not just the ones that are needed, as they are needed). The search algorithms and tree-structure format of the tables are also much more efficient and faster with CEF. Table 7.3 compares the three routing methods.

TABLE 7.3 **Process Switching, Fast Switching, and CEF Compared**

Efficiency Gain	Process Switching	Fast Switching	CEF
Saves data link headers previously used for Layer 2 encapsulation of packets	No	Yes	Yes
Uses additional tables, with faster lookup time, before reverting to a process-switched routing table lookup	No	Yes	Yes
Tables built using tree structures and very fast search algorithms, meaning less time to route packets	No	No	Yes

Passive Interfaces

Passive interface is a method that a network engineer can use to suppress a particular interface from fully participating in the routing process. Making a router interface passive means that it will not send out hello messages, it will ignore hello messages it receives, and it will not form neighbor relationships. However, the network that the passive interface connects to can still be advertised by the routing protocol. Passive interface can be configured in both OSPF and EIGRP, and are detailed later in those sections.

Cram Quiz

Examine the following partial entries from the route table:

192.168.0.0/16 via f0/0 192.168.1.0/24 via f0/1 192.168.1.128/25 via f1/0 192.168.1.192/26 via f1/1 0.0.0.0/0 via g0/0

1. Which interface will forward a packet sent to 192.168.11.129?

   ❍ **A.** f0/0

   ❍ **B.** f0/1

   ❍ **C.** f1/0

   ❍ **D.** f1/1

   ❍ **E.** g0/0

2. Will a passive interface send hello packets?

   ❍ **A.** Yes

   ❍ **B.** No

3. Ed's router has a Gigabit Ethernet interface on it. He is concerned that the automatic OSPF metric calculation might not be accurate for his router. What is the default OSPF metric calculation?

   ❍ **A.** (Link bandwidth in bps) × 100,000,000

   ❍ **B.** (Link bandwidth in bps) / 100,000,000

   ❍ **C.** 100,000,000 × (Link bandwidth in bps)

   ❍ **D.** 100,000,000 / (Link bandwidth in bps)

   ❍ **E.** 1000,000,000 / (Link bandwidth in bps)

Cram Quiz Answers

1. Answer A is correct. 192.168.11.129 matches the first 16 bits of that entry; it does not match the first 24, 25, or 26 bits of the next three entries, and although it matches the default route entry, there is a longer match that will be preferred.
2. No. Passive interface suppresses routing protocol communications while still allowing the network to be advertised.
3. Answer D is correct. Even a router with a Gigabit Ethernet interface will use the default IP OSPF cost calculation.

Inter-VLAN Routing

CramSaver

1. Which of the following correctly sets up router on a stick?
   - **A. interface f0/1 ip address 192.168.1.1 255.255.255.0 ! interface f0/1.110 encapsulation dot1q 110 ip address 192.168.110.1 255.255.255.0 ! interface f0/1.220 encapsulation dot1q 220 ip address 192.168.220.1 255.255.255.0**
   - **B. interface f0/1 ip address 192.168.1.1 255.255.255.0 ! interface f0/1.110 encapsulation 802.1q 110 ip address 192.168.110.1 255.255.255.0 ! interface f0/1.220 encapsulation 802.1q 220 ip address 192.168.220.1 255.255.255.0**
   - **C. interface f0/1 ip address 192.168.1.1 255.255.255.0 ! interface f1/1 encapsulation dot1q 110 ip address 192.168.110.1 255.255.255.0 ! interface f1/0.220 encapsulation dot1q 220 ip address 192.168.220.1 255.255.255.0**

2. Jaden has a Catalyst 2960 that she wants to set up for inter-VLAN routing with SVIs. She enters the following configuration: **interface vlan 1 ip address 192.168.1.1 255.2555.255.0 ! interface vlan 110 ip address 192.168.110.1 255.255.255.0 ! interface vlan 220 ip address 192.168.220.1 255.255.255.0 !**. She is frustrated because the config doesn't seem to be working. What is the problem?
   - **A.** The **encapsulation dot1q** command is missing.
   - **B.** The native VLAN is incorrect.
   - **C.** Extended range VLANs are not supported in a 2960.
   - **D.** The 2960 does not support multiple SVIs; only one at a time.

Answers

1. Answer A is correct. Answer B is wrong because it uses 802.1Q instead of dot1q. C is wrong because it uses a separate physical interface instead of subinterfaces.
2. Answer D is correct; the 2960 only supports one VLAN interface. Answer A is wrong because the **encapsulation dot1q** command is applied at the router trunk interface, not at the switch. Answer B is wrong because the native VLAN is a trunk configuration, not an SVI command. Answer C is incorrect; the 2960 does support extended-range VLANs, but this fact is irrelevant to the question.

VLANs define separate broadcast domains and should be separate IP subnets. The only way to get traffic from one VLAN to another is to route between them (inter-VLAN routing). We have several choices for how to do this: We could have one router for every VLAN, with an Ethernet port on each connected to a switch port in each VLAN, and then interconnect all the routers; the problem here, of course, is that having so many routers and connections gets expensive and complicated, and latency can be bad.

We could get one big router with a lot of Ethernet ports and could connect one to a port in each VLAN on the switch. This is a little simpler, but still expensive and probably not as fast as it could be unless we really spend some money.

Our last two choices are to use router on a stick (honest, that's what it's called; we wouldn't make something like that up) or Layer 3 switching. The next section details router on a stick.

Router on a Stick

This feature takes advantage of trunk links: All VLANs can be transported across a trunk link to be distributed by the neighbor device. Suppose that we built a trunk from a switch to a router. We'd want at least a Fast Ethernet port on the router (because a 10BASE-T interface does not support router on a stick on all routers), and it would have to support either 802.1Q. Now all we need to do is build routable interfaces, one for each VLAN.

We do this by using sub-interfaces. A sub-interface is a virtual interface that is spawned from the physical interface, and uses the physical interface for Layer 1 connectivity. A sub-interface can be given an IP address and mask, can be shut down or enabled, can run routing protocols—in fact, there isn't much that a physical interface can do that a sub-interface can't. So if our router has a FastEthernet interface, we can configure it to run 802.1Q, build a subinterface for each VLAN, give those sub-interfaces IP addresses in the appropriate subnets for each VLAN, and let the router route between the VLANs whose traffic is coming up that trunk link. A frame destined for VLAN 30 could come up the trunk link from VLAN 10 to the router's VLAN 10 sub-interface, get routed to VLAN 30, and leave that same port from the VLAN 30 sub-interface. The hosts in each VLAN will use the sub-interface configured for their VLAN as their default gateway.

The following example configures router on a stick for inter-VLAN routing between VLANs 10 and 30, using 802.1Q trunking on interface FastEthernet 0/1:

```
Router(config)#int fa0/1
Router(config-if)#no ip address
Router(config-if)#interface fa0/1.1
Router(config-if)#ip address 10.1.1.1 255.255.255.0
Router(config-sub-if)#encapsulation dot1q 1 native
!
! Creates subinterface for Native VLAN 1
! (Required for dot1q functionality)
!
Router(config-sub-if)#int fa0/1.10
Router(config-sub-if)#encap dot1q 10
Router(config-sub-if)#ip address 10.10.10.1  255.255.255.0
!
! Creates subinterface for VLAN 10 and
! applies IP address in VLAN10's subnet
!
Router(config-sub-if)#int fa0/1.30
Router(config-sub-if)#ip address 10.30.30.1  255.255.255.0
Router(config-sub-if)#encap dot1q 30
!
! Creates subinterface for VLAN 30 and
! applies IP address in VLAN30's subnet
!
```

Figure 7.7 illustrates a typical router-on-a-stick application. Note that the IP addressing is different, just to help you separate the addressing from the configurations.

Why is it called router on a stick, anyway? Just because the router looks like a lollipop on the end of the trunk "stick." Yes, that's really why.

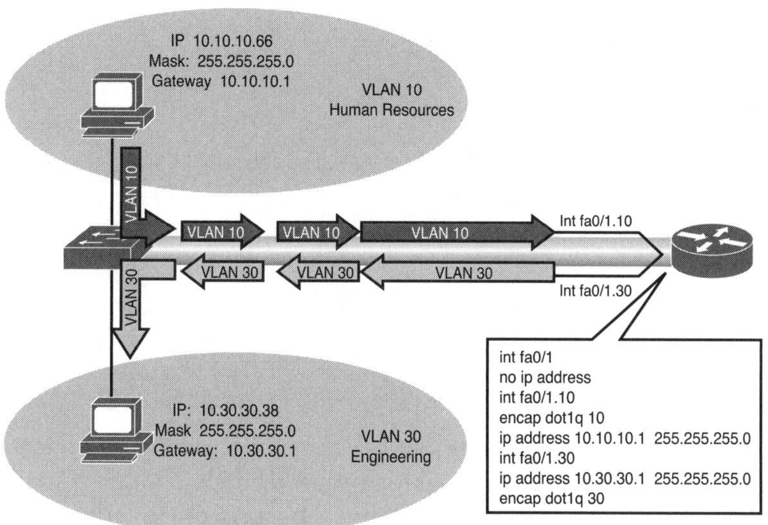

FIGURE 7.7 **Router on a stick.**

L3 Switching

A Layer 3 switch has the capability to create a virtual routed interface (a VLAN interface) for each VLAN, and route between those switched virtual interfaces(SVIs) for inter-VLAN routing. It's similar in function to router on a stick, except that there is no stick, and the router is internal to the switch and extremely fast. If you are routing a lot of inter-VLAN traffic, buying and configuring a Layer 3 switch will bring you serious gains in throughput.

Not every switch is Layer 3 capable; the lowly 2960 cannot do it, but a 3550 will. Layer 3 switches are more expensive than Layer 2 switches, but are much more capable.

Here is a sample configuration of inter-VLAN routing for the same network, using SVIs instead of router on a stick:

```
Switch(config)#ip routing
!
! Enables the Layer 3 capability of the switch
!
Switch(config)#vlan 10
Switch(config)#vlan 30
!
! Creates the VLANs
!
```

```
Switch(config)#interface vlan 10
Switch(config-if)#ip address 10.10.10.1  255.255.255.0
Switch(config-if)#no shut
!
Switch(config-if)#interface vlan 30
Switch(config-if)#ip address 10.30.30.1  255.255.255.0
Switch(config-if)#no shut
!
! Creates the SVIs, complete with IP addresses
!
!
```

Upstream Routing

Upstream routing is one of the CCNA exam topics, but there really isn't much to it. All it means is that having configured inter-VLAN routing using router on a stick or SVIs on a Layer 3 switch, don't forget about routing to other parts of the network that are "upstream" (toward the core) from the access layer where the VLANS are. Upstream routing can be done with static, default, and dynamic routing.

Cram Quiz

1. What are some advantages of Router on a stick? Choose all that apply.
   - ❍ **A.** Use of separate physical interfaces improves performance.
   - ❍ **B.** Use of single physical interface may save hardware upgrade costs.
   - ❍ **C.** Router security mechanisms can be implemented to control traffic between VLANs.
   - ❍ **D.** Traffic is automatically routed between VLANs because of connected networks.
   - ❍ **E.** All VLANs supported by the switch can be routed.

2. What are some disadvantages of router on a stick? Choose all that apply.
   - ❍ **A.** Single point of failure: If router interface fails, all inter-VLAN traffic fails.
   - ❍ **B.** Potential for congestion on single router interface.
   - ❍ **C.** CEF is typically slower than SVI routing on a Layer 3 switch.
   - ❍ **D.** The encryption used for router on a stick cannot be used outside the United States.
   - ❍ **E.** Deploying router on a stick may cause the Toronto Maple Leafs to make it to the second round of the NHL playoffs.

3. If you have already deployed router on a stick, what is the primary advantage of using SVIs on a Layer 3 switch instead?

   ❍ **A.** Higher speed / less congestion

   ❍ **B.** Lower cost of equipment

   ❍ **C.** Greater security

   ❍ **D.** Single point of failure

Cram Quiz Answers

1. Answers B, C, D, and E are correct. Answer A is incorrect because only a single physical interface is used; in fact, that's kind of the point of it.
2. Answers A, B, and C are correct. Answer D is incorrect because router on a stick does not use any encryption. Answer E is incorrect because nothing is likely to cause the Leafs to make it to the second round.
3. Answer A is correct. Answer B is incorrect because, generally speaking, you will pay more for a Layer 3 switch than a router with a Fast Ethernet interface. Answer C is incorrect; there is no more and no less security in using SVIs over router on a stick. Answer D is incorrect; having a single point of failure is not an advantage.

OSPF

CramSaver

1. Which of the following are true statements about OSPF?
   - **A.** OSPF can use hierarchical routing to reduce router load.
   - **B.** OSPFv2 supports both IPv4 and IPv6 routes.
   - **C.** OSPFv3 does not support IPv4 routes.
   - **D.** OSPF performs automatic route summarization.

2. Which of the following is a valid OSPF configuration?
   - **A.** **router ospf 100 network 192.168.1.0 0.0.0.255 network 10.0.0.0 0.255.255.255**
   - **B.** **router ospf 1 network 192.168.1.0 255.255.255.0 area 0 network 10.0.0.0 255.0.0.0 area 0**
   - **C.** **router ospf 99 network 192.168.1.0 0.0.0.255 network 10.0.0.0 0.255.255.255**
   - **D.** **router ospf 200 network 0.0.0.0 0.0.0.0 area 0**

3. How is the OSPF router ID determined? Choose all that apply.
   - **A.** The highest IP address on any physical or virtual interface at the moment of OSPF startup
   - **B.** The first interface to be activated for OSPF on the router
   - **C.** The lowest IP address on any physical or virtual interface at the moment of OSPF startup
   - **D.** The last interface to be activated for OSPF on the router
   - **E.** Manually using the **router-id** command

Answers

1. Answers A and C are correct. OSPFv2 and v3 can be configured as multi-area to reduce router load. Answer B is wrong; OSPFv2 supports only IPv4 routing, just as OSPFv3 supports only IPv6 routing. Answer D is wrong because OSPF supports only manual summarization.
2. Answer D is correct; it may look weird, but it is valid. The other answers are either missing the required area ID or use a normal mask instead of a wildcard mask. This config essentially says, "Put all my interfaces, regardless of IP, into area 0."
3. Answers A and E are correct. The physical interface with the highest IP will be chosen as the router ID—unless there is a loopback interface, in which case the highest IP on any loopback will be chosen—unless the **router-id** command is used, in which case the specified IP will be used as the router ID.

The Open Shortest Path First (OSPF) protocol was developed by the Internet Engineering Task Force (IETF) in 1988 as a more scalable solution than RIP. OSPF is an open standard and is not Cisco proprietary. It uses the Shortest Path First (SPF) algorithm developed by Edgar Dijkstra. It is a link-state routing protocol, which means that it sends updates only when there is a change in the network, and instead of sending routing updates, it sends link state advertisements (LSAs) instead.

Characteristics

OSPF is a polite protocol. Unlike chatty RIP, which broadcasts out its entire routing table every 30 seconds regardless of whether other routers want to hear it, OSPF takes a more refined approach to routing. First, OSPF sends out hello messages to neighboring routers to announce itself as an OSPF router and discover who its neighbor routers are. Routers have to agree on certain parameters (such as timers and being on a common subnet) before they can become neighbors. After its neighbor routers are discovered, the router determines whether it should exchange routes with those neighbors. (If they decide to do so, they become *adjacent*.) If they are adjacent, they begin to exchange information about networks (links) it knows about, using messages called link state advertisements (LSAs). After exchanging all routes, the routers send out updates only when there is a change, and they send information only for that affected link, not the entire routing table. Routers take the LSAs heard from other routers and place those routes in its link-state database (similar to the topology database in EIGRP). Routers then run the SPF algorithm to determine the best route to a destination and place that route in the routing table.

To determine the best path, OSPF uses a metric called *cost*, which Cisco defines as 108 / Bandwidth. If you had a 100Mbps link, the cost would be 1 because 100,000,000 / 100,000,000 = 1. Here are some other common costs:

- **10Mbps:** 10
- **1.544Mbps (T1):** 64
- **64Kbps:** 1562

These examples are not included just to impress you with the authors' math abilities. You should know the formula to determine the cost of a link. Given the bandwidth of an interface, know how to calculate the OSPF cost.

The bandwidth costs are based on a bandwidth reference of 100Mb. If you have faster links in your enterprise, such as Gigabit Ethernet, you can change what OSPF bases its cost on by using the **auto-cost reference-bandwidth** command. For example, to change your OSPF to use 109 / Bandwidth (1,000,000 or Gb), type the following command under the router process configuration mode:

```
Router(config-router)#auto-cost reference-bandwidth 1000
```

To maintain consistency throughout your network, you should set the same bandwidth reference across on all your routers.

The SPF algorithm places each router as the *root* of a tree and calculates the shortest path from itself to each destination. The shortest path then gets put into the routing table and is used to route packets to their destination.

Hierarchical Routing

An important concept to grasp with OSPF is that it is a hierarchical protocol. Hierarchical routing protocols break up your autonomous system into multiple areas and summarize routes between areas. If summarized wisely, you can cut down a significant portion of routing updates by advertising only the summarized route. Figure 7.8 shows a multi-area OSPF system for reference.

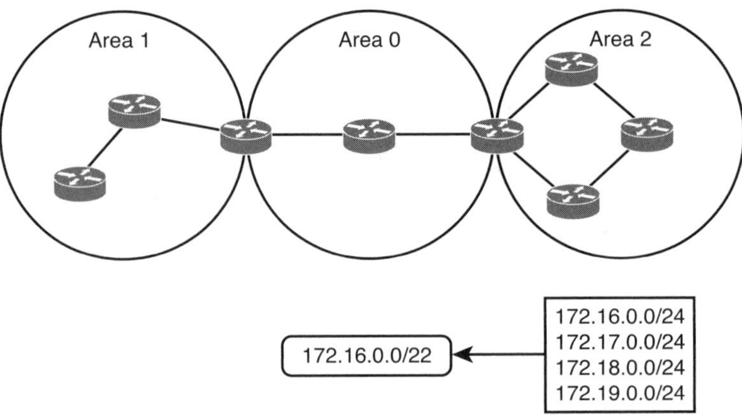

FIGURE 7.8 **Multi-area OSPF example.**

As the number of networks increases in your domain, the amount of processing required on each router increases. Multi-area OSPF routers send special *summary LSA* messages between areas that greatly reduce the amount of routing detail that the routers have to process. This is a built-in feature of OSPF. Summary LSAs should not be confused with manual route summarization, though. To lower the amount of processing required even further, you can also use route summarization in addition to the summary LSAs functionality. Route summarization looks for the same sequence of bits used in multiple subnet IDs and creates a less-explicit summary route, which is then advertised to other routers. Being able to provide summary route information between areas provides several benefits:

- **Less processing on routers:** Fewer networks to advertise and store in the database, less calculations for route changes.
- **Instability hidden from other routers:** If a single network goes down in area 2, it will not affect the routers in area 0 and area 1.
- **Fast convergence:** Because fewer routes are sent to area 0, the routers in areas 0 and 1 can converge faster.
- **Less bandwidth overhead:** There is less bandwidth because only one route is sent, so the advertisement is smaller.
- **Greater control over routing updates:** Because you gain control over routing updates, you can control what routes get sent from one area to another.

You might have noticed that both area 2 and area 1 are connected via area 0. Area 0 is the *backbone* area in OSPF, and all other areas must be connected to it. Routes are then summarized into your backbone area, and from the backbone into other areas.

We will cover multi-area OSPF in more detail in Chapter 13.

Designated Router and Backup Designated Router

Summarizing is an excellent way to conserve your precious bandwidth. On networks that contain more than two routers, OSPF can also conserve bandwidth by electing a designated router for that network that all routers communicate with. Routers exchange information with a designated router instead of each other. This cuts down significantly on the number of advertisements.

The process of using a designated router is somewhat complex, so let's go through it one step at a time. First, the designated router (DR) is elected on only two types of networks:

- **Broadcast multiaccess:** Ethernet, Token Ring
- **Nonbroadcast multiaccess:** Frame Relay, ATM, X.25

On a point-to-point network with only two routers, there is no need for this type of election. Remember that on a point-to-point network, there is no point (of having a DR).

Second, the DR is not the only type of router elected on these types of networks. A backup designated router (BDR) is used in the event that a DR should fail.

The DR and BDR election is as follows:

1. The router with the highest priority becomes the DR. The router with the second-highest priority becomes the BDR. Priority is a number between 0 and 255 and is configured on an interface with the command **ip ospf priority** *priority_number*. The default priority is 1, and if the router is set to priority 0, it will never become a DR or BDR.
2. In the case of a tie, such as when every router's priority is left to the default of 1, the tiebreaker is the router with the highest router ID.

Every router has an identifier called a router ID (RID) that is used to identify itself in its messages. The router ID is an IP address and is assigned as follows:

- The router ID can be configured with the **router-id** command under the OSPF routing process. You can choose a valid IP address that you are using on the router or make up a new one.
- If the **router-id** command is not used, the numerically highest IP address on any loopback interface is chosen as the router ID. A loopback interface is a virtual, software-only interface that can never fail if the IOS is running (although they can be shut down on purpose).
- If you do not have any loopback interfaces configured, the highest IP address on any active physical interface is chosen as the router ID.

See whether you can determine the router ID given the following IP addresses on a router:

Serial 0/0: 192.168.100.19

FastEthernet 0/0: 10.0.0.1

Loopback 0: 172.16.201.200

Although the highest IP address is the one configured on the serial interface, a loopback interface takes precedence over any physical interfaces. Therefore, the router ID would be 172.16.201.200.

ExamAlert

The **router-id** command is common in the real world; however, for the test make sure that you know the process the router uses to select a router ID if the **router-id** command is not used. It first looks at the highest IP address on any logical (loopback) interface, and if no loopback interfaces exist, it looks at the highest IP address on any active physical interface.

Let's review. On broadcast and nonbroadcast multiaccess networks, a DR and BDR are elected. The election is done by first choosing the routers with the highest priority value or, if the priorities are same, choosing the routers with the highest router ID. The router ID is chosen by the highest IP address on any loopback interface or, if no loopback interfaces are configured, the highest IP address on any active physical interface. Whew! That's a lot of work, but in the end it will conserve a significant amount of bandwidth by minimizing the number of link-state messages.

Now that we have elected a DR and BDR, the next phase is ready to begin. In Figure 7.9, you see five routers. The Mocha router is the DR, and the Latte router is the BDR. Instead of all routers sending LSAs to each other, they send out messages only to the DR and BDR. Messages are sent to the multicast address of 224.0.0.6; both the DR and BDR belong to this multicast group address.

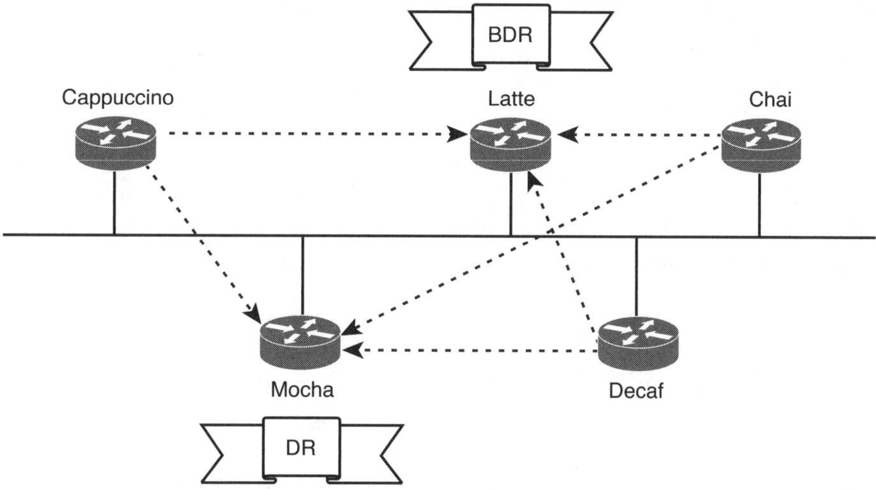

FIGURE 7.9 **OSPF DR/BDR operation.**

Next, the Mocha router, which is the DR, takes the information it learned from the other routers and sends it back out to all routers, as shown in Figure 7.10. Messages are sent to the AllSPFRouter multicast address of 224.0.0.5; all routers running OSPF are members of this multicast group address.

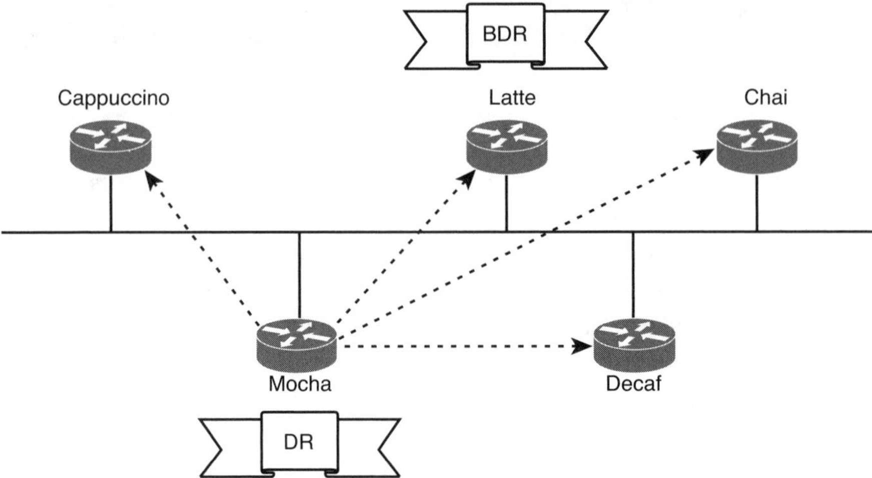

FIGURE 7.10 **DR sends to 224.0.0.6.**

Configuring Single-Area OSPFv2

Understanding the complexities involved in OSPF is the difficult part; configuring it is fairly straightforward. The process is the same as with the other protocols. First, we enable the routing protocol. This is done with the command **router ospf** *process-id*. The process ID can be any number you prefer between 1 and 65,535. If you know something about EIGRP already, you should note that this process ID is *not* the same as the autonomous system number found in EIGRP. Here, the process ID is local to the router and does not need to match other routers.

The next step is to activate OSPF on your interfaces and advertise your networks. This is done with the **network** command. The syntax is as follows:

```
network <ip_address> <wildcard_mask> area <area-id>
```

Note that you specify a wildcard mask in the configuration. Wildcard masks are covered in Chapter 9, "IP Access Lists." Here, wildcard masks are used to match the IP address that is being used on an interface.

Take a look at Figure 7.11. This is the same simple scenario with Router1 and Router2, but now we are configuring single-area OSPF.

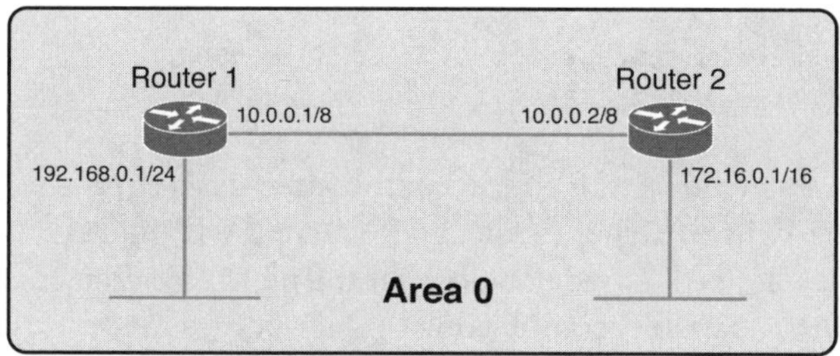

FIGURE 7.11 **OSPF scenario.**

Given this example, the configurations for Router1 and Router2 would be as follows:

```
!
! Configuration for Router 1:
!
Router1(config)#router ospf 100
Router1(config-router)#network 10.0.0.0 0.255.255.255 area 0
Router1(config-router)#network 192.168.1.0 0.0.0.255 area 0
!

!
! Configuration for Router2:
!
Router2(config)#router ospf 200
Router2(config-router)#network 10.0.0.0 0.255.255.255 area 0
Router2(config-router)#network 172.16.0.0 0.0.255.255 area 0
!
```

The wildcard mask used in these statements is matching the IP address on the interface. Here, we are matching the entire network, of which the IP address is a part. For example, on Router1, the command **network 192.168.1.0 0.0.0.255 area 0** tells the router to match all addresses that begin with 192.168.1.X. The last octet, which has 255 in the wildcard mask, is ignored. The router examines the IP addresses of its directly connected interfaces and activates OSPF on those interfaces that match the statement.

Because you are using wildcard masks to match the IP address on your directly connected interfaces, you could also use the wildcard mask of 0.0.0.0 to match the exact address. Just as with IP access lists, a wildcard mask of 0.0.0.0 would match a specific address. For example, if Router1 had the IP address of 192.168.1.1 on one interface and 192.168.50.1 on another interface, you could configure Router1 using a wildcard mask of 0.0.0.0:

```
Router1(config)#router ospf 100
Router1(config-router)#network 192.168.1.1 0.0.0.0 area 0
Router1(config-router)#network 192.168.50.1 0.0.0.0 area 0
```

Using a wildcard mask that matches the IP address of the interface is equivalent to using a wildcard mask that matches the network where the IP address resides. For the exam, you will need to understand what the network statement really means: The *<ip_address>* variable, combined with the wildcard mask, defines a range of IP addresses that are activated in a particular area. Therefore, if a router has multiple interfaces, you might be able to make a **network** command that activates OSPF on some and not others.

Suppose a router has the following IP addresses on its various interfaces:

172.16.0.13

172.16.0.17

172.16.0.21

172.16.0.25

172.16.0.29

You are supposed to activate OSPF on all interfaces, putting them in area 0—all except for 172.16.0.13. And, just to make it interesting, you have to do it with only one **network** statement. You can see fairly easily that the **network** command is going to have to be something like this:

```
network 172.16.0.???  0.0.0.??? area 0
```

We are really just doing that summarization trick again, matching 1s and 0s that are the same. So, let's take the octet where the numbers are varying (the fourth in this case) and break it into binary:

13 = 00001101

17 = 00010001

21 = 00010101

25 = 00011001

29 = 00011101

Look how quickly the pattern emerges: The first 4 bits, 0001, match in all the IPs except 13, the first one. That means that if we set the wildcard mask bits to 0 for those first 4 bits, and set the remaining mask bits to 1, we can match any address that matches the bit pattern of 0001 in the first 4 bits of the fourth octet.

The wildcard mask, then, would look like this:

00000000.00000000.00000000.00001111 (or 0.0.0.15 in decimal wildcard format)

"Exactly match the first three octets, and match only the first 4 bits of the fourth octet. The last 4 bits of the fourth octet can be anything."

Now we need something to match it against. The convention is that we choose the lowest binary value that matches the bit pattern we are specifying: In this case, with the pattern matching ending at the fourth bit, the value we would use is 16. So, the **network** statement would look like this:

```
network 172.16.0.16  0.0.0.15 area 0
```

"Exactly match 172, and 16, and 0, but only the first four bits of the binary pattern of 16."

That's kind of long and complicated.

ExamAlert

The syntax for OSPF differs slightly from other routing protocols. Make sure that you feel comfortable configuring OSPF. Remember, it uses a process ID, not an autonomous system (which you will learn about later). Also, OSPF uses wildcard masks and not subnet masks in its configuration.

You should be familiar with some optional commands for the exam, including the following:

- **ip ospf priority** *priority number*: This interface command is used to change the priority of an interface for the DR/BDR election.
- **ip ospf cost** *cost*: This interface command is used to manually change the cost of an interface.
- **passive-interface** *interface*: This command, performed at the config-router prompt, suppresses OSPF interaction on the specified interface while still allowing the connected network to be advertised. The command may also be set up in the following way:
    - **passive-interface default:** Sets all interfaces to passive by default.
    - **no passive-interface** *interface*: Reverts specified interface to nonpassive.
- **default-information originate:** Causes routers to inject configured default routes into the OSPF system. This is great for a typical scenario where one router connects to the ISP and has a static default route configured; **default-information originate** causes the router to add the default route to its OSPF updates so that other routers learn the default route to the Internet.

Configuring Single-Area OSPFv3

When comparing OSPFv2 (which we just covered) with OSPFv3, there are just a few differences to be aware of:

- OSPFv2 does not support IPv6 routes and OSPFv3 does not support IPv4 routes. Therefore, if you have a dual-stack router (one which uses both IPv4 and IPv6 addressing), you must run both versions of OSPF.
- The characteristics and behavior of OSPFv3 are the same as for OSPFv2. There are some differences in the details of the LSA structure, but that level of detail (the actual guts of the LSA) is well beyond the scope of CCNA.
- The configuration of OSPFv3 is a little bit different; the following section details the differences.

Using the same network diagram, we must first configure IPv6 addressing. Figure 7.12 shows our test system with IPv6 addresses applied.

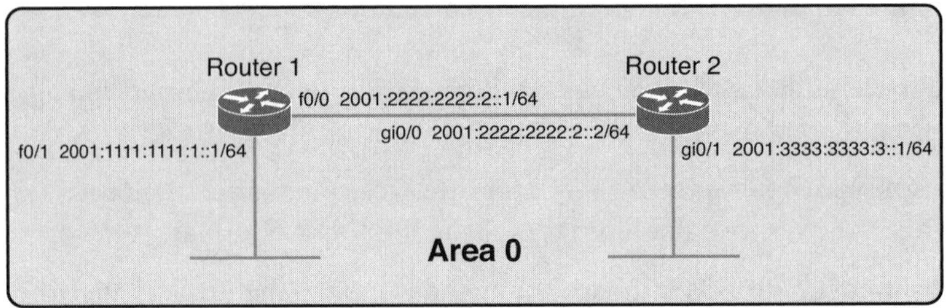

FIGURE 7.12 **IPv6 addressing for OSPF.**

The first task, then, is to set up IPv6 addressing (the concepts of IPv6 addressing were covered in Chapter 3. We have selected very simple addresses to help keep things clear. The following outputs show the IPv6 addressing configuration for Router1 and Router2:

```
!
Configuration for Router1
!
Router1(config)#interface FastEthernet0/0
 ip address 10.0.0.1 255.0.0.0
 ipv6 address 2001:2222:2222:2::1/64
!
interface FastEthernet0/1
 ip address 192.168.1.1 255.255.255.0
 ipv6 address 2001:1111:1111:1::1/64
!
```

```
!
Configuration for Router2
!
interface GigabitEthernet0/0
 ip address 10.0.0.2 255.0.0.0
 ipv6 address 2001:2222:2222:2::2/64
!
interface GigabitEthernet0/1
 ip address 172.16.0.1 255.255.0.0
 ipv6 address 2001:3333:3333:3::1/64
!
```

Setting up OSPFv3 for IPv6 routing is quite simple, even though it is a little different from configuring OSPFv2. The first task is to enable IPv6 routing using the **ipv6 unicast-routing** global config command. The global config command **ipv6 router ospf** *process-id* starts the OSPFv3 process. You may be prompted to define a router ID manually; you may want to do so regardless of being prompted. In either case, the command to manually define the router ID is the same as in OSPFv2: **router-id** *ip_address*, at the router config. Then, at each interface, configure OSPFv3 with the **ipv6 ospf** *process-id* **area** *area-id* interface command.

Those commands are not terribly difficult or complex; just remember that the routing process is created globally, then activated at each interface. The basic configurations for OSPFv3 on Router1 and Router2 look like this:

```
!
!  Configuration for Router1
!
Router1(config)#ipv6 unicast-routing
Router1(config)#ipv6 router ospf 100
May 23 14:20:45.241: %OSPFv3-4-NORTRID: OSPFv3 process 100 could not
pick a router-id,
please configure manually
Router1(config-rtr)#router-id 1.1.1.1
Router1(config-rtr)#interface f0/0
Router1(config-if)#ipv6 ospf 100 area 0
Router1(config-rtr)#interface f0/1
Router1(config-if)#ipv6 ospf 100 area 0
!

!
!  Configuration for Router2
!
Router2(config)#ipv6 unicast-routing
Router2(config)#ipv6 router ospf 200
```

```
May 23 14:22:31.308: %OSPFv3-4-NORTRID: OSPFv3 process 200 could not
pick a router-id,
please configure manually
Router2(config-rtr)#router-id 2.2.2.2
Router2(config-rtr)#interface g0/0
Router2(config-if)#ipv6 ospf 200 area 0
Router2(config-rtr)#interface g0/1
Router2(config-if)#ipv6 ospf 200 area 0
!
```

Verifying and Troubleshooting OSPF

For verification, you can use **show ip protocols** and **show ip route**. Other commands you can use to verify your configuration include the following:

- **show ip ospf interface:** This command displays area ID and DR/BDR information. Here is an output of **show ip ospf interface** from Router2:

```
Router2#show ip ospf interface
GigabitEthernet0/0 is up, line protocol is up
  Internet Address 10.0.0.2/8, Area 0
  Process ID 200, Router ID 172.16.0.1, Network Type BROADCAST, Cost: 1
  Topology-MTID    Cost    Disabled    Shutdown      Topology Name
        0           1         no          no            Base
  Transmit Delay is 1 sec, State BDR, Priority 1
  Designated Router (ID) 192.168.1.1, Interface address 10.0.0.1
  Backup Designated router (ID) 172.16.0.1, Interface address 10.0.0.2
  Timer intervals configured, Hello 10, Dead 40, Wait 40, Retransmit 5
    oob-resync timeout 40
    Hello due in 00:00:07
  Supports Link-local Signaling (LLS)
  Cisco NSF helper support enabled
  IETF NSF helper support enabled
  Index 1/1, flood queue length 0
  Next 0x0(0)/0x0(0)
  Last flood scan length is 1, maximum is 1
  Last flood scan time is 0 msec, maximum is 0 msec
  Neighbor Count is 1, Adjacent neighbor count is 1
    Adjacent with neighbor 192.168.1.1  (Designated Router)
  Suppress hello for 0 neighbor(s)
```

- **show ip ospf neighbor:** This command displays neighbor information:

```
Router2#show ip ospf neighbor

Neighbor ID     Pri   State       Dead Time   Address       Interface
192.168.1.1       1   FULL/DR     00:00:39    10.0.0.1      GigabitEthernet0/0
```

You can use the **debug ip ospf events** command to troubleshoot OSPF. This command is helpful to troubleshoot why routers are not forming a neighbor relationship with each other. OSPF routers form neighbor relationships before becoming "adjacent," which is the point at which they can exchange routing information. Several items must line up, however, for a neighbor relationship to be established:

- Timers must be the same on both routers. OSPF uses Hello timers that define how often they send out Hello messages and Dead timers that define how long after a router stops hearing a Hello message does it declare its neighbor as down.
- Interfaces connecting the two routers must be in the same area.
- Password authentication, if being used, must be the same.
- Type of area must be the same.

Neighbors are formed automatically or can be established through the use of the **neighbor** command done under the routing process. Sometimes the neighbor adjacency does not form, and the **debug ip ospf events** command can help you to troubleshoot what is going wrong. The following **debug** output shows an example of an adjacency not forming because of two routers having different timers configured. Note that in the output "Dead R 40 C 30" R 40 is the timer of the connected router and "C 30 is the local dead timer:

```
Router1#deb ip ospf events
OSPF events debugging is on
Router1#Sep 17 01:32:31.536: OSPF: Send hello to 224.0.0.5 area 0 on
FastEthernet0/0 from 10.0.0.1
Sep 17 01:32:31.536: OSPF: Send hello to 224.0.0.5 area 1 on
FastEthernet0/1 from 192.168.1.10
Sep 17 01:32:35.148: OSPF: Rcv hello from 172.16.0.1 area 0 from
FastEthernet0/0 10.0.0.2
Sep 17 01:32:35.148: OSPF: Mismatched hello parameters from 10.0.0.2
Sep 17 01:32:35.148: OSPF: Dead R 40 C 30, Hello R 10 C 10  Mask R
255.0.0.0 C 255.0.0.0
```

Verification of OSPFv3

Then commands for verification of OSPF for IPv6 are quite similar to those for OSPFv2 for IPv4. The **show ipv6 ospf interface** command has similar output to its IPv4 counterpart:

```
Router2#sh ipv6 ospf interface
!  some output omitted for brevity
GigabitEthernet0/0 is up, line protocol is up
```

```
  Link Local Address FE80::216:47FF:FE9A:74B8, Interface ID 3
  Area 0, Process ID 200, Instance ID 0, Router ID 172.16.0.1
  Network Type BROADCAST, Cost: 1
  Transmit Delay is 1 sec, State DR, Priority 1
  Designated Router (ID) 172.16.0.1, local address FE80::216:47FF:FE9A:74B8
  Backup Designated router (ID) 192.168.1.1, local address
FE80::21D:70FF:FEE3:B10C
  Timer intervals configured, Hello 10, Dead 40, Wait 40, Retransmit 5
    Hello due in 00:00:03
  Graceful restart helper support enabled
  Index 1/1/1, flood queue length 0
  Next 0x0(0)/0x0(0)/0x0(0)
  Last flood scan length is 0, maximum is 6
  Last flood scan time is 0 msec, maximum is 0 msec
  Neighbor Count is 1, Adjacent neighbor count is 1
    Adjacent with neighbor 192.168.1.1  (Backup Designated Router)
  Suppress hello for 0 neighbor(s)
```

Likewise, the **show ipv6 ospf neighbor** command is familiar as well:

```
Router2#sh ipv6 ospf neighbor

Neighbor ID    Pri   State       Dead Time    Interface ID   Interface
192.168.1.1      1   FULL/BDR    00:00:33     4              GigabitEthernet0/0
```

There is, of course, a new, separate route table for IPv6 routes. As you might have guessed, the command **show ipv6 route** displays the following on Router2. (Note that the administrative distance and the metric for the OSPFv3-learned routes are the same as for OSPFv2.)

```
Router2#show ipv6 route
IPv6 Routing Table - default - 6 entries
Codes: C - Connected, L - Local, S - Static, U - Per-user Static route
       B - BGP, HA - Home Agent, MR - Mobile Router, R - RIP
       I1 - ISIS L1, I2 - ISIS L2, IA - ISIS interarea, IS - ISIS summary
       D - EIGRP, EX - EIGRP external, NM - NEMO, ND - Neighbor Discovery
       O - OSPF Intra, OI - OSPF Inter, OE1 - OSPF ext 1, OE2 - OSPF ext 2
       ON1 - OSPF NSSA ext 1, ON2 - OSPF NSSA ext 2
O   2001:1111:1111:1::/64 [110/2]
     via FE80::21D:70FF:FEE3:B10C, GigabitEthernet0/0
C   2001:2222:2222:2::/64 [0/0]
     via GigabitEthernet0/0, directly connected
L   2001:2222:2222:2::2/128 [0/0]
     via GigabitEthernet0/0, receive
C   2001:3333:3333:3::/64 [0/0]
     via GigabitEthernet0/1, directly connected
L   2001:3333:3333:3::1/128 [0/0]
     via GigabitEthernet0/1, receive
L   FF00::/8 [0/0]
     via Null0, receive
```

In fact, OSPFv3 for IPv6 is nowhere near as scary as people expect. Table 7.3 shows a nice summary of the verification commands for both OSPFv2 and OSPFv3 and how similar they are.

TABLE 7.3 **OSPF Commands for v2 and v3**

To Show Details of	OSPFv2	OSPFv3
Interfaces active in OSPF	**show ip ospf interface**	**show ipv6 ospf interface**
All routing protocols	**show ip protocols**	**show ipv6 protocols**
Summarized information of active OSPF interfaces	**show ip ospf interface brief**	**show ipv6 ospf interface brief**
Neighbor routers	**show ip ospf neighbor**	**show ipv6 ospf neighbor**
The OSPF link-state database	**show ip ospf database**	**show ipv6 ospf database**
OSPF-learned route table entries	**show ip route ospf**	**show ipv6 route ospf**
The OSPF process	**show ip ospf**	**show ipv6 ospf**

Cram Quiz

1. Which of the following is a valid OSPFv3 configuration?

❍ **A.** Router(config)#**ipv6 unicast-routing** Router(config)#**router ospf 100** Router(config-rtr)#**interface f0/0** Router(config-if)#**ipv6 ospf 100 area 0** Router(config-rtr)#**interface f0/1** Router(config-if)#**ipv6 ospf 100 area 0**

❍ **B.** Router(config)#**ipv4 unicast-routing** Router(config)#**ipv6 router ospf 100** Router(config-rtr)#**interface f0/0** Router(config-if)#**ipv6 ospf 100 area 0** Router(config-rtr)#**interface f0/1** Router(config-if)#**ipv6 ospf 100 area 0**

❍ **C.** Router(config)#**ipv6 unicast-routing** Router(config)#**ipv6 router ospf 100** Router(config-rtr)#**interface f0/0** Router(config-if)#**ipv6 ospf 100 area 0** Router(config-rtr)#**interface f0/1** Router(config-if)#**ipv6 ospf 100 area 0**

❍ **D.** Router(config)#**ipv6 unicast-routing** Router(config)#**ipv6 router ospf 100** Router(config-rtr)#**network 2001:1:1:1::1/64** Router(config-rtr)#**network 2001:2:2:2::1/64**

2. How are the DR and BDR chosen on a point-to-point serial link?

   ❍ **A.** Highest router priority

   ❍ **B.** Highest router ID

   ❍ **C.** Manually using the **ip ospf** [**dr** | **bdr**] command

   ❍ **D.** DR/BDR election does not occur on point-to-point serial links

3. What command lists the area, DR and BDR, process ID, and adjacent neighbors?

   ❍ **A.** **show ip ospf database**

   ❍ **B.** **show ip ospf interface**

   ❍ **C.** **show ipv6 router**

   ❍ **D.** **show ip protocols**

   ❍ **E.** **show ip ospf neighbor**

Cram Quiz Answers

1. Answer C is correct. Answer A is incorrect because **router ospf 100** is the OSPF(v2) command. Answer B is incorrect because the **ipv4 unicast-routing** command is invalid. Answer D is incorrect because OSPFv3 is not configured using network statements.
2. Answer D is correct. DR and BDR elections only occur on broadcast and non-broadcast multiaccess networks, and are not required on point-to-point links.
3. Answer B is correct.

Review Questions

1. How is the router ID chosen in OSPF? Choose all that apply.
   - ❍ **A.** Highest loopback IP address
   - ❍ **B.** Highest physical IP address if no loopback exists
   - ❍ **C.** Lowest loopback IP address
   - ❍ **D.** Lowest physical IP address if no loopback exists

2. OSPF supports hierarchical routing. What benefits do you gain from using a routing protocol that supports hierarchical routing? Choose all that apply.
   - ❍ **A.** Hierarchical routing speeds up the time for all routers to converge.
   - ❍ **B.** Hierarchical routing requires less configuration.
   - ❍ **C.** Hierarchical routing reduces the amount of routing overhead.
   - ❍ **D.** Hierarchical routing hides network instability from routers in other areas.
   - ❍ **E.** Hierarchical routing requires less design considerations.

3. What is the cost of a 128K link in OSPF?
   - ❍ **A.** 1562
   - ❍ **B.** 64
   - ❍ **C.** 781
   - ❍ **D.** 10

4. You have a serial interface with the IP address of 192.168.22.33/30. How would you add this link to area 0 in the OSPF process?
   - ❍ **A.** Router(config-router)#**network 192.168.22.32 0.0.0.3 area 0**
   - ❍ **B.** Router(config-router)#**network 192.168.22.32 255.255.255.252**
   - ❍ **C.** Router(config-router)#**network 192.168.22.33 0.0.0.3**
   - ❍ **D.** Router(config-router)#**network 192.168.22.33 255.255.255.252 area 0**

For questions 5 and 6, refer to Figure 7.13.

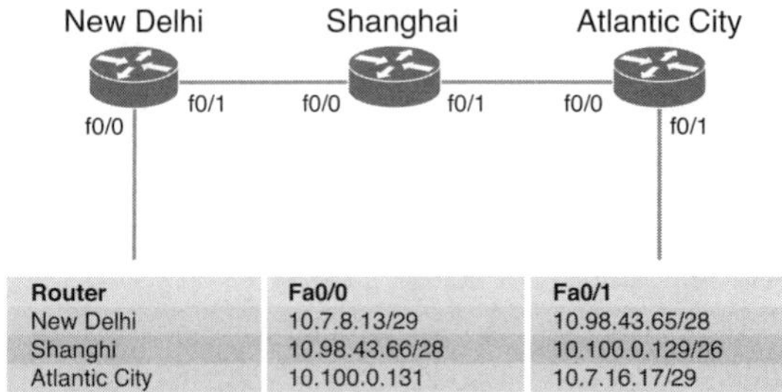

Router	Fa0/0	Fa0/1
New Delhi	10.7.8.13/29	10.98.43.65/28
Shanghi	10.98.43.66/28	10.100.0.129/26
Atlantic City	10.100.0.131	10.7.16.17/29

FIGURE 7.13 **Network topology for Questions 5 and 6.**

5. What would be the syntax to create a static route to the Atlantic City Fa0/1 network from the New Delhi router?

❍ **A.** Router(config)#**ip route 10.7.16.16/29 Fastethernet0/1**

❍ **B.** Router(config)#**ip route 10.7.16.16 255.255.255.248 fastethernet0/0**

❍ **C.** Router(config)#**ip route 10.7.16.16 255.255.255.248 10.98.43.66**

❍ **D.** Router(config)#**ip route 10.7.16.16 mask 255.255.255.248 gw 10.98.43.66**

❍ **e.** Router(config)#**ip route 10.7.16.16 255.255.240 fa0/1**

6. What is the command to enter a default route on Shanghai's router to send all traffic to the New Delhi router?

❍ **A.** Router(config)#**ip default-route fastethernet0/0**

❍ **B.** Router(config)#**ip route default fastethernet0/0**

❍ **C.** Router(config)#**ip route 0.0.0.0 fasthernet0/0**

❍ **D.** Router(config)#**ip route 0.0.0.0 0.0.0.0 fastethernet0/0**

❍ **E.** Router(config)#**ip route 0.0.0.0 255.255.255.255 fastethernet0/0**

7. Your network is running EIGRP, OSPF, RIP, and static routes. Which routing source will be the least preferred?

❍ **A.** EIGRP

❍ **B.** OSPF

❍ **C.** RIP

❍ **D.** Static

For questions 8 through 10, refer to the following figure and output.

Router	Fa0/0	Fa0/1
Botswana	10.7.18.5/30	10.0.23.33/27
Ukraine	10.0.23.34/27	10.202.114.129/28
Tanzania	10.202.114.130/28	10.5.5.0/24

FIGURE 7.14 **Network topology for Questions 8 through 10.**

```
Botswana
router ospf 1
 network 10.7.18.4 0.0.0.30 area 1
 network 10.0.32.32 0.0.0.31 area 0

Ukraine
router ospf 1
 network 10.0.23.32 0.0.0.31 area 0
 network 10.202.114.128 0.0.0.15 area 0

Tanzania
router ospf 11
 network 10.202.114.128 0.0.0.15 area 2
 network 10.5.5.0 0.0.0.255 area 3
```

8. What is wrong with the Botswana configuration?

❍ **A.** The network specified for FastEthernet0/1 in the router config is incorrect.

❍ **B.** The wildcard mask for the network on the FastEthernet0/1 interface is incorrect.

❍ **C.** The OSPF process ID is incorrect.

❍ **D.** Area 1 is not directly connected to area 0.

❍ **E.** The network on fastethernet0/1 is in the wrong area.

9. What is wrong with the Ukraine configuration?

- ❍ **A.** The wildcard mask for the network on the FastEthernet0/0 interface is incorrect.
- ❍ **B.** The wildcard mask for the network on the FastEthernet0/1 interface is incorrect.
- ❍ **C.** The OSPF process ID is incorrect.
- ❍ **D.** The network on FastEthernet0/0 is in the wrong area.
- ❍ **E.** The network on FastEthernet0/1 is in the wrong area.

10. What is wrong with the Tanzania configuration?

- ❍ **A.** The wildcard mask for the network on the FastEthernet0/0 interface is incorrect.
- ❍ **B.** The wildcard mask for the network on the FastEthernet0/1 interface is incorrect.
- ❍ **C.** The OSPF process ID is incorrect.
- ❍ **D.** Area 3 is not directly connected to area 0.
- ❍ **E.** The network on FastEthernet0/1 is in the wrong area.

Answers to Review Questions

1. Answers A and B are correct. OSPF chooses the highest IP address of any logical loopback interfaces or, if no loopback interfaces are configured, the highest IP address on any physical interface that is active at the moment the OSPF process begins. Answers C and D are incorrect because they imply that the lowest IP address is used, which is not the case with OSPF's router ID.
2. Answers A, C, and D are correct. When you hear the term hierarchical routing, think areas and route summarization. OSPF, which supports hierarchical routing, allows you to summarize networks from one area into another. Instead of routers needing to know about all the individual networks in another area, they need to know only about the summary route. The fewer routes result in faster convergence and less routing overhead and, should a network in an area go down, it will not affect routers in other areas. Answer B is incorrect because OSPF will cause additional configuration to be performed. Answer E is incorrect because OSPF typically requires more design than non hierarchical routing protocols such as RIP to ensure an addressing scheme that allows for summarization between areas.
3. Answer C is correct. Cost is defined as 108 / Bandwidth. Thus, 100,000,000 / 128,000 equals 781. Answer A is incorrect because this is the cost to a 64K link. Answer B is incorrect because this is the cost of a 1.544 T1 link. Answer D is incorrect because this is the cost of a 10MB link.
4. Answer A is correct. The IP address of the interface is 192.168.22.33/30, which is on network 192.168.22.32. Although you could have entered 192.168.22.33 0.0.0.0 area 0, this was not a valid option. Only answer A has the correct network and wildcard mask. This is tricky because it requires you to determine both the network address and the correct OSPF syntax. Answer B uses a subnet mask and not a wildcard mask, so it is incorrect. Answer C is incorrect because it does not list the correct network address. Answer D is also incorrect because it does not list the correct address and because it uses a subnet mask in which a wildcard mask is required.
5. Answer is C. The syntax for a static route is ip route <destination network address> [subnet mask] {next-hop-address | interface] [distance]. Answer A is wrong because you cannot use slash notation (/29) in the command. Answer B is wrong because the wrong interface is being used. Answer D is wrong because it is using the wrong syntax. Finally, Answer E is incorrect because it is using the wrong subnet mask.
6. Answer D is correct. A default route has 0.0.0.0 for the network and 0.0.0.0 for the mask to specify any network and any mask. Answers A and B are incorrect because they are not valid commands. Answer C is incorrect because it is missing a subnet mask. Answer E is incorrect because it is using the wrong subnet mask value.
7. Answer C is correct. RIP has the highest administrative distance so it is the least preferred routing information source. Answers A, B, and D are incorrect because their administrative distances are lower than that of RIP.

8. Answer A is correct. The network statement matches 10.0.32.32/27, but the actual network is 10.0.23.32/27. There is nothing wrong with the rest of the configuration, so Answers B, C, D, and E are all incorrect.

9. Answer E is correct. This is a tricky one that requires a process of elimination. Answers A and B are incorrect because the wildcard masks are correct for the networks on those interfaces. Answer C is incorrect because a router's process ID is unique to that router and can be different from other routers. Answer D is incorrect because it is in area 0 and it is connected to another router (Botswana) that also has an attached interface (Fa0/1) in area 0. For answer E, you have to compare the Tanzania configuration, which has its FastEthernet0/0 in area 2. You must be in the same area as the interface that you are attaching to and these areas do not match. Either Tanzania or Ukraine has the incorrect area, but nothing in the diagram or output will tell you which router is improperly configured. However, by using process of elimination you can eliminate the other wrong answers and are left with only Answer E as the correct answer. Ruling out the wrong answers is a great technique to use on the exam if you get stuck.

10. Answer D is correct. The rules of OSPF state that all areas must have a connection to the backbone area 0. In this configuration, Tanzania has its FastEthernet0/1 interface in area 3 and its FastEthernet0/0 interface in area 2. Area 2 is connected to the Ukraine, which has a connection to area 0. However, area 3 does not have a connection to area 0. There is nothing wrong with the remaining configuration, so Answers A, B, C, and E are all incorrect.

CHAPTER EIGHT

Visualizing Data Flow Between Two Hosts on a Network

This chapter covers the following official CCNA Routing and Switching 200-120 exam topics:

- ▶ Recognize the purpose and functions of various network devices such as routers, switches, bridges, and hubs.
- ▶ Describe the purpose and basic operation of the protocols in the OSI and TCP/IP models.
- ▶ Predict the data flow between two hosts across a network.
- ▶ Describe the technological requirements for running IPv6 in conjunction with IPv4 such as dual stack.

Imagine opening up the hood of your car and listening to the engine. As you listen closely, you hear a slight tick tick tick as the belt moves along the pulleys. Now here's the question: Is that a problem or is that normal? Without knowledge of what that engine is supposed to sound like, we really don't know about that sound that we're hearing. When designing, configuring, or troubleshooting a computer network, being able to predict what the data looks like as it passes over various parts of our network and how all those networked devices will interact with those packets and frames of data is an important skill. In this chapter, we take an inside look at the details of packets and frames as they move across the network.

Host-to-Host Direct Communications

CramSaver

If you can correctly answer these questions before going through this section, save time by skimming the Exam Alerts in this section and then completing the Cram Quiz at the end of the section.

1. What protocol would be the first one used if two computers, connected via an Ethernet crossover cable, were just powered on and were going to send an IPv4 pint packet to the other?
2. What is the protocol used in IPv6 to learn the Layer 2 MAC address of another host that is on the same network?

Answers

1. Computers would need to learn the Layer 3 to Layer 2 mappings for each other (IP to MAC address mappings) before the PING could begin. If these computers were just powered on, they wouldn't have those mappings for each other yet and the first protocol they would use is ARP (Address Resolution Protocol), to learn those addresses from each other.
2. IPv6 uses the Neighbor Discovery Protocol (NDP) to learn the Layer 3 to Layer 2 mappings for other devices in the same network that they want to communicate with. ARP is not used in IPv6.

Let's begin by considering the topology with two computers, directly connected, as shown in Figure 8.1.

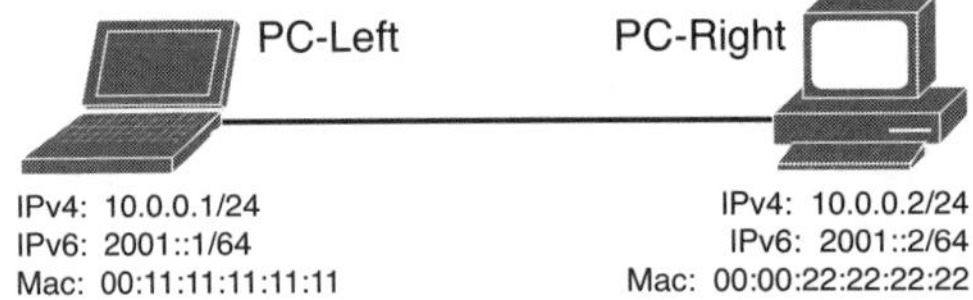

FIGURE 8.1 **Two computers connected via a crossover Ethernet cable.**

We should be prepared to know what the data looks like on the crossover cable connecting the PC on the left to the PC on the right. This will help in troubleshooting and in understanding how to implement network security. For example, if the PC-Left was going to run a Telnet application, to connect to a Telnet server that was running on PC-Right, we should be able to answer the following questions about the Layer 2 headers, Layer 3 headers, and Layer 4 headers:

- What are the Layer 2 source and destination addresses?
- What are the Layer 3 source and destination addresses?
- What are the Layer 4 protocol and destination port number?

We should also anticipate what protocols in addition to Telnet may be used (or needed) for this conversation to occur.

For a direct connection between like devices (in this case, two PCs), we would use a crossover cable that connects the send pair of wires on one end to the receive pair on the other end.

To telnet from the PC on the left to the computer on the right using an IPv4 address, the computers would need to know each other's Layer 2 MAC addresses. This would be done through Address Resolution Protocol (ARP) in IPv4 and would use Neighbor Discovery Protocol (NDP) in IPv6. IPv6 NDP uses Internet Control Message Protocol Version 6 (ICMPv6) for its communications.

Once they know each other's Layer 2 MAC addresses, the PC on the left would send out a frame that includes the information from the wire capture (from a protocol analyzer) of the initial Telnet packet directed to the PC on the right, as shown in Figure 8.2.

```
Ethernet II, Src: Intel_11:11:11 (00:11:11:11:11:11), Dst: VisualTe_22:22:22 (00:00:22:22:22:22)
Internet Protocol Version 4, Src: 10.0.0.1 (10.0.0.1), Dst: 10.0.0.2 (10.0.0.2)
Transmission Control Protocol, Src Port: 25970 (25970), Dst Port: telnet (23), Seq: 0, Len: 0
```

FIGURE 8.2 **Packet capture of IPv4 going to the Telnet server.**

The first row in Figure 8.2 shows the source and destination Layer 2 addresses. The second row shows the source and destination Layer 3 IPv4 addresses. The third row shows the well-known destination TCP port of Telnet, which is 23. The source port would be some high (above number 1023) unused open port that the PC on the left randomly chooses for the TCP session. If this is the very first packet for the TCP session, it would include a synchronization request, as the beginning of a three-way TCP handshake.

If that session had been started using IPv6, the Layer 2 source and destination MAC addresses would be the same, the Layer 3 source and destination IPv6 addresses would be as they are shown in Figure 8.3, and the TCP destination port would still be port 23.

```
Ethernet II, Src: Intel_11:11:11 (00:11:11:11:11:11), Dst: VisualTe_22:22:22 (00:00:22:22:22:22)
Internet Protocol Version 6, Src: 2001::1 (2001::1), Dst: 2001::2 (2001::2)
Transmission Control Protocol, Src Port: 41153 (41153), Dst Port: telnet (23), Seq: 0, Len: 0
```

FIGURE 8.3 **Packet capture of IPv6 going to the Telnet server.**

Once again, for the source port the computer initiating this session would choose some unused high-numbered port and allocate that TCP port for this session.

Reply traffic that is going from the computer on the right back to the computer on the left would show the exact opposite of the addresses and ports regarding source and destination. For example, the return traffic would have the source port of 23 and a destination port of 41153, as well as a source IPv6 address of 2001::2 and a destination IPv6 address of 2001::1.

Cram Quiz

1. What type of cable is required when connecting two similar Ethernet devices together (for example, two routers back to back, or two PCs back to back)?

   ❍ **A.** Null modem cable

   ❍ **B.** Rollover cable

   ❍ **C.** Crossover cable

   ❍ **D.** DTE/DCE cable

2. What is used in IPv4 to resolve the Layer 3 IP address to the Layer 2 MAC address on an Ethernet network?

   ❍ **A.** Neighbor Discovery Protocol (NDP) that uses ICMP for communications

   ❍ **B.** Address Resolution Protocol (ARP)

   ❍ **C.** ICMP

   ❍ **D.** DNS

Cram Quiz Answers

1. Answer C is correct. To connect two like devices together, such as two routers or two PCs or two switches, a crossover cable is needed. This allows the send pair on one end to be linked to the receive pair on the other end. Roll over cables are used for console connections, and DTE/DCE cables are used for serial interfaces, but don't apply to Ethernet.
2. Answer B is correct. IPv4 uses the ARP to identify which Layer 2 MAC addresses are associated with local IPv4 addresses on an Ethernet network. IPv6 uses protocols within NDP to provide a similar resolution between a Layer 3 IPv6 address and a MAC address on the local network. ICMP in IPv4 is not used for the ARP process. DNS is used to map names to IP addresses (for both IPv4 and IPv6 protocols).

Host to Host Through a Switch

CramSaver

If you can correctly answer these questions before going through this section, save time by skimming the Exam Alerts in this section and then completing the Cram Quiz at the end of the section.

1. What changes will a switch make to the Layer 2 source and destination addresses that are in the frames it is forwarding?
2. How does the switch know which ports are associated with which MAC addresses?

Answers

1. The switch doesn't modify any Layer 2 or higher addresses (source or destination) in the frames it forwards.
2. The switch dynamically looks at the Layer 2 source addresses of incoming frames and associates that source address with the port the frame came in on.

Consider the topology shown in Figure 8.4.

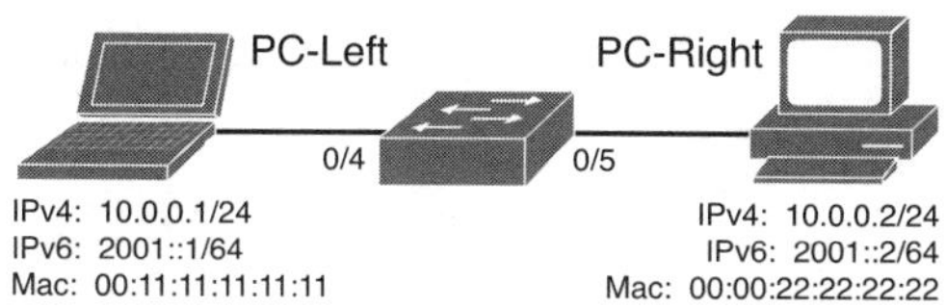

FIGURE 8.4 **Two computers connected using a Layer 2 switch.**

If we use the same scenario with the PC on the left starting a Telnet session to the PC on the right, but this time the PC on the left is connected to port 0/4 on a Layer 2 transparent switch, and the PC on the right is connected to port 0/5 on that same switch, and both switch ports are in the same VLAN, we would expect to see the identical Layer 2, Layer 3, and Layer 4 information in the headers, including some high-numbered unused TCP source port. That's because the transparent switch isn't going to modify the addresses at Layer 2 or anything at Layer 3 or higher.

On the switch, if we issue the command **show mac address-table dynamic**, we see that the switch has learned the source MAC addresses and the associated port, as shown in Example 8.1.

EXAMPLE 8.1 MAC Address Table for Switch Connecting the Two PCs

```
Switch#show mac address-table dynamic

          Mac Address Table

-------------------------------------------

Vlan    Mac Address       Type        Ports

----    -----------       --------    -----

   1    0011.1111.1111    DYNAMIC     Gi0/4

   1    0022.2222.2222    DYNAMIC     Gi0/5
```

Cram Quiz

1. What would be the source L2 address used in a frame sent by a PC on the network.

   ❍ **A.** The PC's default gateway address

   ❍ **B.** The IP address assigned to the PC via DHCP

   ❍ **C.** The router's local Layer 2 address

   ❍ **D.** The PC's MAC address

2. If the destination address in a frame is 00:12:34:56:78:9a, and that frame is sent through a Layer 2 switch, what will be the destination address of that frame as it is forwarded out another interface of that same Layer 2 switch?

   ❍ **A.** It will be the IP address of the default gateway.

   ❍ **B.** It will be the IP address of the management interface of the switch.

   ❍ **C.** It will be the same Layer 2 destination address.

   ❍ **D.** It will be the source address of the Layer 2 switch.

Cram Quiz Answers

1. Answer D is correct. The source address of a Layer 2 frame on Ethernet will be the MAC address of the device that has encapsulated the data and sent it. In the case of a PC that is sending a Layer 2 frame, the source MAC address would be the MAC address of the network interface card on that PC.
2. Answer C is correct. A transparent Layer 2 switch doesn't alter the source or destination Layer 2 addresses (nor does it modify the source or destination Layer 3 IP addresses) for frames that it is forwarding. A transparent switch simply forwards frames based on its MAC address table. Frames with an unknown Layer 2 destination address are flooded out of all other ports in the same VLAN.

Host to Host Through a Router

CramSaver

If you can correctly answer these questions before going through this section, save time by skimming the Exam Alerts in this section and then completing the Cram Quiz at the end of the section.

1. When a local host on subnet A is sending a packet to a remote computer or server located on subnet B, what will the destination MAC address be in the frame sent by the local host?
2. Will a local host use ARP or NDP to resolve the Layer 2 address of a remote host?

Answers

1. The destination address of a Layer 2 frame would be the MAC address of the computer's default gateway.
2. This is a bit of a trick question because local hosts do not need (and won't resolve) the Layer 2 address of a remote (nonlocal network) host. So, neither IPv4's ARP or IPv6's NDP would be used because the local host won't try to resolve the remote Layer 2 address of the destination. A local host would resolve the Layer 2 address of its default gateway, if needed. In IPv4, it would use ARP. In IPv6, it would use NDP.

Consider the topology shown in Figure 8.5.

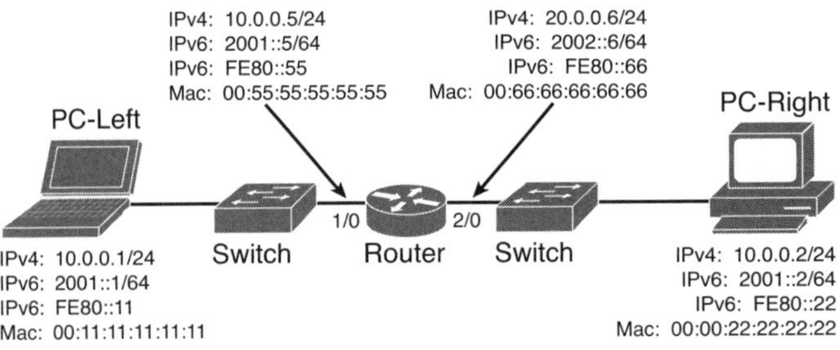

FIGURE 8.5 **Host to host through a router.**

Visualizing the traffic flow between two hosts that are on separate VLANs, or on different IP subnets, is much different than our previous scenarios where both hosts were on the same IP network.

One of the things that is going to change inside the headers as a packet crosses networks is the Layer 2 source and destination addresses. The Layer 2 source and destination addresses are going to change every time we cross a router on the path from the source computer to its final destination.

In this scenario, as shown in Figure 8.5, the PC on the left is going to start a Telnet session from itself to the PC on the far right. If the user knows and is using an IP address for this connection, regardless whether it is IPv4 or IPv6, we do not need to use DNS. If we did need to use DNS (because the user is using a name instead of an IP address), a DNS request (to resolve the name to a Layer 3 address) would be used by the computer that is initiating the Telnet session.

The PC on the left, when attempting to initiate a Telnet session to the computer on the far right looks at the destination IP address of the target and compares that IP address to its own network address. Because the source computer is on the 10.0.0.0/24 network and because the destination's first three octets are not 10.0.0, the computer on the left believes that the target is not on the local subnet. As a result, the PC on the left realizes that it needs to use a default gateway on its own local network to assist it in getting the data moved. It is very likely that the PC on the left learned its default gateway from the DHCP server. At Layer 3, the packet that is about to be sent will have the source IP address of the PC on the left and the destination IP address of the PC on the right. However, at Layer 2, the source Layer 2 address will be the PC on the left's MAC address, and the destination Layer 2 address in the frame about to be sent will be the default gateway Layer 2 address. If the PC on the left does not have that Layer 2 address cached, in IPv4 it will issue an ARP request to resolve that and learn the Layer 2 address of its default gateway. In IPv6, NDP is used for the resolution of the Layer 2 address of the default gateway. With the Layer 2 resolution done, the packet/frame that the computer on the left would send includes the source and destination addresses, as shown in Figure 8.6.

```
Ethernet II, Src: Intel_11:11:11 (00:11:11:11:11:11), Dst: 00:55:55:55:55:55 (00:55:55:55:55:55)
Internet Protocol Version 4, Src: 10.0.0.1 (10.0.0.1), Dst: 20.0.0.2 (20.0.0.2)
Transmission Control Protocol, Src Port: 61691 (61691), Dst Port: telnet (23), Seq: 0, Len: 0
```

FIGURE 8.6 **Packet capture of IPv4 between PC-Left and the router.**

If IPv6 were used, and the Layer 2 resolution was done already (via NDP), the first frame/packet sent by the computer on the left to initiate the Telnet session to the computer on the right would include the Layer 2, Layer 3, and Layer 4 header information similar to what is shown in Figure 8.7.

```
Ethernet II, Src: Intel_11:11:11 (00:11:11:11:11:11), Dst: 00:55:55:55:55:55 (00:55:55:55:55:55)
Internet Protocol Version 6, Src: 2001::1 (2001::1), Dst: 2002::2 (2002::2)
Transmission Control Protocol, Src Port: 59106 (59106), Dst Port: telnet (23), Seq: 0, Len: 0
```

FIGURE 8.7 **Packet capture of IPv6 between PC-Left and the router.**

With either IPv4 or IPv6, the source port would be some high-number, random, unused port number (greater than 1023) selected by the client that is starting the TCP session.

The part that many people guess incorrectly is about the Layer 2 destination address being the address of the default gateway. Layer 2 addresses are only important for communicating the same VLAN or the same subnet. A host on network A will not have any need or reason to learn the Layer 2 address of a host on network B. ARP requests and NDP to learn Layer 2 addresses are always going to be on the local subnet, with regard to learning about local hosts.

Now to get the packet over to the PC on the right, the router also has to do some work. If there were a switch that connected the PC on the left to the router, the frame would be switched based on Layer 2 forwarding, and the switch would forward the frame to the router interface 1/0. When the router receives a frame, it looks at that destination Layer 2 address and recognizes that the destination address is the router's own MAC address on 1/0. As a result, the router decapsulates the frame (removes the Layer 2 header information) to take a look at the Layer 3 IP destination address (which is 20.0.0.2). The router realizes that the destination IP address doesn't belong to the router, but the router does understand by looking at its routing table that it can reach that destination network where the host 20.0.0.2 is connected. In our example, the router is directly connected to the 20.0.0.0/24 network. Because the router is directly connected, if it knows the Layer 2 address of the PC on the right (00:22:22:22:22:22), the router could go ahead and re-encapsulate the packet and include its source Layer 2 address (interface 2/0 of 00:66:66:66:66:66) as the source Layer 2 address and the PC on the right's Layer 2 address (00:22:22:22:22:22) as the destination. This same process is used for IPv4 or IPv6. If the router does not know the Layer 2 address of the PC on the right, it uses ARP in the case of IPv4 and NDP in the case of IPv6 to learn it. When the router sends an IPv4 frame out of its 2/0 interface, the headers at Layers 2, 3, and 4 include the addresses and destination port, as shown in Figure 8.8.

```
Ethernet II, Src: 00:66:66:66:66:66 (00:66:66:66:66:66), Dst: Schaffne_22:22:22 (00:22:22:22:22:22)
Internet Protocol Version 4, Src: 10.0.0.1 (10.0.0.1), Dst: 20.0.0.2 (20.0.0.2)
Transmission Control Protocol, Src Port: 61691 (61691), Dst Port: telnet (23), Seq: 0, Len: 0
```

FIGURE 8.8 **IPv4 packet capture between the router and PC-Right.**

If IPv6 is used, the Layer 2 information about the addresses is similar to what it was in IPv4, but at Layer 3 we have the IPv6 source address of the PC on the left and the IPv6 destination address is the PC on the right, as shown in Figure 8.9. The source and destination Layer 3 (IP) addresses don't change on the path between the source and destination.

```
Ethernet II, Src: 00:66:66:66:66:66 (00:66:66:66:66:66), Dst: Schaffne_22:22:22 (00:22:22:22:22:22)
Internet Protocol Version 6, Src: 2001::1 (2001::1), Dst: 2002::2 (2002::2)
Transmission Control Protocol, Src Port: 59106 (59106), Dst Port: telnet (23), Seq: 0, Len: 0
```

FIGURE 8.9 **IPv6 packet capture between the router and PC-Right.**

Regarding the data moving from the router to PC-Right, the switch receiving a frame from the router makes a Layer 2 forwarding decision and delivers that frame to PC-Right, which when looking at the frame will recognizes its own MAC address as the destination address in the frame and will decapsulate to take a look at the Layer 3 destination address. PC-Right will also recognize this address as belonging to itself, which will cause it to continue to decapsulate and take a look at the Layer 4 information. The requested destination service is TCP port 23, and if PC-Right has a Telnet server running, it can process an acknowledgment back to PC-Left as part of the three-way TCP handshake. The reply traffic has the source and destination addresses and ports reversed or swapped (compared to the initial incoming frame/packet). The Layer 2 addresses change every time the packet crosses a router.

Cram Quiz

1. When a host sends a packet to a remote server, and that packet is routed by two routers (all over Ethernet) before being delivered to the server, how many different Layer 2 destination addresses are used in the entire path between the host and the server?

   ❍ **A.** 1

   ❍ **B.** 2

   ❍ **C.** 3

   ❍ **C.** 4

2. Which Layer 2 destination address (on an Ethernet network) is used by a router delivering a frame to a server that is attached to same subnet as the router?

   ❍ **A.** The server's IP address

   ❍ **B.** The router's MAC address on the interface sending the frame

   ❍ **C.** The router's IP address on the interface sending the frame

   ❍ **D.** The server's MAC address assigned to the network interface card

3. If a Windows host on an Ethernet network has the IP address of 10.67.82.45 255.255.252.0 and tries to send a packet to a server at 10.67.83.46, which Layer 2 address is used as a destination address in the Layer 2 frame sent from the Windows host?

   ❍ **A.** It uses the MAC address of the server.

   ❍ **B.** It uses the MAC address of its default gateway.

   ❍ **C.** It uses the IP address of the server.

   ❍ **D.** It uses the IP address of the default gateway.

Cram Quiz Answers

1. Answer C is correct. The Layer 2 destination of the first router, the second router, and the final server are all used, for a total of three different Layer 2 addresses used.
2. Answer D is correct. The server is the final destination, so the router directly connected to the same subnet as the server uses the server's MAC address as the Layer 2 destination address when encapsulating the frame and sending it toward the server.
3. Answer A is correct. This is a tricky question because you first need to determine whether the server's address is local or remote to the Windows host. The Windows host is on the 10.67.82.0/22 subnet, which has a range of 10.67.82.1 to 10.67.83.254, which means that the server is on the same local subnet. (It is within the same range.) Because the server is local, ARP would be used (if not already cached by the Windows host), and the Layer 2 destination address used in the Layer 2 header would be the MAC address of the server.

Review Questions

Answer these questions. The answers follow the last question. If you cannot answer these questions correctly, consider reading this chapter again until you can.

For all of these questions, the PCs have a correctly configured default gateway for both IPv4 or IPv6, respectively. Refer to Figure 8.10 for all questions (where referenced).

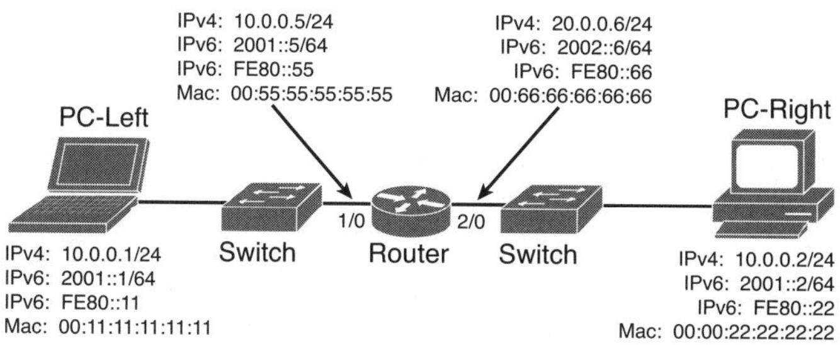

FIGURE 8.10 **Topology for Review Questions.**

1. If the PC on the left is trying to pint the router at 20.0.0.6, which Layer 2 destination Layer 2 address is used in the frame sent by the PC?

   ❍ **A.** FE80::55

   ❍ **B.** 00:55:55:55:55:55

   ❍ **C.** 00:66:66:66:66:66

   ❍ **D.** FE80::66

   ❍ **E.** 2001::5

2. When does a host use ARP or NDP to resolve the Layer 2 address of a server that is not connoted to the same local network as the host?

   ❍ **A.** Whenever the destination IP address is in the same class as the host.

   ❍ **B.** When a default gateway was statically configured the host.

   ❍ **C.** The host won't resolve a remote Layer 2 address.

   ❍ **D.** When the nonlocal Layer 2 mapping isn't already in the ARP cache.

   ❍ **E.** When the nonlocal Layer 2 mapping isn't in the IPv6 neighbor table.

3. What is the source Layer 4 TCP port number for a packet being sent from a Telnet server to a Telnet client?

   ❍ **A.** 23.

   ❍ **B.** The high-numbered port the client originally chose as a source port.

   ❍ **C.** There isn't enough information provided to know for sure.

   ❍ **D.** 1024.

4. Consider the topology in Figure 8.10. What address would be the Layer 2 destination address in a packet being sent from the PC on the right to the PC on the left as it leaves the PC on the right?

   ❍ **A.** 00:11:11:11:11:11

   ❍ **B.** 00:55:55:55:55:55

   ❍ **C.** 00:66:66:66:66:66

   ❍ **D.** 00:22:22:22:22:22

5. PC-Right is sending a packet to PC-Left. As the packet leaves the 1/0 interface of the router, what will the source Layer 3 address be in the packet?

   ❍ **A.** 2002::6

   ❍ **B.** 10.0.0.5

   ❍ **C.** 00:22:22:22:22:22

   ❍ **D.** 2002::2

   ❍ **E.** FE80::5

6. The switch between PC-Left and the router 1/0 interface will modify which of the addresses?

   ❍ **A.** Layer 2 source address, if the frame is being sent from the router to the PC.

   ❍ **B.** Layer 2 destination address, if the frame is being sent from the PC to the router.

   ❍ **C.** Layer 3 source address for any packets being sent from the PC to anywhere else.

   ❍ **D.** No Layer 2 or Layer 3 source or destination addresses will be modified by the switch.

7. PC-Right is attempting to send a ping to the address of 2001::1. Which of the following may happen as a result?

❍ **A.** ARP for 20.0.0.6

❍ **B.** ARP for 10.0.0.1

❍ **C.** ARP for 20.0.0.6 and 10.0.0.1

❍ **D.** NDP for 2002::6

❍ **E.** NDP for 2001::1

❍ **F.** NDP for 2002::6 and 2001::1

8. PC-Left is about to send a packet to 10.0.0.5. Which of the following is true?

❍ **A.** The PC will use NDP to learn the Layer 2 address of the router.

❍ **B.** The PC will consider the destination Layer 3 address to be local.

❍ **C.** The PC will consider the destination Layer 3 address to be remote.

❍ **D.** None of the answers provided are true.

9. When does a device, when it receives an IPv6 packet encapsulated in a frame, decapsulate it?

❍ **A.** Hosts (client computers) always decapsulate packets from frames, regardless of the Layer 2 destination address in the frame.

❍ **B.** It won't. Decapsulation applies only to IPv4.

❍ **C.** It won't, unless the Layer 2 destination address is of interest to the host (such as the destination address matching the receiving host's MAC address).

❍ **D.** When the device is a router, because routers always decapsulate regardless of the Layer 2 destination address in the frame.

10. When a switch receives a frame of data, how does it know which interface to forward the frame out of?

❍ **A.** It generates ARP to dynamically learn the ports where MAC addresses are located.

❍ **B.** It generates NDP neighbor solicitations to learn the ports where MAC addresses are located.

❍ **C.** It uses DHCP snooping as its mechanism to learn where the MAC addresses are located (only when the switch is acting as a DHCP server).

❍ **D.** The switch pays attention to the source MAC addresses in frames as they enter the switch and associates the source MAC address with the port the frame was received on.

Answers to Review Questions

1. Answer B is correct. When the destination IP address is not on the local subnet, the computer uses its default gateway. This involves creating a Layer 2 header that has the destination MAC address of the local router interface as the destination Layer 2 address.
2. Answer C is correct. Computers don't need to learn the Layer 2 address of a device that is not on their local subnet. When trying to reach a remote device, it would need the Layer 2 address of its default gateway.
3. Answer A is correct. When a client connects to a Telnet server, the destination well-known port for Telnet is TCP port 23. A reply packet going back to the client from the server would have a source TCP port number of 23, and the destination TCP port would be the high-numbered port the client shows when it started the TCP session.
4. Answer C is correct. When the PC on the right considers sending a packet to the PC on the left which is in a different IP subnet, it uses its local default gateway to forward the packet. In that process, the PC on the right includes the routers local MAC address as the Layer 2 destination address, which will let the switch forward the frame to the router where the router can decapsulate, making routing decision and re-encapsulate as it forwards the data on to its final destination.
5. Answer D is correct. The Layer 3 addresses do not change between the source and destination. So, as the packet leaves the interface 1/0 of the router on its way to PC-Left, the source IP address will still be the IP address of the PC on the right. Out of all the choices given, the only IP address from the choices (that belong to PC-Right) is 2002::2.
6. Answer D is correct. A Layer 2 transparent switch will never modify the source or destination addresses in any of the frames/packets that are sent through that switch.
7. Answer F is correct. IPv6 uses NDP to resolve Layer 3 to Layer 2 mappings. If not already cached, this would need to be done by the PC on the right for the Layer 2 address of the router. And if not already cached, it would need be done by the router for the Layer 2 address of the PC on the left.
8. Answer B is correct. The PC on the left is on network 10.0.0.0/24 if it was sending a packet to 10.0.0.5. Because the first three octets match its own network address, it would believe the destination is local, and as a result the PC on the left would try to resolve the Layer 2 address of the local address that is using 10.0.0.5. In this case, that happens to be the IP address of the router.
9. Answer C is correct. Computers running either IPv6 or IPv4 won't decapsulate a Layer 2 frame unless that Layer 2 frame is of interest to that device. Interesting layer to destination addresses could include the receiving device's own MAC address, broadcast addresses, and multicast addresses for multicast groups which that device has joined.

10. Answer C is correct. A transparent Layer 2 switch dynamically learns which ports are associated with MAC addresses by paying attention to the source MAC addresses used in frames that are received on the switch ports. It stores these dynamic entries in its MAC address table. When a frame enters the switch, the switch uses its MAC address table to determine which interface (associated with the destination MAC address) to forward on. Frames that are unknown (not in the table, which include broadcast and multicast destination frames) are forwarded to all other ports that are associated with the same VLAN.

What Next?

If you want more practice on this chapter's exam topics before you move on, remember that you can access all of the Cram Quiz questions on the CD. You can also create a custom exam by topic with the practice exam software. Note any topic you struggle with and go to that topic's material in this chapter.

CHAPTER NINE

IP Access Lists

This chapter covers the following officialCCNA Routing and Switching 200-120 exam topics:

- Describe the types, features, and applications of ACLs.
- Named IP ACLs.
- Numbered IP ACLs.
- Log option.
- Configure and verify ACLs in a network environment.
- Behavior of the different components when the license server is lost.
- How to install the license server.

Access control lists (ACLs) have many uses on Cisco routers. This chapter describes their use as packet filters by which you can filter traffic coming from one network into another. However, keep in mind that an ACL can also be used for the following purposes:

- **Classifying and organizing traffic for quality of service:** You can use an ACL to categorize and prioritize your traffic with quality of service (QoS).
- **Filtering routing updates:** ACLs can be used with routing protocols to control what networks are advertised. Routing protocols are discussed further in Chapter 7, "Basic Routing," and in Chapter 13, "Advanced Router Operation."
- **Defining interesting traffic for dial-on-demand routing (DDR):** ACLs can be used to configure what traffic will dial a remote router when using Integrated Services Digital Network (ISDN).
- **Network Address Translation (NAT):** ACLs are used to identify inside local addresses when configuring NAT. NAT is discussed in greater detail in Chapter 16, Advanced Troubleshooting."

ExamAlert

This chapter focuses on using ACLs as packet filters, but make sure that you do not forget that ACLs are used for a lot more than just packet filtering. The exam will test your knowledge of the various uses of ACLs.

IP Access Lists as Packet Filters

CramSaver

1. Which of the following are possible uses for access lists? Choose all that apply.
   - **A.** To authenticate network users
   - **B.** To perform data encryption
   - **C.** To classify traffic for QoS
   - **D.** To filter traffic as it enters or leaves a router
   - **E.** To identify "interesting" traffic for NAT
   - **F.** To enhance the security of vty lines

2. Which of the following statements are true, when considering the best-practices guidelines for implementing ACLs as traffic filters on an interface? Choose 2.
   - **A.** Standard IP ACLs should be placed as close to the source of traffic as possible.
   - **B.** Standard IP ACLs should be placed as close to the destination of traffic as possible.
   - **C.** Extended IP ACLs should be placed as close to the source of traffic as possible.
   - **D.** Extended IP ACLs should be placed as close to the destination of traffic as possible.

Answers

1. Answers C, D, E, and F are correct. A is incorrect; ACLs do not perform user authentication. B is incorrect; the ACL does not perform data encryption. You could argue that an ACL can identify interesting traffic that would be encrypted by a VPN, but that's too much of a stretch for this question.
2. Answers B and C are correct. Because standard lists have so little precision, putting them near the source can filter more traffic than desired. Extended lists, being very precise, can filter exactly what you want and are consequently better placed near the source to avoid needlessly routing traffic only to drop it later.

When used as a packet filter, ACLs can be used to filter traffic as it passes through a router. For example, suppose that Andrew wants to block Mike from being able to communicate to the web server (see Figure 9.1).

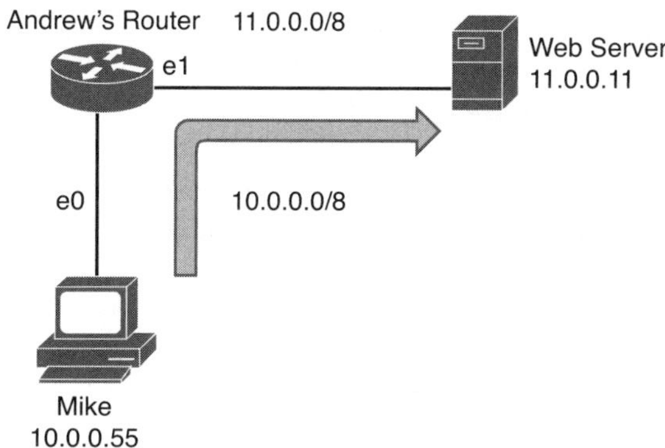

FIGURE 9.1 **ACL example.**

Andrew could go on his router and configure an ACL that would prevent Mike from communicating to the server while allowing all other traffic to pass through the router. ACLs then get applied on an interface in the inbound or outbound direction. When applied inbound, you are filtering as the traffic comes into the incoming interface on the router. When applied in the outbound direction, you are filtering traffic as it leaves the outgoing interface.

In Figure 9.1, the ACL can be applied inbound on Ethernet 0 or outbound on Ethernet 1. This is because Mike's traffic would come inbound on Ethernet 0 and exit on Ethernet 1. If applied inbound on interface Ethernet 0, the ACL would filter the traffic before the router could examine its routing table to determine the outgoing interface; if applied outbound on Ethernet 1, the ACL would filter Mike's traffic after the router looked in its routing table and forwarded the traffic to Ethernet 1. Later in this chapter, you learn some general rules about where you should apply ACLs.

No matter where you apply the ACL, the list will process the packets and check them against your list in the order that you put the statements in. For this reason, you must be careful about the order of the statements. After you have configured your ACL, there is no way to reorder your statements. If Figure 9.1 is our example, and if you wanted to prevent Mike from accessing the web server but allow everyone else on the 10.0.0.0/8 network to access the web server, your ACL would need statements to first deny Mike's computer and then allow everyone else on the network.

ACLs test each packet, going through the rules in top-down order. If the first rule does not match, the second is tested, until a rule is exactly matched. When a rule matches, its "permit" or "deny" action is taken immediately, and no further rules are tested. If the packet is checked against each entry in the ACL and there is no match, the default action is to drop the packet, because there is an implicit deny any at the end of every ACL that will drop any packet that does not match an entry in the ACL. Therefore, all traffic is denied except for what you explicitly permit. Figure 9.2 illustrates the logic of an access list that is configured to first deny Mike's computer at 10.0.0.55 and then permit all other traffic from the 10.0.0.0/8 network. (The syntax for this list is shown later in the chapter.)

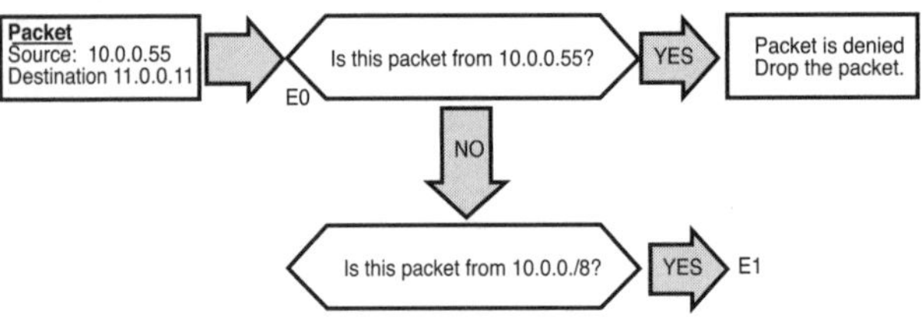

FIGURE 9.2 **ACL logic.**

If the order of ACL statements were reversed, and you first permitted the 10.0.0.0/8 network and then denied Mike, Mike would never be denied because the ACL would check Mike's packet and see that he belongs to the 10.0.0.0/8 network and is therefore permitted. The ACL would never get to the deny statement. Figure 9.3 illustrates the logic behind a poorly written ACL that first permitted the 10.0.0.0/8 network and then denied Mike's computer.

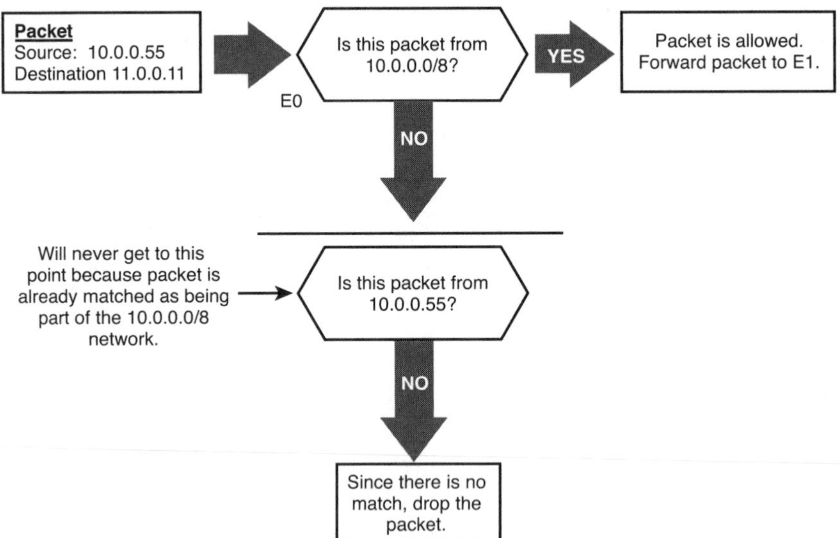

FIGURE 9.3 **ACL logic of a poorly designed access list.**

Likewise, if your ACL denied Mike's computer but did not permit the rest of the network, any other traffic would be denied because it was not implicitly permitted. You must have at least one permit statement in your ACL. If you do not, all traffic is dropped by the ACL.

Types of ACLs

The previous examples illustrate the use of IP ACLs. You can create many types of ACLs, including IP, AppleTalk, IPX, MAC addresses, NetBIOS, and other protocols. However, for the CCENT exam, you can breathe a sigh of relief because you only need to be familiar with configuring and troubleshooting IP ACLs.

No matter what type of ACL you use, though, you can have only one ACL per protocol, per interface, per direction. For example, you can have one IP ACL inbound on an interface and another IP ACL outbound on an interface, but you cannot have two inbound IP ACLs on the same interface.

The two types of IP ACLs that you can configure are as follows:

- Standard IP ACLs
- Extended IP ACLs

When you create an access list, you assign it either a number or a name. (Named lists are discussed a little later.) There are predefined ranges for each type of access list. Table 9.1 shows the predefined ranges for IP standard and extended ACLs.

TABLE 9.1 **Access List Ranges**

Type	Range
IP standard	1–99
IP extended	100–199
IP standard expanded	1300–1999
IP extended expanded	2000–2699

Standard ACLs

A standard IP ACL is simple; it filters based on source address only. You can filter a source network or a source host, but you cannot filter based on the destination of a packet, the particular protocol being used such as the

Transmission Control Protocol (TCP) or the User Datagram Protocol (UDP), or on the port number. You can permit or deny only source traffic. This is analogous to entering a new country and having customs only check your passport to verify that you (being the source) are allowed to pass through customs.

Extended ACLs

An extended ACL gives you much more power than just a standard ACL. With an extended ACL, you can filter your traffic based on any of the following criteria:

- Source address
- Destination address
- Protocol—TCP, UDP, Internet Control Messaging Protocol (ICMP), and so on
- Source port (if using TCP or UDP)
- Destination port (if protocol is TCP or UDP)
- ICMP message (if protocol is ICMP)

An IP extended access list is analogous to passing through customs, but this time the customs agent verifies not only your identity, but also asks about your destination and the purpose of your stay.

Named ACLs

One of the disadvantages of using IP standard and IP extended ACLs is that you reference them by number, which is not too descriptive of their use. With a named ACL, this is not the case because you can name your ACL with a descriptive name. The ACL named DenyMike is a lot more meaningful than an ACL simply numbered 1. There are both IP standard and IP extended named ACLs.

Another advantage to named ACLs is that they allow you to remove individual lines out of an ACL. With numbered ACLs, you cannot delete individual statements. Instead, you have to delete your existing access list and re-create the entire list.

Cram Quiz

1. Which of the following are attributes of standard IP ACLs?

    ❍ **A.** Numbered range 1 to 99

    ❍ **B.** Numbered range 100 to 199

    ❍ **C.** Filter based on destination IP

    ❍ **D.** Filter based on source IP

    ❍ **E.** Can selectively permit or deny individual protocols such as ICMP, TCP, UDP, and so on

    ❍ **F.** Permit or deny only the entire IP protocol

2. Which of the following are advantages of named IP ACLs? Choose all that apply.

    ❍ **A.** Because all named IP ACLs are extended, traffic filtering is more precise.

    ❍ **B.** Individual ACL lines can be added or removed at any point in the ACL using the command line.

    ❍ **C.** Creating a named ACL requires fewer command lines.

    ❍ **D.** Named ACLs can be given a name that describes what function they perform.

3. Duncan instructs you to create IP access list 10 to block ICMP Echo from reaching the server at 10.1.1.8. You tell him that you cannot. Why can't you?

    ❍ **A.** Because ACLs cannot block ICMP Echo

    ❍ **B.** Because an ICMP ACL is required instead

    ❍ **C.** Because a named ACL is required to block ICMP Echo

    ❍ **D.** Because IP ACL 10 is a standard IP ACL, which cannot match on the ICMP Echo protocol

Cram Quiz Answers

1. Answers A, D, and F are correct. Standard IP ACLs use the number range 1 to 99, filter based on source IP only, and permit or deny the entire IP protocol, not subprotocols.
2. Answers B and D are correct. Named ACLS allow adding or removing an individual line at the CLI; numbered lists only allow adding an additional line at the bottom of the list. Answer A is incorrect: A named list may be either standard or extended. Answer C is wrong; making a named list actually takes more command lines.
3. Answer D is correct. IP ACL 10 is in the standard range, so it cannot filter based on protocol or destination. Answer A is wrong; extended ACLs can block ICMP Echo. Answer B is incorrect; there is no such thing as an ICMP ACL. Answer C is wrong; A numbered extended ACL can block ICMP Echo.

Configuring and Implementing

CramSaver

1. What is wrong with the following syntax? Choose all that apply.

```
access-list 1 deny tcp 10.1.1.8 0.0.0.0 host 192.168.1.5 eq
tftp
```

   A. Nothing; the config line is correct.

   B. The ACL number is not in the extended range.

   C. The ACL number is correct but the operand **tftp** is invalid.

   D. The list denies TCP but TFTP uses UDP.

   E. The syntax “host 192.168.1.5” is invalid.

   F. The mask of 0.0.0.0 is invalid.

2. What will the following access list do?

```
access-list 100 deny tcp host 10.1.1.1 192.168.1.0 0.0.0.255
eq 23 access-list 100 deny
tcp 10.1.1.1 0.0.0.0 192.168.1.0 0.0.0.255 eq ftp
access-list 100 deny tcp
10.1.1.1 0.0.0.0192.168.1.0 0.0.0.255 eq ftp-data
access-list 100 deny udp any any eq 69
```

   A. Block Telnet traffic from 10.1.1.1 to the 192.168.1.0 network.

   B. Block TCP traffic from 10.1.1.1 to the 192.168.1.0 network with the destination port of 20.

   C. Block TCP traffic from 10.1.1.1 to the 192.168.1.0 network with the destination port of 21.

   D. Block all hosts from using TFTP to reach any host.

   E. Deny all traffic.

3. Duncan wants to prevent you from using Telnet to reach the router at 172.16.20.254. He creates the following ACL and applies it inbound to all router interfaces:

```
access-list 172 deny tcp any eq 23 host 172.16.20.254 permit
ip any any
```

   Did Duncan achieve his objective?

   A. Yes, he blocked all traffic.

   B. Yes, he blocked Telnet but not Telnet-Data.

   C. No, he failed to block Telnet to the router.

   D. No, he blocked Telnet only to one interface of the router.

Answers

1. Answers B and D are correct. Answer A is wrong for several reasons explained here. Answer C is wrong because the ACL number must be in the extended range to filter on specific protocol and destination. Answers E and F are incorrect; that syntax is valid in both cases.
2. Answer E is correct. Although all the other answers are correct, too, this is a classic case of "choose the best answer." An IP ACL with no "permit" line denies all traffic.
3. Answer C is correct. Answer A is incorrect because he has **permit ip any any** in the list. Answer B is incorrect; there is no such thing as Telnet-Data. Answer D is tricky: Because he named only one interface, he might well have blocked only that interface from Telnet, except that the list does not block Telnet as desired because the **eq 23** operator/operand is in the source, not the destination clause.

In this next section, you learn how to configure standard, extended, and named ACLs.

Configuring Standard ACLs

Because a standard access list filters only traffic based on source traffic, all you need is the IP address of the host or subnet you want to permit or deny. ACLs are created in global configuration mode and then applied on an interface. The syntax for creating a standard ACL is as follows:

```
access-list {1-99 | 1300-1999} {permit | deny} <source-address>
[wildcard-mask]
```

For example, if you want to deny Mike's computer at 10.0.0.55 but permit all other hosts on the 10.0.0.0/8 network, you configure the following ACL:

```
Router(config)#access-list 1 deny 10.0.0.55 0.0.0.0
Router(config)#access-list 1 permit 10.0.0.0 0.255.255.255
```

Next, you need to apply the access list on an interface. Because you have no way of specifying the destination or application of your traffic, you should apply the access list as close to the destination as possible. Given Figure 9.1 as our example, interface Ethernet 1 is closest to the destination (the web server). Traffic is leaving this interface heading for the web server, so you should apply this access list outbound on Ethernet 1. The syntax for applying your IP access list on an interface is as follows:

```
ip access-group {number | name} {in | out}
```

Because you want to apply this access list outbound on Ethernet 1, the syntax from global configuration is as follows:

```
Router(config)#interface ethernet 1
Router(config-if)#ip access-group 1 out
```

The Wildcard Mask

Wildcard masks define how much of an address needs to be looked at for there to be a match. For example, in the previous example, you wanted to deny Mike's computer (10.0.0.55) but allow all other hosts on that network (10.0.0.0/8). So, you want the router to check every bit of the source address as it passes through the router to verify that it matches the complete address 10.0.0.55. Therefore, you need a wildcard mask that tells your router to check every bit. For matching the 10.0.0.0/8 network, however, you need only your router to check the first 8 bits because you need to check only the network portion (the 10.0.0.0/8 network) and the source host address will vary.

Wildcard masks use 0s to designate what bits you want to match and 1s to designate those bits that you do not want the router to examine. If you want to match the 10.0.0.55 host, you need the wildcard mask of all 0s to indicate to your router that it needs to check every bit to verify that it matches 10.0.0.55 exactly. This would be a wildcard mask of 0.0.0.0. If you want to match the 10.0.0.0/8 network, your wildcard mask would be all 0s in the first octet to match the 10 network and all 1s in the remaining 24 bits to tell your router not to examine the host bits. This wildcard mask, shown in Figure 9.4, would be 0.255.255.255.

Let's review the syntax you saw earlier. The complete commands to create and apply the ACL are as follows:

```
Router(config)#access-list 1 deny 10.0.0.55 0.0.0.0
Router(config)#access-list 1 permit 10.0.0.0 0.255.255.255
Router(config)#interface ethernet 1
Router(config-if)#ip access-group 1 out
```

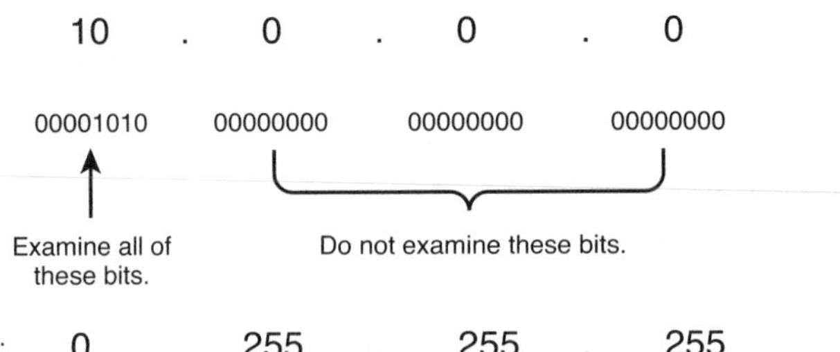

FIGURE 9.4 **Wildcard mask for 10.0.0.0/8.**

This example shows matching a default Class A network. If you want instead to match a default Class B network, the wildcard mask is 0.0.255.255 to match the first two octets. If you want to match a default Class C network, the wildcard mask is 0.0.0.255. Notice that the wildcard mask, when used to match a network, is the inverse of the subnet mask. For this reason, the wildcard mask is often called the *inverse mask*.

Now look at what happens when you begin subnetting your networks. Take the 192.168.12.64/28 network, for example. This is a subnetted Class C network, which falls on the 16-bit boundary in the last octet. You need to match the first three octets entirely and the first 4 bits of the last octet because they compose the network portion of this address. By writing out the subnetwork and drawing a line at the bit boundary, you can determine how many 0s and 1s you need to make up the wildcard mask. Adding up the 1s in binary gives you the final wildcard mask of 0.0.0.15 to match the 192.168.12.64 subnetwork.

```
Increments:    128 64 32 16  | 8 4 2 1
Subnetwork       0  1  0  0  | 0 0 0 0
Wildcard mask  0   0  0   0  | 1 1 1 1
```

If you dislike working with binary and want a shortcut, you can also take the original subnet mask and subtract it from 255.255.255.255. In this example, the subnet mask would be 255.255.255.240 (/28). Subtracting this from 255.255.255.255 gives you the wildcard mask of 0.0.0.15.

Note at this point that the wildcard mask does not care about or actually recognize subnets; it is simply doing a bit-for-bit match between the packet IP (source/destination) and the ACL rule entry. We can certainly define a wildcard mask that will match every IP in a given subnet and nothing else, but the key here is that the ACL rule matches a range of IP addresses (whether they represent a subnet or a group of IPs in a larger network). For example, 192.168.1.16 0.0.0.15 matches the range of 192.168.1.16 to 192.168.1.31 inclusive (16 hosts), regardless of whether they are on that subnet or part of the group of 254 hosts in the 192.168.1.0/24 classful network.

Sometimes you do not want to match a network or subnet, such as when you want to match a specific host or, on the other extreme, permit or deny every host regardless of their network. You can use special wildcard masks and keywords to refer to these unique situations.

To match a specific host such as 10.0.0.55, you need the router to examine every bit. This can be represented with the wildcard mask of 0.0.0.0. Alternatively, you can use the keyword **host** before the host address and not specify any wildcard mask. Thus, the following two commands accomplish the same thing:

```
Router(config)#access-list 1 deny 10.0.0.55 0.0.0.0
Router(config)#access-list 1 deny host 10.0.0.55
```

If you want to match all hosts regardless of the network they are on, you can use the designation of an unspecified network (0.0.0.0) with a wildcard mask that does not examine any bits (255.255.255.255). Alternatively, you can use the keyword **any**. The following two commands are functionally equivalent:

```
Router(config)#access-list 1 permit 0.0.0.0 255.255.255.255
Router(config)#access-list 1 permit any
```

Configuring Extended ACLs

As mentioned earlier, extended ACLs allow you to filter based on the following criteria:

- Source address
- Destination address
- Protocol (IP, TCP, UDP, ICMP, and so on)
- Source port (if TCP or UDP is the protocol)
- Destination port (if TCP or UDP is the protocol)
- ICMP message (if ICMP is the protocol)

The syntax of the command varies slightly if you are filtering for general IP traffic, TCP/UDP ports, or ICMP messages. For just filtering IP traffic, the syntax is as follows:

```
access-list access-list-number {deny | permit}  ip source source-
wildcard destination destination-wildcard
```

For example, if you want to prevent all IP traffic coming from the host 10.0.0.55 to a server with the address of 11.0.0.11 while allowing all other traffic on the 10.0.0.0/8 to access the server, you use the following syntax:

```
Router(config)#access-list 100 deny ip host 10.0.0.55 host 11.0.0.11
Router(config)#access-list 100 permit ip 10.0.0.0 0.255.255.255 host
11.0.0.11
```

Note the use of the keyword **host** before 10.0.0.55 and 11.0.0.11. This is equivalent to using a wildcard mask of 0.0.0.0.

Because you can specify both the source and destination in the extended ACL, you generally want to apply an IP extended ACL as close to the source as possible so that it is filtered as soon as possible. Using Figure 9.1 as our example, you would apply the access list inbound on interface Ethernet 0 because that is closest to the source of your traffic. The syntax for this is as follows:

```
Router(config)#interface ethernet 0
Router(config-if)#ip access-group 100 in
```

You can also filter based on TCP or UDP port number. The syntax for filtering based on port number is the same but, instead of IP, you specify if the traffic is TCP or UDP and what the port numbers are. You have the option of specifying source ports and destination ports. Remember, if you are filtering traffic going to a destination, you are going to filter based only on the destination port number and not the source port. Because source ports are typically dynamically assigned, it is not as common to specify the source port number. The syntax for an IP extended ACL that filters TCP or UDP ports is as follows:

```
access-list access-list-number {deny | permit} {tcp | udp} source
source-wildcard [operator [port-number(s)]] destination
destination-wildcard [operator [port-number(s)].
```

Common operator values include the following:

- **eq:** Match any traffic that equals this port number.
- **gt:** Match any traffic that is greater than this port number.
- **lt:** Match any traffic that is less than this port number.
- **range:** Match any traffic within this range of port numbers (requires you to specify a beginning and ending port number).

For the port number, you can either enter the port number or enter the keyword for that protocol. Cisco routers provide keywords for many common protocols such as WWW, FTP, FTP-Data, Telnet, and more.

Using Figure 9.1 again as our example, you can configure an extended ACL to prevent Mike's computer at 10.0.0.55 from sending web traffic to the web server at 11.0.0.11 while allowing everyone else on the 10.0.0.0/8 network web access to the web server. Because this is an IP extended ACL, you apply it closest to the source as possible, which would be inbound on interface Ethernet 0. The syntax for this ACL is as follows:

```
Router(config)#access-list 100 deny tcp host 10.0.0.55 host
11.0.0.11 eq 80
```

```
Router(config)#access-list 100 permit tcp 10.0.0.0 0.255.255.255 host
11.0.0.11 eq 80
Router(config)#interface ethernet 0
Router(config-if)#ip access-group 100 in
```

For ICMP, the syntax is similar, except now you have the option of specifying an ICMP message. The two most common ICMP messages (and the ones to know for the exam) are Echo and Echo Replies. These messages are used when sending pings to a host. Echo, sometimes called an Echo Request, is sent by the sending host, and Echo Replies are sent by the recipient of the ping message to indicate that the host is up. The syntax for an IP extended ACL that filters ICMP is as follows:

```
access-list access-list-number {deny | permit}  icmp source
source-wildcard destination destination-wildcard [ICMP code |
message].
```

Because many computer attacks use ICMP (such as the Ping-of-Death denial-of-service attack and ICMP tunneling), it is common for network administrators to block ICMP at their perimeter firewall. ICMP is a helpful tool for troubleshooting, however, so some administrators like to block only ICMP Echo (ICMP type 8) messages from coming into their networks but still allow Echo Replies (ICMP type 0) in. This configuration allows them to ping outbound and get an Echo Reply back, but prevents others from pinging into their network. For example, if you want to block ICMP Echo messages from the 10.0.0.0/8 network from going to the destination network of 11.0.0.0/8 while allowing all other IP traffic from anywhere to anywhere, you use the following syntax:

```
Router(config)#access-list 100 deny icmp 10.0.0.0 0.255.255.255
11.0.0.0 0.255.255.255 echo
Router(config)#access-list 100 permit ip any any
Router(config)#interface ethernet 0
Router(config-if)#ip access-group 100 in
```

This ACL blocks all ICMP type 8 Echo messages from entering into the 11.0.0.0/8 network while allowing all other traffic. Note that in this example if ICMP pings are coming from any other network to the 11.0.0.0/8 network, they would be allowed; only the 10.0.0.0/8 network is prevented from sending pings to the 11.0.0.0/8 network in this example.

Filtering Telnet and SSH Access

The ACLs shown so far help you to filter traffic as it passes through the router. In this next example, you learn how to filter traffic to the router itself.

Routers are a critical component of any network. If a malicious hacker were to compromise one of your routers, he could reconfigure it to prevent anyone from being able to communicate across your enterprise. Therefore, it is common to use ACLs to control who is allowed Telnet or Secure Shell (SSH) access to your router.

For example, if you want to allow only Mike the ability to telnet or SSH to Andrew's router (see Figure 9.1) but prevent everyone else access, you could create an ACL that allows only Mike's IP address (10.0.0.55). Remember, you do not need to add a statement to block everyone else, because all traffic is denied by default unless it is explicitly permitted. Because you are controlling Telnet and SSH access to the router and not traffic passing through the router, you need to apply your ACL on the virtual teletype (vty) lines and not on an interface. Because vty lines are used for remote connectivity to your router and are therefore inherently Telnet (TCP port 23) and SSH (TCP port 22) traffic, you do not need an extended ACL. Instead, use an IP standard ACL to control what source hosts are allowed Telnet and SSH access to your router. To allow Mike's computer (10.0.0.10) Telnet or SSH access but deny everyone else, use the following syntax:

```
Router(config)#access-list 1 permit host 10.0.0.55
```

Applying this ACL is different from how you applied ACLs on an interface. When applying an ACL on a vty line, the syntax is as follows:

```
Router(config-line)#access-class access-list-number {in | out}
```

Because you are controlling Telnet and SSH access to the router, you should apply this ACL inbound on the vty lines. The complete syntax to create this access list and apply it on all five vty lines is as follows:

```
Router(config)#access-list 1 permit host 10.0.0.55
Router(config)#line vty 0 4
Router(config-line)#access-class 1 in
```

Advanced vty Access List Options

In the previous section, you learned how to permit or deny Telnet or SSH access to your router. You can specify whether you are using SSH or Telnet on your vty line with the **transport input** command. For example, if you want to allow only SSH access, type the following command from the vty line:

```
Router(config-line)#transport input ssh
```

If you want to allow both SSH and Telnet, type the following:

```
Router(config-line)#trasnport input telnet ssh
```

You can even go so far as to specify certain hosts SSH access while others are allowed Telnet access by using extended access lists. For example, if you want to allow the 10.0.0.5 host SSH access but allow the 10.0.0.6 Telnet access, you can use the following access list:

```
Router(config)#access-list 100 permit tcp host 10.0.0.5 any eq 22
Router(config)#access-list 100 permit tcp host 10.0.0.6 any eq 23
Router(config)#line vty 0 4
Router(config-line)#access-class 100 in
```

Notice that you do not need to specify the destination address in the access list because the router itself is the destination.

You should see now that extended access lists are very flexible. Be careful, though, because an ACL on a vty line could leave you locked out of your own router if you mistype an IP address. If you have ever locked yourself out of your house or car, you know the feeling.

Advanced Options

You can add a few additional keywords to the end of an ACL to enable advanced options:

- **log**
- **log-input**
- **established**

The **log** keyword, when added to the end of an ACL, logs the source and destination addresses, the protocol and port every time a match is made. If you log to buffered memory (enabled with the global configuration command **logging buffered**), you can view these log entries with the command **show logging**. The logging is limited, however, because it logs only the first packet and then logs again in 5-minute intervals. The log option is available for both standard and extended ACLs.

The **log-input** keyword is similar to the **log** keyword, but it also logs the Layer 2 address of the source host being matched. In the case of Ethernet networks, this would be the MAC address. The **log-input** keyword can be added only to the end of extended ACLs.

The **established** keyword is another advanced feature that will allow traffic through only if it sees that a TCP session is already established. A TCP session is considered established if the three-way handshake is initiated first. This keyword is added only to the end of extended ACLs that are filtering TCP traffic.

You can use TCP established to deny all traffic into your network except for incoming traffic that was first initiated from inside your network. This is commonly used to block all originating traffic from the Internet into a company's network except for Internet traffic that was first initiated from users inside the company. The following configuration would accomplish this for all TCP-based traffic coming in to interface serial 0/0 on the router:

```
access-list 100 permit tcp any any  established
interface serial 0/0
 ip access-group 100 in
```

Although the access list is using a permit statement, all traffic is denied unless it is first established from the inside network. If the router sees that the ACK flag is set in inbound packets (meaning that it is part of an already-established TCP session), it will then begin to allow traffic through.

Configuring Named ACLs

Up to this point, you have learned how to configure numbered ACLs. This section teaches you how to configure named ACLs.

As mentioned earlier, named ACLs provide the benefit of using descriptive names for your ACLs and the capability to both add (at any position in the list) and remove individual lines. If you attempt to remove an individual line from a numbered access list, it will delete the entire list; with named ACLs, this is not the case. You can add a line at any point you want, or delete any line from the list, all without duplicating or deleting the list itself.

The syntax for named ACLs is similar to that of numbered lists. Instead of using a number, you will give it a name. Remember, though, that the number indicates what type of access list you are using (IP, IPX, and so on) and whether it is standard or extended. Because you are using a named ACL, you will need to configure your router so that it knows what type of ACL you want to create and whether it is to be standard or extended. The syntax for an IP named ACL is as follows:

```
ip access-list {standard | extended}  name
```

After entering this global configuration command, you are presented with the named access control list (NACL) mode, where you can enter your permit or deny statements.

For example, to create an extended NACL called DenyMike that blocks the host 10.0.0.55 from sending web traffic (TCP port 80) to the web server at 11.0.0.11 but allows everyone else, you use the following syntax:

```
Router(config)#ip access-list extended DenyMike
Router(config-ext-nacl)#deny tcp host 10.0.0.55 host 11.0.0.11 eq 80
Router(config-ext-nacl)#permit ip any any
Router(config-ext-nacl)#interface ethernet 0
Router(config-if)#ip access-group DenyMike in
```

Named ACLs provide clarity through descriptive names and ease of configuration because of the capability of both inserting and deleting individual lines. Although named ACLs might be more attractive for real-world usage, make sure that you feel comfortable with numbered ACLs as well.

Cram Quiz

1. Which ACL configuration will prevent the host at 192.168.1.11 from using Telnet to reach the server at 10.11.11.11, while allowing all other traffic? (Consider only the ACL syntax; assume that the ACL has been applied correctly to the appropriate interface in the appropriate direction.)

   ❍ **A.** **access-list 99 deny host 192.168.1.11 access-list 99 permit any**

   ❍ **B.** **access-list 101 deny tcp 10.11.11.11 0.0.0.0 192.168.1.11 0.0.0.0 eq 23 access-list 101 permit ip any any**

   ❍ **C.** **access-list 101 deny tcp host 192.168.1.11 host 10.11.11.11 eq 23 access-list 101 permit ip any any**

   ❍ **D.** **access-list 101 permit ip any any access-list 101 deny tcp 192.168.1.11 0.0.0.0 10.11.11.11 0.0.0.0 eq 23**

2. Will the following ACL configuration prevent 192.168.1.75 from using Telnet to reach the router at 10.1.1.1?

   ```
   access-list 1 deny 192.168.1.75 0.0.0.0 access-list 1 permit any
   ! line vty 0 4    ip
   access-group 1 in
   ```

   ❍ **A.** Yes, the configuration is perfect.

   ❍ **B.** No, the ACL is wrong.

   ❍ **C.** No, the destination is not specified.

   ❍ **D.** No, the ACL is correct but the command to apply the ACL is wrong.

   ❍ **E.** Yes, but the ACL must be extended to properly block Telnet.

3. Which ACL configuration correctly prevents hosts in the sixth subnet of 172.16.0.0/20 from using TFTP to send a file to the router at 10.1.1.1, while allowing all other traffic? (Note that the "zero subnets" are available.)

   ❍ A. **access-list 101 permit ip any any access-list 101 deny udp 172.16.0.0 0.0.255.255 10.1.1.1 0.0.0.0 eq 69**

   ❍ B. **access-list 102 deny udp 172.16.80.0 0.0.15.255 host 10.1.1.1 eq 69 log access-list 102 permit IP any any**

   ❍ C. **access-list 103 deny udp 172.16.0.0 0.0.255.255 10.1.1.1 0.0.0.0 eq 69 access-list 103 permit ip any any**

   ❍ D. **access-list 104 deny tcp 172.16.80.0 0.0.15.255 10.1.1.1 0.0.0.0 eq 69 access-list 104 permit ip any any**

Cram Quiz Answers

1. Answer C is correct. Answer A is wrong because it uses a standard IP ACL number and therefore cannot use protocol, destination, or port in the syntax. Answer B is wrong because it reverses the source and destination addresses. Answer D is wrong because it lists the **permit ip any any** line first, meaning that it will not deny any traffic, despite the syntax being correct.

2. Answer D is correct. The ACL syntax is correct, but the command **ip access-group 1 in** is invalid for vty line configuration; it should read **access-class 1 in**. Answer A is incorrect. Answer B is wrong; the ACL is fine. Answer C is wrong because the destination cannot be specified in a standard ACL; furthermore, the destination is not needed because the vty lines are the destination. Answer E is not correct because the vty line configuration does not require that Telnet be specified.

3. Answer B is correct. Don't be thrown off by the **log** keyword, and don't be surprised to find a subnetting question embedded in an ACL question. Answer A is wrong because it puts the **permit ip any any** statement first and will not deny any traffic. Answer C is wrong because it denies the entire network, not just the specified subnet. Answer D is wrong because it denies TCP, not UDP. TFTP uses UDP.

Troubleshooting and Verifying ACL Configurations

In an ideal world, nothing would ever go wrong. If you have been working with computers for any length of time, you know that this is not the case. Inevitably, things do go wrong, and you will need to know how to vary and troubleshoot your configuration. When verifying and troubleshooting IP ACLs, you need to be familiar with three commands :

- **show access-list:** Shows you what ACLs you have configured on your router
- **show ip access-list:** Shows you only the IP ACLs you have configured on your router
- **show ip interface:** Shows you the direction (inbound/outbound) and placement of an ACL

The first two commands show only what ACLs you have configured on your router, but they do not show where they have been applied. The third command, **show ip interface**, shows you where the ACL has been applied and in what direction (inbound or outbound). Following is the output of the **show ip interface** command, with the relevant portions highlighted:

```
Ethernet0 is up, line protocol is up
  Internet address is 10.0.0.1, subnet mask is 255.0.0.0
  Broadcast address is 255.255.255.255
  Address determined by non-volatile memory
  MTU is 1500 bytes
  Helper address is not set
  Directed broadcast forwarding is enabled
  Multicast groups joined: 224.0.0.1 224.0.0.2
  Outgoing access list is not set
  Inbound  access list is 100
  Proxy ARP is enabled
  Security level is default
  Split horizon is enabled
  ICMP redirects are always sent
  ICMP unreachables are always sent
  ICMP mask replies are never sent
  IP fast switching is enabled
  IP fast switching on the same interface is disabled
  IP SSE switching is disabled
  Router Discovery is disabled
  IP output packet accounting is disabled
```

```
IP access violation accounting is disabled
TCP/IP header compression is disabled
Probe proxy name replies are disabled
```

From this output, you can see that ACL 100 is applied inbound on interface Ethernet 0.

ExamAlert

Anytime you configure an ACL, you should execute the **show access list** (or **show ip** ACLs) and **show ip interface** commands to verify the configuration.

Cram Quiz

1. Which of the following applies to numbered extended IP access lists? Choose all that apply.

   ❍ **A.** Permit/deny the entire protocol

   ❍ **B.** Usually applied (as packet filters) as close to the source of traffic as possible

   ❍ **C.** Usually applied (as packet filters) as close to the destination of traffic as possible

   ❍ **D.** Permit/deny based on protocol, address, port, source, and destination

   ❍ **E.** Permit/deny based solely on source address

   ❍ **F.** Allow insertion or removal of a line at any point in the list

2. Which of the following applies to numbered standard IP access lists? Choose all that apply.

   ❍ **A.** Permit/deny the entire protocol

   ❍ **B.** Usually applied (as packet filters) as close to the source of traffic as possible

   ❍ **C.** Usually applied (as packet filters) as close to the destination of traffic as possible

   ❍ **D.** Permit/deny based on protocol, address, port, source, and destination

   ❍ **E.** Permit/deny based solely on source address

   ❍ **F.** Allow insertion or removal of a line at any point in the list

3. Examine the command line given. True or False: The following syntax achieves the goal of denying HTTP traffic while allowing all other traffic?

   ```
   access-list 101 deny tcp any any eq 80
   access-list 101 permit tcp any any
   ```

Cram Quiz Answers

1. Answers B and D are correct. Answers A, C, and E are wrong because those are characteristic of standard IP ACLs. Answer F is wrong because that is a feature only of named ACLs.
2. Answers A, C, and E are correct. Answers B and D are characteristic of extended IP ACLs, and Answer F is a feature only of named ACLs.
3. False. The ACL does deny HTTP traffic, but only permits TCP, which is a subset of the remaining traffic, not "all" of it.

Review Questions

1. Examine the following figure. What will the following ACL do? Select the best answer.

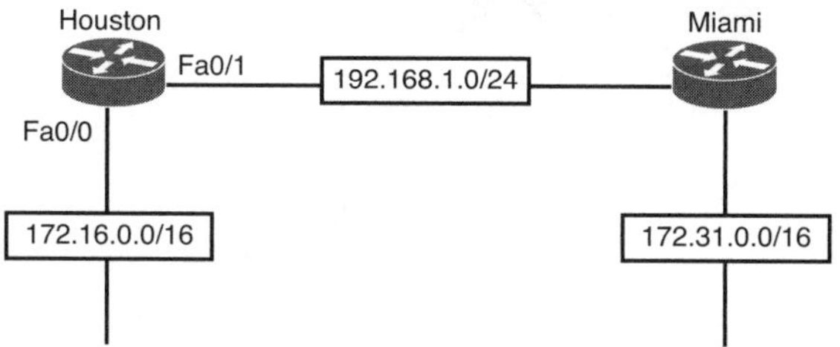


```
Houston(config)#access-list 114 deny tcp 172.16.0.0 0.0.255.255
172.31.0.0 0.0.255.255 eq 25
Houston(config)#access-list 114 deny tcp 172.16.0.0 0.0.255.255
172.31.0.0 0.0.255.255 eq 80
Houston(config)#access-list 114 permit tcp 172.16.0.0 0.0.255.255
172.31.0.0 0.0.255.255 eq 25
Houston(config)#access-list 114 permit tcp 172.16.0.0 0.0.255.255
172.31.0.0 0.0.255.255 eq 80
Houston(config)#interface fastethernet0/0
Houston(config-if)#ip access-group 114 in
```

- ❍ **A.** Deny SMTP and WWW traffic sourced from Houston's Ethernet network and destined for Miami's Ethernet network.
- ❍ **B.** Permit SMTP and WWW traffic sourced from Houston's Ethernet network and destined for Miami's Ethernet network.
- ❍ **C.** Nothing. This is an invalid ACL.
- ❍ **D.** Deny all traffic.

2. What is true about named ACLs? Choose all that apply.

- ❍ **A.** Named ACLs allow you to remove individual lines; numbered ACLs do not.
- ❍ **B.** The name of the access list must be limited to eight characters or fewer.
- ❍ **C.** You must specify whether the access list is standard or extended.
- ❍ **D.** Named ACLs cannot be used with NAT.
- ❍ **E.** You do not need to specify the protocol if you are using an extended named access list to filter IP traffic.

3. Examine the following figure. Which of the following configurations would allow Telnet access to the Tokyo router for the user named Ross but deny all other Telnet access? Choose all that apply.

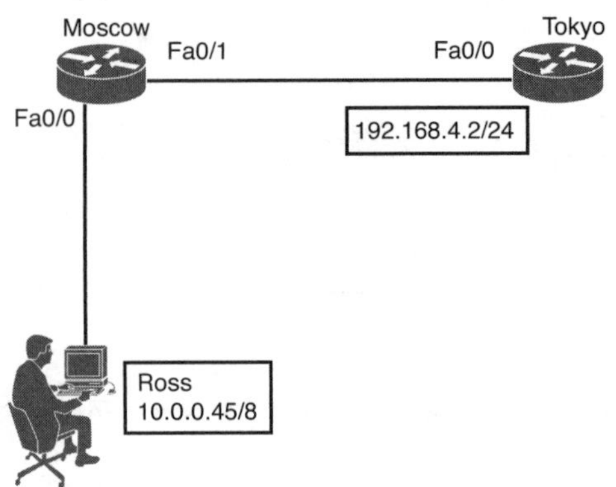

❍ **A.** Moscow(config)# **access-list 100 deny ip any any**

Moscow(config)#**access-list 100 permit tcp host 10.0.0.45 host 192.168.4.2 eq 23**

Moscow(config)#**interface fastethernet 0/0**

Moscow(config-if)#**ip access-group 100 in**

❍ **B.** Moscow(config)#**access-list 199 permit tcp host 10.0.0.45 192.168.4.2 0.0.0.0 eq 23**

Moscow(config)#**interface fastethernet 0/0**

Moscow(config-if)#**ip access-group 199 in**

❍ **C.** Moscow(config)#**access-list 125 permit tcp 10.0.0.45 0.0.0.0 host 192.168.4.2 eq Telnet**

Moscow(config)#**interface fastethernet0/1**

Moscow(config-if)#**ip access-group 125 out**

❍ **D.** Tokyo(config)#**access-list 173 permit tcp host 10.0.0.45 host 192.168.4.2 eq 23**

Tokyo(config)#**interface fastethernet0/0**

Tokyo(config-if)#**ip access-group 173 in**

❍ **E.** Tokyo(config)#**access-list 40 permit host 10.0.0.45**

Tokyo(config)#**line vty 0 4**

Tokyo(config-line)#**access-class 40 in**

❍ **F.** Tokyo(config)#**access-list 87 permit host 10.0.0.45**

Tokyo(config)#**line vty 0 4**

Tokyo(config-line)#access-class 1 in

4. Examine the following figure. Based on the figure, you want to configure an access list that prevents users on the 172.16.32.0/21 and 172.17.32.0/21 networks from sending pings to the 172.18.32.0/21 network. You still, however, want to send pings out from the 172.18.32.0/21 network. What commands would you enter on the Blue router to make this work?

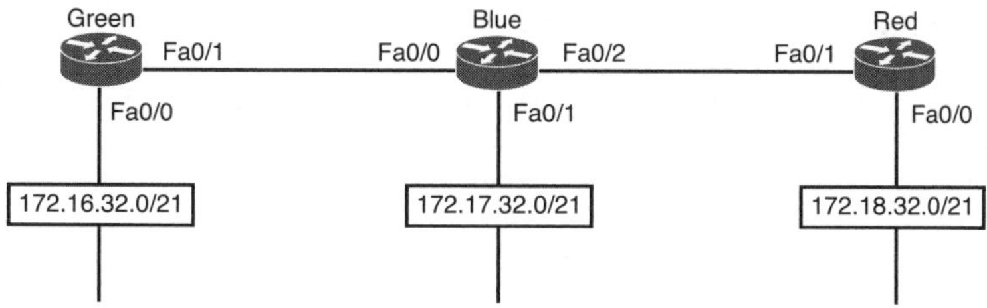

❍ **A.** Blue(config)#**access-list 100 deny icmp 172.16.32.0 0.0.7.255 172.18.32.0.0 0.0.7.255 echo**

Blue(config)#**access-list 100 deny icmp 172.17.32.0 0.0.7.255 172.18.32.0 0.0.7.255 echo**

Blue(config)#**access-list 100 permit ip any any**

Blue(config)#**interface fastethernet 0/2**

Blue(config-if)#**ip access-group 100 out**

❍ **B.** Blue(config)#**access-list 100 deny icmp 172.16.32.0 0.0.15.255. 172.18.32.0 0.0.15.255 echo**

Blue(config)#**access-list 100 deny icmp 172.17.32.0 0.0.15.255 172.18.32.0 0.0.15.255 echo**

Blue(config)#**access-list 100 permit ip any any**

Blue(config)#**interface fastethernet 0/2**

Blue(config-if)#**ip access-group 100 out**

❍ **C.** Blue(config)#**access-list 100 deny icmp 172.16.32.0 0.0.7.255 172.18.32.0.0 0.0.7.255 echo**

Blue(config)#**access-list 100 deny icmp 172.17.32.0 0.0.7.255 172.18.32.0 0.0.7.255 echo**

Blue(config)#**access-list 100 permit ip any any**

Blue(config)#**interface fastethernet 0/1**

Blue(config-if)#**ip access-group 100 in**

❍ **D.** Blue(config)#**access-list 100 deny icmp 172.16.32.0 0.0.15.255. 172.18.32.0 0.0.15.255 echo**

Blue(config)#**access-list 100 deny icmp 172.17.32.0 0.0.15.255 172.18.32.0 0.0.15.255 echo**

Blue(config)#**access-list 100 permit ip any any**

Blue(config)#**interface fastethernet 0/1**

Blue(config-if)#**ip access-group 100 in**

5. You want to filter FTP access sourced from the 192.168.99.192/27 network yet allow all other traffic to pass. You do not care about the destination. You enter the following command on your router, yet FTP traffic coming from the 192.168.99.192/27 network is still allowed. Why?

```
Router(config)#access-list 100 deny tcp any 192.168.99.192
     0.0.0.31 eq 20
Router(config)#access-list 100 deny tcp any 192.168.99.192
     0.0.0.31 eq 21
Router(config)#access-list 100 permit ip any any
Router(config)#interface serial 0/0
Router(config-if)#ip access-group 100 in
```

❍ **A.** The port numbers are wrong.
❍ **B.** FTP uses UDP, not TCP.
❍ **C.** The source and destination are backward.
❍ **D.** The permit statement should be first.

6. What types of ACLs are processed after the router examines the routing table and sends the packet to the outgoing interface? Choose all that apply.

❍ **A.** IP standard inbound
❍ **B.** IP extended inbound
❍ **C.** IP standard outbound
❍ **D.** IP extended outbound

7. What command can you enter to verify that an access list has been applied on your interface?

❍ **A.** **show ip interface brief**
❍ **B.** **show access-list**
❍ **C.** **show ip access-list**
❍ **D.** **show ip interface**

8. Following best-practice guidelines for ACLs as traffic filters, where should you apply your ACLs? Choose all that apply.

❍ **A.** Standard ACLs should generally be applied closest to the source.
❍ **B.** Standard ACLs should generally be applied closest to the destination.
❍ **C.** Extended ACLs should generally be applied closest to the source.
❍ **D.** Extended ACLs should generally be applied closest to the destination.

9. What does the following named access list do?

```
Router(config)#ip access-list extended QueACL
Router(config-ext-nacl)#permit tcp any 192.168.15.8 0.0.0.3 eq
119
Router(config-ext-nacl)#interface fastethernet1/3
Router(config-if)#ip access-group QueACL in
```

❍ **A.** Allows NNTP traffic coming into the Fa1/3 interface to the 192.168.15.8 255.255.255.252 network, but denies everything else

❍ **B.** Allows SMTP traffic coming into the Fa1/3 interface to the 192.168.15.8 host, but denies everything else

❍ **C.** Allows NNTP traffic coming into the Fa1/3 interface to the 192.168.15.8 host, but denies everything else

❍ **D.** Allows SMTP traffic coming into the Fa1/3 interface to the 192.168.15.8/30 network, but denies everything else

❍ **E.** Allows all traffic to pass because no deny statement is given

Answers to Review Questions

1. Answer D is correct. ACLs are top-down, meaning that they check the packet against your statements in the order that you enter them. In this example, the access list would first deny SMTP and WWW traffic sourced from Houston's Ethernet network and destined for Miami's Ethernet network. Following this, the access list permits SMTP and WWW traffic. However, because this traffic was first denied, the packet will never get permitted. In addition, because all traffic is denied by default unless explicitly permitted, all other traffic will be denied. Thus, this access list denies all traffic. Answer A, although technically correct, is not the best answer because all traffic is being denied, not just SMTP and WWW traffic. Answer B is incorrect because SMTP and WWW traffic is being denied first. Answer C is incorrect because this is a perfectly acceptable, albeit poorly written, access list.
2. Answers A and C are correct. Answer B is wrong because named ACLs can be longer than eight characters. Answer D is wrong because you can use named ACLs with NAT. Answer E is wrong because you do always need to specify the protocol when using a named access list.
3. Answers B, C, and E are correct. Answer B configures the access list using the host keyword for the 10.0.0.45 host. Answer C configures the access list using the host keyword for the 192.168.4.2 host. Answer E configures the access list using the host keyword for both the 192.168.4.2 and the 10.0.0.45 host. Answer A is incorrect because the first deny statement would block all traffic, including the Telnet traffic. Answer D is incorrect because this would block Telnet traffic going through the Tokyo router and not traffic going to the Tokyo router. (ACLs applied to an interface are for traffic passing through the router and never for traffic destined to the router.) Answer F is incorrect because the wrong access list is applied on the vty lines.
4. Answer A is correct. The correct wildcard mask is 0.0.7.255 for all networks. You can apply this access list inbound on Fa0/1 and Fa0/0 or outbound on Fa0/2. Although the general rule is to apply extended ACLs inbound closest to the source, none of the answers did this correctly (making this a tricky question). Answer B is incorrect because the wildcard masks are wrong. Answers C and D are incorrect because they are applied inbound on Fa0/1. The 172.16.32.0/21 network would still have been allowed through. Answer D is additionally wrong because the wrong wildcard mask is used.
5. Answer C is correct. Answer A is wrong because the port numbers are correct. Answer B is wrong because FTP does use TCP. Answer D is wrong because if the permit statement is first, all traffic is allowed through. (ACLs are top-down.)
6. Answers C and D are correct. Outbound ACLs are processed after the routing table is checked and the outbound interface is chosen. Answers A and B are incorrect because they are both inbound.
7. Answer D is correct. The command show ip interface will verify the direction and placement of an access list on an interface. Answer A is incorrect because this shows only brief output that does not include access list information. Answers B and C are incorrect because they do not show where the ACL is applied.

8. Answers B and C are correct. Standard ACLs should generally be applied outbound closest to the destination of the traffic because you have no other way of referencing the destination. Extended ACLs should generally be applied inbound closest to the source because you can specify the destination and you want to filter the traffic as early as possible. Answers A and D are incorrect because the directions are the opposite from what they should be.
9. Answer A is correct. TCP port 119 is used by NNTP, and the wildcard mask 0.0.0.3 matches the 192.168.15.8 255.255.255.252 (/30) subnet. Answers B and D are wrong because this access list permits NNTP, not SMTP. Answer C is wrong because this access list permits traffic to the 192.168.15.8 host, in addition to 192.168.15.9, 192.168.15.10, and 192.168.15.11. Answer E is wrong because no deny statement is necessary; all traffic is implicitly denied, except for what is explicitly permitted.

What Next?

If you want more practice on this chapter's exam topics before you move on, remember that you can access all of the Cram Quiz questions on the CD. You can also create a custom exam by topic with the practice exam software. Note any topic you struggle with and go to that topic's material in this chapter.

CHAPTER TEN
IP Services

This chapter covers the following official CCNA Routing and Switching 200-120 exam topics:

- Identify the basic operation of NAT.
- Configure and verify NAT for given network requirements.
- Configure and verify NTP as a client.
- Configure and verify DHCP (IOS router).

(For more information on the official CCNA exam topics, see the "About the CCNA Exam" section in the Introduction.)

In this chapter we examine the three main implementations of Network Address Translation (NAT) on Cisco routers, along with the applications, advantages, and disadvantages of the NAT service, and finally the configuration commands to implement, verify, and troubleshoot it.

We will examine the theory and configuration of Network Time Protocol (NTP) on IOS routers. NTP is a standards-based IP protocol used to synchronize the clocks on multiple networked devices.

Dynamic Host Control Protocol (DHCP) is a well-known IP protocol that provides client addressing. In this section, we examine the configuration of the IOS router as both DHCP client and server.

Network Address Translation

CramSaver

If you can correctly answer these questions before going through this section, save time by skimming the Exam Alerts in this section and then completing the Cram Quiz at the end of the section.

1. Which of the following best describes PAT?

   A. Multiple inside local IP addresses are translated to a single inside global IP address, with multiple translations to the same IP distinguished by random source port selection.

   B. Multiple inside local IP addresses are translated to a single outside global IP address, with multiple translations to the same IP distinguished by random TCP source port selection.

   C. Inside local IP addresses are translated to multiple outside global IP addresses.

   D. Inside local IP addresses are translated to multiple inside global IP addresses.

2. Which four of the following are required for a PAT configuration?

   A. **ip nat inside source static 192.168.1.0 10.1.1.18**

   B. **ip nat outside**

   C. **access-list 1 permit 192.168.1.0 0.0.0.255**

   D. **ip nat pool Internet 192.168.1.20 192.168.1.100 netmask 255.255.255.0**

   E. **ip nat inside**

   F. **ip nat inside source list 1 interface serial 0/1 overload**

Answers

1. Answer A is correct. Answers B and C are wrong because inside global addresses are translated to inside global addresses, not outside global. Answer D is wrong because it describes NAT, not PAT.
2. Answers B, C, E, and F are correct. They create a typical PAT config. Answer A is a static NAT. Answer D creates a pool that, although optional, is not required for PAT (and in this case, the PAT config does not reference this pool).

NAT has become a generic term for several related but different processes. The basic principle involves changing the source IP of a host in the packet header as its traffic crosses the NAT device. The following sections detail the NAT implementations supported on a Cisco router.

NAT Terminology

A number of unfortunately confusing terms are associated with NAT that in a typically evil plot are usually testable. Figure 10.1 diagrams a typical, simple NAT setup and accurately locates the terms you need to know.

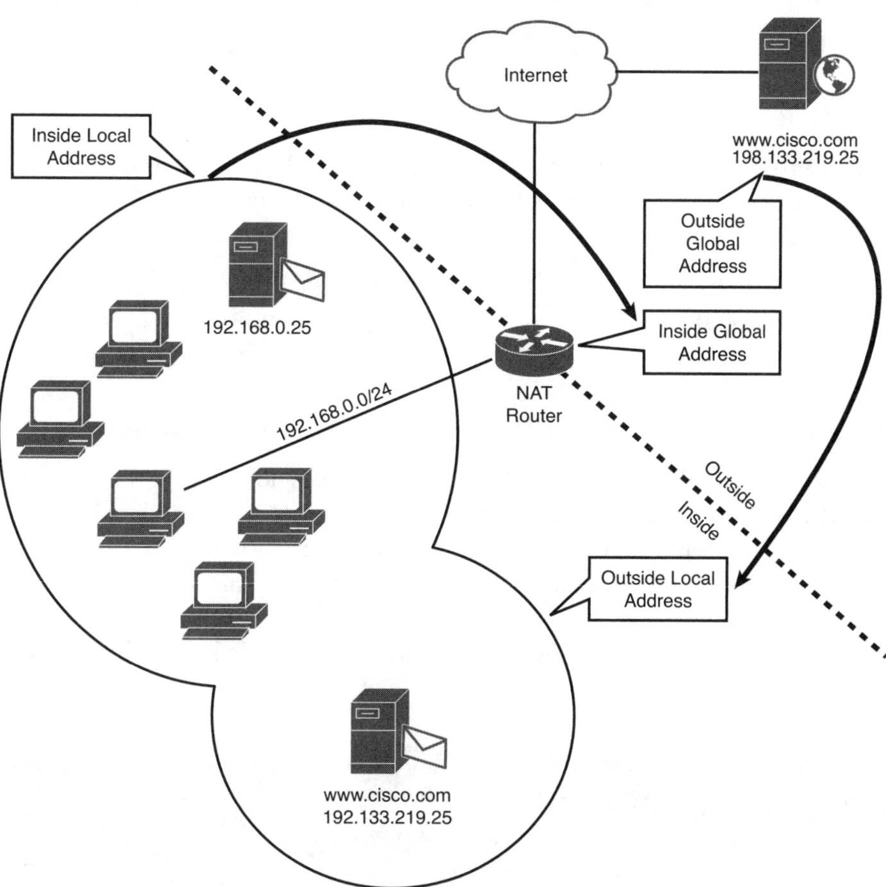

FIGURE 10.1 **NAT terminology put into context.**

You need to be familiar with the following terms:

- **Inside:** This refers (usually) to the private side of the network, usually the source of addresses that are being translated.
- **Outside:** This is "everything else" that is not "inside": typically the public side of the network, the address space to which inside hosts are being translated.
- **Inside local:** These addresses are assigned to inside hosts and are the ones being translated. Inside local IPs are often RFC 1918 private IPs such as 192.168.x.x, 172.16.x.x through 172.31.x.x, and 10.x.x.x, but this is by no means a requirement.
- **Inside global:** These are the addresses to which inside locals get translated (often registered IPs obtained from the Internet service provider [ISP]).
- **Outside global:** These are usually registered IPs assigned to web servers, mail servers, or any host that is reachable on the public network (Internet, usually) itself.
- **Outside local:** These are the addresses of outside global hosts as they appear on the inside network; they might or might not have been translated from outside to inside, depending on the configuration.

These terms are confusing, and explaining them tends to make things worse.

As a simplification, start with local and global: Local addresses are most often the RFC 1918 private ones that we are so familiar with; these will be on the private side of an Internet router. Global addresses are usually real, live, registered IPs, such as www.cisco.com, which at the time of this writing was 198.133.219.25. From this toehold on the terms, you should be able to reconstruct the others—an outside host with a local IP, an inside host with a global IP, and so on.

ExamAlert

You must know these terms and where they fit in the NAT system. Furthermore, you must be able to apply these terms to the output of some of the NAT verification and troubleshooting commands.

Applications, Advantages, and Disadvantages of NAT

NAT has three main applications:

- If you have more inside hosts than you have outside IP addresses, the NAT service can translate multiple inside local host IPs to a single inside global IP. The two most common scenarios for this are a typical Internet access router, where all the hosts on the inside are granted Internet access using very few—or even just one—outside IP address, or a modification of that example in which a lot of IPs are available, but not enough for our requirements. In both cases, the problem that NAT solves is the depletion of IP addresses. The fact is that very few registered IPs are available any more, so being able to "reuse" them by NATing many hosts to a few of them is very helpful in extending the lifespan of the Internet address space.
- NAT can be used to solve two related and vexing network issues: The overlapping address space and the well-meaning admin error. The *overlapping address space* happens when we connect to another network that uses the same IP address range as we do; sometimes this happens when we merge with another company. The problem is that we will have duplicate routes in different locations when the routers start updating each other, leading to instability, misrouting, and general mayhem.

  The *well-meaning admin error* happens when the person responsible for the network design either fails to plan for future growth of his network, or simply makes a mistake because of ignorance or arrogance. This most often takes the form of a private network being addressed with public IPs that belong to someone else.

  A real-world example of this occurred when a representative from the ISP told their customer (a credit union where I worked) to use the address space of 191.168.0.0 /24 for the inside network. This worked fine until Internet connectivity was required; at which time, it was pointed out that the 191.168.0.0 network was a registered Internet range belonging to an insurance firm in the Carolinas. This did cause some issues (for example, when one wanted to ping a domain controller in the head office in Vancouver, the replies came back from a large router somewhere on the East Coast), but the problem was largely hidden by the NAT service, which translated all those inside local IPs (which were incorrectly using registered Internet addresses) to appropriate outside global addresses.

- NAT can also be used to give a whole cluster of machines (each with different inside local IPs) a single IP address that the clients can use. This is called load distribution, and works well for high-volume server clusters such as databases or web servers in which all the clients can use a single virtual IP to reach the service, and that single IP is NATed to all the real IPs of the physical servers.

The advantages of NAT are first and foremost that it conserves the registered IP address space. There is a critical shortage of IPs now, so being able to connect hundreds of hosts to the Internet through a single address is a huge benefit. NAT also provides a certain degree of security because it hides the originating IP address and, if configured properly, prevents bad guys on the Internet from connecting to inside hosts. (The usual caveats here: NAT alone does not provide adequate security, but it can form a part of a secure configuration.) It also helps as a workaround alternative to having to readdress entire networks when address schemes overlap and makes it easy to change ISP addresses without having to re-address all the inside hosts.

The disadvantages of NAT are primarily that by its very nature it changes the source IP of traffic from the actual IP of the host to the inside global IP to which it is translated. Some applications do not like this loss of end-to-end IP traceability and stop working. NAT also makes it more difficult when troubleshooting because of that source IP change—and you might be NATed a couple times or more on the journey through the internetwork. Last, the NAT process introduces a certain delay in the transmission of packets as they are rewritten and the translation information is looked up. Spending more money on your NAT box might help speed this up. Call your authorized Cisco value-added reseller (VAR), quick!

ExamAlert

Know the applications, advantages, and disadvantages of NAT.

Let's look now at the three main NAT implementations.

Static NAT

Static NAT refers to the creation of a one-to-one mapping of an inside local IP to an inside global IP. Note that this type of NAT does not conserve IP addresses at all because we need one outside IP for every inside IP. Static NAT gives hosts, such as mail or web servers, access to the Internet even though they are actually on the private network. Perhaps more importantly, it allows us to access that web server from the Internet by creating a static NAT entry from the server's inside local IP to an inside global IP, which is reachable from the Internet.

Configuring a static NAT entry is easy. The only trick is to make sure that you get NAT working in the right direction: You must be very clear when identifying the inside interface and the outside. Figure 10.2 shows a simple network that we use to learn NAT configuration.

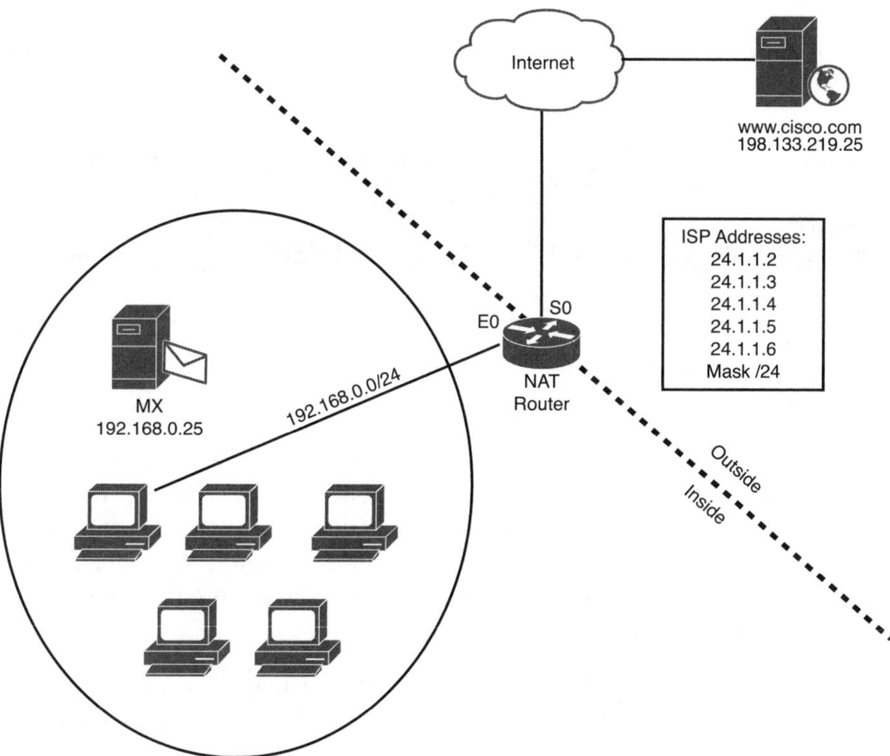

FIGURE 10.2 **Sample NAT network.**

Let's create a static NAT entry for the MX (Mail Exchanger) server with the IP of 192.168.0.25. The ISP has told us that we can use a block of IP addresses as shown, from 24.1.1.2 through 24.1.1.6, for our inside global addresses. We have decided to use 24.1.1.2 for the inside global IP of the MX host.

The global-config static NAT command uses fairly logical syntax:

```
ip nat inside source static <inside_local_IP> <inside_global_IP>
```

For our example, the command to enter on the NAT router would look like this:

```
NAT(config)#ip nat inside source static 192.168.0.25  24.1.1.2
```

Next, we have to identify the inside and outside interfaces:

```
NAT(config)#interface e0
NAT(config-if)#ip nat inside
NAT(config-if)#interface s0
NAT(config-if)#ip nat outside
```

And that's all there is to creating a static NAT entry. Remember that static NAT entries use up one outside IP for every inside IP, so they do not conserve the IP address space at all.

ExamAlert

Be very familiar with the static NAT syntax, including the command prompt level at which it is used.

Dynamic NAT

Dynamic NAT enables an inside host to get an outside address when needed; this saves us the trouble of creating multiple static maps, one for each host that wants to use the Internet. Dynamic NAT entries still don't conserve IPs, because we still need one IP for every host that wants to connect to the Internet. Remember that if you have more hosts than outside IPs, some hosts will not get a translation entry and will not be capable of using the Internet. For this reason, it is not used much for Internet connectivity.

One of the interesting concepts introduced with dynamic NAT is that of the NAT pool: A pool is a defined group of addresses that are available for translation. Configuring dynamic NAT involves identifying which hosts are to be translated, and to which addresses they should be translated. It is common to use an access list to define the inside source and a pool for the outside addresses. The syntax to build a NAT pool looks like this:

```
ip nat pool [pool-name] [first-IP] [last-IP] netmask [mask]
```

The pool name is arbitrary. You can pick something that is meaningful to you. The *first-IP* and *last-IP* are the first and last IPs in the pool range, and the *mask* is the subnet mask of the network those outside IPs are on. Note that you must have the word **netmask** in the syntax! Here's what this command would look like if we used the same network shown in Figure 10.2 and wanted to use the last four IPs in the range that the ISP gave us:

```
NAT(config)#ip nat pool MyPool 24.1.1.3 24.1.1.6 netmask
255.255.255.0
```

Next, we need to identify what hosts get to be translated; this is commonly done with a standard access list:

```
NAT(config)#access-list 1 permit 192.168.0.0 0.0.0.255
```

This list permits any address that starts with 192.168.0.x. Note that in this case the list is not permitting traffic to or from the hosts; rather, it is identifying those hosts that can be translated.

Tip

It is a good idea (a best practice) to specifically deny any hosts that you do not want translated, using your access list. For example, because we already have a static NAT entry for the MX server in our example, we don't want it to get another dynamic translation, so we would start the access list with the following line:

```
NAT(config)#access-list 1 deny host 192.168.0.25
NAT(config)#access-list 1 permit 192.168.0.0  0.0.0.255
```

So at this point, we have built the pool of addresses that we will be translating to, we have identified which hosts can be translated (and possibly those that cannot), and all that is left is to configure the NAT process itself:

```
NAT(config)#ip nat inside source list 1 pool MyPool
NAT(config)#interface e0
NAT(config-if)#ip nat inside
NAT(config-if)#interface s0
NAT(config-if)#ip nat outside
```

The first line tells the router to use List 1 (which we built previously) to identify which hosts can be translated (these are the inside source addresses), and then identifies the pool called **MyPool** as the addresses to which the Inside Source Addresses should be translated.

The next lines, as before, tell the router which interface should be inside and outside. Remember, if you get these backward, you could translate the Internet into your private network; that could be bad.

Note that with a pool of only four addresses, the first four hosts who request a translation will get one (which they keep for 24 hours by default), and any additional hosts who request a translation will not be able to get one. The next section shows how Port Address Translation (PAT) resolves this limitation.

ExamAlert

Know the syntax to create a pool of addresses to which hosts can be translated!

PAT

Port Address Translation (PAT), also known as an *extended NAT entry*, leverages the nature of TCP/IP communication by using the source ports of hosts to distinguish them from each other when they are all being translated, possibly to a single outside address.

With PAT, an inside host is given a translation entry that uses not only the host's IP address but also its source port. Figure 10.3 illustrates the process as three inside hosts are translated to a single outside IP address as they contact different web servers.

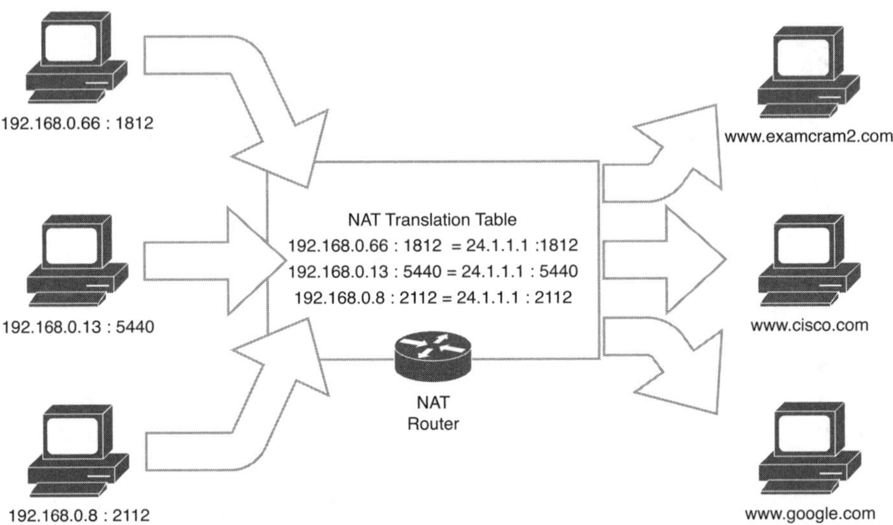

FIGURE 10.3 **The mechanics of PAT.**

So, you can see now how PAT can hugely extend the registered Internet address space: We could in theory translate thousands of private IPs to a single IP (often, the IP assigned to our outside interface) using PAT by extending the inside local IP with the randomly generated source port and mapping that to the inside global IP extended by the same port number. With more than 64,000 ports available for this *extended translation entry*, the chances of two hosts randomly choosing the same source port are slim. If it does happen, the conflicting hosts choose a different port number. We can further reduce the chances of this conflict happening by using a pool for PAT, which makes it very unlikely indeed that two hosts would get the same port *and* inside global IP from the pool.

The Cisco term for PAT is *overload* because we are overloading a single inside global IP with many inside local + port mappings.

Configuring PAT is easy; the commands are similar to dynamic NAT, with the addition of the keyword **overload**, as shown:

```
NAT(config)#access-list 1 permit 192.168.0.0 0.0.0.255
NAT(config)#ip nat inside source list 1 interface serial 0 overload
NAT(config)#interface e0
NAT(config-if)#ip nat inside
NAT(config-if)#interface s0
NAT(config-if)#ip nat outside
```

Note that we have used the parameters **interface serial 0 overload** at the end of the NAT command; the keyword **overload** turns on PAT, and the **interface serial 0** parameter simply instructs the NAT service to use the existing IP of Serial 0 as the inside global IP for the translation. Here is a sample configuration that ties together a static NAT entry, creates a pool, and overloads that pool to enable PAT:

```
NAT(config)#access-list 1 deny host 192.168.0.25
NAT(config)#access-list 1 permit 192.168.0.0 0.0.0.255
NAT(config)#ip nat inside source static 192.168.0.25  24.1.1.2
NAT(config)#ip nat pool MyPool 24.1.1.3 24.1.1.6 netmask
255.255.255.0
NAT(config)#ip nat inside source list 1 pool MyPool overload
NAT(config)#interface e0
NAT(config-if)#ip nat inside
NAT(config-if)#interface s0
NAT(config-if)#ip nat outside
```

ExamAlert

This configuration, because it is such a fundamental and important one for Internet-connected networks, is highly tested. You should practice entering this configuration on a real router or router sim until you are totally comfortable with the commands.

Verification and Troubleshooting NAT and PAT

The main command used to verify that your NAT configuration is working is **show ip nat translations**. The following sample output demonstrates which could have come from the NAT router in our previous examples.

```
NAT#show ip nat translations
Pro  Inside Global   Inside Local       Outside Local     Outside Global
tcp  24.1.1.1:1812   192.168.0.66:1812  63.240.93.157     63.240.93.157
tcp  24.1.1.1:5440   192.168.0.13:5440  198.133.219.25    198.133.219.25
tcp  24.1.1.1:2112   192.168.0.8:2112   64.233.187.104    64.233.187.104
```

Note that all three inside hosts have been translated to the same inside global IP (which likely means that we have overloaded the S0 interface). We have proved that the PAT service is functioning because we can see the different port number extensions listed for each host. Note that the outside global and outside local IPs are the same; this is because we are not translating those IPs back into our inside network. If we were trying to solve the overlapping address space problem, those two IPs would be different for each outside host.

The command **show ip nat statistics** gives us a snapshot of how many translations have been performed, a general overview of how the NAT device is configured, and how much of our pool has been used, as demonstrated in the following output:

```
NAT#show ip nat statistics
Total translations:  3 (0 static, 0 dynamic, 3 extended)
Outside interfaces:  Serial0
Inside interfaces:  Ethernet)
Hits: 38  Misses:  3
Expired Translations:  0
Dynamic Mappings:
-- Inside source
access-list 1 pool MyPool refcount 3
Pool MyPool:  netmask 255.255.255.0
Start 24.1.1.3 end 24.1.1.6
Type generic, total addresses 4, allocated 3 (75%), misses 0
```

If you can successfully ping a remote host, chances are good that your NAT/PAT config is at least partially functional.

If you do run into problems, it is possible to clear the NAT translations from the router, using **clear ip nat translation***. This command clears all dynamic and extended translation entries. To clear a static entry, you must remove the command from your running config.

Cram Quiz

The Acme Giant Magnet Company recently contracted a small wild animal to configure PAT for Internet access on their router. Their requirements are as follows:

- The two LAN subnets connected to f0/0 and f0/1 must both be configured for Internet access using PAT.
- The Internet connection uses GigabitEthernet1/0. The router's g1/0 is a DHCP client of the ISP, so the IP address is not static, but it is within the subnet 204.174.65.16/28.
- A pool of addresses should be used for the NAT translations.

Examine the following partial router config. Then, identify the configuration issues, choosing all problems that apply from the following answers:

```
interface f0/0
 ip address 192.168.1.1 255.255.255.128
 ip nat outside
!
interface f0/1
 ip address 192.168.1.129 255.255.255.128
 ip nat outside
!
interface g1/0
 ip address dhcp
 speed 100
 duplex full
 ip nat outside
!
access-list 7 permit 192.168.1.0  255.255.255.0
!
ip nat inside source list 1 interface g1/0
!
ip nat pool Acme 204.174.65.1  204.174.65.15 netmask 255.255.255.240
!
```

1. Identify the possible issues with this configuration. Choose all that apply.
   - ❍ **A.** The access list specifies the wrong source address and has an invalid configuration.
   - ❍ **B.** The access list specifies the correct source address but has an invalid configuration.
   - ❍ **C.** The LAN interfaces are not correctly configured for PAT.
   - ❍ **D.** The Internet interface is not correctly configured for PAT.
   - ❍ **E.** The NAT pool specifies the wrong mask.
   - ❍ **F.** The NAT pool specifies the wrong subnet.
   - ❍ **G.** The NAT pool is not being used.
   - ❍ **H.** The **ip nat inside source** command specifies the correct access list but is incorrectly configured for PAT.
   - ❍ **I.** The **ip nat inside source** command specifies the wrong access list but is correctly configured for PAT.
   - ❍ **J.** The **ip nat inside source** command specifies the wrong access list and is incorrectly configured for PAT.

Rejean has recently joined the help desk at the Acme Giant Magnet company. Shortly after 9 a.m. on Monday, when most of the users have arrived for work, picked up a cup of coffee, and have logged in and begun surfing the Web, the help desk line begins ringing almost continually. Soon Rejean has more than 50 tickets in the queue, all of them from users complaining that they cannot access the Internet. Rejean does some troubleshooting, and discovers that several people can access the Internet, but many cannot. Rejean suspects that there may be an issue with the Internet router that also performs NAT for the company. He checks the help desk communication log for the past couple days to see whether there were any changes made. He notes that one of the Kardashian sisters was in on Saturday night to update the router after the ISP changed the subnet address used on the Internet segment to 24.12.1.16/28 and assigned Acme the IP address range of 24.12.1.18 through 24.12.1.29 in the same subnet for NAT purposes. Unfortunately, these are the only Internet IP addresses available to Acme from this ISP. Rejean looks at the router config:

```
interface f0/0
 description Office LAN
 ip address 192.168.0.1 255.255.255.0
 ip nat inside
!
interface g1/0
 description MetroGig Internet
 ip address 24.12.1.18 255.255.255.240
 ip nat outside
!
access-list 1 permit 192.168.0.0 0.0.0.255
ip nat pool Shamalamadingdong 24.12.1.18 24.12.1.29 netmask
255.255.255.248
ip nat inside source list 1 pool Shamalamadingdong
!
```

2. What is wrong, and what can be done to fix it? Spot the issue and select the best solution from the list.
   - ❍ **A.** The inside and outside interfaces are reversed. Unreverse them.
   - ❍ **B.** The pool addresses are wrong. Use the correct address range.
   - ❍ **C.** The pool mask is wrong. Use a wildcard mask.
   - ❍ **D.** The pool is not large enough. Add more addresses to the pool.
   - ❍ **E.** The pool is not being overloaded. Implement PAT.
   - ❍ **F.** The access list is incorrect. Fix the source address.
   - ❍ **G.** The access list is incorrect. Fix the mask.

Cram Quiz Answers

1. Answers B, C, F, G, and J are correct. (The "invalid configuration" is that the wildcard mask does not correctly identify the networks to be translated; it looks more like the decimal mask format.) Answer A is incorrect: Although the access list does not specify the two individual subnets as source addresses, it does specify a valid network address that would include both subnets (if the mask were right). Answer D is wrong because the Internet interface is set up correctly. Answer E is wrong because the pool mask is correct; the subnet address is wrong. Answers H and I are wrong because J is correct. The NAT command should specify **list 7**, and should have the **overload** command at the end to configure PAT.
2. Answer E is correct. All other answer are self-explanatory; there is nothing else wrong. However, I amsure that some of you went for Answer D as a possibility. If you did, you are wrong because you can't add more addresses to the pool. The entire subnet has already been used up: 24.12.1.17 for our router, .18 through .29 for the pool, and .30 presumably for the ISP router.

Network Time Protocol

CramSaver

1. What is the purpose of NTP?
    - **A.** To elect a time authority
    - **B.** To obtain the true time from the Ultimate True Clock (UTC)
    - **C.** To measure the variation of quartz crystal oscillators and choose a median clock value
    - **D.** To synchronize the clocks of various networked devices to a highly accurate true time source
    - **E.** To track time field distortions and compensate for them

2. What are two advantages of using NTP?
    - **A.** Automatically discovers all NTP-capable devices on the network and synchronizes their clocks
    - **B.** Automatically adjusts for detected local time zone
    - **C.** Makes comparison of time-stamped logs simpler
    - **D.** Ensures daylight savings time is correctly observed
    - **E.** Ensures clock consistency and accuracy on multiple networked devices

Answers

1. Answer D is correct. Answer A is wrong; there are no elections in NTP. Answer B is wrong; there is no such thing as the Ultimate Time Clock; UTC stands for universal time coordinated. Answer C is wrong because I just made that up. Answer E is wrong; I think I got that from a *Star Trek* episode.
2. Answers C and E are correct. Answer A is wrong because NTP does not have a discovery capability. Answer B is wrong because NTP send the correct time in UTC; local time zone must be adjusted by the local device administrator. Answer D is incorrect because DST is a local time zone-dependent configuration.

Network Time Protocol (NTP) is a standards-based IP protocol that synchronizes the time on networked devices.

Why is time synchronization important? Other than the commonsense view that clocks should all tell the correct time, imagine a few other scenarios.

You send an email at 10 a.m., and it arrives at 9:58 a.m. because the sending and receiving servers' clocks are out of sync.

You are comparing the logs between two systems to determine what the sequence of events was in a particular incident; if the time is not synchronized between those systems, the sequence of events is difficult—if not impossible—to determine because they clocks are not synchronized.

Voice over IP (VoIP) systems time stamp each voice packet to better track delay, for both real-time (jitter) quality of service (QoS) policing and log trend analysis.

So, accepting that NTP is important, how does it work? Here are some of the features of NTP.

NTP uses external reference clocks (usually highly accurate atomic or GPS clocks accessible over the Internet). All devices using NTP set their internal clocks to the *true time* provided by these clocks.

NTP clocks are organized by *stratum*. A *stratum 1* clock is the most authoritative (and presumed the most accurate). Each hop away from the stratum 1 clock adds to the stratum number; thus, if your router is three hops away from the stratum 1 clock, it is a stratum 4 clock. Cisco's NTP does not support stratum 1 service, meaning that Cisco devices are not usually directly attached to NTP source clocks. (There are some recent GPS clock implementations, but that is not relevant to CCNA.)

NTP propagates the correct time using universal time coordinated (UTC). Devices can offset their own clocks to the correct local time zone if desired; often they are left at UTC so that all time-stamped entries use the same time zone, making it much easier to compare log files.

NTP is scalable and redundant. If one clock source is unreachable, another can be checked. Multiple sources can be compared to get the best accuracy of time. Time sources that are identified as *insane* (a great word to describe sources that are temporarily or permanently unreliable) can be ignored and deleted.

NTP is very accurate: Time is resolved to less than a nanosecond.

A Cisco device can be an NTP client (getting its time from an NTP source clock) or an NTP server (providing the true time to other devices as a source). CCNA is concerned only with setting up a router as a client.

Configuring an IOS Router as an NTP Client

NTP is disabled by default, and for CCNA purposes the client can be configured with a single global config command:

```
Router1(config)# ntp server <ip_address> [version]
```

One command to set up Router1 to get the correct time via NTP (using NTPv4) from 10.3.3.125 is as follows:

```
Router1(config)# ntp server 10.3.3.125 version 4
```

Verification of NTP

How do you know whether your router is correctly configured and using NTP? The two basic commands CCNAs need to know are **show ntp status** and **show ntp associations**. Sample output of those two commands is shown here:

```
Router1# show ntp status
Clock is synchronized, stratum 4, reference is 10.3.3.125
nominal freq is 250.0000 Hz, actual freq is 250.0000 Hz, precision is
2**21
ntp uptime is 2800 (1/100 of seconds), resolution is 4000
reference time is D42BDAF2.4C2F31A4 (21:11:30.481 UTC Thu Jun 27 2012)
clock offset is -0.00228 msec, root delay is 1.15 msec
root dispersion is 3234.21 msec, peer dispersion is 121.41 msec
loopfilter state is 'CTRL' (Normal Controlled Loop), drift is
0.000000000 s/s
system poll interval is 64, last update was 21 sec ago.
!
Router1# show ntp associations

 address      ref clock     st  when  poll reach  delay  offset disp
*10.3.3.125   127.127.1.1   3   28    64   1      1.048  -0.001 4928.4

* sys.peer, # selected, + candidate, - outlyer, x falseticker,
configured
```

Cram Quiz

1. Which configuration sets up the router as an NTP client of the GPS clock at 216.234.161.11?

   ❍ **A.** Router(config)#**ntp server 216.234.161.11 version 4**

   ❍ **B.** Router(config)#**ntp client 216.234.161.11 version 4**

   ❍ **C.** Router(config-if)#**ntp server 216.234.161.11 version 4**

   ❍ **D.** Router(config-if)#**ntp client 216.234.161.11 version 4**

2. How would you verify whether your router is getting NTP information from an NTP server?

   ❍ **A.** **show ntp service**

   ❍ **B.** **show ntp server**

   ❍ **C.** **show ntp source**

   ❍ **D.** **show ntp status**

3. How would you verify all the NTP servers your router is configured to use?

   ❍ **A.** **show ntp status**

   ❍ **B.** **show ntp associations**

   ❍ **C.** **show ntp server**

   ❍ **D.** **show ntp stratum**

Cram Quiz Answers

1. Answer A is correct. Answers B, C, and D are wrong because they aren't Answer A.
2. Answer D is correct. Answer A is not a real command. Answer B is not a real command. Answer C displays the configured NTP source address, if the router is itself an NTP server.
3. Answer B is correct. Answer A is wrong because the command will show one server, but not all the ones to which the router is associated. Answers C and D are not real commands.

DHCP

CramSaver

1. Several hosts use static IP addresses on the network. What command will prevent DHCP from handing out addresses that are already in use?
   - **A.** **no ip dhcp conflict**
   - **B.** **ip dhcp conflict-resolve**
   - **C.** **ip dhcp excluded-address**
   - **D.** **ip dhcp address-exclude**
2. What **dhcp pool** command defines the default gateway address for DHCP clients?
   - **A.** **ip default-gateway**
   - **B.** **default-router** *<default_gateway_ip>*
   - **C.** **default-gateway**
   - **D.** None of these answers are correct.

Answers

1. Answer C is correct. Answers A, B, and D are not real commands.
2. Answer B is correct. Answer A is the command to set the gateway on a switch. Answer C is not a valid command, and Answer D is incorrect.

Your router can be both a DHCP server, to hand out addresses to hosts, and a DHCP client, to obtain a DHCP address for one of its interfaces. The DHCP service is quite simple, but provides reliable DHCP functionality for small deployments.

Configuring an IOS Router as a DHCP Client

The client setup is easy. The basic command (entered at the interface that should obtain its address from DHCP) is as follows:

```
Router(config-if)#ip address DHCP
```

While there are several options to modify how the client operates, they are beyond the scope of CCNA.

Configuring an IOS Router as a DHCP Server

DHCP server configuration is a little more complex, but by no means difficult. A DHCP server should provide the following to clients:

- A valid IP address from a defined range within the requesting subnet
- The correct subnet mask for the subnet
- The default gateway IP

In addition, the DHCP server may also provide the following:

- DNS server IP (primary and possibly secondary)
- TFTP server IP (Option 150) or hostname (Option 66)

DHCP servers are configured with a range of IPs to hand out. The range is variously called a *scope*, a *subnet*, or in the case of the IOS, a *pool*. The pool will specify the subnet address, the mask, the default gateway, and usually the DNS addresses too. Other options such as the TFTP server address (which is, incidentally, critically important to a Cisco Unified Communications IP Phone deployment) may optionally be included in the pool.

Most networks have some IP addresses that are already in use: The routers and switches, the servers, the printers—these devices are often given a static IP instead of using DHCP. It would be a bad idea to have DHCP hand out these addresses again to a different device, so we must also configure a set of excluded IP addresses, to prevent the router from handing them out along with the other addresses in the pool.

The router will test to see whether the address it will offer is already assigned to a host by pinging the address three times. If a conflict is detected, the address is marked as conflicting and a different address will be offered and tested.

A typical configuration would look something like the following. (The commands have been annotated to explain their function.)

```
ip dhcp excluded-address 192.168.1.1 192.168.1.10
ip dhcp excluded-address 192.168.2.1 192.168.2.10
! specifies which IP address ranges may NOT be assigned to hosts
!
ip dhcp pool North-Pavilion-Subnet
network 192.168.1.0 255.255.255.0
!
```

```
! Creates the pool named North-Pavilion-Subnet, defines the addresses
! to assign and the correct subnet mask
!
dns-server 10.8.8.7 10.8.8.8
! Defines Primary and Secondary DNS server IP address
default-router 192.168.1.1
! Defines the Default Gateway IP
lease 4 0 0
! Sets the DHCP address lease time to 4 days, 0 hours, 0 minutes
domain-name examcram2.com
! Sets the domain name suffix for hosts
!
ip dhcp pool South-Pavilion-Subnet
network 192.168.2.0 /24
dns-server 10.8.8.7 10.8.8.8
default-router 192.168.2.1
lease 4 0 0
domain-name examcram2.com
! Similar configurations specific to South Pavilion subnet
```

Verification of DHCP Operation

The commands available to verify your DHCP include the following:

- **show ip dhcp binding:** Lists which IPs have been leased to hosts, expiration of lease, and lease type
- **show ip dhcp pool <*pool_name*>:** Lists the utilization details of the specified pool

Examples of these two verification commands are shown here. In the example, note that the **show ip dhcp binding** output indicates that 192.168.1.11 has been leased. (Note that this is the first IP available outside of the excluded range.) The **show ip dhcp pool** output indicates that one address has been leased and which one will be leased next, along with some other basic pool data:

```
Router1#show ip dhcp binding
Bindings from all pools not associated with VRF:
IP address        Client-ID/            Lease expiration        Type
                  Hardware address/
                  User name
192.168.2.11/24   0063.6973.636f.2d64.  Jul 1 2013 04:36 AM     Automatic
                  656d.6574.6572.2d47.
                  4c4f.4241.4c
```

```
Router1# show ip dhcp pool South-Pavilion-Subnet
Pool South-Pavilion-Subnet:
Utilization mark (high/low) : 100 / 0
Subnet size (first/next) : 0 / 0
Total addresses : 254
Leased addresses : 1
Pending event : none
1 subnet is currently in the pool :
Current index  IP address range              Leased addresses
192.168.2.12   192.168.2.1 - 192.168.2.254   1
```

Cram Quiz

Use the following DHCP config to answer the Cram Quiz questions:

```
ip dhcp excluded-address 192.168.1.1 192.168.1.10
ip dhcp excluded-address 192.168.2.1 192.168.2.10
!
ip dhcp pool North-Pavilion-Subnet
network 192.168.1.0 255.255.255.0
dns-server 10.8.8.7 10.8.8.8
default-router 192.168.1.1
lease 4 0 0
domain-name examcram2.com
!
ip dhcp pool South-Pavilion-Subnet
network 192.168.2.0 /24
dns-server 10.8.8.7 10.8.8.8
default-router 192.168.2.1
lease 4 0 0
domain-name examcram2.com
```

1. True or False: DHCP will offer the IP of 192.168.1.10 to a DHCP client.
2. What happens when Gary statically assigns the IP of 192.168.1.11/24 to his laptop?
   - ❍ **A.** The DHCP router will offer a client the same address, and a conflict will ensue.
   - ❍ **B.** The DHCP router will ping 192.168.1.11 once, and if there is a reply, it will not offer an address.
   - ❍ **C.** The DHCP router will ping 192.168.1.11 three times, and if there is a reply, it will force that host to perform a DHCP release/renew.
   - ❍ **D.** The DHCP router will ping 192.168.1.11 three times, and if there is a reply, it will mark that address as in conflict. It will then offer the next available address in the pool.

Cram Quiz Answers

1. False. The excluded range includes that address; the DHCP router will start with offering 192.168.1.11.

2. Answer D is correct. Answer A is wrong because there is a conflict-detection mechanism in the router DHCP service. Answer B is wrong because it pings three times, marks the address as in conflict, and offers the next available address instead. Answer C is wrong because there is no capability to force a DHCP release/renew on a client.

Review Questions

Use the following NAT config to answer the next three questions:

```
interface f0/0
description Office LAN
ip address 192.168.0.1 255.255.255.0
ip nat inside
no shut
!
interface g1/0
description MetroGig Internet
ip address 24.12.1.18 255.255.255.248
ip nat outside
no shut
!
access-list 1 permit 192.168.0.0 0.0.0.255
ip nat pool Shamalamadingdong 24.12.1.19 24.12.1.29 netmask
255.255.255.248
ip nat inside source list 1 pool Shamalamadingdong overload
!
```

1. Which of the following would you expect to see as an inside local address?

❍ **A.** 192.168.1.10

❍ **B.** 192.168.0.25

❍ **C.** 192.168.1.0

❍ **D.** 24.12.1.29

❍ **E.** 24.12.1.1

❍ **F.** 24.12.1.30

2. What type of configuration is this?

❍ **A.** NAT

❍ **B.** Dynamic NAT

❍ **C.** PAT

❍ **D.** Static NAT

3. True or False: All possible translations will use the same inside local address.

4. True or False: NTP requires Internet connectivity to function.

5. What is the primary benefit of NTP?

❍ **A.** Synchronization of clocks on multiple networked devices

❍ **B.** Automatic Time Zone detection and setting

❍ **C.** Implementation of ISO Metric Time

❍ **C.** All of the above

6. Which command sets your router to use the Internet-accessible time server at 216.234.161.11?

❍ **A.** Router(config-if)#**ntp server 216.234.161.11 version 4**

❍ **B.** Router(config)#**ntp client 216.234.161.11 version 4**

❍ **C.** Router(config)#**ntp server 216.234.161.11 version 4**

❍ **D.** Router(config-if)#**ntp client 216.234.161.11 version 4**

7. What can be learned from the command **show ntp status**?

❍ **A.** Current NTP server in use

❍ **B.** Stratum level of the NTP server

❍ **C.** Stratum level of this router

❍ **D.** All of the above

8. The Montreal Canadiens hockey club has hired you to set up the DHCP service on their router. They would like to know which of the following statements is true of the IOS DHCP service.

❍ **A.** Multiple subnets can be served by one router.

❍ **B.** Options that can be specified to clients include default gateway, DNS servers, TFTP server, IP address and subnet mask.

❍ **C.** IP address conflicts cannot be resolved if using IOS DHCP.

❍ **D.** There is no way to verify which hosts have been assigned which DHCP addresses.

9. What command enables you to determine what DHCP address was leased to a particular host?

❍ **A.** **show ip dhcp binding**

❍ **B.** **show ip dhcp assigned**

❍ **C.** **show ip dhcp lease**

❍ **D.** **show ip dhcp conflict**

10. What command excludes certain IP addresses from being offered to DHCP clients?

❍ **A.** **ip dhcp pool**

❍ **B.** **ip address dhcp**

❍ **C.** **ip dhcp conflict-avoid auto**

❍ **D.** **ip dhcp excluded-address**

Answers to Review Questions

1. Answer D is correct. Inside local addresses are what the hosts get translated to. The config **line ip nat pool Shamalamadingdong 24.12.1.19 24.12.1.29 netmask 255.255.255.248** shows that the hosts will be translated to addresses in the range of 24.12.1.19 24.12.1.29.
2. Answer C is correct. The **overload** term at the end of the NAT command activates PAT.
3. False. Because a pool is being overloaded, multiple translations will happen on multiple addresses in the pool.
4. Answer C is correct. Although the use of an Internet-accessible NTP server is typical and desirable, you can use your router (and some switches) as an internal NTP source, perhaps in an isolated lab. It's not recommended to do so in a production environment, unless you happen to have your own atomic or GPS clock.
5. Answer A is correct. NTP is not time zone aware (it uses the UTC time format), and there is no such thing as metric time, even in Canada.
6. Answer C is correct. The other answers are either at the wrong config prompt or use the wrong command syntax.
7. Answer D is correct.
8. Answers A and B are correct. There is a conflict-prevention mechanism in the IOS DHCP service, and the command **show ip dhcp binding** will list the addresses leased to hosts.
9. Answer A is correct. The command **show ip dhcp binding** will list the addresses leased to hosts.
10. Answer D is correct.

CHAPTER ELEVEN

Troubleshooting

This chapter covers the following official CCNA Routing and Switching 200-120 exam topics:

- Troubleshoot and resolve Layer 1 problems.
- Troubleshoot and resolve VLAN problems.
- Troubleshoot and resolve trunking problems on Cisco switches.
- Troubleshoot and correct common problems associated with IP addressing and host configurations.
- Troubleshoot and resolve ACL issues.

Troubleshoot Layer 1 Problems

CramSaver

If you can correctly answer these questions before going through this section, save time by skimming the Exam Alerts in this section and then completing the Cram Quiz at the end of the section.

1. What is likely to cause CRC errors? Choose two.

   A. Speed mismatch

   B. Duplex mismatch

   C. Damaged cables

   D. Electromagnetic interference

2. What command should be used to view counters for collisions, runts, and giants?

   A. show variance

   B. show version

   C. show interface

   D. show errors

Answers

1. Answers C and D are correct. EMI, damaged cables, and cables that are too long can cause CRC errors.
2. Answer C is correct. The command **show interface** can be used to view the counters for collisions, runts and giants. The other commands are either incorrect IOS syntax, or do not show the information about collisions, runts, or giants.

Problems with the Wiring

If Layer 1 isn't working or functioning, Layer 2 doesn't have a chance. This section focuses our troubleshooting efforts on Layer 1 issues.

If a cable is damaged, so badly that it can no longer carry the bits that are being transmitted on that media, that would be a physical layer problem. If the cable is fiber, and is bent too sharply, that can cause problems do to allowing light to escape, or causing problems with the reflection that should normally occur inside the cable. Another problem with fiber may be due to poor or incorrect splicing or termination of the fiber. Problems such as CRC errors may be reported from the **show interfaces** command as a result of a damaged cable.

With copper cables, if the incorrect type of cable is used or if there is a large source of electromagnetic interference (EMI), that can also disrupt the signal and cause a failure on the network.

Duplex

In a high-speed network, we will usually use full duplex. With full duplex, devices on the network can both send and receive at the same time. The duplex settings should match between two directly connected devices such as a switch and a host connected to a switch. If one of these devices believes it should be operating at half duplex (due to an incorrect configuration setting or an error in negotiating the speed and duplex) and the other device believes it's okay to operate at full duplex, this will cause a significant slowdown when the half-duplex device thinks that collisions are occurring every time it receives data while it's also sending data.

Finding the Errors

The **show interface** command can assist us by showing the interface status, duplex in use, the line protocol status, the link state, in addition to indicating noise, collisions, and late collisions that are occurring, as shown in Example 11.1:

EXAMPLE 11.1 **Output from the show interface Command**

```
Switch#show interfaces Gi0/2
GigabitEthernet0/2 is up, line protocol is up (connected)
  Hardware is Gigabit Ethernet, address is 001c.b148.1e82 (bia 001c.
b148.1e82)
  MTU 1504 bytes, BW 100000 Kbit, DLY 100 usec,
     reliability 255/255, txload 1/255, rxload 1/255
  Encapsulation ARPA, loopback not set
  Keepalive set (10 sec)
  Half-duplex, 100Mb/s, media type is 10/100/1000BaseTX
  input flow-control is off, output flow-control is unsupported
  ARP type: ARPA, ARP Timeout 04:00:00
  Last input 00:00:00, output 00:00:00, output hang never
  Last clearing of "show interface" counters never
  Input queue: 0/75/0/0 (size/max/drops/flushes); Total output drops:
0
  Queueing strategy: fifo
  Output queue: 0/40 (size/max)
  5 minute input rate 2000 bits/sec, 4 packets/sec
  5 minute output rate 0 bits/sec, 0 packets/sec
```

continues

EXAMPLE 11.1 **Continued**

```
     429 packets input, 33084 bytes, 0 no buffer
     Received 429 broadcasts (423 multicasts)
     12 runts, 0 giants, 0 throttles
     6 input errors, 6 CRC, 0 frame, 0 overrun, 0 ignored
     0 watchdog, 423 multicast, 0 pause input
     0 input packets with dribble condition detected
     276 packets output, 19502 bytes, 0 underruns
     65 output errors, 55 collisions, 5 interface resets
     0 babbles, 25 late collision, 0 deferred
     0 lost carrier, 0 no carrier, 0 PAUSE output
     0 output buffer failures, 0 output buffers swapped out
```

Determine the Link State

From the very first line of the output of Example 11.1, we can learn the interface status and line protocol status. The combination of these results in the link state of the interface being looked at. Table 11.1 shows an example of the resulting link states.

TABLE 11.1 **Link State as a Result of Interface and Line Protocol Status**

Interface Status	Line Protocol Status	Resulting Link State
Up	Up (connected)	Functional/working
Up	Down	Problem at Layer 2
Down	Down	Unplugged, or other end of connection is not enabled or on
Administratively down	Down	Locally shut down / disabled

The interface and line protocol status roughly equate to Layer 1 and Layer 2, respectively. Layer 2 problems could be created by an encapsulation mismatch, such as one end of a serial link being configured for PPP and the other side using the Cisco default of High-Level Data Link Control (HDLC). Both ends of the link should be enabled and configured to use the same Layer 2 encapsulation. Additional reasons of an up/down state could include clock rate, missing keepalives, PPP authentication failures, or a router at one end of a Frame Relay private virtual circuit (PVC) being shut down, which may cause an up/down status at the router at the other end of the PVC.

The output of the **show interfaces** command shown in Example 11.1 can also indicate problems with noise (from EMI) and collisions (potentially from a duplex mismatch). Table 11.2 lists noise and collision indicators, along with how to resolve the issues.

TABLE 11.2 **Reasons for Noise and Collisions**

Noise	Collisions	Late Collisions
Excessive cyclic redundancy check (CRC) errors can be caused by incorrect cabling, damaged cables, or large sources of EMI near copper Ethernet cabling. Verify that correct and working cabling is present, and remove excessive EMI that may be harming the transmission of bits on the copper media.	These are expected in half-duplex networks using hubs. However, if using full-duplex Ethernet, there shouldn't be many collisions. If they are seen in large numbers, a duplex issue likely exists. To resolve this issue, verify that both sides are configured to use full duplex.	This is likely due to a duplex mismatch with one end seeing the link as full and the other seeing it as half duplex. Correct the duplex issue. In half-duplex networks, if the Ethernet lengths are exceeded, this may also cause late collisions.

A CRC error is caused by a checksum being different (for the same frame) between the device that sent the frame and the device that received the frame. A runt is an Ethernet frame that is less than 64 bytes (the legal limit), and a giant is a frame that is larger than 1518 bytes. In some environments, seeing a giant (frame) is not necessarily bad; for example, it is common to see giant frames in Multiprotocol Label Switching (MPLS) networks, or in other environments where the maximum frame size is intentionally larger than 1518 bytes.

For troubleshooting the issues mentioned in Table 11.2, the primary command is the **show** *interface(s)* command. CDP, if enabled, can also generate a duplex mismatch message when it detects that the duplex of the local device is different than its CDP neighbor at the other end of the link.

Cram Quiz

1. If a switch port is administratively shut down, what would be the status of a router, whose interface connected to that port is configured with an IP address and is administratively up?

   ❍ **A.** Up/up

   ❍ **B.** Up/down

   ❍ **C.** Down/down

   ❍ **C.** Administratively down

2. Which ends of an Ethernet connection would show excessive collisions if there is a duplex mismatch?

   ❍ **A.** The end configured as half duplex

   ❍ **B.** The end configured as full duplex

   ❍ **C.** The end configured with a clock rate

   ❍ **D.** The end configured with the DTE cable connection

Cram Quiz Answers

1. Answer C is correct. The router, because it is not receiving a link signal from the shutdown switch port, would show as being down/down, which loosely relates to the Layer 1 and Layer 2 status of the interface. When a shutdown command is used, the interface will show administratively down.
2. Answer A is correct. The side configured as half duplex would believe a collision has happened when the other side sends data at the same time the half-duplex side is trying to send data, and that is where the collisions would be seen. The full-duplex side would have collision detection turned off, because it believes that full duplex won't need to check for collisions. Clock rate commands and DTE interfaces apply to serial connections, not to Ethernet.

Verify and Troubleshoot VLANs and Port Membership

CramSaver

If you can correctly answer these questions before going through this section, save time by skimming the Exam Alerts in this section and then completing the Cram Quiz at the end of the section.

1. What is the traditional/common relationship between a Layer 2 VLAN and a Layer 3 IP subnet?
   - **A.** There is a two to one correlation: two VLANs per subnet.
   - **B.** There is a one to two correlation: one VLAN to two subnets.
   - **C.** There is a one to one correlation: one VLAN to a single subnet.
   - **D.** There is a one to three correlation: one VLAN to an IPv4, IPv6, and OSPF subnet.

2. What may cause two devices that have IP addresses in the same subnet to not be able to communicate with each other?
   - **A.** They have the same mask.
   - **B.** They have different IP host addresses.
   - **C.** They are in different VLANs.
   - **D.** They are in the same VLAN.

Answers

1. There are normally a one to one correlation between broadcast domains (VLANs) and IP subnets. Although multiple subnets of the same protocol could be associated to a single subnet, this isn't usually done. IPv4 and IPv6 can use the same VLAN, but in Answer D, OSPF is a routing protocol, not an network address type.
2. If two devices that have IP addresses in the same subnet can't communicate with each other, they may have (in error) been placed into different VLANs. Devices with IP addresses in the same subnet range should also be in the same Layer 2 broadcast domain (VLAN).

Troubleshooting VLANs

A VLAN is a Layer 2 broadcast domain. If two customers connected to Ethernet are in the same IP subnet, they both need to be in the same VLAN as well. Controlling which VLAN a host belongs to is managed by the switch at the switch port where a host is connected. There are several ways of verifying which VLANs ports are assigned to. One method is to use the command **show VLAN** (brief), as shown in Example 11.2.

EXAMPLE 11.2 **Verifying Port Assignments with show vlan**

```
Switch#show vlan brief

VLAN Name                             Status    Ports
---- -------------------------------- --------- -------------------------------
1    default                          active    Gi0/1, Gi0/3, Gi0/4, Gi0/5
                                                Gi0/6, Gi0/7, Gi0/8, Gi0/9
                                                Gi0/10, Gi0/11, Gi0/12, Gi0/13
                                                Gi0/14, Gi0/15, Gi0/16, Gi0/17
                                                Gi0/18, Gi0/19, Gi0/20, Gi0/21
                                                Gi0/22, Gi0/23, Gi0/24, Gi0/25
                                                Gi0/26, Gi0/27, Gi0/28
2    VLAN0002                               active
3    VLAN0003                               active
4    VLAN0004                               active
5    VLAN0005                               active
11   VLAN0011                               active
12   VLAN0012                               active
55   VLAN0055                               active    Gi0/2
<snip>
```

In the output, devices connected to ports G0/1 and G0/3-28 all are in the same VLAN (VLAN 1). Port G0/2 is the only port allocated to VLAN 55. Unless there is also a default gateway that supports VLAN 55, the host connected to G0/2 won't be able to communicate with other hosts connected to this switch.

Another useful command that can show how a port is configured as well as how it is currently operating is the command **show interface switchport**, which will show how a port is administratively configured, in addition to how it is currently operating. In Example 11.3, we can see the details for a specific port g0/2 as we look at the details provided by the command **show interface g0/2 switchport**.

EXAMPLE 11.3 **Viewing Switch Port Details**

```
Switch#show interface g0/2 switchport
Name: Gi0/2
Switchport: Enabled
Administrative Mode: static access
Operational Mode: static access
Administrative Trunking Encapsulation: negotiate
Operational Trunking Encapsulation: native
Negotiation of Trunking: Off
Access Mode VLAN: 55 (VLAN0055)
Trunking Native Mode VLAN: 1 (default)
Administrative Native VLAN tagging: enabled
<snip>
```

From this output, we can see that this switch port is administratively configured as an access port, and is also operating as an access port. We can also see the current access mode VLAN of 55.

To configure a switchport as an access port (not a trunk) and assign the VLAN of 55, we use the commands shown in Example 11.4.

EXAMPLE 11.4 **Commands to Configure an Access Port in VLAN 55**

```
! Enter configuration mode
Switch#conf t
! Move to the interface you want to configure
Switch(config)#interface GigabitEthernet0/2
! Specify the mode
Switch(config-if)#switchport mode access
! Specify the VLAN assignment
Switch(config-if)#switchport access vlan 55
```

Cram Quiz

Answer these questions. The answers follow the last question. If you cannot answer these questions correctly, consider reading this section again until you can.

1. What are the two steps required for creating and using smaller broadcast domains? Choose two.

   ❍ **A.** Creating more VLANs

   ❍ **B.** Assigning one or more port from existing VLANs to the new VLAN

   ❍ **C.** Creating more collision domains

   ❍ **D.** Assigning one or more ports from existing collision domains to the new collision domains.

2. What would cause a host with an IP address of 10.1.1.14/28 to not be able to ping another host that has the address of 10.1.1.2/28 if both interfaces are up and connected to the same physical switch?

   ❍ **A.** The two IP addresses are in different subnets, and would require a default gateway for the hosts to reach each other.

   ❍ **B.** The ports the hosts are connected to are in different VLANs.

   ❍ **C.** The mask isn't valid.

   D. The default gateways used by the hosts don't have a route mto the other network.

Cram Quiz Answers

1. Answers A and B are correct. A VLAN is a Layer 2 broadcast domain. By default there is only one, which all ports belong to. To create smaller broadcast domains, new VLANs should be created, and some of the ports that were in the default VLAN (originally) should be move to the new VLAN. If there are no ports in a VLAN, it will be an unused broadcast domain. The original default VLAN will be come a smaller broadcast domain as some of the ports are moved to the new VLANs.

2. Answer B is correct. The hosts have IP addresses in the same subnet. If the ports the hosts were connected to were not in the same VLAN (different broadcast domains for each host), that would prevent the two devices (that from an IP subnet perspective are local to each other in the same network) from being able to reach each other.

Verify Trunk Configuration and Operation

CramSaver

If you can correctly answer these questions before going through this section, save time by skimming the Exam Alerts in this section and then completing the Cram Quiz at the end of the section.

1. What is the difference between operational and administrative modes on a switch port?
2. If a switch receives a tagged frame on a trunk port, what does it do with that frame if it doesn't know about the VLAN listed in the 802.1Q header?

Answers

1. Administrative mode is how a port has been configured, whereas operational mode is how the switch port is currently operating. (The two may differ from each other.)
2. Switches that receive a tag for an unknown VLAN will drop the frame.

Is the Link Up and Configured?

When troubleshooting a trunk port, we would first verify that we have basic connectivity, and then secondly verify that both ends of the link are either configured for or have successfully negotiated a truck. The commands **show interfaces** and **show CDP neighbors** can verify the link, and the command **show interface trunk** can verify whether the trunk is functioning.

VLANs Must Exist for the Trunk to Support Them

Another problem that may come up is that a switch cannot forward frames across the trunk for a VLAN that it does not know about. For example, if a switch receives a tagged frame that indicates the frame is for VLAN 9, but the switch doesn't have VLAN 9 in its configuration, it simply drops that frame and does not forward it, even if it has other trunk links.

Administrative Versus Operational

The verification of a trunk can be done using the commands **show interfaces** along with the **switchport** or **trunk** options, as shown in Examples 11.5 and 11.6.

EXAMPLE 11.5 **Checking the Administrative and Operational Modes**

```
Switch#show int g0/2 switchport
Name: Gi0/2
Switchport: Enabled
Administrative Mode: trunk
Operational Mode: trunk
Administrative Trunking Encapsulation: dot1q
Operational Trunking Encapsulation: dot1q
Negotiation of Trunking: On
Access Mode VLAN: 1 (default)
Trunking Native Mode VLAN: 1 (default)
Administrative Native VLAN tagging: enabled
Voice VLAN: none
Administrative private-vlan host-association: none
Administrative private-vlan mapping: none
Administrative private-vlan trunk native VLAN: none
Administrative private-vlan trunk Native VLAN tagging: enabled
Administrative private-vlan trunk encapsulation: dot1q
Administrative private-vlan trunk normal VLANs: none
Administrative private-vlan trunk associations: none
Administrative private-vlan trunk mappings: none
Operational private-vlan: none
Trunking VLANs Enabled: ALL
Pruning VLANs Enabled: 2-1001
Capture Mode Disabled
Capture VLANs Allowed: ALL
<snip>
```

The Operational Mode output indicates that this interface is currently operating as a trunk port.

The verification of the trunk, its encapsulation, and native VLAN (which should both match between the two devices which have connected interfaces that are doing trunking) can be seen by using the command **show interfaces trunk**, as shown in Example 11.6

EXAMPLE 11.6 **Verifying the Trunk**

```
Switch#show int g0/2 trunk

Port        Mode             Encapsulation  Status        Native vlan
Gi0/2       on               802.1q         trunking      1

Port        Vlans allowed on trunk
Gi0/2       1-4094

Port        Vlans allowed and active in management domain
Gi0/2       1-5,11-12,55

Port        Vlans in spanning tree forwarding state and not pruned
Gi0/2       1-5,11-12,55
```

The Mode indicates whether trunking was negotiated or configured (in this example, on indicates it was configured), and the status indicates that trunking is active.

The last two sections in the output, "Vlans allowed and active in management domain" and "Vlans in spanning tree forwarding state and not pruned," should be identical unless spanning tree is blocking on any of the switches' trunk ports or VLAN Trunking Protocol (VTP) pruning is preventing some of the traffic from being forwarded.

Cram Quiz

Answer these questions. The answers follow the last question. If you cannot answer these questions correctly, consider reading this section again until you can.

1. What does a switch do when it receives a tagged frame on a trunk interface, and the switch doesn't have the VLAN (identified by the tag) configured?

   ❍ **A.** It forwards the frame out of all other interfaces for all VLANs.

   ❍ **B.** It discards the frame.

   ❍ **C.** It converts the frame to a unicast and forwards the frame to its default gateways Layer 2 address.

   ❍ **D.** It assumes the frame is for the same VLAN as the "native" VLAN configured on the trunk.

2. What could cause a VLAN to be allowed on a trunk port, but currently not be allowed to be forwarded on that same trunk port? Choose two.

   ❍ **A.** The VLAN doesn't exist on the switch.

   ❍ **B.** Spanning Tree Protocol is currently blocking on that trunk port for the VLAN.

   ❍ **C.** The native VLAN isn't the default VLAN of 1

   ❍ **D.** The native VLAN for the trunk is the same VLAN as the frame being sent.

Cram Quiz Answers

1. Answer B is correct. If a switch receives a frame that is tagged with an unknown VLAN, the receiving switch will drop/discard the frame.

2. Answers A and B are correct. If a VLAN doesn't exist on a switch, it won't forward that VLAN over a trunk port. Spanning Tree Protocol (STP) could also prevent the forwarding on a trunk, if there were redundant paths and the trunk port (in the question) was currently blocking for VLAN. The native VLAN on a trunk would not by itself have relevance on whether a specific VLAN could be forwarded on a trunk. Frames for the VLAN that matches the native VLAN configured on the trunk are sent without any 802.1Q tags at all over the trunk.

Troubleshoot Problems with IP Addressing and Host Configurations

CramSaver

If you can correctly answer these questions before going through this section, save time by skimming the Exam Alerts in this section and then completing the Cram Quiz at the end of the section.

1. Will a host at 10.65.0.1/10 be able to ping a host at 10.63.0.2/10 if there is no default gateway configured?

   A. Yes

   B. No

   C. It depends if IPv6 is running

2. Which of the following ways is the most efficient to discover and change an IP address that you suspect is incorrectly configured on a router (in the wrong subnet) but is in the same VLAN as the local router you are connected to, when the only connectivity to the other router is over IP?

   A. Ping every address in the subnet until you find out what the configured IP address is.

   B. Use CDP to discover the IP address of the peer, change the local router IP to be in the same subnet, remotely access the router, and then change the Windows address back to the correct subnet as well.

   C. Use CDP to discover the IP address of the peer, telnet to the router, and change the IP address.

   D. This can't be done over IP. A console connect must be used to correct the IP addressing problem on the router.

Answers

1. Answer B is correct. These two addresses are in different subnets, which would require a default gateway to be used. The two subnets are 10.64.0.0/10 and 10.0.0.0/10. A default gateway is required for hosts in one subnet to reach hosts in another subnet.
2. Answer C is correct. CDP could be used to discover the Layer 3 address of the peer. CDP operates at Layer 2 and could still function even when incorrect Layer 3 addresses are used. The local router could be manually configured to be in the same subnet as the router, and then remote access via telnet or Secure Shell (SSH) could be used to access the other router (from the local router). Once the router IP is changed, the local router should be changed back to the correct subnet address as well.

Verify Hosts Have Correct IP Addresses

When two computers are connected to the same Layer 2 broadcast domain (VLAN), they should both have IP addresses from the same IP Layer 3 address space (IP network or subnet). One of the most common problems with IP addressing arises from an administrator not realizing the boundaries for an IP subnet. One way of see whether IP addresses belong to the same subnet is to identify the first and last valid IP address in any given subnet and make sure that all the devices in that VLAN have addresses within the same IP subnet (including the default gateway that will be used by the hosts in that subnet). To learn how to calculate the ranges of IP subnets, see Chapter 3, "Concepts in IP Addressing."

How to Remotely Change a Cisco IP Address

If you are working with Cisco devices, you can leverage CDP to see the Layer 3 address of a directly connected Cisco device, (but the mask is not shown as part of the CDP information). If you use CDP and learn that the directly connected device is using the address of 10.0.0.1 and that the local device that you are on is using 172.16.0.2, for example, you could temporarily change your own local IP address to put it on the same network as your peer, and then remotely connect to that device. Be aware, though, that once remotely connected to that second device the moment we change its IP address and press Enter we are going to lose our current session to that device and may have to reconnect to the new IP address we just configured on that device.

Making Sure That We Have a Default Gateway on Hosts

Hosts on the subnet need to be configured with a default gateway that can and is willing to route traffic for those devices (when those devices need to communicate with other devices outside of the subnet). A default gateway could be a multilayer switch, a dedicated router, or a router on a stick. In any of those scenarios, the clients need a local default gateway (where the gateway's address is on the same local subnet of the client). On a Windows computer, the command **ipconfig** can be used to see the IP address and the default gateway. The command **ipconfig /all** enables you to include additional information such as the DHCP server (if one was used by the client).

Troubleshooting NAT

Another item that involves IP addresses and is often in need of troubleshooting is Network Address Translation (NAT)

Table 11.3 describes the commands most effective in troubleshooting NAT.

TABLE 11.3 **Useful NAT related commands**

Useful Command	Purpose
show ip nat translations	Shows any current NAT translations in place. If you have dynamic NAT configured, and no traffic going through the router yet, there may not be any translations in place.
show ip nat statistics	Verifies whether the interfaces are configured to support NAT (and additional details about the number of translations).
debug ip nat	Can provide insight to what is (or isn't) happening regarding NAT on the router.
show access-list	If an ACL is used as part of the configuration for NAT, verifying that the ACL is correct (matching the desired source traffic as an example) is a good troubleshooting step.

It is also important to verify that the outside networks (from NAT's perspective) have a route back to the inside global addresses used in NAT (meaning that the reply packets from the outside networks will be returned through the NAT device). Routing on the NAT device should be verified as well. If the NAT device doesn't have a route for a destination network, it will not trigger the NAT process for a packet trying to go to that destination network.

Cram Quiz

Answer these questions. The answers follow the last question. If you cannot answer these questions correctly, consider reading this section again until you can.

1. What is the term for the NAT address that is a routable global address, and maps to an inside address using NAT?

 ❍ **A.** Outside local

 ❍ **B.** Outside global

 ❍ **C.** Inside local

 ❍ **D.** Inside global

2. Which of the following addresses would belong to a DHCP pool of 123.58.24.0/21? Choose all that apply.

   ❍ **A.** 123.58.23.50

   ❍ **B.** 123.58.25.50

   ❍ **C.** 123.58.29.50

   ❍ **D.** 123.58.33.50

Cram Quiz Answers

1. Answer D is correct. A NAT inside global address is an outside globally routable address that maps to the IP address of an inside host.

2. Answers B and C are correct. The subnet 123.58.24.0/21 has a block size of 8, so the subnets are 123.58.0.0/21, 123.58.8.0/21, 123.58.16.0/21, 123.58.24.0/21, 123.58.32.0/21, and so on. The range for the 24 subnet is 123.58.24.1 to 123.58.31.255. The two correct answers fall within that range.

Troubleshoot ACL Issues

CramSaver

If you can correctly answer these questions before going through this section, save time by skimming the Exam Alerts in this section and then completing the Cram Quiz at the end of the section.

1. What happens when an ACL that doesn't exist in the running configuration is applied to an interface?

   A. All traffic is filtered based on the direction the ACL is applied.

   C. If applied outbound, all traffic except for traffic sourced from the router is denied outbound on that interface.

   C. All traffic if permitted in the ACL is applied, inbound or outbound.

   D. The IOS won't accept the command, and the ACL name/number won't be applied to the running configuration.

2. Consider the following ACL:

```
access-list 100 permit tcp 10.1.2.0 0.0.0.255 host 5.5.5.5
eq 80
access-list 100 deny ip host 34.2.1.99 host 5.5.5.5
access-list 100 permit icmp 10.1.2.3 0.0.0.0 host 5.5.5.5
access-list 100 permit tcp 34.2.1.0 0.0.0.0.255 5.5.5.0
0.0.0.255 eq 443
```

   When applied outbound on a router interface, which of the following are true?

   A. All hosts on the 34.2.1.0/24 subnet are allowed HTTPS access to the hosts on the 5.5.5.0/24 network.

   B. All hosts on the 10.1.2.0/24 network can send ICMP ping requests to the device at 5.5.5.5.

   C. The host at 10.1.2.3 can connect to a web server at 5.5.5.5.

   D. All hosts on subnet 34.2.1.0/24 can connect to HTTP services running on 5.5.5.5.

Answers

1. Answer D is correct. A mistyped ACL (when applying it to an interface) won't have any effect if there isn't at least one entry (access control entry or ACE) present in the ACL. It will be as if there is no ACL applied from a traffic flow perspective. The running configuration will show that the ACL is applied, but there will be no denying traffic as a result of it.

2. Answer C is correct. ACLs are processed from top down. The first ACL entry that a packet matches is acted on (permit or deny), and the rest of the ACL entries aren't considered. The host at 10.1.2.3 can access TCP port 80 because of the first line of the ACL. Not all hosts on the 34.2.1.0/24 subnet are allowed HTTP access to the hosts on 5.5.5.0/24, because there is no permit statement for that and because there is an implicit deny all at the end of an ACL. The same is true about all hosts on 10.1.2.0/24 not being all able to send ICMP ping requests. The deny statement for host 34.2.1.99 prevents the last option (fourth provided possible answer) from being true.

Table 11.4 describes the most common problems with access control lists.

TABLE 11.4 **Common ACL Problems and Solutions**

Problem	Solution
Implied deny (at the end) for all traffic that doesn't match earlier in the ACL	Add a permit entry for the traffic you want to be permitted by the ACL. Forgotten items often include management and routing protocols, being denied inbound on a router interface.
Deny statements not denying traffic	Move the deny statements higher up in the ACL so that they are processed first. ACLs are processed from top to bottom, in order. The first match found is used. If a deny statement is after (below) a statement that permits matched traffic, the traffic will be permitted (as it was matched first). In general, more specific matches (permit or deny) should be placed higher in the lists before the more general statements.
ACL not working	Make sure that the name/number of the ACL is correct (spelling counts) when applying it to an interface, and that it is being applied in the correct direction on the interface. An ACL that doesn't exist (typo in the name) that is applied to an interface is as if there is no ACL applied at all.

By using the hit counts that are shown with the **show access-list** command, you can see which entries in the ACLs have matches. Adding a **deny any** command at the end of an ACL won't improve performance, but will give an indication of how many packets are being denied at the end of the ACLs because of the hit counts associated with that explicit ACL entry.

A strategy for troubleshooting ACLs is to consider a specific packet, against each line of the ACL, from top to bottom, and see which of the entries (if any) are a match. When a match is seen, the permit or deny (based on that entry) will be applied by the router. At the end of the ACL there is an implied deny all.

Cram Quiz

1. What is the default behavior in an ACL when there is a match on a deny statement in an ACL?

   ❍ **A.** The rest of the ACL is processed, in order, to run other permit statements.

   ❍ **B.** The rest of the ACL is processed, in order, to run other deny statements.

   ❍ **C.** The implicit permit overrides the explicit deny in the matched entry.

   ❍ **D.** No other processing of the ACL, for the packet being considered, is performed.

2. Consider the following ACL:

```
access-list 102 deny icmp any any
access-list 102 permit tcp any any eq 80
access-list 102 permit udp any any eq 53
```

   After you apply an access list to the outside interface of the router, the internal clients can still ping devices on the Internet. What would explain this? Choose two.

   ❍ **A.** Ping uses UDP port 53.

   ❍ **B.** Ping uses TCP port 80.

   ❍ **C.** The ACL wasn't applied to the correct interface.

   ❍ **D.** The incorrect ACL number was applied to the correct interface.

Cram Quiz Answers

1. Answer D is correct. In an ACL, when there is a match of an entry, no further processing of the ACL for the packet being analyzed will be performed. If the match is a deny, the packet will be denied. If the match is an entry, the packet will be permitted.
2. Answer C and D are correct. If the incorrect ACL is applied to the interface (for example, an ACL number or name that doesn't exist in the configuration), it is as if there is no ACL applied at all. If the ACL is applied to the wrong interface, that also explain why it isn't denying the traffic that it should be denying. Ping uses ICMP, and not UDP or TCP.

Review Questions

Answer these questions. The answers follow the last question. If you cannot answer these questions correctly, consider reading this section again until you can.

1. Consider Figure 11.1 and partial output from the **show interface** command.

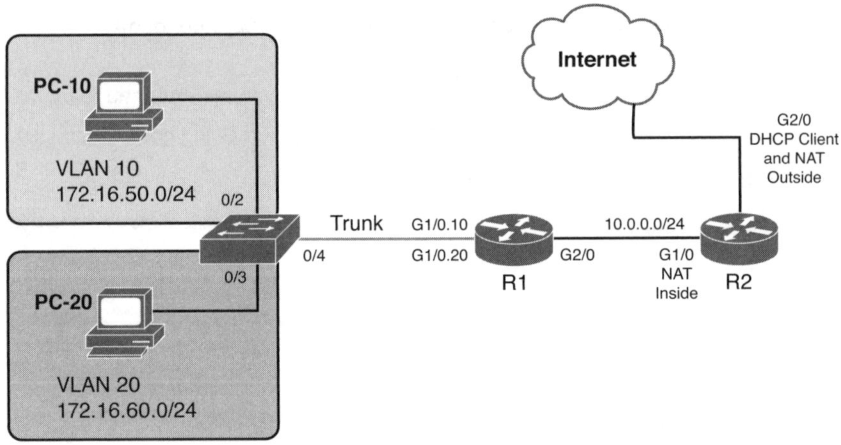

FIGURE 11.1 **Network topology for Question 1**

```
switch#show int g0/3
GigabitEthernet0/3 is down, line protocol is down (notconnect)
  Hardware is Gigabit Ethernet, address is 001c.b148.1e83 (bia
001c.b148.1e83)
  MTU 1504 bytes, BW 10000 Kbit, DLY 1000 usec,
     reliability 255/255, txload 1/255, rxload 1/255
  Encapsulation ARPA, loopback not set
  Keepalive set (10 sec)
  Auto-duplex, Auto-speed, media type is 10/100/1000BaseTX
  input flow-control is off, output flow-control is unsupported
```

The user at PC 20 has called the help desk and is complaining that he can't access the Internet. Which of the following statements is correct?

- ❍ **A.** The switch port autonegotiated a speed of 10Mbps.
- ❍ **B.** This switchport belongs to the default VLAN of 1.
- ❍ **C.** The switchport is administratively disabled.
- ❍ **D.** The cable between the switch and PC 20 isn't connected.

2. Refer to Figure 11.1 and this partial output from the switch:

```
Switch#show interfaces Gi0/2
GigabitEthernet0/2 is up, line protocol is up (connected)
  Hardware is Gigabit Ethernet, address is 001c.b148.1e82 (bia 001c.
b148.1e82)
  MTU 1504 bytes, BW 100000 Kbit, DLY 100 usec,
     reliability 255/255, txload 1/255, rxload 1/255
  Encapsulation ARPA, loopback not set
  Keepalive set (10 sec)
  Half-duplex, 100Mb/s, media type is 10/100/1000BaseTX
  input flow-control is off, output flow-control is unsupported
  ARP type: ARPA, ARP Timeout 04:00:00
  Last input 00:00:00, output 00:00:00, output hang never
  Last clearing of "show interface" counters never
  Input queue: 0/75/0/0 (size/max/drops/flushes); Total output drops: 0
  Queueing strategy: fifo
  Output queue: 0/40 (size/max)
  5 minute input rate 2000 bits/sec, 4 packets/sec
  5 minute output rate 0 bits/sec, 0 packets/sec
     7423429 packets input, 1145833084 bytes, 0 no buffer
     Received 29 broadcasts (23 multicasts)
     0 runts, 0 giants, 0 throttles
     0 input errors, 0 CRC, 0 frame, 0 overrun, 0 ignored
     0 watchdog, 20 multicast, 0 pause input
     0 input packets with dribble condition detected
     3221276 packets output, 1456219502 bytes, 0 underruns
     2635128 output errors, 675211 collisions, 25 interface resets
     0 babbles, 23654 late collision, 0 deferred
     0 lost carrier, 0 no carrier, 0 PAUSE output
     0 output buffer failures, 0 output buffers swapped out
```

The user at PC 10 is complaining that the network seems slow while accessing the Internet. Which one of the following is the most likely reason for this user's experience?

❍ **A.** The Internet servers may be overloaded.

❍ **B.** Excessive EMI is present somewhere on the link.

❍ **C.** The cable between the PC and the switch is too long.

❍ **D.** The cable between the PC and the switch is faulty.

❍ **D.** There is a duplex mismatch between the PC and port 0/3 on the switch.

3. Refer to Figure 11.1 and the partial output from the switch:

```
switch#show vlan brief

VLAN Name                 Status    Ports
---- -------------------- --------- -------------------------------
1    default              active    Gi0/1, Gi0/4, Gi0/5, Gi0/6
                                    Gi0/7, Gi0/8, Gi0/9, Gi0/10
                                    Gi0/11, Gi0/12, Gi0/13, Gi0/14
                                    Gi0/15, Gi0/16, Gi0/17, Gi0/18
                                    Gi0/19, Gi0/20, Gi0/21, Gi0/22
                                    Gi0/23, Gi0/24, Gi0/25, Gi0/26
                                    Gi0/27, Gi0/28
10   sales                active
11   VLAN0011             active
12   VLAN0012             active
20   engineering          active    Gi0/2, Gi0/3
55   VLAN0055             active
```

The user at PC 10 can access the Internet, but is having problems accessing a network printer that is located in the common work area next to his office. Based on the information provided, what is the cause of the problem?

❍ **A.** The printer is turned off.

❍ **B.** PC 10 isn't connected to the network.

❍ **C.** PC 10 is in the incorrect Layer 2 broadcast domain and IP subnet.

❍ **D.** The printer isn't connected to VLAN 10.

4. Refer to Figure 11.1 and the switch output to answer the following question:

```
switch#show interfaces g0/2 switchport
Name: Gi0/2
Switchport: Enabled
Administrative Mode: trunk
Operational Mode: trunk
Administrative Trunking Encapsulation: dot1q
Operational Trunking Encapsulation: dot1q
Negotiation of Trunking: On
Access Mode VLAN: 10
Trunking Native Mode VLAN: 1 (default)
Administrative Native VLAN tagging: enabled
Voice VLAN: none
Administrative private-vlan host-association: none
Administrative private-vlan mapping: none
Administrative private-vlan trunk native VLAN: none
Administrative private-vlan trunk Native VLAN tagging: enabled
Administrative private-vlan trunk encapsulation: dot1q
Administrative private-vlan trunk normal VLANs: none
```

```
Administrative private-vlan trunk associations: none
Administrative private-vlan trunk mappings: none
Operational private-vlan: none
Trunking VLANs Enabled: ALL
Pruning VLANs Enabled: 2-1001
Capture Mode Disabled
Capture VLANs Allowed: ALL
```

The user at PC 10 cannot access devices in VLAN 20. Based on the information provided, what is the cause?

❍ **A.** ACL at the default gateway that PC 10 is using.

❍ **B.** The switch port connecting PC 10 to the network is operating as a trunk.

❍ **C.** The VLAN assignment for port g0/2 is incorrect for VLAN 10.

❍ **D.** The switch port is administratively disabled.

5. Refer to Figure 11.1 and the partial output from the switch:

```
switch#show int trunk

Port       Mode           Encapsulation   Status        Native vlan
Gi0/4      desirable      802.1q          trunking      1

Port       Vlans allowed on trunk
Gi0/4      1-4094

Port       Vlans allowed and active in management domain
Gi0/4      1-5,10-12,20,55

Port       Vlans in spanning tree forwarding state and not pruned
Gi0/4      1-5,10-12,20,55
```

Users on VLAN 10 cannot access the Internet, but users on VLAN 20 can. What could be causing this problem?

❍ **A.** The trunk was negotiated between the switch and R1.

❍ **B.** VLAN 1 user traffic will include an 802.1Q tag of 1 (for VLAN 1).

❍ **C.** You cannot trunk between a switch and a Layer 3 router.

❍ **D.** The subinterface on R1 may be down or have an incorrect IP address.

6. Refer to Figure 11.1 and the switch output to answer this question:

```
switch#show int g 0/4 switchport
Name: Gi0/4
Switchport: Enabled
Administrative Mode: static access
Operational Mode: static access
Administrative Trunking Encapsulation: dot1q
Operational Trunking Encapsulation: native
Negotiation of Trunking: Off
Access Mode VLAN: 10
Trunking Native Mode VLAN: 10 (default)
Administrative Native VLAN tagging: enabled
Voice VLAN: none
```

Several of the users on the internal VLANs are complaining that there is no access to the Internet. What would be causing this, based on the information provided?

❍ **A.** NAT is not being performed.

❍ **B.** The connection between the switch and R1 isn't a trunk.

❍ **C.** ACLs are blocking traffic.

❍ **C.** The PCs aren't adding the correct 802.1Q tags to the frames as they send them.

7. Refer to Figure 11.1 as part of this question.

Which of the following would be valid addresses for the default gateway to use?

❍ **A.** 172.16.0.1 for both VLAN 10 and VLAN 20

❍ **B.** 172.16.51.1 for VLAN 10 and 172.16.61.1 for VLAN 20

❍ **C.** 172.16.50.10 for VLAN 10 and 172.16.50.20 for VLAN 20

❍ **D.** 172.16.60.254 for VLAN 20 and 172.16.50.1 for VLAN 10

8. Which of the following usable host addresses would reside on the same IP subnet as the host 172.29.161.172/23 ?

   ❍ **A.** 172.29.160.1

   ❍ **B.** 172.29.161.255

   ❍ **C.** 172.29.162.5

   ❍ **D.** 172.29.163.97

9. Refer to Figure 11.1 as part of this question. Consider the following partial configuration on router R1:

```
access-list 105 permit tcp host 172.16.50.25 eq ssh host
172.16.60.1 eq ssh
access-list 105 permit icmp 172.16.0.0 0.0.255.255 172.16.0.0
0.0.255.255
access-list 105 deny tcp 172.16.0.0 0.0.255.255 172.16.0.0
0.0.255.255
access-list 105 permit tcp 172.16.0.0 0.0.255.255 any

interface g1/0.10
ip access-group 105 in
```

   Which of the following are true? Choose two.

   ❍ **A.** The PC at 172.16.50.25 in VLAN 10 will be able to establish an SSH session with the host 172.16.60.1 which is in VLAN 20.

   ❍ **B.** Pings are allowed between VLAN 10 and VLAN 20 addresses.

   ❍ **C.** External DNS servers wouldn't be accessible to VLAN 10 hosts.

   ❍ **D.** VLAN 10 hosts could access Internet web servers based on URLs and names.

10. Refer to Figure 11.1 and the output from R1 and R2:

```
R1#show ip route
O*E2  0.0.0.0/0 [110/1] via 10.0.0.2, 00:39:32,
GigabitEthernet2/0
      10.0.0.0/8 is variably subnetted, 2 subnets, 2 masks
C        10.0.0.0/24 is directly connected, GigabitEthernet2/0
L        10.0.0.1/32 is directly connected, GigabitEthernet2/0
      172.16.0.0/16 is variably subnetted, 4 subnets, 2 masks
C        172.16.50.0/24 is directly connected,
GigabitEthernet1/0.10
L        172.16.50.1/32 is directly connected,
GigabitEthernet1/0.10
C        172.16.60.0/24 is directly connected,
GigabitEthernet1/0.20
L        172.16.60.1/32 is directly connected,
GigabitEthernet1/0.20

R2#show ip protocols
Routing Protocol is "ospf 1"
 Outgoing update filter list for all interfaces is not set
 Incoming update filter list for all interfaces is not set
 Router ID 2.2.2.2
 It is an autonomous system boundary router
 Redistributing External Routes from,
 Number of areas in this router is 1. 1 normal 0 stub 0 nssa
 Maximum path: 4
 Routing for Networks:
  10.0.0.0 0.0.0.255 area 0
 Routing Information Sources:
  Gateway          Distance      Last Update
  172.16.60.1           110      00:36:24
 Distance: (default is 110)
```

Which of the following, if not included in an inbound ACL applied to R1's G2/0 interface, could cause a routing failure for both VLAN 10 and VLAN 20 hosts attempting to access Internet web servers?

- ❍ **A. permit icmp any any**
- ❍ **B. permit ospf any any**
- ❍ **C. permit tcp any any**
- ❍ **D. permit udp any any**

Answers to Review Questions

1. Answer D is correct. The cable between the switch and PC 20 isn't connected. The down/down status indicates that there is an unplugged cable. Another cause of this status could be that the interface (in this case, on the PC) is disabled. An administratively disabled port would indicate that it was administratively down. The switch port autonegotiation settings or VLAN membership wouldn't have an impact on the interface Layer 1/Layer 2 status.

2. Answer E is correct. A duplex mismatch would result in counters for collisions and late collisions to be very high. In a half-duplex environment, we would expect collisions, but not late collisions. Internet servers being overloaded, all of them, is not likely at the same. If there was excessive EMI or the cable was too long, that could create some errors on the interface and would likely cause a failure of the link (with extreme interference or faulty cable), but not provide overall slowness to all of the Internet.

3. Answer C is correct. Based on the diagram and the output from the switch, it shows that PC 10 (port g0/2) is assigned to VLAN 20 (instead of VLAN 10). The other options are possibilities, but not able to be determined in this question, based on the information provided, and the question asks you to make a decision based on the information provided.

4. Answer B is correct. From the output of the switch, it shows the link to the customer is acting as a trunk. Hosts on the network won't be providing 802.1Q tagging, and the native VLAN on the trunk is not the same VLAN as the host computer. When a frame is sent over a trunk, but doesn't include a tag, the receiving device assumes that the frame belongs to the same VLAN as the "native" VLAN configured for the trunk. As a result, the user wouldn't have access to the network using this port. If the switch port were disabled, it would show as down in the output.

5. Answer D is correct. The subinterface on R1 may be down or may have an incorrect IP address. You can trunk between a router and a switch; that is what router on a stick does. There is no tag by default on the native VLAN on a trunk. The trunk was negotiated, but that wouldn't cause a problem. Ruling out all of these, the only option left is that perhaps the subinterface of the router supporting VLAN 10 may be down or may have an incorrect address (by process of elimination from the choices given).

6. Answer B is correct. The operational mode (the mode that it is currently using) indicates an access port. The connect to the router performing as a router on a stick (ROAS) needs to be a trunk. That would cause a failure for network users attempting access their default gateway, which is across that link. Based on the information provided, that would be the cause instead of NAT or ACLs. PCs, by default, don't add or use 802.1Q tags on frames they send or receive.

7. Answer D is correct. The default gateway for any VLAN needs to be in the same subnet as the host addresses in those VLANs. The two subnets are 172.16.50.0/24 and 172.16.60.0/24. Any IP addresses within those respective subnets could be used as the address of the default gateway. Host machines would need to know what their default gateway was, and this would likely be communicated through DHCP.

8. Answer A is correct. The host at 172.29.161.172/23 is on subnet 172.29.160.0/23 whose range of IPs would then be 172.29.160.1 to 172.29.161.254. The correct address of 172.29.160.1 is the first (and only one of the answers) in that range. The other answers are incorrect as they are not in the same range.
9. Answers B and C are correct. The SSH wouldn't be able to form, because a source port would not be 22, but rather would be some high-numbered source port, so the first entry wouldn't permit it, and the third entry is denying. All ICMP is allowed between the two VLANs' IP address space, and DNS isn't being allowed from VLAN 10's address space (implicitly), so DNS wouldn't work outside the VLAN. Because of the default deny all at the end of the ACLs, any traffic not explicitly permitted would be denied.
10. Answer B is correct. Based on the information provided, OSPF is being used between R1 and R2, including the learning of a default route on R1. If an inbound ACL on R1 g2/0 didn't permit the inbound OSPF messages, R1 would lose the default route, and a routing failure related to Internet traffic would occur. OSPF doesn't use ICMP, TCP, or UDP for its messages, and for that reason all the other choices provided are incorrect.

CHAPTER TWELVE

Advanced Switching Concepts

This chapter covers the following official 200-101 ICND2 and 200-120 CCNA exam topics:

- Identify enhanced switching technologies: RSTP, PVSTP, EtherChannel.
- Configure and verify PVSTP operation.

This chapter details the Spanning Tree Protocol (STP) and reviews some of its enhanced features, including Per-VLAN Spanning Tree Protocol and Rapid Spanning Tree Protocol. We then examine the theory and configuration of EtherChannel.

Spanning Tree Protocol

CramSaver

1. We create redundant switched networks by connecting multiple switches together using multiple links. What is the primary purpose of Spanning Tree Protocol in a redundant switched network?
   - **A.** To create logical layer two loops for redundancy
   - **B.** To suppress broadcast traffic when redundant loops are in use by data traffic
   - **C.** To allow use of looped redundant links for additional bandwidth
   - **D.** To eliminate logical layer two loops

2. The operation of spanning tree involves several steps. In one of the first steps, all switches examine BPDUs to determine who the root bridge is. Which switch becomes the root?
   - **A.** The switch with the lowest bridge ID. Bridge ID is a combination of IP address and MAC.
   - **B.** The switch with the lowest bridge ID. Bridge ID is a combination of priority and MAC.
   - **C.** The switch with the highest priority.
   - **D.** The switch with the highest MAC.

3. Each switch examines BPDUs to determine its root port. Which of the following are true of the root port?
   - **A.** It has the lowest path cost to the root switch.
   - **B.** It has the highest path cost to the root switch.
   - **C.** Each switch will have multiple root ports.
   - **D.** Each switch will have only one root port, with the exception of the root switch, which will have none.
   - **E.** The port that has the highest speed will always be the root port.
   - **F.** The port that has the lowest interface number port (for example, Fa0/1 versus Fa0/12) will always be the root port.

Answers

1. Answer D is correct. STP eliminates logical layer two loops in redundant switched topologies. Answer A is wrong because loops are undesirable. Answer B is incorrect; STP solves the problems caused by broadcast storms, but it does not actively suppress broadcasts. Answer C is incorrect; if there are loops in the topology, without STP to eliminate them the topology is almost unusable.

2. Answer B is correct. The lowest bridge ID becomes the root. Bridge ID is a combination of STP priority (default = 32768 or 0x8000) and MAC address.
3. Answers A and D are correct. Each switch will have one root port (except the root itself which has none); the root port has the lowest path cost to the root switch.

Earlier, we mentioned that one of the functions of a switch was Layer 2 loop removal. This is a critical feature, because without it many switched networks would completely cease to function. Either accidentally or deliberately in the process of creating a redundant network, the problem arises when we create a looped switched path. A loop can be defined as two or more switches (or perhaps a switch and a hub) that are interconnected by two or more physical links.

There is an important distinction to make between the physical loop (the cables connecting switches and hubs that create the physical loop) and the logical loop, which is the looped path taken by the frames around the physical loop. STP eliminates the logical loop by preventing certain frames from traversing the physical loop.

Switching loops create three major problems:

- **Broadcast storms:** Switches must flood broadcasts, so a looped topology will create multiple copies of a single broadcast and perpetually cycle them through the loop.
- **MAC table instability:** Loops make it appear that a single MAC address is reachable on multiple ports of a switch, and the switch is constantly updating the MAC table.
- **Duplicate frames:** Because there are multiple paths to a single MAC, it is possible that a frame could be duplicated to be flooded out all paths to a single destination MAC.

All these problems are serious and will bring a network to an effective standstill unless prevented.

Figure 12.1 illustrates a looped configuration causing a broadcast storm.

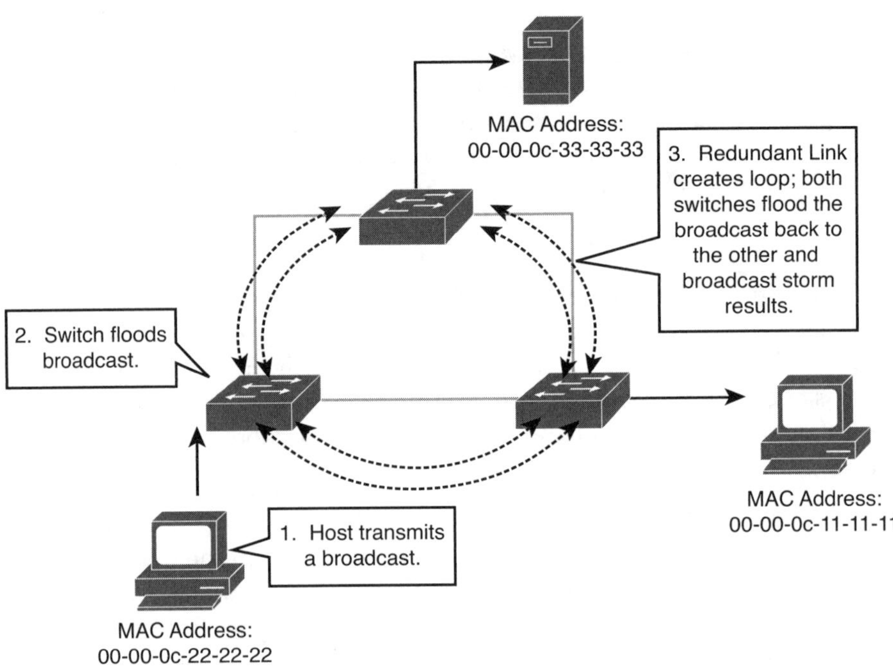
MAC Address:
00-00-0c-33-33-33
3. Redundant Link creates loop; both switches flood the broadcast back to the other and broadcast storm results.
2. Switch floods broadcast.
MAC Address:
00-00-0c-11-11-11
1. Host transmits a broadcast.
MAC Address:
00-00-0c-22-22-22

FIGURE 12.1 **A Layer 2 (switching) loop.**

Other than simple error, the most common reason that loops are created is because we want to build a redundant or fault-tolerant network. By definition, *redundancy* means that we have a backup, separate path for data to follow in the event the first one fails. The problem is that unless the backup path is physically disabled—perhaps by unplugging it—the path creates a loop and causes the problems mentioned previously. We like redundant systems; we do not like loops and the problems they cause. We need a mechanism that automatically detects and prevents loops so that we can build the fault-tolerant physical links and have them become active only when needed. The mechanism is called the Spanning Tree Protocol (STP). STP is a protocol that runs on bridges and switches to find and block redundant looped paths during normal operation. STP was originally developed by the Digital Equipment Corporation (DEC), and the idea was adopted and modified by the IEEE to become 802.1d. The two are incompatible, but it is exceedingly rare to find a DEC bridge these days, so the incompatibility is not usually a problem.

ExamAlert

STP eliminates Layer 2 loops in switched networks with redundant paths.

Root Election

STP's basic function is to create a loop-free path to a root bridge. The root bridge is the bridge or switch that is the root of the spanning tree, with the branches being loop-free paths to the other switches in the system. The root is the switch with the lowest bridge ID; the ID is determined by a combination of an administrative priority and the MAC address of the switch. The priority is set to 32,768 (8000 hex) by default; if we leave the priority at the default, whatever switch has the lowest MAC will be the root. Figure 12.2 illustrates a simple root selection when all switches are using the default priority.

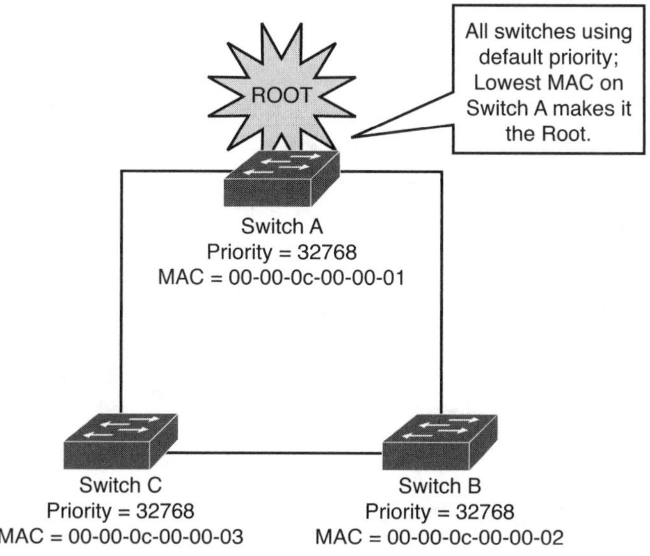

FIGURE 12.2 **Root bridge selection with the default priority.**

We cannot change the MAC address of a switch. So, what happens if Switch A in the previous example happens to be an old, slow Catalyst 1900? It might get elected the root because it has a low MAC address, but we really don't want it to be the root: Usually, we would choose a big, fast switch at the core of the network as the root. Let's say that Switch C is a hot new switch and we want it to be our root. How do we override the existing election? The answer is to change the default priority. Remember, the lowest ID wins the election, and the ID is the priority prepended to the MAC. The ID is one long string, so lowering the priority makes the ID lower. So, if we change the priority of Switch C to a low value, it will win the election despite the fact that it has a higher MAC than Switch A. Figure 12.3 illustrates this.

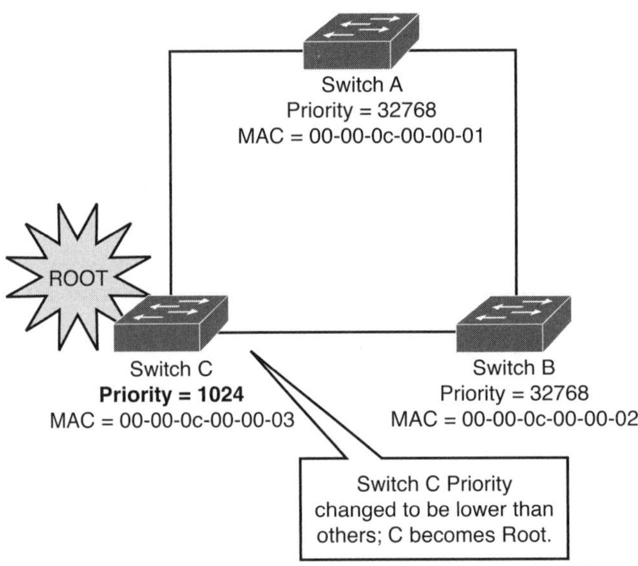

FIGURE 12.3 **Root election with a modified priority.**

> **ExamAlert**
>
> The root is elected based on the bridge ID and the priority. The switch with the lowest priority will always be the root.

STP Communication with BPDUs

To determine the presence of loops and to block loops, switches must be capable of communicating with each other about the various connections they have. This communication in STP is carried out by the exchange of bridge protocol data units (BPDUs). The 802.1d BPDU is multicasted every 2 seconds and includes information the switches need to decide whether there are loops, how to fix them, and which switch is the root. Figure 12.4 shows the fields in an 802.1d BPDU. Note the fields for the bridge ID, the root ID, and the root path cost.

Port Types

STP assigns different ports on a switch to different roles, depending on where the root is and where the loops are in the topology. The sections that follow describe the port roles and how they are selected.

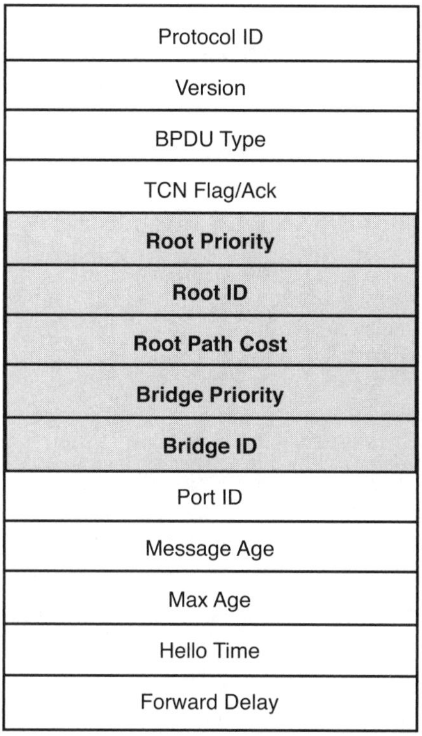

Protocol ID
Version
BPDU Type
TCN Flag/Ack
Root Priority
Root ID
Root Path Cost
Bridge Priority
Bridge ID
Port ID
Message Age
Max Age
Hello Time
Forward Delay

FIGURE 12.4 **Detailed contents of 802.1d BPDU packet.**

Root

The root port on a switch is the one port that has the lowest-cost path to the root switch. Path cost is calculated based on the bandwidth of the links. Table 12.1 lists the IEEE-defined values for STP path cost. Note that there are old (1998) and new (2004) values. The new values were defined because of the increasingly widespread availability of multi-gigabit link speeds and future requirements for terabit speeds.

Note

This text, like many others, will commonly refer to the 1998 cost values in the text and diagrams.

TABLE 12.1 **STP Path Costs**

Link Speed	2004 STP Cost	1998 STP Cost
10Mbps	2000000	100
100Mbps	200000	19
1Gbps	20000	4
10Gbps	2000	2
100Gbps	200	Not defined
1Tbps	20	Not defined
10Tbps	2	Not defined

After the switches have elected the root for the system, each switch must then decide which port it will use to reach the root. Some switches will have only one port that can reach the root at all; some might have several, depending on the number and location of uplinks between the switches in the system. The exchange of BPDUs that decides the root election also tells each switch about the path costs to reach the root (as indicated by the value of the Root Path Cost field in the BPDU). Each switch adds its own path cost to the path cost received from the neighboring switch and chooses the port with the lowest cost as the root port. Figure 12.5 illustrates root port selection in a simple switched network.

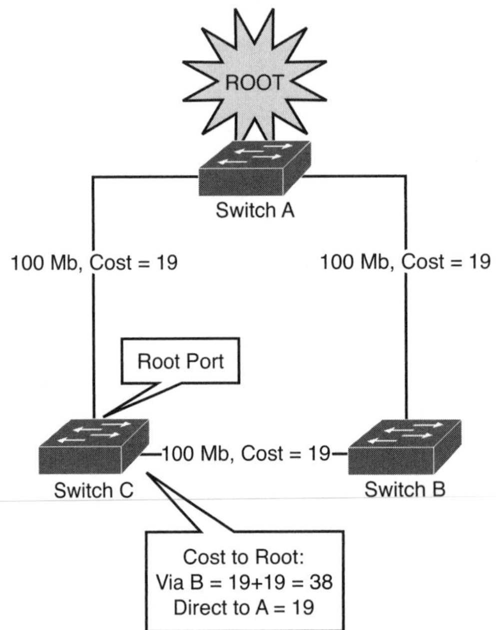

FIGURE 12.5 **The root port is the one with the lowest root path cost.**

Note that the root itself does not have any root ports: It does not need to reach the root; it is the root!

Designated

For each LAN segment, there must be one designated port. This is the port that will forward traffic to and from the root from the LAN segment. The designated port is the port that has the least cost path to the root from the LAN segment.

The root switch has only designated ports. Because it *is* the root, it won't have a root port, and it can't block any of the ports that connect to other switches (because that would make the other switch's root ports not work).

In Figure 12.6, our three switches have already elected the root and chosen their root ports. Switch A is the root, so all of its ports are designated. Switches B and C must next choose which port will block and which port will be designated on the link between them.

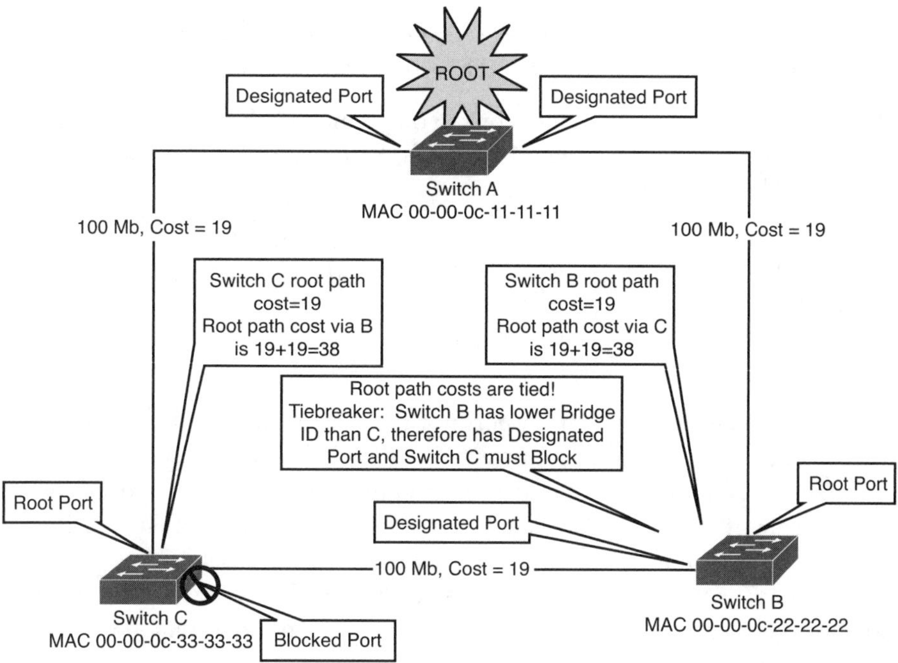

FIGURE 12.6 **The designated port selection process.**

The first criterion examined is which switch has the lowest root path cost. In our setup here, B and C each connect to the root with a 100Mbps connection, with an STP cost of 19. By examining each other's BPDUs, B and C realize that they are tied for root path cost.

This is a common scenario in modern networks where switches are directly connected over full-duplex crossover cables. One of the switches must block its port to stop the loop. The second criterion (the first tiebreaker) is the lower bridge ID: In this case, Switch B wins, and Switch C must block its port.

As we get into more complex switched systems, we get into situations where additional criteria (tiebreakers) are needed. The full list is examined in the next section.

Port Role Selection

The order of criteria a switch goes through when deciding its root and designated ports is as follows:

1. The port with the lowest cumulative root path cost will be the root port/designated port.
2. If tied between multiple ports, the port that connects to the neighboring switch with the lowest bridge ID becomes the root port/designated port.
3. If there are multiple connections to that same switch, the port with the lowest received (from the other switch) STP priority will be the root port/designated port.
4. If tied, the port with the lowest received (from the other switch) hardware number (Fa0/1 is lower than Fa0/2) will be the root port/designated port.

Blocked

A blocked port is neither the root port nor the designated port, but is still an important part of the redundant links between switches. It lost in the election to choose the active root or designated ports, but it might take over one of these roles if the active port failed. A blocked port is the one that actually stops the loop, so it is just as important as the root or designated. A blocked port does not send or process received data, but it will process received BPDUs both as a keepalive mechanism and the STP failover mechanism.

Convergence

Convergence is the term used to describe the process STP goes through to achieve a stable, loop-free network. (The same term is used with reference to routing information stability as well.) When all switches have elected the root and decided on their root, designated, and blocked ports, the system is said to be converged.

Port States

With 802.1d STP, each port on each switch goes through four distinct port states in the process of convergence:

1. **Blocking**: When a switch boots, all ports start in the listening state. This is to prevent loops during the time that the STP topology is converging. A port that is a link between switches will transition to blocking unless it becomes a root or designated port. Blocked ports send no data at all (not even BPDUs), but they do listen for (receive) BPDUs from other switches.

   If a switch dies or a link between switches fails, the other switches connected to it wait for a specific time until they begin the STP convergence process. This interval is called the Max Age Timer, and by default it is 20 seconds. Effectively, it means that a switch will wait until it has missed 10 BPDUs (which are sent every 2 seconds) from a connected switch before it kicks in the STP recalculation process, which by default takes a further 30 seconds to complete (15 seconds for listening and 15 seconds for learning).

2. **Listening**: The listening state enables a blocked port to begin sending BPDUs. By default, the listening state is 15 seconds.

3. **Learning**: The learning state is when the switch begins populating its MAC address table. It is not yet forwarding any frames, but it is getting ready to forward by building as complete a MAC table as it can. The listening state is also 15 seconds by default. The listening and learning states together are called the forward delay.

4. **Forwarding**: The forwarding state, as its name implies, is when the port starts forwarding frames. This is simply normal operation for a port that is not blocked.

If you take a quick look at these states and their timers, you can see that in 802.1d STP, reaching convergence can take anywhere from 30 to 50 seconds (Forward delay [15 + 15]+ MaxAge[20] = 50 seconds). Understand that during this 30 to 50 seconds, no data frames are being forwarded at all; no data is being sent anywhere because every port on every switch is either blocking, listening, or learning. (BPDUs are being sent, however.) This is, of course, detrimental to the productivity and utility of a network, especially a modern, busy one. A 50-second delay every time a topology change happens is unacceptable, so Cisco (and then the IEEE) created several enhancements to 802.1d STP to speed up the process of convergence. Some of these enhancements are discussed in the following section.

ExamAlert

In a converged STP system, all ports are either blocking or forwarding.

Know the four STP port states and what exactly the port is doing in each one!

RSTP Enhancements

The Rapid Spanning Tree protocol (RSTP, IEEE 802.1w; remember, 802.1w is *Wapid Spanning Twee*) has many of its roots in Cisco-created enhancements to ordinary 802.1d STP. The primary goal of these enhancements is to speed up convergence. RSTP relies less on timers; instead, the BPDU becomes much more detailed and informative so that switches can gather more information with greater accuracy. New port states have been defined, as shown in Table 12.2.

TABLE 12.2 **RSTP Port States**

802.1d STP	802.1w RSTP
Blocking	Discarding
Listening	Discarding
Learning	Learning
Forwarding	Forwarding

Switches wait for only three missing BPDUs before commencing the spanning-tree recalculation process. The process of convergence is itself much more rapid because new port states have been defined as well. In addition to the root and designated port states in STP, RSTP defines the alternate and backup port states. The alternate port is the port that will become the root port if the primary root port fails. The backup port is the port that will become the designated port if the primary designated port fails. The BPDUs in RSTP convey information about these port states to neighboring switches. This enhanced communication allows for quicker convergence, without relying on the 30-second to 50-second timers in STP.

Another significant improvement in convergence speed comes from the Rapid Transition to Forwarding (RTF) features of edge ports and link types. *Edge ports* are ports that are connected to non-STP-capable devices such as PCs, servers, or routers. These devices will not normally create STP loops, so there is no need for them to transition to discarding (block) to prevent loops. This function is enabled by Cisco's **portfast** command feature. With PortFast configured, a switch port will stop sending BPDUs and transition to the forwarding state almost immediately. This is useful to get frames moving through the switch so hosts can get on with business. Picture a database server and a PC connected to the same switch; they would not have to wait the 50 seconds for STP convergence if PortFast were configured on both ports. In addition, if a port configured for PortFast does receive a BPDU (perhaps because someone plugged a switch in), by default it will disable PortFast and start STP on that port to prevent loops. You can also optionally configure the switch port with BPDU Guard to shut down the port if it receives a BPDU. This is more secure because it prevents the unauthorized installation of switches.

The interface-configuration syntax to configure a Catalyst switch port with PortFast looks like this:

```
Switch(config-if)#spanning-tree portfast
```

Or, to set all nontrunking ports to use PortFast by default, use the global configuration command:

```
Switch(config)#spanning-tree portfast default
```

To turn PortFast off, simply use **no spanning-tree portfast**.

Link types refers to a port setting of either full duplex or half duplex. If a port is set for full duplex, RSTP assumes that it is a candidate for rapid transition because there can be only one other device at the end of such a connection. If it is set for half duplex, however, it is conceivable that there could be multiple STP-capable devices on that segment. So by default, the RTF functions are disabled. It is possible to override this default.

Understanding Per-VLAN Spanning Tree (PVST)

PVST (sometimes abbreviated PVSTP; you may also see older references to PVST+, but the + has been dropped recently) is a Cisco proprietary improvement on 802.1d STP. The improvement is pretty straightforward: Instead of having one instance of STP running on the switch, Cisco switches can run one STP instance per VLAN. (The name choice becomes pretty clear at this point.)

The advantage is that each VLAN can now have an optimal switched environment set up, instead of just one optimization for all VLANs (which might not be optimal for most of the VLANs). The assumption is that the traffic patterns for each VLAN are going to differ from the others, so forcing all VLANs to use the same single STP-determined switching path doesn't make sense. PVST allows us to make the root switch different in each VLAN, to adjust the STP settings so that traffic is switched the way we want, and generally make optimizations for each VLAN independently of all the others. It can, if well thought out, also allow us to make use of all the redundant links we have (still without loops). Imagine a simple scenario: We have just two VLANs, numbered 1 and 99. We have two redundant uplinks from a single switch to the distribution layer. STP will block one of those links to prevent the looping problems, and we only get the bandwidth of one link.

But if we run PVST instead, we can have one of those redundant links forwarding for VLAN 1, and the other for VLAN 99 (at the same time). We can now use the full bandwidth of both links, and PVSTP is running in each VLAN to prevent loops. Figure 12.7 illustrates this scenario.

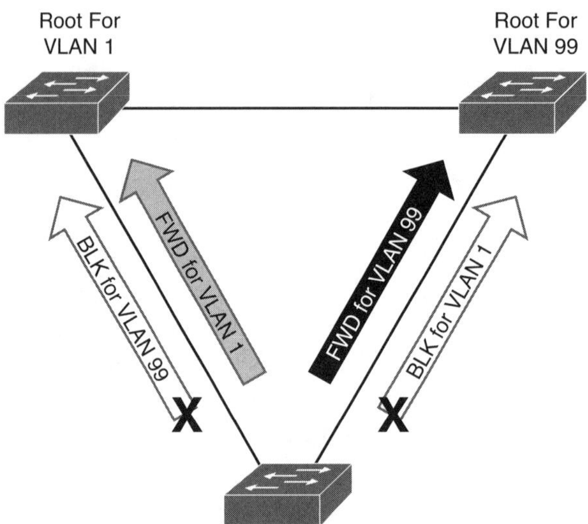

FIGURE 12.7 **PVST optimization.**

PVST is a good improvement, and it's just as easy as STP to use. If you spend the time on design and implementation, it can make a big improvement in how fast and how efficiently your network switches frames, compared to single-instance 802.1d STP. Of course, you will probably prefer to run RPVSTP, the Rapid Spanning Tree version of PVST, which is another Cisco proprietary improvement, this time to RSTP.

Setting the Spanning-Tree Mode

It is simple to set the spanning-tree mode on your switch. On most switches, the default is PVST. If you need to reset the mode to PVST, use the global configuration command **spanning-tree mode pvst**. To set the mode to RPVSTP, the command is **spanning-tree mode rapid-pvst**.

Because CCNA focuses almost exclusively on PVST, we will look at only PVST commands. We'll be tossing in a few extras for interest's sake, of course.

Configuring and Verifying PVST

Beyond setting the STP mode as just explained, you will want to adjust the various STP settings so that you can tune the topology optimizations exactly the way you want. In CCNA land, you can modify the following settings to alter how STP operates:

- **Bridge ID:** Affects root selection
- **Port Cost:** Affects root port selection and designated port selection
- **PortFast:** Limits participation in STP

Other STP guards, including BPDU Guard, Root Guard, and Loop Guard, enforce your STP configurations

Changing the Bridge ID

Remember that the root switch is elected based on the bridge ID, which is a combination of STP priority and MAC address. We can't change the MAC; it is "burned in" at the factory. But we can change the priority. The global config command is simple: **spanning-tree vlan** *vlan_id* **priority** *priority*. (Remember we are dealing with PVST, so note that we can set the priority to be different for each VLAN; that's how we can have a different root for each VLAN.)

There is just a bit of weirdness in the **priority** *priority* part of that command. The acceptable range is 0 to 65535 because we are changing the value of what was (in 802.1d STP) a 16-bit number. But to get a separate bridge (switch) ID for each VLAN in its proprietary PVST, Cisco took the first 4 bits of that number as the priority value and used the last 12 bits for the VLAN ID. Clever, but it makes it a little goofy for configuration: Because you are changing the first 4 bits of a 16-bit string, the last of those 4 bits has a value of 4096, so the priority value you enter must be a multiple of 4096. The 12-bit VLAN ID part is called the *system ID extension*; it's automatically configured by the priority command when you specify the VLAN ID (number).

Looking back at Figure 12.7, here's a sample config that would set up Switch1 at the top left and Switch2 at the top right as the root switches for VLANs 1 and 99, respectively:

```
Switch1(config)#spanning-tree vlan 1 priority 4096
Switch1(config)#spanning-tree vlan 99 priority 8192
Switch2(config)#spanning-tree vlan 99 priority 4096
Switch2(config)#spanning-tree vlan 1 priority 8192
```

Note that the example also shows that we can set the priority for the other VLAN in our example to be quite low (relative to other switches not seen in the diagram), which means we can set up Switch2 as the *secondary root* for VLAN 1, and Switch1 as the *secondary root* for VLAN 99. That way if the primary root fails, we have more control over what the topology does by influencing the selection of the new root.

Sometimes Cisco realizes that complexity isn't always cool and gives us a way easier command to work with. The command **spanning tree** *vlan_id* **root** [**primary** | **secondary**] lets us identify the switches we want to be the primary root and secondary root very simply, without calculating multiples of 4096 or keeping track of multiple priority settings on multiple switches. Here's an example of setting up Switch1 and Switch2 using the simpler command:

```
Switch1(config)#spanning-tree vlan 1 root primary
Switch1(config)#spanning-tree vlan 99 root secondary
Switch2(config)#spanning-tree vlan 99 root primary
Switch2(config)#spanning-tree vlan 1 root secondary
```

What's going on in the background with the **root primary** command? The STP priority value is being automatically set to the lowest value that will (almost) guarantee it becoming the root. Specifically, if the STP priority is set to anything higher than 24576, it is reset to 24576. If the STP priority is set to anything lower than 24576, it is reset to the highest multiple of 4096 that will guarantee it becomes the root. The **root secondary** command does something similar, but sets the STP priority so that it will always be the second-lowest value in the system after the primary root. (Note that if the **priority** command forces the STP priority to 0, that will override the **root primary** command—hence the "almost guarantee.")

This command is so simple, and guarantees the specified primary and secondary so well, that Cisco recommends its use over the earlier priority command. You, of course, need to know both.

Changing the Port Cost

By default, the STP port cost is calculated based on the speed of the port. As a reminder, Table 12.3 lists the default STP port costs.

TABLE 12.3 **Default STP Port Costs**

Interface Type	Default STP Cost
10Mbps Ethernet	100
100Mbps Fast Ethernet	19
1Gbps Gigabit Ethernet	4
10Gbps 10 Gigabit Ethernet	2

Sometimes we want to manually override the default cost, to influence how STP selects the root port, designated port, or alternate port. It is not difficult; the difficult part, as always, is in the planning. At the interface config prompt, the command is **spanning-tree vlan** *vlan_ID* **cost** *cost*.

Let's take an example of three switches connected together as shown in Figure 12.8. The figure shows that Switch3 is the root, with all its ports designated. Switch2 uses its f0/3/0 as its root port, and its f0/3/2 as the designated port for the segment between itself and Switch1. The figure also shows why Switch3 became the root switch. With the priorities at the default, the lowest MAC of Switch3 becomes the tiebreaker.

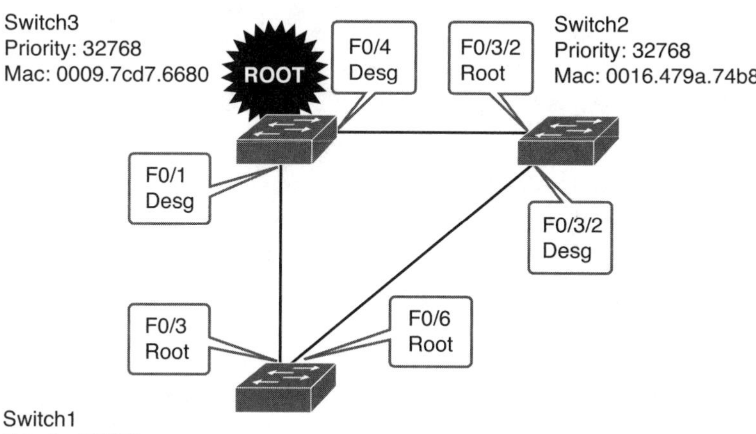

FIGURE 12.8 **STP example system.**

If we look at the output of **show spanning-tree** on each switch, we can see the information that we need to create the diagram in Figure 12.8. It's a fairly intimidating command output, especially when we have multiple VLANs to work with, but it is one you will need to be able to understand completely. See whether you can find the info about who is the root, which port roles have been assigned, and the bridge IDs. The goal is to be able to draw the same diagram just from using the output.

Note

The outputs differ slightly between the three switches because they are different switch platforms. Switch1 is a 2960, so that is the format you should expect on the exam. It is not a bad thing to learn what other output formats look like for the real world, though!

```
! Output from Switch1:
Switch1#show spanning-tree

VLAN0001
  Spanning tree enabled protocol ieee
  Root ID     Priority     32768
              Address      0009.7cd7.6680
              Cost         19
              Port         3 (FastEthernet0/3)
              Hello Time    2 sec  Max Age 20 sec  Forward Delay 15 sec

  Bridge ID   Priority     32769  (priority 32768 sys-id-ext 1)
              Address      001c.f65e.8200
              Hello Time    2 sec  Max Age 20 sec  Forward Delay 15 sec
              Aging Time   300 sec

Interface            Role Sts Cost      Prio.Nbr Type
-------------------- ---- --- --------- -------- --------------------------
Fa0/3                Root FWD 19        128.3    P2p
Fa0/6                Altn BLK 19        128.6    P2p
! Output from Switch2:
switch2#show spanning-tree brief

VLAN1
  Spanning tree enabled protocol ieee
  Root ID     Priority     32768
              Address      0009.7cd7.6680
              Cost         19
              Port         31 (FastEthernet0/3/0)
              Hello Time    2 sec  Max Age 20 sec  Forward Delay 15 sec
```

```
  Bridge ID  Priority    32768
             Address     0016.479a.74b8
             Hello Time   2 sec  Max Age 20 sec  Forward Delay 15 sec
             Aging Time 300

Interface                                   Designated
Name                 Port ID Prio Cost  Sts Cost  Bridge ID            Port ID
-------------------- ------- ---- ----- --- ----- -------------------- -------
FastEthernet0/3/0    128.31   128    19 FWD     0 32768 0009.7cd7.6680 128.16
FastEthernet0/3/2    128.33   128    19 FWD    19 32768 0016.479a.74b8 128.33
! Output from Switch3:
Switch3#sh spanning-tree brief

VLAN1
  Spanning tree enabled protocol IEEE
  ROOT ID    Priority 32768
             Address 0009.7cd7.6680
             This bridge is the root
             Hello Time   2 sec  Max Age 20 sec  Forward Delay 15 sec

  Bridge ID  Priority    32768
             Address     0009.7cd7.6680
             Hello Time   2 sec  Max Age 20 sec  Forward Delay 15 sec


Port                            Designated
Name    Port ID Prio Cost Sts   Cost  Bridge ID      Port ID
------- ------- ---- ---- ---   ----  -------------- -------
Fa0/1   128.13  128  19    FWD  0     0009.7cd7.6680 128.13
Fa0/4   128.16  128  19    FWD  0     0009.7cd7.6680 128.16
```

Notice the highlighted sections that show the key info: Who is the root, which port connects to the root, what the port states are and the port costs.

Now, let's try to force Switch 1 to become the root, using the **spanning tree vlan 1 root primary** command, and look at the **show spanning-tree** output changes:

```
! Output from Switch1
Switch1(config)#spanning-tree vlan 1 root primary
!
Switch1#show spanning-tree

VLAN0001
  Spanning tree enabled protocol ieee
  Root ID    Priority    24577
             Address     001c.f65e.8200
             This bridge is the root
             Hello Time   2 sec  Max Age 20 sec  Forward Delay 15 sec
```

```
  Bridge ID  Priority    24577  (priority 24576 sys-id-ext 1)
             Address     001c.f65e.8200
             Hello Time   2 sec  Max Age 20 sec  Forward Delay 15 sec
             Aging Time  15  sec

Interface            Role Sts Cost      Prio.Nbr Type
------------------- ---- --- --------- -------- --------------------
-----------
Fa0/3                Desg FWD 19        128.3    P2p
Fa0/6                Desg FWD 19        128.6    P2p
```

You can see that not only has Switch1 become the root, it has also changed both its root and alternate ports to designated.

Cram Quiz

1. What is the purpose of PortFast?
   - ❍ **A.** To promote eligible ports to root status
   - ❍ **B.** To allow ports that may cause Layer 2 loops to rapidly transition to forwarding state
   - ❍ **C.** To allow ports that will not cause layer two loops to rapidly transition to forwarding state
   - ❍ **D.** To decrease the speed of STP convergence on trunk links

2. What are the key differences between STP and RSTP? Choose all that apply.
   - ❍ **A.** STP uses timers, while RSTP uses enhanced BPDU data to perform port state transitions.
   - ❍ **B.** RSTP defines new port roles so that when a transition is necessary it happens much more quickly.
   - ❍ **C.** RSTP includes additional rapid transition to forwarding features.
   - ❍ **D.** RSTP is not standards based.

3. What are the possible port states in STP?
   - ❍ **A.** Learning
   - ❍ **B.** Blocking
   - ❍ **C.** Forwarding
   - ❍ **D.** Discarding
   - ❍ **E.** Listening
   - ❍ **F.** Alternate

4. What are the possible port states in RSTP?

❍ **A.** Learning

❍ **B.** Blocking

❍ **C.** Forwarding

❍ **D.** Discarding

❍ **E.** Listening

❍ **F.** Alternate

Cram Quiz Answers

1. Answer C is correct. PortFast can be applied to edge ports that will not cause layer two loops. Answer A is wrong; PortFast has nothing to do with root status. Answer B is incorrect; be careful of deliberately tricky wording. Answer D is incorrect because PortFast decreases convergence time, not increases it.
2. Answers A, B, and C are correct. Answer D is wrong; RSTP is standardized as 802.1w.
3. Answers A, B, C, and E are correct. The other answers are not valid for STP.
4. Answers A, C, and D are valid port states for RSTP. The others are not.

EtherChannel

Cram**Saver**

1. What is the definition of EtherChannel?
   - **A.** Special high-bandwidth fiber-channel cards provide high-speed uplinks using Ethernet emulation.
   - **B.** Multiple Ethernet interfaces provide higher aggregate bandwidth provided that STP is disabled.
   - **C.** Multiple Ethernet links are paired for redundancy; bandwidth is not aggregated, but STP treats the EtherChannel as one link.
   - **D.** Multiple Ethernet links are aggregated for higher bandwidth; STP sees the EtherChannel as one link.

2. What is the maximum number of links that can be bound to a single PAgP channel group?
   - **A.** 2
   - **B.** 4
   - **C.** 8
   - **D.** 16
   - **E.** 32

3. Which command binds an interface to port channel 1?
   - **A.** (config-if)#**b port-channel 1 member**
   - **B.** (config-if)#**port-channel group 1**
   - **C.** (config)#**channel-group 1 mode on**
   - **D.** (config-if)#**channel-group1 mode on**

Answers

1. Answer D is correct. Answer A is wrong; no special hardware is required, just two to eight Ethernet links. Answer B is incorrect because STP does not have to be disabled; the fact that STP sees the channel as one link is an important feature of EtherChannel. Answer C is wrong because the bandwidth is aggregated.
2. Answer C is correct; a maximum of eight individual links can be bound to a single channel group.
3. Answer D is correct. Answers A and B are not valid commands; Answer C is valid but at the wrong configuration prompt.

According to Cisco's website, EtherChannel is "a technology-leveraging, standards-based Fast Ethernet used in parallel to provide the additional bandwidth network backbones require today. It provides flexible, scalable bandwidth with resiliency and load sharing across links for switches, router interfaces and servers. Supports up to eight links per channel." EtherChannel can be used with Gig Ethernet too.

Note

Cisco's wording appears to imply that EtherChannel is standards based. I think what they mean is that Fast Ethernet is the standard. Make no mistake: EtherChannel is Cisco proprietary when using its native Port Aggregation Protocol (PAgP). If you need a true standard technology for interoperation between Cisco and non-Cisco gear, Cisco also supports the IEEE standard Link Aggregation Control Protocol (LACP, 802.3ad). In addition, some third-party vendors are licensed to support EtherChannel. So, for example, you could connect a Cisco switch to an Intel network interface card (NIC) that supports EtherChannel.

So, what does that rather dense wording in the first paragraph mean? Let's break it down:

- **Bandwidth:** Multiple (up to eight) parallel Ethernet links between devices (switches, routers, servers) are "bundled" to get aggregated bandwidth of up to eight times the bandwidth of one link. Using eight Fast Ethernet links, the max aggregate bandwidth of the EtherChannel would be 800Mbps full duplex, with four links 400Mbps, and so on.
- **Fault Tolerance:** If one of the links in the EtherChannel fails, the others carry on without it. Aggregate bandwidth is reduced, of course.
- **Spanning tree:** Because an EtherChannel is a "bundle" of individual links, STP sees the bundle as a single link. This is important, because otherwise STP would block all but one of the links; it also means that when one of the links fails, STP does not waste time reconverging, because the bundle is still active.
- **Transparency to the network:** All network adapters that are part of the EtherChannel use the same MAC, so networked applications, users, and devices are not aware of the individual links, just that there is a link.

Configuring EtherChannel

EtherChannels are more complicated than they really ought to be. In truth, it's pretty easy to configure them and make them work, but it is way easier to screw up the config and make them not work!

ExamAlert

Make sure that you get very comfortable with the EtherChannel section in Chapter 16, "Advanced Troubleshooting"!

The key to understanding EtherChannel is to understand the names used in the IOS:

- **EtherChannel** refers to both the technology and the virtual interface it creates.
- **Port channel** is the virtual EtherChannel interface (bundle). Individual physical interfaces are bound to the port channel using the **channel-group** command. The port channel is seen as a single virtual interface by STP.
- **Channel-group** *number* **mode** [**on** | **auto** | **desirable** | **active** | **passive**] is the command that binds a physical interface to a port-channel (virtual interface) bundle.
- **Interfaces** are assigned to a channel group. All interfaces with the same channel group binding can become part of the port channel bundle (but there are several requirements, as covered later).

Note

Okay, here is the first weird bit: The terms EtherChannel, *port channel*, and *channel group* all mean the same thing. Think of them as synonyms. You will see that you use the **channel-group** command to create the bundle, but the command to verify it is **show etherchannel**, and in the output of the command it is identified as a **PortChannel**. Bang head here.

Figure 12.9 shows the relationship between these elements.

There are two ways to build an EtherChannel: manually and dynamically. Let's begin with manual configuration.

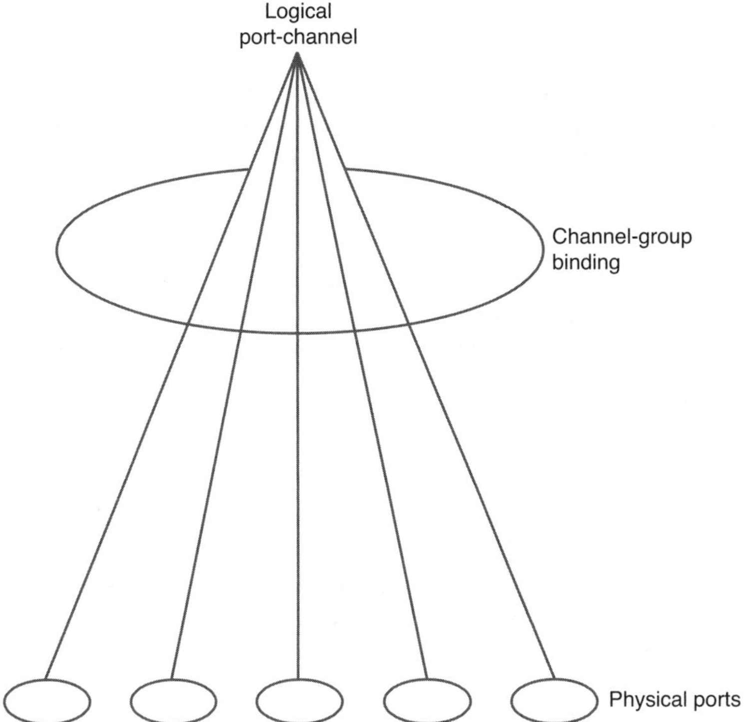

FIGURE 12.9 **Elements of EtherChannel.**

Manual Configuration of EtherChannel

The (surprisingly simple) steps are as follows:

1. At the interface config prompt for each of the physical interfaces you want to add to the EtherChannel, use the **channel-group** *number* **mode on** command.
2. Use the channel group same number for all interfaces that should join the same port channel. You can have multiple port channels; each must use a different number. The number assigned on Switch1 does not have to match the number used on Switch2.

The **channel-group** command, as it is applied to the physical interface, automatically creates the port channel interface. If the partner switch has a compatible configuration, the port channel becomes active. The automatically created port channel interface shows up in the **show interfaces** and **show ip interface brief** commands.

Dynamic Configuration of EtherChannel

This is where you can get into trouble if you are not paying attention. As mentioned earlier, it is easy to configure, but much easier to mess it up. Here's where the problems come from: Cisco supports two EtherChannel negotiation protocols: PAgP and LACP. (Any time I see the word *negotiate*, I get suspicious. Negotiation always carries the possibility of failure.) These two protocols are, of course, incompatible.

Let's go back to the manual configuration for a sec. We used the command **channel-group** *number* **mode on** in the config. The **mode on** keywords tell the switch "Don't negotiate, just do PAgP." As long as both switches use the **mode on** keyword, "it just works."

Negotiation Using PAgP

Negotiation requires that at least one switch begin the negotiation. In PAgP, the negotiation options are **desirable** and **auto**. Desirable begins the negotiation, and Auto waits for it. Table 12.4 shows the interaction of the two settings; a check mark indicates the negotiations will succeed (and the EtherChannel will form), and an X indicates that it will fail.

TABLE 12.4 **EtherChannel Negotiation with PAgP**

Near End	Far End	Success?
Auto	Auto	X
Auto	Desirable	✔
Desirable	Desirable	✔
Desirable	Auto	✔

As you can see, it isn't difficult to make PAgP work. Your confusion will probably be with the keyword **auto**. It seems like Auto should automatically work, but it will not. It gets more confusing when you get it mixed up with the settings for trunk negotiation using DTP. Stay focused.

Negotiation Using LACP

You can use LACP on two Cisco switches if you want, but it's more likely that you will use it to get a Cisco switch to work with a non-Cisco device. With LACP, your negotiation options are **mode active** and **mode passive**. As you might have guessed, Active begins the negotiation, but Passive will not. One end of the link needs to be Active. Table 12.5 shows the interaction of these two settings; a check mark indicates the negotiations will succeed (and the EtherChannel will form), and an X indicates that it will fail.

TABLE 12.5 **EtherChannel Negotiation with LACP**

Near End	Far End	Success?
Passive	Passive	X
Passive	Active	✔
Active	Active	✔
Active	Passive	✔

That's pretty much what you would expect, and quite similar to what happens with PAgP. Here's the difficult part, though: You can mix the negotiation protocols. They won't work together, of course, but there is nothing to stop you from misconfiguring it. Table 12.6 lists all the possible options in a matrix of successes and failures. (Remember that **mode on** really means that "negotiation is off; just do it.")

TABLE 12.6 **The EtherChannel Negotiation Matrix**

	On	Desirable	Auto	Active	Passive
On	✔	X	X	X	X
Desirable	X	✔	✔	X	X
Auto	X	✔	X	X	X
Active	X	X	X	✔	✔
Passive	X	X	X	✔	X

ExamAlert

As the table graphically shows, we have more ways to make EtherChannel *not* work than we do to make it work. By this point, you are probably beginning to realize that the exam loves this kind of situation. You might want to get comfy with Table 12.6.

Verifying EtherChannel

The commands available for verifying EtherChannel operation include the following:

- **show EtherChannel:** Lists the channel groups, how many ports are in each one, and their current state. An example is shown in Example 12.1.

- **show EtherChannel summary:** Lists the number of EtherChannels in use, the port channel identifiers, which ports are in each one and their current state, and the protocol used (if any). An example is shown in Example 12.2.
- **show EtherChannel detail:** Lists detailed information about channel groups and member interfaces. An example is shown in Example 12.3.
- **show spanning-tree:** This is of interest because the port channel in Example 12.4, Po1, appears as the STP root port, demonstrating that STP sees it as a single high-bandwidth link (and therefore that it is operational).

EXAMPLE 12.1 **show EtherChannel Command Output**

```
Switch1#show EtherChannel
                Channel-group listing:
                ----------------------

Group: 1
----------
Group state = L2
Ports: 4   Maxports = 8
Port-channels: 1 Max Port-channels = 1
Protocol:    -
Minimum Links: 0
```

EXAMPLE 12.2 **show EtherChannel summary Command Output**

```
Switch1#show EtherChannel summary
Flags:  D - down        P - bundled in port-channel
        I - stand-alone s - suspended
        H - Hot-standby (LACP only)
        R - Layer3      S - Layer2
        U - in use      f - failed to allocate aggregator

        M - not in use, minimum links not met
        u - unsuitable for bundling
        w - waiting to be aggregated
        d - default port


Number of channel-groups in use: 1
Number of aggregators:           1
```

```
Group  Port-channel  Protocol    Ports
------+-------------+-----------+-----------------------------------
-----------
1      Po1(SU)           -        Fa0/3(P)    Fa0/4(P)    Fa0/5(P)
                                  Fa0/6(P)
```

EXAMPLE 12.3 **show EtherChannel detail Command Output**

```
Switch1#show EtherChannel detail
                Channel-group listing:
                ----------------------

Group: 1
----------
Group state = L2
Ports: 4   Maxports = 8
Port-channels: 1 Max Port-channels = 1
Protocol:    -
Minimum Links: 0
                Ports in the group:
                -------------------
Port: Fa0/3
------------

Port state    = Up Mstr In-Bndl
Channel group = 1           Mode = On        Gcchange = -
Port-channel  = Po1         GC   =   -       Pseudo port-channel = Po1
Port index    = 0           Load = 0x00      Protocol =    -

Age of the port in the current state: 0d:15h:18m:26s

Port: Fa0/4
------------

Port state    = Up Mstr In-Bndl
Channel group = 1           Mode = On        Gcchange = -
Port-channel  = Po1         GC   =   -       Pseudo port-channel = Po1
Port index    = 0           Load = 0x00      Protocol =    -

Age of the port in the current state: 0d:15h:13m:49s

Port: Fa0/5
------------

Port state    = Up Mstr In-Bndl
Channel group = 1           Mode = On        Gcchange = -
Port-channel  = Po1         GC   =   -       Pseudo port-channel = Po1
Port index    = 0           Load = 0x00      Protocol =    -
```

```
Age of the port in the current state: 0d:15h:13m:48s

Port: Fa0/6
------------

Port state    = Up Mstr In-Bndl
Channel group = 1           Mode = On         Gcchange = -
Port-channel  = Po1         GC   =   -        Pseudo port-channel = Po1
Port index    = 0           Load = 0x00       Protocol =    -

Age of the port in the current state: 0d:15h:18m:27s

                Port-channels in the group:
                ---------------------------

Port-channel: Po1
------------

Age of the Port-channel   = 0d:15h:31m:06s
Logical slot/port   = 2/1          Number of ports = 4
GC                  = 0x00000000      HotStandBy port = null
Port state          = Port-channel Ag-Inuse
Protocol            =    -
Port security       = Disabled

Ports in the Port-channel:

Index   Load   Port     EC state        No of bits
------+------+------+------------------+-----------
  0     00     Fa0/3    On                   0
  0     00     Fa0/4    On                   0
  0     00     Fa0/5    On                   0
  0     00     Fa0/6    On                   0

Time since last port bundled:    0d:15h:13m:48s    Fa0/5
Time since last port Un-bundled: 0d:15h:18m:36s    Fa0/6
```

EXAMPLE 12.4 **show spanning-tree Command Output**

```
Switch1#show spanning-tree

VLAN0001
  Spanning tree enabled protocol ieee
  Root ID     Priority    32768
              Address     0009.7cd7.6680
              Cost        8
              Port        64 (Port-channel1)
              Hello Time   2 sec  Max Age 20 sec  Forward Delay 15 sec
```

```
  Bridge ID  Priority    32769  (priority 32768 sys-id-ext 1)
             Address     001c.f65e.8200
             Hello Time   2 sec  Max Age 20 sec  Forward Delay 15 sec
             Aging Time  300 sec

Interface           Role Sts Cost      Prio.Nbr Type
------------------- ---- --- --------- -------- --------------------
-----------
Fa0/1               Desg FWD 19        128.1    P2p
Fa0/8               Desg FWD 19        128.8    P2p
Po1                 Root FWD 8         128.64   P2p
```

Cram Quiz

Examine the following excerpts from the running config outputs from Switch1 and Switch2:

```
! Output from Switch1
!
interface FastEthernet0/3
 switchport mode trunk
 speed 100
 duplex full
 channel-group 1 mode on
!
interface FastEthernet0/4
 switchport mode trunk
 speed 100
 duplex full
 channel-group 1 mode on
!
interface FastEthernet0/5
 switchport mode trunk
 speed 100
 duplex full
 channel-group 1 mode on
!
interface FastEthernet0/6
 switchport mode trunk
 speed 100
 duplex full
 channel-group 1 mode on
!
! Output from Switch2
!
interface FastEthernet0/3
 switchport mode trunk
 speed 100
```

```
 duplex full
 channel-group 2 mode auto
!
interface FastEthernet0/4
 switchport mode trunk
 speed 100
 duplex full
 channel-group 2 mode auto
!
interface FastEthernet0/5
 switchport mode trunk
 speed 100
 duplex full
 channel-group 2 mode active
!
interface FastEthernet0/6
 switchport mode trunk
 speed 100
 duplex full
 channel-group 2 mode active
!
```

1. Will the EtherChannel configuration succeed using all four links as desired? Why or why not?
   - ❍ **A.** Yes, all the configurations are compatible.
   - ❍ **B.** No, because Switch2 uses a different channel group number.
   - ❍ **C.** No, because EtherChannels cannot be formed on trunk links.
   - ❍ **D.** No, because the negotiation will fail on two of the links.
   - ❍ **E.** No, because the negotiation will fail on all four links.

2. Ewan and Charley are arguing about EtherChannel negotiation protocol compatibility. When considering whether two negotiation configurations will successfully make a link part of the port channel, which of the following are compatible configurations? Choose all that apply.
   - ❍ **A.** **channel-group 1 mode on** and **channel-group 5 mode on**
   - ❍ **B.** **channel-group 1 mode active** and **channel-group 5 mode desirable**
   - ❍ **C.** **channel-group 1 mode active** and **channel-group 1 mode passive**
   - ❍ **D.** **channel-group 1 mode on** and **channel-group 5 mode desirable**
   - ❍ **E.** **channel-group 1 mode auto** and **channel-group 5 mode auto**
   - ❍ **F.** **channel-group 1 mode auto** and **channel-group 5 mode desirable**

3. Based on the following output, is the EtherChannel functioning, and, if so, how many ports is it using?

```
Switch1#show EtherChannel summary
Flags:  D - down          P - bundled in port-channel
        I - stand-alone s - suspended
        H - Hot-standby (LACP only)
        R - Layer3        S - Layer2
        U - in use        f - failed to allocate aggregator

        M - not in use, minimum links not met
        u - unsuitable for bundling
        w - waiting to be aggregated
        d - default port


Number of channel-groups in use: 1
Number of aggregators:           1

Group  Port-channel  Protocol    Ports
------+-------------+-----------+-------------------------------
----------------
1      Po1(SU)         -         Fa0/3(P)    Fa0/4(P)    Fa0/5(P)
                                 Fa0/6(P)
```

❍ **A.** No, it is not functioning.

❍ **B.** Yes, with two ports.

❍ **C.** Yes, with four ports.

❍ **D.** Yes, with eight ports.

❍ **E.** Cannot be determined from this output.

Cram Quiz Answers

1. Answer E is correct. Switch1 uses the **mode on** setting, which does not negotiate. Therefore, the only compatible setting on Switch2 would be **mode on** as well. None of the ports on Switch2 use **mode on**, so negotiation fails on all four ports.
2. Answers A, C, and F are correct. Refer to Table 12-6 for the EtherChannel negotiation compatibility matrix.
3. Answer C is correct. The last line of the output indicates **Po1 (SU)**, which indicates the EtherChannel is operational as a Layer2 link, and the four ports (F0/3,4,5 and 6) each have the **(P)** code, which indicates they are bundled in port channel.

Review Questions

1. What is the function of 802.1d STP?
   - ❍ **A.** Prevents routing loops in redundant topologies
   - ❍ **B.** Prevents Layer 2 loops in networks with redundant switched paths
   - ❍ **C.** Prevents frame forwarding until all IP addresses are known
   - ❍ **D.** Enables the use of multiple routed paths for load sharing
   - ❍ **E.** Allows the propagation of VLAN information from a central source

2. What defines the root switch in an STP system? Choose two.
   - ❍ **A.** The switch with the lowest bridge ID
   - ❍ **B.** The switch with the highest bridge ID
   - ❍ **C.** The fastest switch
   - ❍ **D.** The switch with the most connections to other switches
   - ❍ **E.** The first switch to send out a BPDU
   - ❍ **F.** The switch with the lowest priority
   - ❍ **G.** The switch with the highest priority

3. Which one of the following statements describes a converged STP system?
   - ❍ **A.** All switches are running STP.
   - ❍ **B.** All ports are blocking.
   - ❍ **C.** All ports are forwarding.
   - ❍ **D.** All ports that are not forwarding are blocking.

4. Which one of the following is true of the spanning-tree root path cost?
   - ❍ **A.** It is the cost of the exit port to the root.
   - ❍ **B.** It is the bandwidth of the exit port to the root.
   - ❍ **C.** It is the delay in data transmission to the root.
   - ❍ **D.** It is the cumulative cost, based on number of hops, to the root.
   - ❍ **E.** It is the cumulative cost, based on bandwidth, of all links on the path to the root.

Given the diagram in Figure 12.10, answer the following questions.

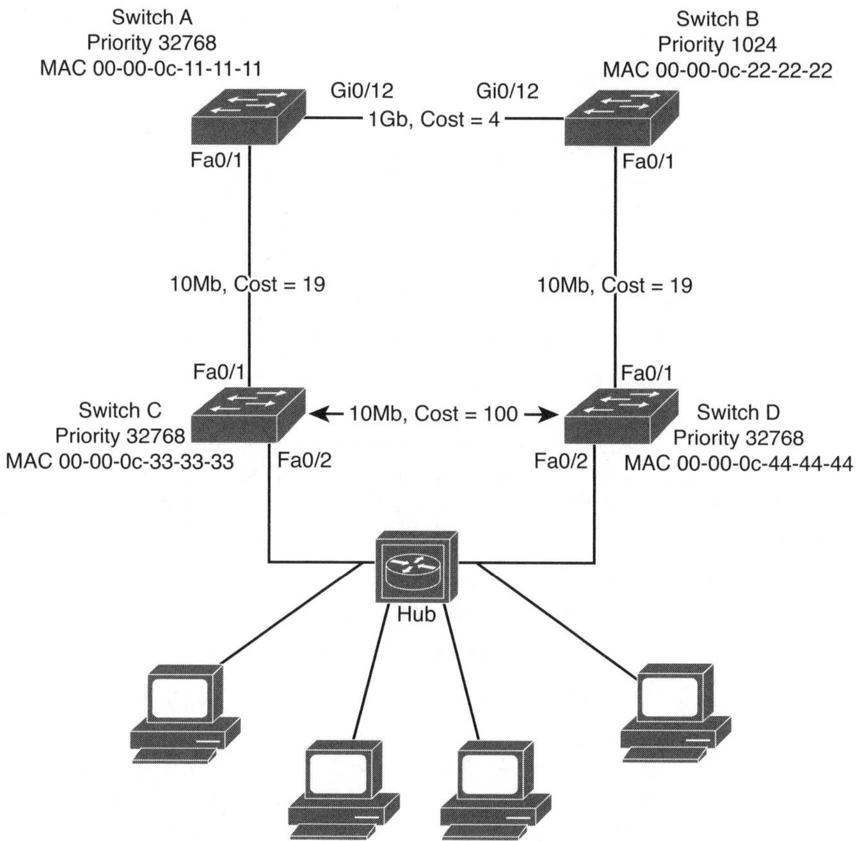

FIGURE 12.10 **Network topology for Questions 5 and 6.**

5. Which switch will become the root?

❍ **A.** Switch A

❍ **B.** Switch B

❍ **C.** Switch C

❍ **D.** Switch D

6. Which of the following will be the designated port for the Ethernet segment between switches C and D?
   - ❍ **A.** Switch C, Fa0/1
   - ❍ **B.** Switch C, Fa0/2
   - ❍ **C.** Switch D, Fa0/1
   - ❍ **D.** Switch D, Fa0/2

7. What is the command to activate a Rapid Spanning Tree instance for each VLAN?
   - ❍ **A.** Switch(config-if)#**spanning-tree mode rapid-pvst**
   - ❍ **B.** Switch(config)#**spanning-tree mode rapid-pvst**
   - ❍ **C.** Switch(config)#**spanning-tree mode pvrst**
   - ❍ **D.** Switch(config)#**spanning-tree mode pvst rapid**

8. Wayne and Garth need to connect a server to the network. They are concerned that STP will cause significant service outages to the server. What two settings will optimize the switching environment and minimize service outages for the new server? Choose two.
   - ❍ **A.** Switch(config)#**spanning-tree mode rapid-pvst**
   - ❍ **B.** Switch(config-if)#**spanning-tree portfast**
   - ❍ **C.** Switch(config)#**spanning-tree vlan 1 root secondary**
   - ❍ **D.** Switch#**show spanning-tree vlan 1**

9. Which if the following are true statements about EtherChannel?
   - ❍ **A.** EtherChannel requires specialized hardware accelerator modules to provide the necessary aggregation computation power.
   - ❍ **B.** 10BASE-T links cannot be aggregated by EtherChannel.
   - ❍ **C.** Gigabit Ethernet links cannot be aggregated by EtherChannel.
   - ❍ **D.** A maximum of four links can be aggregated by EtherChannel.
   - ❍ **E.** A maximum of eight links can be aggregated by EtherChannel.
   - ❍ **F.** All links in an EtherChannel must be added to the same channel group.
   - ❍ **G.** The channel group number on each switch must be the same.

10. Two of these commands are compatible and will place a link into a functional EtherChannel. Which two?
    - ❍ **A.** **channel-group 2 mode active**
    - ❍ **B.** **channel-group 2 mode on**
    - ❍ **C.** **channel-group 2 mode desirable**
    - ❍ **D.** **channel-group 2 mode dynamic-auto**
    - ❍ **E.** **channel-group 2 mode auto**

Answers to Review Questions

1. Answer B is correct. STP prevents Layer 2 loops if redundant paths exist. Answers A, C, D, and E are incorrect; STP is not concerned with routing loops, IP addresses, routing in general, or VLAN administration.
2. Answers A and F are correct. The bridge ID is the priority prepended to the MAC address of the switch. The switch with the lowest bridge ID becomes the root; therefore, the switch with the lowest priority will always be the root. Answers B, C, D, E, and G are incorrect; the winning bridge ID and priority will be the lowest. The speed of the switch has no bearing on whether it will be the root if left to default settings. The number of connections to other switches has no impact either.
3. Answer D is correct. Convergence in STP means that all ports are either blocked to prevent loops or forwarding to allow data transmission. (However, if all ports are blocking, the system has not converged yet.) Answers A, B, and C are incorrect; all switches must run STP or run the risk of loops destabilizing the network.
4. Answer E is correct. The root path cost is the accumulated cost of all the links on the path to the root. The cost is calculated based on the bandwidth of the links. Answers A, B, C, and D are incorrect. You must add the STP cost of all the links on the path to the root; cost has nothing to do with delay or hop count.
5. Answer B is correct; Switch B will become the root because it has the lowest priority. Remember that even though A has a lower MAC, the priority overrides this, and the switch with the lowest priority will be the root. Answers A, B, and C are incorrect.
6. Answer D is correct. Because D has the lower root path cost (at 19) than C (at 23), D will make its port the designated port—even though C has a lower bridge ID. Answers A, B, and C are incorrect; the designated ports must be connected to the Ethernet segment, and the switch with the lowest root path cost will host the DP. Only if there is a tie for root path cost will bridge ID become a deciding factor.
7. Answer B is correct. Answer A is at the wrong command prompt, although the command is correct. Answers C and D are not valid commands.
8. Answers A and B are correct. Setting the mode to Rapid PVST will speed up STP convergence and enable RTF features, including PortFast, which will achieve the goal of optimization and minimizing outages. Answer C is a valid command, but we do not have enough information to decide whether it will help with optimization. Answer D is an STP verification command; it will have no impact on optimization, although it may inform decisions that we might make about optimizations.
9. Answers B, E, and F are correct. EtherChannel does not require any specialized hardware; it aggregates the bandwidth of up to eight Fast Ethernet, Gigabit Ethernet or 10 Gigabit Ethernet links. All links must use the same channel group number to be aggregated in a single port channel. Multiple port channels are allowed on a single switch, using different numbers. The port channel numbers do not have to match across switches.
10. Answers C and E are correct. Refer to Table 12.6 for the EtherChannel negotiation compatibility matrix.

CHAPTER THIRTEEN

Advanced Router Operation

This chapter covers the following official 200-101 ICND2 and 200-120 CCNA exam topics:

- Manage Cisco IOS files.
- Configure and verify OSPF (single area).
- Configure and verify EIGRP (single autonomous system).

In Chapter 7, "Basic Routing," you learned about static, default, and basic OSPF routing. These solutions work well for networks that are not very large and that are not prone to frequent changes. For larger and more complex networks, you need a scalable solution. Open Shortest Path First (OSPF) Protocol can scale and successfully route in large environments when additional features are utilized. Enhanced Interior Gateway Routing Protocol (EIGRP), Cisco's proprietary advanced distance vector protocol, is likewise able to scale to complex environments if properly implemented. In this chapter, we explore some more advanced capabilities and configurations for OSPF and introduce EIGRP.

Before we get to the heavy lifting, though, we cover the fundamentals of IOS and configuration file management.

Router IOS and Configuration File Management

CramSaver

1. Which command will create a backup of your IOS image file to a TFTP server?
   - **A. copy ios tftp**
   - **B. backup ios tftp**
   - **C. copy tftp flash**
   - **D. copy flash tftp**
2. Which command will restore or upgrade your IOS image file using TFTP?
   - **A. copy flash tftp**
   - **B. copy tftp flash**
   - **C. restore ios flash /overwrite**
   - **D. restore factory default**
3. Bob is attempting to upgrade his IOS image file. Yvette warns him to check that there is enough space in flash for the new, larger file. What command will show how much room is left in the flash directory?
   - **A. show flash**
   - **B. show version**
   - **C. show memory**
   - **D. show run**

Answers

1. Answer D is correct. Answers A and B are not valid commands. Answer C reverses the command order.
2. Answer B is correct. Answer A reverses the command order. Answer C is not a valid command. Answer D is valid, but only on a Cisco Unity Express module, not the router IOS.
3. Answer A is correct. Answer B is wrong because **show version** will not show you how much flash is available, just how much there is in total. Answer C lists detailed RAM memory allocations, not flash utilization. D is wrong because **show run** will not list flash memory utilization.

Understanding your IOS, how to back up and restore it, and how it is licensed are things you might overlook, thinking that configuration is more important and demanding. True enough; you will spend more time and effort on learning the complexities of configuration and features. But the exam will test you on a few of these seemingly mundane topics—and never forget what my first boss told me: "He who laughs last made a backup."

Back Up and Restore IOS

At some point in your career, you will need to back up, restore, or upgrade your IOS. You can use Trivial File Transfer Protocol (TFTP), FTP, or RCP to transfer an IOS image to or from a server. TFTP is the most common, so that is covered here. (It is also covered on the CCNA exams.)

With TFTP (unlike FTP), there is no means of authenticating with a username or password or navigating directories. To back up your IOS, you use the **copy** command from within privileged exec mode. The syntax of this command is **copy** *source destination*. So, if you want to copy an IOS from your flash to a TFTP server, the syntax is **copy flash tftp**. After executing this command, you are prompted with a number of questions asking for such things as the IOS filename and IP address of the TFTP server. Following is the output of this command. The TFTP server in this example is located at the IP address 172.16.0.254:

```
Router#copy flash tftp
Source filename [c2800nm-adventerprisek9-mz.151-3.T.bin]?
Address or name of remote host []? 192.168.1.111
Destination filename [c2800nm-adventerprisek9-mz.151-3.T.bin]?
!!!!!!!!!!!!!!!!!!!!!!!!!!!!!!!!!!!!!!!!!!!!!!!!!!!!!!!!!!!!!!!!!!!!!!
!!!!!!!!!!!!!!!!!!!!!!!!!!!!!!!!!!!!!!!!!!!!!!!!!!!!!!!!!!!!!!!!!!!!!!
!!!!!!!!!!!!!!!!!!!!!!!!!!!!!!!!!!!!!!!!!!!!!!!!!!!!!!!!!!!!!!!!!!!!!!
!!!!!!!!!!!!!!!!!!!!!!!!!!!!!!!!!!!!!!!!!!!!!!!!!!!
66483320 bytes copied in 118.036 secs (563246 bytes/sec)
```

To restore or upgrade your IOS from a TFTP server to a router, the syntax is **copy tftp flash**.

Remember the following troubleshooting steps if you are having difficulties using TFTP:

- Verify that the TFTP server is running.
- Verify cable configurations. You should use a crossover cable between a router and a server, or, if you have a switch, use a straight-through cable from the router to the switch and from the switch to the server.
- Verify that your router is on the same subnet as your TFTP server or has a means to route to it somehow (static route or routing protocol).

Cram Quiz

1. What does the command **copy tftp flash** do?
   - ❍ **A.** Restores the IOS from a TFTP server
   - ❍ **B.** Backs up the IOS to a TFTP server

2. What does the command **copy flash tftp** do?
   - ❍ **A.** Restores the IOS from a TFTP server
   - ❍ **B.** Backs up the IOS to a TFTP server

Cram Quiz Answers

1. Answer A is correct.
2. Answer B is correct.

OSPF

CramSaver

1. Four entries in the Hello messages between two OSPF routers must match for the two routers to become neighbors. Which four of the following are they?
   - **A.** Process ID
   - **B.** Area ID
   - **C.** Router ID
   - **D.** Stub Area Flag
   - **E.** Authentication
   - **F.** OSPF timers
   - **G.** Subnet mask

2. On a multiaccess networks like Ethernet, in which state will an OSPF router remain with a neighbor router that is not the DR or BDR?
   - **A.** Down
   - **B.** Attempt
   - **C.** Init
   - **D.** 2-way
   - **E.** Exstart
   - **F.** Loading
   - **G.** Full

3. What are three benefits of configuring multi-area OSPF? Choose three.
   - **A.** Lower hardware costs due to fewer routers
   - **B.** Reduced RAM and CPU utilization on routers internal to an area
   - **C.** Reduced size of topology and route tables
   - **D.** Detailed information propagated about network problems in a remote area
   - **E.** Route instability in one area is hidden from other areas

4. What is the definition of an ABR?
   - A. A router that has had the **ip ospf abr** command entered at one or more interfaces
   - B. The Area Broadcast Redirect feature, which prevents excessive broadcast traffic on multiaccess networks in a given area
   - C. A router with all interfaces in a border area
   - D. A router with one interface in each of two (or more) areas
   - E. A router with one interface in area 0 and at least one interface in another area (not area 0).

Answers

1. Answers B, D, E, and F are correct.
2. Answer D is correct.
3. Answers B, C, and E are correct. Answer A is incorrect; router count is not necessarily increased or decreased as a result of using multi-area OSPF. Answer D is incorrect because it describes essentially the opposite of what multi-area OSPF does.
4. Answer E is correct. Answer A is not a valid command. Answer B is complete fiction. Answer C is incorrect because there is no such thing as a "border area." Answer D is very close, but does not specify that one of the interfaces must be in area 0.

Chapter 7 introduced OSPF and some of its key characteristics. You also learned how to configure it for basic single-area operation. In this section, we go a little deeper, including a better understanding of adjacency, OSPF router states, and different link-state advertisement (LSA) types. We discuss multi-area configuration and examine some of the details of the OSPF process. We close out OSPF by examining OSPF Version 3 advanced implementation.

Advanced OSPF Concepts

This section covers what adjacency really means and how OSPF routers get there, the different states an OSPF router can be in, the different LSA types, and the concepts behind multi-area OSPF.

Adjacency

OSPF routers go through a series of steps to achieve what is commonly called *adjacency*. The odd thing is, adjacent isn't really an official OSPF state, it's just a commonly used word to describe when two routers recognize each other and are prepared to exchange route information. You will encounter the term *fully adjacent*, as well, which is when the routers have completed exchanging route information and are converged.

Let's back up a little and go over the OSPF steps that the routers go through to become adjacent or fully adjacent:

1. When you configure OSPFv2 on a router, you switch on the routing process for a particular interface in a specific OSPF area, using the **network** command (or possibly the interface command **ip ospf** *process-id* **area** *area #*). You can verify the configuration of this command with the **show running-config** command.
2. The interfaces begin sending (usually via multicast) Hello messages so that the router can discover other neighbor routers and announce itself to other OSPF routers. You can verify the configuration with the **show ip ospf interface** [*type number* | **brief**] command.
3. When the router receives a Hello message from another router and sees its own IP address in the other router's neighbor list (and assuming the required parameters are compatible; authentication, stub area flag, area number, and timers), the two routers become neighbors. At this point, the routers are adjacent. You can verify the neighbor relationships with the **show ip ospf neighbor** [*type number*] command.
4. Once the adjacency is established, the routers flood LSAs that describe the links that they are advertising to the other OSPF routers. The LSAs are used to build the topology database (a.k.a. the link-state database). When all information about all the links has been exchanged, the routers are fully adjacent. You can verify the contents of the LSDB using the **show ip ospf database** command.
5. When the topology database is complete, each router runs the Shortest Path First (SPF) algorithm to determine the best routes to each known network and places these routes into the route table. You can verify the content of the routing table using the **show ip route** command.

Note

There are some exceptions and clarifications to this list of steps, depending on the network type (primarily whether it is point-to-point network type such as a T1 line or multiaccess like Ethernet or Frame Relay).

ExamAlert

The verification commands in the preceding list are those you should know and be able to recognize and interpret the output from.

OSPF States

A router may progress through eight "official" OSPF states on its way to what we popularly call *full adjacency*. (I say *may* because some states do not happen on some types of networks.) The following descriptions have been adapted for clarity and simplicity from Cisco's web page about OSPF neighbor states at http://www.cisco.com/en/US/tech/tk365/technologies_tech_note09186a0080093f0e.shtml.

Down

This is the first OSPF neighbor state. No hellos have been received from this neighbor, but Hello packets could still be sent to the neighbor in this state. (This would happen only if the neighbor were statically defined.)

If a router that is fully adjacent with a neighbor router doesn't receive a Hello packet from that neighbor within the Dead timer (The Dead timer is four times the Hello timer by default), or if a statically defined neighbor is deleted, the neighbor state changes from full to down.

Attempt

This state is valid only for statically defined neighbors in a nonbroadcast multiaccess (NBMA) environment. In the attempt state, the router sends unicast Hello packets to a statically defined neighbor from which Hellos have not been received (within the Dead interval).

Init

The init state occurs when a router receives a Hello packet from a neighbor but the receiving router's own router ID is not listed in it. In other words, I see your Hellos, but apparently you have not yet seen my Hellos.

2-Way

As soon as I receive a Hello from a neighbor and I see my own router ID listed in it, I change the state between us to 2-way.

Note

Four values in the Hello message must match for two OSPF routers to become neighbors: the Hello and Dead intervals (timers), the area ID, the stub area flag, and the authentication type and password (if used). Any mismatch and the neighbor relationship will not be established.

In the 2-way state, I determine whether I should become adjacent with this neighbor. On Ethernet and NBMA networks, a router moves to the full state only with the designated router (DR) and the backup designated router (BDR); it stays in the 2-way state with all other (DRother) neighbors. On point-to-point and point-to-multipoint networks, a router moves to the full state with all connected routers.

During this stage, the DR and BDR are elected. (For more information on the DR election process, see the section on DR/BDR elections in Chapter 7.)

Note

Receiving a database descriptor (DBD) packet from a neighbor in the init state will also a cause a transition to 2-way state.

Exstart

Once the DR and BDR are elected, the actual process of exchanging link-state information can start between the routers and their DR and BDR.

In this state, the routers and their DR and BDR establish a master-slave relationship and choose the initial sequence number for adjacency formation. The router with the higher router ID becomes the master and starts the exchange, and as such is the only router that can increment the sequence number. You might expect that the DR/BDR with the highest router ID will become the master during this process, but remember that the DR/BDR election might be determined by a higher priority configured on the router instead of highest router ID. Therefore, it is possible that a DR could become the slave. Also note that master/slave selection is on a per-neighbor basis; one might be a master with neighbor A but a slave with neighbor B.

Exchange

In the exchange state, OSPF routers exchange DBD packets. Database descriptors contain LSA headers only—not the details of the link as in a full LSA—and describe the contents of the entire link-state database. (You can think of these

DBDs as a checklist: Got this link? Got that link?) Each DBD packet has a sequence number that can be incremented only by the master router and that is explicitly acknowledged by the slave. Routers also send link-state request packets and link-state update packets (which contain the entire LSA) in this state. The contents of the DBD received are compared to the information contained in the router's link-state database to check whether new or more current link-state information is available with the neighbor.

Loading

In this state, the actual exchange of link-state information occurs. Based on the information provided by the DBDs, routers send link-state request packets: "Tell me more about this link!" The neighbor then provides the requested link-state information in link-state update (LSU) packets. During the adjacency, if a router receives an outdated or missing LSA, it requests that LSA by sending a link-state request packet. All LSU packets are acknowledged.

Full

In this state, routers are fully adjacent with each other. All the router and network LSAs are exchanged, and the routers' databases are fully synchronized.

Full is the normal state for an OSPF router. If a router is stuck in another state, it's an indication that there are problems in forming adjacencies. The only exception to this is the 2-way state, which is normal in a multiaccess network such as Ethernet, where routers achieve the full state with their DR and BDR only. Neighbors always see each other as 2-way.

> **Note**
>
> This section started by talking about *adjacent* and *fully adjacent*. So, where exactly do these familiar terms fit into the official OSPF states? Essentially, the exstart state is adjacent, and the full state is fully adjacent.

Maintaining the Neighbor Relationship

Once the routers have converged, OSPF calms down and is very quiet. The routers send Hellos (based on the Hello interval, which defaults to every 10 seconds for Ethernet and every 30 seconds for nonbroadcast networks like Frame Relay), and listen for Hellos from other routers. As long as a Hello is received from a neighbor router within the Dead interval timer, the neighbor relationship is maintained. (The Dead interval is four times the Hello interval by default—40 seconds for Ethernet and 120 seconds for nonbroadcast networks.)

If any link state changes, the source router floods an updated LSA to other neighbors, or if a DR/BDR has been elected, only to the DR and BDR. This behavior really underlines the importance of the DR/BDR: Without the DR/BDR, there would be much more flooding of LSAs to every neighbor router, causing a lot more OSPF traffic and overhead.

Each LSA has a lifetime of 30 minutes by default. If nothing changes, no LSA updates are sent out for 30 minutes. But, when that 30-minute timer expires, a new LSA is flooded to replace the expired one, and the 30-minute lifetime starts over.

Multi-Area OSPF

Within a area, each router floods LSAs to its neighbor routers. With each new LSA, the topology database might change, and the SPF algorithm might have to be rerun to determine the best routes. That might mean quite a bit of work for the routers as the routed system grows or becomes busier. In a big system, we want to reduce that work load and make room for other more important activities—such as routing and actually moving business data around. We do that by using multiple areas in the OSPF system.

Benefits of Multi-Area OSPF

If we split up the system into separate OSPF areas, the routers' behavior doesn't change all that drastically; each router still floods LSAs to its neighbor routers. The big difference is that routers in different areas cannot be neighbors, so most LSA floods are immediately reduced to occurring only between routers within the same area. The Area Border Router (ABR) actually creates a special LSA (Type 3), which identifies subnets in other areas and identifies itself as the advertising router. These Type 3 LSAs contain less detail about the subnets they describe and make it seems that the subnets are all directly connected to the ABR. This combination of less detail and less path calculation info to deal with makes much less work for the routers in the area into which the ABR is injecting the Type 3 LSAs. That's the first benefit of multi-area OSPF.

The next benefit is easy to see: If the routers within an area know detailed information only about other routers and links within the same area, there is less data in the topology database and therefore less RAM usage (in addition to reduced CPU utilization for SPF recalculation). That translates into less work for the routers.

The last benefit comes from the special role played by ABRs. An ABR has (at least) one interface in area 0 (the backbone area), and one or more interfaces in one or more other areas. The ABR sends out only summary information about links in other areas, basically making it seem as though it is directly connected to everything that is not in the local area. So, a router in area 1 knows all the detail about the links and routers within area 1, but sees everything else in all other areas as simply being directly connected to the ABR for area 1. As a bonus, if a link in area 51 is unstable (*flapping* was the term we used to use), that instability is hidden from area 1 because area 1 isn't getting the details, just the fact that the link exists and can be reached through Router1. That all means less information being sent between areas, again reducing the workload for the routers.

So, when do you really need to go with a multi-area configuration instead of a single area 0 setup? Not for a while; it really depends on what the RAM and CPU load is on your routers, which is hard to predict without getting into data modeling using some network specifics. However, a few guidelines apply; most seem to suggest that if you get to about 50 routers in area 0 you might want to start splitting up the system. Because it is impossible to be specific until we have specifics to model from, the best you will see is "The maximum number of routers in a single OSPF area is 50 to 100." Some service providers have more than 350 routers in a single area, but you can bet that is a highly optimized environment. Cisco also suggests that you not have more than 200 subnets within a single area, because it is the subnets (links) that actually increase the OSPF load the most.

ExamAlert

Be familiar with the benefits of multi-area (hierarchical) OSPF routing:

- Type 1 and 2 LSAs are flooded only to routers within a single area, reducing LSA traffic and workload on internal routers.
- Detailed knowledge of only the links within a given area reduces the size and complexity of the LSDB and SPF recalculation, reducing RAM and CPU load for the routers within each area.
- The ABR and ASBR routers send in only summarized information about subnets in other areas into a given area, reducing LSDB size and complexity, and hiding instability in another area that could cause constant route updates.

Multi-Area OSPF LSA Types

We have seen that the ABRs automatically reduce the clutter of detailed info sent between areas. So, how is that done?

So far, we have talked in generic terms about LSAs. In fact, there are seven types of LSA defined in OSPF (although Cisco does not support Type 6), and it is the information contained (or omitted) in each type that determines how much and what kind of information is propagated between areas. The following points give you some idea of what the LSAs are and what they do:

- Type 1 LSAs, called router LSAs, are sent by every router to other routers within the same area. They describe the router, giving the router ID, all its IP addresses and masks, and the state of its interfaces. OSPF can create a fairly accurate model of the network using these LSAs. Type 1 LSAs do not leave the area.
- Type 2 LSAs, called network LSAs, are sent only by the DR for each segment that has one (but only if that DR has at least one neighbor). Type 2 LSAs describe the network itself, including the subnet and mask. When Type 2 LSAs exist, the Type 1 LSAs refer to the Type 2 LSAs. The odd thing is that the Network LSA is treated as a node in the OSPF network model; the network becomes an entity. This allows the OSPF process to finish the mathematical model of the network because it knows which Router LSAs are associated with which network LSAs.
- Type 3 LSAs, called summary LSAs, are sent by the ABR and describe subnets in other areas. Don't be confused by the word *summary*; these are not necessarily route summarizations (although OSPF can certainly perform route summarization). Instead, think of the ABR as saying, "Attention routers in area 51: I know about these subnets in some other area. Don't worry about the details; just send traffic for those subnets to me and I will handle it."

You need to know about LSA Types 1, 2, and 3. There are other types, some of which are not even supported by Cisco and some of which are only supported by Cisco, but none of which need concern you at this time. Table 13.1 summarizes all the LSA types. Don't panic; you only need to know the first three for CCNA. I have thrown in the others just to impress you, and to show you that there is even more to OSPF (stuff that you might learn about in a CCNP routing course).

TABLE 13.1 **All OSPF LSA Types**

LSA Name	Number (Type)	Originated By	Purpose/Content
Router LSA	1	All routers in an area	Describe directly connected links (intra-area routes); Type 1 LSAs do not leave the area.
Network LSA	2	DR on broadcast or nonbroadcast network	Describes neighbor routers on the segment. Type 2 LSAs do not leave the area.
Summary LSA	3	ABR	Describes routes in another area (interarea routes).
Summary LSA	4	ABR	Describes routes to an ASBR to neighbors outside the area.
External LSA	5	ASBR	Describes routes being redistributed into OSPF from another routing protocol. Listed as E1 or E2 in the route table.
Multicast LSA	6	Not supported on Cisco routers	N/A
NSSA external LSA	7	ASBR	Describes routes redistributed into a not-so-stubby area (NSSA). Translated into a Type 5 LSA by ABR as it leaves the NSSA. These appear in the route table as N1 or N2.

Implementing Multi-Area OSPFv2

Take a look at Figure 13.1, in which we have Router1, Router2, Router3, and Router4 set up for multi-area OSPF.

In this setup, we want to put Router1's Fa0/0 into area 0, and Fa0/1 into a new area we will call area 1. Router 2's G0/0 is in area 0, and G0/1 is in area 51. (If we have to talk about areas, we have to have an area 51.)

Implementing this multi-area design is simple; the hard part is in the planning and design, and then making sure that you implement your design correctly. This example is really simple, so it didn't even take long to design or implement.

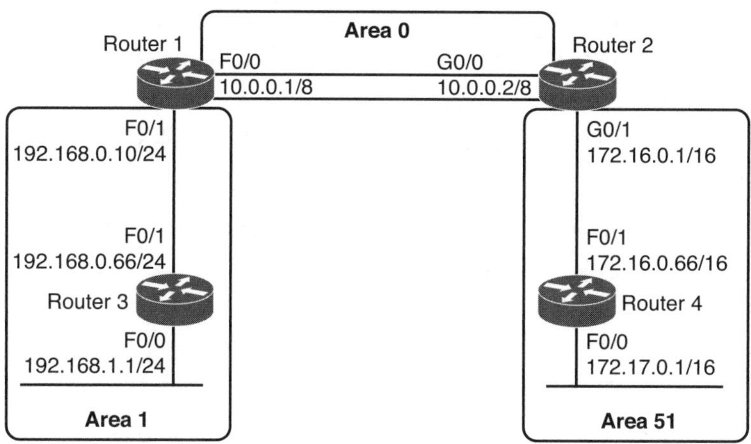

FIGURE 13.1 **Multi-area OSPF.**

Remember the original single-area configuration discussed in Chapter 7? In that example, all interfaces were in area 0. Take a look at the configurations for the new multi-area design. You will see that simply changing the area assignment for the appropriate interfaces is all that's required:

```
! Config for Router 1:
!
Router1(config)#router ospf 100
Router1(config-router)#network 10.0.0.1  0.0.0.0 area 0
Router1(config-router)#network 192.168.0.0  0.0.0.255 area 1
!
! Config for Router2:
!
Router2(config)#router ospf 200
Router2(config-router)#network 10.0.0.2  0.0.0.0 area 0
Router2(config-router)#network 172.16.0.0  0.0.255.255 area 51
!
! Config for Router3:
!
Router3(config)#router ospf 300
Router3(config-router)#network 192.168.0.0 0.0.0.255 area 1
Router3(config-router)#network 192.168.1.0 0.0.0.255 area 1
!
! Config for Router4
Router4(config)#router ospf 400
Router4(config-router)#network 172.16.0.0  0.0.255.255 area 51
Router4(config-router)#network 172.17.0.0  0.0.255.255 area 51
!
```

OSPF does the rest, determining what types of LSAs each router interface must send out, electing DR/BDR routers, and so on. All the same rules apply for valid configurations:

- The OSPF process ID does *not* have to match between routers; but it can be the same if you want.
- The **network** command activates OSPF on any interface that falls within the address/wildcard mask range.
- The Hello/Dead timers must be the same on neighbor routers. (They will be the same by default, unless you or someone else changes them, like maybe on an exam question.)
- The area number must match between neighbor routers. If you somehow manage to misconfigure OSPF so that two routers' interfaces on the same segment and in the same subnet have different area IDs, they will not become neighbors.
- The wildcard mask used in the **network** statements can match the IP address on the interface, the subnet mask, or the entire network of which the IP address is a part. For example, on Router1, the command **network 192.168.0.0 0.0.0.255 area 1** tells the router to match all addresses that begin with 192.168.0. The last octet, which has 255 in the wildcard mask, is ignored. The router examines the IP addresses of its directly connected interfaces and activates OSPF on those interfaces that match the statement.

Because you are using wildcard masks to match the IP address on your directly connected interfaces, you could also use the wildcard mask of 0.0.0.0 to match the exact address. Just as with IP access lists in Chapter 9, "IP Access Lists," a wildcard mask of 0.0.0.0 would match a specific address. For example, on Router1, we configured the following:

```
Router1(config)#router ospf 100
Router1(config-router)#network 10.0.0.1  0.0.0.0 area 0
```

Using a wildcard mask that matches the IP address of the interface is equivalent to using a wildcard mask that matches the network where the IP address resides. Note that Router1 and Router2 use different masks for the different **network** commands but that the masks match with the corresponding neighbor routers.

ExamAlert

Make sure that you feel comfortable configuring OSPF. Remember, it uses a process ID that does not have to match that used on other routers. Also, OSPF uses wildcard masks and not subnet masks in its configuration.

You should be familiar with two optional commands for the CCNA exam. These commands, configured under the interface, are as follows:

- **ip ospf priority** *priority_number***:** This is used to change the priority of an interface for the DR/BDR election.
- **ip ospf cost** *cost***:** This is used to manually change the cost of an interface.

Verifying and Troubleshooting OSPFv2

For verification, you can use the **show ip protocols** and **show ip route** as before. Other commands you can use to verify your configuration are as follows:

- **show ip ospf interface**: This command displays area ID, timer settings, and DR/BDR information.

```
Router1#show ip ospf interface
FastEthernet0/0 is up, line protocol is up
  Internet Address 10.0.0.1/8, Area 0
  Process ID 100, Router ID 192.168.1.10, Network Type BROADCAST, Cost: 1
  Transmit Delay is 1 sec, State DR, Priority 1
  Designat`ed Router (ID) 192.168.1.10, Interface address 10.0.0.1
  Backup Designated router (ID) 172.16.0.1, Interface address 10.0.0.2
  Timer intervals configured, Hello 10, Dead 40, Wait 40, Retransmit 5
    oob-resync timeout 40
    Hello due in 00:00:07
  Supports Link-local Signaling (LLS)
  Cisco NSF helper support enabled
  IETF NSF helper support enabled
  Index 1/1, flood queue length 0
  Next 0x0(0)/0x0(0)
  Last flood scan length is 2, maximum is 2
  Last flood scan time is 0 msec, maximum is 0 msec
  Neighbor Count is 1, Adjacent neighbor count is 1
    Adjacent with neighbor 172.16.0.1  (Backup Designated Router)
  Suppress hello for 0 neighbor(s)
```

- **show ip ospf interface brief**: This command displays summary interface-specific OSPF information.

```
Router1#show ip ospf interface brief
Interface      PID    Area    IP Address/Mask     Cost  State Nbrs F/C
Fa0/0          100    0       10.0.0.1/8          1     DR    1/1
Fa0/1          100    1       192.168.1.10/24     1     DR    0/0
```

- **show ip ospf neighbor**: This command displays neighbor information.

```
Router1#show ip ospf neighbor
Neighbor ID    Pri  State        Dead Time  Address    Interface
172.16.0.1       1  FULL/BDR     00:00:37   10.0.0.2   FastEthernet0/0
```

You can use the **debug ip ospf events** command to troubleshoot OSPF. This command is helpful to troubleshoot why routers are not forming a neighbor relationship with each other. OSPF routers form neighbor relationships before exchanging any routing information. Remember those four items in the Hello packet that must match for a neighbor adjacency to be established:

- Timers must be the same on both routers. OSPF uses Hello timers that define how often they send out Hello messages and Dead timers that define how long after a router stops hearing a Hello message does it declare its neighbor as down.
- Interfaces connecting the two routers must be in the same area.
- Password authentication, if being used, must be the same.
- Type of area must be the same. (This last item is beyond the scope of the CCNA test, but it is covered on the CCNP Routing exam.)

Neighbors are formed automatically or can be established through the use of the **neighbor** command, entered under the routing process. Sometimes the neighbor adjacency does not form, and the **debug ip ospf events** command can help you to troubleshoot what is going wrong. The following **debug** output shows an example of an adjacency not forming because of two routers having different Dead interval timers configured. Note the highlighted part, in which *R* means received and *C* means configured:

```
Router1#debug ip ospf events
OSPF: Mismatched hello parameters from 10.0.0.2
OSPF: Dead R 40 C 30, Hello R 10 C 10  Mask R 255.0.0.0 C 255.0.0.0
```

Configuring Multi-Area OSPFv3

Other than the fact that OSPFv3 routes IPv6 and is configured a little differently, there is one weird little difference that could be the perfect topic for one of those really picky exam questions. As far as the neighbor relationships go, all the requirements are the same as for OSPFv2, with the strange exception that two routers do *not* need to be in the same subnet to become neighbors. So, to become neighbors in OSPFv3

- Interfaces must be up/up.
- No access control lists (ACLs) blocking OSPFv3 protocol traffic.
- Each router ID must be unique.
- Authentication (if used) must succeed.
- Hello and Dead timers must match.
- Interfaces do *not* have to be in the same subnet.

Remember that last weird one!

Setting up OSPFv3 for multi-area operation using IPv6 is just as simple as it was for OSPFv2. Here is a refresher on the IPv6 addressing configuration we used back in Chapter 7:

```
!
Configuration for Router1
!
Router1(config)#interface FastEthernet0/0
 ip address 10.0.0.1 255.0.0.0
ipv6 address 2001:2222:2222:2::1/64
!
interface FastEthernet0/1
 ip address 192.168.1.1 255.255.255.0
ipv6 address 2001:1111:1111:1::1/64
!

!
Configuration for Router2
!
interface GigabitEthernet0/0
 ip address 10.0.0.2 255.0.0.0
ipv6 address 2001:2222:2222:2::2/64
!
interface GigabitEthernet0/1
 ip address 172.16.0.1 255.255.0.0
ipv6 address 2001:3333:3333:3::1/64
!
```

To configure OSPFv3 to route IPv6 in a multi-area environment, all we need to do is change the area ID assignments to match the design shown back in Figure 13.1, as follows:

```
!
!  Configuration for Router1
!
Router1(config)#ipv6 unicast-routing
Router1(config)#ipv6 router ospf 100
May 23 14:20:45.241: %OSPFv3-4-NORTRID: OSPFv3 process 100 could not
pick a router-id,
please configure manually
Router1(config-rtr)#router-id 1.1.1.1
Router1(config-rtr)#interface f0/0
Router1(config-if)#ipv6 ospf 100 area 0
Router1(config-rtr)#interface f0/1
Router1(config-if)#ipv6 ospf 100 area 1
!

!
!  Configuration for Router2
!
Router2(config)#ipv6 unicast-routing
Router2(config)#ipv6 router ospf 200
May 23 14:22:31.308: %OSPFv3-4-NORTRID: OSPFv3 process 200 could not
pick a router-id,
please configure manually
Router2(config-rtr)#router-id 2.2.2.2
Router2(config-rtr)#interface g0/0
Router2(config-if)#ipv6 ospf 200 area 0
Router2(config-rtr)#interface g0/1
Router2(config-if)#ipv6 ospf 200 area 51
!
```

That's all there is to it. All the other multi-area information—the various LSA types, how they behave, the router roles (ABR, ASBR, and so on)—is exactly the same.

Verification of OSPFv3

The verification commands for OSPFv3 are similar to those for OSPFv2, with the consistent change of replacing **ip** with **ipv6**:

- **show ipv6 ospf:** This command lists router ID, areas, and the number of interfaces in each area.
- **show ipv6 ospf interface** [**brief**]**:** This command displays area ID, timer settings, and DR/BDR information.

- **show ipv6 ospf neighbor:** This command displays neighbor information.
- **show ipv6 ospf database:** This command lists the contents of the IPv6 OSPF topology database.
- **show ipv6 protocols:** This command lists the IPv6 routing protocols in use, on which interfaces, and configured features such as redistribution and passive interface.
- **show ipv6 route** [**ospf**]**:** This command shows the IPv6 route table. The **ospf** switch limits the output to OSPFv3-learned routes only.

Note

All of these commands also work for OSPFv2 if you substitute **ip** for **ipv6**.

ExamAlert

Recognize the output of, and know how to interpret, all of these commands, both for OSPFv2 and v3.

Cram Quiz

1. True or False: An OSPF router will always be in the full state with all neighbor routers.

2. What confirms the establishment of our neighbor relationship with another router?

   ❍ **A.** Receipt of a Hello packet from the neighbor

   ❍ **B.** Receipt of a Hello packet from the neighbor with matching values for area ID, authentication, and stub area flag

   ❍ **C.** Receipt of a Hello packet from the neighbor with matching values for area ID, authentication, stub area flag, and timers

   ❍ **D.** Receipt of a Hello packet from the DR identifying neighbor routers on the link

3. What would cause you to consider implementing multi-area OSPF?

   ❍ **A.** Multi-area is simpler to configure and understand.

   ❍ **B.** Excessive router load due to frequent LSA flooding and SPF recalculation.

   ❍ **C.** Excessive broadcast traffic from LSA floods and Hello traffic.

   ❍ **D.** Too few routers in the backbone area.

Examine the following output to answer the remaining questions:

```
FastEthernet0/0 is up, line protocol is up
  Internet Address 10.0.0.1/8, Area 0
  Process ID 100, Router ID 192.168.1.10, Network Type BROADCAST, Cost: 1
  Transmit Delay is 1 sec, State DR, Priority 1
  Designated Router (ID) 192.168.1.10, Interface address 10.0.0.1
  No backup designated router on this network
  Timer intervals configured, Hello 10, Dead 30, Wait 30, Retransmit 5
    oob-resync timeout 40
    Hello due in 00:00:06
  Supports Link-local Signaling (LLS)
  Cisco NSF helper support enabled
  IETF NSF helper support enabled
  Index 1/1, flood queue length 0
  Next 0x0(0)/0x0(0)
  Last flood scan length is 2, maximum is 2
  Last flood scan time is 0 msec, maximum is 0 msec
  Neighbor Count is 0, Adjacent neighbor count is 0
  Suppress hello for 0 neighbor(s)
```

4. What command generated this output?

❍ **A. show interface**

❍ **B. show ip ospf neighbor**

❍ **C. show ip ospf interface brief**

❍ **D. show ip ospf interface**

❍ **E. show ip protocols**

❍ **F. show ip ospf database**

5. Assuming all other routers are using the default OSPF settings, what does this output suggest might be the reason are there no neighbor routers?

❍ **A.** Interface problem.

❍ **B.** No BDR has been elected.

❍ **C.** Incorrect Hello timer.

❍ **D.** Incorrect Dead timer.

Cram Quiz Answers

1. False. An OSPF router may stay in the 2-way state with a neighbor router on multiaccess media if that neighbor is not the DR or BDR.

2. Answer C is correct. Answers A and B are not the best answers, because all the specific conditions must be met. Answer D is incorrect; the DR has no influence on neighbor state between other routers.

3. Answer B is correct. Answer A is incorrect because multi-area is somewhat more complex to configure, not less. Answer C is incorrect because OSPF does not broadcast LSA or Hello traffic, it multicasts. Answer D is incorrect; having too many routers in the backbone, not too few, is one reason to consider moving to multi-area.
4. Answer D is correct.
5. Answer D is correct. The default Dead timer is 40 (or 120 depending on OSPF network type); the output shows 30 for this router. Answer A is wrong because the interface shows up/up. Answer B is wrong because a BDR is not needed before we can form a neighbor relationship with another router. Answer C is incorrect; the default Hello timer is 10 (or 30 depending on OSPF network type).

EIGRP

CramSaver

1. EIGRP is similar to OSPF in which of the following ways? Choose all that apply.
   - **A.** Standards-based protocol
   - **B.** Incremental route updates
   - **C.** Metric references link bandwidth
   - **D.** Hierarchical routing using areas
   - **E.** Uses multicast for Hello and route updates

2. What is a feasible successor?
   - **A.** The backup router in a redundant router configuration
   - **B.** The best route; installed in the route table
   - **C.** The metric for EIGRP
   - **D.** The second-best route; installed in the route table if the best route fails

3. Which command is valid?
   - **A.** Router(config)#**router eigrp**
   - **B.** Router(config)#**router eigrp 100**
   - **C.** Router#**router eigrp 1**
   - **D.** Router(config)#**router eigrp 0**

4. Which commands would be valid to activate EIGRP on the interface with IP address 192.168.1.1/24? Choose two.
   - **A.** Router(config-router)#**network 192.168.1.1 0.0.0.0**
   - **B.** Router(config)#**network 192.168.1.1 0.0.0.0**
   - **C.** Router(config-router)#**network 192.168.1.0**
   - **D.** Router(config-if)#**network 192.168.1.0**

Answers

1. Answers B, C, and E are correct. Answer A is wrong; EIGRP is Cisco proprietary. Answer D is incorrect; EIGRP does not use areas, although it has some advanced features that provide similar control over route updates to certain parts of the network.

2. Answer D is correct. Answer A is wrong; the feasible successor refers to a backup route, not a backup router. Answer B is wrong; the best route is called the successor route. Answer C is wrong; the metric is called the feasible distance.
3. Answer B is correct. Answer A is missing the autonomous system number. Answer C is at the wrong command prompt. Answer D is wrong because the valid range for autonomous system numbers is 1 through 65535.
4. Answers A and C are correct. Answers B and D are at the wrong command prompt.

EIGRP is a hybrid or advanced distance vector routing protocol developed by Cisco in the 1990s to replace Interior Gateway Routing Protocol (IGRP). EIGRP uses a composite metric and sends updates only when there is a change in the network, making it quite sophisticated and very efficient. EIGRP and OSPF are the two main competitors for interior gateway protocols in modern enterprise networks; they are pretty much equal in capability and scalability, with the key difference being that EIGRP is Cisco proprietary while OSPF is, of course, standards based.

Characteristics of EIGRP

EIGRP uses the bandwidth and delay of an interface by default, with the option of factoring in interface reliability and load. EIGRP maintains three tables, as shown in Figure 13.2, in a similar way to OSPF:

- Neighbor table
- Topology table
- Routing table

EIGRP begins by sending hello packets out all active interfaces. The router listens for hello packets from other routers. From the hello packets, the router learns of neighboring routers, which get listed in the neighbor table.

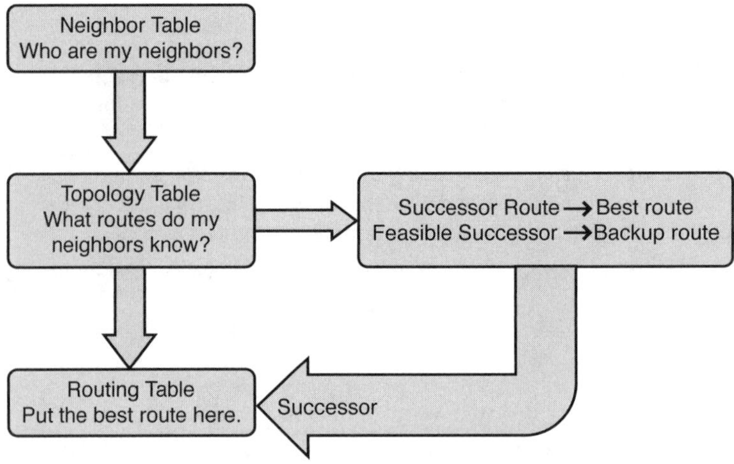

FIGURE 13.2 **EIGRP tables.**

The EIGRP neighbor relationship is similar in many ways to that in OSPF; neighbors are discovered and maintained using hello packets, and there are criteria that must match for the neighbor relationship to form:

- The neighboring interfaces must be in the same subnet.
- The autonomous system number must match (more on this a little later).
- Authentication (if used) must be successful.

K-values (the constant values used to activate other components of the EIGRP composite metric) must be the same. The theory and configuration of the K-values is beyond the official scope of CCNA, but you should file this point under "might be worth remembering."

ExamAlert

Know the neighbor conditions (including the K-value match). Remember that while OSPF neighbors require that the Hello and Dead timers must match, EIGRP routers do not.

The neighbor discovery and establishment process is much simpler in EIGRP than it is in OSPF. There are far fewer states that an EIGRP router goes through with potential neighbors. Once the initial checks are made, the routers move from not being neighbors to being neighbors and start exchanging route information. Route information is exchanged using the Reliable Transport Protocol (RTP) (not to be confused with the Real-time Transport Protocol, also RTP). EIGRP's RTP allows each message to be acknowledged and its originator seen, which means that EIGRP routers can tell whether there is a routing loop and ignore the looped update.

After the router knows of its neighbors, it begins exchanging routes with its neighbors. These routes go into the topology table, which is similar to a routing table, but contains all known routes, not just the best routes. Instead, the topology table is used to build a map of the network based on the metrics of all known links. The DUAL algorithm is run against the topology table, and two routes are determined as a result:

- **Successor route:** This is the best route as determined by the DUAL algorithm. This route gets injected into the routing table and is the one used when packets are routed.
- **Feasible successor route:** This is the next best route and is kept in the topology table. It is used only in the event that the primary successor route goes down.

By having a feasible successor route, the router is ready to instantly inject another route into the routing table should the successor ever go down. This makes convergence very rapid with EIGRP.

What defines a feasible successor? It isn't as simple as "the second-best route." There is a mathematical test that a route must pass to be a feasible successor, but it takes a little bit of background explanation.

Let's say that Router2 advertises a link with a metric of 25 to Router1. When Router1 fills in its topology table, it lists the advertised distance (that's the EIGRP term for the metric that Router2 reported), and it also fills in the feasible distance. The feasible distance is the metric from Router1's point of view (the full metric, which includes the metric advertised by Router2, plus the metric from Router1 to get to Router2). Take a look at Figure 13.3 to get a picture of what is happening.

The mathematical test that a route must pass is as follows: For a valid path to a given network to qualify as a feasible successor, the advertised distance must be less than the feasible distance of the successor route (not equal to; less than).

Now, suppose that there is a second path to that same advertised network shown in the figure. It is a valid path, and the advertised metric (advertised distance) is 100. Because the advertised distance (100) is less than the feasible distance of the successor (200), this other path qualifies as a feasible successor, and it will be immediately moved to the route table as the new successor if the original successor route fails.

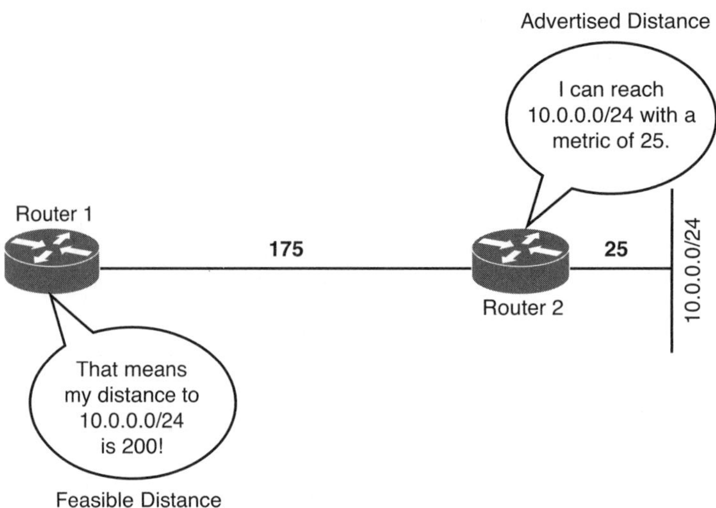

FIGURE 13.3 **EIGRP advertised distance and feasible distance.**

But what about routes that are valid for a given network, but not qualified as feasible successors? They will exist in the topology table, but can't be immediately moved to the route table when the successor fails because they are not feasible successors. When this happens, EIGRP marks these potential routes as *active*, which means the router is actively sending out queries to other EIGRP neighbors to see whether they have a better route to the network. The other routers send reply messages confirming that the route is still valid, and the querying router marks the route as the new successor and changes its status to passive in the topology table.

In addition to being a rapid-convergence protocol, EIGRP is the only routing protocol that supports multiple Layer 3 protocols (namely IP, AppleTalk, and IPX). All the other routing protocols mentioned in this chapter support only IP or IPv6. This, of course, is not as big a deal as it once was (especially for CCNAs) because IP is almost universally used and the CCNA exams no longer ask anything about IPX or AppleTalk.

EIGRP routers initially flood their route updates to new neighbors, which could conceivably be a significant use of bandwidth. To mitigate the impact of that, an EIGRP router by default is only allowed to use 50% of the bandwidth on any interface for transmitting EIGRP updates. Once the initial flood of route information is done, EIGRP routers send only partial (incremental) updates when changes occur, or when old information expires and must be refreshed.

Another distinction of EIGRP is its use of two administrative distance values. EIGRP uses administrative distance 90 for routes learned through EIGRP. Routes can also be redistributed into EIGRP from another routing protocol. When this occurs, redistributed routes get an administrative distance of 170. Internal routes are best described as those that are direct testimony, or trusted the most, whereas external routes are like hearsay and are therefore trusted less.

ExamAlert

Remember the main characteristics of EIGRP:

Hybrid (advanced distance vector) protocol

- Uses a sophisticated composite (sometimes called compound) metric that factors in bandwidth and delay by default in calculating the metric, but can also factor in reliability and load if manually configured to do so.
- Uses successor and feasible successor route definitions. Successors (best routes) go directly to the route table, whereas feasible successors are immediately promoted to successors and put in the route table if the original successor fails.
- Uses acknowledged updates to eliminate routing loops.

Implementing EIGRP

Basic EIGRP configuration is not difficult at all. Just remember to specify an autonomous system number that defines your routing domain. The autonomous system number is assigned globally for the routing process and can be any number in the range of 1 to 65535, but that same number must be used on all routers. Routing updates will not be exchanged between routers with different autonomous numbers. Because the exam focuses heavily on troubleshooting, make sure that you always check that the autonomous numbers match in the exam scenarios.

The following example shows how to configure EIGRP for a router connected to networks 192.168.10.0/24 and 192.168.20.0/24. The autonomous system number is 1 and is specified when entering the routing process.

```
Router(config)#router eigrp 1
Router(config-router)#network 192.168.10.0
Router(config-router)#network 192.168.20.1 0.0.0.0
```

Notice that you can use a different syntax in the **network** command: The first entry uses the classful network ID, and the second specifies the interface IP with a wildcard mask, a little bit like OSPF. You can enter the **network** statements using either syntax, or even both.

Similar to OSPF, EIGRP is a classless routing protocol (supporting variable-length subnet masking [VLSM] and discontiguous subnets).

ExamAlert

In contradiction with some other CCNA or EIGRP texts you may have read, since IOS v15.0 EIGRP is no longer classful by default. It used to be; and with the old default settings, EIGRP had trouble with discontiguous subnets, so you had to watch for that scenario on your exam. Since IOS 15 (which is the version CCNA is based on), to enable classless routing you no longer have to type the following command under the routing process:

```
Router(config-router)#no auto-summary
! This command is now the default in IOS 15.0
```

The old default "classful" capability, the command to make EIGRP classless, and the scenarios where you had to recognize that as an issue were all very testable concepts. Keith and I, and our technical editors Brian and Andrew, are suspicious types. We hope that you will not see any questions about the older defaults, but it might be worth keeping in the back of your mind.

Verifying and Troubleshooting EIGRP

The most common **show** command when verifying your routing configuration is **show ip route**. This is the first command to use to see whether your routing table is being populated as expected.

You can also use **show ip protocols** and **show ip eigrp topology** to troubleshoot EIGRP. The first command, **show ip protocols**, is helpful to see your autonomous system number and the networks you are advertising:

```
Router#show ip protocols
Routing Protocol is "eigrp 100"
  Outgoing update filter list for all interfaces is not set
  Incoming update filter list for all interfaces is not set
  Default networks flagged in outgoing updates
  Default networks accepted from incoming updates
  Redistributing: eigrp 100
  EIGRP-IPv4 Protocol for AS(100)
    Metric weight K1=1, K2=0, K3=1, K4=0, K5=0
    NSF-aware route hold timer is 240
    Router-ID: 172.16.0.1
    Topology : 0 (base)
      Active Timer: 3 min
      Distance: internal 90 external 170
      Maximum path: 4
      Maximum hopcount 100
      Maximum metric variance 1
```

```
  Automatic Summarization: disabled
  Maximum path: 4
  Routing for Networks:
    1.0.0.0
    10.0.0.0
    172.16.0.0
  Routing Information Sources:
    Gateway         Distance      Last Update
    10.0.0.1              90      4w6d
  Distance: internal 90 external 170
```

Table 13.2 summarizes the important lines of this command.

TABLE 13.2 **Summary of show ip protocols Output**

Entry	Meaning
Outgoing/incoming filters	Used to filter routing updates between routers.
Redistributing	Covered in the Cisco Certified Network Professional (CCNP) exam. This pertains to redistributing information between different routing protocols and is outside the scope of this exam.
Automatic network summarization is in effect	Whether the **no auto-summary** command has been applied. In this example, the command has not been applied, and EIGRP is doing classful routing.
Routing for networks	Which networks your router is advertising to other routers.
Routing information sources	This defines which routers are sending your EIGRP routes, the administrative distance for those routes, and the last time your router received an update from other routers.
Distance	The administrative distance for internal and external routes.

The second command is **show ip eigrp topology**. As the command suggests, this outputs your topology table. Your topology table contains all the routes your router knows about. Here is where you will also see your successor (best routes) and your feasible successor (backup routes):

```
Router#show ip eigrp topology

IP-EIGRP Topology Table for process 77

Codes: P - Passive, A - Active, U - Update, Q - Query, R - Reply,
       r - Reply status

P 172.16.0.0 255.255.0.0, 2 successors, FD is 36251776
         via 172.16.17.1 (36251776/36226176), Ethernet0
```

```
          via 172.16.18.1 (36251776/36226176), Ethernet1
P 172.20.0.0 255.255.0.0, 1 successors, FD is 307200
          via 172.16.81.28 (307200/281600), Ethernet1
          via 172.16.19.5 (702311/295210), Ethernet2
```

From this output you can begin to get an idea of the topology of your network. Notice that for the 172.16.0.0/16 network you have two successors. This is because the metric is the same for both networks and, subsequently, you will load balance across two networks. The metric that is put in the routing table is the first number in parenthesis (36251776 in this example) and is the feasible distance (FD).

The 172.20.0.0 network has only one successor route out Ethernet1 that is learned from a router with the IP address 172.16.81.28. You also have a backup route (feasible successor) out Ethernet2 that is learned from a router at 172.16.19.5.

For the exam, make sure that you are comfortable analyzing the output of these **show** commands.

Active Versus Passive Routes

You will notice in the output of the **show ip eigrp topology** command that the routes begin with a P for passive. According to the legend at the beginning of this output, a route can also be A for active. A passive route is when your routing table has fully converged. An active route is when a route has changed and your routers are querying other routers to discover the change in the topology. Ideally, your routes should be in passive mode.

Cram Quiz

1. What is the mathematical test that qualifies a known route as a feasible successor?

   ❍ **A.** AD < FD of successor

   ❍ **B.** AD > FD of successor

   ❍ **C.** FD ≤ AD of successor

   ❍ **D.** FD ≥ AD of successor

2. Kathy is puzzled because her EIGRP routers are not sending routing updates about some of the subnets in her network, and consequently some traffic is being dropped because there is no route to its destination in the route tables. What could be the problem?

   ❍ **A.** Timer mismatch between neighbor routers.

   ❍ **B.** Autonomous System number mismatch.

   ❍ **C.** Solar flares with coronal mass ejection.

   ❍ **D.** The **no auto-summary** command is missing.

3. Colonel Chris Hadfield, the first Canadian to command the International Space Station, recently did not tweet some facts about EIGRP. If those tweets had happened, what facts might they have included? Choose all that apply.

   ❍ **A.** EIGRP is a hybrid protocol, or an "advanced distance vector protocol with some link-state features."

   ❍ **B.** EIGRP autonomous system numbers do not have to match between routers for them to exchange routes.

   ❍ **C.** All EIGRP traffic is unicast.

   ❍ **D.** EIGRP, like OSPF, can only route IPv4 traffic.

Cram Quiz Answers

1. Answer A is correct: The AD must be less than (not equal to) the FD of the successor route.

2. Answer D is correct. If subnets are in use, without very restrictive subnet allocation there will be convergence problems. Use the **no auto-summary** command to force EIGRP to advertise subnets with the mask to converge around poorly-designed subnet allocation. Answer A is wrong because EIGRP does not require timers to match. Answer B is wrong, because if the autonomous system numbers do not match, no routes will be exchanged at all. (The routers will not even become neighbors.) Answer C is wrong; solar flares with CME can cause EMI on copper and wireless media, but not in a way that it would selectively suppress routes.

3. Answer A is the only correct answer. Answer B is wrong; autonomous system numbers must match. Answer C is wrong because most EIGRP traffic is multicast, although it can switch to unicasting under certain circumstances. Answer D is wrong; EIGRP can also route IPX and AppleTalk, not that anyone cares any more.

Review Questions

1. Which fields in the hello packet for EIGRP must match for two routers to form a neighbor relationship? Choose all that apply.

   ❍ **A.** Timers

   ❍ **B.** AS number

   ❍ **C.** K-values

   ❍ **D.** Subnet

   ❍ **E.** Authentication

2. How is the router ID chosen in OSPF? Choose all that apply.

   ❍ **A.** Highest loopback IP address

   ❍ **B.** Highest physical IP address if no loopback exists

   ❍ **C.** Lowest loopback IP address

   ❍ **D.** Lowest physical IP address if no loopback exists

3. True or False: EIGRP fully supports VLSM, subnets and classless routing.

4. OSPF supports hierarchical routing. What benefits do you gain from using a routing protocol that supports hierarchical routing? Choose all that apply.

   ❍ **A.** Hierarchical routing speeds up the time for all routers to converge.

   ❍ **B.** Hierarchical routing requires less configuration.

   ❍ **C.** Hierarchical routing reduces the amount of routing overhead.

   ❍ **D.** Hierarchical routing hides network instability from routers in other areas.

   ❍ **E.** Hierarchical routing requires less design considerations.

5. Examine the following partial output of **show ip eigrp** topology:

```
P 172.20.0.0 255.255.0.0, 1 successors, FD is 307200
          via 172.16.81.28 (307200/281600), Ethernet1
          via 172.16.19.5 (702311/295210), Ethernet2
```

   Is the route via 172.16.19.5 a feasible successor? (Yes/No)

6. You have a serial interface with the IP address of 192.168.22.33/30. You are instructed to use the exact subnet address and wildcard mask syntax to activate this interface in area 0 for OSPF. Which command achieves this specific goal?

   ❍ **A.** Router(config-router)#**network 192.168.22.32 0.0.0.3 area 0**

   ❍ **B.** Router(config-router)#**network 192.168.22.32 255.255.255.252**

   ❍ **C.** Router(config-router)#**network 192.168.22.33 0.0.0.3 area 0**

   ❍ **D.** Router(config-router)#**network 192.168.22.33 255.255.255.252 area 0**

7. When would an OSPF DRother router stop at the 2-way state with a neighbor?

   ❍ **A.** When Hello message values do not match.

   ❍ **B.** When the neighbor is on a different subnet.

   ❍ **C.** When authentication has failed.

   ❍ **D.** When the neighbor is also a DRother.

   ❍ **E.** When the neighbor is a DR.

For questions 8–10, refer to the following figure and configuration:

Router	Fa0/0	Fa0/1
Botswana	10.7.18.5/30	10.0.23.33/27
Ukraine	10.0.23.34/27	10.202.114.129/28
Tanzania	10.202.114.130/28	10.5.5.0/24

```
Botswana
router ospf 1
 network 10.7.18.4 0.0.0.30 area 1
 network 10.0.23.32 0.0.0.63 area 0

Ukraine
router ospf 1
 network 10.0.23.32 0.0.0.31 area 0
 network 10.202.114.128 0.0.0.15 area 0

Tanzania
router ospf 11
 network 10.202.114.128 0.0.0.15 area 2
 network 10.5.5.0 0.0.0.255 area 3
```

8. What is wrong with the Botswana configuration?

   ❍ **A.** The wildcard mask for the network on the Fastethernet0/0 interface is incorrect.

   ❍ **B.** The wildcard mask for the network on the Fastethernet0/1 interface is incorrect.

   ❍ **C.** The OSPF process ID is incorrect.

   ❍ **D.** Area 1 is not directly connected to area 0.

   ❍ **E.** The network on fastethernet0/1 is in the wrong area.

9. What is wrong with the Ukraine configuration?

❍ **A.** The wildcard mask for the network on the Fastethernet0/0 interface is incorrect.

❍ **B.** The wildcard mask for the network on the Fastethernet0/1 interface is incorrect.

❍ **C.** The OSPF process ID is incorrect.

❍ **D.** The network on Fastethernet0/0 is in the wrong area.

❍ **E.** The network on Fastethernet0/1 is in the wrong area.

10. What is wrong with the Tanzania configuration?

❍ **A.** The wildcard mask for the network on the Fastethernet0/0 interface is incorrect.

❍ **B.** The wildcard mask for the network on the Fastethernet0/1 interface is incorrect.

❍ **C.** The OSPF process ID is incorrect.

❍ **D.** Area 3 is not directly connected to area 0.

❍ **E.** The network on Fastethernet0/1 is in the wrong area.

Answers to Review Questions

1. Answers B, C, D, and E are correct. In EIGRP, the timers do not have to match (unlike OSPF).
2. Answers A and B are correct. OSPF chooses the highest IP address of any logical loopback interfaces, or if no loopback interfaces are configured, the highest IP address on any physical interface that is active at the moment the OSPF process begins. Answers C and D are incorrect because they imply that the lowest IP address is used, which is not the case with OSPF's router ID.
3. True. EIGRP, with autosummarization turned off, sends the mask with every route update, therefore fully supporting VLSM, classless routing, and discontiguous subnet designs.
4. Answers A, C, and D are correct. When you hear the term *hierarchical routing*, think areas and reduced workload for routers. OSPF, when using hierarchical routing, reduces the amount and detail of routing information sent from one area into another. Instead of routers needing to know about all the individual networks in another area, they need to know only that the route to the other networks is through the ABR. The reduced detail results in faster convergence and less routing overhead, and should a network in an area go down it will not affect routers in other areas. Answer B is incorrect because OSPF will cause additional configuration to be performed. Answer E is incorrect because OSPF usually requires more design than nonhierarchical routing protocols such as RIP to ensure an addressing scheme that allows for summarization between areas.
5. Yes, it is, because the FD (295210) is less than the AD (307200) of the successor.
6. Answer A is correct. The IP address of the interface is 192.168.22.33/30, which is on network 192.168.22.32. Although you could have entered 192.168.22.33 0.0.0.0 area 0, this was not the instruction, nor an available choice. Only Answer A has the correct network and wildcard mask. This is tricky because it requires you to determine both the network address and the correct OSPF syntax. Answer B uses a subnet mask and not a wildcard mask, so it is incorrect. Answer C is incorrect because it does not list the correct network address, as the question specified. Answer D is also incorrect because it does not list the correct address and because it uses a subnet mask in which a wildcard mask is required.
7. Answer D is correct. On networks where a DR/BDR exist, routers only get to the full state with the DR and BDR. All DRother routers remain at 2-way with each other. Answers A, B, and C would prevent the neighbor relationship from forming at all. Answer E is wrong because if the neighbor is the DR, they should proceed to the full state.
8. Answer A is correct. When matching a subnet, the wildcard mask is the inverse of the subnet mask. Fastethernet0/0 is a /30 network that in dotted notation is 255.255.255.252. The inverse of this is 0.0.0.3, not 0.0.0.30. There is nothing wrong with the rest of the configuration, so Answers B, C, D, and E are all incorrect.

9. Answer E is correct. This is a tricky one that requires a process of elimination. Answers A and B are incorrect because the wildcard masks are correct for the networks on those interfaces. Answer C is incorrect because a router's process ID is unique to that router and can be different from other routers. Answer D is incorrect because it is in area 0 and it is connected to another router (Botswana) that also has an attached interface (Fa0/1) in area 0. For answer E, you have to compare the Tanzania configuration, which has its Fastethernet0/0 in area 2. You must be in the same area as the interface that you are attaching to and these areas do not match. Either Tanzania or Ukraine has the incorrect area, but nothing in the diagram or output will tell you which router is improperly configured. However, by using process of elimination you can eliminate the other wrong answers and are left with only Answer E as the correct answer. Ruling out the wrong answers is a great technique to use on the exam if you get stuck.

10. Answer D is correct. The rules of OSPF state that all areas must have a connection to the backbone area 0. In this configuration, Tanzania has its Fastethernet0/1 interface in area 3 and its Fastethernet0/0 interface in area 2. Area 2 is connected to the Ukraine, which has a connection to area 0. However, area 3 does not have a connection to area 0. There is nothing wrong with the remaining configuration, so Answers A, B, C, and E are all incorrect.

CHAPTER FOURTEEN

Advanced IP Services

This chapter covers the following official 200-101 ICND2 and 200-120 CCNA exam topics:

- Recognize high availability (FHRP).
- Configure and verify syslog.
- Describe SNMP v2 and v3.
- Utilize NetFlow data.

It is interesting that the published objectives from Cisco include the words *recognize*, *utilize*, and *describe* for most of the topics in this chapter, with the word *configure* used only for syslog. So, to be ready for the exam, you should be prepared to describe the characteristics and functionality of all the items listed, and the configuration of syslog as well.

First-hop redundancy protocols (FHRPs) are simply a method of providing a virtual default gateway so that even if one of our real routers fails, the virtual default gateway address they are using will still work.

Syslog, Simple Network Management Protocol (SNMP), and NetFlow are useful methods to collect information from network devices.

Recognize High Availability (FHRP)

CramSaver

If you can correctly answer these questions before going through this section, save time by skimming the Exam Alerts in this section and then completing the Cram Quiz at the end of the section.

1. A user on the network has been given an IP address via DHCP. During that process, the user was also given a default gateway address to use. What method can be used to provide fault tolerance for this user, as well as other users in the same subnet, and allow two or more routers to load balance this networks traffic?
2. What Cisco proprietary protocol is used for high availability and uses only a single router, at any given time, to forward packets for a single subnet?

Answers

1. Gateway Load Balancing Protocol (GLBP) is the protocol that allows multiple routers to load balance as they route traffic off of a single network. This is done by some of the routers forwarding for a portion of the devices in the network and other routers forwarding for others in the same subnet.
2. Hot Standby Router Protocol (HSRP) uses a singe active router at any one time to forward traffic from a given subnets. The other routers in the HSRP group are standby devices that only forward for that subnet in the event of a failure of the active router.

Hot Standby Router Protocol

Let's begin by considering the topology as shown in Figure 14.1.

The computers that are located in VLAN 10 will need to use a default gateway to communicate with computers on other networks. If the default gateway fails, so does the customer's ability to reach remote networks. HSRP can be used to provide a single IP address that the clients can use as a default gateway, so that if either of the routers on their local network fail, the IP address they are using it as a default gateway can continue to function. This can provide high availability (HA) for the first hop (or router) that the customers will use to reach remote networks. To implement this, the administrator selects an unused IP address for a subnet and configures DHCP so that clients will use this IP address as a default gateway. In our example, we are using the address 10.0.0.254; this IP address is often referred to as a virtual IP address, and in HSRP there is a corresponding virtual MAC address as well.

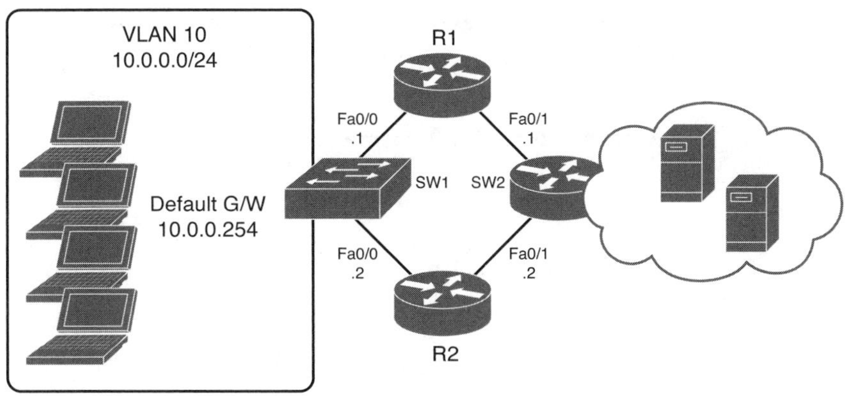

FIGURE 14.1 **Network with two routers connected.**

The routers that are connected to the 10.0.0.0/24 subnet and that are participating in HSRP will decide among themselves which one of the routers should be the active router. The active router takes the responsibility of responding to ARP requests for the virtual address, and the active router replies with the corresponding virtual MAC address. The other routers in the group act as standby routers. In the background, a hello, which includes a function of a keepalive message, is sent to let the active and standby routers know that all the routers are available and reachable on that subnet. If for whatever reason the active router no longer appears to be online, a standby router is promoted to the active router role and assumes responsibility for the virtual IP address and MAC address. From the customer's perspective, they are using the same IP address for a default gateway, and the Layer 2 mapping for that address remains the same on the client computers. Table 14.1 describes some common labels used with HSRP.

TABLE 14.1 **Common Labels in HSRP**

HSRP Label	What It Means
HSRP group (also called a *standby group*)	The group of routers that are working together in the same subnet to support the virtual IP address the clients are using as a default gateway.
Active router	This is the router in the group that is taking an active role in responding on behalf of the Layer 3 virtual IP address, (and corresponding Layer 2 address). Only one router can be the active router at any given time for a subnet. Other routers in the group will act as standby routers.
Standby router	This is a router in the group that is not the active router but is monitoring the availability of the active router and has the potential to become the active router if the active router fails.

To see the details of the HSRP group, you can issue the command **show standby**, as shown in Example 14.1.

EXAMPLE 14.1 **Viewing HSRP Status Information**

```
R1#show standby
FastEthernet0/0 - Group 1
  State is Active
    2 state changes, last state change 00:00:49
  Virtual IP address is 10.0.0.254
  Active virtual MAC address is 0000.0c07.ac01
    Local virtual MAC address is 0000.0c07.ac01 (v1 default)
  Hello time 3 sec, hold time 10 sec
    Next hello sent in 1.156 secs
  Preemption disabled
  Active router is local
  Standby router is 10.0.0.2, priority 100 (expires in 7.608 sec)
  Priority 105 (configured 105)
  Group name is "hsrp-Fa0/0-1" (default)
```

If we have routers with interfaces in multiple VLANs (either physical interfaces, subinterfaces, or VLAN interfaces), it is possible for two routers to be connected to dozens of subnets and both be part of multiple HSRP groups (one for each subnet). One router could be responsible as the active router for half of the groups (each group representing a subnet), and the other router could be responsible (be the active router) for the other half of the groups (each group representing a subnet). By modifying the priority, the administrator can control which of the two devices will be the active router for a given group (subnet) when both routers are available. The key to remember is that for any single group (subnet) there will be only a single active router at any given time.

Another factor that could influence our decision on which router should be the active router is regarding its other interfaces. Consider Figure 14.1. If R1 is the active router on VLAN 10, but its interface Fa0/1 fails, it really won't be able to function as a very good router because it lost its connectivity to the rest of the network. To solve that problem, the interface tracking feature can be enabled in conjunction with HSRP, which can track other interfaces on the same router (in our example, we might want to track the R1 Fa0/1 interface). If that tracked interface fails, we could influence the decision about who should be the active router for VLAN 10.

Gateway Load Balancing Protocol (GLBP)

One of the challenges of HSRP is that it doesn't fully utilize the resources (in our example, the routers that are both connected to LAN 10). That's because only one router can be active for a group (subnet) at any given time. To solve this challenge, Cisco came up with another proprietary protocol named Gateway Load Balancing Protocol. The biggest difference is that GLBP can do load balancing between multiple routers for the same subnet. Using the same topology as shown in Figure 14.1, if we were to use GLBP, we would still use a virtual IP address that the clients would use as a default gateway. There would, however, be multiple virtual MAC addresses associated with that virtual IP address. In the case of two routers there would be two virtual MAC addresses, one used by each router. Both of these routers would be an active virtual forwarder (AVF) for any frames sent to the virtual Layer 2 address that they manage. One of the two routers would take on an additional role in responding to Address Resolution Protocol (ARP) requests from the virtual IP of 10.0.0.254. This role is called the active virtual gateway (AVG). As these ARP requests come in from clients, the AVG will reply with the virtual Layer 2 addresses that are being managed by the forwarders (in our example, the two routers connected to VLAN 10). Because these are handed out in a round-robin fashion, some of the clients will be using the Layer 2 address managed by R1, and other clients will be using the Layer 2 address managed by R2 as the clients forward frames to the Layer 2 address that they believe is associated with the default gateway (based on the replies they got from their ARP requests).

We can verify the status of GLBP by using the command **show glbp**, as shown in Example 14.2.

EXAMPLE 14.2 **Verifying the Status of GLBP**

```
R1#show glbp
FastEthernet0/0 - Group 1
  State is Active
    2 state changes, last state change 00:00:41
  Virtual IP address is 10.0.0.254
  Hello time 3 sec, hold time 10 sec
    Next hello sent in 0.060 secs
  Redirect time 600 sec, forwarder timeout 14400 sec
  Preemption disabled
  Active is local
  Standby is 10.0.0.2, priority 100 (expires in 9.280 sec)
  Priority 105 (configured)
  Weighting 100 (default 100), thresholds: lower 1, upper 100
  Load balancing: round-robin
```

```
  Group members:
    0011.1111.1111 (10.0.0.1) local
    0022.2222.2222 (10.0.0.2)
  There are 2 forwarders (1 active)
  Forwarder 1
    State is Active
      1 state change, last state change 00:00:31
    MAC address is 0007.b400.0101 (default)
    Owner ID is 0011.1111.1111
    Redirection enabled
    Preemption enabled, min delay 30 sec
    Active is local, weighting 100
  Forwarder 2
    State is Listen
    MAC address is 0007.b400.0102 (learnt)
    Owner ID is 0022.2222.2222
    Redirection enabled, 598.744 sec remaining (maximum 600 sec)
    Time to live: 14398.744 sec (maximum 14400 sec)
    Preemption enabled, min delay 30 sec
    Active is 10.0.0.2 (primary), weighting 100 (expires in 8.740 sec)
```

Virtual Router Redundancy Protocol (VRRP)

VRRP is an industry standard method of implementing first-hop redundancy, and is similar to HSRP in both configuration and function. To verify the status of VRRP, you use the command **show vrrp**, as shown in Example 14.3.

EXAMPLE 14.3 **Verifying VRRP Status**

```
R1#show vrrp
FastEthernet0/0 - Group 1
  State is Master
  Virtual IP address is 10.0.0.254
  Virtual MAC address is 0000.5e00.0101
  Advertisement interval is 1.000 sec
  Preemption enabled
  Priority is 105
  Master Router is 10.0.0.1 (local), priority is 105
  Master Advertisement interval is 1.000 sec
  Master Down interval is 3.589 sec
```

Cram Quiz

1. How do Cisco routers that both belong to an HSRP group know that the other router is present on the same subnet and a member of the HSRP group?
   - ❍ **A.** They use ICMP messages.
   - ❍ **B.** They must be running the same routing protocol.
   - ❍ **C.** They send periodic hello messages.
   - ❍ **D.** They are administratively configured to point to the other router as an HSRP peer.

2. Which FHRP can have two routers both forwarding packets as the default gateway for a single subnet at the same time?
   - ❍ **A.** HSRP
   - ❍ **B.** GLBP
   - ❍ **C.** VRRP
   - ❍ **D.** OSPF

Cram Quiz Answers

1. Answer C is correct. HSRP uses periodic hello messages that are used to identify other routers in the HSRP group. HSRP routers don't have to be statically configured with the peer's IP address, nor does HSRP use ICMP to discover the devices belonging to the group. Although the two routers may be running the same routing protocol, the routing protocol is not used by HSRP to identify members of the HSRP group.
2. Answer B is correct. Gateway Load Balancing Protocol can have multiple virtual forwarders, simultaneously, for the same subnet. HSRP and VRRP don't have that feature. OSPF is a routing protocol, and not an FHRP.

Configure and Verify Syslog

CramSaver

If you can correctly answer these questions before going through this section, save time by skimming the Exam Alerts in this section and then completing the Cram Quiz at the end of the section.

1. How is severity used in combination with a centralized syslog server ?
2. What does the command **logging trap warning** do ?

Answers

1. The severity level controls the level of syslog messages that are being sent to a configured destination syslog server. The level specified implies that level (and below that level, which represents that level and messages numerically lower, which are more severe messages) of syslog messages will be sent to the syslog server.
2. The command **logging trap warning** will send syslog level 4 (and numerically lower through 0 as well) messages to any configured syslog destination servers.

Syslog is a protocol that can be used to communicate events that are happening. Syslog messages generated by a router or switch can be sent to various lines, such as the console and vty, in addition to servers that are prepared to receive the syslog messages (often referred to as syslog servers). Example 14.4 provides syslog message examples.

EXAMPLE 14.4 **Syslog Message Examples**

```
R1#
%VRRP-6-STATECHANGE: Fa0/0 Grp 1 state Init -> Backup
R1#
%SYS-5-CONFIG_I: Configured from console by console
R1#
%LINK-3-UPDOWN: Interface FastEthernet0/0, changed state to up
R1#
%LINEPROTO-5-UPDOWN: Line protocol on Interface FastEthernet0/0,
changed state to up
R1#
%VRRP-6-STATECHANGE: Fa0/0 Grp 1 state Backup -> Master
R1#
%OSPF-5-ADJCHG: Process 1, Nbr 3.0.0.2 on FastEthernet0/0 from LOADING
to FULL, Loading Done
```

Syslog messages may or may not contain, based on how the router or switch is configured, the elements shown in Table 14.2.

TABLE 14.2 **Syslog Message Elements**

Syslog Message Element	Description
Sequence number	Sequence numbers are optional, but when configured will show up as part of the syslog messages.
Time stamp	Time stamps are optional, but when configured will show up as part of the syslog messages. Network Time Protocol (NTP) is important to ensure that the accurate time is used when time stamps are enabled.
Facility	The category that this syslog message fits into, such as UPDOWN, CONFIG, and so on.
Severity	A number from 0 to 7.
Mnemonic	Text string that uniquely describes the message.
Description	Text string containing detailed information about the event being reported.

The severity levels also have names associated with each of them, and the configuration commands generally will accept either the number or the name as part of a syslog configuration. Table 14.3 contains a listing of the levels along with their common name.

TABLE 14.3 **Syslog Levels**

Severity Level Name	Severity Level Number
7	Debugging
6	Informational
5	Notification
4	Warning
3	Error
2	Critical
1	Alert
0	Emergency

Level 0 is the most severe, and level 7 is the least severe.

Logging of syslog messages to the console is a default behavior on most Cisco devices. If you are connected via a vty line via SSH or Telnet, you use the command **terminal monitor**, which would then enable you to see syslog messages from your vty session.

Configure the router to send its syslog messages to a syslog server is a two-step process. First, you must identify the IP address of a syslog server that you want to send these messages to. Second, you identify what level of events (syslog messages) you want to send. These two elements are configured as shown in Example 14.5.

EXAMPLE 14.5 **Configuring a Syslog Destination and the Level of Messages to be Sent to That Destination**

```
R1(config)#logging 172.16.10.5
R1(config)#logging trap ?
  <0-7>          Logging severity level
  alerts         Immediate action needed           (severity=1)
  critical       Critical conditions               (severity=2)
  debugging      Debugging messages                (severity=7)
  emergencies    System is unusable                (severity=0)
  errors         Error conditions                  (severity=3)
  informational  Informational messages            (severity=6)
  notifications  Normal but significant conditions (severity=5)
  warnings       Warning conditions                (severity=4)
  <cr>

R1(config)#logging trap notifications

R1(config)#do show log
<snip>
Trap logging: level notifications, 47 message lines logged
        Logging to 172.16.10.5  (udp port 514,  audit disabled,
             authentication disabled, encryption disabled, link down),
             0 message lines logged,
             0 message lines rate-limited,
             0 message lines dropped-by-MD,
             xml disabled, sequence number disabled
             filtering disabled
```

Syslog messages sent to syslog server will be sent at the level specified in the command **logging trap** followed by the level. In our example, we selected the notifications level, which is level 5. This means that levels 5, 4, 3, 2, 1, and level 0 will all be sent. The level selected and lower levels are sent.

The benefit of having all these syslog messages sent from multiple devices to a single centralized syslog server is that you can now correlate network events from multiple devices and see those in one location. Data from the syslog server can be exported into programs, which can further enable you to use the information in ways that are meaningful as to network events that are happening.

Cram Quiz

1. If configured to send syslog messages at level 3 to a syslog server, which levels will the syslog server send when they occur on the router? Choose all that apply.

   ❍ **A.** 5

   ❍ **B.** 4

   ❍ **C.** 3

   ❍ **D.** 2

   ❍ **E.** 1

   ❍ **F.** 0

2. What does the 5 represent in the following syslog output?

   ```
   %OSPF-5-ADJCHG
   ```

   ❍ **A.** This is a level 5 syslog message.

   ❍ **B.** This is the fifth syslog message of this type.

   ❍ **C.** This is an LSA type 5.

   ❍ **D.** This is a time stamp.

Cram Quiz Answers

1. Answers C, D, E, and F are correct. Levels 3 and numerically lower (lower also representing more severe) syslog messages will be sent when the logging level is set to level 3.
2. Answer A is correct. The 5 represents the syslog level for the event.

Describe SNMP v2 and v3

CramSaver

If you can correctly answer these questions before going through this section, save time by skimming the Exam Alerts in this section and then completing the Cram Quiz at the end of the section.

1. Which flavor of SNMP provides authentication, confidentiality, and data integrity?
2. What is the purpose of a MIB in SNMP?

Answers

1. SNMPv3 provides authentication, confidentiality, and data integrity.
2. A MIB is a directory of specific objects within an SNMP agent that can be addressed (queried) from an SNMP manager.

SNMP is the Simple Network Management Protocol. It's used between a device that is acting as an agent (for example, a router or a switch running SNMP) and a management station, also referred to as an SNMP manager. The agent has a list of items that can either be requested as information or perhaps set or changed remotely by the manager through SNMP. The individual elements that can be viewed or managed via SNMP vary by platform, but the items that can be seen or managed is referred to as a Management Information Base (MIB). An SNMP management station will have the appropriate MIB installed and configured to properly work with devices it is managing.

An SNMP management program may periodically send requests to determine the health or status of a network component, such as an interface on a router. SNMP has three major versions: v1, v2c, and v3. Versions 1 and 2c are not considered secure. They use something called a community string as a password, which is often sent as plain text without encryption. Version 3 supports encryption for confidentiality, data integrity, and authentication, and when supported by both the SNMP manager and a router or switch being managed, it should be used instead of the older versions (which use less security).

An example of configuring a simple community string which will allow both reads and writes (RW) from an SNMP manager as long as the IP address of that manager is permitted in access list 55 is demonstrated here:

```
R1(config)#snmp-server community MyPaSsWoRd! RW 55
```

A community string may be set up to allow read only access (RO) or read write access (RW). with an SNMP manager configured with the appropriate community strings, it can gather information using the RO community strings, as well as change the settings on elements in the MIB on devices using the RW community string.

Cram Quiz

1. What does the 55 mean in the following configuration?

```
snmp-server community MyPaSsWoRd! RW 55
```

- ❍ **A.** That is the password for read write.
- ❍ **B.** That is the ACL controlling access.
- ❍ **C.** That is the line number where this line belongs in the configuration.
- ❍ **D.** That is a MIB identifier.

Cram Quiz Answers

1. Answer B is correct. An access control list may be created and applied as part of an SNMP configuration to control the permitted source addresses that may access the SNMP-managed device using SNMP.

Utilize Netflow Data

CramSaver

If you can correctly answer these questions before going through this section, save time by skimming the Exam Alerts in this section and then completing the Cram Quiz at the end of the section.

1. What would be a reason to use NetFlow in addition to syslog and SNMP information collection?
2. What are the two main components of the NetFlow system?

Answers

1. NetFlow allows the collection of application-specific traffic internetwork, including source IP addresses, destination IP addresses, the ports in use, and other details. Syslog and SNMP cannot provide that level of detail.
2. The two main components of NetFlow are the devices that can gather the information and export it and a NetFlow collector that can receive the gathered NetFlow data.

NetFlow is an IOS feature that can enable you to collect detailed information about the traffic flows going through your routers. Syslog can tell us what events are happening, and SNMP can tell us the status of a device and its properties, NetFlow collects and reports the information about the sessions, IP addresses, size of packets, and so on regarding the traffic.

The information gathered through NetFlow can help us identify who's using which resources on the network, assist us in analyzing the applications and services that are currently in use, help us with planning, and can provide accounting information about utilization.

The two major components in NetFlow are the network device that supports NetFlow and can pay attention to and collect this information and a destination device called a collector that can compile all the information it receives and assist us in putting it into meaningful reports. A syslog server is to syslog what a NetFlow collector is to NetFlow.

There are several versions of NetFlow, but the common elements that can be collected include the following:

- Source IP address
- Destination IP address

- Source port
- Destination port
- Layer 3 protocol type
- Type of service
- Interface information

An example of configuring NetFlow information gathering, both inbound and outbound on an interface, along with the sending of that information to a NetFlow collector at a.b.c.d using UDP port 9996, is shown in Example 14.6.

EXAMPLE 14.6 **NetFlow Configuration**

```
R3(config)#int fa 0/0
R3(config-if)#ip flow ingress
R3(config-if)#ip flow egress
R3(config-if)#exit
R3(config)#ip flow-export destination 172.16.10.55 9996
R3(config)#ip flow-export version 9
```

To verify the NetFlow settings, we can use the commands shown in Example 14.7.

EXAMPLE 14.7 **Verifying NetFlow Settings**

```
R3#show ip flow export
Flow export v9 is enabled for main cache
  Export source and destination details :
  VRF ID : Default
    Destination(1)  172.16.10.55 (9996)
  Version 9 flow records
  3 flows exported in 1 udp datagrams
  0 flows failed due to lack of export packet
  1 export packets were sent up to process level
  0 export packets were dropped due to no fib
  0 export packets were dropped due to adjacency issues
  0 export packets were dropped due to fragmentation failures
  0 export packets were dropped due to encapsulation fixup failures

R3#show ip cache flow
IP packet size distribution (384 total packets):
   1-32   64   96  128  160  192  224  256  288  320  352  384  416
448  480
   .000 .765 .000 .020 .000 .000 .000 .000 .000 .000 .002 .000 .020
.000 .000
```

```
    512   544   576 1024 1536 2048 2560 3072 3584 4096 4608
   .000  .000  .190 .000 .000 .000 .000 .000 .000 .000 .000

IP Flow Switching Cache, 278544 bytes
  2 active, 4094 inactive, 4 added
  134 ager polls, 0 flow alloc failures
  Active flows timeout in 30 minutes
  Inactive flows timeout in 15 seconds
IP Sub Flow Cache, 25800 bytes
  2 active, 1022 inactive, 4 added, 4 added to flow
  0 alloc failures, 0 force free
  1 chunk, 1 chunk added
  last clearing of statistics never
Protocol    Total     Flows    Packets Bytes  Packets Active(Sec) Idle(Sec)
--------    Flows      /Sec      /Flow  /Pkt     /Sec     /Flow     /Flow
ICMP            2       0.0          4   100      0.0       0.1      15.0
Total:          2       0.0          4   100      0.0       0.1      15.0

SrcIf       SrcIPaddress     DstIf        DstIPaddress     Pr SrcP DstP  Pkts

SrcIf       SrcIPaddress     DstIf        DstIPaddress     Pr SrcP DstP  Pkts
Fa0/1       20.0.0.2         Fa0/0*       10.0.0.50        06 0017 595B   163
Fa0/0       10.0.0.50        Fa0/1        20.0.0.2         06 595B 0017   225
```

A version of NetFlow called Flexible NetFlow uses the concept of NetFlow *records* to define which fields to consider as part of a flow. It also uses NetFlow *monitors*, which are applied to an interface to perform NetFlow monitoring, and NetFlow *exporters* to send the collected data to a remote system for analysis.

Cram Quiz

1. Which of the following NetFlow components would be applied to an interface?

   ❍ **A.** NetFlow record

   ❍ **B.** NetFlow monitor

   ❍ **C.** NetFlow exporter

   ❍ **D.** NetFlow analyzer

Cram Quiz Answers

1. Answer B is correct. A NetFlow monitor is applied to an interface in Flexible NetFlow to perform NetFlow monitoring.

Review Questions

You can find the answers to these questions at the end of the chapter.

1. Consider the following partial output:

```
R1#show standby
FastEthernet0/0 - Group 1
  State is Active
    2 state changes, last state change 00:00:49
  Virtual IP address is 10.0.0.254
  Active virtual MAC address is 0000.0c07.ac01
    Local virtual MAC address is 0000.0c07.ac01 (v1 default)
  Hello time 3 sec, hold time 10 sec
    Next hello sent in 1.156 secs
  Preemption disabled
  Active router is local
  Standby router is 10.0.0.2, priority 100 (expires in 7.608 sec)
  Priority 105 (configured 105)
  Group name is "hsrp-Fa0/0-1" (default)
```

How many routers will be able to forward traffic, simultaneously using the protocol shown, for the specific subnet that Fa0/0 is connected to?

❍ **A.** 2

❍ **B.** 1

❍ **C.** Depends on how many routers are in the group

❍ **D.** 3

❍ **E.** 4

2. Consider the following partial output:

```
R1#show glbp
FastEthernet0/0 - Group 1
  State is Active
    2 state changes, last state change 00:00:41
  Virtual IP address is 10.0.0.254
  Hello time 3 sec, hold time 10 sec
    Next hello sent in 0.060 secs
Group members:
    0011.1111.1111 (10.0.0.1) local
    0022.2222.2222 (10.0.0.2)
  There are 2 forwarders (1 active)
  Forwarder 1
    State is Active
      1 state change, last state change 00:00:31
    MAC address is 0007.b400.0101 (default)
    Owner ID is 0011.1111.1111
    Redirection enabled
    Preemption enabled, min delay 30 sec
    Active is local, weighting 100
  Forwarder 2
    State is Listen
    MAC address is 0007.b400.0102 (learnt)
    Owner ID is 0022.2222.2222
    Redirection enabled, 598.744 sec remaining (maximum 600 sec)
    Time to live: 14398.744 sec (maximum 14400 sec)
    Preemption enabled, min delay 30 sec
    Active is 10.0.0.2 (primary), weighting 100 (expires in 8.740 sec)
```

Based on the output provided, how many virtual MAC addresses are being used?

- ❍ **A.** 4
- ❍ **B.** 3
- ❍ **C.** 2
- ❍ **D.** 5
- ❍ **E.** 6

3. VRRP more closely resembles which Cisco proprietary protocol?

- ❍ **A.** HSRP
- ❍ **A.** GLBP
- ❍ **B.** EIGRP
- ❍ **C.** NetFlow

4. Consider the following partial output:

```
R1(config)#do show log
<snip>
Trap logging: level notifications, 47 message lines logged
      Logging to 172.16.10.5  (udp port 514,  audit disabled,
            authentication disabled, encryption disabled, link down),
            0 message lines logged,
```

Which of the following are true?

❍ **A.** Syslog messages level 6 and lower will be sent to the syslog server.

❍ **B.** Syslog messages level 7 and lower will be sent to the syslog server.

❍ **C.** Syslog messages level 5 and lower will be sent to the syslog server.

❍ **D.** Syslog debug messages and lower will be sent to the syslog server.

5. which of the following commands could be used to send level 4 syslog messages to a configured syslog destination server?

❍ **A.** **logging trap critical**

❍ **B.** **logging trap alert**

❍ **C.** **logging trap error**

❍ **D.** **logging trap warning**

❍ **E.** **logging trap emergency**

6. What command enables you to see syslog messages when connected via an SSH session on a vty line?

❍ **A.** **logging ssh**

❍ **B.** **logging trap vty**

❍ **C.** **logging vty**

❍ **D.** **terminal monitor**

7. Review the following output :

```
R1(config)#snmp-server community MyPaSsWoRd! RW 55
```

Which of the following are true?

❍ **A.** The password for the community string is RW.

❍ **B.** The string just before it is the RW community string,

❍ **C.** There are 55 simultaneous read/write commands allowed.

❍ **D.** The RW is a typo; it should be RO.

❍ **E.** Only a source address in the ACL 55 can ping this device.

8. Which SNMP version supports encryption and data integrity?

❍ **A.** SNMPv2c

❍ **B.** SNMPv3

❍ **C.** SNMPv3.5

❍ **D.** None of these answers

9. Consider the following partial output:

```
R3#show ip flow export
Flow export v9 is enabled for main cache
  Export source and destination details :
  VRF ID : Default
    Destination(1)  172.16.10.55 (9996)
  Version 9 flow records
```

What is the UDP port used by the collector?

❍ **A.** 53

❍ **B.** 9

❍ **C.** 9996

❍ **D.** Can't tell from this output

10. Consider the following partial output:

```
R3(config)#int fa 0/0
R3(config-if)#ip flow ingress
R3(config-if)#ip flow egress
```

Which IOS application is being implemented through these commands?

❍ **A.** CEF

❍ **B.** PBR

❍ **C.** HSRP

❍ **D.** NetFlow

Answers to Review Questions

1. Answer B is correct. With HSRP, only one router at any given time will be the active and forwarding router for a single subnet. If the active router fails, a standby router is promoted to continue providing support for the virtual IP address that is being managed by the active router.
2. Answer C is correct. GLBP uses the concept of active virtual forwarders, where each member of the group will have its own virtual MAC address. In the example shown, there are two forwarders, so there'd be exactly two virtual MAC addresses.
3. Answer A is correct. VRRP most resembles Cisco HSRP; it uses a similar method, configuration, and service as HSRP. VRRP doesn't do per subnet load balancing like GLBP, and NetFlow is an IOS application that collects flow-based information crossing the network.
4. Answer C is correct. Notifications is level 5 in the world of syslog. If we are doing traps at level 5, that means everything at that level and lower will be sent to the syslog destination configured. Debugging is at level 7, and level 7 as well as level 6 will not be included because of the settings shown in the question.
5. Answer D is correct. The command **trap level warning** will cause level 4 syslog messages to be sent to any destination syslog servers. The other options of error, critical, alert, and emergency are lower than 4 and would not cause level 4 messages to be sent.
6. Answer D is correct. By default, sessions on the vty lines, such as SSH, will not see syslog messages. To enable this feature while using SSH on a vty line, use the command **terminal monitor**. To stop logging to your session, use the command **terminal no monitor**.
7. Answer B is correct. The RW refers to read and write, and it means the community string that is listed just before this will allow both read and write privileges if used. The 55 is an access control list, and the SNMP manager must be coming in from a source IP address that is permitted in this access list. However, the question was asking about the RW and what it meant, not asking about the ACL 55.
8. Answer B is correct. SNMPv3 provides encryption, data integrity, and authentication. Version 3.5 isn't a valid version, and the older SNMP doesn't have as much security as SNMPv3.
9. Answer C is correct. 9996 is the destination port for the collector. In this output, NetFlow uses UDP to the port specified from the router sending the data to the NetFlow collector. UDP 53 is DNS.
10. Answer D is correct. The **ip flow** command is used to implement the NetFlow function on a router. In addition, a collector must be identified for this router to send the information to over UDP to the port specified in the configuration, which needs to match a listening port on the collector.

CHAPTER FIFTEEN

WAN Operation

This chapter covers the following official 200-101 ICND2 and 200-120 CCNA exam topics:

- ▶ Identify different WAN technologies.
- ▶ Configure and verify a basic WAN serial connection.
- ▶ Configure and verify a PPP connection between Cisco routers.
- ▶ Configure and verify Frame Relay on Cisco routers.
- ▶ Implement and troubleshoot PPPoE.

A WAN is a network that spans a broad geographic area and includes such technologies as Asynchronous Transfer Mode (ATM), Frame Relay, digital subscriber link (DSL), (TV) cable, leased lines, Integrated Services Digital Network (ISDN), cellular data, and satellite. These wide-area networking services are usually leased from providers because of the prohibitive cost and trouble of setting them up for private use.

WAN Technologies

CramSaver

If you can correctly answer these questions before going through this section, save time by skimming the Exam Alerts in this section and then completing the Cram Quiz at the end of the section.

1. What is the default Layer 2 encapsulation on a Cisco serial interface?

   A. HDLC

   B. PPP

   C. ATM

   D. Frame Relay

2. What are some of the advantages of PPP? Choose all that apply.

   A. Cisco proprietary format provides additional features

   B. Standards-based protocol for wide compatibility

   C. Can perform link features such as compression, callback, multilink, and authentication

   D. Encapsulates multiple Layer 3 protocols

   E. Default encapsulation on all Cisco serial interfaces (simple "do nothing" implementation)

3. Your router's hostname is millennium, with a username of Solo and a password of Falcon. What should the router at the opposite end of the PPP link between them use as the username?

   A. Millennium

   B. Falcon

   C. Solo

   D. millennium

4. Your Frame Relay provider has assigned you DLCI 400 to connect to 10.40.0.1, and DLCI 200 to connect to 10.20.0.1. You have decided to avoid Inverse ARP and create static maps to support your EIGRP implementation. Which of the following commands is correct?

   A. **no ip split-horizon**

   B. **frame relay map ip 10.40.0.1 200**

   C. **frame relay map ip 10.40.0.1 400**

   D. **frame relay map ip 400 10.40.0.1 broadcast**

   E. **frame relay map ip 10.40.0.1 400 broadcast**

Answers

1. Answer A is correct. The other protocols must be manually selected.
2. Answers B, C, and D are correct. Answer A is wrong because PPP is standards based. Answer E is wrong because HDLC, not PPP, is the default encapsulation on Cisco serial interfaces.
3. Answer D is correct. The router hostname becomes the connecting router's username; both the username and the password are case sensitive.
4. Answer E is correct. Answer A has nothing to do with creating static maps. Answer B names the wrong DLCI. Answer C does not include the broadcast parameter, which will be needed for EIGRP to multicast into the Frame Relay network. Answer D reverses the syntax, incorrectly placing the DLCI before the IP address.

In its simplest definition, wide-area networking can be broken down into three categories:

- ▶ Dedicated (leased) line
- ▶ Switched
- ▶ Internet

Dedicated (usually leased line) WAN solutions use synchronous serial interfaces to connect two sites together. This is the easiest to configure and provides the best reliability. However, this is also the most expensive over long distances.

The second option is switched technologies. This category is further broken down: Circuit-switched solutions typically use either modems connected to asynchronous interfaces, or ISDN telephony-based technologies. With circuit-switched solutions, you establish a circuit between two sites using a telephone/data provider, and often tear down that circuit when you are finished sending the data (Many ISDN circuits are more or less permanently up).

The second switched category is packet-switched technologies, which also use synchronous serial interfaces similar to leased-line solutions, but with these a virtual circuit is established between two or more sites and your data packets are switched across a service provider's network. The service provider's network is transparent to the customer; you will not be able to see any of your provider's equipment. Packet-switched technologies include Frame Relay, ATM, and X.25. They are commonly used when leased-line solutions become cost prohibitive.

These traditional WAN services have evolved over time to reflect changes in technology and customer demand. One important development came in the form of Point-to-Point Protocol over Ethernet (PPPoE), which provides the benefits of the PPP encapsulation (specifically, IP address assignment and authentication) on top of the ubiquitous high-speed simplicity of Ethernet, all in a telco DSL environment that would otherwise not support point-to-point links. PPPoE is one of the big "win-win" solutions of the Internet age: Telcos are happy because they can use DSL, and Internet service providers (ISPs) are happy because they can still control the customer IP and conditionally authenticate the connection (and all the customer has to do is plug in a phone and an Ethernet jack).

More recently, the use of Ethernet over Multiprotocol Label Switching (EoMPLS) has provided enterprise customers with a relatively simple, flexible, and versatile way of accessing high-speed WAN services. MPLS is a provider system that offers IP connectivity over almost any Layer 2 link that can transport IP. (EoMPLS, of course, uses Ethernet at Layer 2 to connect to the provider MPLS cloud, but customers can use T1 or Frame Relay or a variety of other connection options.) MPLS service can also provide important features such as privacy and quality of service (QoS).

In areas where copper or fiber connectivity is not available (or not cost effective), satellite links offer a workable solution under most conditions. VSAT (Very Small Aperture Terminal) uses a dish of unobtrusive and manageable size to provide moderate bandwidth in otherwise inaccessible locations. Poor weather, unfortunately, can significantly degrade the signal. The overall cost of these systems is pretty low, considering how useful they are, but high bandwidth gets very expensive because of the shortage of satellite capability.

Of course, no chapter on WAN technologies could skip over mentioning the Internet as a WAN option. Regardless of how you access the Internet (and pretty much any technology described in this chapter or elsewhere in the book will get you there), the Internet represents the ultimate WAN: accessible from almost anywhere, with increasingly useful bandwidth (even from 3G/4G/LTE cellular access), effective security options, and low to moderate cost. Many small to medium-size businesses find that they can do away with all traditional WAN services and use a suitable Internet connection to greater advantage for less.

Encapsulation Types

With each WAN solution, there is an encapsulation type. Encapsulations wrap an "information envelope" called a *frame* around your data; it is used to transport your data traffic. If you use leased line as your wide-area networking choice, you will probably encapsulate your data inside a High-Level Data Link Control (HDLC) frame or Point-to-Point Protocol (PPP) frame. For packet-switched networks, you will probably use Frame Relay or Asynchronous Transfer Mode (ATM). (ATM and Frame Relay actually have multiple encapsulation types that you could use.) Finally, in circuit-switched environments you might have HDLC or PPP. It is more common to use PPP because of the options available with PPP that are designed for use with telephone-based circuit-switched networks. These options include such things as authentication, multilinking, callback, and compression.

Cisco HDLC

The default encapsulation on a serial interface is HDLC. The original HDLC encapsulation was defined by the International Organization for Standards (ISO), those same folks who developed the OSI model. The ISO version of HDLC had one shortcoming, however; it had no options to support multiple Layer 3 routed protocols. As a result, most vendors have created their own form of HDLC. Cisco is no exception; it has its own proprietary form of HDLC to support various Layer 3 protocols such as IPX, IP, and AppleTalk. Figure 15.1 illustrates the difference between the ISO and Cisco HDLC frame formats.

ExamAlert

Vendors love to test your knowledge of the default settings for their products. Make sure that you know that HDLC is the default encapsulation on a serial interface.

Cisco HDLC

Flag	Address	Control	Proprietary Field to support multiple protocols	Data	FCS	Flag

ISO HDLC

Flag	Address	Control	Data	FCS	Flag

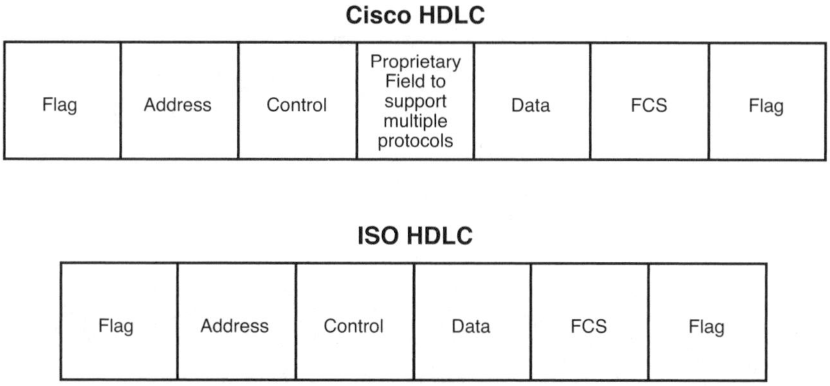

FIGURE 15.1 **Cisco and ISO HDLC formats.**

PPP

Point-to-Point Protocol (PPP), defined in RFC 1661, is used to encapsulate network layer protocols over point-to-point links. PPP can be used over asynchronous, synchronous, or ISDN links.

Components

PPP has two sublayers called Network Control Protocol (NCP) and Link Control Protocol (LCP).

NCP is responsible for supporting multiple Layer 3 protocols. Each protocol has its own NCP, such as the IPCP for IP communication and IPXCP for IPX communication. Think of NCP as the "packager," as it is responsible for packaging, or encapsulating, your packets into a control protocol that is readable by PPP.

The Link Control Protocol is used for establishing the link and negotiating optional settings. These options include the following:

- **Compression:** You can compress your data to conserve bandwidth across your wide-area network. Options for compression are Stacker and Predictor.
- **Callback:** With callback, you dial in to a router using a modem or ISDN and then disconnect. The other router then calls you back at a predefined number. This option is used for centralized billing and security reasons.
- **Multilink:** Multilink allows you to bundle together more than one link to create more bandwidth. (Traffic will load balance across the links.) For example, you can bundle two 64K channels together to get a combined 128K.
- **Authentication:** You can use authentication to verify a router's identity when it is connecting into your router. Options for authentication include Challenge Handshake Authentication Protocol (CHAP) and Password Authentication Protocol (PAP).

You can think of LCP as the "negotiator" because it is responsible for negotiating these options between two routers.

ExamAlert

Know the various options of PPP. Remember CCMA (sounds like CCNA), which stands for compression, callback, multilink, and authentication.

Authentication with PAP and CHAP

The two types of authentications you can use with PPP (that are of interest to CCNA candidates) are as follows:

- Password Authentication Protocol (PAP)
- Challenge Handshake Authentication Protocol (CHAP)

PAP uses a two-way authentication process where the username and password are sent followed by a response message indicating successful or failed authentication. CHAP, however, is much more strict about authentication. It performs a three-way authentication process, as shown in Figure 15.2, which takes place not only at the beginning of a connection, but also at any time afterward. As if that wasn't paranoid enough, CHAP never sends the password across the link. Instead, a message digest 5 (MD5) algorithm hash of the password is sent.

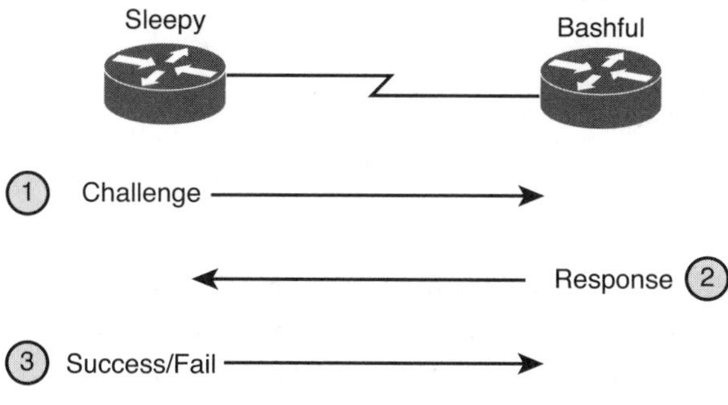

FIGURE 15.2 **CHAP authentication.**

Configuration of PPP Authentication

Configuring PPP authentication is a four-step process:

1. Configure your hostname.
2. Configure the username and password list for other routers to authenticate to your router.
3. Enable PPP encapsulation.
4. Enable PAP or CHAP authentication.

The hostname takes on a special significance with PPP because it is used as the username to authenticate to another router. For example, suppose that you have two routers named Sleepy and Bashful, as shown in Figure 15.3. For

Sleepy, its hostname is used as the username to authenticate to Bashful. For Bashful, its hostname is used as the username to authenticate to Sleepy. Use the hostname command to configure the hostname on each router.

Sleepy:

```
Router(config)#hostname Sleepy
```

Bashful:

```
Router(config)#hostname Bashful
```

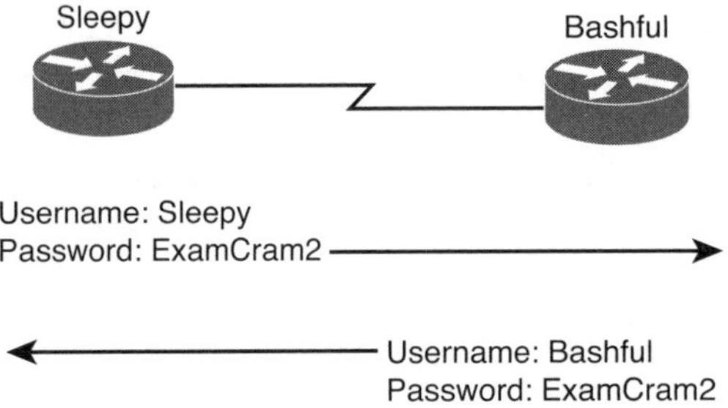

FIGURE 15.3 **PPP configuration example.**

Next, configure the username and password for other routers to authenticate to you. For the Sleepy router, you need to configure a username and password for the Bashful router to authenticate to it. Likewise, you need to configure a username and password for the Sleepy router to authenticate to the Bashful router. Both routers must use the same password. Use the global configuration **username** command to configure your username and password. The syntax for this command is as follows:

```
username name password password
```

For example, on Sleepy:

```
Sleepy(config)#username Bashful password ExamCram2
```

Next, on Bashful:

```
Bashful(config)#username Sleepy password ExamCram2
```

ExamAlert

The hostnames and passwords are case sensitive. The hostname Sleepy is different from the hostname sleepy. Make sure that you check the case of your letters when configuring PPP authentication.

The third step in configuring PPP is to enable PPP encapsulation on the interface using the **encapsulation** command. For example, to configure PPP encapsulation on the Serial 0 interface, type the following:

```
Sleepy(config)#interface serial 0

Sleepy(config-if)#encapsulation ppp
```

Finally, you will need to configure your authentication. The interface level command to do this is as follows:

```
ppp authentication [chap | chap pap | pap]
```

If you choose the **chap pap** option, it will try CHAP authentication first, and if that fails, it will try PAP. Starting with IOS Version 12.3, Cisco supports Extensible Authentication Protocol (EAP), Microsoft CHAP (MS-Chap), and MS-Chap Version 2. Following is the final configuration for the two routers using CHAP authentication:

Sleepy:

```
Router(config)#hostname Sleepy
Sleepy(config)#username Bashful password ExamCram2
Sleepy(config)#interface serial0
Sleepy(config-if)#encapsulation ppp
Sleepy(config-if)#ppp authentication chap
```

Bashful:

```
Router(config)#hostname Bashful
Bashful(config)#username Sleepy password ExamCram2
Bashful(config)#interface serial0
Bashful(config-if)#encapsulation ppp
Bashful(config-if)#ppp authentication chap
```

Verification and Troubleshooting

Verifying and troubleshooting PPP can be done with two commands:

```
show interfaces

debug ppp authentication
```

The **show interfaces** command will show you if the line protocol is up or down and the state of LCP. LCP will report in the "closed" state if it was unable to establish a connection to another router. Following is output from the Sleepy router:

```
Sleepy(config)#show interfaces serial0
```

```
serial0 is up, line protocol is up
Hardware is QUICC
  MTU 1500 bytes, BW 64 Kbit, DLY 20000 usec, rely 255/255, load 1/255
  Encapsulation PPP, loopback not set, keepalive not set
 LCP Open
Closed: IPXCP
Listen: CCP
Open: IPCP, CDPCP
<...output omitted...>
```

The **debug ppp authentication** command will show your authentication as it happens. Following is the output of this command on a router using CHAP authentication:

```
Sleepy#debug ppp authentication
PPP serial0: Send CHAP challenge id=34 to remote
PPP serial0: CHAP challenge from Bashful
PPP serial0: CHAP response received from Bashful
PPP serial0: CHAP response id=34 received from Bashful
PPP serial0: send CHAP success id=34 to remote
```

Configuring PPPoE

Okay, maybe I should clarify the title of this section a little. It should be more like "*Recognize* the configuration of PPPoE," because the exam isn't going to make you do much beyond that.

The important things are to remember to translate the key concepts from PPP into the config for PPPoE. PPP uses a dialer interface, which is a virtual interface whose configuration is activated as required for connectivity (in the old days, for dialup links, in this context for establishing the PPPoE link). PPPoE quite literally creates a tunnel using Ethernet, with the tunnel encapsulating PPP, which in turn encapsulates IP. In other words, Ethernet transports PPP to the ISP router, where it is decapsulated and the PPP process can begin. The extra overhead of the PPPoE encapsulation must be accommodated by lowering the maximum transmission unit (MTU) to 1492, from the default of 1500.

A typical dialer interface config is shown, with annotations to help you identify critical parts for the exam. In this example we are looking at the customer router config; the ISP router is configured to authenticate as user Spock, sending an MD5 hash of the password Kirk.

```
! PPP configuration applied to Dialer interface:
! "IP Address Negotiated" allows ISP to assign an available public IP
to the interface
!
```

```
interface dialer 2
 encapsulation ppp
 ip address negotiated
!
! Inbound authentication with CHAP:
! ISP will authenticate as user "Spock" with MD5 hash of password
"Kirk"
 ppp chap hostname Spock
 ppp chap password Kirk
!
! Dialer pool number (99) must match the one referenced at Gi0/1
below:
 mtu 1492
 dialer pool 99
!
! Interface references matching dialer pool number (99):
interface GigabitEthernet0/1
 no ip address
 pppoe-client dial-pool-number 99
```

Frame Relay

Frame Relay is a scalable WAN solution that is often used as an alternative to leased lines when leased lines prove to be cost prohibitive. With Frame Relay, you can have a single serial interface on a router connecting into multiple remote sites through virtual circuits.

Concepts and Terminology

You should be familiar with many terms when working with Frame Relay. The following sections introduce you to these terms and their definitions.

Virtual Circuits and Network Design

Your virtual circuits can be either permanent or switched. A permanent virtual circuit (PVC) is always connected and, once up, operates very much like a leased line. A switched virtual circuit (SVC) is established only when it is needed. Of these two, PVCs are much more common.

DLCI

Circuits are identified by data-link connection identifiers (DLCIs). DLCIs are assigned by your provider and are used between your router and the Frame Relay provider. In other words, DLCIs are locally significant.

For example, in Figure 15.4, there are three routers: Sleepy, Grumpy, and Bashful. The Sleepy router is connected to a Frame Relay provider that provides permanent virtual circuits to both the Bashful and Grumpy routers. DLCI 100 defines the PVC to Bashful, and DLCI 200 defines the PVC to Grumpy. Although it is not shown in the figure, Bashful and Grumpy will likewise have DLCIs to define their PVCs back to Sleepy.

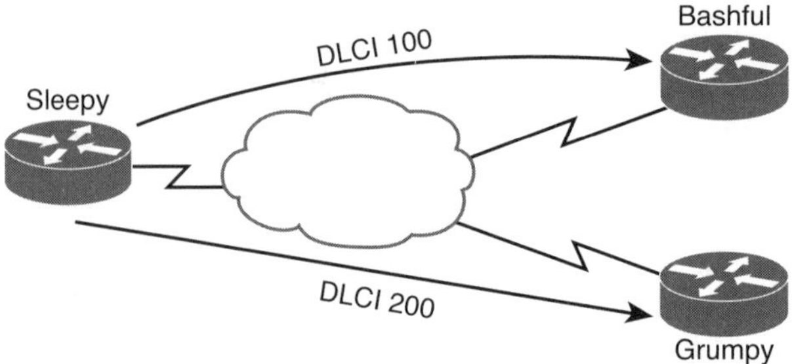

FIGURE 15.4 **Frame Relay PVCs.**

As an analogy, DLCIs are like shipping docks. If you work for a shipping company, you might have several ships attached to docks that are each going to a different destination. When you have a package to ship, you just need to take it to the ship headed for the destination. It is the captain's job to know how to reach the destination.

DLCIs are like these docks. They are significant only on your side. You send your packet out the relevant DLCI, and the provider's job is to figure out how to get that frame to its destination.

LMI

Behind the scenes is a little helper called the local management interface (LMI) that works as a status enquiry and reporting message. LMI messages are sent between your router and the Frame Relay provider's equipment to verify and report on the status of your PVC. Your PVC can be in three possible states:

- **Active:** Active is good. Active means that everything is up and operational.
- **Inactive:** Inactive is bad. Inactive means that you are connected to your Frame Relay provider, but there is a problem with the far-end connection. The problem is most likely between the far-end router and its connection to the Frame Relay provider. You should contact your provider to troubleshoot the issue.

- **Deleted:** Deleted is also bad. Deleted means that there is a problem between your router and the Frame Relay provider's equipment. You should contact your provider to troubleshoot this issue.

Because of the frequency of LMI messages sent between your router and the Frame Relay provider, LMI is also used as a keepalive mechanism. Should your router stop hearing LMI messages it will know that there is a problem with your PVC.

There are three types of LMI. These can be manually configured (discussed later in the configuration section) or, with IOS 11.2 and later, can be auto-detected. The LMI type must match between your router and the provider's Frame Relay switch, but the router-switch link at the other end of the circuit could use a different LMI type. The three types of LMI are as follows:

- Cisco
- ANSI
- Q933A

CIR

The committed information rate (CIR) is the guaranteed rate at which you are allowed to pass data for a particular PVC. When ordering a PVC, you will request a local access rate (the bandwidth of the physical connection) and the CIR for a PVC. For example, you may order a T1, which has a local access rate of 1.544Mb for the Sleepy router, and a CIR of 128K for the PVC to Bashful, and a CIR of 512K for Grumpy.

BECN and FECN

Frame Relay is generous with its bandwidth. If there is no congestion on your link, you are allowed to burst above the CIR rate. Any traffic sent above your CIR is marked as being Discard Eligible (DE) and, in the event of congestion, will be dropped.

When congestion does occur, congestion notification messages are sent out to notify both the sending and the receiving routers that congestion has occurred and that they should slow down their transmission rates. A Backward Explicit Congestion Notification (BECN) is sent back to the sender and a Forward Explicit Congestion Notification (FECN) is sent forward to the destination to notify them of congestion.

A BECN message is only sent back to the source when the destination sends a frame back. Because the provider must wait for a message to return to set the BECN bit in the frame header, the FECN bit is sent to the destination to request some traffic to be sent back in the reverse direction. Without this, the source might never know that congestion has occurred.

In Figure 15.5, traffic is congested going from the Sleepy router to the Bashful router. A FECN is sent to the Bashful router, and a BECN is sent back to the Sleepy router.

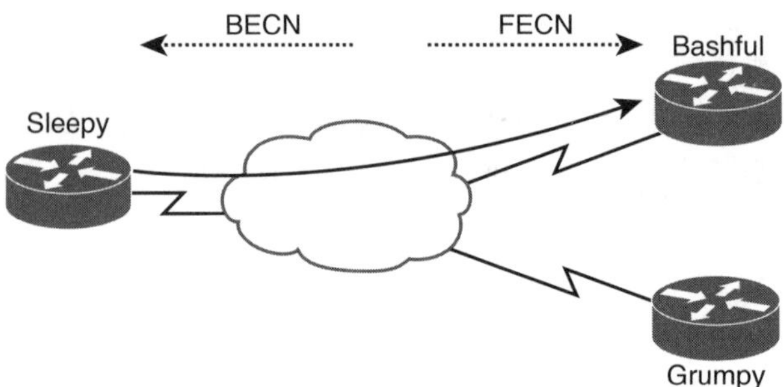

FIGURE 15.5 **Congestion on a Frame Relay network.**

Inverse ARP

Frame Relay needs a mechanism to map Layer 3 addresses with Layer 2 Frame Relay DLCIs. This can be done through a static map command (shown later in the configuration section) or through Inverse ARP (IARP). Just like Ethernet ARP, Inverse ARP is used to map a Layer 3 address to a Layer 2 address. However, Ethernet ARP maps an IP address to a MAC address and Inverse ARP works to map an IP address (or other protocol) to a DLCI.

In Figure 15.6 Sleepy will need a Layer 3 to Layer 2 map to connect to Bashful, which has IP address 10.0.0.2. Using Inverse ARP, Sleepy will automatically create a map telling it to use DLCI 100 to get to IP address 10.0.0.2.

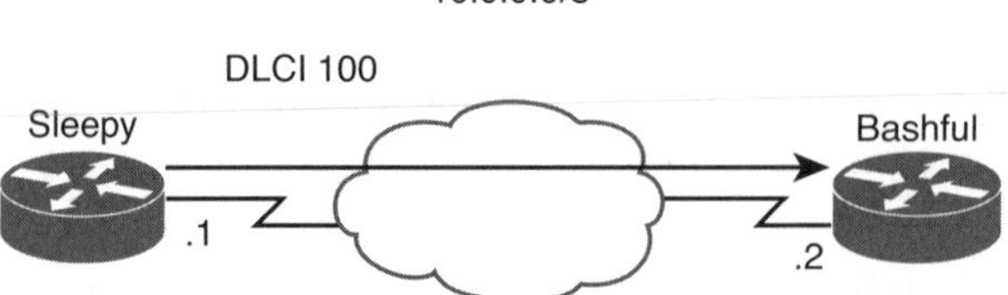

FIGURE 15.6 **Inverse ARP example.**

NBMA

Frame Relay is a nonbroadcast multiaccess (NBMA) medium, which means that broadcast traffic is not allowed to traverse Frame Relay traffic. There are ways, however, to circumvent the NBMA nature of Frame Relay to simulate broadcasts into the Frame Relay cloud. These are discussed in the configuration section.

The Split-Horizon Problem

The split-horizon rule states that a route learned on an interface should not be advertised back out that same interface. This poses a problem in NBMA networks where multiple circuits can connect to a single interface in a hub-and-spoke topology.

Hub-and-spoke topologies are commonly used to connect multiple branch offices to a headquarters office. For example, in Figure 15.7, the Bashful and Grumpy routers have circuits to the Sleepy router but not to each other. In this example, Sleepy is operating as the headquarters office. When Grumpy advertises its 13.0.0.0/8 network to the Sleepy router, it is sent into serial 0/0, but the Sleepy router is not allowed to send it back out serial 0/0. This causes a problem because serial 0/0 is also connected to the Bashful router. As a result, the Bashful router will never know about the 13.0.0.0/8 network.

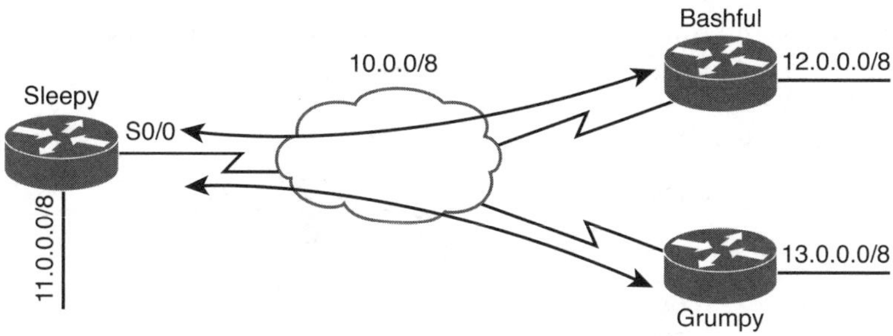

FIGURE 15.7 **Split-horizon problem.**

You have four options to get around the split horizon problem:

- Disable split horizon with the **no ip split-horizon** command. If you are not careful, this could create a loop.
- Have a fully meshed topology where every router has a PVC to every other router. This can get expensive.

- Use static routes instead of dynamic routing protocols. This is not a scalable solution.
- Use subinterfaces. This is your best option.

Subinterfaces

A *subinterface* is a subset of an existing physical interface. As far as the router is concerned, the subinterface is a separate interface. By creating subinterfaces, each circuit can be on its own subnet.

There are two types of subinterfaces:

- **Point to point:** This maps a single IP subnet to a single subinterface and DLCI.
- **Multipoint:** This maps a single IP subnet to multiple DLCIs on a subinterface.

Of these two, only point-to-point subinterfaces address the issue of split horizon. In Figure 15.8, subinterfaces are used on the Sleepy router. Subinterface serial 0/0.1 is connected to the Bashful router and subinterface serial 0/0.2 is connected to the Grumpy router. Now when Grumpy advertises the 13.0.0.0/8 network to Sleepy, it is sent to the subinterface. Sleepy can forward that information on to the Bashful router because the Bashful router is connected to a different subinterface—a logically (but not physically) different interface.

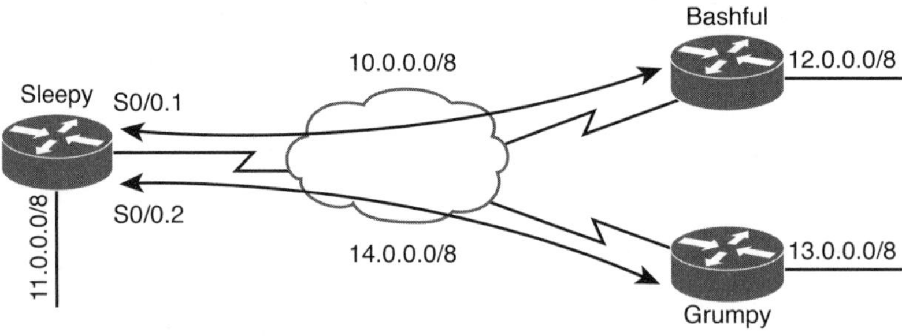

FIGURE 15.8 **Split horizon with subinterfaces.**

Configuration

Configuring Frame Relay involves the following steps:

1. Changing the encapsulation for Frame Relay
2. Configuring the LMI type (optional)
3. Configuring the Frame Relay map (optional in most cases)
4. Configuring subinterfaces (optional)
5. If using a point-to-point subinterface, configuring your DLCI

To begin, select the Frame Relay encapsulation on the interface. There are two types of Frame Relay encapsulations: Cisco and IETF. Cisco is the default. The syntax to set your encapsulation is as follows:

```
encapsulation frame-relay [ietf]
```

Next, you can configure the LMI type. The three LMI types are Cisco, ANSI, and Q933a. Since IOS 11.2, the LMI type is automatically detected. To manually set the LMI type, enter the following command under the interface:

```
frame-relay lmi-type [cisco | ansi | q933a]
```

The third option, configuring a static Frame Relay map, is optional unless you are using point-to-point subinterfaces. (In that case, the **interface-dlci** command is used.) The Frame Relay map will map a Layer 3 address to a local DLCI. This step is optional because Inverse ARP will automatically perform this map for you. The syntax for a Frame Relay map is as follows:

```
frame-relay map protocol address dlci [broadcast] [cisco | ietf]
```

Table 15.1 describes each of these parameters.

TABLE 15.1 **Frame Relay map Command**

Parameter	Description
protocol	Layer 3 protocol (IP, IPX).
address	The Layer 3 address of the remote router (the IP or IPX address).
dlci	Local DLCI number, defining your PVC to the remote router.
broadcast	Optional. This allows for broadcasts and multicasts to traverse your NBMA Frame Relay network.
cisco | **ietf**	Optional. This allows you to change your Frame Relay encapsulation per DLCI.

For example, if you were connected to another router using DLCI 100 and the router had the IP address of 10.0.0.2, your Frame Relay **map** statement would be as follows:

```
Router(config-if)#frame-relay map ip 10.0.0.2 100
```

If you want to use a routing protocol across your Frame Relay network, you will probably need to add the keyword **broadcast** to the end of this command. Routing protocols use broadcasts and multicasts by default, and Frame Relay does not enable broadcasts and multicasts without the use of the broadcast keyword. If you are using Inverse ARP to create your maps for you, Inverse ARP assumes that you want to use routing protocols and adds the broadcast feature for you.

ExamAlert

Watch for a routing protocol configuration in a Frame Relay environment that looks properly configured, but just isn't working. The **broadcast** keyword could be the solution the question is testing for.

If you are using a routing protocol in a hub-and-spoke topology, you will probably want to use subinterfaces to avoid the split-horizon problem. To configure a subinterface, remove the IP address off the main interface and put it under the subinterface. Configuring a subinterface involves assigning it a number and specifying the type. The following command creates point-to-point subinterface serial 0/0.1:

```
Router(config)#interface serial0/0.1 point-to-point
```

To create a multipoint subinterface, enter **multipoint** instead:

```
Router(config)#interface  serial0/0.1 multipoint
```

After entering one of these commands you will be taken to the subinterface configuration mode, where you can enter your IP address:

```
Router(config-subif)#ip address 10.0.0.2 255.0.0.0
```

If you are using a multipoint subinterface, you must configure Frame Relay maps and you cannot rely on Inverse ARP.

If you are using a point-to-point subinterface, you need to assign a DLCI to the subinterface. This is only for point-to-point subinterfaces; this is not needed on the main interface or on multipoint subinterfaces. To assign a DLCI to a point-to-point subinterface, enter the following command under the subinterface:

```
frame-relay interface-dlci dlci
```

Now let's put the entire configuration together. The following configuration will configure Frame Relay for the Sleepy router using a point-to-point subinterface to connect to the Bashful router and a multipoint subinterface to connect to the Grumpy router. (A point-to-point could also have been used, but we'll use multipoint so you can see both methods.) Figure 15.9 shows the topology for the configuration.

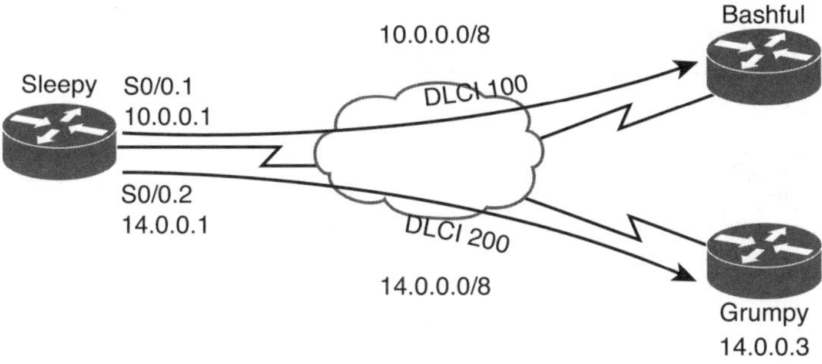

FIGURE 15.9 **Frame Relay configuration.**

```
interface serial 0/0
encapsulation frame-relay
!
! Take the IP address off the main interface:
no ip address
!
! Configure the connection to the Bashful router
interface serial 0/0.1 point-to-point
ip address 10.0.0.1 255.0.0.0
frame-relay interface-dlci 100
!
! Configure the connection to the Grumpy router
interface serial 0/0.2 multipoint
ip address 14.0.0.1 255.0.0.0
frame-relay map ip 14.0.0.3 200 broadcast
```

Many engineers like to configure their subinterface number to be the same as the DLCI. For example, if you had a subinterface connected to DLCI 100, your subinterface may be serial 0/0.100. You don't *have* to do it this way, but it's a nice way to keep your mind clear(er).

Verification and Troubleshooting

You should be familiar with three verification commands and one troubleshooting command for the exam.

The three commands you can use to verify your configuration are as follows:

- **show frame-relay lmi**
- **show frame-relay pvc**
- **show frame-relay map**

The output of **show frame-relay lmi** (displayed in the following) shows LMI statistics, including the number of status enquiries sent and received. Because the status enquiries and responses are used as continuous keepalives, these should be incrementing:

```
LMI Statistics for interface Serial1 (Frame Relay DTE) LMI TYPE = ANSI
  Invalid Unnumbered info 0             Invalid Prot Disc 0
  Invalid dummy Call Ref 0              Invalid Msg Type 0
  Invalid Status Message 0              Invalid Lock Shift 0
  Invalid Information ID 0              Invalid Report IE Len 0
  Invalid Report Request 0              Invalid Keep IE Len 0
  Num Status Enq. Sent 140              Num Status msgs Rcvd 139
  Num Update Status Rcvd 0              Num Status Timeouts 0
```

The output of **show frame-relay pvc** (displayed in the following) will inform you to the status of your PVC. The status should read ACTIVE. This is also where you will see if your router is receiving BECN and FECN messages:

```
DLCI = 100, DLCI USAGE = LOCAL, PVC STATUS = ACTIVE, INTERFACE =
Serial0/0

   input pkts 120            output pkts 70           in bytes 5122
   out bytes 3366           dropped pkts 0            in FECN pkts 0
   in BECN pkts 0           out FECN pkts 0           out BECN pkts 0
   in DE pkts 0             out DE pkts 0
   out bcast pkts 7          out bcast bytes 1366
   pvc create time 1d04h, last time pvc status changed 00:30:32
```

The output of **show frame-relay map** (displayed in the following) will show you any static maps configured and maps created by Inverse ARP. This command will also show you the status of your PVC:

```
Serial0/0 (up): ip 10.0.0.1 dlci 100(0x64,0x1840), dynamic,
              broadcast,, status defined, active
```

ExamAlert

Remember the three show Frame Relay commands and what they do. **show frame-relay lmi** shows your LMI statistics, and **show frame-relay pvc** and **show frame-relay map** show your PVC status.

For troubleshooting, you can execute the **debug frame-relay lmi** command. This command shows you LMI messages in real time:

```
Serial 0/0 (out) : StEnq, clock 202121241, myseq 120, mineseen,
119, yourseen 140, DTE up
PVC IE 0x64, length 0x6, dlci 100, status 0, bandwidth 64000
```

Cram Quiz

Answer these questions. The answers follow the last question. If you cannot answer these questions correctly, consider reading this section again until you can.

1. Which command will show you whether Inverse ARP and static maps are configured correctly?

❍ **A.** **show inverse-arp**

❍ **B.** **show map**

❍ **C.** **show frame-relay map**

❍ **D.** **show map static**

2. What is the main advantage of using point-to-point subinterfaces in Frame Relay?

❍ **A.** This is the only method of allowing routing protocols to broadcast/multicast into Frame Relay.

❍ **B.** Point-to-point subinterfaces are less expensive.

❍ **C.** Complex configurations provide ultimate engineering control.

❍ **D.** Eliminates problems caused by split-horizon rule.

3. Which of the following are true about CHAP authentication? Choose all that apply.

❍ **A.** Password is encrypted and sent across the link securely.

❍ **B.** User name is not case sensitive.

❍ **C.** Password is case sensitive.

❍ **D.** Password is hashed using MD5, and the hash is sent across the link.

❍ **E.** Authentication is repeated for each packet.

❍ **F.** Authentication is performed once only.

❍ **G.** Authentication is performed initially, then again at any time after initial success.

Cram Quiz Answers

1. Answer C is correct. The other answers are not valid commands.
2. Answer D is correct. Answer A is wrong because using the “broadcast” parameter in a static map will also allow broadcasts and multicasts into the Frame Relay network. Answer B is incorrect; in fact, it is possible that the provider could charge more for multiple P2P PVCs. Answer C is wrong because complexity is rarely an advantage.
3. Answers C, D, and G are correct. Answer A is wrong (because Answer D is correct). The password is not encrypted and sent; it is hashed, and the hash is sent This is more secure because the information used to create the hash is not revealed in transit. Answer B is wrong; the username is case sensitive. Answers E and F are wrong because Answer G is correct.

Review Questions

1. Frame Relay NBMA networks present problems with split horizon if the topology is not a full mesh. What could you do to get around issues of split horizon in Frame Relay networks? Select the best answer.

   ❍ **A.** Enable the command **split-horizon frame-relay** on each serial interface.

   ❍ **B.** Create subinterfaces at the main site and put each DLCI on its own subinterface.

   ❍ **C.** Disable routing protocols on Frame Relay interfaces.

   ❍ **D.** Create static routes on your spoke routers.

2. Which of the following are components of the LCP phase of PPP? Choose all that apply.

   ❍ **A.** Compression

   ❍ **B.** Authentication

   ❍ **C.** QoS

   ❍ **D.** Multilink

3. What are the three Frame Relay LMI types? Choose three.

   ❍ **A.** HDLC

   ❍ **B.** Cisco

   ❍ **C.** Q933A

   ❍ **D.** IETF

   ❍ **E.** ANSI

4. There is an error in the following configuration. What is it?

```
router eigrp 100
network 10.0.0.0
network 11.0.0.0
!
interface fastethernet0/0
ip address 10.0.0.1 255.0.0.0
!
interface serial0/0
ip address 11.0.0.1 255.0.0.0
encapsulation frame-relay
frame-relay map ip 11.0.0.2 255.0.0.0
```

   ❍ **A.** EIGRP configuration is incorrect.

   ❍ **B.** IP addresses are incorrect.

   ❍ **C.** The **frame-relay map** statement is incorrect.

   ❍ **D.** Configuration is missing a static route statement.

5. You have a Cisco router with a serial interface set to the default encapsulation. You connect it to a Juniper router running HDLC encapsulation. Why are the two routers unable to communicate?

❍ **A.** The default encapsulation on the Cisco router is PPP. You must change it to HDLC.

❍ **B.** The default encapsulation on the Cisco router is IETF. You must change it to HDLC.

❍ **C.** Cisco's HDLC implementation is proprietary and is therefore incompatible with other vendor's HDLC implementations.

❍ **D.** Cisco routers can connect only to other Cisco routers. You must replace the Juniper router with a Cisco router.

6. What commands can you enter to check the state of your Frame Relay PVC? Choose all that apply.

❍ **A.** **show frame-relay lmi**

❍ **B.** **show frame-relay pvc**

❍ **C.** **show frame-relay map**

❍ **D.** **show frame-relay status**

❍ **E.** **show frame-relay**

Answers to Review Questions

1. Answer B is correct. You should create a subinterface at the main site for each DLCI. This will require a different subnet on each subinterface, but you resolve split-horizon issues. Answer A is incorrect because there is not a **split-horizon frame-relay** command. Answers C and D would technically resolve your problem, but they would limit the functionality of your routers. Therefore, Answers C and D are not the best answers.

2. Answers A, B, and D are correct. The LCP phase is responsible for the initial link setup and negotiating options, such as compression, callback, multilink, and authentication. Answer C is incorrect because this is not a component of LCP.

3. Answers B, C, and E are correct. Answer A is incorrect because HDLC is a wide-area network Layer 2 encapsulation, not a Frame Relay LMI type. Answer D is incorrect because IETF is a Frame Relay encapsulation type, not a Frame Relay LMI type.

4. Answer C is correct. The correct syntax for the frame-relay map command is frame-relay map {protocol protocol-address dlci} Answer A is incorrect because EIGRP is configured correctly. Answer B is incorrect because the IP addresses are correct. Answer D is incorrect because the router is running EIGRP and does not need a static route.

5. Answer C is correct. Cisco's HDLC contains a proprietary data field that makes it incompatible with other vendor's implementation of HDLC. Answers A and B are incorrect because the default encapsulation is HDLC, not PPP or IETF. Although answer D would make some Cisco salespeople happy, Answer D is not the correct answer either. Cisco can communicate with other vendors but not with the default encapsulation.

6. Answers B and C are correct. Answer A is incorrect because show frame-relay lmi shows your LMI statistics and not your PVC status. Answers D and E are incorrect because these are invalid commands.

CHAPTER SIXTEEN

Advanced Troubleshooting

This chapter covers the following official 200-101 ICND2 and 200-120 CCNA exam topics:

- Troubleshoot and resolve spanning tree operation issues.
- Troubleshoot and resolve routing issues.
- Troubleshoot and resolve OSPF problems.
- Troubleshoot and resolve EIGRP problems.
- Troubleshoot and resolve inter-VLAN routing problems.
- Troubleshoot and resolve WAN implementation issues.
- Monitor NetFlow statistics.
- Troubleshoot EtherChannel problems.

When everything is working, and traffic is moving successfully between source and destination, there isn't too much troubleshooting to be done. However, when the packets don't make it, you should ask the following questions:

- Is the physical connectivity okay along the path?
- Is the default gateway correct?
- Is the switching and routing correct?
- Is name resolution working (when applicable)?
- Is there any type of access control list (ACL) blocking the path either to the destination or on the return path?

This chapter focuses on the troubleshooting topics specified in the Cisco published objectives, as listed in the chapter opening.

Troubleshoot and Resolve Spanning Tree Operation Issues

CramSaver

If you can correctly answer these questions before going through this section, save time by skimming the Exam Alerts in this section and then completing the Cram Quiz at the end of the section.

1. SwitchA is the root of spanning tree, and has two working connections (both operating at 100Mbps to SwitchB). Port 15 on SwitchA is connected to port 16 on SwitchB, and port 16 on SwitchA is connected to port 15 on switch B. Which port on SwitchB will be the root port?
2. Why would Switch1, that has a lower bridge ID than Switch2, not be the STP root of VLAN 5?

Answers

1. SwitchB would choose its local port of 16 to be the root, even though it is not the local lowest-numbered interface. In the event of multiple equal-cost paths to the root, through the same neighbor switch, the advertiser's lowest-numbered port will chosen when all other cost factors are equal.
2. If Switch1 doesn't have VLAN 5 defined, it won't have spanning tree running for that VLAN. Another issue that could cause this would be that STP has been disabled for VLAN 5.

Spanning tree's job is to prevent layer two loops, and if left to its defaults shouldn't cause any problems on its own; however, the Spanning Tree Protocol (STP) topology might be different that you think, if there is a physical link that is down. To verify a directly connected connection to another Cisco device, use the **show cdp neighbors** command. If the resulting output shows a neighbor, that confirms the physical connection is present as CDP works at Layer 2. To see the details of spanning tree for a specific VLAN, you can issue the **show spanning-tree vlan** *vlan-id* command, as demonstrated in Example 16.1. You should compare the current state of the STP against the expected state to assist in determining where a problem may be occurring.

EXAMPLE 16.1 **Output of show spanning-tree vlan 10**

```
SW1#show spanning-tree vlan 10

VLAN0010
  Spanning tree enabled protocol ieee
  Root ID     Priority     32778
              Address      1833.1234.0e80
              This bridge is the root
              Hello Time    2 sec   Max Age 20 sec   Forward Delay 15 sec

  Bridge ID   Priority     32778   (priority 32768 sys-id-ext 10)
              Address      1833.1234.0e80
              Hello Time    2 sec   Max Age 20 sec   Forward Delay 15 sec
              Aging Time   300 sec

Interface           Role Sts Cost      Prio.Nbr Type
------------------- ---- --- --------- -------- ---------------------
-----------
Fa0/17              Desg FWD 19        128.11   P2p Edge
Gi0/1               Desg FWD 4         128.25   P2p
Gi0/2               Desg FWD 4         128.26   P2p
```

The output from **show spanning-tree vlan** *vlan-id* will provide you with the following information:

- Version of STP
- Root ID: Bridge ID (BID: priority and MAC address) of the root bridge.
- Cost for this local switch to reach the root bridge (for a nonroot switch)
- Timers set by the root bridge
- Bridge ID: Bridge ID (BID: priority and MAC address) of local bridge
- Local interfaces, their roles, status, and local cost

From this information, you can quickly determine the following.

If the root ID and the bridge ID are the same, that means the switch you are looking at is the root bridge for the VLAN you specified with the *vlan-id* parameter. If this is the case, the cost to reach the root will also be 0, and all the interfaces will be in a forwarding status, and will have the role of designated.

The root bridge will have the lowest BID. If the device you thought was the root isn't, and you have already verified the connectivity between switches, and the VLAN exists on all the switches, then it is possible that some other device has a lower BID.

To find the root bridge, follow the root port on the local switch until you find the root bridge. You can do so by identifying the root port and then identifying which switch that root port connects to. If the next immediate switch (**show cdp neighbor** can help you determine the next switch that is connected) isn't the root, continue to follow that next switch's root port until you find the root. The root will have the lowest BID, and that is why it is the root bridge. The output in Example 16.2 shows Gi0/15 as the root port.

EXAMPLE 16.2 **Following the Path to the Root**

```
SW-1#show spanning-tree vlan 11

VLAN0011
  Spanning tree enabled protocol ieee
  Root ID    Priority    24587
             Address     0011.92a4.0880
             Cost        4
             Port        15 (GigabitEthernet0/15)
             Hello Time   2 sec  Max Age 20 sec  Forward Delay 15 sec

  Bridge ID  Priority    32779  (priority 32768 sys-id-ext 11)
             Address     001c.b148.1e80
             Hello Time   2 sec  Max Age 20 sec  Forward Delay 15 sec
             Aging Time  15  sec

Interface           Role Sts Cost      Prio.Nbr Type
------------------- ---- --- --------- -------- --------------------
-----------
Gi0/3               Desg FWD 4        128.3    P2p Edge
Gi0/4               Desg FWD 4        128.4    P2p Edge
Gi0/13              Altn BLK 4        128.13   P2p
Gi0/15              Root FWD 4        128.15   P2p
Gi0/17              Desg FWD 4        128.17   P2p
```

Nonroot bridges will have exactly one root port leading toward the root bridge for a VLAN. In Example 16.2, you see this as port Gi0/15. Parallel paths that lead toward the root bridge are blocked on all but the single root port to prevent loops. To determine which port is the root port (when multiple exist going towards the root), the one with the overall lowest cost will be chosen. Cost is a combination of the advertised cost from the designated port advertising the root path and the local port cost of the interface hearing the BPDU. In Example 16.2, the root bridge is directly connected to Switch 1's Gi0/15. The advertised cost of 0 is being received on Switch 1's Gi0/15 and the local cost of this port on Switch 1 is 4, for a total cost of 4 (0 + 4 = 4). If two different switches are advertising the same exact cost, and the receiving interfaces also have the same cost, the tiebreaker will be choosing the advertising switch that has the lowest BID. If the local switch has two or more connections to the designated switch, the cost and the BID of the advertising switch is the same (due to it being the same switch with multiple ports), the advertisements that contain the lowest numeric priority will be chosen by the local switch as the root port. If the priority values advertised are the same, the advertising switch's interface number (lower being preferred) will be the tiebreaker. In this case, the local switch will make its local root port, the one connected to the neighbor's lowest-numbered port (not its own lowest-numbered port).

In the event of parallel Layer 2 paths, and STP failing (due to being turned off for example), symptoms include the following:

- Broadcast storm, as frames are looped over and over, which will cause a very high load on the switch. LEDs for all ports in the VLAN will continuously rapidly flash.
- High CPU as the switch forwards frames at its maximum ability to do so.
- Most devices on that VLAN will not be reachable, because of the very high load while the loop is present.

An immediate solution is to remove one or more cables that are providing the redundant path (leave at least one cable for each desired path), and then investigate to see why STP wasn't preventing the Layer 2 loops. You should correct this issue before restoring the physical parallel path; otherwise, a loop will return after the parallel path is available.

Cram Quiz

1. Which command enables you to verify Layer 1 and Layer 2 connectivity, and identify a directly connected Cisco device and which port you are connected to on that device?

   ❍ **A.** **ping**

   ❍ **B.** **show cdp neighbors detail**

   ❍ **C.** **traceroute**

   ❍ **D.** **show ip ospf neighbor**

2. If you are at the console of a nonroot switch, how do you identify the neighboring switch that is connected through the local switch's root port?

   ❍ A. Use **show spanning-tree** and **traceroute**.

   ❍ B. Use **show spanning-tree** and **show interface**.

   ❍ C. Use **show spanning-tree** and **show cdp neighbors**.

   ❍ D. Use **show spanning-tree** and **telnet**.

Cram Quiz Answers

1. Answer B is correct. **show cdp neighbors detail** shows the name of the directly connected CDP-enabled Cisco device, along with the port it is using for the connection. The **ping**, **traceroute**, and **show ip ospf neighbor** commands will not reveal that level of detail.

2. Answer C is correct. The **show spanning-tree** and **show cdp neighbors** commands enable you to determine the root port, and then the **cdp** command will allow you to see the information for the device connected to the root port.

Troubleshoot and Resolve Routing Issues

CramSaver

If you can correctly answer these questions before going through this section, save time by skimming the Exam Alerts in this section and then completing the Cram Quiz at the end of the section.

1. What would be the problem of a computer with the IP address of 10.1.1.2/24 had a default gateway of 10.1.2.1?
2. If a router is receiving routes from several neighbors, with the exception of one, what may be causing that problem?

Answers

1. If a client is on the 10.1.1.0/24 network, it should also have a default gateway on that same network. Having a default gateway that is not local to the directly connected network is not useful for a host.
2. Reasons for not learning routes from a specific neighbor include interfaces being down, routing protocols not being enabled on a specific interface, the IP address and mask being incorrect on interface, access control lists filtering inbound packets and incorrect routing protocol configuration (for example, the wrong area for OSPF).

For a router to forward a packet, it first has to have that packet. If the client doesn't have a correct default gateway configured, or has a physical problem accessing the network, the router may never get a packet to forward from that client. First things to check when troubleshooting routing issues include that the client has a valid IP address in the correct subnet and has a correct default gateway configured. You can verify the configuration by using the **ipconfig** command on the Windows platform or **ifconfig** on a Linux or Macintosh platform. The client should also be configured to use a Domain Name System (DNS) server for name resolution. Without DNS, the client might not ever try to send an IP packet if they cannot resolve the name to an IP address. Problems for the client could include not being able to reach a DHCP server or having incorrect static configurations for IP information.

You can test connectivity to the default gateway using the **ping** command. You can test with the **nslookup** command.

When the router receives a packet, it looks at the destination IP address in the Layer 3 header and makes a forwarding decision based on its routing table. The longest route in the table that matches the destination IP address will be used. Several issues can cause a routing failure, as outlined in Table 16.1.

TABLE 16.1 **Reasons Routing Could Fail (and How to Check Them)**

Item to Check	How to Check
Interfaces are not up/up.	**show ip interface brief**
Interfaces have misconfigured IP.	**show running-config**, **show ip interface**
Sub-interfaces with incorrect VLAN.	**show vlans**, **show running-config**
Switch interface not configured correctly.	**show interface** *port/num* **switchport**, **show interface switchport**, **show running-config**
Incorrect native VLAN on switch.	**show interface trunk, show interface** *port/num* **switchport**
Switchport in err-disable state.	**show interfaces status err-disabled**, **show interfaces status**
Routing configuration errors or missing routes.	**show ip protocols, show ip route**, **show ip ospf interface**, **show ip eigrp interfaces**
ACLs filtering routing protocols.	**show ip interface**, **show ip protocols**
Layer 2 encapsulation configuration errors.	**Show interface**

Cram Quiz

1. A new router has been configured with a routing protocol and IP addresses on each interface. The router can't ping the IP address of another router on the local network. Which of the following should be checked first?

   ❍ **A.** Routing protocol being used

   ❍ **B.** Interface status

   ❍ **C.** Subnet mask being used

   ❍ **D.** Router neighbor status

2. What command enables you to verify the state of an interface on a switch, including its administrative and operational status?

   ❍ **A.** **show interface status**

   ❍ **B.** **show interface switchport**

   ❍ **C.** **show ip interface brief**

   ❍ **D.** **show interface status err-disabled**

Cram Quiz Answers

1. Answer B is correct. Router interfaces are shut down by default. If the interface status is administratively down, that would prevent ping and any other network connectivity from the router interface.
2. Answer A is correct. **show interface status** will show the status of the interface, including how it is administratively configured and how it is operationally functioning.

Troubleshoot and Resolve OSPF Problems

CramSaver

If you can correctly answer these questions before going through this section, save time by skimming the Exam Alerts in this section and then completing the Cram Quiz at the end of the section.

1. What command enables you see the network statements that were included in OSPF router configuration mode?
2. Which of the following could prevent an OSPF neighbor relationship from forming if not matched?
   - **A.** Area number
   - **B.** Timers
   - **C.** Router names
   - **D.** Authentication

Answers

1. **show ip protocols** is the command that enables you to see which network statements were included in the running configuration. A **show run** would also reveal the information regarding the configuration.
2. Answer D is correct. An OSPF neighbor relationship would be prevented from forming if the authentication were different between two neighbors, if the masks or networks were different, if the timers were different, or if the area ID were different. Any one of those would cause a failure. Router names do not need to match for the routers to become OSPF neighbors.

To work properly, OSPF needs to be running. OSPF will not start without a router ID. The router ID will be the configured router ID; if that is not configured as the highest IP address on a loopback interface, and in the absence of a loopback interface, it will use the highest IP address on any other up interface. If there are no IP version 4 addresses and the router ID is not been configured, the OSPF process will not function.

To learn any new routes, an OSPF router must become a neighbor with another OSPF router. To do that, the Hello and Dead intervals must match, the area ID must match, and their authentication methods must match each other as well. The network, including the length of the mask, must match for the neighbor relationship to form. A lack of connectivity or any of these items could cause a neighbor relationship to fail.

When troubleshooting OSPF, you have many things to check and validate. Table 16.2 outlines some of the most common commands, including what they can reveal about the current OSPF configuration and operation. Examples of each of these commands are included after the table.

TABLE 16.2 **Verifying OSPF Configuration and Operation**

Command	What It Verifies	Supporting Output Example
show ip ospf neighbor	Established neighbor relationships	Example 16.3
show ip ospf interface	IP address/mask, area, adjacencies, timers	Example 16.4
show ip protocols	The network statements used in the router configuration, filter lists, information about routers that we have learned from	Example 16.5
show ip route ospf	The routes learned from OSPF	Example 16.6

EXAMPLE 16.3 **Verifying OSPF neighbors**

```
R1#show ip ospf neighbor

Neighbor ID     Pri   State      Dead Time   Address         Interface
172.16.20.1       0   FULL/  -   00:00:37    10.0.0.2        Serial1/2
172.16.10.10      1   FULL/DR    00:00:35    172.16.10.10    GigabitEthernet2/0
172.16.30.1       0   FULL/  -   00:00:37    10.0.0.6        Serial1/3
```

EXAMPLE 16.4 **Verifying Addresses and OSPF-Related Interface Information**

```
R1#show ip ospf interface
Serial1/2 is up, line protocol is up
  Internet Address 10.0.0.1/30, Area 0
  Process ID 1, Router ID 172.16.10.1, Network Type POINT_TO_POINT,
Cost: 64
  Topology-MTID    Cost    Disabled    Shutdown      Topology Name
        0           64        no          no            Base
  Transmit Delay is 1 sec, State POINT_TO_POINT
  Timer intervals configured, Hello 10, Dead 40, Wait 40, Retransmit 5
    oob-resync timeout 40
    Hello due in 00:00:04
  Supports Link-local Signaling (LLS)
  Cisco NSF helper support enabled
  IETF NSF helper support enabled
  Index 1/1, flood queue length 0
```

```
  Next 0x0(0)/0x0(0)
  Last flood scan length is 1, maximum is 1
  Last flood scan time is 0 msec, maximum is 0 msec
  Neighbor Count is 1, Adjacent neighbor count is 1
    Adjacent with neighbor 172.16.20.1
  Suppress hello for 0 neighbor(s)
GigabitEthernet2/0 is up, line protocol is up
  Internet Address 172.16.10.1/24, Area 0
  Process ID 1, Router ID 172.16.10.1, Network Type BROADCAST, Cost: 1
  Topology-MTID    Cost    Disabled    Shutdown     Topology Name
        0           1         no          no            Base
  Transmit Delay is 1 sec, State BDR, Priority 1
  Designated Router (ID) 172.16.10.10, Interface address 172.16.10.10
  Backup Designated router (ID) 172.16.10.1, Interface address
172.16.10.1
  Timer intervals configured, Hello 10, Dead 40, Wait 40, Retransmit 5
    oob-resync timeout 40
    Hello due in 00:00:03
  Supports Link-local Signaling (LLS)
  Cisco NSF helper support enabled
  IETF NSF helper support enabled
  Index 4/4, flood queue length 0
  Next 0x0(0)/0x0(0)
  Last flood scan length is 1, maximum is 1
  Last flood scan time is 0 msec, maximum is 4 msec
  Neighbor Count is 1, Adjacent neighbor count is 1
    Adjacent with neighbor 172.16.10.10  (Designated Router)
  Suppress hello for 0 neighbor(s)
Serial1/3 is up, line protocol is up
  Internet Address 10.0.0.5/30, Area 0
  Process ID 1, Router ID 172.16.10.1, Network Type POINT_TO_POINT,
Cost: 64
  Topology-MTID    Cost    Disabled    Shutdown     Topology Name
        0           64        no          no            Base
  Transmit Delay is 1 sec, State POINT_TO_POINT
  Timer intervals configured, Hello 10, Dead 40, Wait 40, Retransmit 5
    oob-resync timeout 40
    Hello due in 00:00:04
  Supports Link-local Signaling (LLS)
  Cisco NSF helper support enabled
  IETF NSF helper support enabled
  Index 2/2, flood queue length 0
  Next 0x0(0)/0x0(0)
  Last flood scan length is 1, maximum is 1
  Last flood scan time is 0 msec, maximum is 4 msec
  Neighbor Count is 1, Adjacent neighbor count is 1
    Adjacent with neighbor 172.16.30.1
  Suppress hello for 0 neighbor(s)
```

EXAMPLE 16.5 **Verifying Routing OSPF Configuration**

```
R1#show ip protocols
Routing Protocol is "ospf 1"
  Outgoing update filter list for all interfaces is not set
  Incoming update filter list for all interfaces is not set
  Router ID 172.16.10.1
  Number of areas in this router is 1. 1 normal 0 stub 0 nssa
  Maximum path: 4
  Routing for Networks:
    10.0.0.0 0.255.255.255 area 0
    172.16.0.0 0.0.255.255 area 0
  Routing Information Sources:
    Gateway         Distance      Last Update
    172.16.30.1          110      00:05:45
    172.16.20.1          110      00:02:19
  Distance: (default is 110)
```

EXAMPLE 16.6 **Verifying the Routes Learned from OSPF**

```
R1#show ip route ospf
Codes: L - local, C - connected, S - static, R - RIP, M - mobile, B - BGP
       D - EIGRP, EX - EIGRP external, O - OSPF, IA - OSPF inter area
       N1 - OSPF NSSA external type 1, N2 - OSPF NSSA external type 2
       E1 - OSPF external type 1, E2 - OSPF external type 2
       i - IS-IS, su - IS-IS summary, L1 - IS-IS level-1, L2 - IS-IS level-2
       ia - IS-IS inter area, * - candidate default, U - per-user static route
       o - ODR, P - periodic downloaded static route, + - replicated route

Gateway of last resort is 10.0.0.2 to network 0.0.0.0

      10.0.0.0/8 is variably subnetted, 5 subnets, 2 masks
O        10.0.0.8/30 [110/128] via 10.0.0.6, 00:06:39, Serial1/3
                     [110/128] via 10.0.0.2, 00:03:03, Serial1/2
      172.16.0.0/16 is variably subnetted, 4 subnets, 2 masks
O        172.16.20.0/24 [110/65] via 10.0.0.2, 00:03:03, Serial1/2
O        172.16.30.0/24 [110/65] via 10.0.0.6, 00:06:29, Serial1/3
```

It is strongly recommended that you practice these commands either in a simulator, an emulator, or on live gear to assist you in preparing for any simulations that you may encounter on the live exam.

If a remote router has failed to include one of its interfaces in OSPF, it won't be advertising that interface (or rather the network to which that interface is connected), which would result in a missing route on the other OSPF routers. A router with an interface that isn't enabled for OSPF won't be peering with another OSPF router directly on that interface.

Cram Quiz

1. You suspect a timers mismatch preventing OSPF routers from becoming neighbors. Which command enables you to verify the timers in use for the ospf interfaces?

   ❍ **A.** **show ip ospf interface brief**

   ❍ **B.** **show ip ospf interface**

   ❍ **C.** **show ip ospf neighbor**

   ❍ **D.** **show ip ospf**

2. What command can you use to determine which network statements were used with OSPF?

   ❍ **A.** **show ip ospf interface brief**

   ❍ **B.** **show ip ospf interface**

   ❍ **C.** **show ip ospf neighbor**

   ❍ **D.** **show ip protocols**

Cram Quiz Answers

1. Answer B is correct. **show ip ospf interface** will reveal the OSPF timers on the interfaces.
2. Answer D is correct. **show ip protocols** will show the network statements used in router configuration mode.

Troubleshoot and Resolve EIGRP Problems

CramSaver

If you can correctly answer these questions before going through this section, save time by skimming the Exam Alerts in this section and then completing the Cram Quiz at the end of the section.

1. What will be the results of router 1 using the autonomous system number of 6, and router 2 using the autonomous number of 7?
2. What command will display the results of the network statements that were used in the router configuration for EIGRP?

Answers

1. A neighbor relationship between the two routers would not form if they're using different autonomous system numbers. The autonomous system numbers must match
2. The command **show IP protocols** will reveal the details about the network statements that were used in router configuration mode. The command **show ip eigrp interface** will confirm which interfaces are participating in EIGRP.

EIGRP must form a neighbor relationship with another EIGRP router to learn routes via Enhanced Interior Gateway Routing Protocol (EIGRP). Things that could prevent a neighbor relationship from forming could include the following:

- Interfaces that are shut down.
- Interfaces that are not enabled for EIGRP.
- A misconfigured EIGRP such as a different a autonomous system number (which must match between neighbors). The K values must also match between neighbors.

Common factors that could prevent basic connectivity between two routers may include bad or missing cabling, or routers being in different VLANs. These basic connectivity issues would lead to EIGRP failure between two neighbors.

Missing routes could be a result of missing EIGRP neighbors, interfaces that are not included in the EIGRP network statements, or from summarization done either manually or automatically at classful boundaries.

When troubleshooting EIGRP, you should look at several EIGRP-related configuration items. Table 16.3 describes commonly used commands, including what they do and which of the corresponding examples (following the table) you can refer to see their output.

TABLE 16.23 **Verifying EIGRP Configuration and Operation**

Command	What It shows	Example
show ip protocols	Autonomous system number, filters in place, metric weights, summarization in place, network statements, neighbors you have learned from	Example 16.7
show ip eigrp interfaces	Verifies which interface are participating in EIGRP	Example 16.8
show ip eigrp neighbors	Show EIGRP neighbors	Example 16.9
show ip route eigrp	Shows routes learned via EIGRP	Example 16.10

EXAMPLE 16.7 **show ip protocols Command Output**

```
R1#show ip protocols
Routing Protocol is "eigrp 1"
  Outgoing update filter list for all interfaces is not set
  Incoming update filter list for all interfaces is not set
  Default networks flagged in outgoing updates
  Default networks accepted from incoming updates
  Redistributing: eigrp 1
  EIGRP-IPv4 Protocol for AS(1)
    Metric weight K1=1, K2=0, K3=1, K4=0, K5=0
    NSF-aware route hold timer is 240
    Router-ID: 172.16.10.1
    Topology : 0 (base)
      Active Timer: 3 min
      Distance: internal 90 external 170
      Maximum path: 4
      Maximum hopcount 100
      Maximum metric variance 1

  Automatic Summarization: disabled
  Maximum path: 4
  Routing for Networks:
    10.0.0.0
    172.16.0.0
```

```
  Routing Information Sources:
    Gateway          Distance      Last Update
    10.0.0.2               90      00:00:12
    10.0.0.6               90      00:00:12
    172.16.10.10           90      00:00:05
  Distance: internal 90 external 170
```

EXAMPLE 16.8 **show ip eigrp interfaces Command Output**

```
R1#show ip eigrp interfaces
EIGRP-IPv4 Interfaces for AS(1)
                     Xmit Queue   Mean   Pacing Time  Multicast   Pending
Interface    Peers  Un/Reliable  SRTT   Un/Reliable  Flow Timer  Routes
Se1/2          1        0/0       105       0/15         471          0
Se1/3          1        0/0       101       0/15         443          0
Gi2/0          1        0/0        60       0/1          240          0
```

EXAMPLE 16.9 **show ip eigrp neighbors Command Output**

```
R1#show ip eigrp neighbors
EIGRP-IPv4 Neighbors for AS(1)
H   Address             Interface        Hold Uptime    SRTT    RTO  Q   Seq
                                         (sec)          (ms)         Cnt Num
2   172.16.10.10        Gi2/0              13 00:02:35    60    360  0   4
1   10.0.0.6            Se1/3              12 00:02:40   101    606  0   14
0   10.0.0.2            Se1/2              12 00:02:40   105    630  0   13
```

EXAMPLE 16.10 **show ip route eigrp Command Output**

```
R1#show ip route eigrp
Codes: L - local, C - connected, S - static, R - RIP, M - mobile, B - BGP
       D - EIGRP, EX - EIGRP external, O - OSPF, IA - OSPF inter area
       N1 - OSPF NSSA external type 1, N2 - OSPF NSSA external type 2
       E1 - OSPF external type 1, E2 - OSPF external type 2
       i - IS-IS, su - IS-IS summary, L1 - IS-IS level-1, L2 - IS-IS level-2
       ia - IS-IS inter area, * - candidate default, U - per-user static route
       o - ODR, P - periodic downloaded static route, + - replicated route

Gateway of last resort is 10.0.0.2 to network 0.0.0.0

      10.0.0.0/8 is variably subnetted, 5 subnets, 2 masks
D        10.0.0.8/30 [90/2681856] via 10.0.0.6, 00:03:15, Serial1/3
                     [90/2681856] via 10.0.0.2, 00:03:15, Serial1/2
      172.16.0.0/16 is variably subnetted, 4 subnets, 2 masks
D        172.16.20.0/24 [90/2170112] via 10.0.0.2, 00:03:13, Serial1/2
D        172.16.30.0/24 [90/2170112] via 10.0.0.6, 00:03:13, Serial1/3
```

Cram Quiz

1. You are looking for a specific route that should have been learned via EIGRP. What method can you use to see only EIGRP learned routes?

   ❍ **A.** **show ip eigrp route**

   ❍ **B.** **show ip route eigrp**

   ❍ **C.** **show ip route**

   ❍ **D.** **show ip route | eigrp**

2. How do you verify which EIGRP neighbors a router has?

   ❍ **A.** **show running-config**

   ❍ **B.** **show ip eigrp interface**

   ❍ **C.** **show ip eigrp neighbor**

   ❍ **D.** **show ip eigrp database**

Cram Quiz Answers

1. Answer B is correct. **show ip route eigrp** will show just the routes learned via EIGRP.
2. Answer C is correct. **show ip eigrp neighbor** will show the current EIGRP neighbors.

Troubleshoot and Resolve Inter-VLAN Routing Problems

CramSaver

If you can correctly answer these questions before going through this section, save time by skimming the Exam Alerts in this section and then completing the Cram Quiz at the end of the section.

1. Which type of interface is used on a router to support router on a stick?
2. How would a switch port be configured to support a router that is supporting multiple VLANs on a single interface?

Answers

1. The router would use a subinterface, one for each of the VLANs that it is supporting.
2. The switch port that connects to the router would need to be configured as a trunk port.

Routing between VLANs, which is really just routing between different subnets or networks, can be done several different ways. An external router can be used with multiple interfaces, each connected to a switch port that is assigned to the respective VLAN that interface belongs to. To reduce the number of physical interfaces required on both the router and the switch, you could use a single interface connected to a switch port and have that switch port configured as a trunk. This is often referred to as a *router on a stick*. On the router side, you would use subinterfaces, with each subinterface configured to support a specific VLAN. Each subinterface would be configured with an appropriate IP address for the subnet with which the subinterface is associated.

In troubleshooting this setup, you want to ensure that Layers 1 and 2 are functioning, that the switchport is configured for trunking, and that the router subinterfaces are correctly configured. On the switch to verify the port configuration, you could issue the **show interface** *mod/port* **switchport** command; that would display the details regarding how that port is administratively configured and, more important, how it's operationally functioning. You could also issue the **show interface trunk** command on the switch to verify that trunking is operational and that the VLANs required by the router are being forwarded on that trunk link. On a router that is configured to support multiple VLANs on a single interface, you could use the **show vlans** command to display the details about the subinterfaces involved, the VLAN supported, and the IP address configured on that subinterface.

If the router is becoming a neighbor with other routers, it can learn additional routes through a neighbor relationship with another router that is running a routing protocol. Troubleshooting EIGRP or OSPF has been addressed earlier in this chapter. The clients on each of the VLANs should be configured either statically or through DHCP to use a local router as their default gateway. Any one of these not working could cause a problem with inter-VLAN routing.

Another way to perform inter-VLAN routing is to use a multilayer switch, which is common in today's high-speed networks. In this case, you want to verify that IP routing is enabled on the multilayer switch, verify that each VLAN is supported by at least one switch virtual interface (a VLAN interface), and that the clients are using that switch virtual interface as a default gateway.

Cram Quiz

1. How many physical interfaces will a router use when supporting three VLANs using router on a stick?

   ❍ **A.** 1

   ❍ **B.** 2

   ❍ **C.** 3

   ❍ **D.** 4

2. What should the switch port be configured as when supporting an external router on a stick?

   ❍ **A.** Access port

   ❍ **B.** Trunk

   ❍ **C.** Layer 3

   ❍ **D.** Administratively shut down

Cram Quiz Answers

1. Answer A is correct. Only 1 physical interface is required when doing router on a stick. Logical sub interfaces are created to support multiple VLANs.
2. Answer B is correct. The switch port to support an external router doing router on a stick should be configured as a trunk port.

Troubleshoot and Resolve WAN Implementation Issues

CramSaver

If you can correctly answer these questions before going through this section, save time by skimming the Exam Alerts in this section and then completing the Cram Quiz at the end of the section.

1. If router 1 is using PPP at the headquarters location, what is the appropriate branch site encapsulation for the wide-area network link?
2. What command enables you to verify the type of serial cable connected and to identify whether clocking signals are present?

Answers

1. If router 1 is using PPP, the branch side should be PPP. The routers of both ends of a point-to-point connection could use either PPP or HDLC, but it needs to match at both ends.
2. You can use the **show controllers** command to validate the type of cable as well as to indicate whether clocking signals are present.

The same problems that can come up between two routers over an Ethernet network can also happen between two routers connected over a WAN connection, plus there is additional configuration above and beyond what Ethernet has that could cause it to fail.

The encapsulation of High-Level Data Link Control (HDLC) is the default on WAN serial interfaces. If either of the two peers in a point-to-point connection aren't using the same encapsulation type, there will be loss of connectivity at Layer 2, between them. Options for Layer 2 encapsulation of a leased line include HDLC and PPP. In Frame Relay, you want all the routers connected to the Frame Relay network to use the Frame Relay encapsulation method.

The command **show interface** *type mod/port* can reveal the status of the interface, in addition to the encapsulation being used.

Example 16.11 shows that status of a WAN link as up/down, implying that Layer 1 is okay but Layer 2 is not. This is due to the local router using PPP and the remote router using a Layer 2 encapsulation protocol of HDLC.

EXAMPLE 16.11 **Verifying WAN Link Status**

```
R1#show int ser1/2
Serial1/2 is up, line protocol is down
  Internet address is 10.0.0.1/30
  MTU 1500 bytes, BW 1544 Kbit/sec, DLY 20000 usec,
     reliability 255/255, txload 1/255, rxload 1/255
  Encapsulation PPP, LCP REQsent, crc 16, loopback not set
  Keepalive set (10 sec)
  Restart-Delay is 0 secs
  Last input 00:00:00, output 00:00:00, output hang never
  Last clearing of "show interface" counters 00:03:18
  Input queue: 0/75/0/0 (size/max/drops/flushes); Total output drops: 0
  Queueing strategy: weighted fair
  Output queue: 0/1000/64/0 (size/max total/threshold/drops)
     Conversations  0/1/256 (active/max active/max total)
     Reserved Conversations 0/0 (allocated/max allocated)
     Available Bandwidth 1158 kilobits/sec
  5 minute input rate 0 bits/sec, 0 packets/sec
  5 minute output rate 0 bits/sec, 0 packets/sec
     27 packets input, 1203 bytes, 0 no buffer
     Received 0 broadcasts, 0 runts, 0 giants, 0 throttles
     0 input errors, 0 CRC, 0 frame, 0 overrun, 0 ignored, 0 abort
     93 packets output, 1302 bytes, 0 underruns
     0 output errors, 0 collisions, 9 interface resets
     27 unknown protocol drops
     0 output buffer failures, 0 output buffers swapped out
     9 carrier transitions     DCD=up  DSR=up  DTR=up  RTS=up  CTS=up
```

In a Frame Relay network, you would want to verify that the mappings of L3 addresses to L2 addresses (the data-link connection identifier [DLCI] to use) are correct. You can verify this with the **show frame-relay map** command. The mapping should reflect the local DLCI (which identifies the local end of a single PVC) that should be used to send frames to the remote devices IP address as shown in Example 16.12.

EXAMPLE 16.12 **Verifying L3 to L2 Address Mappings**

```
R1#show frame map
Serial1/0.123 (up): ip 10.0.0.2 dlci 102(0x66,0x1860), static,
              broadcast,
              CISCO, status defined, active
Serial1/0.123 (up): ip 10.0.0.3 dlci 103(0x67,0x1870), static,
              broadcast,
              CISCO, status defined, active
```

Another challenge that could arise is the lack of a clocking signal on a serial interface. On traditional serial connections, the clocking is provided by the carrier (the service provider). In a lab environment, you might have a back-to-back serial connection without any real WAN service provider, and in this case you would need to add a **clock rate** command to the router that had the DCE side of the back to back serial connection. You can use the **show controllers** *type mod/port* command to verify the type of cable (including DCE versus DTE connection) and the presence or absence of clocking. In Example 16.13, the output reflects that there is a DTE V.35 cable connected and that clocking is being seen.

EXAMPLE 16.13 **Verifying That Clocking Is in Place**

```
Router#show controllers serial
MK5 unit 0, NIM slot 1, NIM type code 7, NIM version 1
idb = 0x6150, driver structure at 0x34A878, regaddr = 0x8100300
IB at 0x6045500: mode=0x0108, local_addr=0, remote_addr=0
N1=1524, N2=1, scaler=100, T1=1000, T3=2000, TP=1
buffer size 1524
DTE V.35 serial cable attached, clock present
RX ring with 32 entries at 0x45560 : RLEN=5, Rxhead 0
```

Cram Quiz

1. A router is using the default encapsulation at the HQ site for a point-to-point serial connection to a branch office. What is the correct encapsulation to use at the branch office on the serial interface?

   ❍ **A.** Frame Relay

   ❍ **B.** HDLC

   ❍ **C.** SDLC

   ❍ **D.** PPP

2. Three branch offices are connected to the central site using Frame Relay WAN connectivity. What is the relationship between the IP and the DLCI in the local Frame Relay mappings?

   ❍ **A.** The local DLCI is used, and the local IP is used.

   ❍ **B.** The remote DLCI is used, and the remote IP is used.

   ❍ **C.** The local DLCI is used, and the a remote IP is used.

   ❍ **D.** The remote DLCI is used, and the local IP is used.

Cram Quiz Answers

1. Answer B is correct. The default encapsulation on a Cisco router is HDLC for its serial WAN interfaces. As a result, the branch office should also use HDLC.
2. Answer C is correct. In a Frame Relay mapping, the local DLCI for a PVC is used and associated with the IP address of a remote device, which is reachable over that PVC.

Monitor NetFlow Statistics

Cram**Saver**

If you can correctly answer these questions before going through this section, save time by skimming the Exam Alerts in this section and then completing the Cram Quiz at the end of the section.

1. What command enables you to validate the IP address of the NetFlow collector?
2. What command enables you to see a summary of NetFlow accounting statistics on the local router?

Answers

1. The **show ip flow export** command provides the status and statistics about NetFlow data export, including the IP address of the NetFlow collector.
2. To display a summary of NetFlow accounting statistics on the router, you can issue the command **show ip cache flow**.

NetFlow is a terrific application for providing details about packet flows to the network. For example, if you are having some type of congestion issue at some point in your network, it might be difficult to clearly identify which source and destination traffic going through that part of the network is causing the congestion. You could use NetFlow to collect the information about the source IP addresses, the destination IP addresses, the port numbers involved, and more. The information provided by NetFlow could then be used to identifying exactly what traffic is on the network at the time of congestion. Based on that, you can take further steps to either increase the throughput by using EtherChannel or perhaps implementing quality of service (QoS) so that latency-sensitive traffic is prioritized through the network.

If NetFlow is not configured properly, of course, you cannot collect the data from NetFlow. To verify that an interface has been configured for NetFlow, you can use the **show ip interface** and **show ip cache flow** commands to get information about NetFlow.

If it turns out that NetFlow is enabled on the interfaces, it is possible that the NetFlow information is not being correctly exported. To verify NetFlow destinations, you can use the **show ip flow export** command. The output from this command will also provide you with information about NetFlow data export, including the IP address of the NetFlow collector to which you are (or should be) sending data.

To display a summary of NetFlow accounting statistics on the router, you can issue the **show IP cache flow** command.

Cram Quiz

1. How do you verify that you are sending NetFlow data to the correct IP address of a NetFlow collector?

   ❍ **A. show ip interface**

   ❍ **B. show ip flow export**

   ❍ **C. show ip cache flow**

   ❍ **D. show ip flow cache**

2. You have verified that the correct NetFlow export IP address is being used but want to verify you have connectivity to the server. Which command could you use for that? Choose all that apply.

   ❍ **A. netflow check**

   ❍ **B. ping**

   ❍ **C. traceroute**

   ❍ **D. test netflow**

Cram Quiz Answers

1. Answer B is correct. The **show ip flow export** command enables you to verify the IP address to which you are sending NetFlow information.
2. Answers B and C are correct. You could use the **traceroute** or **ping** commands to validate IP connectivity to the server to which you are sending NetFlow information.

Troubleshoot EtherChannel Problems

CramSaver

If you can correctly answer these questions before going through this section, save time by skimming the Exam Alerts in this section and then completing the Cram Quiz at the end of the section.

1. What command enables you to display a single one line summary per channel group?
2 What command enables you to display specific information about a port channel interface, its status, the protocols used, and which interfaces were included in the port channel, along with the age of the channel?

Answers

1. The **show etherchannel summary** command provides a one-line summary per channel group.
2. The **show etherchannel port-channel** command could be used to display specific information about a port channel interface, about its status, the protocols used, and which interfaces were included in the port channel, along with the age of the channel.

The typical problems with EtherChannel are that the two sides don't agree on the following configured parameters, which should match:

- Speed and duplex of the interfaces on both sides.
- Same VLAN membership or same trunk configuration on both sides.
- Protocol for EtherChannel needs to match, such as LACP or PAgP, or both set to On.

If you change the parameters, make sure that you make the identical changes to both switches on each end of the EtherChannel. Making changes to individual ports that are part of a channel, making them different from other ports in the same EtherChannel, will cause problems. Changes after the EtherChannel is in place should be done on the logical port channel interface, which allows the changes to be inherited by the physical ports involved. For a new EtherChannel, a best practice is to default the interfaces in the range, shut down those same interfaces, apply all the configurations (in range mode for the ports, to confirm the exact same configurations), and after all configuration commands have been applied, on *both* switches, then do a **no shutdown** for the ranges of port on both switches.

The commands **show etherchannel summary** and **show etherchannel port-channel** are the two primary commands to verify that the EtherChannel is working, as demonstrated in Example 16.14 and Example 16.15.

EXAMPLE 16.14 **show etherchannel summary Command Output**

```
SW-1#show etherchannel summary
Flags:  D - down        P - bundled in port-channel
        I - stand-alone s - suspended
        H - Hot-standby (LACP only)
        R - Layer3      S - Layer2
        U - in use      f - failed to allocate aggregator

        M - not in use, minimum links not met
        u - unsuitable for bundling
        w - waiting to be aggregated
        d - default port


Number of channel-groups in use: 1
Number of aggregators:           1

Group  Port-channel  Protocol    Ports
------+-------------+-----------+-----------------------------------
-----------
1      Po1(SU)         LACP      Gi0/13(P)   Gi0/15(P)
```

EXAMPLE 16.15 **show etherchannel port-channel Command Output**

```
SW-1#show etherchannel port-channel
                Channel-group listing:
                ----------------------


Group: 1
----------
                Port-channels in the group:
                ---------------------------


Port-channel: Po1    (Primary Aggregator)

------------

Age of the Port-channel   = 0d:00h:00m:34s
Logical slot/port   = 2/1          Number of ports = 2
```

```
HotStandBy port = null
Port state            = Port-channel Ag-Inuse
Protocol              =    LACP
Port security         = Disabled

Ports in the Port-channel:

Index    Load    Port      EC state         No of bits
------+------+------+-----------------+-----------
  0       00      Gi0/13    Active              0
  0       00      Gi0/15    Active              0

Time since last port bundled:     0d:00h:00m:26s    Gi0/15
```

If ports are missing from an EtherChannel, it may be due to a configuration error, which should be corrected. For an EtherChannel that is not functioning, ports in err-disable or other nonforwarding states may be the reason. Performing an interface range **shutdown**, followed by a **no shutdown** on the ports in the range, on both switches (presuming the configuration is correct), will clear any err-disabled interfaces and allow the EtherChannel to renegotiate and come up. STP will see the bundle as a single logical port and can allow forwarding when the STP has converged. For the 802.1D, that may take up to 30 seconds. For Rapid Spanning Tree (802.1w), it may take only a few seconds.

Cram Quiz

1. Where should changes to an existing EtherChannel be made?

   ❍ **A.** On the individual ports belonging to the EtherChannel.

   ❍ **B.** On the logical EtherChannel interface.

   ❍ **C.** They can't. The existing EtherChannel must be taken down and re-created with the new parameters.

   ❍ **D.** Changes should be made within STP.

2. What command shows the interfaces actively involved in a functioning EtherChannel?

   ❍ **A.** **show run**

   ❍ **B.** **show etherchannel summary**

   ❍ **C.** **show interface**

   ❍ **D.** **show etherchannel port-channel**

Cram Quiz Answers

1. Answer B is correct. Changes to an existing EtherChannel should be done to the logical interface, instead of changing all the physical interfaces that make up the EtherChannel.
2. Answers B and D are correct. Both the **show etherchannel summary** and the **show etherchannel port-channel** commands show the interfaces in an active EtherChannel.

Review Questions

Answer these questions. The answers follow the last question. If you cannot answer these questions correctly, consider reading this chapter again until you can.

1. What is the most likely reason for a Layer 2 loop?
   - ❍ **A.** The TTL is too large.
   - ❍ **B.** STP is disabled.
   - ❍ **C.** A routing protocol has failed.
   - ❍ **D.** Too many broadcasts on the network.

2. Two OSPF routers, R1 and R2, have become neighbors. R1 is not seeing all of R2's routes. What is the most likely cause of this?
   - ❍ **A.** An interface is not configured for OSPF on R1.
   - ❍ **B.** OSPF is not enabled on R1.
   - ❍ **C.** An interface is not configured for OSPF on R2.
   - ❍ **D.** The timers do not match between the two routers.

3. An OSPF neighbor relationship is not forming. Which of the following could cause the problem? Choose two.
   - ❍ **A.** A different area between the routers.
   - ❍ **B.** The process ID being different on the two routers.
   - ❍ **C.** A timer mismatch between the routers.
   - ❍ **D.** The autonomous system number differs on the two routers.

4. A Windows client computer is trying to reach the IP address of the remote host. The connection attempt is unsuccessful. Which tool could be used from the client to assist in identifying where in the path the packet is failing?
   - ❍ **A.** **ifconfig**
   - ❍ **B.** **ping**
   - ❍ **C.** **tracert**
   - ❍ **D.** **ipconfig**

5. Which of the following is used by a router to determine the best path to a given network?
   - ❍ **A.** The route with the longest network match in its routing table
   - ❍ **B.** The route with the lowest administrative distance
   - ❍ **C.** The route with the lowest metric or cost
   - ❍ **D.** The route with the highest administrative distance

6. What command in subinterface configuration mode identifies which VLAN the subinterface is going to be supporting?
   - ❍ **A.** **interface**
   - ❍ **B.** **ip address**
   - ❍ **C.** **duplex**
   - ❍ **D.** **encapsulation**

7. Two routers running EIGRP are not becoming neighbors. EIGRP is configured on both routers. Which of the following reasons would prevent the neighbor relationship? Choose two.
   - ❍ **A.** Different router IDs
   - ❍ **B.** Mismatched EIGRP autonomous system numbers
   - ❍ **C.** Different router names
   - ❍ **D.** Different K values

8. Which of the following would prevent two routers connected over a WAN leased line to fail due to a Layer 2 issue?
   - ❍ **A.** Using the incorrect TCP port.
   - ❍ **B.** Running the incorrect routing protocol.
   - ❍ **C.** Mismatched encapsulation.
   - ❍ **D.** Being in the incorrect subnet.

9. What could be used to identify the source of congestion at a specific point in the network?
   - ❍ **A.** Access control list logs
   - ❍ **B.** Syslog messages
   - ❍ **C.** NetFlow
   - ❍ **D.** **show interface** commands

10. What command can be used to verify which interfaces are used and currently working as part of an EtherChannel?
   - ❍ **A.** **show ip interface**
   - ❍ **B.** **show etherchannel summary**
   - ❍ **C.** **show channel summary**
   - ❍ **D.** **show portchannel summary**

Answers to Review Questions

1. Answer B is correct. The most likely reason for a Layer 2 loop is that spanning tree has been disabled. There is no TTL (Time To Live) mechanism used at Layer 2, and a routing protocol would have no impact on a Layer 2 loop. During a Layer 2 loop, a single broadcast is escalated into a broadcast storm as a result of that loop.
2. Answer C is correct. If two OSPF routers become neighbors, and a route is missing, it is likely because the other router (in this case, R2) does not have that interface (connected to the missing network) enabled for OSPF, which is preventing the advertisement of that network. If OSPF was not enabled on one of the routers, there would be no neighbor relationship to begin with. If the timers did not match between the two routers, they would not have formed a neighbor relationship to begin with.
3. Answers A and C are correct. If the connection between two OSPF routers is not being assigned the same area by both routers, those routers will not form a neighbor relationship. A timer mismatch on the interface between the two routers would also prevent a neighbor relationship. The process ID does not have to match between the two routers, and OSPF does not use an autonomous system number (like EIGRP does).
4. Answer C is correct. A Windows client trying to validate the path to a given destination can use the command **tracert**. **ifconfig** is used on a Macintosh or Linux platform to see what the IP address is. On Windows, **ipconfig** us used to see the configured IP address. The **ping** command doesn't, by default, record the path between the source and destination.
5. Answer A is correct. A router will choose the route with the longest match from the routing table when making a forwarding decision. If there are multiple identical routes, administrative distance is used (lowest being preferred), and in the case of multiple identical routes, the route with the best (lowest) metric/cost is chosen.
6. Answer D is correct. The **encapsulation** command is used to indicate which VLAN the subinterface will be servicing. Although the IP address used on the subinterface should be compatible with the other IP addresses in that same VLAN, the IP address itself is not what causes the dot1q tags to be looked at. Duplex is a physical layer characteristic.
7. Answers B and D are correct. To be neighbors, two routers running EIGRP must have identical autonomous system numbers, and they must also have matching K values.
8. Answer C is correct. WANs over a leased line must have compatible/matching encapsulation at each end. Encapsulation is a Layer 2 issue, as mentioned in the question. Subnets, TCP ports, and routing protocols all operate at higher levels of the protocol stack.
9. Answer C is correct. NetFlow can provide detailed traffic patterns which can assist in identifying the source of traffic that may be causing congestion. NetFlow also provides additional details such as the destination addresses and the protocols in use. Access control list logs, syslog messages, and **show interface** commands would not provide the same level of detail as NetFlow.

10. Answer B is correct. The **show etherchannel summary** command enables you to verify which interfaces are participating in an EtherChannel. The other commands listed as options to this question are either invalid syntax or would not display the same information about the EtherChannel.

Practice Exam 1

If you are reading this, you likely feel ready to tackle the CCNA exam and need to assess your skills to see whether you can spot any weaknesses. As you take this practice exam, the authors recommend the following test-taking tips:

- **Read each question twice:** There is a big difference between reading a question that you think reads, "Which of the following are true," but really reads, "Which of the following are not true." Be sure to read each question carefully so that you can fully understand the question.
- **Read the answers starting from the bottom:** When you read the answers from the bottom, you force yourself to carefully read each answer. If you read the answers from the top, you might find yourself quickly selecting an answer that looks vaguely right and skipping over the other answers that might have been a better answer.
- **Time yourself:** The CCNA exam is a 90-minute exam. Time yourself during this practice exam to make sure that you stay within this time limit.
- **If you do not know the answer to a question, make a note of it:** Go back and review any trouble areas later. You should be interested not only in finding the answer to the question, but also in mastering that particular topic in its entirety. If you are unsure about one aspect of a topic, chances are you might be unsure about other areas related to that same topic.
- **Mentally get yourself in the frame of mind to take a test:** To properly assess yourself, take this practice exam as you would take the real exam. This means that you should find yourself a quiet place without any distractions so that you can focus on each question. (Yes, that includes turning off the television.) You can have some scratch paper to write on, but calculators are not allowed on the real exam, so do not use them on the practice exam.

- **If you cannot determine the correct answers, begin eliminating the incorrect answers:** If there are four options and you know that three are absolutely wrong, the fourth option has to be the correct one.
- **Continue taking this practice exam until you get a perfect score:** When you can consistently score high on these practice exams, you are ready to take the real exam.
- **Don't despair:** Should you not do so well on the practice exam, do not worry. It only means that you need to continue studying. Be glad that you are able to spot your weak areas now and not after taking the real exam. Go back through and review your problem areas.

We wish you the best of luck in your pursuit of the coveted CCNA certification.

1. A branch office has ordered a leased line for Internet connectivity. The service provider is providing the WAN circuit only (no switch). The branch office has 25 users connected to an Ethernet Layer 2 switch. You have been asked to assist them in getting connected to the Internet through the leased line. Which of the following would be needed for this connectivity?

   ❍ **A.** An adapter to connect an existing Ethernet port on their switch to the leased line
   ❍ **B.** A new Layer 2 switch with a crossover cable
   ❍ **C.** A router with two Ethernet interface
   ❍ **D.** A router with two serial interfaces with the correct cables
   ❍ **E.** A router with one Ethernet interface and one serial interface with the correct cables

2. A user at a computer is accessing a web server on the Internet. Which of the following from the TCP/IP protocol suite would be used at the application layer?

   ❍ **A.** SMTP
   ❍ **B.** TCP
   ❍ **C.** IP
   ❍ **D.** UDP
   ❍ **E.** HTTP

3. When a computer is making a DNS request, what protocol is being used at OSI Layer 3?

   ❍ **A.** TCP
   ❍ **B.** UDP
   ❍ **C.** IP
   ❍ **D.** DNS
   ❍ **E.** Ethernet

4. Which of the following is an application layer service that allows the reliable sending and receiving of files?

   ❍ **A.** DNS
   ❍ **B.** DHCP
   ❍ **C.** Telnet
   ❍ **D.** NTP
   ❍ **E.** TFTP
   ❍ **F.** FTP

5. You have been given the following networks:

   100.16.0.0

   100.17.0.0

   100.18.0.0

   100.19.0.0

   Which of the following would be the most accurate summary of these four networks?

   ❍ **A.** 10.16.0.0/13
   ❍ **B.** 10.16.0.0 255.252.0.0
   ❍ **C.** 10.16.0.0/15
   ❍ **D.** 10.16.0.0 255.240.0.0

6. Which subnet does the host 172.19.52.228/21 belong to?

   ❍ **A.** 172.19.32.0 /21
   ❍ **B.** 172.19.40.0 /21
   ❍ **C.** 172.19.48.0 /21
   ❍ **D.** 172.19.56.0 /21

7. What is the first valid host on the subnetwork that the node 10.30.139.178/23 belongs to?

   ❍ **A.** 10.30.136.1
   ❍ **B.** 10.30.138.1
   ❍ **C.** 10.30.140.1
   ❍ **D.** 10.30.142.1

8. What is the range of addresses for the subnet that host 10.26.15.95/23 is connected to?

   ❍ **A.** 10.26.14.1–10.26.15.254
   ❍ **B.** 10.26.12.1–10.26.13.254
   ❍ **C.** 10.26.16.1–10.26.17.254
   ❍ **D.** 10.26.18.1–10.26.19.254

9. What NetFlow functions are applied directly to an interface?

   ❍ **A.** NefFlow record
   ❍ **B.** NetFlow monitoring
   ❍ **C.** NetFlow export
   ❍ **D.** NetFlow importing

10. Consider the following network topology. CDP is enabled on all the devices that support it. Which CDP devices will Switch 2 see in the output of **show cdp neighbors**?

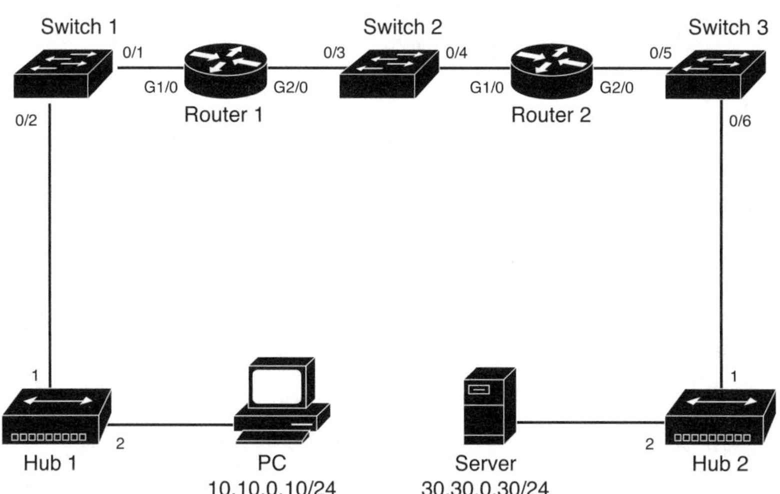

❍ **A.** Router 1 and Router 2 only.

❍ **B.** Switch 1, Router 1, Router 2 and Switch 3.

❍ **C.** Switch 1, Router 1, Router 2 and Switch 3, Hub 1 and Hub 2.

❍ **D.** Switch 1, Router 1, Router 2 and Switch 3, Hub 1, Hub 2 and the Server running Identity Services Engine (ISE).

❍ **E.** CDP runs on only routers, so the transparent switch would not show any neighbors.

11. Where is the startup config file stored?

❍ **A.** Flash

❍ **B.** NVRAM

❍ **C.** ROMmon

❍ **D.** Config register

12. You want to store the password to enter privileged mode, and have the system store it using MD5. Which command would do that?

❍ **A.** **enable password Cisco123**

❍ **B.** **enable secret Cisco123**

❍ **C.** **enable Cisco123 Secret**

❍ **D.** **service password-encryption**

13. What command triggers user authentication during an SSH session to a router?

❍ **A.** The generation of a RSA key pair

❍ **B.** The specification of a domain name

❍ **C.** **login local** at the vty lines

❍ **D.** Permitting the SSH protocol at the vty lines

14. An end user has connected another switch to his access port to allow more devices in his office to join the network. Which switch specific security measure could be implemented to prevent him overloading the network with multiple source MAC addresses?

❍ **A.** Access control lists

❍ **B.** BPDU filtering

❍ **C.** SSH

❍ **D.** Port security

15. Which three statements are true about Ethernet?

❍ **A.** Using full duplex, network devices do not have to wait to see if the media is available.

❍ **B.** Full duplex uses CSMA/CD.

❍ **C.** Hubs operate at half duplex.

❍ **D.** Only one side, either the switch or the host, needs to support full duplex for it to work.

❍ **E.** A dedicated switch port is needed for each full-duplex device.

16. Consider the following network topology. The PC is sending several ping requests to the server and is getting replies. Which of the devices shown in the topology will use only the destination address in the Layer 2 header to make a forwarding decision for the third pint request sent?

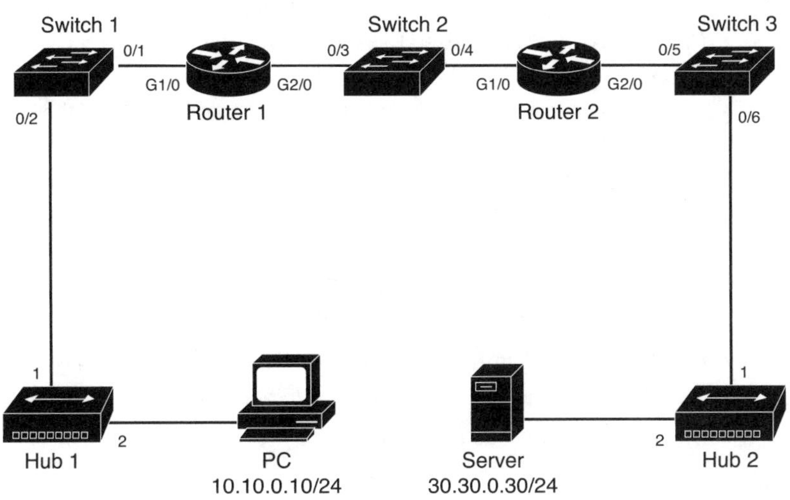

- ❍ **A.** All the hubs
- ❍ **B.** All the switches
- ❍ **C.** Only Switch 3 (the last switch in the path)
- ❍ **D.** The PC
- ❍ **E.** The server

17. Customers on VLAN 3 want access to devices on VLAN 4. What is required for that access?

- ❍ **A.** Customers must be moved over to access ports in VLAN 4.
- ❍ **B.** They must use a router.
- ❍ **C.** An access list must be created.
- ❍ **D.** VLAN 3 devices can't access VLAN 4 devices, because it is a different logical network.

18. How does Switch 1, connected to Switch 2 using a trunk port, communicate which VLAN a frame is associated with?

- ❍ **A.** When sending a frame, the switch assumes the receiving switch will look at the destination IP address in the header and map that IP subnet to the corresponding destination VLAN.
- ❍ **B.** The native VLAN is used to send all user traffic, so the receiving switch always uses the VLAN ID of the native VLAN.
- ❍ **C.** ISL is used as an industry standard for tagging frames as they are sent down a trunk.
- ❍ **D.** When sending a frame, the switch adds an 802.1Q header, which includes the VLAN ID for the frame.

19. Which of the following is true about an access port?

- ❍ **A.** Uses the concept of a native VLAN
- ❍ **B.** Sends and receives 802.1Q tags for the VLAN is it is associated with
- ❍ **C.** Uses a crossover cable to connect to a router
- ❍ **D.** Carries traffic for a single VLAN

20. Consider the following network topology. R1 is routing a packet from the server at 172.16.30.32 the PC at 172.16.10.10. What does R1 do with a packet that it receives? (Choose 2.)

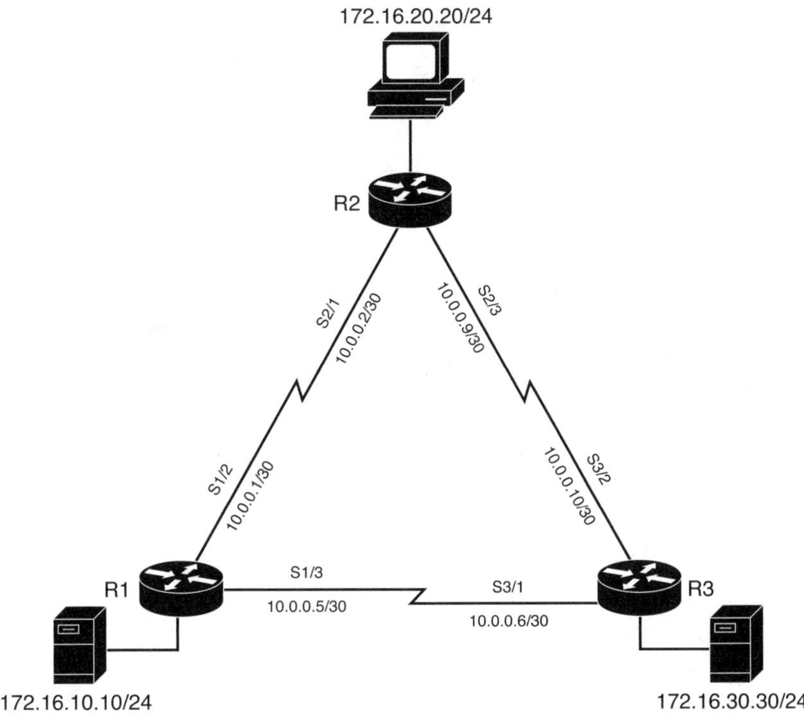

❍ **A.** Does a route lookup to determine which interface to send the packet

❍ **B.** Swaps out the source IP address with its own IP address

❍ **C.** Updates the outgoing frame with the original senders Layer 2 address

❍ **D.** Sends the packet out of the appropriate egress interface

21. What will the router use as an OSPF router ID when all options are present?

❍ **A.** Highest loopback address

❍ **B.** ID specified by the **router-id** command

❍ **C.** Highest IP address on a physical interface

❍ **D.** Serial number of the BIOS on the router

22. On a new router, you have brought up the interfaces and configured them as shown in the diagram. You are adding the following commands to the router:

```
Router(config)#router ospf 1
Router(config-router)#network 10.0.0.0 0.0.0.255 area 0
Router(config-router)#interface g1/0
```

When attempting to enter the next command

```
Router(config-if)#ipv6 ospf 1 area 0
```

You receive an error.

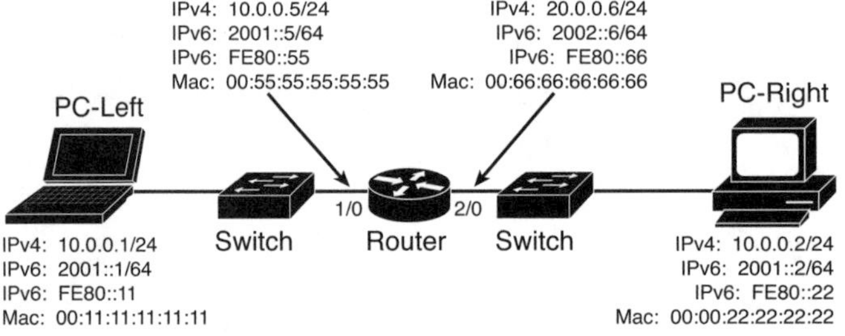

What should be added to the configuration?

- ❍ **A.** Enable unicast routing for IPv6.
- ❍ **B.** Add network statements to include interface 2/0.
- ❍ **C.** Configure a router ID in OSPFv2.
- ❍ **D.** Configure a router ID in OSPFv3.

23. Consider the following output:

```
Router#show ipv6 ospf int brief
Interface    PID   Area          Intf ID    Cost   State Nbrs F/C
Gi2/0        1     0             6          1      DOWN  0/0
Gi1/0        1     0             5          1      DR    0/0
```

Based on this output, which of the following is true?

❍ **A.** The interface Gi2/0 is shut down or not connected to the Ethernet network.

❍ **B.** OSPFv3 hasn't been enabled on Gi2/0.

❍ **C.** A network statement should be added to include Gi2/0 in OSPFv3.

❍ **D.** The router ID needs to be configured for IPv6 OSPFv3 to fully start.

❍ **E.** OSPFv3 has been enabled on Gi2/0, but there are no neighbors, so that is why it is in a DOWN state.

24. Consider the following diagram.

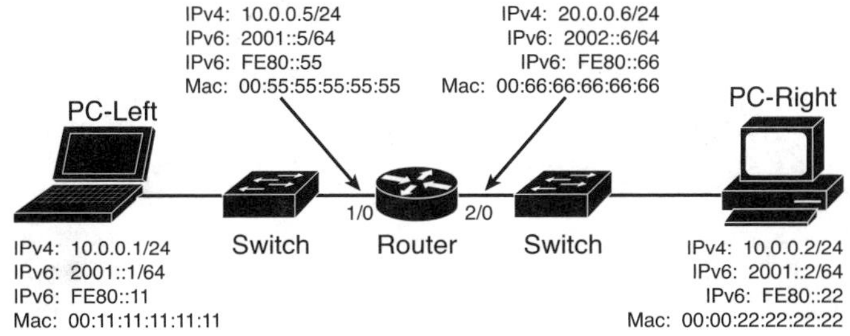

If the PC on the left sends a packet to the IP address of the PC on the right, what will be the physical source address in the frame when it reaches the destination PC?

❍ **A.** 10.0.0.1

❍ **B.** 10.0.0.5

❍ **C.** 20.0.0.6

❍ **D.** 00:11:11:11:11:11

❍ **E.** 00:55:55:55:55:55

❍ **F.** 00:66:66:66:66:66

25. Consider the following network topology. If the server connected to R3 is sending a reply to the PC connected to R1, what will the source IP address be when that packet exits R1?

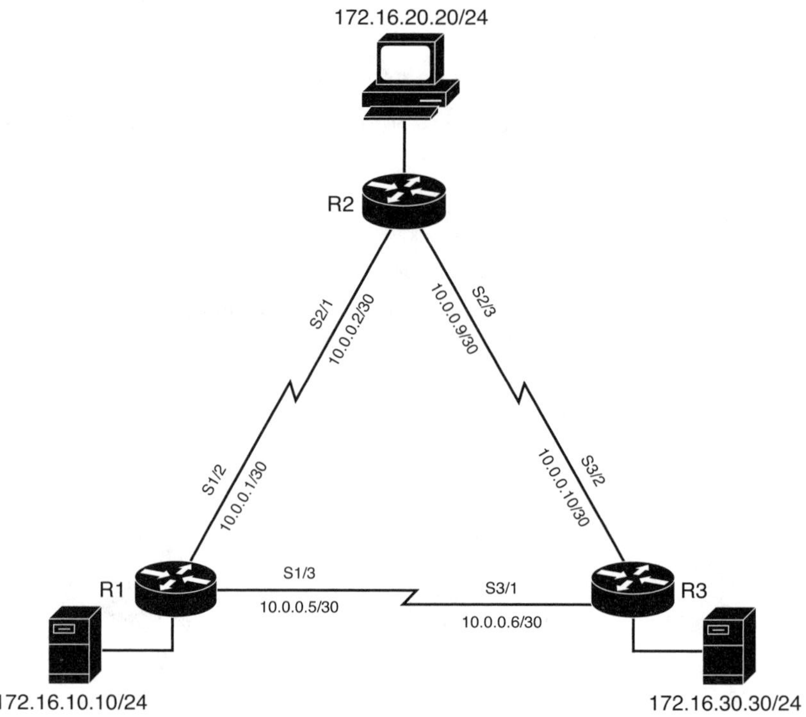

❍ **A.** 10.0.0.2

❍ **B.** 10.0.0.1

❍ **C.** 10.0.0.10

❍ **D.** 10.0.0.6

❍ **E.** 172.16.30.30

26. Consider the following diagram.

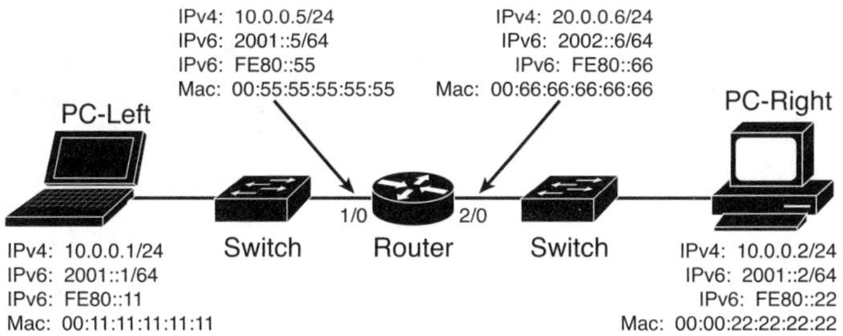

The computers are configured to use the router as their default gateway. If the PC on the left wanted to ping the PC on the right, and didn't have any ARP entries in its ARP cache, which IP address would the PC on the left ARP for before sending a packet to 20.0.0.2?

❍ **A.** 20.0.0.2

❍ **B.** 10.0.0.5

❍ **C.** fe08::55

❍ **D.** fe80::22

27. Which is true, as a general recommendation, about ACLs?

❍ **A.** Standard ACLs should be placed close to the destination.

❍ **B.** Named standard ACLs should be placed close to the source.

❍ **C.** Extended ACLs should be place close to the destination.

❍ **D.** Named extended ACLs should be place close to the destination.

28. Consider the following network topology.

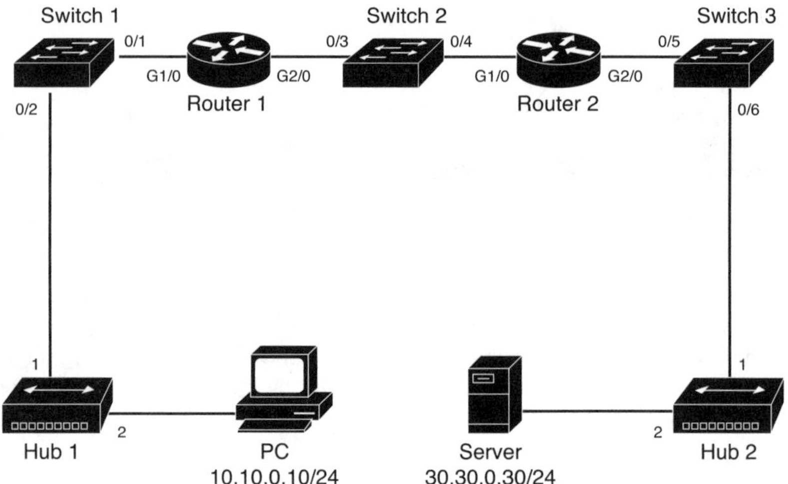

The PC has used a browser and is connected using HTTP to the web server at 30.30.0.30. Which ACL entry applied outbound on Router 2 G1/0 would match return traffic from the server to the PC?

- ❍ **A.** **access-list 100 permit tcp host 30.30.0.30 eq 80 10.0.0.0 0.255.255.255**
- ❍ **B.** **access-list 100 permit tcp host 30.30.0.30 10.0.0.0 0.255.255.255 eq 80**
- ❍ **C.** **access-list 100 permit tcp 30.30.0.0 0.0.255.255 eq 80 10.0.0.0 0.0.0.255**
- ❍ **D.** **access-list 100 permit tcp 30.0.0.0 0.0.0.255 10.0.0.0 0.255.255.255 eq 80**

29. Consider the diagram shown.

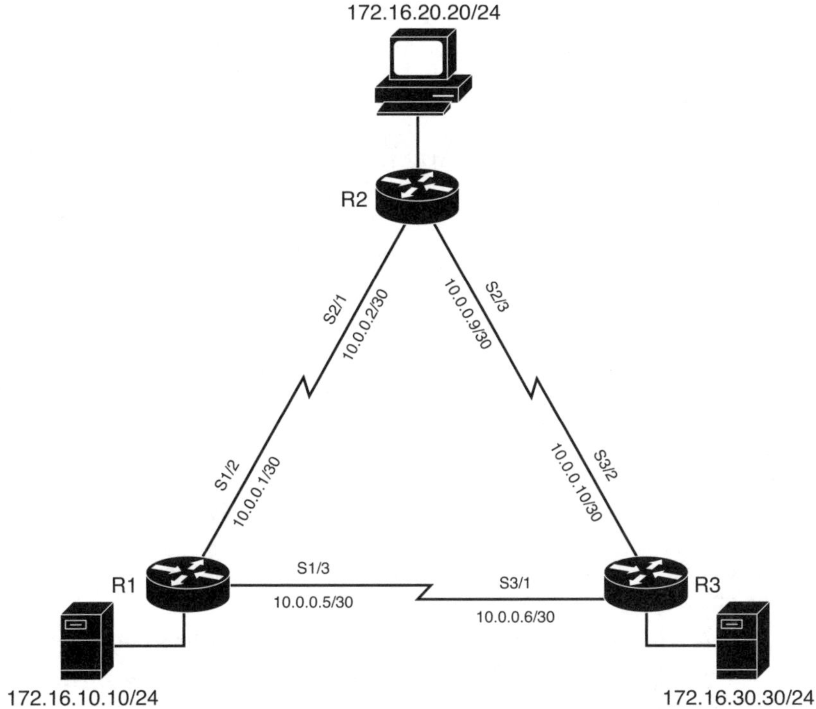

The link between R1 and R2 is 64Kbps, and the other two WAN links are 1.54Mbps. All interfaces are aware of the actual bandwidth on each of the links. OSPF is enabled on all routers and all interfaces. The computer connected to R1 sends a packet to 172.16.20.20. Which path will the packet take?

- ❍ **A.** R1 to R2 to 172.16.20.20.
- ❍ **B.** R1 to R3 to R2 to 172.16.20.20.
- ❍ **C.** The packet will loop back and forth between R1 and R3 until the TTL expires.
- ❍ **D.** A static route must be added because of the WAN link speed differences.

30. Review the topology diagram and the following partial output.

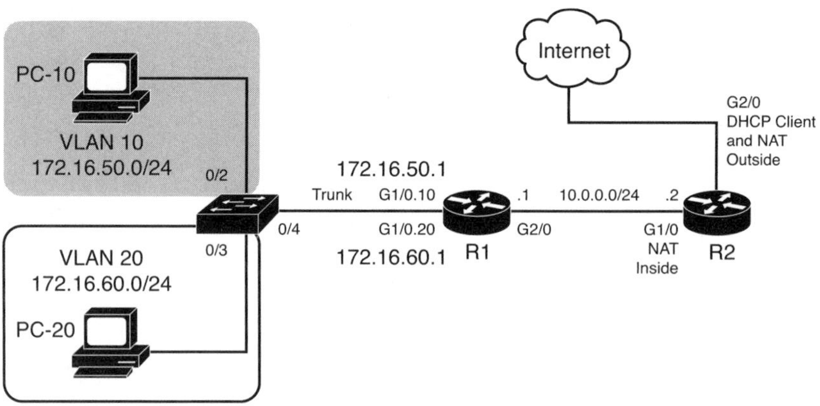


```
R2#show ip nat translations
Pro Inside global      Inside local       Outside local      Outside global
udp 23.15.1.28:123  172.16.50.3:123   65.55.56.206:123  65.55.56.206:123
```

Which of the following NAT commands could have been used that could result in the output shown? (Choose 2.)

- ❍ **A. ip nat inside source list 2 interface GigabitEthernet2/0 overload**
- ❍ **B. ip nat inside source list 1 interface GigabitEthernet2/0 overload**
- ❍ **C. access-list 2 permit 172.16.0.0 0.0.0.255**
- ❍ **D. ip nat inside source list 1 interface GigabitEthernet1/0 overload**
- ❍ **E. access-list 1 permit 172.16.0.0 0.0.255.255**
- ❍ **F. ip nat inside source list 2 interface GigabitEthernet1/0 overload**

31. What is the required interface configuration command for a router to be a DHCP client to receive both an IP address and default gateway (if provided) by a DHCP server?

- ❍ **A. ip address dhcp**
- ❍ **B. ip dhcp client**
- ❍ **C. ip dhcp pool-member**
- ❍ **D.** Nothing, if the interface comes up and not IP address is configured, the interface will automatically become a DHCP client and issue a DHCP discover packet.

32. You have set up a Cisco IOS router as a DHCP server. You are not sure whether static IP addresses are already in use on the network that may be in the range of the DHCP pool you intend to use. You use the pool anyway. How can you see details regarding duplicate addresses that the router tried to hand out?

- ❍ **A.** **show ip dhcp binding**
- ❍ **B.** **show ip dhcp server statistics**
- ❍ **C.** **show dhcp binding**
- ❍ **D.** **show dhcp server statistics**
- ❍ **E.** **show ip dhcp conflict**

33. Reviewthe partial output shown:

```
R1(config)#ntp server 204.2.134.163
R1(config)#do ping 204.2.134.163
Type escape sequence to abort.
Sending 5, 100-byte ICMP Echos to 204.2.134.163, timeout is 2 seconds:
!!!!!
Success rate is 100 percent (5/5), round-trip min/avg/max = 52/64/76 ms
```

How would you verify the time is synchronized to the time server?

- ❍ **A.** **show ntp status**
- ❍ **B.** **show clock**
- ❍ **C.** **show clock detail**
- ❍ **D.** **show ntp associations detail**

34. Consider the diagram and the partial output that follows.

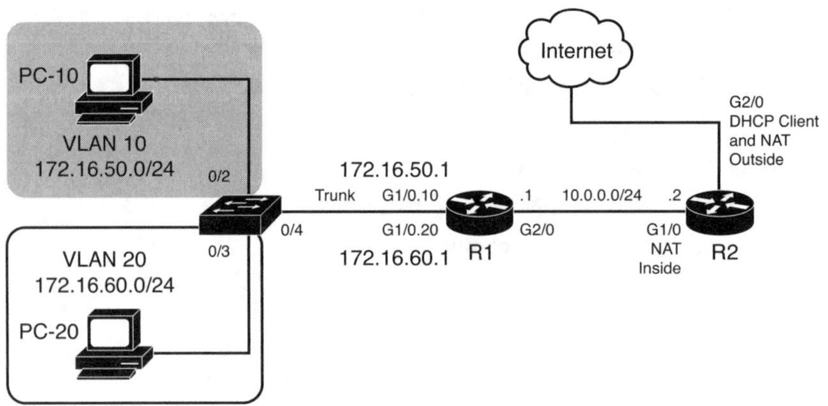


```
switch#show vlan brief
VLAN Name                             Status    Ports
---- -------------------------------- --------- -------------------------------
1    default                          active    Gi0/1, Gi0/5, Gi0/6
                                                Gi0/7, Gi0/8, Gi0/9,
                                                Gi0/11, Gi0/12, Gi0/13, Gi0/14
                                                Gi0/15, Gi0/16, Gi0/17, Gi0/18
10   VLAN0010                         active    Gi0/20
20   VLAN0020                         active    Gi0/3
55   VLAN0055                         active    Gi0/2
R1#show ip dhcp pool
Pool subnet50-pool :
 Utilization mark (high/low)    : 100 / 0
 Subnet size (first/next)       : 0 / 0
 Total addresses                : 254
 Leased addresses               : 0
 Pending event                  : none
 1 subnet is currently in the pool :
 Current index        IP address range                    Leased addresses
 172.16.50.1          172.16.50.1      - 172.16.50.254     0
Pool subnet60-pool :
 Utilization mark (high/low)    : 100 / 0
 Subnet size (first/next)       : 0 / 0
 Total addresses                : 254
 Leased addresses               : 0
 Pending event                  : none
 1 subnet is currently in the pool :
 Current index        IP address range                    Leased addresses
 172.16.60.1          172.16.60.1      - 172.16.60.254     1
R1#show run
<snip>
```

```
ip dhcp pool subnet50-pool
   network 172.16.50.0 255.255.255.0
   default-router 172.16.50.1
   dns-server 8.8.8.8
!
ip dhcp pool subnet60-pool
   network 172.16.60.0 255.255.255.0
   dns-server 8.8.8.8
   default-router 172.16.60.1
<snip>
```

The user at PC-10 is calling to say he can't connect to the Internet. PC-20 isn't having any problems. Based on the information provided, what is the problem?

❍ **A.** The incorrect DHCP pool is being used at the router.

❍ **B.** The incorrect default gateway is being handed out via DHCP.

❍ **C.** The physical connection between the router and the switch has failed.

❍ **D.** The PC is connected to the wrong VLAN.

❍ **E.** The incorrect DNS information is being handed out from the DHCP server.

35. Review the diagram and the partial output that follows.

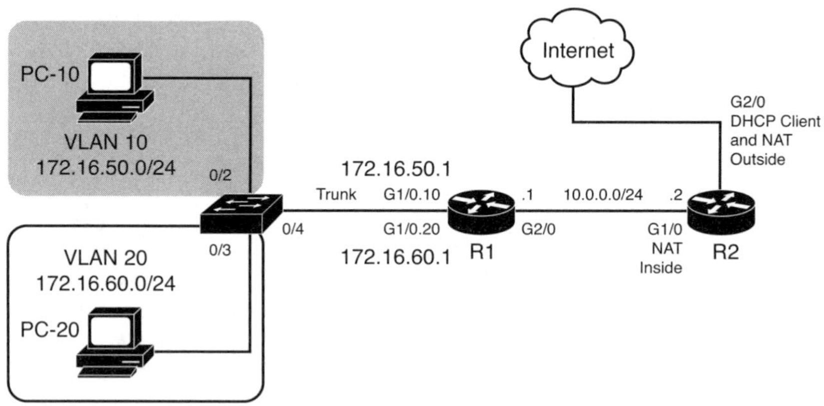


```
switch#show int trunk
Port        Mode             Encapsulation  Status        Native vlan
Gi0/5       desirable        802.1q         trunking      1
Port        Vlans allowed on trunk
Gi0/5       1-4094
Port        Vlans allowed and active in management domain
Gi0/5       1-5,10-12,20,55
Port        Vlans in spanning tree forwarding state and not pruned
Gi0/5       1-5,10-12,20,55
R1#show vlans
Virtual LAN ID:  1 (IEEE 802.1Q Encapsulation)
   vLAN Trunk Interface:   GigabitEthernet1/0
GigabitEthernet1/0
Virtual LAN ID:  10 (IEEE 802.1Q Encapsulation)
   vLAN Trunk Interface:   GigabitEthernet1/0.10
   Protocols Configured:   Address:          Received:    Transmitted:
           IP              172.16.50.1               0               0
       Other                                         0               0

Virtual LAN ID:  20 (IEEE 802.1Q Encapsulation)
   vLAN Trunk Interface:   GigabitEthernet1/0.20
   Protocols Configured:   Address:          Received:    Transmitted:
           IP              172.16.60.1               0               0
       Other                                         0               0
   0 packets, 0 bytes input
   0 packets, 0 bytes output
```

```
R1#show ip dhcp pool
Pool subnet50-pool :
 Utilization mark (high/low)    : 100 / 0
 Subnet size (first/next)       : 0 / 0
 Total addresses                : 254
 Leased addresses               : 0
 Pending event                  : none
 1 subnet is currently in the pool :
 Current index        IP address range                    Leased addresses
 172.16.50.1          172.16.50.1      - 172.16.50.254     0
Pool subnet60-pool :
 Utilization mark (high/low)    : 100 / 0
 Subnet size (first/next)       : 0 / 0
 Total addresses                : 254
 Leased addresses               : 0
 Pending event                  : none
 1 subnet is currently in the pool :
 Current index        IP address range                    Leased addresses
 172.16.60.1          172.16.60.1      - 172.16.60.254     0
```

Users in VLAN 10 are not able to browse the Internet. Based on the information provided, what is the cause?

❍ **A.** Switch interface g0/4 isn't trunking.

❍ **B.** DHCP services aren't configured on the router.

❍ **C.** The router hasn't configured sub-interfaces to support the VLANs.

❍ **D.** The IP addresses on the router's interfaces aren't correct.

36. Consider the topology and the following partial output.

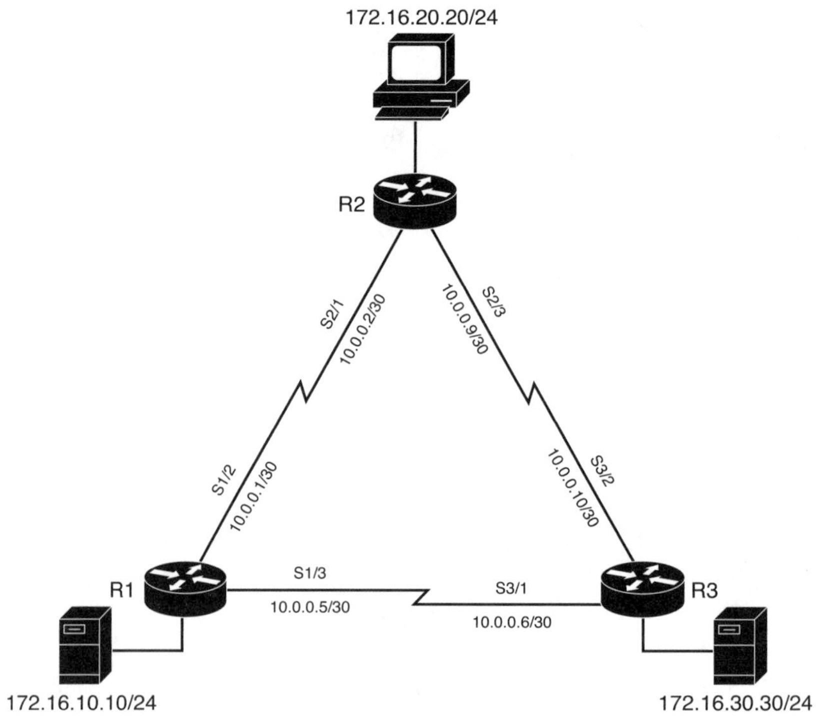


```
R1#show ip int brief
Interface                  IP-Address      OK? Method Status         Protocol
Serial1/2                  10.0.0.1        YES manual up             up
Serial1/3                  10.0.0.5        YES manual up             up
GigabitEthernet2/0         172.16.10.1     YES manual up             up
R1#show ip route
       10.0.0.0/8 is variably subnetted, 5 subnets, 2 masks
C         10.0.0.0/30 is directly connected, Serial1/2
L         10.0.0.1/32 is directly connected, Serial1/2
C         10.0.0.4/30 is directly connected, Serial1/3
L         10.0.0.5/32 is directly connected, Serial1/3
O         10.0.0.8/30 [110/128] via 10.0.0.6, 00:04:52, Serial1/3
                      [110/128] via 10.0.0.2, 00:06:46, Serial1/2
       172.16.0.0/16 is variably subnetted, 3 subnets, 2 masks
C         172.16.10.0/24 is directly connected, GigabitEthernet2/0
L         172.16.10.1/32 is directly connected, GigabitEthernet2/0
O           172.16.20.0/24 [110/65] via 10.0.0.2, 00:08:41, Serial1/2
```

```
R2#show ip int brief
Interface              IP-Address      OK? Method Status      Protocol
GigabitEthernet1/0     172.16.20.1     YES manual up          up
Serial2/1              10.0.0.2        YES manual up          up
Serial2/3              10.0.0.9        YES manual up          up
R2#show ip route
      10.0.0.0/8 is variably subnetted, 5 subnets, 2 masks
C        10.0.0.0/30 is directly connected, Serial2/1
L        10.0.0.2/32 is directly connected, Serial2/1
O        10.0.0.4/30 [110/128] via 10.0.0.10, 00:04:52, Serial2/3
                     [110/128] via 10.0.0.1, 00:08:40, Serial2/1
C        10.0.0.8/30 is directly connected, Serial2/3
L        10.0.0.9/32 is directly connected, Serial2/3
      172.16.0.0/16 is variably subnetted, 3 subnets, 2 masks
O        172.16.10.0/24 [110/65] via 10.0.0.1, 00:08:40, Serial2/1
C        172.16.20.0/24 is directly connected, GigabitEthernet1/0
L        172.16.20.1/32 is directly connected, GigabitEthernet1/0
R3#show ip int brief
Interface              IP-Address      OK? Method Status      Protocol
GigabitEthernet1/0     172.16.30.1     YES manual up          up
Serial3/1              10.0.0.6        YES manual up          up
Serial3/2              10.0.0.10       YES manual up          up
R3#show ip route
      10.0.0.0/8 is variably subnetted, 5 subnets, 2 masks
O        10.0.0.0/30 [110/128] via 10.0.0.9, 00:04:49, Serial3/2
                     [110/128] via 10.0.0.5, 00:04:49, Serial3/1
C        10.0.0.4/30 is directly connected, Serial3/1
L        10.0.0.6/32 is directly connected, Serial3/1
C        10.0.0.8/30 is directly connected, Serial3/2
L        10.0.0.10/32 is directly connected, Serial3/2
      172.16.0.0/16 is variably subnetted, 4 subnets, 2 masks
O        172.16.10.0/24 [110/65] via 10.0.0.5, 00:04:49, Serial3/1
O        172.16.20.0/24 [110/65] via 10.0.0.9, 00:04:49, Serial3/2
C        172.16.30.0/24 is directly connected, GigabitEthernet1/0
L        172.16.30.1/32 is directly connected, GigabitEthernet1/0
```

Users connected to R1 and R2 complain that the Server at 172.16.30.30 isn't reachable. Based on the output, what is causing the problem?

- ❍ **A.** R3 isn't including its interface connected to 172.16.30.0/24 in OSPF.
- ❍ **B.** R3 doesn't have routes back to the PC networks connected to R1 and R2.
- ❍ **C.** R3 hasn't formed OSPF neighbor relationships with R1 and R2.
- ❍ **D.** R3 serial interfaces are down.
- ❍ **E.** R3 has the wrong addresses on its serial interfaces.

37. Consider the following output:

```
SW4#show spanning-tree vlan 1
VLAN0001
  Spanning tree enabled protocol rstp
  Root ID     Priority     32769
              Address      1234.210E.47B3
              Cost         19
              Port         5(FastEthernet0/5)
              Hello Time   3 sec  Max Age 20 sec  Forward Delay 15 sec
  Bridge ID   Priority     32769  (priority 32768 sys-id-ext 1)
              Address      1234.210F.47B3
              Hello Time   3 sec  Max Age 20 sec  Forward Delay 15 sec
              Aging Time   20
Interface          Role Sts Cost       Prio.Nbr Type
---------------- ---- --- --------- -------- ------------------------
--------
Fa0/4              Altn BLK 19         128.4    P2p
Fa0/5              Root FWD 19         128.5    P2p
Fa0/3              Desg FWD 19         128.3    P2p
```

Which of the following are true?

- ❍ **A.** This switch has a lower bridge ID then the current root.
- ❍ **B.** This switch is the root bridge.
- ❍ **C.** This switch has a higher MAC address than the root bridge.
- ❍ **D.** The timers that are being learned from the root are the default timers for spanning tree.

38. Consider the diagram shown.

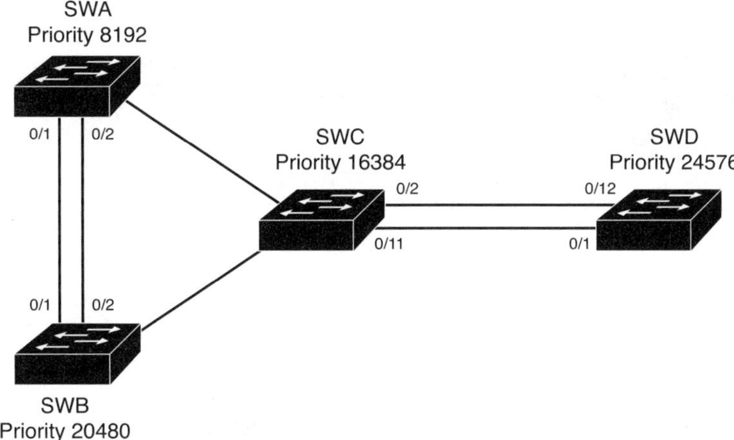

Regarding VLAN 1, the priorities have been set as shown in the diagram, and Rapid Spanning Tree has been enabled on all switches. All other spanning tree properties are using their default settings. Based on the information provided, which of the following are true? (Choose all that apply.)

- ❍ **A.** Switch A is discarding frames on 0/2.
- ❍ **B.** Switch B is discarding frames on 0/1.
- ❍ **C.** Switch C is discarding frames on 0/11.
- ❍ **D.** Switch C is discarding frames on 0/2.
- ❍ **E.** Switch D is discarding frames on 0/12.
- ❍ **F.** Switch D is discarding frames on 0/1.

39. Consider the following diagram.

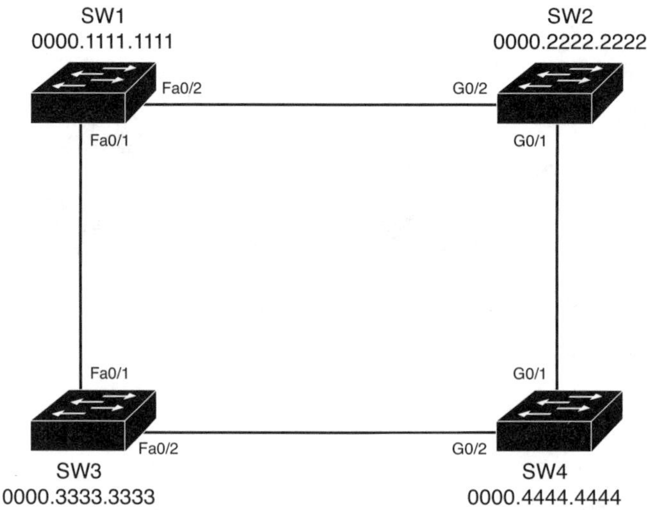

If switches are using the defaults for spanning tree, and the base MAC addresses are as shown in the topology, which port will perform the discarding/blocking function for VLAN 1?

❍ **A.** Switch 2, 0/1

❍ **B.** Switch 4, 0/1

❍ **C.** Switch 4, 0/2

❍ **D.** Switch 3, 0/2

40. Which of the following are accurate statements about the configuration and operation of VLANs? (Choose 2.)

❍ **A.** There is usually a one-to-one correlation between IP networks and VLANs.

❍ **B.** A Layer 2 switch is required to forward frames between two different VLANs.

❍ **C.** The switch builds a separate MAC address table for each VLAN.

❍ **D.** No ports are assigned to any VLANs until the VLANs are created and an administrator assigns ports.

41. Which type of Layer 2 ports should be configured between two switches that are supporting multiple VLANs?

❍ **A.** Access ports

❍ **B.** Trunk ports

❍ **C.** EtherChannel

❍ **D.** Routed ports

❍ **E.** None of these other answers

42. A data packet is being sent over a trunk link but does not include any VLAN tagging information. What would cause this? (Choose 2.)

❍ **A.** The trunk is misconfigured as an access port.

❍ **B.** The traffic being sent is belongs to the native VLAN for the trunk.

❍ **C.** The trunk is not operating at full duplex.

❍ **D.** The trunk is been configured to dynamically negotiate as desirable on both ends.

43. What is the result of creating more VLANs?

❍ **A.** The number of broadcast domains increases, while the size of each decreases.

❍ **B.** The number of broadcast domains decreases, while the size of each increases.

❍ **C.** The number of collision domains increases, while the size of each decreases.

❍ **D.** The number of collision domains decreases, while the size of each increases.

44. You have been asked to configure a multilayer switch to become a default router for multiple VLANs. Which items should be configured on the switch? (Choose all that apply).

❍ **A.** Configure the switch to be a DHCP client.

❍ **B.** Enable IP routing.

❍ **C.** Enable a default gateway for the switch.

❍ **D.** VLAN interfaces.

45. Consider the following output:

```
R1#show ip eigrp topology
IP-EIGRP Topology Table for AS 1
Codes: P - Passive, A - Active, U - Update, Q - Query, R - Reply,
       r - Reply status
<snip>
P 4.4.4.4/32, 1 successors, FD is 131072
         via 10.12.0.2 (131072/130816), GigabitEthernet0/0
         via 10.13.0.3 (2298112/130816), Serial0/0/0
```

What is the feasible distance regarding network 4.4.4.4/32 that would be seen on the router being used as a successor?

❍ **A.** 130816

❍ **B.** 131072

❍ **C.** 2298112

❍ **D.** Not enough information provided to know

46. Which of the following methods should be used to protect access to the vty lines on a Cisco router?

❍ **A.** Disable SSH, while permitting and enabling Telnet.

❍ **B.** Use access control lists on all Ethernet interfaces to control access to the vty lines.

❍ **C.** Apply an access control list to the vty lines using the **access-class** command.

❍ **D.** The vty lines should be disabled.

47. Which of the following is true about a router performing router on a stick? (Choose 2.)

❍ **A.** It can use a single physical interface.

❍ **B.** It must use multiple physical interfaces.

❍ **C.** The switch connecting to the router must be configured as an access port.

❍ **D.** The switch connecting to the router must be configured as a trunk port.

48. If two routers running OSPF are booted at the same time and are using the defaults, which of the following are true with regard to who will be the designated router?

❍ **A.** The router on a serial point-to-point interface that has the highest router ID.

❍ **B.** The router on a serial point-to-point interface that has the lowest router ID.

❍ **C.** The router on an Ethernet network that has the lowest router ID.

❍ **D.** The router on an Ethernet network that has the highest router ID.

49. Which of the following about routing protocols and their operations are true? (Choose 2.)

❍ **A.** Classful routing protocols send the mask along with the networks in advertisements.

❍ **B.** Classless routing protocols send the mask along with the networks in advertisements.

❍ **C.** On a discontiguous network, using autosummarization at classful boundaries could cause loss of connectivity in your network.

❍ **D.** EIGRP is classful and proprietary.

❍ **E.** OSPF is classless and proprietary.

❍ **F.** None of the other answers provided are accurate.

50. If a router is running three different routing protocols (EIGRP, OSPF, and RIPv2), and a specific route has been learned by each of these three routing protocols, which route or routes will be put in the routing table?

❍ **A.** All three routes will be in the routing table as equal-cost routes.

❍ **B.** A router will equal-cost load balance across two equal-cost routes, so two of the three routes would be in the routing table.

❍ **C.** The OSPF route would be in the routing table and the others would not.

❍ **D.** The route learned from the routing protocol that the local router believes to have the lowest administrative distance will be put into the routing table, and the other two routes will not be put into the routing table.

❍ **E.** The route learned from the routing protocol that the local router believes to have the highest administrative distance will be put into the routing table, and the other two routes will not be put into the routing table.

51. What is the default behavior when a switch port using port security has a violation message?

❍ **A.** Packet is dropped, but port remains enabled for learned MAC addresses.

❍ **B.** SNMP and syslog messages are generated, and port is disabled.

❍ **C.** Packet is forwarded, but SNMP and Syslog messages are generated.

❍ **D.** Packet is dropped, and the port is rate limited for all future traffic ingress on that port.

52. Which of the following would provide detail similar to the level of that found on a telephone bill, regarding duration, protocols involved, addresses used, and so on?

❍ **A.** Syslog

❍ **B.** CDP

❍ **C.** SNMP

❍ **D.** NetFlow

53. Which FHRP uses an AVG and an AVF?

❍ **A.** HSRP

❍ **B.** GLBP

❍ **C.** VRRP

❍ **D.** EIGRP

54. Why are interfaces that are not connected to HSRP networks tracked?

❍ **A.** To influence which router will be the active HSRP router.

❍ **B.** To increase priority of an HSRP router.

❍ **C.** HSRP doesn't support tracking, but GLBP does.

❍ **D.** To provide a single IP address as an alternate default gateway.

55. R1 and R2 have been configured to connect over their Serial 0/0/0 interfaces. Review the configuration:

```
R1(config)#username R2 password cisco
R1(config)#int ser 0/0/0
R1(config-if)#encap ppp
R1(config-if)#ppp authen chap
R2(config)#username R1 password cisco
R2(config)#int ser 0/0/1
R2(config-if)#encap ppp
R2(config-if)#ppp authen chap
```

The two routers are not able to connect. What is the problem with the configuration?

❍ **A.** Wrong interface

❍ **B.** Wrong username

❍ **C.** Wrong password

❍ **D.** Wrong encapsulation

❍ **E.** Wrong authentication type

56. Which of the following is the Cisco default LMI type for Frame Relay?

❍ **A.** ANSI

❍ **B.** Cisco

❍ **C.** Q933a

❍ **D.** IEEE

❍ **E.** 802.1Q

57. Consider the following output:

```
R2#show int ser 2/0
Serial2/0 is up, line protocol is up
  Hardware is M8T-X.21
  Internet address is 10.23.0.1/30
  MTU 1500 bytes, BW 1544 Kbit/sec, DLY 20000 usec,
     reliability 255/255, txload 1/255, rxload 1/255
  Encapsulation FRAME-RELAY, crc 16, loopback not set
  Keepalive set (10 sec)
  Restart-Delay is 0 secs
  LMI enq sent  41, LMI stat recvd 41, LMI upd recvd 0, DTE LMI up
  LMI enq recvd 0, LMI stat sent  0, LMI upd sent  0
  LMI DLCI 1023  LMI type is CISCO  frame relay DTE
```

Which of the following would be acceptable to configure on the router on the other side of this WAN connection?

❍ **A.** **ppp authentication chap**

❍ **B.** **encapsulation hdlc.**

❍ **C.** **Encapsulation ppp.**

❍ **D.** **ip address 10.23.0.5 255.255.255.252**

❍ **E.** **frame map ip 10.23.0.1 65 broadcast**

58. Which allows a dynamic Frame Relay mapping betwee a remote IP address to a local DLCI?

❍ **A.** DHCP

❍ **B.** Inverse ARP

❍ **C.** HDLC

❍ **D.** SLAAC

59. You want to use a VPN protocols for site-to-site and remote-access secure connectivity. Which of the following are open standards that can be used to provide VPN services such as authentication, confidentiality, and data integrity?

❍ **A.** HDLC

❍ **B.** IPsec

❍ **C.** SSL

❍ **D.** PPP

❍ **E.** Frame Relay

60. What connection type does Frame Relay use to logically allow point-to-point connections between two WAN routers that is up regardless of whether it is being used?

❍ **A.** PVC
❍ **B.** SVC
❍ **C.** Cell switching
❍ **D.** Circuit switching

61. Which command enables you to learn the IP address of a directly connected switch?

❍ **A.** **show cdp neighbor**
❍ **B.** **show cdp neighbor detail**
❍ **C.** **show cdp neighbor status**
❍ **D.** **show cdp neighbor address**

62. In the routing table, what does the letter *D* represent?

❍ **A.** EIGRP-learned route
❍ **B.** Default route
❍ **C.** Static route
❍ **D.** OSPF-learned route
❍ **E.** Directly connected route

63. Your network uses a centralized DHCP server. Existing subnets are functioning. On a brand new subnet, clients can't obtain a DHCP address, but do have a link indicator on their network card. What is the likely problem?

❍ **A.** Layer 2 switch is powered off.
❍ **B.** Layer 2 switch have a default gateway.
❍ **C.** Local router doesn't have DHCP relay configured.
❍ **D.** Local router isn't a DHCP client.

64. Consider the following output and consider a packet being sent to the router with the following:

Source Layer 2 address: ca01.159c.001c

Destination Layer 2 address: 0000.1212.1212

Source Layer 3 address: 10.12.0.2

Destination Layer 3 address: 10.15.0.5

```
R1#show arp
Protocol  Address         Age (min)  Hardware Addr   Type  Interface
Internet  10.12.0.1             -    0000.1212.1212  ARPA  GigabitEthernet1/0
Internet  10.12.0.2             4    ca01.159c.001c  ARPA  GigabitEthernet1/0
Internet  10.13.0.1             -    0000.1313.1313  ARPA  GigabitEthernet2/0
Internet  10.13.0.3            16    ca02.1bb0.001c  ARPA  GigabitEthernet2/0
Internet  10.14.0.1             -    0000.1414.1414  ARPA  GigabitEthernet3/0
Internet  10.14.0.4             3    ca03.1bb0.001c  ARPA  GigabitEthernet3/0
Internet  10.15.0.1             -    0000.1515.1515  ARPA  GigabitEthernet4/0
Internet  10.15.0.5             7    ca04.19bc.001c  ARPA  GigabitEthernet4/0
```

What would the router do?

❍ **A.** Decapsulate the packet, then reencapsulate using the L2 source address of 0000.1515.1515.

❍ **B.** Decapsulate the packet, then reencapsulate using the L3 source address of 10.15.0.1.

❍ **C.** Decapsulate the packet, then reencapsulate using the L2 destination address of 0000.1515.1515.

❍ **D.** Decapsulate the packet, then reencapsulate using the L3 destination address of 10.12.0.2.

❍ **E.** It would drop the packet.

65. You are troubleshooting the MAC address table on a switch. Which command will show the current entries, along with the VLANs the MAC addresses are associated with on the switch?

❍ **A.** **show interface**

❍ **B.** **show mac-table**

❍ **C.** **show cam address-table**

❍ **D.** **show mac-address-table**

❍ **E.** **show run**

66. Which Frame Relay DLCI does a router concern itself with?

- ❍ **A.** A remote DLCI that maps to a remote IP address
- ❍ **B.** A local DLCI that maps to a local IP address
- ❍ **C.** A remote DLCI that maps to a local IP address
- ❍ **D.** A local DLCI that maps to a remote IP address

67. What is true about the mapping between a DLCI and an IP address?

- ❍ **A.** A local DLCI that maps to a remote IP address.
- ❍ **B.** A local DLCI that maps to a local IP address.
- ❍ **C.** A remote DLCI that maps to a remote IP address.
- ❍ **D.** A remote DLCI that maps to a local IP address.

Answer Key to Practice Exam 1

Answers at a Glance to Practice Exam 1

1. E
2. E
3. C
4. F
5. B
6. C
7. B
8. A
9. B
10. A
11. B
12. B
13. C
14. D
15. A, C, E
16. B
17. B
18. D
19. D
20. A, D
21. B
22. A
23. A
24. F
25. E
26. B
27. A
28. A
29. B
30. B, E
31. A
32. E
33. A, D
34. D
35. A
36. A
37. C
38. F
39. C
40. A, C
41. B
42. A, B
43. A
44. B,D
45. A
46. C
47. A, D
48. D
49. B, C
50. D
51. B
52. D
53. B
54. A
55. A
56. B
57. E
58. B
59. B, C
60. A
61. B
62. A
63. C
64. A
65. D
66. D
67. A

Answers with Explanations

1. Answer E is correct. A leased line represents a serial interface, so the network device to connect the branch to the Internet would need an Ethernet connection to connect to their existing switch and a serial interface with the appropriate cable to connect to the service provider's leased line. The router would also need to be configured with Network Address Translation and appropriate IP addressing to function. A Layer 2 switch does not have routing capability, which would be needed for connecting the branch to the Internet. A Layer 2 switch also does not have a serial interface that would be suitable for connectivity to a leased line. A router with only two Ethernet interfaces would not have the serial interface required to connect to leased line. A router with two serial interfaces would not have the Ethernet connectivity to connect to the existing Layer 2 switch.
2. Answer E is correct. The application layer protocol for accessing a web server is HTTP. SMTP is an application layer protocol used for sending email. TCP is a transport layer protocol. IP is a network layer / Internet layer protocol. UDP is a transport layer protocol.
3. Answer C is correct. IP is the OSI Layer 3 protocol used on the Internet today. TCP is an OSI layer 4 connection-oriented transport protocol. UDP is a connectionless OSI Layer 4 transport protocol. DNS is an application layer protocol. Ethernet is not an OSI Layer 3 protocol.
4. Answer F is correct. FTP is the File Transfer Protocol, which can reliably send and retrieve files. It uses TCP as transport layer for reliable communications. DNS is a name resolution protocol. DHCP is the dynamic host configuration protocol used to assign IP addresses and other parameters to devices on the network. Telnet is a remote access application layer service that can give us command-line interface access to a remote device (although it is not secure). NTP is the Network Time Protocol, and TFTP is the Trivial File Transfer Protocol, which uses UDP at the transport layer, which is nonreliable.
5. Answer B is correct. The first 14 bits are the same for all networks, so the summary would be the value of those first 14 bits, along with a mask of 14, which represented in decimal is the mask 255.252.0.0. All the other options have a mask that is too long, and not accurately summarizing the networks, or to short, which is an oversummarization.
6. Answer C is correct. With a 21-bit mask, the block size is increments of 8. The subnet 172.19.48.0 has a range of valid host from 172.19.48.1 to 172.19.55.254. The IP address in the question is in that range. All the other subnets don't include that range.
7. Answer B is correct. With a mask of /23, the block size is 2. Subnets would include (in the third octet) 136, 138, 140, 142, and so on. The host in question is on the 138 subnet. The valid host range for subnet 138 would be 10.30.138.1 to 10.30.139.254, with a broadcast address of .255 for that subnet. All the other answers are incorrect because they are not the first address in subnet 138.

8. Answer A is correct. A mask of /23 provides a block size of 2, including 12, 14, 16, 18, and so on as subnets in the third octet. The host is in subnet 14, which has a range of 10.26.14.1 to 10.26.15.254. All the other answers are incorrect.
9. Answer B is correct. The command for basic interface monitoring in NetFlow is **ip flow**. Exporting is a global configuration to send collected data to an external is a global command. In NetFlow Version 9, custom configurations can be used, including a NetFlow record that describes what makes up a flow, a NetFlow monitor that describes where to collect the data (this is applied directly to an interface), and a NetFlow export object to identify where to send the collected data. Version 9 is also referred to as Flexible NetFlow.
10. Answer A is correct. CDP will only show directly connected Cisco devices that are running CDP. Switch 2 would see both Router 1 and Router 2 as neighbors. CDP isn't routed or forwarded beyond the directly connected network, so all the other answers presented are incorrect. ISE doesn't advertise CDP, and hubs are Layer 1 devices that can't create any Layer 2 information to send out.
11. Answer B is correct. The startup configuration file is stored in NVRAM. Flash is where the IOS image is stored. ROMmon is a low-level tool to use when troubleshooting a router or switch. The config register stores information about how to boot and what files to use when booting.
12. Answer B is correct. The command **enable secret Cisco123** will automatically store the privileged mode password of Cisco123 using MD5. The **enable password** command doesn't store a password using MD5, and the **service password-encryption** command adds some security to plain-text passwords, but not MD5.
13. Answer C is correct. The command **login local** in vty line configuration mode is what triggers the user to be prompted for a username and password. The keyword **local** refers to the local database, which is the running configuration on the router or switch. This applies to both Telnet and SSH. The generation of a key pair, configuring a domain name, and allowing SSH at the vty lines are important for SSH to operate, but they are not the reason for the interactive prompt for user authentication.
14. Answer D is correct. Port security can limit the number of MAC addresses allowed in on the switch port. The default value, when implemented, is one MAC address. ACLs are not a switch specific technical control. BPDU filtering would prevent STP BPDUs, but would not limit the number of MAC addresses on the switch port. SSH is a secure remote-access protocol, but is not specific to switch port security.
15. Answers A, C, and E are correct. Using full duplex, each node is allocated dedicated bandwidth and access to media, which means that there is no need to wait to see whether the media is free. To implement full duplex, every node on the network will be connected to its own switch port, which means a dedicated switch port is required for each full-duplex device. Full duplex doesn't use carrier sensing multiple access with collision detection. In full duplex, collision detection is disabled on the network adapters. Hubs operate at half duplex. Both the switch and the host both need to support full duplex for it to operate.

16. Answer B is correct. Layer 2 switches make their forwarding decisions based on only the Layer 2 destination address that is in the header of the frame. Hubs operate at the physical layer and do not understand any of the addressing in the headers of Layer 2 or higher. The PC and the server are both considering Layer 2 and Layer 3 address information when making forwarding decisions. Because this isn't the first packet being sent, it is presumed that the switches would have learned and put into their tables all the needed MAC addresses.

17. Answer B is correct. A router is required to make Layer 3 forwarding decisions between Layer 2 broadcast domains/VLANs. The devices in each VLAN will use an IP subnet addressing plan, and normally there will be a relationship of one subnet per VLAN. Customers don't have to move to the new VLAN to reach servers there; they simply need to forward traffic to their default gateway and allow that Layer 3 device to route the traffic to the new subnet/VLAN. No ACLs are implemented by default, so no ACL is required to permit traffic to be routed to and from another VLAN.

18. Answer D is correct. Trunks include 802.1Q headers to add information about the VLAN membership for each of the frames that are sent. By default, traffic from all VLANs is allowed on the trunk ports. Traffic that is associated with the native VLAN is not tagged. The switches don't look at the IP addresses to map the packets to specific VLANs. ISL is a proprietary Cisco standard, which is seldom used anymore.

19. Answer D is correct. Access ports carry the traffic for a single VLAN. No trunking occurs on an access port. There are no 802.1Q tags on traffic sent to or from an access port. Access ports connect to devices such as routers, printers, computers, and so forth using a straight-through cable—not a crossover cable. Native VLANs play a role in trunk ports (where traffic on the Native VLAN isn't tagged), but it doesn't play a role in an access port.

20. Answers A and D are correct. When a router receives a packet that needs to be forwarded, it will consult its routing table to determine which interface it should route the packet out of. It then switches the packet (internally) to that egress or exit interface, and then re-encapsulates the packet into a Layer 2 frame using its own Layer 2 address as the source and including the next hop and its Layer 2 address as the Layer 2 destination address. The router does not alter the source IP address (with the exception if it is doing network address translation). As the router sends a frame, it will not use the source address of the sender of the packet, but rather it will use its own Layer 2 address as the source MAC address on the interface that it's using to send the frame.

21. Answer B is correct. The router will use the configured router ID in OSPF. If that is not configured, it will use the highest IP address on a loopback interface. If there are no loopback interfaces, it will use the highest IP address on the physical interface at the time OSPF is started. OSPF will not use a serial number from the BIOS.

22. Answer A is correct. By default, IPv6 unicast routing is not enabled on many IOS routers. Without this enabled, the router will not forward IPv6 traffic on behalf of its customers (the PCs in this example). IPv6 doesn't use a **network** statement

to enable interfaces for OSPF, it uses the interface commands instead. Both OSPFv2 and OSPFv3 will use an IP address already configured on the router as an OSPF router ID in the event that there isn't a configured router ID or any loopbacks with IPv4 addresses when OSPF begins.

23. Answer A is correct. The interface is enabled for OSPFv3; otherwise, it wouldn't show up in this list. The down state is due to the interface being administratively shut down. OSPFv3 doesn't use **network** statements to enable interfaces, it uses interface commands. A router ID doesn't have to be configured; if there is at least one IPv4 address configured on the same router, it will use that. Because G1/0 is in OSPFv3, that confirms that OSPFv3 has selected a router ID and is running. If there were no neighbors on a link, the output would show the state of the Ethernet interface as DR.

24. Answer F is correct. The router is the last device in this Ethernet network that is forwarding the frame to the PC on the right. As a result, when the router encapsulates the packet and puts it into a frame and sends it out its 2/0 interface, its source Layer 2 address (also referred to as the hardware address) will be used in the Layer 2 header as the source MAC address. The PC in the left would initially place its own Layer 2 address as a source as it sends the frame to the router. When the router receives a frame and makes a routing decision, it will re-encapsulate the frame as it sends the frame to the PC on the right. The IP addresses shown are Layer 3 addresses. The router will use the source Layer 2 address on the interface that is being used to send the frame.

25. Answer E is correct. The source address of an IP packet (with the exception of a network address translation) will stay the same from the source all they way to the destination. In this example, the server at 172.16.30.30 is sending a packet to 172.16.10.10, so the source address of the packet, when it leaves the Ethernet interface R1 headed toward the PC, will still have the source IP address of 172.16.30.30. All the other choices given are not the source IP address of the server.

26. Answer B is correct. The router would ARP for the Layer 2 address of its local gateway (the router), which is on the local subnet with the PC on the left. IPv6 doesn't use ARP, and ARP is only used within a subnet/VLAN.

27. Answer A is correct. Standard ACLs, both named and numbered, can filter based only on source IP address. Placing them too close to the source may prevent traffic to more destinations than intended. So, standard ACLs, when used for filtering traffic, should be placed close to the destinations they are intended to protect. Extended ACL, both named and numbered, can granularly filter on source, destination, and even ports. As a result, extended ACLs can be placed very close to the source because they will still allow traffic that needs to be forwarded and at the same time deny traffic that shouldn't be allowed. A side benefit is that we deny this traffic early (near the source), so it is less of a burden on the rest of the network.

28. Answer A is correct. Answer B has the incorrect destination port, which would be the high-numbered source port the client used to initiate the connection. Answer C has the wrong destination network of 10.0.0.0/24, and Answer D has the incorrect source address and incorrect destination port.

29. Answer B is correct. The path would go from the computer at 172.16.10.10 to R1 to R3 to R2 to 172.16.20.20. The OSPF routes learned by R1 would indicate that the better path is through R3, and not directly through the interface that goes to R2. OSPF will use the total cost of the path to determine the best path. No static routes would be required, and there would not be a loop between R1 and R3. If R1 sent a packet to R3, R3 would use its routing table and know that it should forward the packet to 172.16.20.20 through its s3/2 interface to R2.

30. Answers B and E are correct. The correct entries would be the creation of access list 1, which identifies any source IP addresses beginning with 172.16.x.x. The **ip nat** statement using access list 1 and using PAT on the 2/0 interface is the other correct statement. The other incorrect answers either use the wrong interface or incorrect source IP addresses.

31. Answer A is correct. The correct interface command to make a router interface a DHCP client is **ip address dhcp**. The other commands offered as incorrect answers are not valid IOS command syntax. The non-IP-configured Cisco IOS router interface does not automatically become a DHCP client without the proper configuration to cause that.

32. Answer E is correct. **show ip dhcp conflict** shows information about an IP address that the router was going to lease, before the router discovered that the proposed IP address was already in use on the network. The command **show ip dhcp binding** shows active DHCP leases from the DHCP server service running on the router. The command **show ip dhcp server statistics** displays statistics about memory usage and the number of DHCP messages and what types, but doesn't show any leased IP addresses specifically. The two incorrect options that begin **show dhcp** are both incorrect syntax on the Cisco IOS.

33. Answers A and D are correct. The commands **show ntp status** and **show ntp associations detail** will both include synchronization information. The command **show clock** doesn't mention NTP, and the command **show clock detail** will mention that NTP is configured, but not indicate whether the time is synchronized.

34. Answer D is correct. The PC is connected to VLAN 55 on port 0/2, instead of VLAN 10. Because the user in VLAN 20 is working, the router and connection to the switch are working. Comparing the pool for VLAN 10 and VLAN 20, we could suppose that the DHCP services for VLAN 20 are fine, it is just that the client needs to connect to that VLAN.

35. Answer A is correct. The switch, based on the diagram, connects to the router on switch port 0/4. The output shows that this is not currently a trunk. The output confirms that DHCP services are configured, as well as has subinterfaces that match the topology, including correct addresses.

36. Answer A is correct. R3 isn't advertising the 172.16.30.0/24 network in OSPF, likely due to not including that interface in either an OSPF **network** statement or interface configuration on that connected interface (either way would add the network to OSPF). R3 shows routes back to both of the 172.16.x.0/24 subnetworks, learned via OSPF, which implies the OSPF neighbor relationship is working. Because the OSPF neighbors are present, that implies the interfaces are up on R3. The output reflects the correct IP addressing used on R3's interfaces.

37. Answer C is correct. This switch has the same priority as the root, but its base MAC address is higher, which makes for an overall higher bridge ID for this switch, which is causing it not to be the root switch. This switch is not the root; a root switch would have all designated ports, and the output would state that this switch is the root (if it were). The timers are learned from the root switch, and the default hello time is 2 seconds, and the output is showing 3.

38. Answer F is correct. Switch D is discarding frames on 0/1. Switch A because of its low priority will be the root of spanning tree. As a result all the ports on switch A, it will be in a designated/forwarding state. Switch B has two equal-cost paths to the root, and when using the defaults will choose a root port based on the lowest cost to get to the root. Because the cost of both paths is equal, the tiebreaker is the advertised priorities that are sent in the BPDUs. The BPDU sent from the root's 0/1 will be preferred over the BPDUs sent from the root's 0/2 (with lower being better). This means that switch B will be forwarding on 0/1. Switch C will be forwarding on all ports, (because its bridge ID is better than switch B's), and 0/2 and 0/11 will both be designated because the cost for switch C is better than switch D. When switch D sees the BPDUs from switch C (on both interfaces), it knows that there is a loop. The cost is equal for both sets of BPDUs, so it boils down again to the advertising switches' port numbers, with lower being better. For that reason, the advertisements out of 0/2 that are seen by switch D on its 0/12 would be preferred over the BPDUs sent from switch C's 0/11 (which are being received on switch D's 0/1).

39. Answer C is correct. When using the defaults, the root for the spanning tree will be based on the lowest MAC address. This would make switch 1 become the root for VLAN 1. Switch 3 and switch 2 will both be forwarding on all ports, and switch 4 will set its root port to the switch that has best (lowest cost). If the costs were equal, the switch with the lowest bridge ID (between SW2 and SW3) would be chosen. The gigabit ports connected to Fast Ethernet will autonegotiate to 100Mbps. The cost advertised by SW2 will be 19, and the cost advertised by switch 3 will be 19. However, because the g0/2 operating at 100Mbps will add a local cost of 19, while int g0/1 at 1000Mbps will add a cost of only 4 more, the overall cost of 23 through switch 2 is a better cost than 38 going through switch 3.

40. Answers A and C are correct. Typically, every Layer 2 broadcast domain/VLAN will be associated with a separate IP network or subnetwork. The switch maintains a MAC address table that associates which ports in which MAC addresses are associated with those ports for each VLAN that is on that switch. To route packets between VLANs, a Layer 3 device is used. This Layer 3 device could be an external router or an internal Layer 3 function on a multilayer switch. By default, VLAN 1 exists on a new switch, and all ports are assigned to that VLAN by default.

41. Answer B is correct. To support multiple VLANs crossing a link, the interfaces between the two switches need to be configured as a trunk. This makes the answer of access ports incorrect. EtherChannel may be used to support a single VLAN or a trunk, but by itself without trunk configuration or dynamically negotiating a trunk, it would not support multiple VLANs. A Layer 3 routed port would not meet the requirement of the question listed here, which is about Layer 2 ports.

42. Answers A and B are correct. If the trunk were configured accidentally as an access port, or if traffic crossing a working trunk were traffic for the native VLAN, both of those conditions would result in no tagging being present on the frames sent over the trunk. Although it is likely that the duplex should be full, which is optimal, if for some reason it were set to half duplex, that would not affect the tagging. If negotiation had been set to desirable on both ends, that setting should result in a successful trunk where tagging data frames for all except the native VLAN should be happening.

43. Answer A is correct. A VLAN is a Layer 2 broadcast domain. If more are created, there will be more VLANs, but the number of devices in each VLAN will decrease. For example, if there are 3 switches, with 36 ports, all using 1 VLAN, and then we add more VLANs and distribute the ports, we could have 3 VLANs with 12 ports each (size of each VLAN decreasing).

44. Answers B and D are correct. To support inter-VLAN routing, a multilayer switch would need a VLAN interface for each subnet/VLAN being supported, as well as having IP routing enabled on the switch. The switch would not need to be a DHCP client, and a default gateway wouldn't be used by the switch, because IP routing is enabled (a default IP route would be used instead).

45. Answer A is correct. In EIGRP, each router advertises its own feasible distance regarding a route. Router 1 is showing a feasible distance of 131072 for network 4.4.4.4/32. On the line that says via 10.12.0.2, it then shows the FD followed by the advertised (reported) distance from 10.12.0.2. This reported/advertised distance is the FD on that router.

46. Answer C is correct. Access control lists applied to the logical vty lines using the **access-class** command to control which source IP addresses are allowed to attempt a login is considered a best practice for security. Telnet should be disabled, while allowing only SSH. Access control lists on physical interfaces used for filtering may be a good idea, but it doesn't completely control access to the vty lines, because there are also serial interfaces that may be present, and in the future when new interfaces are put into service, they would also have to have the access control lists added there. By having access control on the logical vty lines, it doesn't matter which physical interfaces are used, or if new interfaces show up, because the control is on the vty line. The vty lines are an important access method for the CLI and should not be disabled, but rather should be protected.

47. Answers A and D are correct. For a router to perform as a router on a stick, it needs to be connected to a trunk port, and as a result it may use a single physical interface to accomplish this. The router will use multiple logical subinterfaces to support the VLANs, using a single subinterface and IP address per VLAN supported.

48. Answer D is correct. By default, the router on an Ethernet network that has the highest router ID compared to other OSPF devices that are all booting at the same time will become the designated router for that segment. This is not a preemptive election. If a new router comes online and sees that there is already an established OSPF designated router, it will not supersede the existing one that is currently there. On serial point-to-point networks, a designated router is not used.

49. Answers B and C are correct. Classless routing protocols, such as OSPF and EIGRP include the network mask along with the prefixes/networks that they are advertising in routing updates. This allows us to use VLSM, which means that we can use different length of masks in different parts of our networks and that the routing protocol can advertise all the details about those different length masks. Classful summarization can hide the details of subnets, and if not planned correctly could lead to loss of connectivity to some of your networks because the routers are not clear about where those subnets exist (after receiving summaries from multiple routers advertising the same summary routes). EIGRP is classless and proprietary. OSPF is classless but it is not proprietary; it is an open standard.

50. Answer D is correct. A tiebreaker regarding routes to the same network is the administrative distance. The lower the administrator distance, the better the route appears to the local router. OSPF and EIGRP have different administered distances based on the type of route (for example, internal versus external). The route with the lowest administered distance will be the single route that is placed in the routing table. All three routes will not make it because the default administrator distance is not the same for each of the routing protocols. By default, a router that has equal-cost routes can load balance up to four and can be configured to use more if desired. An equal-cost route would have equal metrics in addition to equal administrative distance.

51. Answer B is correct. The default action for a port security violation is to shut down the port. It will also generate an SNMP message (when SNMP is configured), and it will also generate a syslog message by default about the violation. Rate limiting is not one of the three port security violation actions.

52. Answer D is correct. NetFlow provides detail flow information that can include addresses, protocols, and more. Syslog and SNMP can provide event information, but don't collect the details of flows through the network like NetFlow. CDP is a neighbor discovery protocol.

53. Answer B is correct. GLBP uses an Active Virtual Gateway (AVG) to reply to ARP requests, and the Active Virtual Forwarders (AVFs) perform the forwarding. HSRP and VRRP don't use those terms or exact methods. EIGRP isn't an FHRP, it is a routing protocol.

54. Answer A is correct. Tracking other interfaces provides the opportunity to lower the active HSRPs priority when those tracked interfaces go down. Those tracked interfaces may be the path that would have been used to forward packets out of the HSRP network. By lowering the active routers priority (through tracking) and configuring preempt on the other routers, another router could take over the responsibility of being the active HSRP router.

55. Answer A is correct. Both routers should be using serial 0/0/0. R2 is incorrectly configured on its serial 0/0/1 interface.

56. Answer B is correct. The 3 LMI types supported by Cisco routers are ANSI, Cisco, and Q933a. The default is Cisco. IEEE is a standards group, and 802.1Q is the IEEE standard for Ethernet trunking.

57. Answer E is correct. The frame map would be appropriate, as long as the local DLCI on the remote router was 65. Because R2 is using Frame Relay encapsulation, none of the PPP or HDLC options would be appropriate for the other router. The IP address of R2 is on the 10.23.0.0/30 subnet, and the proposed IP for the other side is on the 10.23.0.4/30 subnet, and if used, they wouldn't be on the same logical IP subnet as each other.

58. Answer B is correct. Inverse ARP can be used to dynamically assign the IP to DLCI mapping. A static mapping can also be administratively configured. DHCP is used to assign IP address to DHCP clients. SLAAC is an automatic addressing mechanism used by IPv6 and isn't tied to Frame Relay. HDLC is a Layer 2 protocol, and is not used when frame Relay encapsulation is being used.

59. Answers B and C are correct. IPsec and SSL are open standard security protocols that can be used as part of VPN solutions. Layer 2 WAN protocols include Cisco's proprietary HDLC as well as industry standards of PPP and Frame Relay.

60. Answer A is correct. A permanent virtual circuit (PVC) is the mechanism that allows a logical point-to-point path through the service provider's network. SVCs are on-demand circuits that are built when needed and taken down when not needed. Cell switching is done for ATM, and circuit switching isn't used by Frame Relay.

61. Answer B is correct. The command **show cdp neighbor detail** will reveal the Layer 3 address of a directly connected CDP device. The other commands are either incorrect syntax or wouldn't provide the detail about the Layer 3 address asked for in the question.

62. Answer A is correct. *D* represents an EIGRP learned route. Default routes can be learned via a routing protocol or statically configured. A directly connected route will have a *C*, and OSPF will have an *O* (and possibly other characters as well) to indicate it is an OSPF-learned route. Static routes have an *S*.

63. Answer C is correct. When using a centralized DHCP server, the local router needs to forward DHCP client requests that it sees (from clients) to the central DHCP server. If the switch is powered off, the clients do not receive a link signal. The local router does not have to be a DHCP client to be a DHCP relay, which is what is causing the problem here. The switch is operating only as a Layer 2 switch, and therefore will not be involved with the Layer 3 routing (or DHCP relay services) of the local router on that same subnet.

64. Answer A is correct. The Layer 2 destination address is the router's own MAC address, so it would de-encapsulate to look at the Layer 3 header. The packet is destined to a host 10.15.0.5, which based on the ARP information is directly connected to the router G4/0 interface. The router would forward the packet by re-encapsulating the packet into a Layer 2 frame using the source MAC address of g4/0 (0000.1515.1515, based on the ARP cache information), with a destination MAC address of the host at 10.15.0.5, which from the ARP cache on the router we can see is the Layer 2 address of ca04.19bc.001c.

65. Answer D is correct. The command **show mac-address-table** shows the MAC addresses currently known by the switch, along with which VLAN those MAC addresses are associated with. The other commands are either invalid syntax or will not show the content of the MAC address table. On some IOS versions, the command **show mac address-table** will also correctly show the table.

66. Answer D is correct. The local DLCI is the only DLCI the local router will care about. The Frame Relay mapping maps a local DLCI (like the onramp to a freeway) that leads to a remote IP address at the other end of the PVC. All the other options provided are incorrect.

67. Answer A is correct. The local DLCI is the only DLCI the local router will care about. The Frame Relay mapping maps a local DLCI (like the onramp to a freeway) that leads to a remote IP address at the other end of the PVC. All the other options provided are incorrect.

Practice Exam 2

If you are reading this, you likely feel ready to tackle the CCNA exam and need to assess your skills to see whether you can spot any weaknesses. As you take this practice exam, the authors recommend the following test-taking tips:

- **Read each question twice:** There is a big difference between reading a question that you think reads, "Which of the following are true," but really reads, "Which of the following are not true." Be sure to read each question carefully so that you can fully understand the question.
- **Read the answers starting from the bottom:** When you read the answers from the bottom, you force yourself to carefully read each answer. If you read the answers from the top, you might find yourself quickly selecting an answer that looks vaguely right and skipping over the other answers that might have been a better answer.
- **Time yourself:** The CCNA exam is a 90-minute exam. Time yourself during this practice exam to make sure that you stay within this time limit.
- **If you do not know the answer to a question, make a note of it:** Go back and review any trouble areas later. You should be interested not only in finding the answer to the question, but also in mastering that particular topic in its entirety. If you are unsure about one aspect of a topic, chances are you might be unsure about other areas related to that same topic.
- **Mentally get yourself in the frame of mind to take a test:** To properly assess yourself, take this practice exam as you would take the real exam. This means that you should find yourself a quiet place without any distractions so that you can focus on each question. (Yes, that includes turning off the television.) You can have some scratch paper to write on, but calculators are not allowed on the real exam, so do not use them on the practice exam.

- **If you cannot determine the correct answers, begin eliminating the incorrect answers:** If there are four options and you know that three are absolutely wrong, the fourth option has to be the correct one.
- **Continue taking this practice exam until you get a perfect score:** When you can consistently score high on these practice exams, you are ready to take the real exam.
- **Don't despair:** Should you not do so well on the practice exam, do not worry. It only means that you need to continue studying. Be glad that you are able to spot your weak areas now and not after taking the real exam. Go back through and review your problem areas.

We wish you the best of luck in your pursuit of the coveted CCNA certification.

1. Why is a router required to connect a branch office (currently using a Layer 2 switch) to the Internet when using a leased line from a service provider for WAN services?

   ❍ **A.** A router is not required, a Layer 2 switch could be connected directly to the leased line.

   ❍ **B.** Routing capabilities are required, along with Ethernet and serial networking interfaces.

   ❍ **C.** A router has higher Ethernet speeds, compared to the switch, which is required for the leased line.

   ❍ **D.** Layer 2 forwarding is required by the device connected to the leased line.

2. A user at a computer is accessing a remote router using SSH. Which of the following from the TCP/IP protocol suite would be used at the transport layer?

   ❍ **A.** ARP

   ❍ **B.** TCP

   ❍ **C.** IP

   ❍ **D.** UDP

   ❍ **E.** SNMP

3. Which of the following is an application layer service that allows the translation of a website name to an IP address?

   ❍ **A.** DNS

   ❍ **B.** DHCP

   ❍ **C.** Telnet

   ❍ **D.** NTP

   ❍ **E.** TFTP

   ❍ **F.** FTP

4. Which of the following devices can understand and make forwarding decisions based on IP addresses? (Choose 2.)

   ❍ **A.** Hub

   ❍ **B.** Router

   ❍ **C.** Layer 2 switch

   ❍ **D.** Bridge

   ❍ **E.** Multilayer switch

   ❍ **F.** Network interface card

5. Which of the following IP addresses are valid on the same subnet as the host 172.30.255.0/12 (Choose 2.)
   - ❍ **A.** 172.10.0.1
   - ❍ **B.** 172.20.0.1
   - ❍ **C.** 172.30.0.1
   - ❍ **D.** 172.40.0.1

6. If using a mask of 255.255.255.224 on a Class C address space, how many subnets of that class C address could be created?
   - ❍ **A.** 2
   - ❍ **B.** 4
   - ❍ **C.** 8
   - ❍ **D.** 16
   - ❍ **E.** 32

7. You are trying to apply the IP addresses of 20.33.0.1/11 and 20.63.0.1/11 to two different interfaces on the same router. Which of the following statements are true?
   - ❍ **A.** Those two address can't be applied to the same router because they will be overlapping addresses. They are both from subnet 20.32.0.0/11.
   - ❍ **B.** Those two address can be applied to the same router (to two separate interfaces).
   - ❍ **C.** Those two address can't be applied to the same router because they will be overlapping addresses. They are both from subnet 20.32.0.0/11.
   - ❍ **D.** One of those addresses is the network address, and won't allow you to apply it to a router interface.

8. Which of the following can be used to identify directly connected Cisco devices?
   - ❍ **A.** NTP
   - ❍ **B.** CDP
   - ❍ **C.** ICMP
   - ❍ **D.** Telnet

9. Consider the following diagram. CDP is enabled on all the devices that support it. Which CDP devices will Router 1 see in the output of **show cdp neighbors**?

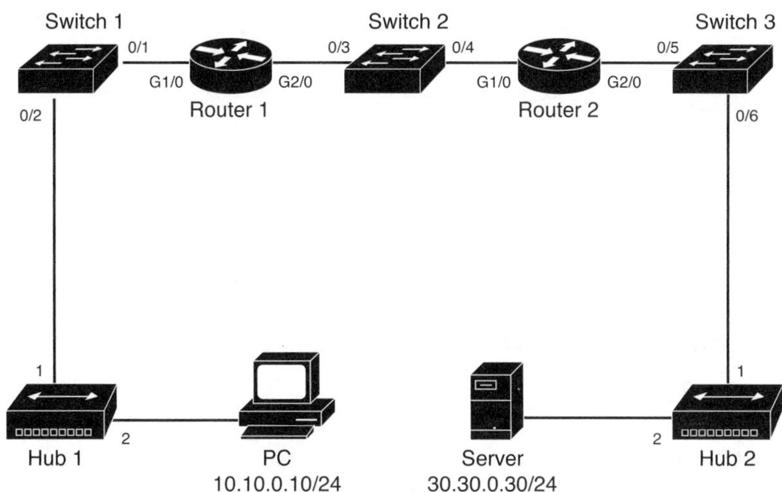

- ❍ **A.** Router 2 only.
- ❍ **B.** Switch 1, Router 2, and Switch 3.
- ❍ **C.** Switch 1, Router 2 only.
- ❍ **D.** Switch 1, Switch 2 only.
- ❍ **E.** CDP runs on only switches, so the router would not show any neighbors.

10. Which of the following would require the use of a crossover cable?

- ❍ **A.** PC to switch
- ❍ **B.** Hub to Switch
- ❍ **C.** Hub to router
- ❍ **D.** Server to hub
- ❍ **E.** PC to PC

11. What command can be used to encrypt plain-text passwords in the configuration of the router?

- ❍ **A.** **service-password-encryption**
- ❍ **B.** **service-password encryption**
- ❍ **C.** **service password encryption**
- ❍ **D.** **service password-encryption**

12. What is the default number of MAC addresses allowed with switch port security is enabled on a port?

❍ **A.** 1

❍ **B.** 2

❍ **C.** 3

❍ **D.** 4

❍ **E.** 5

13. What is the default action in a port security violation?

❍ **A.** Shut down

❍ **B.** Protect

❍ **C.** Restrict

❍ **D.** Warn

14. Which statement is *not* true about Ethernet?

❍ **A.** Full duplex disables CSMA/CD.

❍ **B.** Only one side, either the switch or the host, needs to support full duplex for it to work.

❍ **C.** Hubs operate at half duplex.

❍ **D.** Using full duplex, network devices do not have to wait to see if the media is available.

❍ **E.** A dedicated switch port is needed for each full-duplex device.

15. Consider the following diagram. The PC is sending several ping requests to the server and is getting replies. When the third ping request is sent, what does Switch 2 use to make a forwarding decision?

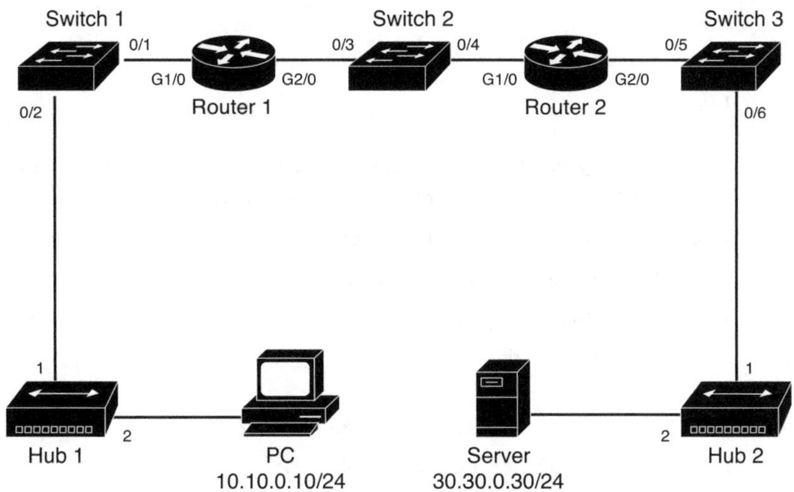

- ❍ **A.** The Layer 3 address of source
- ❍ **B.** The Layer 2 address of the source
- ❍ **C.** R2's g1/0 hardware address
- ❍ **D.** The server's hardware address
- ❍ **E.** R1's G2/0 hardware address

16. What does a Layer 2 switch do when it receives a broadcast frame on one of its interfaces? (Choose 2.)

- ❍ **A.** The frame is dropped.
- ❍ **B.** The switch adds the source MAC address to his table, if it's not already there.
- ❍ **C.** The switch will make a Layer 3 routing decision based on the IP destination address.
- ❍ **D.** The switch will always forward the frame to all the other ports that are in the same VLAN as the port that received the frame.

17. Which device in the network controls VLAN assignment?

- ❍ **A.** PC
- ❍ **B.** NIC
- ❍ **C.** Hub
- ❍ **D.** Switch
- ❍ **E.** Router

18. You want to manipulate STP on a switch to make it become the root of the spanning tree. Which item, when changed, would have the desired result?

- ❍ **A.** Lower the IP to a lower number.
- ❍ **B.** Raise the IP to a higher number.
- ❍ **C.** Lower the priority number.
- ❍ **D.** Raise the priority number.

19. Which of the following is *not* true about a trunk port?

- ❍ **A.** Carries traffic for a single VLAN
- ❍ **B.** Uses the concept of a native VLAN
- ❍ **C.** Sends and receives 802.1Q tags for the VLAN a frame is associated with
- ❍ **D.** Uses a crossover cable to connect to another switch

20. Consider the following diagram. No dynamic routing protocols have been configured in any of the routers. All the WAN links shown in the topology are of equal speed. Each client has been configured to use its local router as a default gateway. What would the correct static route be on R1 to reach the R2's local Ethernet network using the most efficient path?

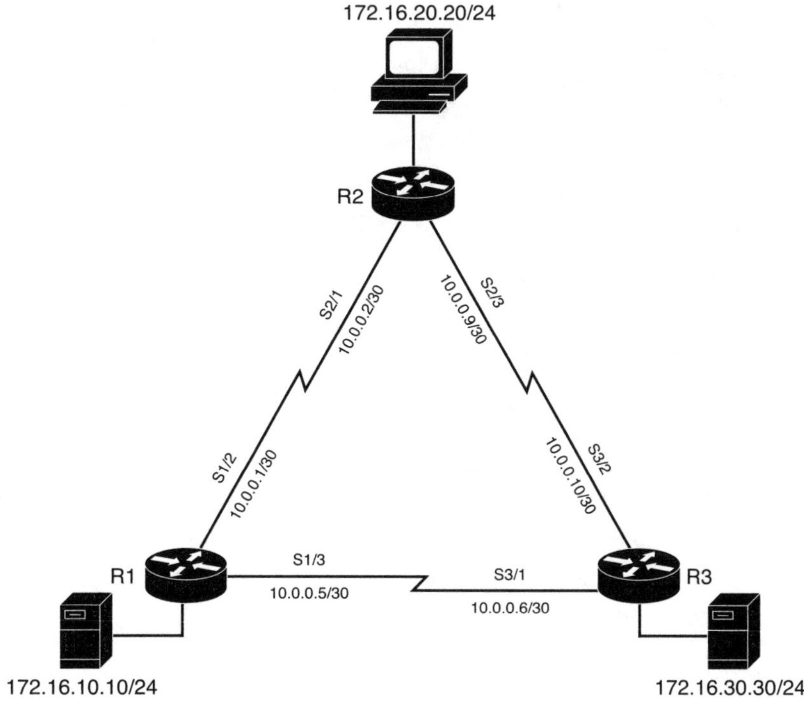

- ❍ **A.** **ip route 0.0.0.0 0.0.0.0 10.0.0.6**
- ❍ **B.** **ip route 172.16.0.0 255.255.0.0 serial 2/1**
- ❍ **C.** **ip route 172.16.30.0 255.255.0.0 serial 1/2**
- ❍ **D.** **ip route 172.16.0.0 255.255.0.0 serial 1/2**
- ❍ **E.** **ip route 172.16.0.0 255.255.0.0 serial 1/3**

21. Consider the following configuration command:

```
ip route 0.0.0.0 0.0.0.0 192.168.1.1
```

Which of the following is true about this command?

- ❍ **A.** This is not a default route.
- ❍ **B.** The exit interface on the local router for this route is 192.168.1.1.
- ❍ **C.** This route command is not valid because it requires an interface to be included in the command.
- ❍ **D.** Packets for unknown networks will be forwarded to 192.168.1.1.

22. On a new router, you have brought up the interfaces and configured them as shown in the diagram. IPv6 unicast routing has been enabled. You have added the following commands to the router.

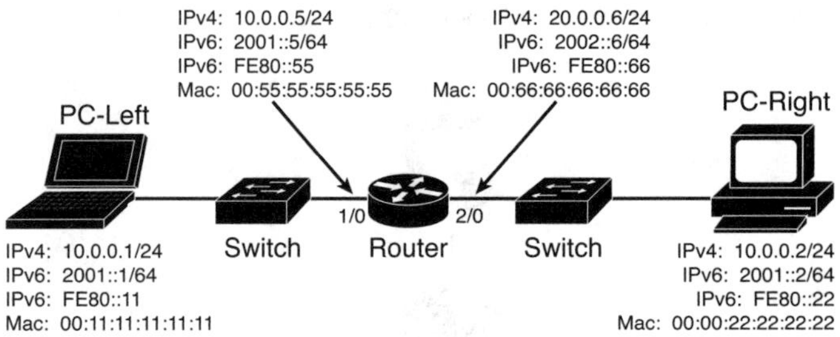


```
Router(config)#router ospf 1
Router(config-router)#exit
Router(config-router)#interface g1/0
Router(config-if)#ospf 1 area 0
Router(config-if)#int g 2/0
Router(config-if)#ospf 1 area 0
```

The PC on the left cannot ping the IPv6 addresses of the PC on the right. What should be added to the configuration?

- ❍ **A.** Add network statements to include the interfaces.
- ❍ **B.** Configure a loopback with an IPv4 address on it.
- ❍ **C.** Verify the clients are both running IPv6.
- ❍ **D.** Configure a router ID in OSPFv3.

23. When configuring a router on a stick, which of the following are true? (Choose 2.)

- ❍ **A.** The router connected to the switch must be connected to a switch trunk port.
- ❍ **B.** Subinterfaces, because of trunking, can use overlapping IP addresses from the same subnets.
- ❍ **C.** The router creates 802.1Q encapsulated subinterfaces, which are assigned IP addresses.
- ❍ **D.** The router connected to the switch must be connected to a switch access port.

24. Consider the diagram shown. All WAN links are 1.54Mbps. OSPF is enabled on all routers and all interfaces. The PC at 172.16.20.20 wants to send an ICMP ping request to the server at 172.16.30.30. Before the ping is sent, the WAN link connecting R2 to R3 fails. What are the results?

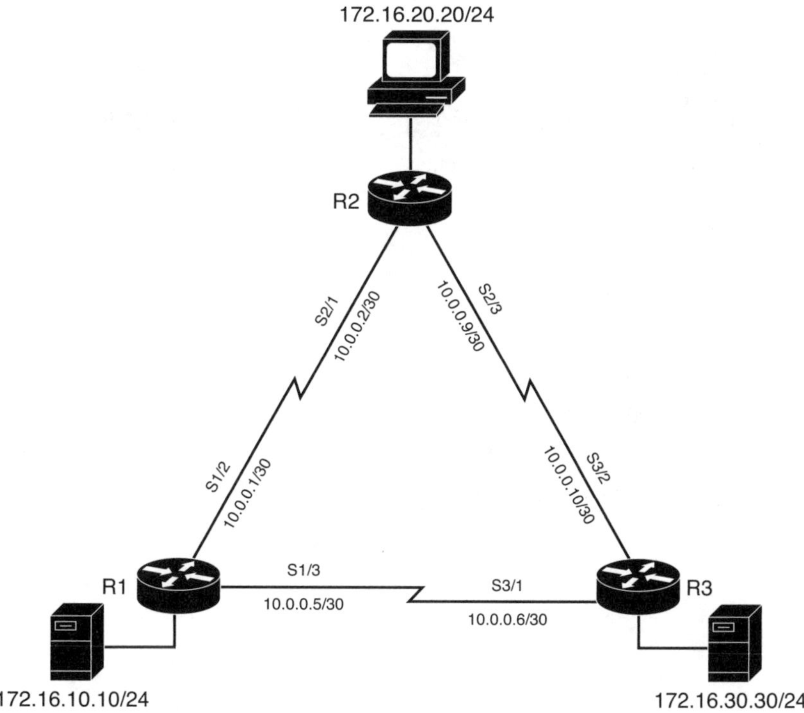

❍ **A.** After OSPF converges, it will use a new route, through R1, to reach 172.16.30.0/24.

❍ **B.** A static route will need to be added to indicate that R2 is the next hop to reach 172.16.30.0/24.

❍ **C.** Because it is a point-to-point WAN link, access to the server won't be available until the link is back up.

❍ **D.** Because OSPF is a distance vector protocol, it will automatically reroute the traffic.

25. Consider the following diagram. If the PC on the right sends a packet to the IP address of the PC on the left, what will be the Layer 2 destination address be in the frame when the router receives it?

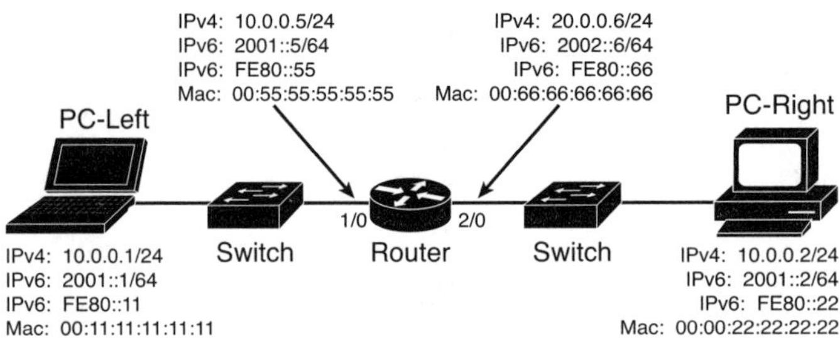

❍ **A.** 10.0.0.1

❍ **B.** 10.0.0.5

❍ **C.** 20.0.0.2

❍ **D.** 00:11:11:11:11:11

❍ **E.** 00:55:55:55:55:55

❍ **F.** 00:66:66:66:66:66

26. Consider the following diagram. The PC is using an SSH session to connect to R2. If we look at the packet as Switch 2 is switching it, which of the following would be true?

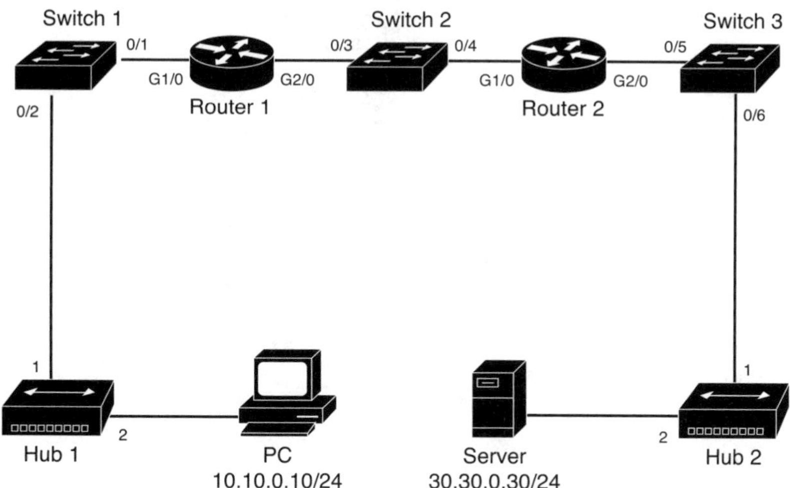

- ❍ **A.** The source IP address would be R1's G2/0 address.
- ❍ **B.** The Layer 2 destination address would be the PC's address.
- ❍ **C.** The source Layer 2 address would be Switch 1's address.
- ❍ **D.** The source Layer 2 address would be R1's G2/0 address.
- ❍ **E.** The destination Layer 2 address would be R2 G1/0.
- ❍ **F.** The source Layer 2 address would be the PCs address.

27. How does a computer know whether the destination it wants to send a packet to is local or remote?

- ❍ **A.** It compares the destination address against the network address the local client is connected to.
- ❍ **B.** It compares the its local mask to the mask of the destination.
- ❍ **C.** It asks the router with a Router Solicitation to ask whether the destination is local or remote; the router should know.
- ❍ **D.** The local client doesn't know. All traffic, local or remote, is forwarded to the router for processing.

28. Consider the following diagram. Following best practices, you want to place an ACL to deny the PC at 172.16.10.10 from accessing the server at 172.16.30.30. All other traffic should be permitted. Which of the following should you do?

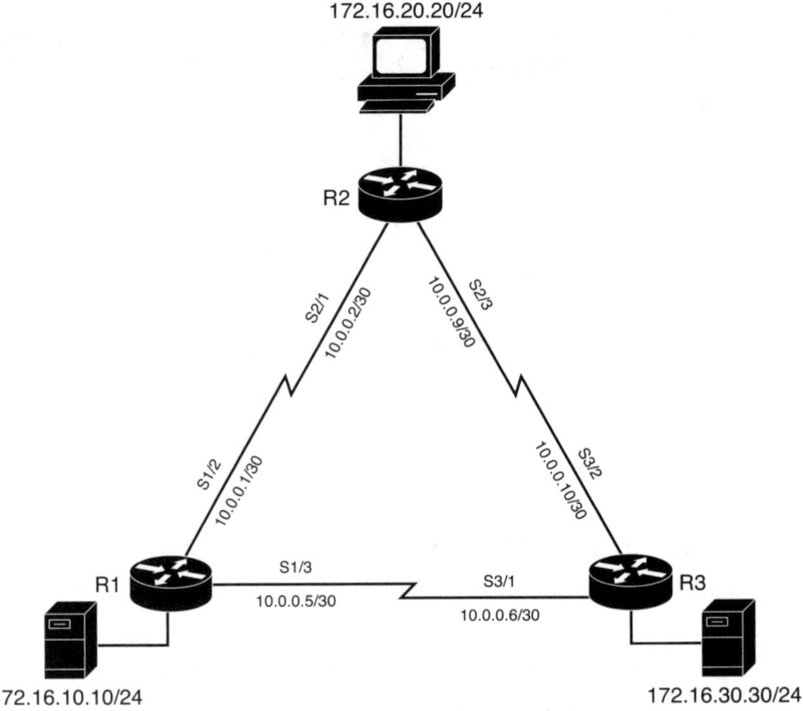

❍ **A.** Place an extended ACL on R1, inbound on the router interface connecting to the PC, to filter traffic from the PC to the server and permit everything else.

❍ **B.** Place a standard ACL on R1, inbound on the router interface connecting to the PC, to filter traffic from the PC to the server.

❍ **C.** Place an extended ACL on R2, outbound on the router interface connecting to the server, to filter traffic from the PC to the server and permit everything else.

❍ **D.** Place standard named ACL on R2, outbound on the router interface connecting to the server, to filter traffic from the PC to the server, and permit everything else.

29. When are wildcards used in Cisco IOS routers? (Choose 2.)

❍ **A.** In network statements

❍ **B.** In static routes

❍ **C.** Never

❍ **D.** In ACLs

❍ **E.** In interface configuration

30. Which are practical ways of securing access to the router over its logical vty lines?

❍ **A.** Remove the console cable.

❍ **B.** Don't allow any IP connectivity to the router.

❍ **C.** Use an ACL as a filtering device on the interface using **access-class** commands.

❍ **D.** Use an ACL as a filtering device on the lines using the **access-class** commands.

❍ **E.** There isn't a practical method of securing the vty lines.

31. Review the diagram and the partial output provided from the configuration on R2.

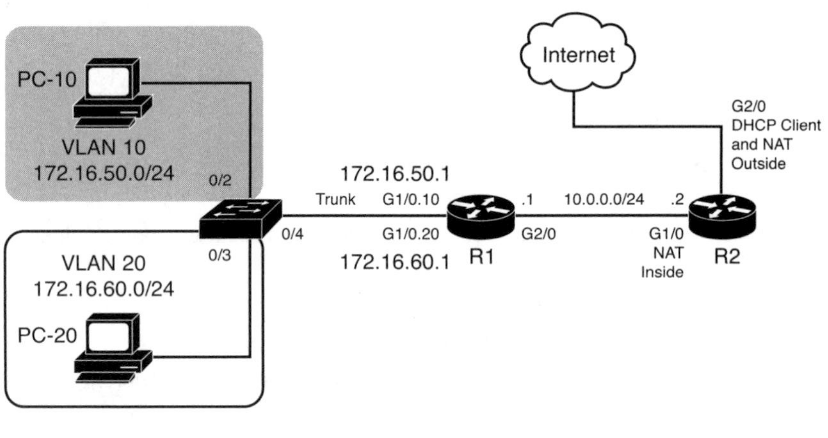


```
interface GigabitEthernet1/0
 ip address 10.0.0.2 255.255.255.0
 ip nat inside
 ip virtual-reassembly
!
interface GigabitEthernet2/0
 ip address dhcp
 ip nat outside
 ip virtual-reassembly
!
!
router ospf 1
 log-adjacency-changes
 network 10.0.0.0 0.0.0.255 area 0
 default-information originate always
!
ip nat inside source list 1 interface GigabitEthernet2/0 overload
!
```

What is required to make this a working NAT/PAT configuration?

- ❍ **A.** The outside NAT interface can't be a DHCP client.
- ❍ **B.** The router can't advertise an OSPF default route on the NAT inside interface.
- ❍ **C.** Create access list 1, which permits the source addresses of the devices that may be translated through NAT/PAT.
- ❍ **D.** The NAT configuration must be on R1 (connected to the clients), not on R2.

32. You have set up a Cisco IOS router as a DHCP server. After a week, you need to find out how many DHCP discover packets have been received by the router. Which command should you use?

❍ **A.** **show ip dhcp binding**

❍ **B.** **show ip dhcp server statistics**

❍ **C.** **show dhcp binding**

❍ **D.** **show dhcp server statistics**

❍ **E.** **show ip dhcp conflict**

33. Review the partial output provided:

```
R2#show ntp associations
  address         ref clock       st   when   poll reach  delay  offset   disp
 * sys.peer, # selected, + candidate, - outlyer, x falseticker, ~ configured
```

What is indicated by this output?

❍ **A.** No NTP is configured on this router.

❍ **B.** NTP may be configured, but it is not currently working.

❍ **C.** This router is willing to be an NTP peer.

❍ **D.** This output only will report NTP association errors; at the moment, there aren't any.

34. Consider the diagram and the partial output that follows.

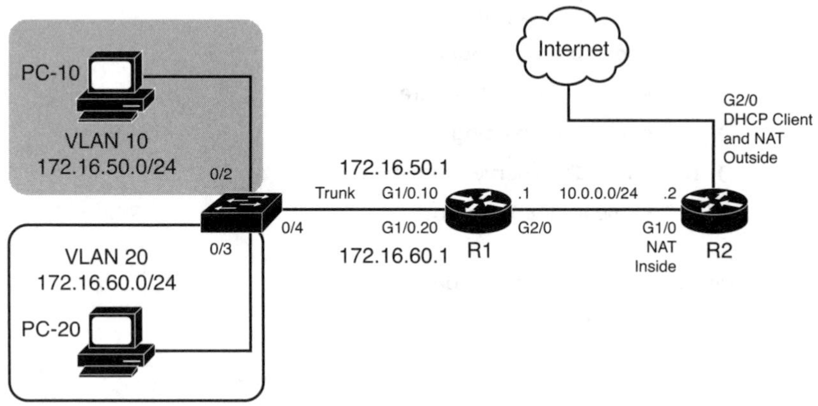


```
switch#show vlan brief

VLAN Name                             Status    Ports
---- -------------------------------- --------- -------------------------------
1    default                          active    Gi0/1, Gi0/5, Gi0/6
                                                Gi0/7, Gi0/8, Gi0/9,
                                                Gi0/11, Gi0/12, Gi0/13, Gi0/14
                                                Gi0/15, Gi0/16, Gi0/17, Gi0/18
10   VLAN0010                         active    Gi0/2
20   VLAN0020                         active    Gi0/3
30   VLAN0055                         active

R1#show ip dhcp pool

Pool subnet50-pool :
 Utilization mark (high/low)     : 100 / 0
 Subnet size (first/next)        : 0 / 0
 Total addresses                 : 254
 Leased addresses                : 0
 Pending event                   : none
 1 subnet is currently in the pool :
 Current index        IP address range                    Leased addresses
 172.16.50.1          172.16.50.1      - 172.16.50.254     1
```

```
Pool subnet60-pool :
 Utilization mark (high/low)     : 100 / 0
 Subnet size (first/next)        : 0 / 0
 Total addresses                 : 254
 Leased addresses                : 0
 Pending event                   : none
 1 subnet is currently in the pool :
 Current index        IP address range                    Leased addresses
 172.16.60.1          172.16.60.1      - 172.16.60.254     1

R1#show run
<snip>
ip dhcp pool subnet50-pool
   network 172.16.50.0 255.255.255.0
   default-router 172.16.50.1
   dns-server 8.8.8.8
!
ip dhcp pool subnet60-pool
   network 172.16.60.0 255.255.255.0
   dns-server 8.8.8.8
   default-router 172.16.20.1
<snip>
```

The user at PC-20 is calling to say he can't connect to the Internet. PC-10 isn't having any problems. Based on the information provided, what is the problem?

- ❍ **A.** The incorrect DHCP pool is being used at the router.
- ❍ **B.** The incorrect default gateway is being handed out via DHCP.
- ❍ **C.** The physical connection between the router and the switch has failed.
- ❍ **D.** The incorrect DNS information is being handed out from the DHCP server.

35. Consider the diagram and the partial output that follows.

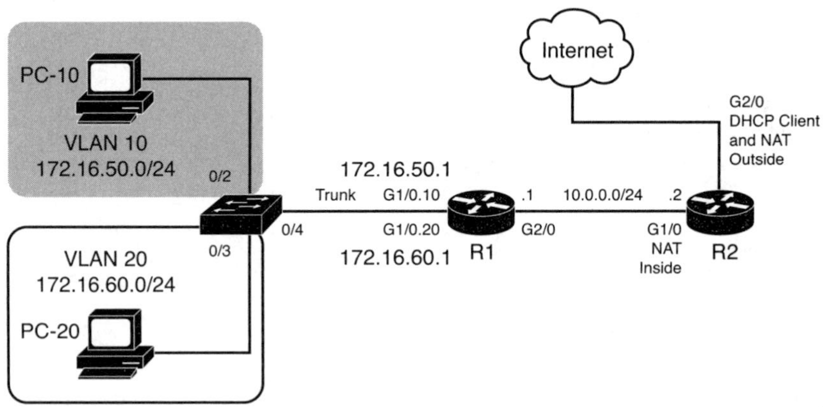


```
switch#show int trunk

Port        Mode              Encapsulation  Status        Native vlan
Gi0/4       desirable         802.1q         trunking      1

Port        Vlans allowed on trunk
Gi0/4       1-4094

Port        Vlans allowed and active in management domain
Gi0/4       1-5,10-12,20,55

Port        Vlans in spanning tree forwarding state and not pruned
Gi0/4       1-5,10-12,20,55

R1#show vlans

Virtual LAN ID:  1 (IEEE 802.1Q Encapsulation)
   vLAN Trunk Interface:   GigabitEthernet1/0
GigabitEthernet1/0

Virtual LAN ID:  10 (IEEE 802.1Q Encapsulation)

   vLAN Trunk Interface:   GigabitEthernet1/0.10

   Protocols Configured:   Address:            Received:        Transmitted:
           IP              172.16.50.1                 0                   0
        Other                                          0                   0
```

```
Virtual LAN ID:  20 (IEEE 802.1Q Encapsulation)

   vLAN Trunk Interface:   GigabitEthernet1/0.20

   Protocols Configured:   Address:            Received:         Transmitted:
           IP              172.16.20.1                 0                    0
        Other                                          0                    0

   0 packets, 0 bytes input
   0 packets, 0 bytes output


R1#show ip dhcp pool

Pool subnet50-pool :
 Utilization mark (high/low)     : 100 / 0
 Subnet size (first/next)        : 0 / 0
 Total addresses                 : 254
 Leased addresses                : 0
 Pending event                   : none
 1 subnet is currently in the pool :
 Current index         IP address range                    Leased addresses
 172.16.50.1           172.16.50.1      - 172.16.50.254     0

Pool subnet60-pool :
 Utilization mark (high/low)     : 100 / 0
 Subnet size (first/next)        : 0 / 0
 Total addresses                 : 254
 Leased addresses                : 0
 Pending event                   : none
 1 subnet is currently in the pool :
 Current index         IP address range                    Leased addresses
 172.16.60.1           172.16.60.1      - 172.16.60.254     0
```

Users in VLAN 20 are not able to browse the Internet. Based on the information provided, what is the cause?

- ❍ **A.** The router interface isn't configured correctly for the 172.16.60.0/24 subnet.
- ❍ **B.** DHCP services aren't configured on the router.
- ❍ **C.** The router hasn't configured subinterfaces to support the VLANs.
- ❍ **D.** The IP addresses on the router's interfaces aren't correct.

36. Consider the diagram and the partial output that follows.

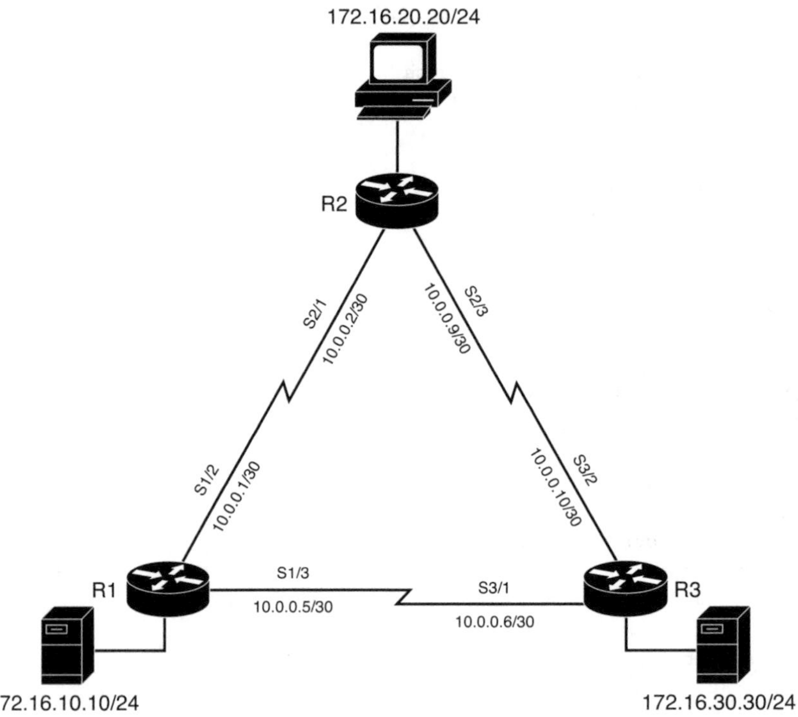


```
R1#show ip nat translations
Pro Inside global      Inside local       Outside local      Outside global
--- 192.168.0.33       172.16.10.10       ---                ---

R1#show ip int brief
Interface                  IP-Address      OK? Method Status        Protocol
Serial1/2                  10.0.0.1        YES manual up            up
Serial1/3                  10.0.0.5        YES manual up            up
GigabitEthernet2/0         172.16.10.1     YES manual up            up
NVI0                       10.0.0.1        YES unset  up            up

R2#show ip route ospf
      10.0.0.0/8 is variably subnetted, 5 subnets, 2 masks
O        10.0.0.4/30 [110/128] via 10.0.0.10, 00:43:57, Serial2/3
                     [110/128] via 10.0.0.1, 00:17:49, Serial2/1
      172.16.0.0/16 is variably subnetted, 4 subnets, 2 masks
O        172.16.10.0/24 [110/65] via 10.0.0.1, 00:49:56, Serial2/1
O        172.16.30.0/24 [110/65] via 10.0.0.10, 00:43:57, Serial2/3
```

Customers on the 172.16.10.0/24 network are complaining that they can't access any of the other remote 172.16.x.0/24 networks? Which commands could be used to correct this problem? (Choose 2.)

- ❍ **A.** On R2, **ip route 0.0.0.0 0.0.0.0 10.0.0.10**
- ❍ **B.** On R3, **ip route 0.0.0.0 0.0.0.0 10.0.0.9**
- ❍ **C.** On R1, **ip route 0.0.0.0 0.0.0.0 10.0.0.2**
- ❍ **D.** On R1, **ip route 0.0.0.0 0.0.0.0 10.0.0.6**
- ❍ **E.** On R2, **ip route 0.0.0.0 0.0.0.0 10.0.0.1**

37. Consider the diagram and the output that follows.

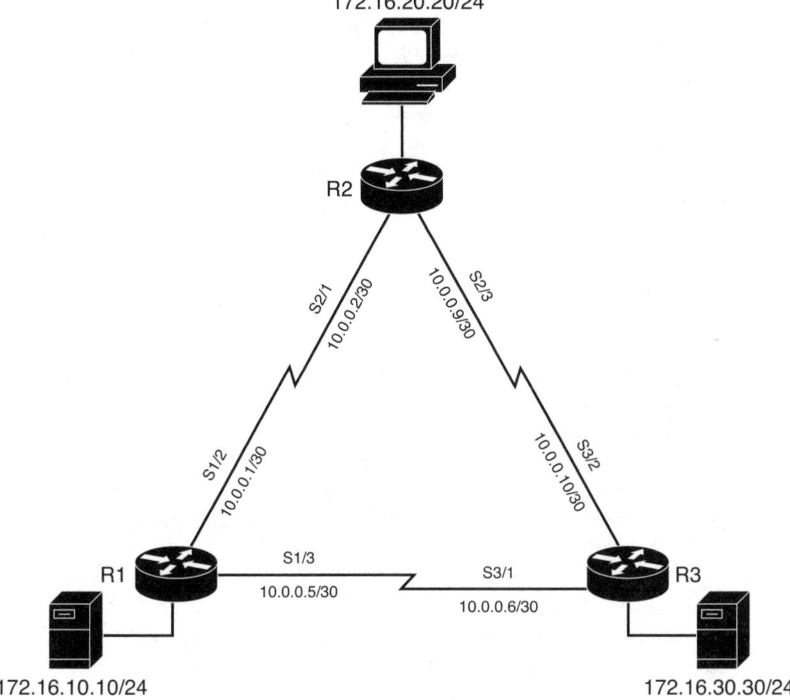

```
R1#show ip ospf neighbor

Neighbor ID     Pri   State           Dead Time   Address         Interface
172.16.30.1       0   FULL/  -        00:00:38    10.0.0.6        Serial1/3

R1#show ip ospf int brief
Interface    PID   Area            IP Address/Mask    Cost  State Nbrs F/C
Se1/2        1     0               10.0.0.1/30        64    DOWN  0/0
Gi2/0        1     0               172.16.10.1/24     1     DR    0/0
Se1/3        1     0               10.0.0.5/30        64    P2P   1/1

R1#show int ser 1/2
Serial1/2 is up, line protocol is down
  Internet address is 10.0.0.1/30
  MTU 1500 bytes, BW 1544 Kbit/sec, DLY 20000 usec,
     reliability 255/255, txload 1/255, rxload 1/255
  Encapsulation PPP, LCP REQsent, crc 16, loopback not set
  Keepalive set (10 sec)
  Restart-Delay is 0 secs
  Last input 00:00:02, output 00:00:01, output hang never
  Last clearing of "show interface" counters 00:02:22
  Input queue: 0/75/0/0 (size/max/drops/flushes); Total output drops: 0
  Queueing strategy: weighted fair
  Output queue: 0/1000/64/0 (size/max total/threshold/drops)
     Conversations  0/1/256 (active/max active/max total)
     Reserved Conversations 0/0 (allocated/max allocated)
     Available Bandwidth 1158 kilobits/sec
  5 minute input rate 0 bits/sec, 0 packets/sec
  5 minute output rate 0 bits/sec, 0 packets/sec
     15 packets input, 360 bytes, 0 no buffer
     Received 0 broadcasts, 0 runts, 0 giants, 0 throttles
     0 input errors, 0 CRC, 0 frame, 0 overrun, 0 ignored, 0 abort
     67 packets output, 938 bytes, 0 underruns
     0 output errors, 0 collisions, 7 interface resets
     15 unknown protocol drops
     0 output buffer failures, 0 output buffers swapped out
     7 carrier transitions     DCD=up  DSR=up  DTR=up  RTS=up  CTS=up

=======
```

```
R2#show ip ospf neighbor

Neighbor ID     Pri   State           Dead Time   Address         Interface
172.16.30.1       0   FULL/  -        00:00:39    10.0.0.10       Serial2/3

R2#show ip ospf int brief
Interface    PID   Area            IP Address/Mask    Cost  State Nbrs F/C
Se2/3        1     0               10.0.0.9/30        64    P2P   1/1
Se2/1        1     0               10.0.0.2/30        64    DOWN  0/0
Gi1/0        1     0               172.16.20.1/24     1     DR    0/0

R2#show int ser 2/1
Serial2/1 is up, line protocol is down
  Internet address is 10.0.0.2/30
  MTU 1500 bytes, BW 1544 Kbit/sec, DLY 20000 usec,
     reliability 255/255, txload 1/255, rxload 1/255
  Encapsulation HDLC, crc 16, loopback not set
  Keepalive set (10 sec)
  Restart-Delay is 0 secs
  Last input 00:00:01, output 00:00:03, output hang never
  Last clearing of "show interface" counters 00:02:08
  Input queue: 0/75/0/0 (size/max/drops/flushes); Total output drops: 0
  Queueing strategy: weighted fair
  Output queue: 0/1000/64/0 (size/max total/threshold/drops)
     Conversations  0/1/256 (active/max active/max total)
     Reserved Conversations 0/0 (allocated/max allocated)
     Available Bandwidth 1158 kilobits/sec
  5 minute input rate 0 bits/sec, 0 packets/sec
  5 minute output rate 0 bits/sec, 0 packets/sec
     61 packets input, 854 bytes, 0 no buffer
     Received 61 broadcasts, 0 runts, 0 giants, 0 throttles
     0 input errors, 0 CRC, 0 frame, 0 overrun, 0 ignored, 0 abort
     13 packets output, 312 bytes, 0 underruns
     0 output errors, 0 collisions, 0 interface resets
     61 unknown protocol drops
     0 output buffer failures, 0 output buffers swapped out
     0 carrier transitions     DCD=up  DSR=up  DTR=up  RTS=up  CTS=up
```

R1 and R2 won't become OSPF neighbors. Based on the information provided, what is causing the problem?

❍ **A.** There is a different mask length on the interfaces connecting R1 and R2.

❍ **B.** There is an OSPF area mismatch between R1 and R2.

❍ **C.** There is an incorrect network address between R1 and R2.

❍ **D.** There is an encapsulation mismatch between R1 and R2.

38. Review the following output:

```
SW4#show spanning-tree vlan 1
VLAN0001
  Spanning tree enabled protocol rstp
  Root ID     Priority     32769
              Address      1234.210E.47B3
              Cost         19
              Port         5(FastEthernet0/5)
              Hello Time   2 sec  Max Age 20 sec  Forward Delay 15 sec

  Bridge ID   Priority     32769  (priority 32768 sys-id-ext 1)
              Address      1234.210F.47B3
              Hello Time   2 sec  Max Age 20 sec  Forward Delay 15 sec
              Aging Time   20

Interface         Role Sts Cost       Prio.Nbr Type
---------------- ---- --- --------- -------- ------------------------
--------
Fa0/4            Altn BLK 19         128.4    P2p
Fa0/5            Root FWD 19         128.5    P2p
Fa0/3            Desg FWD 19         128.3    P2p
```

Which of the following are true?

❍ **A.** The root switch has a lower bridge ID than this switch.

❍ **B.** This switch has the highest bridge ID, which means when spanning tree converges, it will be the root for VLAN 1.

❍ **C.** This switch is blocking on two of its three ports that are participating in spanning tree for VLAN 1.

❍ **D.** The timers that are being learned from the root are the not the default timers for spanning tree.

39. Consider the diagram shown. Regarding VLAN 1, the priorities have been set as shown in the diagram, and Rapid Spanning Tree has been enabled on all switches. All other spanning-tree properties are using their default settings. Why is Switch B port 0/2 in a discarding state?

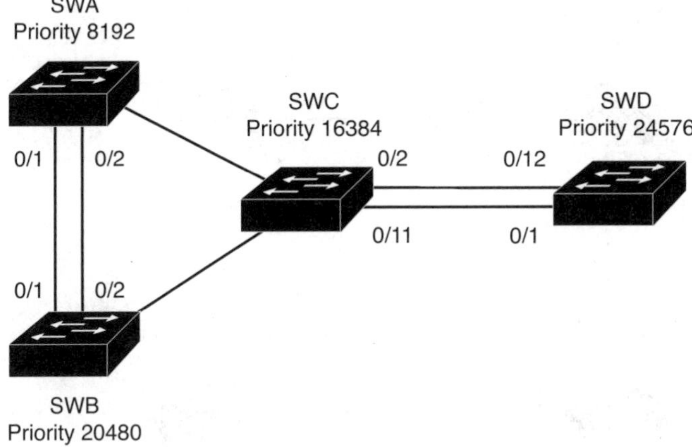

- ❍ **A.** Because Switch C has a better bridge ID.
- ❍ **B.** Because Switch B has a better bridge ID.
- ❍ **C.** Switch B port 0/2 is not in a discarding state, it is forwarding.
- ❍ **D.** Because it has parallel paths to the root switch.

40. Consider the diagram provided. The switches are using the defaults for spanning tree, and the base MAC addresses are as shown in the topology. Which port will perform the discarding/blocking function for VLAN 1 if the cable connection between Switch 1 and Switch 2 becomes disconnected?

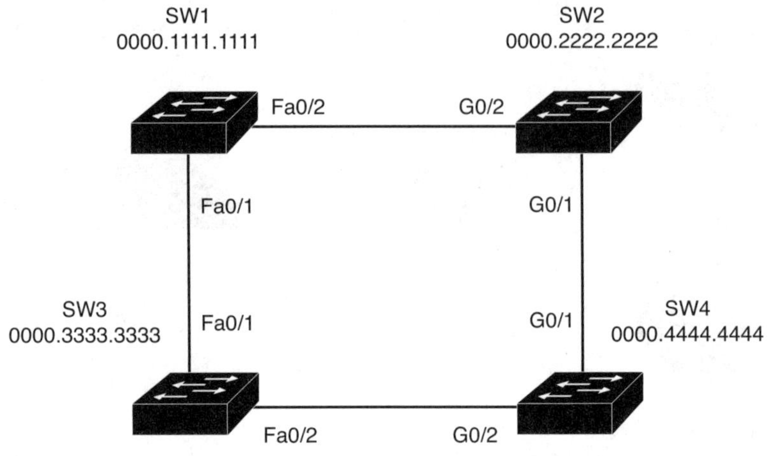

❍ **A.** Switch 2, 0/1.

❍ **B.** Switch 4, 0/1.

❍ **C.** Switch 4, 0/2.

❍ **D.** Switch 3, 0/2.

❍ **E.** None of the ports would be blocking.

41. Which of the following are accurate statements about the configuration and operation of VLANs?

❍ **A.** New VLANs increase the number of broadcast domains available.

❍ **B.** A Layer 2 switch is required to forward frames between two different VLANs.

❍ **C.** Creating new VLANs increases the number of collision domains available on the switch.

❍ **D.** No ports are assigned to any VLANs until the VLANs are created and an administrator assigns ports.

42. Which should be configured between two switches when more throughput is required beyond a single physical link?

❍ **A.** Access ports

❍ **B.** Trunk ports

❍ **C.** EtherChannel

❍ **D.** Routed ports

❍ **E.** None of these answers

43. A data packet is being sent over a trunk link and has VLAN tagging information for VLAN 10. What would cause this? (Choose 2.)

❍ **A.** The trunk is configured as an access port.

❍ **B.** The traffic being sent belongs to the native VLAN.

❍ **C.** The packet was sourced by a host in VLAN 10.

❍ **D.** The packet is destined to a host in VLAN 10.

44. What is the result of adding more switches to an existing infrastructure but not creating more VLANs?

❍ **A.** The number of broadcast domains increases, while the size of the broadcast domain decreases.

❍ **B.** The number of broadcast domains decreases, while the size of the broadcast domain increases.

❍ **C.** The number of collision domains increases, while the size of the broadcast domain decreases.

❍ **D.** The number of collision domains increases, while the size of the broadcast domain increases.

❍ **E.** The number of collision domains decreases, while the size of the broadcast domain increases.

45. If switch A is configured as an EtherChannel that will initiate a negotiation using LACP, which of the options, if used on Switch B, would result in a successful EtherChannel negotiation between the two?

❍ **A.** Auto

❍ **B.** Desirable

❍ **C.** Passive

❍ **D.** On

46. Review the following output:

```
R1#show ip eigrp topology
IP-EIGRP Topology Table for AS 1

Codes: P - Passive, A - Active, U - Update, Q - Query, R - Reply,
       r - Reply status

<snip>
P 4.4.4.4/32, 1 successors, FD is 131072
         via 10.12.0.2 (131072/130816), GigabitEthernet0/0
         via 10.13.0.3 (2298112/130816), Serial0/0/0
```

What is the value of 130816 that is shown twice in the output?

❍ **A.** It is the feasible successor metric on the local router.

❍ **B.** It is the cutoff point for determining feasible successors.

❍ **C.** It is the advertised/reported distance from the neighbors.

❍ **D.** It is the cost to reach each of the next hops.

47. Which of the following methods should be used to protect access to the vty lines on a Cisco router?

❍ **A.** Disable Telnet, while permitting and enabling SSH.

❍ **B.** Use access control lists on all Ethernet interfaces to control access to the vty lines.

❍ **C.** Use passwords only, instead of user accounts that could be compromised.

❍ **D.** The vty lines should be disabled.

48. What does the OSPF configuration command of **default-information originate** do?

❍ **A.** It causes the OSPF router to advertise a default route to its OSPF neighbors regardless of whether the router itself has a default route.

❍ **B.** It causes an OSPF router to advertise a default route to its OSPF neighbors, but only if it has a default route of its own.

❍ **C.** It allows the local router to use one of its OSPF neighbors as a default gateway.

❍ **D.** It allows multiple OSPF processes to run simultaneously on the local router.

49. If a new router running OSPF is added to an existing OSPF network, and the new router has a higher router ID, which of the following are true with regard to who will be the designated router?

❍ **A.** The router on a serial point-to-point interface that has the highest router ID.

❍ **B.** The existing router, which was the OSPF designated router for that segment, will remain the DR.

❍ **C.** The router on a serial point-to-point interface that has the lowest router ID.

❍ **D.** The router on an Ethernet network that has the lowest router ID.

❍ **E.** The router on an Ethernet network that has the highest router ID.

50. Which of the following about routing protocols and their operations are true? (Choose 2.)

❍ **A.** Classful routing protocols send the mask along with the networks in advertisements.

❍ **B.** RIPv2 is an example of a classful routing protocol.

❍ **C.** EIGRP is classless and proprietary.

❍ **D.** OSPF is classful and proprietary.

❍ **E.** None of these answers are accurate.

51. A router is running three different routing protocols (EIGRP, OSPF, and RIPv2), and a specific route has been learned by each of these three routing protocols. Only the route from EIGRP was put in the routing table. What explains this behavior?

❍ **A.** The route learned from the routing protocol that the local router believes to have the lowest administrative distance will be put into the routing table, and the other two routes will not be put into the routing table.

❍ **B.** A router will only equal-cost load balance across multiple equal-cost routes if administratively configured.

❍ **C.** The EIGRP route would be in the routing table due to a shorter metric.

❍ **D.** The route learned from the routing protocol that the local router believes to have the highest administrative distance will be put into the routing table, and the other two routes will not be put into the routing table.

52. What is required to implement OSPFv3?

- ❍ **A.** **ipv6 enable**
- ❍ **B.** A dotted-decimal 32-bit router ID.
- ❍ **C.** **load ipv6**
- ❍ **D.** OSPFv2 is used for IPv6.

53. What command reveals the virtual MAC address used by HSRP?

- ❍ **A.** **show standby**
- ❍ **B.** **show mac hsrp**
- ❍ **C.** **show hsrp mac**
- ❍ **D.** **show vrrp**

54. Which of the following could participate as an active virtual forwarder?

- ❍ **A.** L2 switch running HSRP
- ❍ **B.** L2 switch running GLBP
- ❍ **C.** L3 switch running HSRP
- ❍ **D.** L3 switch running GLBP
- ❍ **E.** None of these answers

55. Which PPP authentication protocol sends hashed messages instead of plain text during authentication?

- ❍ **A.** CHAP
- ❍ **B.** PAP
- ❍ **C.** NCP
- ❍ **D.** LCP

56. Which component of a Frame Relay map indicates that multicast routing updates, such as those from RIPv2, EIGRP, and OSPF, are allowed over the link?

- ❍ **A.** Dynamic
- ❍ **B.** Broadcast
- ❍ **C.** Multicast
- ❍ **D.** Static

57. Review the following output:

```
R3#show frame map
Serial1/0 (up): ip 10.23.0.2 dlci 32(0x20,0x800), dynamic,
               broadcast,
               CISCO, status defined, active
```

Which of the following are true based on this output?

❍ **A.** Multicast traffic is not supported over DLCI 32.

❍ **B.** The local address of the router is 10.23.0.2.

❍ **C.** The remote DLCI for 10.23.0.2 must be 32.

❍ **D.** The local DLCI of 32 can be used to reach the remote IP of 10.23.0.2.

58. Review the following output:

```
R3#show frame map
Serial1/0 (up): ip 10.23.0.2 dlci 32(0x20,0x800), broadcast,
               CISCO, status defined, active
R3#
R3#show ip int brief
Interface              IP-Address      OK? Method Status                Protocol
Serial1/0              10.23.0.2       YES NVRAM  up                    up
```

What is wrong from the output provided? (Choose the single best answer.)

❍ **A.** The **broadcast** keyword shouldn't be present in the mapping.

❍ **B.** The local DLCI of 0x20 is incorrect.

❍ **C.** The interface is not correct.

❍ **D.** The IP address in the mapping is not correct.

59. You want to use a WAN protocol for site-to-site connectivity. Which of the following are Layer 2 WAN protocols?

❍ **A.** HDLC

❍ **B.** IPsec

❍ **C.** SSL

❍ **D.** PPP

❍ **E.** Frame Relay

60. For a WAN connection, you are connecting a local Cisco router to a remote non-Cisco router. Which method could be used to protect the entire session from eavesdropping?

❍ **A.** Frame Relay

❍ **B.** HDLC

❍ **C.** PPP

❍ **D.** IPsec

61. Review the following output:

```
R3#show frame pvc

PVC Statistics for interface Serial1/0 (Frame Relay DTE)

              Active     Inactive      Deleted       Static
  Local          0           1            0             0
  Switched       0           0            0             0
  Unused         0           0            0             0

DLCI = 32, DLCI USAGE = LOCAL, PVC STATUS = INACTIVE, INTERFACE = Serial1/0
```

What would cause the output of the PVC STATUS to show INACTIVE?

❍ **A.** LMI is disabled on the interface.

❍ **B.** The PVC is operational and can transmit packets.

❍ **C.** The PVC is configured but is down.

❍ **D.** There is no status of INACTIVE.

62. Which command generates the partial output provided that follows?

```
Protocol [ip]:
Target IP address: 1.1.1.1
Repeat count [5]:
Datagram size [100]:
Timeout in seconds [2]:
Extended commands [n]: y
Source address or interface:
Type of service [0]:
Set DF bit in IP header? [no]:
Validate reply data? [no]:
Data pattern [0xABCD]:
Loose, Strict, Record, Timestamp, Verbose[none]:
Sweep range of sizes [n]:
```

❍ **A.** Ping
❍ **B.** Extended Ping
❍ **C.** Tracert
❍ **D.** Traceroute
❍ **E.** Extended Traceroute

63. In the routing table, what does the letter *C* represent?

❍ **A.** EIGRP-learned route
❍ **B.** Default route
❍ **C.** Static route
❍ **D.** OSPF-learned route
❍ **E.** Directly connected route

64. Your network uses a centralized DHCP server. Existing subnets are functioning. On a brand new subnet, clients can't obtain a DHCP address, but do have a link indicator on their network card. What is the likely problem?

❍ **A.** Layer 3 switch doesn't have DHCP relay configured.
❍ **B.** Layer 3 switch is powered off.
❍ **C.** Layer 3 switch have a default gateway.
❍ **D.** Layer 3 switch isn't a DHCP client.

65. Consider the following output and consider a packet being sent to the router with the following:

Source Layer 2 address: ca03.159c.001c

Destination Layer 2 address: 0000.2121.2222

Source Layer 3 address: 10.12.0.2

Destination Layer 3 address: 10.15.0.5

```
R1#show arp
Protocol  Address       Age (min)  Hardware Addr   Type   Interface
Internet  10.12.0.1             -  0000.1212.1212  ARPA   GigabitEthernet1/0
Internet  10.12.0.2             4  ca01.159c.001c  ARPA   GigabitEthernet1/0
Internet  10.13.0.1             -  0000.1313.1313  ARPA   GigabitEthernet2/0
Internet  10.13.0.3            16  ca02.1bb0.001c  ARPA   GigabitEthernet2/0
Internet  10.14.0.1             -  0000.1414.1414  ARPA   GigabitEthernet3/0
Internet  10.14.0.4             3  ca03.1bb0.001c  ARPA   GigabitEthernet3/0
Internet  10.15.0.1             -  0000.1515.1515  ARPA   GigabitEthernet4/0
Internet  10.15.0.5             7  ca04.19bc.001c  ARPA   GigabitEthernet4/0
```

What would the router do if the switch forwarded the frame to the router?

- ❍ **A.** Decapsulate the packet, then reencapsulate using the L2 source address of 0000.1515.1515
- ❍ **B.** Decapsulate the packet, then reencapsulate using the L3 source address of 10.15.0.1
- ❍ **C.** Decapsulate the packet, then reencapsulate using the L2 destination address of 0000.1515.1515
- ❍ **D.** Decapsulate the packet, then reencapsulate using the L3 destination address of 10.12.0.2
- ❍ **E.** It would drop the packet

66. A host with a MAC address of 0000.2222.7777 has connected to the switch, but you need to find out what port and VLAN it is connecting on. Which switch command would display that information?

- ❍ **A.** **show mac-address-table**
- ❍ **B.** **show interface**
- ❍ **C.** **show mac-table**
- ❍ **D.** **show cam address-table**
- ❍ **E.** **show run**

67. You have used the **show interface** command and see that the interface is showing up/down. What may cause this?

❍ **A.** A physical cable is not attached to the interface.

❍ **B.** OSPF if not forming a neighbor relationship over that interface.

❍ **C.** An encapsulation mismatch.

❍ **D.** CDP is disabled.

❍ **E.** The interface is shut down.

Answer Key to Practice Exam 2

Answers at a Glance to Practice Exam 2

1. B
2. B
3. A
4. B, E
5. B, C
6. C
7. C
8. B
9. D
10. B
11. D
12. A
13. A
14. B
15. C
16. B, D
17. D
18. C
19. A
20. D
21. D
22. C
23. A, C
24. A
25. F
26. D, E
27. A
28. A
29. A, D
30. D
31. C
32. B
33. A
34. B
35. A
36. B, E
37. D
38. A
39. D
40. E
41. A
42. C
43. C, D
44. D
45. C
46. C
47. A
48. B
49. B
50. C
51. A
52. B
53. A
54. D
55. A
56. B
57. D
58. D
59. A, D, E
60. D
61. C
62. B
63. E
64. A
65. E
66. A
67. C

Answers with Explanations

1. Answer B is correct. A leased line represents a serial interface, so the network device to connect the branch to the Internet would need an Ethernet connection to connect to their existing switch, and a serial interface with the appropriate cable to connect to the service providers leased line. The router would also need to be configured with Network Address Translation and appropriate IP addressing to function. A Layer 2 switch does not have routing capability that would be needed for connecting the branch to the Internet. A Layer 2 switch also does not have a serial interface that would be suitable for connectivity to a leased line. A router with only two Ethernet interfaces would not have the serial interface required to connect to leased line. A router with two serial interfaces would not have the Ethernet connectivity to connect to the existing Layer 2 switch.
2. Answer B is correct. Secure Shell (SSH) uses TCP, which is a reliable connection-oriented transport layer protocol. ARP is used to assist the computer in resolving a Layer 3 to Layer 2 mapping. IP is a network layer protocol. UDP is a transport layer protocol that is unreliable and is not used by SSH. SNMP is a Simple Network Management Protocol application layer service.
3. Answer A is correct. DNS is a name resolution protocol. FTP is the File Transfer Protocol, which can reliably send and retrieve files. It uses TCP as transport layer for reliable communications. DHCP is the Dynamic Host Configuration Protocol used to assign IP addresses and other parameters to devices on the network. Telnet is a remote-access application layer service that can give us command-line interface access to a remote device (although it is not secure). NTP is the Network Time Protocol, and TFTP is the Trivial File Transfer Protocol, which uses UDP at the transport layer which is nonreliable.
4. Answers B and E are correct. Multilayer switches along with routers understand Layer 2 and Layer 3 addresses. A hub is a Layer 1 device and does not understand, recognize, or make forwarding decisions based on Layer 2 or higher. Bridges and Layer 2 switches along with network interface cards understand later 2 addressing.
5. Answers B and C are correct. The mask used in the question is a /12, which means that the subnet values in the second octet are going to be multiples of 16. The subnet the host in the question is on is 172.16.0.0/12, which has a range of 172.16.0.1 to 172.31.255.254. There are two hosts in that range: 172.20.0.1 and 172.30.0.1. All the other answers are not within that range.
6. Answer C is correct. A /27 applied to a Class C address space allows 3 additional bits for custom subnetting. 2 ^ 3 = 8 possible subnets that could be created, using a block size of 32.
7. Answer C is correct. The subnet of 20.32.0.0/11 has a host range from 20.32.0.1 to 20.63.255.254. Both of the proposed interfaces are in that same subnet. As a result, the router won't allow the two interfaces to reside on the same logical IP network on the same router. Neither of the addresses is a network address, and the first one applied would be accepted by the router.

8. Answer B is correct. Cisco Discovery Protocol (CDP) is a proprietary Cisco protocol used to assist network administrators in identifying directly connected Cisco devices. CDP sends periodic messages over Layer 2 networks that support this protocol. NTP is the Network Time Protocol and is an open standard. ICMP is the Internet Control Message Protocol and is also an open standard. LLDP is Link Level Discovery Protocol, which is similar to CDP but isn't proprietary. Telnet is an application layer service for remote access.

9. Answer D is correct. CDP will only show directly connected Cisco devices that are running CDP. Router 1 would see both Switch 1 and Switch 2 as neighbors. CDP isn't routed or forwarded beyond the directly connected network, so all the other answers presented are incorrect.

10. Answer B is correct. When connecting "like" devices, that both send on a specific pair and receive on the same specific pair, a crossover cable is needed to connect the send pair on one device to the receive pair on the other. There are two categories: hub/switch devices and everything else. When connecting two devices directly from the same category, you need a crossover cable.

11. Answer D is correct. The command service password-encryption will take plain-text passwords that are in the configuration or that will be added to the configuration and store them in an encrypted format. The other variants of the command offered as possible answers are not valid syntax.

12. Answer A is correct. The default number of MAC addresses allowed by default with port security is 1 MAC address.

13. Answer A is correct. Shutdown is the default action when a port security violation occurs. Protect and Restrict are optional settings, but not the default. Warn is not a valid port security violation action.

14. Answer B is correct. Both the switch and the host both need to support full duplex for it to operate. Using full duplex, each node is allocated dedicated bandwidth and access to media, which means that there is no need to wait to see whether the media is free. To implement full duplex, every node on the network will be connected to its own switch port, which means that a dedicated switch port is required for each full-duplex device. Full duplex doesn't use carrier sense multiple access with collision detection. In full duplex, collision detection is disabled on the network adapters. Hubs operate at half duplex.

15. Answer C is correct. A switch makes a forwarding decision based on the destination Layer 2 address in a frame. R1 would be sending the frame to the next hop, which is R2, and would have included R2's hardware address as the destination in the Layer 2 header. Because this was not the first packet, it is presumed that Switch 2 would have already learned the required MAC addresses to make the forwarding decision. Switches do not use Layer 3 addresses to make forwarding decisions, nor do they use the source MAC address to make forwarding decisions. Switch 2 is not on the same LAN as the server, so would not use the server's address for its Layer 2 forwarding decision because it's not in the same Layer 2 network as the server.

16. Answers B and D are correct. When a Layer 2 switch receives a frame, it adds that source MAC address that was in the frame to its MAC address table. The switch also makes a forwarding decision based on the destination Layer 2 address. If the destination address is not known (as in the case of a broadcast), the switch forwards the frame out of all the other ports that are associated with that same VLAN (same VLAN as the port the frame came into the switch on). If the switch knows the destination Layer 2 address, it forwards the frame only to the port associated with that MAC address. A Layer 2 switch will not make Layer 3 forwarding decisions.

17. Answer D is correct. The switch controls VLAN membership. On the switch, the ports are assigned to VLAN IDs, such as VLAN 2 and VLAN 3. Computers, routers, and other devices that connect to the switch port become part of the Layer 2 broadcast domain (the VLAN) that the port to which they are connected is assigned. All the devices connected to the same VLAN will normally use Layer 3 IP addresses from the same logical subnet, and will use a default gateway to reach devices that are in different VLANs/subnets.

18. Answer C is correct. Spanning tree makes the decision for who will be the root bridge by using the device with the lowest bridge ID. The bridge ID is made up of two parts: the priority number and the base MAC address (in that order). The device with the lowest bridge ID becomes the root of the spanning tree. Priority has the largest impact on the bridge ID, with the base MAC address portion being the tiebreaker when the priority on two devices is the same. IP address doesn't have a role in the spanning-tree decision process.

19. Answer A is correct. Trunks carry traffic for multiple VLANs. Access ports carry the traffic for a single VLAN. No trunking occurs on an access port. There are 802.1Q tags on traffic sent to or from a trunk port. Switches connect to other switches using a crossover cable. Native VLANs play a role in trunk ports (where traffic on the native VLAN isn't tagged).

20. Answer D is correct. R1 should use its s1/2 interface for forwarding a packet to the 20 subnet. Out of the options provided, the only static route that will cause this is **ip route 172.16.0.0 255.255.0.0 serial 1/2**. All the other options are either the incorrect exit interface or the wrong network or next hop.

21. Answer D is correct. A router using this default route will believe that 192.168.1.1 should be the next hop for any destination networks when no detailed routes match in the routing table. 192.168.1.1 is the next-hop address and not the local IP address of the interface of the router where this command is being implemented. Static routes do not need to include the local interface name that should be used, although specifying the interface is an option and may be useful in a point-to-point serial interface.

22. Answer C is correct. Clients must be running IPv6 to use IPv6. The router is directly connected to both networks, so OSPF isn't required for this scenario to work. IPv6 doesn't use network statement to enable interfaces for OSPF; it uses the interface commands instead. In the commands added, the interfaces were added for OSPFv2 but not IPv6's OSPFv3. Both OSPFv2 and OSPFv3 will use an IP address already configured on the router as an OSPF router ID if there is no configured router ID or any loopbacks with IPv4 addresses when OSPF begins.

23. Answers A and C are correct. The router on a stick uses a router interface connected to a switch trunk port. On the router, logical subinterfaces are created for the VLANs we want the router to participate in. Each subinterface will use 802.1Q tagging for the VLAN they are assigned to, and each subinterface will be given an IP address from the subnet associated with a given VLAN. Each of these logical interfaces must connect to a unique subnet, and no overlapping addresses are allowed.

24. Answer A is correct. After OSPF converges, it will use a new route, through R1, to reach 172.16.30.0/24. One of the benefits of a dynamic routing protocol is that it will adjust to the conditions of the network automatically. A static route would not be required. Although the failed link is a point to point, the characteristic of point to point is not relevant because we have another possible path being advertised by R1. OSPF is a link-state protocol, not distance vector.

25. Answer F is correct. When a frame leaves an interface on an Ethernet network, the source Layer 2 address will be the interface that is sending the frame. The destination Layer 2 address will be the next device on that same Ethernet network that is either receiving the packet for itself or in the case of a router receiving the packets so that they can continue forwarding it. When the router receives a frame from the PC on the right, the destination Layer 2 address will be the router 2/0's Layer 2 address. All the other options given are either IP addresses or incorrect MAC addresses.

26. Answers D and E are correct. Because R1 is forwarding the frame to R2, the source Layer 2 address would be R1's G2/0 interface, because that is the interface R1 is using to forward the frame. The destination Layer 2 address would be R2's G1/0 interface hardware address. The source IP address would be the PC.

27. Answer A is correct. The local computer compares its local network address to the IP address of the destination. If the network portion of the local host matches the same number of bits of the destination, the target is considered to be local on the same subnet, and the router does not need to be used. Traffic to local resources doesn't get sent to the router for forwarding. Router Solicitations in IPv6 don't include queries regarding whether a target is local or remote.

28. Answer A is correct. Extended ACLs should be placed as close to the source as possible. This will deny the traffic that should be stopped (very early before that traffic consumes network resources), but still allow other permitted traffic. Placing the extended ACL close to the server would work, but is not the recommended best practice because the traffic would be routed and forwarded just to be denied right before reaching the server. A standard ACL (named or numbered) does not have the ability to match on a destination address, only source. For that reason, a standard ACL cannot match the requirement in the question.

29. Answers A and D are correct. Wildcard masks are used in ACL creation (if desired) and in network statements for OSPF and EIGRP. Static routes and Interface configurations both use normal masks.

30. Answer D is correct. The practical way of securing access to the router via its vty lines would be to use an ACL and permit only specific address to be able to connect. This is applied using the **access-class** command directly to the vty logical line interfaces. Removing a cable from the console port won't have any effect on the vty lines. No IP connectivity to the router at all is impractical. An ACL applied to an IP interface would use the **access-group** command instead of the **access-class** command.

31. Answer C is correct. There needs to be an ACL 1, which is referred to in the NAT statement. The outside interface can be a DHCP client, and the NAT configuration is pointing to the interface, not a specific IP address. OSPF default route advertisement doesn't prevent an interface from being an inside NAT interface. NAT/PAT can be performed anywhere in the path of a packet between the sender and receiver.

32. Answer B is correct. The command **show ip dhcp server statistics** displays statistics about memory usage and the number of DHCP messages and what types, including number of requests and offers. The command **show ip dhcp conflict** shows information about an IP address that the router was going to lease but then discovered that the proposed IP address was already in use on the network. The command **show ip dhcp binding** shows active DHCP leases from the DHCP server service running on the router. The two incorrect options that begin **show dhcp** are both incorrect syntax on the Cisco IOS.

33. Answer A is correct. If NTP were configured on the router, there would be information about the servers or peers included in this output, even if those peers and servers were not functional NTP associations. This router will not be an NTP server, master, peer, or anything else unless configured.

34. Answer B is correct. The default gateway for DHCP used for VLAN 20 isn't correct. Because the user in VLAN 10 is working, the router and connection to the switch are working. Comparing the pool for VLAN 10 and VLAN 20, we could suppose that the DHCP DNS information for VLAN 20 is fine, because it's the same DNS that VLAN 10 is currently using.

35. Answer A is correct. Based on the output for the VLANs supported by the router, it has an incorrect IP address on G0/1.20; it should be in the 172.16.60.0/24 subnet. The switch, based on the diagram, connects to the router on switch port 0/4. The output shows that this is currently a trunk. The output confirms that DHCP services are configured, as well as has subinterfaces configured (although one of the IPs is incorrect, and that is what is causing the problem).

36. Answers B and E are correct. When R2 and R3 receive a packet from the NAT global address of 192.168.0.33, they don't have a route back to that network (which came from a NAT pool). To correct that, R3 could use R2 as a default route, and R2 could use R1 as a default route, and that would allow the return path for both routers. Any other combination (of two choices) wouldn't provide the routing required from R3 back to the NAT pool.

37. Answer D is correct. There is an encapsulation mismatch between R1 and R2, as shown in the output of the **show interface** command.

38. Answer A is correct. The root switch has a lower bridge ID, which makes this switch were looking at (with a higher bridge ID) not be the root. This switch has the same priority as the root, but its base MAC address is higher, which makes for an overall higher bridge ID for this switch, which is causing it not to be the root switch. This switch is not the root; a root switch would have all designated ports, and the output would state that this switch is the root (if it were). The timers are learned from the root switch, and the default hello time is 2 seconds.

39. Answer D is correct. Switch B has 2 directly connected parallel paths to the root switch. Because the cost is the same, it will use the path with the lowest advertised priority, and by default that would be the root switch 0/1 port advertising a lower (better) priority for the port than on 0/2. When Switch B receives that, it will make 0/1 the root port and discard on 0/2.

40. Answer E is correct. None of the ports would be discarding because there would no longer be a loop.

41. Answer A is correct. Each VLAN is a Layer 2 broadcast domain. So by creating more VLANs, we are increasing the number of broadcast domains available on the switch. Typically, every Layer 2 broadcast domain/VLAN will be associated with a separate IP network or subnetwork. To route packets between VLANs, a Layer 3 device would be used. This Layer 3 device could be an external router or an internal Layer 3 function on a multilayer switch. By default, VLAN 1 exists on a new switch, and all ports are assigned to that VLAN by default. The number of collision domains on a switch is based on how many ports that switch has. Each port on a switch can be a separate collision domain. To increase the number of collision domains, you must add additional ports.

42. Answer C is correct. EtherChannel may be used to support a single VLAN or a trunk to bundle multiple physical links into a larger logical port. All the other options are not used to increase throughput due to bundling links together.

43. Answers C and D are correct. A frame that is crossing a trunk will be tagged so that the receiving switch will know which VLANs the frame belongs to. This would be the case in a data frame being sent either to a device and VLAN 10 or coming from a device in VLAN 10 that was crossing the trunk. If VLAN 10 were the native VLAN, there would be no tagging as the frame passes over the trunk. If the trunk were misconfigured as an access port, there would also be no tagging.

44. Answer D is correct. Adding more switches to the same VLANs will add more collisions domains. Each port on a switch can be a separate collision domain. By adding more ports, the size of the broadcast domain (the same VLAN) will increase, because there are not more devices in that same VLAN.

45. Answer C is correct. The IEEE options for LACP include Active and Passive. Active/Active and Active/Passive will both result in a successful EtherChannel negotiation. Cisco's proprietary PAgP options include Desirable/Desirable and Desirable/Auto as the options that work. Another option is to set both sides to On to avoid negotiation.

46. Answer C is correct. The second number shown is the advertised/reported distance from the neighbor regarding the network in question. That same number would show up on the remote router as its feasible distance for that same network. The feasible successor metric (for the successor route) on the local router would be the number on the left, shown before the reported distance from the neighbor. The cutoff point for determining feasible successors is the current successor metric. An advertised/reported metric must be lower than the current feasible distance to be considered a feasible successor.

47. Answer A is correct. Telnet, because it is unsecure, should be disabled by an administrator in favor of using SSH, which does require a username and password to be configured as long authenticated before allowing access through the vty lines. ACLs applied to the logical vty lines using the **access-class** command to control which source IP addresses are allowed to attempt a login is considered a best practice for security. Telnet should be disabled, while allowing only SSH. Access control lists on physical interfaces used for filtering may be a good idea, but it doesn't completely control access to the vty lines; if in the future new interfaces are added, they also would need access control lists applied. By having access control on the logical vty lines, it doesn't matter which physical interfaces are used, or even whether new interfaces show up, because the control is on the vty line. vty lines are an important access method for CLI and should not be disabled, but rather should be protected.

48. Answer B is correct. The command **default-information originate** causes the OSPF router to advertise a default route using OSPF, but only if that local router has its own default route in the routing table. This makes it a conditional advertisements. This command can be used with the keyword **always**, which would then tell the OSPF router to advertise a default route unconditionally, regardless of whether the local router had its own default route in the routing table. This command does not instruct the router to accept a default route that has been advertised to it through OSPF. This command also has no impact on whether multiple OSPF processes may run simultaneously on the local router.

49. Answer B is correct. The existing router, which was the OSPF designated router for that segment, will remain the DR even if a new router has a better router ID or priority. The election process is not preemptive. By default, the router on an Ethernet network that has the highest router ID compared to other OSPF devices that are all booting simultaneously will become the DR for that segment.

50. Answer C is correct. EIGRP is classless and proprietary. OSPF is classless, but it is not proprietary; it is an open standard. Classless routing protocols, such as OSPF and EIGRP, include in routing updates the network mask along with the prefixes/networks that they are advertising. This allows us to use VLSM, which means that we can use different length of masks in different parts of our networks and the routing protocol can advertise all the details about those different length masks. Classful summarization can hide the details of subnets, and if not planned correctly could lead to loss of connectivity to some of your networks because the routers are not clear about where those subnets exist (after receiving summaries from multiple routers advertising the same summary routes). RIPv2 is classless.

51. Answer A is correct. A tiebreaker for routes to the same network is the administrative distance. The lower the administrative distance, the better the route appears to the local router. OSPF and EIGRP have different administrative distances based on the type of route (for example, internal versus external). The route with the lowest administrative distance will be the single route that is placed in the routing table. All three routes will not make it because the default administrative distance is not the same for each of the routing protocols. By default, a router that has equal-cost routes can load balance up to four and can be configured to use more if desired. An equal-cost route would have equal metrics as well as equal administrative distance. The ADs allow a preference between routing protocols, selecting the lowest AD as the preferred protocol to use.

52. Answer B is correct. A 32-bit router ID is required for OSPFv3 to operate. If one is not configured, the router will use the IPv4 address on a loopback, and if that isn't present, it will use the IPv4 address from a physical or logical interface as the OSPFv3 router ID. The command **IPv6 unicast-routing** is used to enable the IPv6 routing process, and is also required to be in place before IPv6's OSPFv3 may be configured. IPv6 enable can be used to enable IPv6 on an interface, but isn't required if there is an IPv6 address configured on the interface. OSPFv2 is IPv4's OSPF, and **load ipv6** is not valid IOS command syntax.

53. Answer A is correct. The **show standby** command enables you to view the details about the HSRP groups, including the virtual address being used.

54. Answer D is correct. The active virtual forwarder (AVF) is a concept used by GLBP. A Layer 3-capable switch with IP routing enabled and VLAN interfaces created could be an AVF. HSRP doesn't use the AVF, and a Layer 2 switch couldn't participate in any FHRP.

55. Answer A is correct. CHAP uses a hash function based on MD5 for authentication over the network, instead of sending a clear-text password like PAP does. NCP is used to negotiate the Layer 3 protocols that will be used on the PPP connection. LCP negotiates the Layer 2 connection between the PPP peers.

56. Answer B is correct. The **broadcast** keyword, when shown in the output of **show frame map**, indicates that broadcasts and multicasts are allowed over the circuit. **dynamic** or **static** indicates how the Frame Relay map was created.

57. Answer D is correct. The local DLCI of 32 can be used by R3 to send packets to the remote IP address of 10.23.0.2. Broadcasts and multicasts are both supported on this link (as indicated by the **broadcast** keyword). The remote DLCI on the other end of the PVC isn't known and doesn't have to be 32.

58. Answer D is correct. The Frame Relay mapping should indicate the local DLCI to use to reach a remote IP address. The IP address in the mapping shown is also the local routers IP address, which makes it incorrect. The broadcast indicates that broadcasts and multicasts are allowed over a circuit. The DLCI shown is 32, but we don't have enough information to confirm that it is incorrect.

59. Answers A, D, and E are correct. Layer 2 WAN protocols include Cisco's proprietary HDLC and the industry standards of PPP and Frame Relay. IPsec and SSL are open standard security protocols that can be used as part of VPN solutions.

60. Answer D is correct. IPsec could be used to protect the contents of packets as they go back and forth between the two sites. This type of implementation is known as a site-to-site VPN tunnel. PPP is an open standard Layer 2 protocol that can be used between different vendors. Frame Relay, HDLC, and PPP are Layer 2 encapsulation protocols that don't (on their own) provide VPN services.

61. Answer C is correct. If the PVC is configured, but the remote end is not functioning, the LMI could report the status of the PVC as being INACTIVE. If LMI is not being used, the status is STATIC. An operational PVC shows as ACTIVE.

62. Answer B is correct. Extended ping provides the interactive dialog displayed in the output associated with the question. Extended traceroute has a similar (but not identical) dialog. Tracert is a Windows command.

63. Answer E is correct. A directly connected route will have a *C*. The letter *D* represents an EIGRP-learned route. Default routes can be learned via a routing protocol or statically configured. OSPF will have an *O* (and possibly other characters as well) to indicate it is an OSPF-learned route. Static routes have an *S*.

64. Answer A is correct. When using a centralized DHCP server, the local router (or multilayer switch) needs to forward DHCP client requests that it sees (from clients) to the central DHCP server. If the switch were powered off, the clients wouldn't receive a link signal. The local switch doesn't have to be a DHCP client to be a DHCP relay, which is what is causing the problem here. The switch won't use a default gateway command when configured for IP routing. (It would use an IP default network, if configured, but not a default gateway.)

65. Answer E is correct. The Layer 2 destination address is not the router's MAC address, so it would not process the frame any further.

66. Answer A is correct. The **show mac-address-table** command shows the MAC addresses currently known by the switch, along with which VLAN those MAC addresses are associated with. The other commands are either invalid syntax or will not show the content of the MAC address table. In some IOS releases, the **show mac address-table** command also correctly shows the table.

67. Answer C is correct. An encapsulation mismatch would cause a failure at Layer 2, which would result in an up/down status. If no is cable attached, it shows as down/down; and if the interface is shut down, it shows as administratively down. CDP and routing protocols do not affect the Layer 1/Layer 2 status.

Glossary

A

access list Rules applied to a router that will determine traffic patterns for data.

administrative distance A value that ranges from 0 through 255, which determines the priority of a source's routing information.

advanced distance vector protocol A routing protocol that combines the strengths of the distance vector and link-state routing protocols. Cisco Enhanced Interior Gateway Routing Protocol (EIGRP) is considered an advanced distance vector protocol.

application layer The highest layer of the OSI model (Layer 7). It is closest to the end user and selects appropriate network services to support end-user applications such as email and FTP.

ARP (Address Resolution Protocol) A protocol used to map a known logical address to an unknown physical address. A device performs an ARP broadcast to identify the physical address of a destination device. This physical address is then stored in cache memory for later transmissions.

AS (autonomous system) A group of networks under common administration that share a routing strategy.

ATM (Asynchronous Transfer Mode) A dedicated-connection switching technology that organizes digital data into units and transmits them over a physical medium using digital signal technology.

attenuation A term that refers to the reduction in strength of a signal. Attenuation occurs with any type of signal, whether digital or analog. Sometimes referred to as signal loss.

Authentication Header (AH) A header used with IPsec that provides integrity and authentication.

B

bandwidth The available capacity of a network link over a physical medium.

BECN (Backward Explicit Congestion Notification) A Frame Relay message that notifies the sending device that there is congestion in the network. A BECN bit is sent back in the direction from where the frame was sent (the source).

BGP (Border Gateway Protocol) An exterior routing protocol that exchanges route information between autonomous systems.

boot field The lowest four binary digits of a configuration register. The value of the boot field determines the order in which a router searches for Cisco IOS software.

BPDU (bridge protocol data unit) Data messages that are exchanged across the switches within an extended LAN that uses a Spanning Tree Protocol topology.

bridge A device used to segment a LAN into multiple physical segments. A bridge uses a forwarding table to determine which frames need to be forwarded to specific segments. Bridges isolate local traffic to the originating physical segment, but forward all nonlocal and broadcast traffic.

broadcast A data frame that's sent to every node on a local segment.

C

CAM Content-addressable memory is the specialized memory used to store the CAM table—the dynamic table in a network switch that maps MAC addresses to ports. It is the essential mechanism that separates network switches from hubs.

carrier detect signal A signal received on a router interface that indicates whether the physical layer connectivity is operating properly.

CDP (Cisco Discovery Protocol) A Cisco proprietary protocol that operates at the data link layer. CDP enables network administrators to view a summary protocol and address information about other directly connected Cisco routers (and some Cisco switches).

CEF Cisco Express Forwarding is an advanced Layer 3 switching technology used to enhance the performance of routers, by using hardware ASIC chips instead of process-based CPU to make routing decisions.

channel A single communications path on a system. In some situations, channels can be multiplexed over a single connection.

CHAP (Challenge Handshake Authentication Protocol) An authentication protocol for the Point-to-Point Protocol (PPP) that uses a three-way encrypted handshake to force a remote host to identify itself to a local host.

checksum A field that performs calculations to ensure the integrity of data.

CIDR (classless interdomain routing) Implemented to resolve the rapid depletion of IP address space on the Internet and to minimize the number of routes on the Internet. CIDR provides a more efficient method of allocating IP address space by removing the concept of classes in IP addressing. CIDR enables routes to be summarized on powers of 2 boundaries; therefore, it reduces multiple routes into a single prefix.

CIR (committed information rate) The rate at which a Frame Relay link transmits data, averaged over time. CIR is measured in bits per second. This is the committed rate that the service provider guarantees for a Frame Relay connection.

classful addressing Categorizes IP addresses into ranges that are used to create a hierarchy in the IP addressing scheme. The most common classes are A, B, and C, which can be identified by looking at the first three binary digits of an IP address.

classless addressing Classless addressing does not categorize addresses into classes and is designed to deal with wasted address space.

CO (central office) The local telephone company office where all local loops in an area connect.

configuration register A numeric value (usually displayed in hexadecimal form) used to specify certain actions on a router.

congestion A situation that occurs during data transfer if one or more computers generate network traffic faster than it can be transmitted through the network.

console A terminal attached directly to the router for configuring and monitoring the router.

convergence The process by which all routers within an internetwork route information and eventually agree on optimal routes through the internetwork.

counting to infinity A routing problem in which the distance metric for a destination network is continually increased because the internetwork has not fully converged.

CPE (customer premise equipment) Terminating equipment such as telephones and modems supplied by the service provider, installed at the customer site, and connected to the network.

CRC (cyclic redundancy check) An error-checking mechanism by which the receiving node calculates a value based on the data it receives and compares it with the value stored within the frame from the sending node.

CSMA/CA (carrier sense multiple access/collision avoidance) A physical specification used in wireless networks to provide contention-based frame transmission. A sending device first listens to detect if there is any activity and, if it is clear, sends the frame. The sending device will send a signal telling other devices not to transmit.

CSMA/CD (carrier sense multiple access/collision detection) A physical specification used by Ethernet to provide contention-based frame transmission. CSMA/CD specifies that a sending device must share physical transmission media and listen to determine whether a collision occurs after transmitting. In simple terms, this means that an Ethernet card has a built-in capability to detect a potential packet collision on the internetwork.

cut-through switching A method of forwarding frames based on the first 6 bytes contained in the frame. Cut-through switching provides higher throughput than store-and-forward switching because it requires only 6 bytes of data to make the forwarding decision. Cut-through switching does not provide error checking like its counterpart store-and-forward switching.

D

DCE (data communications equipment) The device at the network end of a user-to-network connection that provides a physical connection to the network, forwards traffic, and provides a clocking signal used to synchronize data transmission between the DCE and DTE devices.

de-encapsulation The process by which a destination peer layer removes and reads the control information sent by the source peer layer in another network host.

default mask A binary or decimal representation of the number of bits used to identify an IP network. The class of the IP address defines the default mask. A default mask is represented by four octets of binary digits. The mask can also be presented in dotted-decimal notation.

default route A network route (that usually points to another router) established to receive and attempt to process all packets for which no route appears in the route table.

delay The amount of time necessary to move a packet through the internetwork from source to destination.

demarc The point of demarcation is between the carrier's equipment and the customer premise equipment (CPE).

Diffie-Helman The algorithm used to securely exchange secret shared keys used in IPsec.

discard eligibility bit A bit that can be set to indicate that a frame can be dropped if congestion occurs within the Frame Relay network.

distance vector protocol An interior routing protocol that relies on distance and vector or direction to choose optimal paths. A distance vector protocol requires each router to send all or a large part of its route table to its neighboring routers periodically.

DLCI (data link connection identifier) A value that specifies a permanent virtual circuit (PVC) or switched virtual circuit (SVC) in a Frame Relay network.

DNS (domain name system) A system used to translate fully qualified hostnames or computer names into IP addresses, and vice versa.

dotted-decimal notation A method of representing binary IP addresses in a decimal format. Dotted decimal notation represents the four octets of an IP address in four decimal values separated by decimal points.

DTE (data terminal equipment) The device at the user end of the user-to-network connection that connects to a data network through a data communications equipment (DCE) device.

dynamic route A network route that adjusts automatically to changes within the internetwork.

E

EGP (Exterior Gateway Protocol) A routing protocol that conveys information between autonomous systems; it is widely used within the Internet. The Border Gateway Protocol (BGP) is an example of an exterior routing protocol.

EIGRP (Enhanced Interior Gateway Routing Protocol) A Cisco-proprietary routing protocol that includes features of both distance vector and link-state routing protocols. EIGRP is considered an advanced distance vector protocol.

Encapsulating Security Payload (ESP) An IPsec header that provides confidentiality, authentication, and integrity.

encapsulation Generally speaking, encapsulation is the process of wrapping data in a particular protocol header. In the context of the OSI model, encapsulation is the process by which a source peer layer includes header and trailer control information with a protocol data unit (PDU) destined for its peer layer in another network host. The information encapsulated instructs the destination peer layer how to process the information.

Etherchannel Etherchannel is the Cisco term for switch port aggregation technology that allows the use of two to eight ports in a virtual bundle to provide greater aggregate bandwidth and fault tolerance. An Etherchannel can be created using Fast Ethernet, Gigabit Ethernet or 10-Gigabit Ethernet links.

EXEC The user interface for executing Cisco router commands.

F

FCS (frame check sequence) Extra characters added to a frame for error control purposes. FCS is the result of a cyclic redundancy check (CRC).

feasible successor In EIGRP, a feasible successor route is defined as a valid route whose advertised distance is less than the feasible distance of the successor route.

FECN (Forward Explicit Congestion Notification) A Frame Relay message that notifies the receiving device that there is congestion in the network. An FECN bit is sent in the same direction in which the frame was traveling, toward its destination.

FHRP First-hop redundancy protocols provide default gateway redundancy for hosts on a given subnet. FHRP is actually a feature, not a protocol; the protocols which implement the feature include Hot Standby Router Protocol (HSRP), Virtual Router Redundancy Protocol (VRRP), and Gateway Load Balancing Protocol (GLBP).

flash Router memory that stores the Cisco IOS image and associated microcode. Flash is erasable, reprogrammable ROM that retains its content when the router is powered down or restarted.

flow control A mechanism that throttles back data transmission to ensure that a sending system does not overwhelm the receiving system with data.

Frame Relay A switched data link layer protocol that supports multiple virtual circuits using High-Level Data Link Control (HDLC) encapsulation between connected devices.

frame tagging A method of tagging a frame with a unique user-defined virtual local-area network (VLAN). The process of tagging frames allows VLANs to span multiple switches.

FTP (File Transfer Protocol) A protocol used to copy a file from one host to another host, regardless of the physical hardware or operating system of each device. FTP identifies a client and server during the file-transfer process. In addition, it provides a guaranteed transfer by using the services of the Transmission Control Protocol (TCP).

full duplex The physical transmission process on a network device by which one pair of wires transmits data while another pair of wires receives data. Full-duplex transmission is achieved by eliminating the possibility of collisions on an Ethernet segment, thereby eliminating the need for a device to sense collisions.

G

global configuration mode A router mode that enables simple router configuration commands—such as router names, banners, and passwords—to be executed. Global configuration commands affect the whole router rather than a single interface or component.

H

half duplex The physical transmission process whereby one pair of wires is used to transmit information and the other pair of wires is used to receive information or to sense collisions on the physical media. Half-duplex transmission is required on Ethernet segments with multiple devices.

handshake The process of one system making a request to another system before a connection is established. Handshakes occur during the establishment of a connection between two systems, and they address matters such as synchronization and connection parameters.

HDLC (High-Level Data Link Control) A bit-oriented, synchronous data link layer protocol that specifies data encapsulation methods on serial links.

header Control information placed before the data during the encapsulation process.

hierarchical routing protocol A routing environment that relies on several routers to compose a backbone. Most traffic from non-backbone routers traverses the backbone routers (or at least travels to the backbone) to reach another nonbackbone router. This is accomplished by breaking a network into a hierarchy of networks, where each level is responsible for its own routing.

hold-down The state into which a route is placed so that routers will not advertise or accept updates for that route until a timer expires.

hop count The number of routers a packet passes through on its way to the destination network.

hostname A logical name given to a router.

HSSI (High-Speed Serial Interface) A physical standard designed for serial connections that require high data transmission rates. The HSSI standard allows for high-speed communication that runs at speeds up to 52Mbps.

I

ICMP (Internet Control Message Protocol) A protocol that communicates error messages and controls messages between devices. Thirteen types of ICMP messages are defined. ICMP enables devices to check the status of other devices, to query the current time, and to perform other functions such as ping and traceroute.

IEEE (Institute of Electrical and Electronics Engineers) An organization whose primary function is to define standards for network LANs.

initial configuration dialog The dialog used to configure a router the first time it is booted or when no configuration file exists. The initial configuration dialog is an optional tool used to simplify the configuration process.

inside global The term to describe your inside addresses after they have been translated with Network Address Translation (NAT). Inside global addresses are registered addresses that represent your inside hosts to your outside networks.

inside local The addresses on the inside of your network before they are translated with Network Address Translation (NAT).

interfaces Router components that provide the network connections in which data packets move in and out of the router. Depending on the model of router, interfaces exist either on the motherboard or on separate, modular interface cards.

interior routing protocol A routing protocol that exchanges information within an autonomous system. Routing Information Protocol (RIP) and Open Shortest Path First (OSPF) are examples of interior routing protocols.

Internet Key Exchange A component of IPsec that is used to dynamically and securely exchange secret keys. IKE uses Diffie-Helman to exchange keys.

IP (Internet Protocol) One of the many protocols maintained in the TCP/IP suite of protocols. IP is the transport mechanism for Transmission Control Protocol (TCP), User Datagram Protocol (UDP), and Internet Control Message Protocol (ICMP) data. It also provides the logical addressing necessary for complex routing activity.

IP extended access list An access list that provides a way of filtering IP traffic based on the source IP address, destination IP address, TCP port, UDP port, IP precedence field, TOS field, ICMP-type, ICMP-code, ICMP-message, IGMP-type, and TCP-established connections.

IP standard access list An access list that provides a way of filtering IP traffic on a router interface based on the source IP address or address range.

IPsec A suite of security protocols that is used to provide a secure virtual private network (VPN). IPsec can operate in tunnel mode, where a new IP header is added, or transport mode, where the original IP header is used.

ISL (Inter-Switch Link) A protocol used to enable virtual local-area networks (VLANs) to span multiple switches. ISL is used between switches to communicate common VLANs between devices.

K

keepalive frames Protocol data units (PDUs) transmitted at the data link layer that indicate whether the proper frame type is configured.

L

LAN protocols Protocols that identify Layer 2 protocols used for the transmission of data within a local-area network (LAN). The three most popular LAN protocols used today are Ethernet, Token Ring, and Fiber Distributed Data Interface (FDDI).

LCP (Link Control Protocol) A protocol that configures, tests, maintains, and terminates Point-to-Point Protocol (PPP) connections. LCP is a sublayer of the Point-to-Point Protocol (PPP).

link-state advertisement A packet that contains the status of a router's links or network interfaces.

link-state protocol An interior routing protocol in which each router sends only the state of its own network links across the network, but sends this information to every router within its autonomous system or area. This process enables routers to learn and maintain full knowledge of the network's exact topology and how it is interconnected. Link state protocols use a "shortest path first" algorithm.

LLC (Logical Link Control) sublayer A sublayer of the data link layer. The LLC sublayer provides the software functions of the data link layer.

LMI (Local Management Interface) A set of enhancements to the Frame Relay protocol specifications used to manage complex networks. Some key Frame Relay LMI extensions include global addressing, virtual circuit status messages, and multicasting.

load An indication of how busy a network resource is. CPU utilization and packets processed per second are two indicators of load.

local loop The line from the customer's premises to the telephone company's central office (CO).

logical addressing Network layer addressing is most commonly referred to as logical addressing (versus the physical addressing of the data link layer). A logical address consists of two parts: the network and the node. Routers use the network part of the logical address to determine the best path to the network of a remote device. The node part of the logical address is used to identify the specific host to forward the packet on the destination network.

logical ANDing A process of comparing two sets of binary numbers to result in one value representing an IP address network. Logical ANDing is used to compare an IP address against its subnet mask to yield the IP subnet on which the IP address resides. ANDing is also used to determine whether a packet has a local or remote destination.

M

MAC (Media Access Control) address A physical address used to define a device uniquely.

MAC (Media Access Control) layer A sublayer of the data link layer that provides the hardware functions of the data link layer.

metric The relative cost of sending packets to a destination network over a specific network route. Examples of metrics include bandwidth, delay, and reliability.

MIB (Management Information Base) A database that maintains statistics on certain data items. The Simple Network Management Protocol (SNMP) uses MIBs to query information about devices.

MPLS (Multiprotocol Label Switching) A mechanism in high-performance telecommunications networks that directs data from one network node to the next based on short path labels rather than long network addresses, avoiding complex lookups in a routing table. The labels identify virtual links (paths) between distant nodes rather than endpoints. MPLS can encapsulate packets of various network protocols. MPLS supports a range of access technologies, including T1/E1, ATM, Frame Relay, and DSL.

multicasting A process of using one IP address to represent a group of IP addresses. Multicasting is used to send messages to a subset of IP addresses in a network or networks.

Multi-area OSPF A feature of OSPF which divides the routed system into hierarchical areas, allowing greater control over routing update traffic. Router loads are generally reduced, as is the frequency of SPF recalculation. Multi-area OSPF system can scale to large deployments.

multipath routing protocol A routing protocol that load balances over multiple optimal paths to a destination network when the costs of the paths are equal.

multiplexing A method of flow control used by the transport layer in which application conversations are combined over a single channel by interleaving packets from different segments and transmitting them.

N

NAT (Network Address Translation) The process of translating your multiple internal IP addresses to a single registered IP address on the outside of your network.

NBMA (nonbroadcast multiaccess) A multiaccess network that either does not support broadcasts or for which sending broadcasts is not feasible.

NCP (Network Control Protocol) A collection of protocols that establishes and configures different network layer protocols for use over a Point-to-Point Protocol (PPP) connection. NCP is a sublayer of PPP.

NetBIOS (Network Basic Input/ Output System) A common session layer interface specification from IBM and Microsoft that enables applications to request lower-level network services.

NIC (network interface card) A board that provides network communication capabilities to and from a network host.

NTP Network Time Protocol provides IP network-based synchronization of device clocks, facilitating log and transaction analysis, and improving quality of service (QoS) responsiveness in Voice and Video over IP systems.

NVRAM (nonvolatile random-access memory) A memory area of the router that stores permanent information, such as the router's backup configuration file. The contents of NVRAM are retained when the router is powered down or restarted.

O

OSI (Open Systems Interconnection) model A layered networking framework developed by the International Organization for Standardization. The OSI model describes seven layers that correspond to specific networking functions.

OSPF (Open Shortest Path First) A hierarchical link-state routing protocol that was developed as a successor to the Routing Information Protocol (RIP).

P

packet switching A process by which a router moves a packet from one interface to another.

PAP (Password Authentication Protocol) An authentication protocol for the Point-to-Point Protocol (PPP) that uses a two-way unencrypted handshake to enable a remote host to identify itself to a local host.

passive-interface A routing protocol command that places a router interface into "receive-only" mode; no routing updates are sent out, but those that are received are processed. This allows the passive interface's network to be advertised out other interfaces, without generating unnecessary routing protocol traffic on the passive interface network.

PDU (protocol data unit) A unit of measure that refers to data that is transmitted between two peer layers within different network devices. Segments, packets, and frames are examples of PDUs.

peer-to-peer communication A form of communication that occurs between the same layers of two different network hosts.

ping A tool for testing IP connectivity between two devices. Ping is used to send multiple IP packets between a sending and a receiving device. The destination device responds with an Internet Control Message Protocol (ICMP) packet to notify the source device of its existence.

POP (point of presence) A physical location where a carrier has installed equipment to interconnect with a local exchange carrier.

Port security A system of MAC-based switch port security capabilities that can limit or deny access to certain hosts attempting to connect to an access switch.

PPP (Point-to-Point Protocol) A standard protocol that enables router-to-router and host-to-network connectivity over synchronous and asynchronous circuits such as telephone lines.

presentation layer Layer 6 of the OSI model. The presentation layer is concerned with how data is represented to the application layer.

privileged mode An extensive administrative and management mode on a Cisco router. This router mode permits testing, debugging, and commands to modify the router's configuration.

protocol A formal description of a set of rules and conventions that defines how devices on a network must exchange information.

PSTN (public switched telephone network) The circuit-switching facilities maintained for voice analog communication.

PVC (permanent virtual circuit) A virtual circuit that is permanently established and ready for use.

PVST+ Per-VLAN Spanning Tree Plus is Cisco-proprietary switching technology that creates a separate instance of 802.1d STP for each configured VLAN. Doing so allows for an optimized Layer 2 environment for each VLAN. See also *Rapid-PVSTP+*.

R

RAM (random-access memory) A memory area of a router that serves as a working storage area. RAM contains data such as route tables, various types of caches and buffers, in addition to input and output queues and the router's active configuration file. The contents of RAM are lost when the router is powered down or restarted.

Rapid-PVST+ Rapid Per-VLAN Spanning Tree Plus is Cisco proprietary switching technology that creates a separate instance of 802.1w RSTP for each configured VLAN. Doing so allows for an optimized Layer 2 environment for each VLAN. See also *PVSTP+*.

RARP (Reverse Address Resolution Protocol) This protocol provides mapping that is exactly opposite to the Address Resolution Protocol (ARP). RARP maps a known physical address to a logical address. Diskless machines that do not have a configured IP address when started typically use RARP. RARP requires the existence of a server that maintains physical-to-logical address mappings.

reliability A metric that allows the network administrator to assign arbitrarily a numeric value to indicate a reliability factor for a link. The reliability metric is a method used to capture an administrator's experience with a given network link.

RIP (Routing Information Protocol) A widely used distance vector routing protocol that uses hop count as its metric.

ROM (read-only memory) An area of router memory that contains a version of the Cisco IOS image, usually an older version with minimal functionality. ROM also stores the bootstrap program and power-on diagnostic programs.

ROM Monitor mode A mode on a Cisco router that allows basic functions such as changing the configuration register value or uploading an IOS via Xmodem.

route aggregation The process of combining multiple IP address networks into one superset of IP address networks. Route aggregation is implemented to reduce the number of route table entries required to forward IP packets accurately in an internetwork.

route poisoning A routing technique by which a router immediately marks a network as unreachable as soon as it detects that the network is down. The router broadcasts the update throughout the network and maintains this poisoned route in its route table for a specified period of time.

route table An area of a router's memory that stores the network topology information used to determine optimal routes. Route tables contain information such as destination network, next hop, and associated metrics.

routed protocol A protocol that provides the information required for the routing protocol to determine the topology of the internetwork and the best path to a destination. The routed protocol provides this information in the form of a logical address and other fields within a packet. The information contained in the packet enables the router to direct user traffic. The most common routed protocols include Internet Protocol (IP) and Internetwork Packet Exchange (IPX).

router ID The router identifier used with OSPF. The router ID is selected as the highest IP address among all loopback interfaces. If loopback interfaces are not configured, the router ID is the highest IP address of any active physical interface at the moment that OSPF is initialized.

router modes Modes that enable the execution of specific router commands and functions. User, privileged, and setup are examples of router modes that allow you to perform certain tasks.

routing algorithms Well-defined rules that aid routers in the collection of route information and the determination of the optimal path.

routing loop An event in which two or more routers have not yet converged and are propagating their inaccurate route tables. In addition, they are probably still switching packets based on their inaccurate route tables.

routing protocols Routing protocols use algorithms to generate a list of paths to a particular destination and the cost associated with each path. Routers use routing protocols to communicate among each other the best route to use to reach a particular destination.

RS-232 A physical standard used to identify cabling types for serial data transmission for speeds of 19.2Kbps or less. RS-232 connects two devices communicating over a serial link with either a 25-pin (DB-25) or 9-pin (DB-9) serial interface. RS-232 is now known as EIA/TIA-232.

running configuration file The current configuration file that is active on a router.

RXBoot A router-maintenance mode that enables router recovery functions when the IOS file in flash has been erased or is corrupt.

S

Secure Shell (SSH) A protocol that allows for secure communication between a client and a router. It is a secure alternative to Telnet.

Secure Sockets Layer (SSL) A common method of securing HTTP communication. It is also used for web-based VPNs where users are first authenticated via a web GUI before gaining access to secure web applications.

service set identifier (SSID) A 32-bit unique identifier that is used to name a wireless network.

session layer As Layer 5 of the OSI model, the session layer establishes, manages, and terminates sessions between applications on different network devices.

setup mode The router mode triggered on startup if no configuration file resides in nonvolatile random-access memory (NVRAM).

shortest path first See *link-state protocol.*

sliding windows A method by which TCP dynamically sets the window size during a connection, enabling the receiving device involved in the communication to slow down the sending data rate.

SMTP (Simple Mail Transfer Protocol) A protocol used to pass mail messages between devices, SMTP uses Transmission Control Protocol (TCP) connections to pass the email between hosts.

SNMP Simple Network Management Protocol is a standards-based protocol that allows remote monitoring and management of networked devices.

socket The combination of the sending and destination Transmission Control Protocol (TCP) port numbers and the sending and destination Internet Protocol (IP) addresses defines a socket. Therefore, a socket can be used to define any User Datagram Protocol (UDP) or TCP connection uniquely.

Spanning Tree Protocol A protocol used to eliminate all circular routes in a bridged or switched environment while maintaining redundancy. Circular routes are not desirable in Layer 2 networks because of the forwarding mechanism used at this layer.

split horizon A routing mechanism that prevents a router from sending information that it received about a network back to its neighbor that originally sent the information. This mechanism is useful in preventing routing loops.

startup configuration file The backup configuration file on a router.

static route A network route that is manually entered into the route table. Static routes function well in simple and predictable network environments.

store-and-forward switching A method of forwarding frames by copying an entire frame into the buffer of a switch and making a forwarding decision. Store-and-forward switching does not achieve the same throughput as its counterpart, cut-through switching, because it copies the entire frame into the buffer instead of copying only the first 6 bytes. Store-and-forward switching, however, provides error checking that is not provided by cut-through switching.

subinterface One of possibly many virtual interfaces on a single physical interface.

subnetting A process of splitting a classful range of IP addresses into multiple IP networks to allow more flexibility in IP addressing schemes. Subnetting overcomes the limitation of address classes and allows network administrators the flexibility to assign multiple networks with one class of IP addresses.

SVI A switched virtual interface is a Layer 3 interface defined on a Layer 2 switch. These are also called VLAN interfaces because there is usually one defined for each VLAN, allowing inter-VLAN routing to be performed by a Layer 3 switch instead of by a router. Layer 2 switches can have only one SVI configured, which is used for switch management.

switch Provides increased port density and forwarding capabilities as compared to bridges. The increased port densities of switches enable LANs to be microsegmented, thereby increasing the amount of bandwidth delivered to each device.

syslog A network service that provides centralized log message archiving.

T

TCP (Transmission Control Protocol) One of the many protocols maintained in the TCP/IP suite of protocols. TCP provides a connection-oriented and reliable service to the applications that use it.

TCP three-way handshake A three-step process whereby a TCP session is established. In the first step, the sending device sends the initial sequence number with the SYN bit set in the TCP header. The receiver sends back a packet with the SYN and ACK bits set. In the third and final step, the sender sends a packet with the ACK bit set.

TCP windowing A method of increasing or reducing the number of acknowledgments required between data transmissions. This enables devices to throttle the rate at which data is transmitted.

Telnet A standard protocol that provides a virtual terminal. Telnet enables a network administrator to connect to a router remotely.

TFTP (Trivial File Transfer Protocol) A protocol used to copy files from one device to another. TFTP is a stripped-down version of FTP.

traceroute An IP service that allows a user to utilize the services of the User Datagram Protocol (UDP) and the Internet Control Message Protocol (ICMP) to identify the number of hops between sending and receiving devices and the paths taken from the sending to the receiving device. Traceroute also provides the IP address and DNS name of each hop. Typically, traceroute is used to troubleshoot IP connectivity between two devices.

trailer Control information placed after the data during the encapsulation process. See *encapsulation* for more detail.

transport layer As Layer 4 of the OSI model, it is concerned with segmenting upper-layer applications, establishing end-to-end connectivity through the network, sending segments from one host to another, and ensuring the reliable transport of data.

trunk A switch port that connects to another switch to enable virtual local-area networks (VLANs) to span multiple switches.

tunnel A tunnel takes packets or frames from one protocol and places them inside frames from another network system. See encapsulation.

U

UDP (User Datagram Protocol) One of the many protocols maintained in the TCP/IP suite of protocols, UDP is a Layer 4, best-effort delivery protocol and, therefore, maintains connectionless network services.

user mode A display-only mode on a Cisco router. Only limited information about the router can be viewed within this router mode; no configuration changes are permitted.

V

V.35 A physical standard used to identify cabling types for serial data transmission for speeds up to 4Mbps. The V.35 standard was created by the International Telecommunication Union-Telecommunication (ITU-T) standardization sector.

VLAN (virtual local-area network) A technique of assigning devices to specific LANs based on the port to which they attach on a switch rather than the physical location. VLANs extend the flexibility of LANs by allowing devices to be assigned to specific LANs on a port-by-port basis versus a device basis.

VLSM (variable-length subnet masking) VLSM provides more flexibility in assigning IP address space. (A common problem with routing protocols is the necessity of all devices in a given routing protocol domain to use the same subnet mask.) Routing protocols that support VLSM allow administrators to assign IP networks with different subnet masks. This increased flexibility saves IP address space because administrators can assign IP networks based on the number of hosts on each network.

VTP (VLAN Trunking Protocol) A protocol for configuring and administering VLANS on Cisco network devices. With VTP, an administrator can make configuration changes centrally on a single Catalyst series switch and have those changes automatically communicated to all the other switches in the network.

W

WANs (wide-area networks) WANs use data communications equipment (DCE) to connect multiple LANs. Examples of WAN protocols include Frame Relay, Point-to-Point Protocol (PPP), and High-Level Data Link Control (HDLC).

well-known ports A set of ports between 1 and 1,023 that are reserved for specific TCP/IP protocols and services.

Wired Equivalent Protocol (WEP) A security protocol used in Wi-Fi networks that encrypts packets over radio waves. It offers 40-bit and 104-bit encryption (often referred to 64- and 128-bit encryption because of the added initialization vector in the algorithm).

Wi-Fi Protected Access (WPA)/Wi-Fi Protected Access 2 (WPA) Security protocols for Wi-Fi networks that provide greater security than WEP.

Index

Symbols

A

D

E

F

G

H

I

J - K

L

M

N

O

P

Q

R

S

T

U

V

W - X - Y - Z

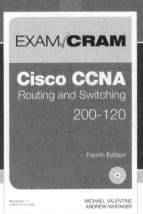